Faith and Family

Ellis Island Series

VOICES FROM SOUTHEAST ASIA
The Refugee Experience in the United States
by John Tenhula

DISTANT MAGNETS
Expectations and Realities in the
Immigrant Experience, 1840–1930
edited by Dirk Hoerder and Horst Rössler

BRANCHING OUT
German-Jewish Immigration to the
United States, 1820–1914
by Avraham Barkai

TIES THAT BIND, TIES THAT DIVIDE
One Hundred Years of Hungarian
Experience in the United States
by Julianna Puskás

Ira Glazier and Luigi de Rosa,
series editors

FAITH AND FAMILY

Dutch Immigration and Settlement in the United States, 1820–1920

Robert P. Swierenga

HM
HOLMES & MEIER
New York/London

Published in the United States of America 2000 by
Holmes & Meier Publishers, Inc.
160 Broadway • New York, NY 10038

Typesetting by BN Typographics West

This book has been printed on acid-free paper.

Library of Congress Cataloging-in-Publication Data

Swierenga, Robert P.
Faith and family : Dutch immigration and settlement in the United States, 1820–1920 / Robert P. Swierenga.
p. cm. — (Ellis Island series)
Includes bibliographical references and index.
ISBN 0-8419-1319-6 (cloth)
1. Dutch Americans—History—19th century. 2. Dutch Americans—History—20th century. 3. Immigrants—United States—History—19th century. 4. Immigrants—United States—History—19th century. 6. Land settlement—United States—History—20th century. 7. United States—Emigration and immigration—History. 8. Netherlands—Emigration and immigration—History. I. Title II. Series.
E184.D9S96 1999
973′.043931—dc21 99-35506
CIP

Manufactured in the United States of America

For

JOHN R. SWIERENGA (1911–1999)
BOUKO (ROBERT) SWIERENGA (1887–1949)
JAN HENDRIKS SWIERENGA (1847–1898)
through whom I trace my roots.
And to my children who carry on:
ROBERT JR., SARAH, CELIA, DANIEL, *and* SUZANNA

CONTENTS

FIGURES

TABLES

ACKNOWLEDGMENTS

For thirty years my research on Dutch immigration has been a pioneering effort, following the pathfinders, Jacob van Hinte and Henry Lucas, who blazed the trail. Herbert Brinks, Elton Bruins, Henry van Stekelenburg, Pieter Stokvis, and Yda Schreuder shared the path and encouraged me to keep focused. Students who stimulated me and opened new trails are Harry Stout (a co-author), Larry Wagenaar, Hans Krabbendam, Annemieke Galema, David Vanderstel, William Van Vugt, Richard Doyle, Suzanne Sinke, and David De Vries. The archives at Calvin College and Hope College opened their rich holdings freely. I thank the staffs for many kindnesses. The Kent State University Department of History, Office of Research and Sponsored Programs, Computer Services, and Inter-library Loan staff facilitated my work in countless ways, notably Bette Sawicki, Eugene Wenninger, Dolly Lowe, Steve Tapp, and Michael Cole. The late Jerome Kemp kindly used his skills to convert older printed texts into machine-readable text by optical scanning. I acknowledge all this assistance with heartfelt gratitude.

My thanks also go to the editors and publishers of the following journals and books for permission to reprint all or part of my essays here:

Chapter 1: "Dutch International Labour Migration to North America in the Nineteenth Century." In *Dutch Immigration to North America*, eds. Mark Boekelman and Herman Ganzevoort, 1–34. Toronto: Multicultural History Society of Ontario, 1983.

Chapter 2: "Socio-Economic Patterns of Migration in the Netherlands in the Nineteenth Century" (with Harry S. Stout). In *Research in Economic History: An Annual Compilation of Research*, vol. 1, ed. Paul Uselding, 298–333. Greenwich, CT: JAI Press, 1976; "Exodus Netherlands, Promised Land America: Dutch Immigration and Settlement in the United States." In *A Bilateral Bicentennial: A History of Dutch-American Relations, 1782–1982*, eds. J. W. Schulte Nordholt and Robert P. Swierenga, 127–47. Amsterdam: Meulenhoff International, New York: Octagon Books, 1982; "Dutch Immigrant Demography, 1820–1880," *Journal of Family History* 5 (Winter 1980): 390–405; and "The Delayed Transition from Folk to Labor Migration: The Netherlands, 1880–1920." *International Migration Review* 27 (Summer 1993): 406–24.

Chapter 3: "Local Patterns of Dutch Migration to the United States in the Mid-Nineteenth Century." In *A Century of European Migrations, 1830–1930*, eds. Rudolph J. Vecoli and Suzanne M. Sinke, 134–57. Urbana: University of Illinois Press, 1991.

Chapter 4: "The Journey Across: Dutch Transatlantic Emigrant Passage to the United States, 1820–1880." In *Connecting Cultures: The Netherlands in Five*

Centuries of Transatlantic Exchange, eds. Rosemarijn Hoefte and Johanna C. Kardux, 101–33. *European Contributions to American Studies*, ed. Rob Kroes. Amsterdam: VU University Press, 1994; and "Dutch Immigration Patterns in the Nineteenth and Twentieth Centuries." In *The Dutch in America: Immigration, Settlement, and Cultural Change*, ed. Robert P. Swierenga, 15–42. New Brunswick, NJ: Rutgers University Press, 1985.

Chapter 5: "Religion and Immigration Behavior: The Dutch Experience." In *Belief and Behavior: Essays in the New Religious History*, eds. Philip R. VanderMeer and Robert P. Swierenga, 164–88. New Brunswick, N.J.: Rutgers University Press, 1991; "Religion and Immigration Patterns: A Comparative Analysis of Dutch Protestants and Catholics, 1835–1880." *Journal of American Ethnic History* 5 (Spring 1986): 23–45; and "Pioneers for Jesus Christ:" Dutch Protestant Colonization in North America as an Act of Faith." In *Sharing the Reformed Tradition: The Dutch–North American Exchange, 1846–1996*, eds. George Harinck and Hans Krabbendam, 35–55. Amsterdam: VU University Press, 1996.

Chapter 6: "Local-Cosmopolitan Theory and Immigrant Religion: The Social Basis of the Antebellum Dutch Reformed Schism." *Journal of Social History* 14 (Fall 1980): 113–35.

Chapter 7: "Dutch Jewish Immigration and Religious Life in the Nineteenth Century." *American Jewish History* 79 (Fall 1990): 56–73; "Samuel Myer Isaacs: The Dutch Rabbi of New York City." *American Jewish Archives* 44 (Fall/Winter 1992): 604–21.

Chapter 8: "Calvinists in the Second City: The Dutch Reformed of Chicago's West Side." In *Rethinking Secularization: Reactions to Modernity*, eds. Gerard Dekker, Donald A. Luidens, and Rodger Rice, 45–61. Washington, DC: University Press of America, 1996; "Religious Diversity and Cultural Localism: The Dutch in Cleveland." *Northwest Ohio Quarterly* 67 (Summer 1995): 1–23; "The Low Countries." In *Peopling of Indiana: The Ethnic Experience*, 2 vols., ed. Robert J. Taylor, Jr., 1:102–23. Indianapolis: Indiana Historical Society, 1996.

Chapter 9: "Dutch International Migration and Occupational Change: A Structural Analysis of Multinational Linked Files." In *Migration Across Time and Nations: Population Mobility in Historical Contexts*, eds. Ira A. Glazier and Luigi De Rosa, 95–124. New York: Holmes & Meier, 1986.

Chapter 10: "The Ethnic Voter and the First Lincoln Election." *Civil War History*, 11 (March 1965): 27–43. Reprinted in *Ethnic Voters and the Election of Lincoln*, ed. Frederick C. Luebke, 129–50. Lincoln: University of Nebraska Press, 1971.

Chapter 11: "Dutch International Migration Statistics, 1820–1880: An Analysis of Linked Multinational Nominal Files." *International Migration Review* 15 (Fall 1981): 445–70; and "Under-Reporting of Dutch Immigration Statistics: A Recalculation." *International Migration Review* 21 (Winter 1988): 1596–99.

Chapter 12: "Het bestuderen van de Nederlandse emigratie naar de Vereenigde Staten." *Jaarboek van het Centraal Bureau voor Genealogie* (The Hague) 36 (1982): 252–68; and "Studying Dutch Immigration to the United States: New Methods and Concepts." *Ethnic Forum: Journal of Ethnic Studies and Ethnic Bibliography* 4 (Spring 1984): 8–20.

Bibliographic Essay: "Dutch Immigrant Historiography," *Immigration History Newsletter*, 11 (Nov. 1979): 1–9; and "Archival Materials and Manuscripts in the Netherlands on Immigration to the United States." In *Guide to the Study of United States History Outside the U.S., 1945–1980*, 6 vols., ed. Lewis Hanke, 3:195–215. Washington, DC: American Historical Association, and Amherst: University of Massachusetts, 1985.

PREFACE

Dutch immigration to the United States has fascinated me ever since my days as a neophyte graduate student at the University of Iowa in the 1960s era of rising ethnic consciousness. Having grown up in a Dutch neighborhood on Chicago's West Side in the cocoon of its Reformed churches, private schools, and social clubs, I also wanted to explore my roots.

Since the "Iowa school" of behavioral political historians dominated the history department, my initial research quite naturally traced the voting behavior of the pioneer Iowa Dutch colony of Pella in the tumultuous decade before the Civil War. Pella, where I was teaching at the time, had long maintained its unique ethnic character and celebrated its heritage with a renowned "Tulip Time" festival each spring. "The Ethnic Voter and the First Lincoln Election," published in *Civil War History* in 1965 (Chapter 10) reported this research and was the first of some thirty-five articles and ten books on Dutch immigration and settlement in the United States.

After completing doctoral studies that year, I joined the history faculty of my alma mater, Calvin College, the college of the (Dutch) Christian Reformed Church, founded in 1886 in Grand Rapids, Michigan, the largest Dutch urban settlement in North America. Calvin's rich historical archives included a complete microfilmed copy of the original Netherlands government emigration lists for the eleven provinces in the years 1847 to 1877. These lists included personal information on 21,000 persons and were tailor-made for my newly acquired expertise in computer-aided research. In keeping with the methodology of social history first developed by James C. Malin in the 1930s, that is, to work "from the bottom up," I decided to create a machine-readable file of the entire population. With the help of data-entry staff at Calvin's computer center and students fluent in the language, funded by the college under the federal work-study program, I soon had the complete nominal file transferred to IBM (Hollerith) cards ready for preliminary "number crunching" in a counter sorter machine. This 1960s technology now graces the Smithsonian Institution.

In 1968 I joined the faculty of Kent State University and took advantage of the superior computing environment and graduate student minds that a research institution affords. The first results of that research were published in 1975 and 1976, co-authored with Harry Stout, who has since gained recognition for seminal studies in American religious history. In 1976 a Fulbright research fellowship at Leiden University enabled me to scour Dutch archives for additional emigration lists in the years before 1847 and after 1877. The augmented file was published in 1983 as *Dutch Emigrants to the United States, South Africa, South America, and Southeast*

Asia, 1835–1880: An Alphabetical Listing by Household Heads and Independent Persons.

By this time I was fully involved in phase two of the research, finding all Dutch-born persons enrolled in the ship passenger manifests collected by U.S. customs agents beginning in 1820. By 1983 more than 55,000 names had been abstracted from more than 1,000 reels of microfilm in the National Archives collection for all Atlantic and Gulf ports through 1880. This information was also published in 1983 as *Dutch Immigrants in U.S. Ship Passenger Manifests, 1820–1880: An Alphabetical Listing by Household Heads and Independent Persons* (two volumes). Currently this file is being extended for the years after 1880. Linking the United States ship passenger manifests with the Netherlands emigration records provided the first reliable critique of the published government statistics. The findings reported in 1981 (Chapter 11) alerted students of immigration to the fact that both Dutch and United States official statistics grossly undercount migration. A comparison of occupations before and after immigration also offered a clear picture of economic mobility in overseas migration (Chapter 9).

Simultaneously with this linkage project, in the late 1970s I began phase three of my research plan, which was to abstract from the U.S. federal population census manuscripts of 1850, 1860, and 1870, the Dutch-born and their children residing throughout the country. The Center for Research Libraries in Chicago lent more than one thousand reels of microfilm through the Kent State Library Inter-library loan department, which tedious clerical task both staffs fulfilled without complaint. The census file of 116,000 names was published in 1987 in three volumes as *Dutch Immigrants in U.S. Population Censuses, 1850, 1860, 1870: An Alphabetical Listing by Household Heads and Independent Persons*. The final step was to link the three files in order to provide a complete profile of Dutch immigrants for the period 1835 to 1870 that identifies households in the village of origin and tracks them to their American destination.

In the United States–Netherlands bicentennial year of 1982 two international conferences, one in Amsterdam and one in Philadelphia, encouraged original research on Dutch-American history. The late J. W. Schulte Nordholt organized the Amsterdam meetings, as I did the Philadelphia sessions. Schulte Nordholt and I co-edited the collection of Amsterdam papers, published as *A Bilateral Bicentennial: A History of Dutch-American Relations, 1782–1982* (1982), and I edited the Philadelphia papers under the title, *The Dutch In America: Immigration, Settlement, and Cultural Change* (1985). Portions of my contributions to both conferences are contained in Chapters 2 and 4.

In 1985 popular interest in the history of the Dutch in America received a boost with the publication in English translation of the seminal 1928 Netherlandic work of Jacob van Hinte, *Netherlanders in America: A Study of Emigration and Settlement in the Nineteenth and Twentieth Centuries in the United States of America*. With the translation expertise of my colleague at Kent State University, Adriaan de Wit, I edited this massive 1,150-page work, which Baker Book House published under the shepherding hand of editor Gordon De Jong.

A second Fulbright research fellowship at Leiden University in 1985 permitted me to complete the archival work begun in 1976 on the emigration records. Subsequent trips filled in lacunae, including research for *The Forerunners: Dutch Jews in the North American Diaspora* (1994), which is the first account of this unique immigration.

This book went to press after I assumed the position of research professor in the newly created A. C. Van Raalte Institute at Hope College, Holland, Michigan. The Institute, named after the clerical leader of the Holland colony, is devoted to the study of the Dutch in North America and provides a fitting venue for my continuing research, which Kent State University supported so generously for twenty-eight years. Now I enjoy the ample support of the Institute and its able director, Elton J. Bruins.

The story of Dutch immigration has been told comprehensively and even brilliantly by others, notably by Jacob van Hinte (1928) and Henry Lucas in *Netherlanders in America: Dutch Immigration to the United States and Canada, 1785–1950* (1955). But the standard narrative accounts, good as they are, suffer from some serious deficiencies. They focus primarily on the study of individual experiences, rather than on the process of immigration, the broader stories of which individual lives were parts. Before asking why people emigrated and the impact of the resettlement on future generations, we must know who emigrated and when, how they transplanted themselves, and which social structural forces were impinging on their decisions.

Previous histories relied almost solely on sources produced by elites, the first-person accounts—often published—of clerics, colonial leaders, and prominent pioneers. These were produced on the various anniversary celebrations of the founding in 1847 of the Holland, Michigan colony, especially the semi-centennial commemoration of 1897. Thus, they bear the marks of fallible memories and the filiopietistic panegyrics such celebrations elicit. Only in the last two decades have Dutch immigrant letters been collected systematically so that the voices of the masses can now be heard.

Until the computer age it was also difficult to treat the immigration story collectively and to weave the multitude of individual stories together to form a coherent pattern. Published immigration statistics, on which previous scholars had to rely, are notoriously unreliable, and this has given rise to erroneous conclusions about the nature of the Dutch immigration.

Finally, earlier historians were emotionally tied to one or another colony or religious community, which produced a distorted picture of the Dutch presence in America. Van Hinte, for example, praised Albertus C. Van Raalte, the founder of the Holland, Michigan colony, but castigated Henry P. Scholte, the founder of the sister colony of Pella, Iowa. Lucas, a native of the Holland colony, gave less attention to the Dutch settlements in New York, New Jersey, and Wisconsin, even though these antedated the settlements in Holland and Pella and played equally important roles in the life of the Dutch in America. Finally, in previous accounts the economic and social forces are subsumed under theological and religious affairs and personalities. As central as religion was in the Dutch immigrant story, it is only one aspect. Agricultural crises in the countryside and social changes also pushed people to seek new opportunities in North America.

New questions must be addressed concerning Dutch immigration. First, were the newcomers colonists or immigrants? Colonists seek to transplant their communities and to keep themselves culturally self-contained; immigrants try to integrate into the cultures of the receiving communities. Did the Dutch need and desire interaction, and if so, to what extent and in what communities? Second, what factors "explain" the Dutch emigration of the nineteenth century? Did more families emigrate from rural peasant communities in the northern Netherlands, or from protoindustrial communities on the Belgian border in the south, or from the western maritime-commercial region around Amsterdam, the Hague, and Rotterdam? Third, what forces directed the migrants to specific destinations? Fourth, did the various communities that the newcomers formed in the United States display different developmental patterns?

In order to reconstruct Dutch immigration patterns at the individual level, I have identified discrete emigrant subgroups of families, friends and neighbors, and congregations in their particular Dutch villages and cities, met them at the ports of departure and entry, traced them to their final destinations in the United States, and observed their initial settlement patterns and work experiences. This approach reveals who emigrated when from each Dutch municipality (*gemeente*), which major routes were used for the transatlantic crossings, the initial settlement places, entry occupations, and the subsequent geographical and social mobility patterns. The United States population censuses illuminated for each Dutch settlement the nature of its economic development, social stratification, education and literacy levels, and family kinship and marriage patterns.

The social statistical side of the immigration story is complementary to the traditional narrative surveys. The expectation is that the meshing of social structural and historical aspects of Dutch immigration will lead to a greater understanding of the complexities and the commonalities of the Dutch diaspora.

Faith and Family

INTRODUCTION

The subject of the migration of peoples has become the central concern in United States social history. As the quintessential "nation of immigrants," international resettlement and community formation are at the crux of the American experience. Although much of the resettlement was unplanned, it was not irrational and chaotic. European immigrants followed in the steps of kith and kin, and none more so than the Dutch, a people legendary for their close-knit family life. In the nineteenth century more Dutch emigrated with family members than did any other nationality group. And the Dutch migration occurred within fixed, narrowly focused geographic bounds. This book explores the salient patterns of that migration experience. It is an attempt to understand the social processes of migration for an entire nationality group, but at the level of individual experiences.

No person has captured the attention of immigrant scholars more than the imaginative British historian Frank Thistlethwaite, since he coined the phrase "anatomy of migration" at an international conference in 1960.[1] Drawing upon the analogy of medical scientists who put tissue under microscopes and break down the undifferentiated mass of cells into a honeycomb of numerous particular cells, Thistlethwaite urged social historians similarly to uncover the "true anatomy of migration" by studying at the individual level the millions of European peasants and artisans who emigrated to North America in the nineteenth and twentieth centuries. This seeming preposterous proposal—to study millions of individual immigrants—caught the immediate fancy of Scandinavian scholars at the conference. Within a few years with the aid of generous university and government funding, they created elaborate research institutes that eventually dissected at the parish level the transatlantic migration patterns of thousands of nondescript rural folk.[2] The Scandinavian research, in turn, spurred and influenced all subsequent migration studies, including this one. But it was the computer revolution of the 1950s that truly made possible the individual-level research on the vast scale required to understand the complexities and "inner secrets" of emigration.

In addition to the excitement sparked by the several Scandinavian groups and the innovations of computer-aided social research, the increasing public interest in ethnic identity in the 1960s led to a resurgence of scholarly research in the subject of immigration, which had languished since the 1920s. Today more than ever before, there is great interest in studying the process of immigration and of community formation in the new land, as well as the effects of migration on both sending and host societies.[3]

Although aggregate statistics abound in official records for the flow of immigration from the mother countries to America, there has been only minimal effort to break down the totals to the more important structural unit of analysis—the individual immigrant. Beyond raw totals and percentages, historians still have relatively little information regarding the large-scale migration of individuals from the Old World to the New World. The major characteristic of the current work in migration studies is that it is "human centered."[4] The goal is to describe how people acted, as well as what they said about themselves. Migration is viewed as a social process that involved the transplanting of individuals and kin groups from specific sending places to specific receiving places in North America. In the interchange, the sending and receiving communities were linked in numerous ways.

To uncover this anatomy of migration, scholars have plundered serial records on both sides of the Atlantic for names of immigrants and biographical information about them. The best sources, of course, are those compiled by governments or churches for various legal and administrative purposes, such as emigration lists, passport journals, ship passenger lists, census and land records, naturalization records, and parish registers. The method is to compile biographical information from *both* sides of the Atlantic on tens of thousands of largely anonymous emigrants who have left only traces of their life patterns in official records. Necessary behavioral facts include last residence or birthplace (in order to consult parish records), birth date, sex, family status, occupation, religion, social class, date of emigrating, destination, and the like.

"Hard" biographical data on individuals, families, and networks of families permit one to address the pressing questions surrounding the immigration experience. First, who migrated? Were the "steady-rooted ones" more likely to remove overseas or the "restless ones"? Did farm laborers join the exodus more than farm owners? Were the poor more mobile than the middle and upper classes? Second, what demographic, economic, and religious developments in the mother country and local parish "pushed" prospective emigrants to depart? Third, what was the nature of the immigration experience? Was it an individual act or did extended family patterns, kinship networks, or religious groups exist, and if so, how long did these persist in America? Fourth, did the process of migration change significantly over the decades? Finally, what happened to the people who migrated? Why did some move up the socioeconomic ladder while others did not? Biographical data on tens of thousands of migrants are examined here to answer these and other questions.

The findings can be summarized under the following headings: cycles and phasing, migration traditions, family and kinship, mobility patterns, and transplanted communities.

Cycles and Phasing

Although migration was an individual decision, it occurred as part of a stream of human action that had an external and internal dimension. The external aspect was the long-run trend or "emigration cycle" in the Atlantic community of nations, which was determined by business conditions and political events such as the

American Civil War. The emigration cycle was virtually the same for every Western European immigrant group, and the Dutch were no exception.[5]

Although the migration flow from each European region was strongly influenced by cyclical forces, it also had a self-generating, internal phasing that was unique to each municipality or region. Each migration area went through several phases, demarcated by changes in the yearly migration rate. In the introductory or pioneering phase, a few venturesome young men or families, faced with declining opportunities at home, chose the alternative of emigration to America. These pioneers sent letters home (the so-called America letters) imploring relatives and friends to join them; but the efforts of the innovators had minimal impact until a major social crisis occurred. Then friends and relatives followed their example and departed in droves.

The exodus increased dramatically in this growth phase, because extended kin networks and church congregations migrated en masse. Soon an emigration mentality saturated many communities, and the decision to leave became a normal action rather than a deviant form of behavior. Transportation and communication links were secured and ethnic communities were able to absorb new workers permanently or as temporary, seasonal labor. Eventually, the saturation phase ended when conditions in Europe and North America changed and the need to emigrate declined or the opportunity to do so passed. This ushered in the final *regressive* phase when the stream of migration ebbed out. For most European countries including the Netherlands, this was the decade of World War I, although there was a brief upsurge of emigration in the post–World War II decades as well.

Migration Traditions

While the emigration cycles and phases provide an overview, the specific characteristic of the migration streams can only be determined by minute local studies on both sides of the Atlantic and by detailed analyses of the interplay between sending and receiving communities. It is generally agreed that the onset of mass migration moved across the map of Europe in the years 1840–1900 from the northwest to the southeast, but it is less well understood that within the various nations emigration was region-specific. Certain communities had extensive out-migration traditions, whereas neighboring communities virtually had none. In the Netherlands less than a third of the municipalities experienced notable overseas out-migration. Moreover, if an emigration tradition was established in a municipality early in the growth phase, the likelihood of continuing heavy migration from that area was strong.

In addition to the relative intensity of emigration, the internal organization differed. The two contrasting types are *chain migration* and *impersonal migration*. In chain migration, family members and close friends follow one another over time and are accommodated in the new land by previous emigrants from their primary social group who had enticed them to leave by sending the famed America letters. Impersonal migration occurred when public or private agencies recruited and assisted immigrants.[6]

Most continental Europeans followed the chain migration path. The reasons for this are clear. Governments in the nineteenth century rarely arranged for the emigration of their citizens. The prospective emigrants, who seldom knew the English language, were thereafter quite helpless unless they could rely on family and friends for assistance. The United States and Canadian governments encouraged such private assistance by raising very few obstacles to free migration before World War I. Chain migration usually included entire families removing together, but after 1880, as poorer families opted to emigrate, fathers and adult sons often left first, and later after working for a time sent passage money for the remainder of the family. Nearly one-half of all Swedish emigrants in the 1880s traveled on prepaid tickets.[7]

Chain migration also had the significant effect of building homogeneous neighborhoods in the New World, because it recruited families from the same Old World villages. Over long periods of time, these primary fields with an early migration tradition would spread outward from the core area through kin and friendship networks until concentrated recruitment fields emerged. These first emigrant villages thus had a "stock effect," or a self-generative effect.[8] In every European nation, a relatively few recruitment fields provided most of the emigrants and those people followed well-defined routes to specific receiving areas. This phenomenon of transplanted communities is the inner mechanism of mass migration that is the main focus of this study.

Family and Kinship

The familial and kinship facets of migration remain least explored. Indeed, it is still not known what proportion of European emigrants relocated as family units. Demographic data provide some clues. The earliest emigrants, the innovators, were usually single males. Families predominated in the group phase, but in the saturation phase, singles again were numerous. Sex ratios follow the same pattern—an early period of male dominance, a growth phase with rising numbers of women and children, and a saturation phase with a more equal sex balance. Regarding family size, some scholars believe that the propensity to emigrate was inversely related to the number of children, yet for Dutch immigrants the number of children was not a deterrent; over 80 percent of all emigrating couples or singles were accompanied by children, mostly of school age.[9]

Mobility Patterns

"America-centeredness," or the estimated proportion of European emigrants who settled in the United States and Canada, has been revised upward in recent years. It was formerly thought that only three out of five European emigrants came to North America and that as many as one-third subsequently returned to their homeland. But recent research places the actual figure of America-centeredness above

85 percent for the Swiss, Dutch, Danes, and Germans, and above 95 percent for Swedish and Norwegian emigrants.[10] Moreover, before 1890 the compensatory counterstream of return migration was less than half of the one-third estimate. And for some groups like Jews, Dutch, and Norwegians, fewer than 5 percent remigrated. Only with the development of an Atlantic migratory labor market after 1890 did the so-called birds of passage become commonplace and that was primarily among southern Europeans. Remigration to the Balkans, for example, was nearly 90 percent in the early twentieth century.

The actual migration patterns of individuals and families to North America can be determined by tracing them in European and American sources. Two aspects of the removal process are of greatest interest: the geographical and the social. Did immigration occur in stages or in one dramatic move? And did immigrants eventually achieve the promise of American life, that is, upward social mobility? Studies of the geography of migration have found a high correlation between emigration overseas and internal mobility in the homeland. Half the newcomers first moved from rural areas in Europe to growing cities, and then after a period of years, removed overseas to a port city or inland staging area, such as Milwaukee for Germans and Chicago for Scandinavians, where they again worked temporarily until they saved enough money to establish themselves on farms. Some remained indefinitely because their money ran out; others found lucrative employment in the cities and stayed there.

Perhaps half of the European immigrants moved in one large step from their ancestral homes to their intended destination in America. Among the Dutch, however, the proportion was above two-thirds because of the strong communal nature of the migration. Indeed, fully 40 percent of the families embarking for the United States reported to Dutch officials a specific state or city as their destination.[11] The number of Dutch who actually went directly to their intended destinations can never be known, of course, but the concentrated settlement in the upper Midwest and the census reports on children's birthplaces indicate that one-stage migration was the norm. No Dutch cities served as staging areas in the old country, and in America major cities along the primary Erie Canal and Great Lakes route from Albany via Rochester and Buffalo to Chicago and Milwaukee served only to a minimum extent as staging areas for Dutch immigrants. Following the initial rooting years, the major colonies of Holland and Pella mothered new colonies, but this provided an outlet primarily for their adult children and for newcomers directly from the Netherlands.

Transplanted Communities

The anatomy of migration is best seen in detailed local studies that trace the transplanting of families from their European mother parishes to daughter colonies in the United States. Since most European immigrants were rural peasant folk from areas generally isolated from the industrial revolution, they valued an ordered, traditional society based on kinship, village, and church. When these people emigrated, they sought to transplant their village cultures, religion, and kin networks. Most were not innovators seeking to break free of their past, but conservatives seeking to maintain their culture in a new environment where they could also enjoy greater economic opportunities. Group identity and the desire for cultural maintenance dictated settlement in segregated communities on the frontier or in urban neighborhoods. The key to success of so many of these efforts was the migration of communities composed of interrelated, church-centered families.

Transplanted communities were the norm rather than the exception. Europeans did not scatter randomly over the American landscape but segregated themselves on the basis of family and village. Immigrant colonies throughout the United States, both rural and urban, were planted by the Dutch, Westfalians, Prussians, Swedes, Norwegians, Finns, Poles, Slovaks, and indeed every nationality.[12] The key to these focused chain migrations is the free information flow between early settlers and family and friends in the old country that created an enduring migration link. This typical migration process was basic to motivating and directing the flow of virtually all immigrant settlement in the United States. Family and neighborhood relationships determined both the decision to emigrate and the choice of final destination. The result was a high degree of ethnic clustering in rural and urban America, such that immigrants were literally surrounded by supportive kin, church, and friendship groups and traditional institutions.

The Dutch experience further illustrates this pattern. The emigration occurred in three distinct eras: the commercial venture at New Amsterdam in the seventeenth century, the "free migration" of the nineteenth century, and the government-sponsored "planned migration" after World War II. The nineteenth century outflow is the most consequential. From 1820 to 1914, some 200,000 Dutch peasants and rural artisans resettled with their families in the United States. The movement began in the 1820s when a few individuals and families responded to the lure of American economic opportunities. The letters these pioneers sent home to attract family and friends fell on fertile soil in the mid-1840s, when a severe potato crop failure caused shortages and when Dutch authorities took legal action against pietistic Calvinists who had seceded from the national church in 1834. These events, coupled with the general problems of overpopulation, land shortage, high taxes, and excessive government regulations and licensing laws, stimulated emigration by large groups of immigrants, especially Calvinist dissenters and Roman Catholics, who were also a suppressed minority.

Following the Civil War, people departed as families rather than as congregations and most left areas earlier affected. The vast majority were day laborers, farmers, and craftsmen from the rural villages and countryside, where economic prospects were dim. Less than one in seven were in white-collar occupations. The populous urban, western region and the culturally traditional but industrializing Catholic region in the South witnessed relatively little overseas migration, in contrast to the Protestant clay-soil areas where emigration was strong. Ninety percent of all Dutch emigrants in the nineteenth century chose to settle in the United States, and the proportion was even higher from rural areas, which is eloquent testimony to the lure of the land.

Notes

1. Frank Thistlethwaite, "Migration from Europe Overseas in the Nineteenth and Twentieth Centuries," in XIe Congrès des Sciences Historiques, *Rapports, V: Historie Contemporaine* (Stockholm: Almquist & Wilsell, 1960), 32–60.
2. Harald Runblom and Hans Norman, eds., *From Sweden to America: A History of the Migration* (Minneapolis: University of Minnesota Press, 1976); Bo Kronborg, Thomas Nilsson, and Andres A. Svalestuen, eds. "Nordic Population Mobility: Comparative Studies of Selected Parishes in the Nordic Countries, 1850–1900," *American Studies in Scandinavia* 9 (1977): 1–156.
3. The literature is large and growing. See John Bodnar, *The Transplanted: The History of Immigrants in Urban America* (Bloomington: Indiana University Press, 1985); Roger Daniels, *Coming to America: A History of Immigration and Ethnicity in American Life* (New York: HarperCollins, 1990); Walter Nugent, *Crossings: The Great Transatlantic Migrations, 1870–1914* (Bloomington: Indiana University Press, 1992); Dudley Baines, *Emigration From Europe, 1815–1930* (Houndmills, Eng.: Macmillan Education Ltd, 1991); Philip A. M. Taylor, *The Distant Magnet: European Migration to the U.S.A.* (New York: Harper & Row, 1971); and Maldwyn Allen Jones, *American Migration* (Chicago: University of Chicago Press, 1960).
4. Kronborg et al., "Nordic Population Mobility," 105.
5. Brinley Thomas, *Migration and Economic Growth: A Study of Great Britain and the Atlantic Economy* (Cambridge: Cambridge University Press, 1954), 87.
6. John S. McDonald and Leatrice D. McDonald, "Chain Migration, Ethnic Neighborhood Formation, and Social Networks," *Milbank Memorial Fund Quarterly* 42 (1964): 82–97.
7. Runblom and Norman, *From Sweden to America*, 184–86.
8. Kronborg et al., "Nordic Population Mobility," 11; Norman, *From Sweden to America*, 31.
9. Kronborg et al., "Nordic Population Mobility," 114, 50.
10. Runblom and Norman, *From Sweden to America*, 117–19; Kristian Hvidt, *Flight to America: The Social Background of 300,000 Danish Emigrants* (New York: Academic Press, 1975), 162; Reine Kero, *Migration from Finland to North America in the Years Between the United States Civil War and the First World War* (Turku, 1974), 241; Walter D. Kamphoefner, *The Westfalians: From Germany to Missouri* (Princeton: Princeton University Press, 1987), 56.
11. Robert P. Swierenga and Harry S. Stout, "Dutch Immigration in the Nineteenth Century, 1820–1877: A Quantitative Overview," *Indiana Social Studies Quarterly* 28 (Autumn 1975): 25.

12. Yda Schreuder, *Dutch Catholic Immigrant Settlement in Wisconsin, 1850–1905* (New York: Garland, 1989), 81–92; Kamphoefner, *The Westfalians*, 70–105, 183–89; Runblom and Norman, *From Sweden to America*, 44–60; Robert C. Ostergren, *A Community Transplanted: The Trans-Atlantic Experience of a Swedish Immigrant Settlement in the Upper Middle West, 1835–1915* (Madison: University of Wisconsin Press, 1988), 134–37; Jon J. Gjerde, *From Peasants to Farmers: The Immigration from Balestrand, Norway to the Upper Middle West* (Cambridge: Cambridge University Press, 1985), 119–67; John G. Rice, *Patterns of Ethnicity in a Minnesota County, 1880–1905* (Department of Geography, University of Umea, Sweden, 1973), 41–48; Josef J. Barton, *Peasants and Strangers: Italians, Rumanians, and Slovaks in an American City, 1890–1950* (Cambridge: Harvard University Press, 1975), 48–63.

PART I

IMMIGRATION PATTERNS

CHAPTER 1

Old Country Environment

THE END OF the Napoleonic wars in 1815, coupled with the rise of free trade doctrines in place of mercantilism and the consolidation of the American nation following the second war with Great Britain, enabled Europeans to take possession of the North American frontier. Between the fall of Napoleon and the outbreak of the First World War in 1914, thirty-five million Europeans streamed across the Atlantic and spread over the vast American landscape. The new transportation and communication systems hastened the process by linking the entire Atlantic world through a network of roads, canals, railways, steamships, and telegraph wires. This made the journey cheaper, safer, and less final.

American economic opportunities, along with social and political freedoms, had a magnetic attraction for Europeans struggling to maintain their standard of living in the face of population pressures and major economic changes. Those with the inclination and means to leave, and the opportunity to do so, joined the exodus. Many others wished to leave, but lacked funds or the necessary information. Having reliable facts about the destination was critical because it reduced uncertainty. The lack of information was more of a hindrance than the lack of money.

Dutch overseas migration during the nineteenth century was not as intense as elsewhere in Europe.[1] Except in a few villages, the Dutch never contracted "American-fever" in the great century of European emigration. No general mass movement emptied a third to a half of the countryside, as happened in Ireland.[2] The "distant magnet" of North America had a limited attraction for Netherlanders. Only 273,000 Dutch emigrated overseas in the one hundred years from 1820 to 1920, and more than a third departed after 1900 (Table 1.1). The national population, on the other hand, increased more than threefold, from 2.0 million in 1815 to 6.9 million in 1920. Dutch labor, as one scholar remarked, "showed little inclination toward long and adventurous voyages."[3]

Among European nations, the Netherlands ranked only tenth in the proportion of their population that emigrated overseas in the nineteenth century, and in the United States the Dutch were seventeenth among foreign-born groups.[4] The migration flow from 1820 to 1920 averaged a moderate 72 per 100,000 population

Table 1.1 Annual Overseas Emigration per 100,000 Netherlands Population, 1820–1920

	Population Dec. 31 (1000s)	Emigration	Rate per 100,000
1820-29	2,424	39 *	2
1830-39	2,737	96 *	4
1840	2,894	107	4
1841	2,931	103	4
1842	2,957	127	4
1843	2,989	296	10
1844	3,020	321	11
1845	3,053	874	29
1846	3,061	2,831	92
1847	3,050	8,090	265
1848	3,055	3,103	102
1849	3,057	3,143	103
1850	3,031	1,299	43
1851	3,080	1,771	57
1852	3,128	1,951	62
1853	3,163	2,653	84
1854	3,195	5,074	159
1855	3,216	3,087	96
1856	3,252	3,050	94
1857	3,282	2,844	87
1858	3,303	1,363	41
1859	3,309	713	22
1860	3,336	1,163	35
1861	3,373	863	26
1862	3,410	931	27
1863	3,453	1,333	39
1864	3,492	1,036	30
1865	3,529	1,814	51
1866	3,553	3,727	105
1867	3,592	4,923	137
1868	3,628	3,520	97
1869	3,580	4,018	112
1870	3,618	2,288	63
1871	3,637	2,520	69
1872	3,675	4,447	121
1873	3,716	5,576	150
1874	3,767	1,719	46
1875	3,810	1,245	33
1876	3,865	875	23
1877	3,925	603	15
1878	3,982	832	21
1879	4,013	1,553	39
1880	4,061	4,670	116
1880	4,061	4,670	116
1881	4,114	7,462	181

TABLE 1.1 *(Continued)*

	POPULATION DEC. 31 (1000s)	EMIGRATION	RATE PER 100,000
1882	4,173	5,975	143
1883	4,225	3,433	81
1884	4,278	2,611	61
1885	4,336	1,782	41
1886	4,391	1,758	40
1887	4,451	4,214	95
1888	4,506	4,461	99
1889	4,511	7,495	166
1890	4,565	3,143	69
1891	4,622	3,825	83
1892	4,670	5,934	127
1893	4,733	5,724	121
1894	4,796	1,357	28
1895	4,859	1,457	30
1896	4,929	2,299	47
1897	5,004	1,543	31
1898	5,075	1,175	23
1899	5,104	1,472	29
1900	5,179	1,548	30
1901	5,263	2,886	55
1902	5,347	3,603	67
1903	5,431	5,296	98
1904	5,510	4,030	73
1905	5,591	3,927	70
1906	5,672	4,958	87
1907	5,747	7,221	126
1908	5,825	4,580	80
1909	5,858	6,769	116
1910	5,945	7,136	120
1911	6,022	7,752	129
1912	6,114	7,774	127
1913	6,213	8,503	137
1914	6,340	6,275	99
1915	6,450	4,131	64
1916	6,583	3,905	59
1917	6,725	1,983	29
1918	6,779	2,182	32
1919	6,831	5,574	82
1920	6,926	11,924	172
TOTALS: 1820–1920	380,104	272,882	72

° Decadal average, U.S. immigrants only: 1820–29=387, 1830–39=958

SOURCE: Emigration totals, 1830–80, are derived from the author's analysis of the landverhuizers records and U.S. ship lists (see chapter 12). Emigration data, 1881-1920, are in *Bijdragen tot de Statistiek van Nederland*, and in *Bijdragen . . . (Nieuw Volgreeks)*. Central Bureau for Statistics, The Hague. Population data are from the *Jaarboekje over . . . 1841–1864, and Bijdragen tot de Statistiek over . . . 1865–1920.*

(Table 1.1), which is indeed low compared to the Irish, English, Scandinavian, German, and Italian immigration. Dutch emigration thus compares with middle-range nations in Europe such as Denmark, Switzerland, France, and Wales.

The causes of the Dutch transatlantic migration are complex and derive from underlying structural problems and specific historical events in the homeland. Economic, social, political and religious forces all contributed in varying degrees to the transplanting. Given the interrelatedness of the Atlantic world, the prospects of land, jobs, and freedom in the United States also enticed the Dutch.

The moderate degree of Dutch emigration indicates that rational choice and pragmatic preference, rather than dire want, led most Dutch to depart. Few Dutch emigrants were driven by a desperate struggle to survive. Most made a conscious calculation that a future in America, where farming or urban jobs awaited them among family and friends, promised more prosperity for them and their children than if they remained in their homeland. Religious and cultural motives were secondary, except among the thousands of Seceders in the 1840s, whose influence should not be minimized. Nor did a failed revolution or political libertarian ideals impel the Dutch to America, as with the German "Forty-Eighters."

The Dutch diaspora was a scattering, a dispersal, of workers at the margins of the economy and religious outsiders who possessed a restless energy and drive to succeed. Mixed among them were the "rolling stones," social misfits, and adventurers that can be found in any mass movement. Hope was the dominant note among the movers who fled the cramped, regimented, and status-bound Dutch society for religious freedom, land for farming, and a modicum of social equality offered in America.

United Netherlands

The Dutch people suffered a series of setbacks between 1800 and 1850 that set the stage for an outward movement.[5] The first blow struck when Napoleon conquered the Netherlands and attempted to rationalize the stagnant, antiquated Dutch economy and integrate it into the larger and more advanced French-Belgian system. Napoleonic bureaucrats fanned out across the Netherlands, compiling the first modern population census (1813) by tabulating civil, demographic, and economic statistics from municipality (*gemeente*) records, and interfering in religious and family life. Government controllers even required each family to adopt a surname that was officially recorded.

Dutch Jews particularly resisted the French-style bureaucracy and its threat to the traditional rabbinic control of the community. Many refused to assume surnames—a Christian custom—and avoided military conscription and new taxes by emigrating to London and to New York, Philadelphia, Baltimore, and other American centers.[6]

Following Napoleon's defeat and two decades of war and blockade, the European powers at the Congress of Vienna in 1815 restored the Dutch monarchy and created the United Netherlands by joining Belgium to Holland, the intent being to form a buffer against French aggression. This ill-fated union required of the Dutch major economic and political adjustments. Belgium was to be the industrial base, Holland the commercial and agricultural power. The Dutch tried to regain lost trading partners and build colonial markets, but the merchant capitalists faced stiff competition from Great Britain's growing industrial might. Belgium coped with the new order better than Holland. Its economy became industrial-oriented, while the Dutch economy remained traditional. The Belgians utilized their coal and iron ore resources, their underemployed rural labor force, and the newly enlarged consumer market of the northern provinces in order to develop textile and metals industries. By 1850 Belgium was one of the most industrialized nations of Europe, whereas the Netherlands, in sharp contrast, suffered from economic stagnation and even decline.

The hybrid nation of the United Netherlands lasted only fifteen years, until 1830 when the Catholic and largely French-speaking Belgians successfully revolted against predominantly Protestant Holland. The North resisted the secession with armed force for nine years until a British trade embargo and the costs of the conflict led the government to the brink of bankruptcy. The European powers in 1839 sanctioned the break up of the United Provinces, leaving the Dutch with little to show for a decade of fighting except high tax burdens and a general feeling of disillusionment and bitterness. They also lost their industrial hinterland, because Belgium readily found new trading partners.

The Belgian debacle, added to other internal problems, so strained the royal house of Orange that in 1840 the aristocratic and strong-willed King Willem I, who headed the restored Dutch monarchy after 1813, abdicated the throne. This caused a constitutional crisis that eventually resulted in Parliament creating a liberal, democratic constitution with the Orangists as titular monarchs. But this transition did not occur before Willem had instigated a massive revolt against the national Reformed Church by his heavy-handed suppression of evangelical reformers in the church.

Religious Developments

Religious protest instigated Dutch emigration and shaped American resettlement for decades.[7] From the beginning of the modern Dutch state in 1648, when the Calvinists triumphed in the Eighty Years War with Spain, the religious geography was fixed. The Protestant majority lived in the central and northern regions (the Seven Provinces) and the Roman Catholic minority controlled the southern two provinces. The long and bitter Calvinist struggle against the Spanish Crown and the hated Inquisition generated such anti-Catholic bigotry that when the Calvinists gained political control they established a national church—the Nederlands Hervormde Kerk—and abolished all Catholic parishes including those in the southern provinces of Noord-Brabant and Limburg.

For nearly 150 years Catholicism was suppressed, until Napoleon conquered Holland and under the Batavian Republic (1795–1813) restored to Catholics a semblance of religious liberty and the ownership of their church property. But it was a short-lived reprieve. In 1816 Willem I centralized control over all religious institutions. Catholics as well as dissenting Protestant groups again lost their local autonomy in church affairs. The aristocratic monarch refused to reinstate the Catholic hierarchy and even banned Catholic parochial schools. Only during the 1820s did Willem liberalize his Catholic policies in an attempt to assuage the Catholic populace of the former Belgian provinces.[8]

But after Belgian independence in 1839 the political constraints were removed and Willem dealt harshly with his Catholic subjects. During the secession struggles of the 1830s, Willem's Catholic subjects had faced a dilemma—to join their Belgian fellow-believers with whom they had historic cultural and religious ties, or to remain with the Protestant North and retain their economic advantages, especially Brabant's benefits from the Dutch colonial trade with the East Indies. Ultimately, the economic interests prevailed, but the Dutch Catholics' ambivalent attitude toward the Belgian Secession made them suspect for generations to the Protestant majority who accordingly treated them as second-class citizens.[9]

An ultra-Calvinist minority in the North were discriminated against even more than the Catholics. These were a largely rural people of pietist tendencies led by a few university professors and their students, who in 1834–35 separated themselves from the Hervormde Kerk over issues of theological liberalism and church polity.[10] The confessional revolt spread quickly throughout the countryside among conservatives who believed that the leaders of the national church were indifferent to historic Reformed orthodoxy and condoned "worldly" conduct among their members. The Seceders also rejected Willem I's structural reorganization of the national church in 1816, which had abolished the historic localistic form of church government and replaced it with a centralized structure in which the monarch appointed all key officials. Within a decade the Seceders numbered over 40,000 adherents throughout the Protestant Netherlands. The movement particularly appealed to the blue-collar workers (small farmers, day laborers, and artisans) in the more isolated, tradition-oriented regions in the North and the Rhine delta.

Dutch authorities, with general public support, moved strongly to suppress the Seceder movement by levying stiff fines on dissenting clerics and unauthorized worship services, which were held in member's homes and barns or at secluded places out in the open. By Dutch law, "secret" (i.e., unauthorized) meetings of more than twenty people were illegal, and if discovered, local authorities disrupted the services and arrested the clerics and lay leaders. Some employers even refused to hire Seceders and customers boycotted Seceder craftsmen and petty merchants. The official persecution ended in 1841, when the more moderate King Willem II (1840–49) came to the throne, but the Seceders suffered from discrimination, social ostracism, and exclusion from community organizations for many decades. In the words of Albertus Pieters: "More than any other element of the population, the members of the separated churches suffered from these conditions [i.e., severe poverty], since they were mostly from the poorer classes, and since the general contempt in which they were held hindered them in securing employment and in every form of enterprise."[11]

That dissenters would be so heavily represented among the early emigrants is understandable, because ardent religious beliefs helped counteract the natural psychological barriers to leaving one's homeland forever. The Dutch Seceders had their counterparts in other countries, who also emigrated because of persecution, such as the German Stundenleute, Norwegian Haugeans, Swedish Janssonists and Old Lutherans, and Mormons from England and Scandinavia.[12]

Such harassment created an emigration mentality. When the potato blight struck in the mid-1840s, Seceder leaders organized colonization societies to bring their congregations to North America. Emigration meant immediate and total emancipation, as well as escape from a sinful nation that was obviously suffering under the judgment of God. The "Groote Trek" was led by a half-dozen Seceder clergymen, notably Albertus C. Van Raalte and Hendrik P. Scholte, who in 1846 and 1847 founded new colonies for hundreds of their followers in Holland, Michigan and Pella, Iowa, respectively. Other thousands of Seceders soon followed.

In the years 1846 through 1850, eighty of every one thousand Separatists departed the Fatherland compared to only four per thousand among Hervormde Kerk adherents.[13] Indeed, one half of all Seceders from 1846 to 1880 departed in the initial decade 1846–57. In some areas, such as the island of Goeree-Overflakkee in the province of Zuid Holland, and the Winterswijk region of eastern Gelderland Province, whole villages were depopulated in a short time.[14] At the provincial level, half of all emigrants from Drenthe were Seceders, as were a third from Groningen and Overijssel and a fifth from Friesland.

The large Seceder migration in the 1840s is readily understandable. The Dutch press and periodicals publicized the unusual mass exodus of congregations, which stimulated others to follow. Although the secession of 1834 was a type of underground movement that split communities, it also transcended local boundaries through the activity of itinerant Seceder preachers. Seceders were intrinsically mobile, as a result of broken familial and social relationships and economic repression. When national economic distress reached its high point in the mid-1840s, those already dislocated people chose overseas emigration.[15]

In terms of official government policy, after 1840 Dutch Catholics as well as dissenting Protestants were grudgingly given more freedoms. King Willem II was more tolerant toward religious minorities, especially Catholics, than his father had been. His government unshackled the Catholic press, allowed convents and monasteries to resume their activities, and permitted the construction of new church buildings. With the foundation of the constitutional monarchy under the new Constitution of 1848, these and all other religious and legal rights were guaranteed to all citizens, including the religious minorities.

The religious configuration in the Netherlands at this time, according to the 1849 national census of the population, showed that the dominant Hervormde Kerk included 55 percent, the Roman Catholics were a strong minority with 38 percent, the Seceders had a minuscule 1.3 percent, and other religious minorities (Jews, Mennonites, Lutherans, etc.) made up the remaining 6 percent. Almost no one admitted having no formal religious affiliation. During the remainder of the nineteenth century, the trend in religious membership was for Catholics to hold their own, and for the Hervormde Kerk to lose steadily its more orthodox members to the Seceders and its more secular members to the ranks of the unchurched. By 1909 the percentage of Catholics had declined slightly to 35 percent, but the Hervormden had dropped more than eleven points to 44 percent, whereas the orthodox Calvinists had grown nearly eightfold from 1.3 to 9.3 percent, and the unchurched went from none to 5 percent.[16]

The major Calvinist accession occurred in 1886 when Abraham Kuyper, a university professor, publicist, and political leader of the conservatives, convinced thousands of dissatisfied Hervormde Kerk members to withdraw from the increasingly heterodox national body. These 1886 Seceders, the so-called "*Doleantie*," joined in 1892 with the 1834 Seceders to form a new Reformed denomination,the Gereformeerde Kerk.[17] With this union, the 1834 Seceders gained respectability and a measure of relief from decades of social contempt and economic impediments.

It was more difficult for the Roman Catholics to achieve full acceptance. The new liberal Constitution of 1848 had not ended religious discrimination and conflict, as they had hoped. When King Willem III (1849–90) and his prime minister Johan Rudolf Thorbecke, the leader of the majority Liberal Party and author of the Constitution, restored the Dutch Catholic hierarchy in 1853, the action sparked such a strong backlash among orthodox Protestants (the "April Movement") that the Thorbecke ministry had to resign. Subsequent governments took the lesson to heart and refrained from making further concessions to the demands for Catholic "rights."[18] Under Guillaume Groen van Prinsterer, a staunch Calvinist and leader of the Anti-Revolutionary Party, the Dutch nation remained committed to its Protestant heritage.

The Protestant-Catholic religious divisions in Dutch society and the Calvinist secessions and Catholic emancipation movements had socioeconomic as well as theological-ecclesiastical roots. The Catholics and orthodox Calvinists lived in the "outer provinces" rather than in the urban centers. They were traditionalists who rejected modernization, and they ranked lower on the socioeconomic scale than the majority Protestants. The Catholic South for two centuries after winning freedom from Spain was politically powerless, heavily taxed, economically hampered, and culturally isolated.[19]

Roman Catholics in the mid-nineteenth century remained oriented to their family, church, and community. They had higher birth rates and larger families, were generally poorer and less educated, and had not been integrated into the modern sectors of the Dutch economy. The agrarian provinces of Limburg and Noord-Brabant were thus the most backward in the nation, populated in Ivo Schöffer's words with "poor cottagers on the land, poor laborers in the industrial centers of Tilburg and Maastricht."[20] Calvinist Seceders form a similar picture. They were concentrated in the northernmost province of Groningen and the isolated heath regions east of the Zuider Zee, and comprised small farmers, rural laborers, artisans, and petty shopkeepers who likewise clung to a local and traditional lifestyle.

The religious protests of the Calvinists and Catholics thus represented, in part, an attempt by the dispossessed to obtain a fairer share of the economic pie and a modicum of political power. The extension of the franchise from one in ten to one in two adult males in the half-century from 1848 to 1900 increased the voice of the lower and middle classes against the ruling liberal bourgeoisie.[21] Acquiring a political voice did not soften the blow in hard economic times, however. In the agricultural depressions of the forties and eighties, it was the orthodox Calvinists who emigrated to North America in numbers far in excess of their share of the population.

The Roman Catholics, on the other hand, emigrated in far fewer numbers than the size of their population in the Netherlands. Their clerical leaders actively discouraged emigration and sought to prevent it. Those who did leave went as singles, nuclear families, or small groups of families. The only Catholic region with a strong group emigration tradition was in northeastern Noord-Brabant, which was a center of Catholic religious life. It was precisely this core region, centered in the municipality of Uden, where Catholic overseas missionary activity in America was launched in the early nineteenth century. These same missionaries, notably Father Theodorus Vanden Broek, later recruited settlers for the Wisconsin frontier, beginning in 1848.[22]

Socioeconomic Developments, 1815–60

Despite the salience of religion in the emigration, socioeconomic rather than politico-religious problems were paramount in Holland.[23] The Napoleonic and Belgian wars left the Netherlands in a weakened state, suffering from high taxes, unemployment, and chronic pauperism. How could the Dutch rebuild their shattered economy? The glory of the golden age, when Dutch merchant traders dominated world markets, had long since faded away. The merchants were on the defensive, isolated and cut off from lucrative markets by new rivals. The Baltic to Mediterranean corn trade, once the exclusive domain of the Dutch, was now dominated by Odessa merchants. British merchants had gained supremacy in the East Indies with the dissolution of the East India Company. Even the once flourishing staple market in Holland had declined.[24]

Dutch merchants and government officials sought desperately to find new sources of income, particularly from the Dutch colonial trade. For the first time in many generations, the government took an active role as promoter of colonial enterprise, but the results were mixed at best. The Dutch economy remained agricultural and commercial.

Manufacturing industry contributed little to the Dutch economy before 1860. Industrial employment lagged behind those in neighboring countries of Belgium, France, and Germany. In 1900 only 32 percent of the Dutch workforce was employed in industry, compared to 44 percent for Great Britain, 42 percent for France, and 47 percent for Germany.[25] In 1849 less than a quarter of the Dutch labor force was employed in manufacturing, whereas nearly half worked in agriculture. Of the manufacturing jobs, only 40,000 out of a labor force of one million were in large concerns—textiles, brickworks, paper, pottery, piping, sugar refining, tobacco, and peat-digging.[26]

These large firms were scattered throughout the country, whereas the vast majority of small-scale industries were concentrated in the eastern and southern rural areas where the farm labor force could be utilized during the off-season. In these sandy-soil regions, plagued by poor arterial road networks, farmers were often forced into subsistence agriculture because national and international markets were inaccessible, unless water transport to port cities was available. Being largely cut off from a money economy, these inland farmers engaged in home industry to supplement their meager cash income from the sale of surplus farm products in nearby market towns.[27]

The products of the rural industries varied depending on raw materials. In flax areas, farm families produced linen textiles. Where there was water power and oak bark for tanning, the leather and shoe industry flourished. In other locales, woolens and cotton textiles were produced for regional and local markets. Thus, Dutch protoindustry played no part in the Atlantic economy, although an estimated 80 percent of the "industrial" labor force in 1859 was employed in small-scale industries located throughout the nation.[28]

Generally, the Dutch economy was stagnant in the middle decades of the nineteenth century. Only the agricultural sector prospered in the soil-rich western and northern coastal regions of specialized dairying and grain production. Great Britain with its growing urban, industrial population provided a strong market for Dutch produce, especially butter and cheese. With good reason was Holland at this time dubbed the "London suburb."[29] While the commercial farmers of the coastal regions benefited most from the British demand, even the more isolated, inland dairy farmers experienced some trickle-down prosperity.

In spite of expansion in commercial agriculture and small-scale rural industries, the modern industrial sector of the Dutch economy did not grow at a rate sufficient to absorb a growing rural population. There were few alternative sources of income for rural families except for home industries. The introduction of the potato into the food diet and use of commercial fertilizers in the sandy-soil regions allowed farmers to subsist on small plots of land, but soon even subdividing did not solve the population problem. Farmers' sons simply had to delay marriage or leave the community.

One contemporary observer, B. W. A. E. Sloet tot Oldhuis, writing in 1866 on the causes of Dutch emigration to the United States, listed several structural, long-term factors that propelled rural residents to depart.[30] Dutch farmers had large families and small farms, but government policy required that the farm be either subdivided equally among sons and daughters, or that one of the children buy the interest of the others and pay the state for the right of redistribution (*soulte*). If none could raise the capital for the estate settlement, the land was sold at auction to richer neighbors or outside land investors, except for the house parcel, and the unmarried members of the family became day laborers or servants, or they migrated to the cities, to neighboring countries, or overseas. Small renters were even worse off. Small farms could only be had on marginal land and leases were customarily renewable annually. If a renter was put off the land, the temptation was great to sell his equipment and possessions and migrate to America.[31]

The license system for craftsmen was another source of discontent, especially in rural areas where craftsmen had to be "jacks of all trades." For example, a village carpenter was forced to buy licenses for wagonmaker, wheelwright, chairmaker, cabinetmaker, footstool maker, and so forth, because villagers brought all their repair work to his shop. In the cities, labor specialization largely obviated this problem. Both officialdom and general taxes were also onerous to the Dutch. They paid for a large standing army, polder and dike levies, poor taxes, real estate and personalty taxes, and compulsory church tithes, in addition to general municipal and national taxes.[32] The revenue supported an army of officials and excisemen, even including gamekeepers who prevented free hunting and fishing on public lands. "There is a continuing, never-ending fight to avoid taxes, on the one hand, and their ever increasing magnitude on the other hand," said Sloet. "With a short sea journey not only could he escape the payment of taxes but also the tax collector, that peace disturbing demon that lives in European society."[33] The tax and licensing systems, according to Sloet, were the result of the rigid, outmoded traditionalism of Dutch society that made America appear, by contrast, as a land of economic freedom, social equality, and political democracy. Virgin land, high wages, low taxes, and individualism were advantages not available in the Old Country.

The Netherlands had a rapid rise in population in the first half of the nineteenth century, especially after 1815.[34] The Dutch population grew from 2 million in 1795 to 3 million in 1850, an increase of 50 percent (Table 1.2). This growth rate was similar to that of Belgium and the Scandinavian countries (Figure 1.1). The growth rate fluctuated with political and economic conditions; and it also varied in the

TABLE 1.2 Population Growth and Density by Dutch Province, 1795–1899

	POPULATION			PERCENTAGE INCREASE		AREA MILE²	POPULATION DENSITY PER MILE²
	1795	1849	1899	1795–1849	1849–1899	1849	1849
DR	40	83	149	109	80	48	1,720
FR	162	247	340	53	38	60	4,146
GE	223	371	567	66	53	94	4,009
GR	115	188	300	64	59	43	4,427
LI	138	205	282	49	37	40	5,111
NB	260	396	554	52	40	93	4,260
NH	408	477	968	17	103	45	10,486
OV	135	216	333	59	54	61	3,514
UT	97	149	351	54	135	25	5,971
ZE	115	160	216	40	35	30	5,300
ZH	386	563	1,144	46	103	55	10,165
TOTALS	2,079	3,057	5,103	47	67	590	5,335

SOURCES: For 1795 census: J. C. Ramaer, *Geschiedkundige Atlas voor Nederland: Het Koninkrijk der Nederlanden (1815–1931)* (The Hague: Martinus Nijhoff, 1931); *Bijdragen tot de Algemene Statistiek van Nederland, 1878, Aflevering 1* (The Hague, 1880); *Statistiek van den loop der bevolking van Nederland over 1899*, 56; H. A. Wijnne, "Statistiek Studiën," *Jaarboekje over 1856*, 273 (for land area).

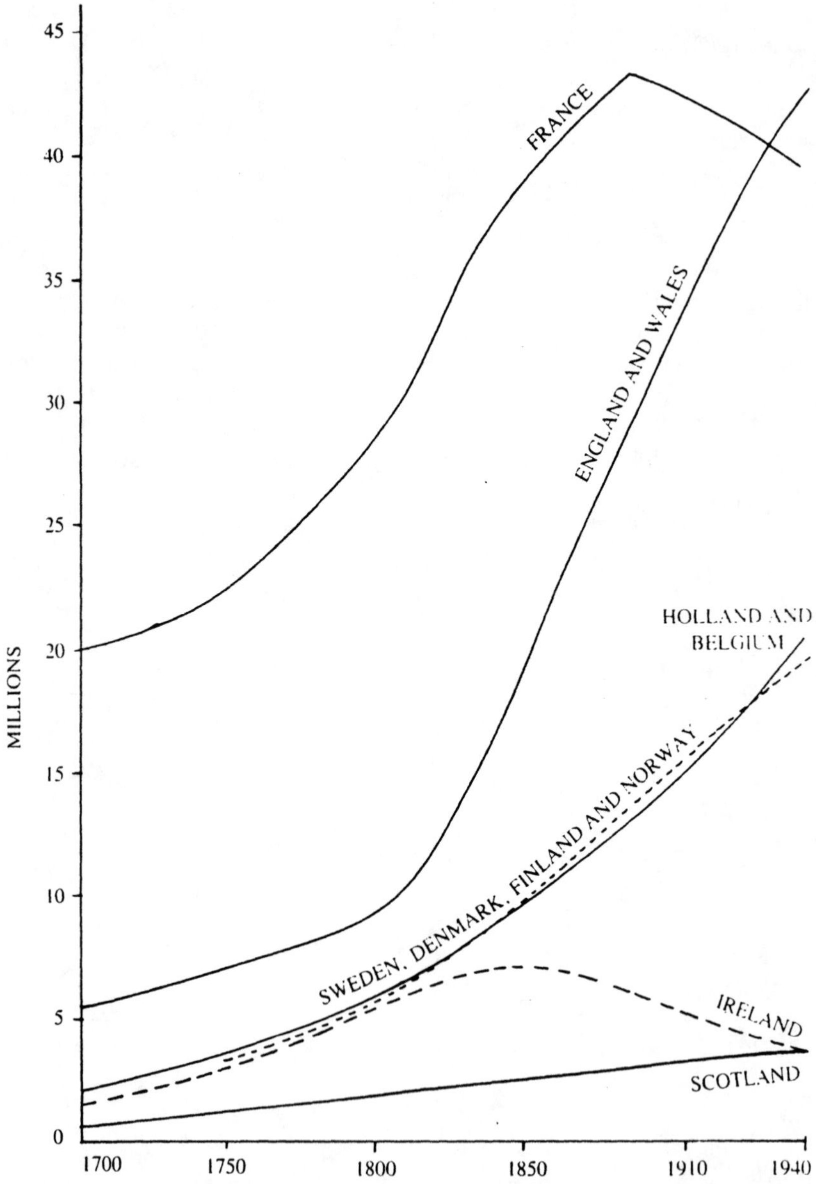

Figure 1.1 Growth of Population, Western European Countries, 1700–1940

SOURCE: N. L. Trantner, *Population Since the Industrial Revolution: The Case of England and Wales* (New York: Barnes & Noble, 1973): 45.

different regions. During the Napoleonic wars the annual rate of population growth was only 4 percent. This figure tripled in the prosperous postwar years, only to decline in the 1830s and 1840s, under the impact of the military mobilization against Belgium, cholera epidemics in 1831 and 1849, and the harvest failure of 1845–47.

In the face of land pressures, commercial farmers hired hands on a cash basis rather than offer yearly contracts. In the new entrepreneurial relationship, the farmer's sense of social responsibility for workers was reduced and laborers became a rural proletariat. The laborers, who had formerly been members of the farmer's family group, became strangers to be hired as needed during peak seasons of planting and harvesting. The workers thus became especially vulnerable to the periodic food crises.

Potato Crisis

The high population growth of the early nineteenth century created severe structural problems in a land scarce nation that had little industrial expansion to absorb the surplus population. The Dutch peasantry were thus in a precarious situation throughout the nineteenth century, subject to crop failures, as in the 1840s, or major market and production dislocations, as in the 1880s and 1890s. Dutch agriculture was determined by the soil (Figure 1.2). The sea (marine) and river-clay regions were fertile, prosperous, and integrated into world markets. But inland sandy soils were relatively infertile before commercial fertilizers came in after 1880, and subsistence farming was the norm. Crop yields in the east were barely half that on the coastal clays, and labor productivity and wages were equally depressed. In the 1820s and 1830s agriculture generally languished, and then the potato blight of 1845–47 undermined the slight improvement earlier in the decade.[35] The failure of the potato crop especially hurt subsistence farmers, rural laborers, and artisans. It brought sharp food price increases and hunger riots and led parts of the countryside to the brink of famine.[36]

As elsewhere in Europe since the late eighteenth century, Dutch working-class families subsisted on potatoes, sometimes eating three potato meals a day. The potato replaced rye as the cheapest food available, and in the agriculturally stagnant years of 1815 to 1850, potato consumption increased rapidly even among the middle classes. The Dutch were second only to Ireland in per capita potato consumption. Potatoes for table use were the major crop in many of the fertile clay-soil regions, although coarse factory and fodder varieties were grown in the higher sandy soils as well. In the northern province of Friesland, for example, potato acreage exceeded that of rye in 1844. Since farm laborers only earned about two guilders a week, many rural families rented a small potato plot to supply their food needs. But demand was so strong that they had to pay a premium of several times the average rent. Potatoes were a dependable crop, and prices remained low and very stable for a half century.

The fungus blight first struck in 1845 and wiped out three quarters of the crop

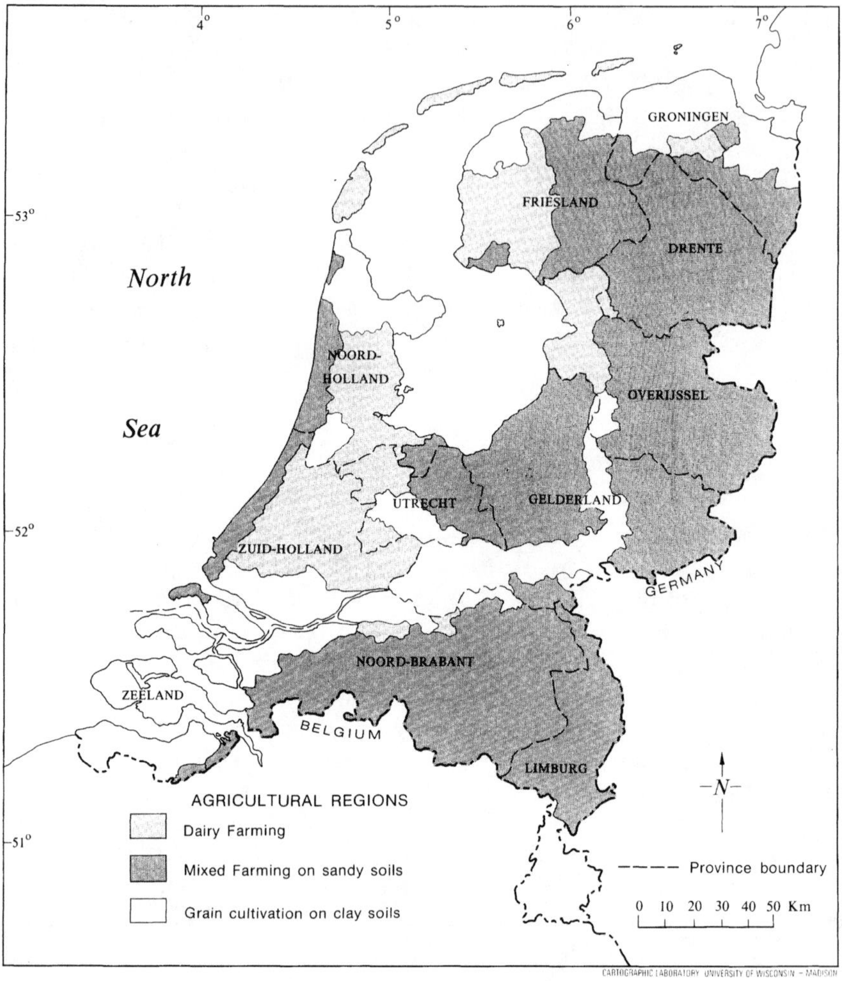

Figure 1.2 Provinces and Agricultural Regions of the Netherlands, 1871
SOURCE: Yda Schreuder, Cartographic Laboratory, University of Wisconsin, Madison.

(Table 1.3). The next year, two-thirds of the crop was destroyed; those harvested were mainly the small early potatoes. Thus, the Dutch situation differed from Ireland, where only half the 1845 crop was lost, but the entire 1846 crop failed. In the Netherlands, the 1846 crop improved slightly, especially in the factory potatoes grown in the inland sandy areas. But in the richest clay-soil regions of Friesland, Groningen, Zuid-Holland, and Zeeland, the yield of edible potatoes was very meager. In addition, rye, the favorite grain of the working classes, was infected with rust in 1846 and the yield was nearly halved. The winter of 1846–47 was also one of the longest and most severe of the decade. Nor could food be imported, because food stocks throughout Western Europe were low after the crop failures of 1845.

The immediate result of the food shortages was a sharp increase in prices and a shift in dietary habits. Potato prices rose two and a half times, even surpassing

TABLE 1.3 Potato Production, The Netherlands, 1842–60 (in thousands of hectoliters)*

YEAR	HECTARES	YEAR	HECTARES
1842	17,140	1851	10,283
1843	17,850	1852	8,527
1844	18,800	1853	7,570
1845	4,450	1854	10,630
1846	5,818	1855	9,912
1847	9,836	1856	13,498
1848	8,217	1857	12,979
1849	11,492	1858	16,979
1850	9,651	1859	11,557
		1860	12,472

* 1 hl (100 mudden)=2.64 Imperial bushels.
SOURCE: B. R. Mitchell, *European Historical Statistics, 1750–1970* (New York: Columbia University Press, 1975), 247; M. Bergman, "Potato Blight," 394.

rye, which doubled in price. Rye once again served as the most popular lower-class food, and potatoes became a delicacy for the upper classes. The longer-range consequences of the crisis were social dislocations and rural protests in market towns, increased pauperism and pillaging in the countryside, and sharply higher national death rates and lower marriage and birth rates.[37]

The number of persons on government poor relief doubled and tripled. In the Zuid-Holland island of Goeree-Overflakkee, which experienced mass emigration to America, over 40 percent of the 21,000 inhabitants received government aid in 1845. In other rural areas, the figures were even higher. National government officials tried to ignore the crisis or downplay its severity, but in 1847 the country had reached such a state of emergency that the government proclaimed by royal decree a day of prayer "for a beginning of deliverance from deep suffering."

The agricultural crisis of 1845–47 affected various social groups and regions differently. To some extent, the crisis shifted resources from consumers to producers, especially large farmers. These commercial farmers were able to cope by switching to grain crops, which brought higher prices because of the scarcity. Export opportunities for dairy and grain farmers also improved during these years. But the potato disease severely hurt marginal farmers, day laborers, and rural artisans, who depended on potatoes for their own food and for a cash income from the sale of surpluses on local markets. Thus, while the commercial farmers prospered, the rest of the rural folk suffered.

The potato disease hit hardest in the clay-soil areas, where the farm laborers had been cut adrift by their employers and where population growth was high (Figure 1.2). Farmers with sufficient capital shifted from potatoes to grains, and potato cultivation moved to the inland sandy-soil regions. For example, between 1845 and 1852 potato growing in Friesland decreased from 12,000 to 7,000 hectares (one hectare equals 2.47 acres), whereas in the sandy-soil province of Noord-Brabant, it increased from 13,000 to 17,000 hectares. Without potato plots, rural laborers in the clay provinces lost their ability to survive without the government dole. Small farmers, laborers, and craftsmen in the inland regions also experienced widespread poverty, but the crisis was less acute there because agriculture was more diversified and less market-oriented. Home industries also provided supplemental income.

Recent studies in Scandinavia and the Netherlands have shown that sudden stressful situations like crop failures and religious persecutions can instigate mass emigration, especially when underlying structural factors have already created an emigration mentality.[38] There are strong indications that the Dutch agricultural crisis of the mid-forties spurred emigration, although the religious-political situation and flight of the Seceders were also significant. In any case the clay-soil areas that specialized in potato growing were precisely the regions that experienced the heaviest overseas emigration of farm laborers and rural artisans.

Agricultural Golden Age, 1850–80

It is undisputed that the agricultural crisis of the forties is highly related to region-specific overseas emigration, notably from the rich clay-soil regions. But general economic insecurity, rather than the immediate distress of food shortages, had a greater impact. Ever since the seventeenth century, the Dutch had enjoyed greater prosperity than all of their neighbors except England. Despite a sharp decline in their relative position in the first half of the nineteenth century, the Dutch at mid-century were one of the richest counties in Europe after the United Kingdom, as measured by per capita income statistics. Not until 1860 did Holland lose its second rank to Belgium and Switzerland.[39]

Thus, it was a feeling of relative deprivation and the prospect of lowered expectations and a declining living standard, rather than the actual fact of poverty and suffering, that prompted many to consider the alternative of emigrating to the United States. Other rural laborers responded to changes in agricultural patterns and mechanized farming by seeking alternative opportunities in the growing industrial sectors of the economy, where wages remained relatively higher than elsewhere in Europe.[40] Between 1860 and 1890 the Netherlands economy developed the preconditions for "take-off," which belatedly occurred after 1890. This greatly improved the food, housing, and social conditions for the working classes and reduced the propensity to emigrate.

Rural living conditions rose markedly in the agricultural golden age after 1860 until the next agricultural crisis in the 1880s. The rise in living standards resulted from changes in government trade, tariff, and tax policies. Government policies extracted more wealth from the Dutch colonies to create capital for building roads, canals, railroads, and other public works. These "social overhead" investments, in turn, served to integrate the Dutch economy on a national and even international scale. Rising colonial income also enabled the Dutch government to reduce the heavy tax burden on basic consumer goods and services that had been necessitated by the Belgian conflict of the 1830s.

Subsequently, the Dutch government gradually modified the tax and tariff laws. They substituted more equitable income taxes for the regressive excise taxes on goods and services, which eliminated one of the major sources of discontent and emigration talk. Additionally, Thorbecke's liberal government followed the general European trend toward free trade, which Great Britain had initiated with the repeal of the Corn Laws in 1846. Germany likewise lifted many of the transport restrictions on the Rhine River trade. Thorbecke abolished a whole series of trade restrictions with Britain and Germany. Sitting astride the crossroads of Europe, the Netherlands benefited greatly from the new unrestricted trade environment and the Dutch economy prospered.

Dutch commercial farmers profited directly from Great Britain's lifting of import restrictions in 1846. Farmers connected by roads and waterways to North Sea ports dramatically increased their beef and dairy exports to the British Isles. England in 1850 absorbed over 90 percent of Dutch butter exports and 55 percent of its cheese.[41] In some areas, such as Noord-Brabant, farmers shifted from grain and potato cultivation to dairying in the 1860s and 1870s. Cattle traders and butter and cheese merchants earned handsome profits from the new production, and some of the prosperity even trickled down to small-scale farmers and village artisans and shopkeepers. Only the poorest subsistence farmers, who barely raised enough to feed their own families, failed to benefit from the new market conditions.

The agricultural improvement was soon reflected in rising land prices and rents, which more than doubled in the years from 1850 to 1870. Land prices rose most markedly in the more commercially-oriented coastal regions of Groningen, Friesland, Noord- and Zuid-Holland, and Zeeland. Agricultural prosperity was clearly greater in the clay soils than in the sandy inland regions where the rural populace continued to rely on supplement income from cottage industries (Figure 1.1).

Dutch Industrial Development, 1850–80

While agricultural prosperity fueled Dutch economic life until the 1880s, industrial expansion was slight.[42] Dutch industry was of the small-scale, handicraft type, located primarily in inland regions and tied to home manufacturing and seasonal labor markets. It supplied local markets in metals, sugar refining, textiles, and papermaking. The small size of the country and the numerous waterways and brick-paved roads also encouraged factories to be set up in the countryside where taxes and wages were lower than in the towns. As Petersen noted: "With this scattering of manufacturing, the country's rural character persisted even after Holland was becoming, according to its labor-force statistics, an industrial nation."[43]

The Dutch industrial sector at mid-century remained starved of capital. Frugal Dutch businessmen, who had accumulated vast capital resources during the heyday of the East Indies trade in the seventeenth century, invested their wealth in Dutch government bonds and foreign enterprises such as American railroads, rather than in local industry. A leading Dutch economic historian has estimated that in 1880 Dutch capitalists sent one-third of national wealth abroad. As a result, new capital for domestic industrial growth did not exceed 10 percent consistently until after 1900.[44]

The high wages of Dutch laborers, which were the highest in all of Europe in the nineteenth century, also retarded the rate of capital accumulation in the modern protoindustrial sector. The high wages were the result of the generous Dutch welfare system that put a floor under wages, a high tax policy, and high agricultural productivity. Thus, the high wage level, Joel Mokyr argues, "was an invisible hand leading the Dutch away from an industrialization not in their [perceived] interest."[45]

Given the inhibiting economic and institutional factors, the Dutch national economy modernized very slowly. The best indicators of change in the period 1850–1914 are the emergence of an integrated transport system to link the major cities by rail and canal, and the shift in the productive labor force among the various branches of industry. The linkage of the large peripheral cities with the Randstad sparked a growing division of labor. The most expansive sectors were metals, chemicals, and public utilities (gas, electric, and waterworks). Foodstuff production increased over three times, due largely to luxury items—cigars, refined sugar, cocoa, butter, and margarine. Consumer industries, such as cabinetmaking, home appliances, and paper and printing, also employed more labor. But the textile and clothing industries, including shoes and leather, suffered greatly from foreign competition and from the replacement of domestic hand industries by factory production.[46]

This competition from foreign imports and the rising urban-based manufacturing of textiles after 1870 threatened the very existence of a rural population dependent on handicraft and home industries. Indeed, the coincidence of the agricultural crisis and the decline in handicrafts in the 1880s and 1890s explains the increasing emigration from the rural Netherlands in those decades.

This general review of economic conditions in the third quarter of the nineteenth century indicates that the second era of heavy Dutch overseas emigration in the period 1865–73 was not caused by "push" factors, as in the first phase before the world economic depression of 1857. Economic conditions in the rural areas had improved after 1850 and oppressive taxes and regulations were lessened. Rather, the second phase emigration was prompted largely by "pull" factors in North America. With the end of the Civil War, the United States economy entered a period of rapid expansion. The Homestead Law of 1862 and the laying of the transcontinental railroads after 1865 opened the "farmers' last frontier" to commercial agriculture.

The land-hungry Dutch wished to be a part of that conquest, and none more so than those with family and friends already settled in the States. Many hastened to follow in a typical chain migration, having been prompted and assisted by relatives. Most of the emigrants in the second wave hailed from the same villages and farming regions as in the forties. Their numbers, as we will explain later, actually exceeded the antebellum group, even though the emigration declined from the most urban provinces of Noord- and Zuid-Holland and Utrecht. For day laborers, American factory jobs were attractive. Labor was scarce and well-paid in the United States, and the social status of workers was much higher than in Europe. Dutch blue-collar workers were understandably attracted by the promise of American life in contrast to the less sanguine prospects at home.

Agricultural Crisis of the 1880s and 1890s

In the last decades of the nineteenth century the Dutch economy experienced dramatic and significant changes that created another emigration wave of massive proportions and fundamentally altered the country's economic and social structures. Two interlocking developments caused the changes—the most severe agricultural depression of the century and a shift in industrial production from rural cottage industries to medium- and large-scale factory production.[47]

Both developments were the result of economic modernization in Western Europe and in the Atlantic trading world. Germany, a nation unified in 1870, for example, entered its age of iron and steel under Otto von Bismarck. As a result, the Dutch increased their Rhine trade with the German hinterland via Rotterdam at the expense of the cross-Channel foodstuffs trade with England. The Dutch economy became even more closely tied to the broader Atlantic economy with the introduction of cargo steamships, the transatlantic telegraph, and the rise of an international grain market. The new technologies and grain marketing patterns affected Dutch farmers as adversely as American farmers in the Great Plains, who joined the Populist protest movement in the 1890s.

The agricultural crisis began in 1878 when wheat prices plummeted in the face of large European imports of cheap North American and Argentinean wheat. Between 1878 and 1896, wheat prices in the Netherlands dropped by half. As farmers switched from wheat to other cash crops, such as potatoes and sugarbeets, prices of these crops also declined. Farmland values skidded to record lows by 1900. In the commercial grain belt of the coastal areas of Groningen and Friesland, the impact was most severe.[48] Grain farmers pared costs by laying off farm laborers and hired hands, and many were forced into bankruptcy. In the inland regions the diversified small family farmers with their pigs and poultry were less affected by the grain glut. Dairymen and beef producers even prospered because prices for meats and dairy products, butter and cheese in particular, actually increased in these years, despite rising competition in the export market from Denmark and France and the threat to butter from the new margarine.[49]

Dutch farmers attempted to cope in various ways with the new international grain marketing system. They increased output by the use of chemical fertilizers, and they turned to new processing and marketing methods, such as farmers' cooperatives in dairy, potatoes, sugarbeets, and even cardboard (from grain straw). Amsterdam became the sugar-refining capital of Europe. But adjustments came slowly. In 1895, for example, factories produced only 27 percent of the total Dutch butter output. Eventually, however, the new agricultural strategies restored a modicum of prosperity to the northern provinces. But not before thousands of excess farm laborers had moved to the cities or emigrated overseas.

Netherlands Economic "Take-off," 1880–1910

Dutch industry entered a period of rapid growth and modernization in the last decades of the nineteenth century. Despite the major agricultural depression, industrial growth in the Randstad was actually stronger than in previous decades. Processing of colonial staples—tobacco, sugar, cocoa, coffee, and rice—expanded in the vicinity of Amsterdam and provided new jobs. Similarly, in the Rotterdam region, the increase in Rhine shipping stimulated the shipbuilding and metalworking industries. The belated introduction of steam engines in manufacturing after 1870 also enabled the Dutch to compete with England and Germany. Mechanization, in fact, was most advanced in the "new" agricultural processing industries: beer, tobacco, cotton textiles, and metals. But as late as 1889, over 75 percent of the total industrial workforce was still employed in small industries (ten or less employees) in the traditional rural protoindustries—textiles, woolens, shoemaking, and clothing.

After 1890, however, industrial production changed rapidly as the Dutch economy underwent "take-off." The machine-building and electro-technical industries expanded sharply, as did chemicals, shipbuilding, and factory-produced foodstuffs (dairy). Small-scale handicraft industries thus declined and large manufacturing industries increased. By 1909 nearly one half of the labor force was employed by large industrial firms.

Progress in industrialization was minimal in the Netherlands from 1850 until the 1880s, and full-blown "take-off" did not begin until the late 1890s. From then until 1914, annual growth in investment capital exceeded 10 percent, foreign trade expanded greatly, and many industrial sectors such as textiles and later metals led the expansion. The Netherlands after 1900 began to emulate the United Kingdom and Germany, which had industrialized a generation or two earlier.[50] Thus, the Dutch economy only belatedly was integrated into the international economy of the Atlantic world. Workers in traditional handicraft and foodstuff industries were forced to adapt to mechanization or suffer a sharp economic decline. Understandably, this group, plus rural day laborers, elected to emigrate to the United States in large numbers, where abundant midwestern farm lands beckoned and wage rates far exceeded those in the old country.

Dutch international labor migration to the United States responded, as one would expect, to structural determinants in both countries resulting from the differing levels of industrialization. Emigration simultaneously alleviated the conditions of labor oversupply, capital scarcity, and food shortages in the Netherlands at mid-century, and in the United States it ameliorated problems of labor scarcity, high wages, and unused lands in the period of rapid economic take-off.

Conclusion

In the Dutch experience, the religious conflict erupted before the promulgation of the liberal constitution of 1848, and the rise of religious liberty lessened the tensions and social ostracism of religious dissenters and minorities. Similarly, population pressure on agricultural resources increased sharply before modern industrialization and urbanization provided alternative economic opportunities at home. The persecuted ones and the pressured ones became the prime candidates for emigration to the United States.

Notes

1. Henry S. Lucas, *Netherlanders in America: Dutch Immigration to the United States and Canada, 1789–1950* (Ann Arbor, MI: University of Michigan Press, 1955; repr. Grand Rapids, MI: Wm. B. Eerdmans, 1989); Jacob van Hinte, *Netherlanders in America: A Study of Emigration and Settlement in the Nineteenth and Twentieth Centuries in the United States of America*, Robert P. Swierenga, ed., Adriaan de Wit, chief trans. (Grand Rapids, MI: Baker Book House, 1985; originally published in 2 vols. in Dutch by P. Noordhoff, Groningen, 1928); Gerald De Jong, *The Dutch in America, 1609–1974* (Boston: Twayne, 1975); Pieter R. D. Stokvis, *De Nederlandse trek naar Amerika, 1846–1847* (Leiden: Universitaire Pers, 1977).
2. Pieter R. D. Stokvis, "Dutch International Migration, 1815–1910" in *The Dutch in America: Immigration, Settlement, and Cultural Change*, ed. Robert P. Swierenga (New Brunswick, NJ: Rutgers University Press, 1985), 43–63; William S. Petersen, *Planned Migration: The Social Determinants of the Dutch-Canadian Movement* (Berkeley: University of California, 1955), 7, 42–43, 60–64; Lucas, *Netherlanders in America*, 44–58.
3. J. Mokyr, "Industrialization and Poverty in Ireland and the Netherlands: Some Notes Toward a Comparative Study," unpublished paper presented to the American Historical Association meeting, San Francisco, 1978, p. 15.
4. Hans Norman, "Emigration from the Nordic Countries: Some Aspects," in *American Immigration in Its Variety and Lasting Imprint*, Rob Kroes, ed. (European Contributions to American Studies, I, 1979), Table 1, 51; *International Migrations*, Walter F. Wilcox, ed., 2 vols. (New York, 1931), vol. 2, Table 1.
5. The best studies of Dutch economic conditions in the first half of the nineteenth century are: Richard T. Griffiths, *Industrial Retardation in the Netherlands, 1830–1850* (The Hague: Martinus Nijhoff, 1979); Joel Mokyr, *Industrialization in the Low Countries, 1795–1850* (New Haven: Yale University Press, 1976); J. A. de Jonge, *De industrialisatie in Nederland tussen 1850 en 1914* (Amsterdam, 1968; repr. Nijmegen: Socialistische Uitgeverij, 1976), summarized in English in J. A. de Jonge, "Industrial Growth in the Netherlands, 1850–1914," *Acta Historiae Neerlandica* 5 (1971), 159–212; J. A. de Jonge, "The Role of the Outer Provinces in the Process of Dutch Economic Growth in the Nineteenth Century," in *Economische ontwikkeling en sociale emancipatie*, eds. P. A. M. Geurts and F. A. M. Messing, II, (The Hague: Martinus Nijhoff, 1977), 51–67; Th. van Tijn and W. M. Zappey, "De negentiende eeuw, 1813–1914" in *De economische geschiedenis van Nederland*, ed. J. H. van Stuijvenberg (Groningen: Wolters-Noordhoff, 1977), ch. 6, 201–59; I. J. Brugmans, *Paardenkracht en mensenmacht: sociaal-economische geschiedenis van Nederland, 1795–1940* (The Hague: Martinus Nijhoff, 1976).

6. Robert P. Swierenga, *The Forerunners: Dutch Jewry in the North American Diaspora* (Detroit: Wayne University Press, 1994), 23–27.
7. The most complete English-language account is Gerrit J. tenZythoff, *Sources of Secession: The Nederlands Hervormde Kerk on the Eve of the Dutch Immigration to the Midwest* (Grand Rapids: Eerdmans, 1987). Cf. Lubbertus Oostendorp, *H.P. Scholte, Leader of the Secession of 1834 and Founder of Pella* (Franeker: T. Wever, 1974).
8. Histories of the Catholic emancipation movement are: W. G. Versluis, *Geschiedenis van de emancipatie der Katholieken in Nederland van 1795-heden* (Utrecht: Decker & Van de Vegt, 1948); M. J. M. van der Heijden, *De dageraad van de emancipatie der Katholieken: de Nederlandsche katholieken en de staatkundige ontwikkelingen uit het laaste kwart van de achttiende eeuw* (Ph.D. diss., University of Nijmegen, 1947); Ludovicus J. Rogier and N. de Rooy, *In vrijheid herboren: Katholiek Nederland, 1853–1953* (The Hague: Uitgeverij Pax, 1953).
9. Yda Schreuder, *Dutch Catholic Immigrant Settlement in Wisconsin, 1850–1905* (New York: Garland Publishing, 1989), 78–81; Van Hinte, *Netherlanders in America*, 73–76.
10. Stokvis, "Dutch Mid-Nineteenth Century Emigration," 41–45; Stokvis, *Nederlandse trek*, 38–52. See also Lucas, *Netherlanders in America*, 42–68; Van Hinte, *Netherlanders in America*, 85–107, 120–30.
11. Albertus Pieters, "Historical Introduction," 16, in *Classis Holland Minutes, 1848–1858* (Grand Rapids, MI: W.B. Eerdmans, 1950).
12. Mack Walker, *Germany and the Emigration, 1816–1885* (Cambridge: Harvard University Press, 1964), 12–18, 78–80; Harald Runblom and Hans Norman, eds., *From Sweden to America: A History of the Migration* (Minneapolis: University of Minnesota Press, 1976), 116, 119–20; Philip A. M. Taylor, *Expectations Westward: The Mormons and the Emigration of the British Converts in the Nineteenth Century* (Edinburgh: Oliver & Boyd, 1965), 148–55; Kristian Hvidt, *Flight to America: The Social Background of 300,000 Danish Emigrants* (New York: Academic Press, 1975), 148–55; Ingrid Semmingsen, *Norway to America: A History of the Migration* (Minneapolis: University of Minnesota Press, 1978), 34–40.
13. These figures are computed from data on Netherlands church affiliation in Stokvis, *Nederlandse trek*, Table 6, 54.
14. Lucas, *Netherlanders in America*, 62.
15. Stokvis, "Dutch Mid-Nineteenth Century Emigration," 45.
16. J. A. de Kok, *Nederland op de breuklijn Rome-Reformatie. Numerieke aspecten van Protestantisering in Katholiek herleving in de noordelijke Nederlanden, 1580–1880* (Assen: Van Gorkum, 1964), 292–93.
17. Ivo Schöffer, *A Short History of the Netherlands* (Amsterdam: Allert de Lange, 1973), 142.
18. Thorbecke headed three cabinets: 1849–53, 1862–66, and 1871–72 (Schöffer, *Short History*, 117–21, 131). Religious developments are in J. P. de Keijser, ed., *De worsteling van het Protestantismus tegen den herstelling der hierarchy in Nederland* (Arnhem, 1853).

19. Johan Goudsblom, *Dutch Society* (New York: Random House, 1967), 59.
20. Schöffer, *Short History*, 142–43.
21. Goudsblom, *Dutch Society*, 25, 83–84; Schöffer, *Short History*, 119–21.
22. Marja Roholl, "A Catholic Wonderland: Pictorial Images of America in *Katholiek Illustratie*, 1867–1942," in *American Photographs in Europe*, eds. David E. Nye and Mick Gridley (Amsterdam: VU University Press, 1994); Schreuder, *Dutch Catholic Emigrant Settlement in Wisconsin*, 77–81.
23. The religious character of the early Dutch emigration has traditionally been given a prominent place by American historians (e.g., Lucas, *Netherlanders in America*, 213–15, 42, 68, 244, 472–73), but Netherlandic scholars stress economic factors. See Stokvis, *Nederlandse trek*, 36–37, 203–05; Van Hinte, *Netherlanders in America*, ch. 4; G. B. van Dijk, "Geloofsvervolging of broodnood: Hollanders naar Michigan," *Spiegel Historiael* (1970): 31–36.
24. De Jonge, "Role of the Outer Provinces," 52.
25. James C. Riley, "The Dutch Economy After 1650: Decline or Growth?" *Journal of European Economic History* 13 (September–December 1984): 521–69, esp. 540, citing Griffiths, *Industrial Retardation*, 38; Paul Gairoch, "Europe's Gross National Product: 1810–1975," *Journal of European Economic History*, 5 (Fall 1976): 286.
26. De Jonge, *Industrialisatie in Nederland*, 237.
27. De Jonge, "Role of the Outer Provinces," 54–55.
28. Ibid., 57; cf. Schreuder, *Dutch Catholic Immigrant Settlement in Wisconsin*, 13–34; and Schreuder, "Dutch Catholic Emigration in the Mid-Nineteenth Century: Noord Brabant, 1847–1871," *Journal of Historical Geography* 11 (Jan. 1985): 48–69.
29. De Jonge, "Industrial Growth," 172.
30. B. W. A. E. Sloet tot Oldhuis, "Over de oorzaken van de landverhuizing der Nederlanders naar de Vereenigde Staten" *Tijdschrift voor Staathuishoudkunde en Statistiek* 25 (3rd ser., 2nd pt., 1866), 87–102. This important pamphlet is translated into English by Dirk Hoogeveen, edited by Robert P. Swierenga, under the title "The Cause of Dutch Emigration to America: An 1866 Account" in *Michigana* 24 (Spring 1979): 56–61; (Summer 1979): 92–97.
31. J. C. Boogman, "The Dutch Crisis in the Eighteen-Forties," in *Britain and the Netherlands: Papers Delivered to the Oxford-Netherlands Historical Conference, 1959*, eds. J. S. Bromley and E. H. Kossmann (London: Chatls & Winders, 1960), 192–203.
32. Griffiths, *Industrial Retardation*, 47–55, discusses the tax structure and its regional impact. For the effect of tax structure on wealth holding, see H. van Dijk, *Wealth and Property in the Netherlands in Modern Times*, (Rotterdam: Erasmus University, 1980).
33. Sloet tot Oldhuis, "Over de oorzaken," 97.
34. These figures include Limburg. E. W. Hofstee, "Population Increase in the Netherlands," *Acta Historiae Neerlandica* 3 (1968): 43–125; William

S. Petersen, "The Demographic Transition in the Netherlands," *American Sociological Review* 25 (June 1960): 334–47; Griffiths, *Industrial Retardation*, 14–17.

35. Michael Wintle, "Modest Growth and Capital Drain in an Advanced Economy: The Case of Dutch Agriculture in the Nineteenth Century," *Agricultural History Review* 39 (1991): 20–21.
36. M. Bergman, "The Potato Blight in the Netherlands and Its Social Consequences," *International Social Science Journal* 12 (1967): 390–431; Frida Terlouw, "De aardappelziekte in Nederland in 1845 en volgende jaren," *Economisch en Sociaal-Historisch Jaarboek* 34 (1971): 263–308. This and the following paragraphs rely heavily on these important articles.
37. Joel Mokyr estimates the famine deaths in 1846–1847 at 60,000 and the "averted births" at 66,000. Mokyr, "Industrialization and Poverty in Ireland and the Netherlands," 24.
38. H. J. Prakke, *Drenthe in Michigan* (Grand Rapids: Wm. B. Eerdmans, 1983), chs. 3–5; Sloet tot Oldhuis, "Over de oorzaken," likewise stress the link between smaller farmers and larger families and emigration.
39. Griffiths, *Industrial Retardation*, 38; Riley, "Dutch Economy After 1650," 540, citing Gairoch, "Europe's Gross National Product," 286.
40. Griffiths, *Industrial Retardation*, 9–14, 28, argues most strongly against the abject poverty thesis of emigration.
41. Ibid., 25.
42. This section relies heavily on the excellent works of De Jonge: *Industrialisatie in Nederland* and "Industrial Growth in the Netherlands, 1850–1914."
43. William Petersen, *Planned Migration: The Social Determinants of the Dutch-Canadian Movement*, 22.
44. De Jonge, "Industrial Growth," 192–95.
45. Mokyr, *Industrialization in the Netherlands*, 165–202, 260.
46. Pim Kooij, "Peripheral Cities and Their Regions in the Dutch Urban System until 1900," *Journal of Economic History* 48 (June 1988): 357–71; H. J. Keuning, *Kaleidoscoop der Nederlandse landschappen. De regionale verscheidenheid van Nederland in historisch-geografisch perspectief* (The Hague: Nijhoff, 1979), esp. Ch. 7.
47. Van Tijn and Zappey, "De negentiende eeuw," 231–34; De Jonge, *Industrialisatie*, 37–257.
48. Hille de Vries, *Landbouw en bevolking tijdens de agrarische depressie in Friesland (1878–1895)* (Wageningen: H. Veenman en Zonen, 1971), and De Vries, "The Labor Market in Dutch Agriculture and Emigration to the United States," in *Dutch in America*, ed. Swierenga, 78–101.
49. This paragraph and the next rely heavily upon De Jonge, "Role of the Outer Provinces," 62–64; and Wintle, "Modest Growth," 24–25.
50. De Jonge, *De industrialisatie in Nederland tussen 1850 en 1914*, 511–13.

CHAPTER 2

Delayed Transition from Folk to Labor Migration

THROUGHOUT THE NINETEENTH century Dutch overseas emigration was overwhelmingly a folk migration of rural families seeking cheap land in the United States. Only after the "closing" of the American frontier in the 1890s and the onset in the Netherlands of industrial "take-off" did the emigration patterns change to a labor migration of single young men and women.

The fluctuations in Dutch emigration follow those of northern Europe generally, even though their economies and societies differed (Figure 2.1). This shows that the American situation was determinative. Once the migrants had weighed the relative advantages and decided to go, they relied on information from family and friends in America to determine when to depart. Their ultimate decision reflects both "push" factors and "pull" factors, but American pull forces exceeded push factors.[1] This is not to deny the importance of the adverse conditions in the homeland, but only to give them a subordinate place.

Allowing for individual lags, the secular trend is cyclical, with the first major peak in the period 1847–57, followed by a second lesser spurt from 1865 to 1873, a third peak—the greatest in the history of the nation—from 1880 to 1893, and a final rise from 1903 to 1913. The intervening troughs, due to economic crises and the American Civil War, were in the years 1857–64, 1874–79, and 1894–99.

Consistently, each of the four peak periods was bimodal, with a steep but brief trough between two high points. In the first cycle, 1847 and 1854 were the years of greatest emigration, with 1850 being the lowest year. In the second up cycle, 1867 and 1873 were the peaks and 1870–71 the low point. In the third cycle, 1881 and 1889 were the peaks, and 1885–86 the trough. In the final cycle, 1907 and 1913 were years of heavy emigration and 1908 was a low point. The meaning of this twin-peak pattern of short cycles within longer cycles is unclear, except that it indicates the extent to which individual migration decisions are sensitive to conditions at home and at the intended destinations.

Although the four migration phases had similar fluctuations over time, each was unique in the composition of the emigrant groups involved. Most notable was the shift from single immigrants to groups to family chain migration. The individual

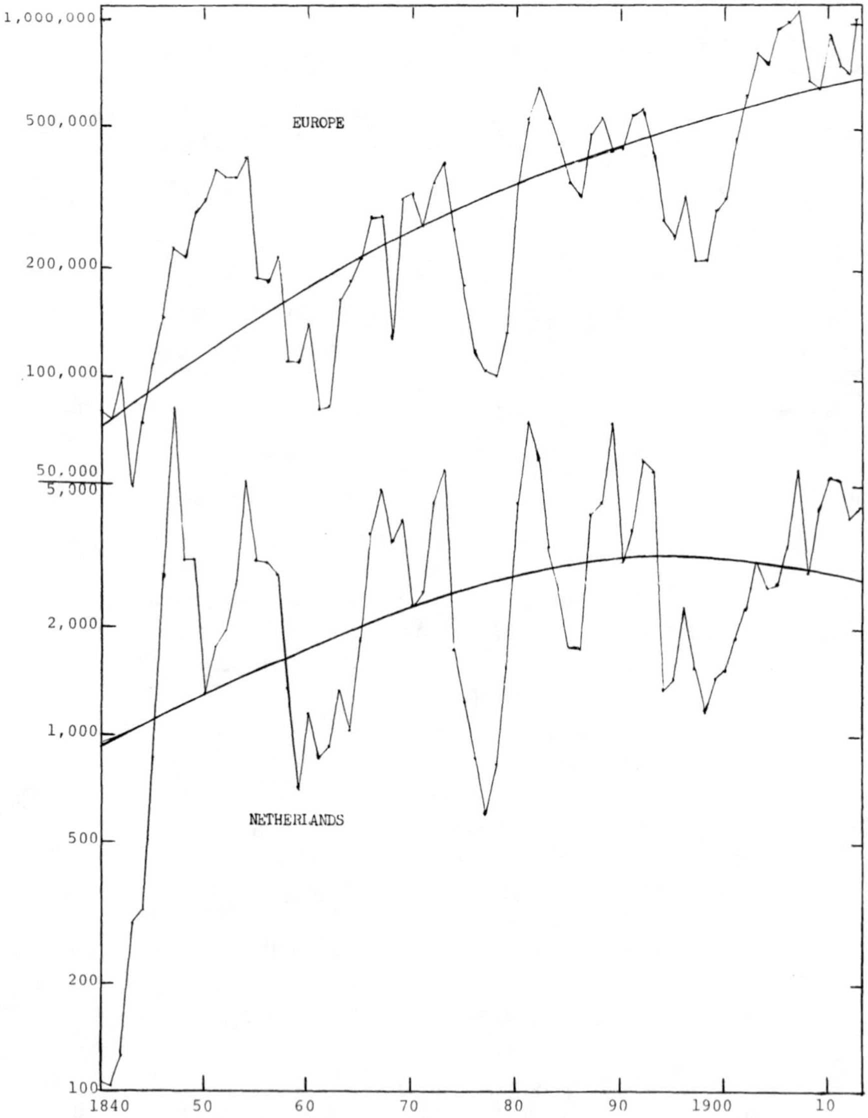

Figure 2.1 Immigration to the United States from Europe and the Netherlands, 1840–1913

SOURCE: Brinley Thomas, *Migration and Economic Growth* (1954), 286; Swierenga study data derived from Netherlands Emigration Records and U.S. Ship Lists.

phase began in the 1820s and 1830s with the departure of a few venturesome persons seeking economic betterment. They were influenced by the emigration of numerous Germans passing down the Rhine River to the port of Rotterdam.[2] Others learned of possibilities in America from their German co-religionists across the border in Graafschap Bentheim and Ost Friesland.[3] Roman Catholics likewise followed the example of the Seceders and formed emigrant associations to promote colonies.[4]

Dutch emigration began in earnest in the mid-1840s following a decade of religious strife, potato crop failures, cholera outbreaks, sharp food price increases, and lengthening relief roles. But this was also a time across the Atlantic of the settling of the upper Middle West, after President Andrew Jackson's Indian removals and congressional liberalization of land policies. During the Mexican War Congress offered soldiers millions of acres of land warrants to induce enlistments or reward those who served.[5] This land paper quickly passed into the hands of dealers who sold it at substantial discounts to prospective buyers of government lands. In the initial Dutch Calvinist colonies of Holland, Michigan, and Pella, Iowa, the leaders stretched their group's supply of Dutch "Willempjes" (silver coins worth $1 US) at the land offices by entering thousands of acres of virgin land with military warrants purchased through dealers at discounts up to 33 percent. Hendrik P. Scholte, Pella's founder, entered nearly all of the colony's 16,000 initial acres of land with warrants.[6]

The onset in 1857 of economic depression and then the Civil War in the United States, together with the improved economic and religious climate in the Netherlands, ended the group migration.[7] During the war prospective emigrants postponed their move until peace was restored. After an eight-year hiatus, in 1865, a second wave of emigrants departed, enticed largely by the American land boom stimulated by the Homestead Act of 1862. They left as nuclear families or single individuals rather than in congregational or community groups. Emigration by the late 1860s was no longer a form of deviant behavior; it had become a normal social action. Much of the post-war migration included families and friends of previous emigrants from the same areas as before 1857. Their letters linked the two localities and encouraged a continuing chain; emigration was now generating more emigration.

Yet a third wave, the greatest in Dutch history except for the decade following the Second World War, began in 1878 when the economic picture in the United States brightened after the nation shook off the effects of the 1873 business panic and ensuing depression, while Congress and the land-grant railroads threw open the farmers' last frontier in the trans-Missouri west. This movement was sustained by an agricultural crisis in the cash grain region of the northern Netherlands caused by a world-wide glut of grain.[8]

This saturation phase, which brought tens of thousands of excess farm workers to America, continued until 1893 when the American economy plunged into yet another four-year depression following a banking panic. Concurrently, the Dutch economy belatedly entered its period of large-scale industrial growth, which provided new jobs for the displaced rural proletariat. But many of these farm laborers wished to continue in agriculture, rather than make a drastic adjustment to factory life. In 1894, Dutch emigration dropped by 80 percent and continued at a low ebb until 1901, when it gradually began to rise, reaching its high point in 1913.

Farmland in America continued to call rural Dutchmen, and to a lesser extent so did cheap land in Canada, South Africa, Indonesia, and South America. Hence, between 1903 and 1913, in the fourth emigration era, some 66,000 Netherlanders left for overseas destinations. This was a rate of over 100 per 100,000 population, which exceeded by a considerable margin the outflow of the previous periods. The First World War, of course, checked this final phase and again diverted Dutch emigrants away from the United States.

In the early 1920s, the flow to the States increased sharply, but the quota limit, imposed first in 1921 and reduced further in 1924, took its toll.[9] Never again, except by special congressional dispensation, could more than 3,100 Dutch annually enter the Unites States, even after the Second World War when there was a lengthy waiting list of 40,000. This dismal prospect encouraged over 80 percent of the nearly one million post-1945 emigrants to settle in Canada, Australia, or elsewhere. In 1965 Congress replaced the national origins law with a quota based on needed skills; this was even more restrictive and admitted only 1,500 Netherlanders per year. Unprecedented prosperity at home in the 1970s also dampened the desire of many to emigrate, although periodically, such as in 1979, inquiries at the Immigration Bureau jumped 100 percent over the previous year and 40 percent more people completed formal applications to emigrate.[10] But no fifth wave materialized.

America-centered

The dramatic changes in the cycles of Dutch emigration coincided with new overseas destinations. During times of troubles in the United States, Dutch emigrants readily shifted their sights to other settlement areas, especially to Dutch colonies in Asia and Latin America. For the most part, at least before 1890, this was not by preference but necessity, since the United States always remained the primary magnet. Java or Capetown or Saramacca might offer advantages to aspiring civil servants, young professionals, and military men, but it was not attractive to rural peasants and craftsmen. For these, the lure of cheap land in America remained irresistible.

Throughout the entire century from 1820 to 1920, three out of four Dutch emigrants chose the United States as their destination. In a number of cycles—1845–57, 1865–73, and 1880–93—the "America-centeredness" consistently exceeded 95 percent (see Figure 2.2). The first exceptional period, when the Dutch emigrant flow was diverted elsewhere, was in the years 1858–66. Latin America (especially Brazil and Surinam) attracted over 1,200 emigrants, South Africa gained 1,000, and nearly 1,000 favored Southeast Asia (see Table 2.1). In 1858, the year after the major American business crisis of 1857, more Dutch emigrants settled in Brazil than in the United States. All were from the province of Zeeland.[11] The return of

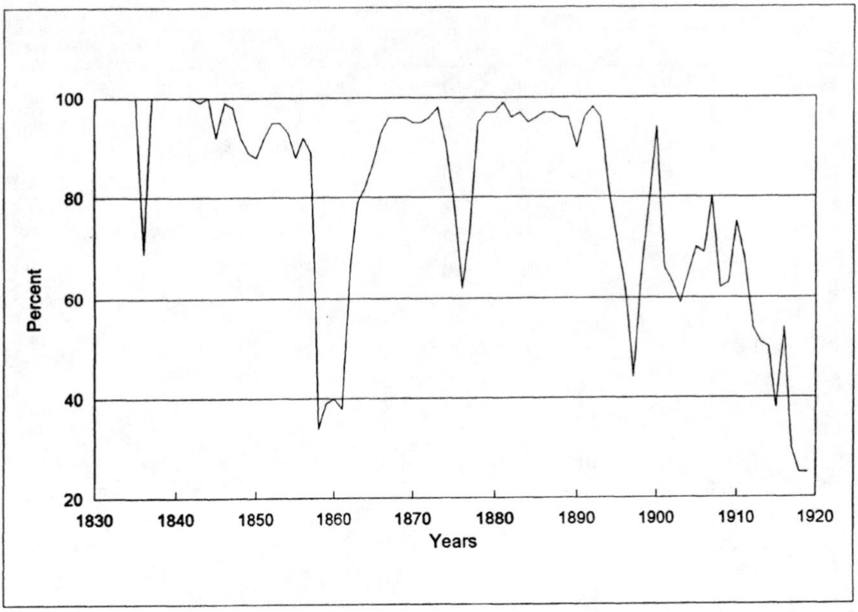

Figure 2.2 North American Destination of Overseas Emigrants, 1835–1920
SOURCE: Swierenga study data derived from Netherlands Emigration Records, 1835–75; *Bijdragen tot de Algemene Statistik van Nederland*, 1876–99; and . . . *Nieuw Volgreets*, 1901–20.

hard times in the United States in 1873 again created a diversion, but it was minor compared to 1857. More than 90 percent of the emigrants in the years 1866–90 went to the United States.

A permanent change in the direction of overseas emigration occurred in the hard times of the 1890s, which was exceeded only by the Great Depression of the 1930s. Prior to 1894, over 97 percent of all Dutch emigrants chose to settle in the States. But in 1894 the preference dropped to 81 percent and it plummeted each year thereafter until it reached a low of 44 percent in 1897 (Table 2.2). Except for the rebound year of 1900, when 94 percent came to the States, never again did the percentage exceed 80; indeed it averaged only 56 percent between 1901 and 1920. Thereafter, the centuries-long American policy of permitting virtually free immigration ended abruptly with the 1921 quota law. In the previous year, 1920, the last when Dutch (or any other) immigrants had freedom of choice, only 40 percent opted for the States. This comparatively low amount was actually an increase over the war-era years 1917–19 when 30, 30, and 25 percent, respectively, of all Dutch emigrants came to the States.

After 1893 and continuing until 1920, at least, more and more Dutch emigrants settled in the Netherlands East Indies or, to a lesser extent, in Canada and South Africa. By 1915 and every year thereafter through 1920, more than one half of all Dutch overseas emigrants went to Asia. In 1918, 68 percent settled there and in 1919, 65 percent. The States had lost their preeminence for the Dutch as the land

Table 2.1 Overseas Emigration by Continent, 1840–80 (Official Statistics)

Year	U.S.A. Number	U.S.A. %	South Africa Number	South Africa %	South America Number	South America %	Asia Number	Asia %	Other Number	Other %	Total° Number
1835–39	29	88	0	0	0	0	4	12	0	0	33
1840	2	100	0	0	0	0	0	0	2	0	2
1841	5	100	0	0	0	0	0	0	0	0	5
1842	23	100	0	0	0	0	0	0	0	0	23
1843	72	99	0	0	1	0	0	0	0	0	73
1844	176	100	0	0	8	0	0	0	0	0	176
1845	445	92	0	0	0	0	30	6	10	2	485
1846	1,059	99	0	0	0	0	0	0	13	1	1,072
1847	3,319	98	0	0	2	0	5	0	75	2	3,401
1848	1,997	92	0	0	22	1	5	0	147	7	2,168
1849	1,855	89	3	0	8	0	8	0	206	10	2,080
1850	680	88	13	2	4	0	16	2	62	8	775
1851	1,113	92	9	1	1	0	2	0	90	7	1,215
1852	1,112	95	10	1	13	1	18	2	23	2	1,176
1853	1,565	95	8	0	0	0	16	1	42	3	1,631
1854	3,365	93	31	1	2	0	37	1	194	5	3,629
1855	1,827	88	26	1	27	1	24	1	161	8	2,065
1856	1,778	92	63	3	1	0	42	2	45	2	1,929
1857	1,475	89	78	5	0	0	26	2	75	5	1,654
1858	406	34	143	12	602	51	26	2	7	0	1,184
1859	193	39	124	3	101	2	71	1	4	0	4,903
1860	341	40	279	33	170	20	65	8	3	0	858
1861	287	38	204	27	164	22	97	13	9	1	761
1862	549	66	144	17	23	3	103	12	13	1	832
1863	833	79	35	3	18	2	124	12	39	4	1,049
1864	603	82	11	1	31	3	78	11	14	2	737
1865	1,464	87	29	2	45	3	144	9	0	0	1,682
1866	3,006	93	4	0	45	1	155	5	11	0	3,221
1867	3,967	96	0	0	30	1	69	2	73	2	4,139
1868	2,883	96	7	0	6	0	46	2	61	2	3,003
1869	3,330	96	10	0	10	0	82	2	48	1	3,480
1870	1,795	95	2	0	3	0	52	3	44	2	1,896
1871	1,828	95	2	0	19	1	28	1	44	2	1,921
1872	3,412	96	18	1	5	0	46	1	67	2	3,548
1873	3,793	98	7	0	13	0	67	2	15	0	3,865
1874	991	91	8	0	3	0	72	7	15	1	1,089
1875	537	79	58	8	10	1	78	11	1	0	682
1876	222	62	48	13	4	0	71	20	11	3	356
1877	180	74	8	3	9	0	48	20	0	0	245
1878	223	95	4	2	0	0	6	3	1	0	234
1879	738	97	3	0	0	0	16	2	6	1	761
1880	2,425	97	12	0	12	0	42	2	19	1	2,510
Totals	55,703	90	1,401	2	1,406	2	1,819	3	1,648	0	62,171

° Includes 15 Middle East, 50 British North America, and 142 West Indies.

Source: Robert P. Swierenga, comp., *Dutch Emigrants to the United States, South America, South Africa, and Southeast Asia, 1835–1880: An Alphabetical Listing by Household Heads and Independent Persons* (Wilmington, DE: Scholarly Resources, 1983). This file is missing 2,933 emigrants in the years 1835–46 and 1877–80. See discussion of sources in Chapter 12.

Table 2.2 Overseas Emigration by Continent, 1881–1920 (Official Statistics)

	North America		South America		Africa		Asia		Australia		Unknown		
Year	Number	%	Number	%	Number	%	Number	%	Number	%	Number	%	Total
1881	7,380	99	+	0	21	0	0	0	0	0	61	1	7,462
1882*	7,230	97	16	0	48	1	6	0	12	0	157	2	7,469
1883*	4,798	98	3	0	52	1	3	0	18	0	26	1	4,900
1884*	3,654	96	4	0	90	2	0	0	7	0	47	1	3,802
1885*	2,121	97	0	0	44	2	0	0	7	0	25	1	2,197
1886*	2,004	97	5	0	37	2	1	0	8	0	24	1	2,079
1887*	5,018	98	0	0	53	1	0	0	0	0	69	1	5,140
1888*	4,298	89	330	7	165	3	0	0	0	0	30	1	4,823
1889*	5,050	54	4,020	43	251	3	0	0	0	0	26	0	9,347
1890*	3,282	87	167	4	308	8	0	0	0	0	24	1	3,781
1891*	3,923	96	0	0	154	4	0	0	0	0	2	0	4,079
1892*	6,211	99	0	0	114	2	0	0	0	0	36	1	6,361
1893	5,476	96	+	0	228	4	0	0	0	0	20	0	5,724
1894	1,102	81	+	0	246	18	0	0	0	0	9	1	1,357
1895	1,036	68	+	0	472	31	1	0	0	0	6	0	1,517
1896	1,445	63	+	0	847	37	2	0	0	0	3	0	2,298
1897	675	44	+	0	863	56	4	0	0	0	1	0	1,543
1898	749	64	+	0	425	36	0	0	1	0	1	0	1,176
1899	1,136	77	+	0	312	21	9	0	9	0	12	1	1,472
1900	1,451	94	+	0	87	6	1	0	1	0	0	0	1,548
Totals 1881–1900	68,039	87	4,545	6	4,817	6	27	0	68	0	579	1	78,075

TABLE 2.2 *Continued*

Year	North America		South America		Africa		Asia		Australia		Unknown		Total
	Number	%	Number	%	Number	%	Number	%	Number	%	Number	%	
1901	1,893	66	89	3	92	3	810	28	2	0			2,886
1902	2,272	63	82	2	399	11	812	24	2	0			3,606
1903	3,133	59	231	4	1,175	22	755	14	1	0			5,296
1904	2,627	65	243	6	384	9	774	19	1	0			4,030
1905	2,733	70	49	2	207	5	866	22	14	0			3,927
1906	3,437	69	275	6	188	4	1,055	21	3	0			4,958
1907	5,778	79	284	4	140	2	1,001	14	18	0			7,221
1908	2,880	62	539	12	144	3	1,113	24	4	0			4,680
1909	4,266	63	923	14	232	3	1,316	20	32	0			6,769
1910	5,350	75	205	3	180	3	1,380	20	21	0			7,136
1911	5,255	68	449	6	251	3	1,729	23	8	0			7,752
1912	4,184	54	840	11	255	3	2,316	32	179	2			7,774
1913	4,338	51	1,251	15	257	3	2,574	31	83	1			8,503
1914	3,134	50	598	10	128	2	2,329	38	86	1			6,275
1915	1,552	38	318	8	62	2	2,171	53	28	0			4,131
1916	1,585	41	245	6	95	2	1,966	51	14	0			3,905
1917	597	30	103	5	26	1	1,252	64	5	0			1,983
1918	541	25	117	5	34	2	1,486	68	4	0			2,182
1919	1,429	25	380	7	141	3	3,615	65	18	0			5,574
1920	4,790	40	656	6	377	3	6,083	51	15	0			11,924
Totals 1901–20	61,755	56	7,924	7	4,767	4	36,041	33	590	0			110,487
Totals 1881–20	129,794	69	12,469	7	9,584	5	36,068	19	658	0	579	0	188,562

° In these years the official statistics in the *Bijdragen tot de Statistiek van Nederland* do not distinguish North and South America; nor do they include migrants to the Dutch colonies, who are not classified as true emigrants. Therefore, I used the figures in Jellinghaus, which are based on harbor embarkations at Rotterdam and Amsterdam, compiled by the Commissie voor toezicht op en doortogt en het vervoer van landverhuizers.

SOURCE: Central Bureau for Statistics, "Statistiek van den loop der bevolking van Nederland. . . 1880–1920," *Bijdragen tot de Statistiek van Nederland*, 1881–1900; *Bijdragen tot de Statistiek van Nederland, Nieuw Volgreeks, 1901–1920*, Gustaaf Marie Willem Jellinghaus, *De staat tegenover de landverhuizing* (The Hague, 1894), Table, p. 134.

of opportunity. The agricultural frontier with its cheap land was gone and urban America seemed less than hospitable to many Dutch peasants.

The key variable in determining the America-centeredness of Dutch immigration was always rurality of origin. Since 80 percent of the emigrants last lived in rural municipalities in the decades from 1835 to 1880, one could expect a strong flow to the United States. Of those who left from rural municipalities, 95 percent went to the States, compared to only 67 percent from urban municipalities. The provinces with the greatest proportion of overseas emigrants embarking for America were the sea clay soil provinces of Friesland, Groningen, Zeeland, plus Drenthe, which ranked from 98 to 95 percent (Table 2.3). Not far behind in the high 80 to low 90 percent range were Gelderland, Limburg, Overijssel, and Zuid-Holland. Conversely, from the populous urban provinces of Utrecht and Noord-Holland only 40 percent and 71 percent, respectively, of all emigrants chose the States.

Quite obviously, the promise of low-priced land in America held greater allure to the Dutch peasant folk than business and professional opportunities in the States appealed to the urban middle class. Only 20 percent of all overseas emigrants were of urban origin and few of these went to America. Consistently the East Indies emigrants originated in the major seaports, commercial centers, and provincial capitals. Upward mobility was difficult in the staid, status-conscious, and rigidly stratified cities. Ambitious sons had to look elsewhere to places like the East Indies, if they hoped to advance into white-collar positions and higher income and

TABLE 2.3 Continental Destination by Province, Household Heads and Single Persons, 1835–80

	North America*		South America		Asia		Africa†		Total‡
Province	Number	%	Number	%	Number	%	Number	%	Number
DR	402	95	3	1	7	2	9	2	421
FR	1,185	98	9	1	8	1	13	1	1,215
GE	3,785	92	82	2	186	5	79	2	4,132
GR	3,051	96	13	0	85	3	16	1	3,165
LI	521	91	4	1	46	8	—	—	571
NB	1,126	89	55	4	71	6	18	1	1,270
NH	1,601	71	41	2	215	10	404	17	2,261
OV	904	93	16	2	29	3	20	2	969
UT	221	40	23	4	254	46	54	10	552
ZE	4,139	96	165	4	13	0	9	0	4,326
ZH	2,104	92	23	1	107	5	65	3	2,299
Totals	19,039	90	434	2	1,021	5	687	3	21,181

* Includes 29 Canada.
† Includes 10 Middle East.
‡ Excludes 64 Western Europe countries.
SOURCE: Robert P. Swierenga, comp., *Dutch Emigrants to the United States, South America, South Africa, and Southeast Asia, 1835–1880: An Alphabetical Listing by Household Heads and Independent Persons* (Wilmington, DE: Scholarly Resources, 1983). This file is missing 2,933 emigrants in the years 1835–46 and 1877–80. See discussion of sources in Chapter 12.

prestige. As a consequence, one-third of all urban emigrants chose not to go to the States, compared to only 5 percent of emigrants from rural areas (*plattenlanden*).[12]

The main point of this review of the timing and termini of Dutch overseas emigration is that prospective emigrants favored the United States, and they responded directly to American conditions until the quota system created artificial barriers. Land booms sparked each emigrant surge, and economic panics and depressions dampened them. In the troughs of the cycle, most prospective immigrants waited at home, although the usual small numbers of white-collar types and the occasional farm family continued to go to the Dutch colonies or to developing countries elsewhere.

Provincial Variations

In addition to cyclical fluctuations and changes in destination, an understanding of the points of origin of the Dutch emigrants is equally important in analyzing migration patterns. Until we know which provinces and even which municipalities in the Netherlands were sending emigrants, and until we know something about the differences between these provinces and municipalities, it is impossible to assess in any systematic way the structure of Dutch emigration. Because the Dutch data provide information on the behavioral characteristics of each emigrant family and single adult by *municipality*, we are in a unique position to understand something of the local dynamics of emigration.

Initially, it is possible to distinguish the eleven Dutch provinces broadly in terms of three major categories: the urban commercial provinces of Noord-Holland, Zuid-Holland, and Utrecht; the agricultural clay provinces of Friesland, Groningen, and Zeeland with their commercial grain production; and the agricultural sand provinces of Drenthe, Overijssel, Gelderland, Limburg, and Noord-Brabant with their general farming. The latter two provinces, as explained earlier, are also the predominant Roman Catholic provinces, which gave them a certain character. Provincial patterns are described in this chapter and the more significant community-level variations are described in Chapter 3.

Beyond land types and economic orientation, it is helpful to analyze Dutch census information and distinguish the provinces on the basis of population patterns. The general urban-rural distinctions come into sharp focus and demonstrate how different the individual provinces stood in terms of total population and average population density per hectare. The most populous in 1849 were the two parts of old Holland province, Noord-Holland and Zuid-Holland, each with more than a half million inhabitants. Noord-Brabant was next with over 400,000, followed by Friesland with 300,000, the eastern provinces of Gelderland and Overijssel with 250,000, Groningen in the north and Limburg in the south with 225,000, Utrecht and Zeeland with 175,000, and isolated Drenthe with 100,000 inhabitants. Although the rural provinces, particularly the sand provinces, underwent little relative increase in population between 1849 and 1869, the urban provinces, notably Zuid-Holland, dramatically increased.

But population size, density, or growth rates had little apparent impact on overseas emigration. Leading in the emigration until 1900 were provinces with relatively low population densities—Zeeland, Gelderland, Groningen, and Friesland after 1880 (Table 2.4).[13] The interior sandy soil provinces of Drenthe and Overijssel never contributed many people for overseas destinations. Neither did the culturally distinct Catholic provinces with their atypically high fertility patterns.[14] Considerably fewer emigrants, relatively, also left the large and populous urban provinces: Noord-Holland, Zuid-Holland, and Utrecht. Collectively, the Randstad, which was the population center of the country and boasted the major seaports and government center, sent out only 13,000 persons, less than one-fourth of the total emigration.

In proportion to population size, Zeeland's emigration rate of 88 per 100,000 in the years 1835–1880 was more than twice that of Groningen (43) and Gelderland (36). The other interior provinces, apart from Gelderland, stood in the second tier, with Drenthe at 18 per 100,000, Friesland at 15, and Overijssel at 13. The Catholic and urban provinces all ranged below 10 per 100,000, except Zuid-Holland at 13. Thus, the urban provinces in the heartland of Holland and the protoindustrial Catholic provinces on the southern flank witnessed less foreign emigration than did the agricultural sea clay provinces where the outflow was strong. These figures show that the causal factors in emigration derive from demographic, economic, and social conditions in the rural villages and countryside rather than in the cities.

The agricultural provinces with consistently high rates of overseas migration in the years 1881–1920 were Friesland, Groningen, and Zeeland (Table 2.5). Between 1881 and 1920 Friesland and Groningen each lost 25,000 inhabitants and Zeeland lost 19,000. During the years 1880 through 1893, Zeeland's rate of overseas emigration was a high 359 per 100,000; Groningen's rate was 344, and Friesland's was 285 (Table 2.5). The rates in all of the other eight provinces were below 100, ranging from 88 for Drenthe to a low of 18 for Noord-Brabant.

The share of the total emigration from the agricultural provinces declined after 1893 (Table 2.4). Friesland's proportion declined from 24 percent in 1894–1900 to 11 percent in 1901–14, and a mere 6 percent in 1914–20. Groningen emigration began to decline already after 1893, falling from 20 to 14 percent after 1894, and to 3 percent by 1920. Zeeland's proportion declined from 17 percent to 2 percent between 1881 and 1920. Conversely, Noord-Holland tripled its percentage in the four periods, from 10 percent to 31 percent; Zuid-Holland's percentage rise was even more pronounced: from 10 percent to 37 percent. The other provinces all held steady at very low levels, except for Gelderland which consistently contributed 9 percent. These figures demonstrate that the structure of Dutch emigration changed fundamentally at the turn of the century when the Dutch economy shifted into industrial high-gear.

In the pre-war period 1901–14, after the lull in emigration in the 1890s when only Friesland surpassed a rate of 100 per 100,000, the three commercial agricultural provinces (Zeeland, Friesland, and Groningen) again experienced high outmigration rates, but with a lower plateau than before 1894 (Table 2.5). Zeeland's

TABLE 2.4 Overseas Emigration by Province by Period, 1835–1920

	Sea Clay Soil						Urban					
	FR		GR		ZE		NH		ZH		UT	
Period	Number	%	Number	%	Number	%	Number	%	Number	%	Number	%
1835–57	1,386	6	1,750	7	6,309	26	1,279	5	2,624	11	526	2
		(5)		(5)		(26)		(3)		(6)		(3)
1858–65	119	2	458	6	1,696	22	1,157	15	1,133	15	302	4
		(0)		(1)		(5)		(3)		(3)		(5)
1866–80	2,360	8	6,491	21	6,225	20	2,970	10	3,517	11	343	1
		(8)		(19)		(19)		(7)		(8)		(5)
Totals 1835–80	3,865	6	8,699	14	14,230	23	5,406	9	7,274	12	1,171	2
1881–93	12,689	22	11,796	20	9,959	17	5,522	10	6,034	10	632	1
		(43)		(35)		(30)		(13)		(13)		(9)
1894–00	2,613	24	1,559	14	1,332	12	1,287	12	1,700	16	637	6
		(9)		(5)		(4)		(3)		(4)		(10)
1901–14	8,810	11	8,145	10	7,139	9	20,513	25	18,830	23	2,409	3
		(34)		(24)		(21)		(49)		(42)		(36)
1915–18	567	4	2,907	20	328	2	3,583	24	4,584	31	813	5
		(2)		(9)		(1)		(9)		(10)		(12)
1919–20	1,001	6	527	3	379	2	5,418	31	6,526	37	1,035	6
		(3)		(2)		(1)		(13)		(14)		(15)
Totals 1881–1920	25,680	14	24,934	14	19,137	11	36,323	20	37,674	21	5,526	3
Grand Total 1835–1920	29,545	12	33,633	14	33,367	14	41,729	17	44,948	18	6,697	3

Table 2.4 *(Continued)*

	Sand Soil						Catholic				
	DR		OV		GE		NB		LI		Total
Period	Number	%	Number	%	Number	%	Number	%	Number	%	Number
1835–57	623	3	1,655	7	5,703	21	1,906	8	112	1	23,873
		(15)		(20)		(20)		(21)		(37)	
1858–65	64	1	253	3	1,033	14	319	4	1,061	14	7,595
		(2)		(3)		(4)		(4)		(28)	
1866–80	825	3	1,013	3	5,731	18	973	3	727	2	31,175
		(20)		(12)		(20)		(11)		(19)	
Totals 1835–80	1,512	2	2,921	5	12,467	20	3,198	5	1,900	3	62,643
1881–93	1,542	3	2,044	4	5,342	9	1,370	2	847	1	57,777
		(36)		(24)		(19)		(15)		(22)	
1894–1900	259	2	265	2	909	8	283	3	48	1	10,892
		(6)		(3)		(3)		(3)		(1)	
1901–14	725	1	2,587	3	7,465	9	3,404	4	784	1	80,811
		(17)		(31)		(26)		(37)		(21)	
1915–18	59	1	237	2	1,258	8	391	3	53	1	14,780
		(1)		(3)		(4)		(4)		(1)	
1919–20	130	1	397	2	1,379	8	500	3	166	1	17,458
		(3)		(5)		(5)		(5)		(4)	
Totals 1881–1920	2,715	1	5,530	3	16,353	9	5,948	3	1,898	1	181,718
Grand Total 1835–1920	4,227	2	8,451	3	28,820	12	9,146	4	3,798	2	244,361

Source: Compiled from Robert P. Swierenga, comp., *Dutch Emigrants to the United States, South Africa, South America, and Southeast Asia, 1835–1880: An Alphabetical Listing by Household Heads and Independent Persons* (Wilmington, DE: Scholarly Resources, 1983); Central Bureau for Statistics, "Statistiek van den loop der bevolking van Nederland. . ., 1880–1920," *Bijdragen tot de Statistiek van Nederland*, 1880–1900; *Bijdragen tot de Statistiek van Nederland, Nieuw Volgreeks*, 1901–20. Data for 1845–47 incomplete.

TABLE 2.5 Overseas Emigration Rates (per 100,000 population) by Province and Period, 1835–1920*

	Sea Clay Soil			Urban			Sand Soils			Catholic		
Period	FR	GR	ZE	NH	ZH	UT	DR	OV	GE	NB	LI	TOT
1835–80	141	413	841	98	116	70	155	125	309	82	97	181
1881–93	285	344	359	49	54	22	88	52	81	18	28	NA
1894–1900	110	76	90	20	22	37	24	12	24	7	3	NA
1901–14	175	179	222	133	98	61	30	49	85	39	17	101
1915–19	41	22	31	87	85	72	8	15	48	15	3	54
1920	205	125	130	272	250	199	53	70	125	47	35	172

* The population base for the period 1835–80 is the average population for the years 1840–78. For the years 1880–1920 the base is the annual average population on December 31.

SOURCE: Compiled from Robert P. Swierenga, comp., *Dutch Emigrants to the United States, South Africa, South America, and Southeast Asia, 1835–1880: An Alphabetical Listing by Household Heads and Independent Persons* (Wilmington, DE: Scholarly Resources, 1983); Central Bureau for Statistics, "Statistiek van den loop der bevolking van Nederland. . ., 1880–1920," *Bijdragen tot de Statistiek van Nederland*, 1880–1900; *Bijdragen tot de Statistiek van Nederland, Nieuw Volgreeks*, 1901–20.

rate was 222 per 100,000, down by 38 percent from the 1880–93 era. Friesland and Groningen had rates of 175 and 179, respectively, in 1901–14. For Groningen the decline was nearly half (46 percent) and the Friesland rate fell 39 percent. The interior mixed-farming regions with a rising small industrial base had the lowest migration rates, ranging from Gelderland's 85 per 100,000 and Utrecht's 61 to only 17 in the southern Catholic province of Limburg. Remarkably, 87 percent of the total Frisian emigration departed after 1880, as did 72 percent of Groningen emigrants. The agricultural depression of the 1880s took a major toll in the north.

The urban provinces of Noord-Holland and Zuid-Holland were in the second rank, with rates of 133 and 98 per 100,000, respectively, in the years 1901–14. In absolute numbers the emigration appears to be more impressive. In the four decades 1881–1920, Zuid-Holland sent out 37,000 persons and Noord-Holland 36,000. Nearly 85 percent of all overseas emigrants in the entire period from 1835 to 1920 departed the Randstad region in these latter decades.

The Great War provided the second severe jolt and overseas emigration fell drastically. The national rate dropped from 101 to 54 per 100,000 in the war years 1915–19. In 1917 and 1918 the rate fell to 29 and 32, respectively, compared to 137 in the last pre-war year of 1913. Only the three urban provinces of Noord-Holland, Zuid-Holland, and Utrecht had above-average rates (of 87, 85, and 72 per 100,000, respectively), but their citizens went to the Dutch East Indies rather than the United States. This was an exodus of urban professionals, civil servants, and businessmen seeking economic opportunities in the colonies.

In 1920, the only post-war year for which specific emigration statistics are available nationwide, the rate rose above pre-war levels. But the traditional America-centeredness did not continue. Economic opportunities in the Dutch colonial empire were more attractive, and the United States immigration quota law of 1921 severely limited the American option. Never again would the United States be the major emigration destination for the Dutch.

In terms of the relative timing of emigration prior to 1880, the province-specific correlations reveal clear patterns. The provinces of Gelderland, Zeeland, Zuid-Holland, Overijssel, Utrecht, Noord-Brabant, and Drenthe sent a far higher proportion of their emigrants overseas in the early period—particularly Utrecht and Noord-Brabant, from which the majority of emigrants left between 1846 and 1857 (Table 2.4). These were the fabled Seceder emigrants led out by the dominies Albertus C. van Raalte, Hendrik P. Scholte, Marten Ypma, Pieter Zonne, and Cornelius Vander Meulen, among other leaders. The Catholic Brabanders followed Father Theodorus Vanden Broek to Little Chute, Wisconsin. The province of Limburg stands out as an anomaly, sending abroad more than one quarter of all its emigrants during the Civil War era (1857–65). The provinces of Noord-Holland, Limburg, and Groningen are distinct because their major migration spurts came late, after 1865.

Between 1880 and 1893, during the agricultural depression in Holland and before the economic depression of the 1890s in the United States, the sea clay provinces of Friesland, Groningen, and Zeeland (in descending order) were dominant emigration fields, together contributing 59 percent to the national total (Table 2.4). All were commercial agricultural regions along the North Sea coast that were throwing off excess farm laborers due to mechanization and land consolidation. The urban provinces of Noord-Holland, Zuid-Holland, and Utrecht (in descending order) totaled 21 percent. The final 20 percent came from the remaining provinces (in descending order): Gelderland, Overijssel, Drenthe, Noord-Brabant, and Limburg. After the American depression hit, the agricultural emigration gave way to an urban emigration from western Holland. Thereafter, Noord-Holland and Zuid-Holland surpassed by wider and wider margins the sea clay agricultural provinces that had long dominated overseas emigration.

In the 1890s the locus shifted dramatically and permanently to Randstad Holland. From the mid-1890s until 1920 a larger proportion of emigrants left the western provinces of Noord-Holland and Zuid-Holland. In the final phase, 1915–20, over two-thirds of all Dutch overseas emigrants hailed from these two urban provinces. Most were white-collar workers departing for the Netherlands colonies.

Migration Within Europe

This discussion of overseas emigration must be viewed in the context of labor migration in general. In theory, short-distance moves always exceed long-distance moves. It was no different with the Dutch, whose laborers traditionally sought temporary work in neighboring countries.[15] In the years 1901 to 1920 nearly 175,000 Dutch moved elsewhere in western Europe and only 110,000 went overseas (Table 2.6). This was a ratio of 2:1 in favor of intra-continental migration. Germany attracted one half the European total and Belgium one third. Most of the remainder went to Great Britain, France, and Switzerland. In the decade before the World War, Germany had the greatest allure, but in the immediate post-war years, Belgium ran a strong second.

During the war when the Netherlands remained neutral while being surrounded by belligerents, the Dutch rate of emigration dropped sharply by two thirds, from a total of 86,000 in the 1910–14 years to only 27,000 from 1915 through 1918 (Table 2.6). In 1918 and 1919, 73 and 78 percent, respectively, remained within Europe (Table 2.7). Nearly one half of those who did depart during the war left Europe for the security of southeast Asia or America. These years were an aberration because Dutch laborers took advantage of rebuilding opportunities in neighboring war-torn countries. During 1919 and 1920, 19,000 Dutch resettled in Belgium to help rebuild the ravaged country, while fewer than 10,000 went to Germany, the pre-war preference. Thus, the war caused a dual dislocation in the emigration stream. It reduced the total outflow by more than two thirds, and it redirected the flow away from Europe by more than 20 percent. However, this was merely an interruption and not a fundamental redirection. In 1920 traditional patterns returned; more than half of the emigrants again went overseas.

TABLE 2.6 Emigration by Destination and Time Periods, Europe and Overseas, 1901–20

EUROPE PERIODS	GERMANY NUMBER	%	BELGIUM NUMBER	%	OTHER NUMBER	%	ALL EUROPE NUMBER
1901–04	14,390	50	10,551	37	3,712	13	28,653
1905–09	29,523	60	14,572	30	4,698	10	48,793
1910–14	26,524	55	15,336	32	6,673	14	48,533
1915–18	8,152	55	3,875	26	2,859	19	14,886
1919–20	9,968	30	19,038	57	4,547	14	33,553
TOTALS	88,558	51	63,372	36	22,488	13	174,418

OVERSEAS ALL PERIODS	U.S.A. NUMBER	%	SOUTH AMERICA NUMBER	%	ASIA* NUMBER	%	SOUTH AFRICA NUMBER	%	OVERSEAS NUMBER
1901–04	9,925	63	645	4	3,195	20	2,050	13	15,815
1905–09	19,094	69	2,114	8	5,424	20	911	3	27,543
1910–14	22,251	59	3,343	9	10,765	29	1,071	3	37,430
1915–18	4,275	60	783	6	6,926	57	217	2	12,201
1919–20	6,210	35	1,039	6	9,731	56	518	3	17,498
TOTALS	61,755	56	7,924	7	36,041	33	4,767	4	110,487

ALL EMIGRANTS† PERIODS	ALL	OVERSEAS %
1901–04	44,468	36
1905–09	76,336	36
1910–14	85,963	44
1915–18	27,087	45
1919–20	51,051	34

* Includes 590 to Australia.

† Excludes 378 of unknown destination.

SOURCE: Central Bureau for Statistics, "Statistiek van den loop der bevolking van Nederland . . . 1880–1920," *Bijdragen tot de Statistiek van Nederland* (The Hague, 1880–1900); *Bijdragen tot de Statistiek van Nederland, Nieuwe Volgreeks* (The Hague, 1901–20).

TABLE 2.7 Emigration by Destination by Year, Europe and Overseas, 1915–20

YEAR	EUROPE NUMBER	%	U.S.A. NUMBER	%	SOUTHEAST ASIA NUMBER	%	SOUTH AMERICA NUMBER	%	SOUTH AFRICA NUMBER	%
1915	4,564	52	1,552	18	2,199	25	318	4	62	1
1916	2,332	37	1,585	25	1,980	32	245	4	95	1
1917	2,045	50	597	15	1,257	31	103	3	26	1
1918	5,945	73	541	7	1,490	18	117	1	34	1
1919	20,349	78	1,420	5	3,633	14	380	1	141	1
1920	13,204	52	4,790	19	6,098	24	659	3	377	2

SOURCE: Central Bureau for Statistics, "Statistiek van den loop der bevolking van Nederland . . . 1880–1920," *Bijdragen tot de Statistiek van Nederland* (The Hague, 1880–1900); *Bijdragen tot de Statistiek van Nederland, Nieuwe Volgreeks* (The Hague, 1901–20).

Demographic Patterns

The demographics of age, sex, and marital status of the immigrants reveal much about the underlying factors of the movement. Demographers rightly begin their studies of population composition with the age-sex factor, since it is a proxy for social structural characteristics and growth patterns.

The age and sex composition of the Dutch immigrants, 1820–80, is portrayed in the population pyramids in Figure 2.3, which are derived from the ship passenger lists for all east coast ports. As expected in an immigrant population, the pyramids display the general shape of a child's top, narrow at the base with a big bulge in the middle, and a noticeable asymmetry due to the large excess of males. This finding confirms one of Ravenstein's "laws of migration," that males ventured on more long-distance moves than did females who stayed closer to home.[16] Crossing the Atlantic to begin life anew was predominantly a male venture.

The age-sex ratios also shifted over time, according to the pattern familiar in immigration research.[17] Adult males dominated almost entirely in the initial phase of mass migration. But the growth phase, which began in the 1840s, included more women and children, and the ratio of males per 1000 families dropped to the lowest point of 133. At this time, entire congregations of Calvinist Seceders and Roman Catholics emigrated to the United States, mainly in families and networks of families. Thereafter, the sex ratio moved toward balance in each successive decade because of strong labor-market forces as immigration approached the saturation period of the 1880s. Finally, in the declining phase the number of males increased again. In the 1820s and 1830s, the number of males per 100 families was a very high 193 and 155, respectively, compared to a national ratio of only 96.[18] Most males were businessmen, gentlemen, and professionals seeking opportunities abroad.

The population pyramids in Figure 2.3 show that the sex discrepancy is least pronounced among "involuntary migrants" (children under 15 years and the aged over 60) and most apparent among "voluntary migrants" (adults 20 to 60 years). The male dominance in the 20–24- and 25–29-year-old groups is clearly demonstrated in the figure. This trend conforms to Scandinavian studies and supports Ravenstein's generalization that males always predominate among age groups whose emigration is heaviest.[19]

The average age of Dutch immigrants also declined in each of the decade cohorts except the 1870s. During the fifty years after 1820, the mean age dropped by nearly 2 years, from a mean of 24.77 years in the 1820s to 22.84 years in the 1860s. In short, the sex and age structure of Dutch immigration in the mid-nineteenth century conforms to Ravenstein's law as stated by William Petersen: "With respect to age differentiation, all migration is one: in both internal and international movements, adolescents and young adults predominate."[20] But more very young and elderly Dutch joined the immigrant stream than was the case with other northern European countries where male "birds of passage" predominated.[21]

Dutch immigration primarily occurred in a family context. Married adults and their dependent children dominated in every decade.[22] In the first and last phases, single adults comprised more than a quarter of the immigrants. During the mass migration of the forties, as few as 15 percent of the immigrants traveled as solitary adults. Until 1880 the proportion of singles hovered around 20 percent, or 25 percent if adult siblings are counted. After 1895 the proportion of singles climbed above 30 percent, reaching 50 percent during the First World War (Figure 2.4). Thus, before 1880 nearly 80 percent of the Dutch immigrated in family units. This figure surpasses by 15 to 30 points the percentage of families in the German and Scandinavian migration, which historians have always characterized as familial.[23] Unlike the remainder of northern Europe, Dutch immigration to America shifted very belatedly from a folk to a labor-type migration.[24] But as late as 1920 two thirds of the Dutch still emigrated with immediate family members.

Even the immigrants who sought industrial work in America emigrated as families, which is a tribute to the traditional familial cohesion in the Netherlands. A Michigan resident, who lived near the Grand Rapids railroad depot and witnessed the arrival of numerous trainloads of Dutch immigrants in the 1880s and 1890s, remarked that "they came to work in the Grand Rapids furniture factories, and they brought along their families."[25]

Few single females emigrated. Dutch women apparently were not yet sufficiently emancipated to take advantage of the increasing American demand for domestic labor and wives. In the 1870s, for example, the proportion of unmarried Dutch emigrant females per 1,000 unmarried emigrant males was less than half that of Swedish emigrant singles (333 compared to 705).[26] From 1900 to 1920 only 28 percent of overseas singles were female; one third of those went to the Dutch colonies and one quarter to the United States.[27]

Family migration was most pronounced in the growth phase of the 1840s. This is confirmed by data on the size and composition of immigrant "units" in the ship lists, which usually consisted of a nuclear family. Two thirds (63 percent) of immigrants traveled in nuclear ("simple") families in the 1840s (Table 2.8). Another 17 percent traveled as extended families (two generation or more), multiple families (with relatives), and with siblings.[28] The family percentage is a lower bound estimate, because in-law linkages often cannot be detected. During the mass migration of the forties, therefore, more than four out of every five Dutch immigrants arrived in family units.

The fertility level of Dutch immigrant women upon arrival in the United States was three times as high as all immigrant women in the United States and nearly equal to that of native American women. According to the 1850 *Report of the Superintendent of the Census*, the native-white birth ratio (i.e., the number of children under ten years of age per 1000 women between fifteen and forty years) was 1,592. For all immigrants the figure was 472, or barely one-third that of native stock.[29] But for Dutch women in the 1840s immigrant cohort, the fertility rate was 1,400 and for all six decades it was 1,346. This was 85 percent of the native American rate. Clearly, Dutch immigrants disembarked with exceptionally large families, compared with all other immigrants. Indeed, over one-third of all Dutch immigrants in the six decades were children below fifteen years of age; and if sons and daughters above age fifteen are included, the number of dependents surpassed 40 percent.

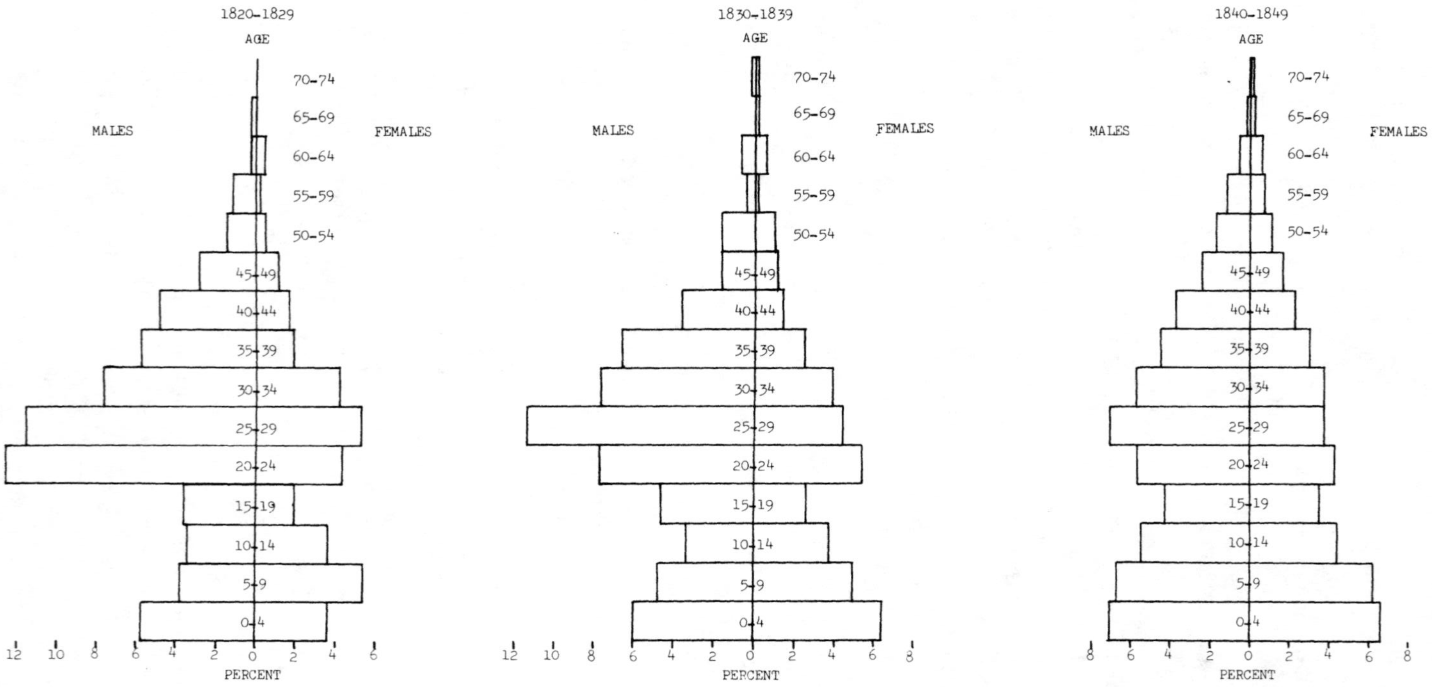

1820-1829
AGE
MALES
FEMALES
70-74
65-69
60-64
55-59
50-54
45-49
40-44
35-39
30-34
25-29
20-24
15-19
10-14
5-9
0-4
12 10 8 6 4 2 0 2 4 6
PERCENT
1830-1839
AGE
MALES
FEMALES
12 10 8 6 4 2 0 2 4 6 8
PERCENT
1840-1849
AGE
MALES
FEMALES
8 6 4 2 0 2 4 6 8
PERCENT

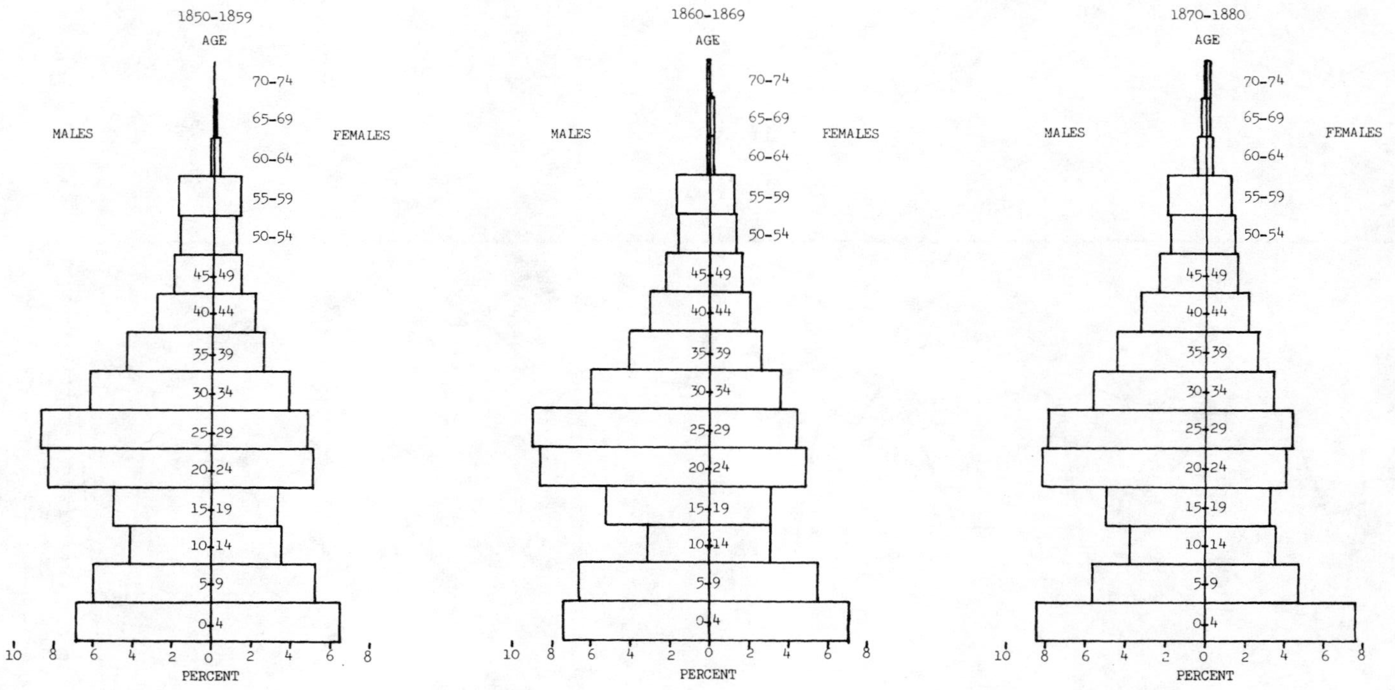

Figure 2.3 Dutch Immigrant Population Pyramids by Decade, 1820–80.

SOURCE: Swierenga study data derived from U.S. ship lists.

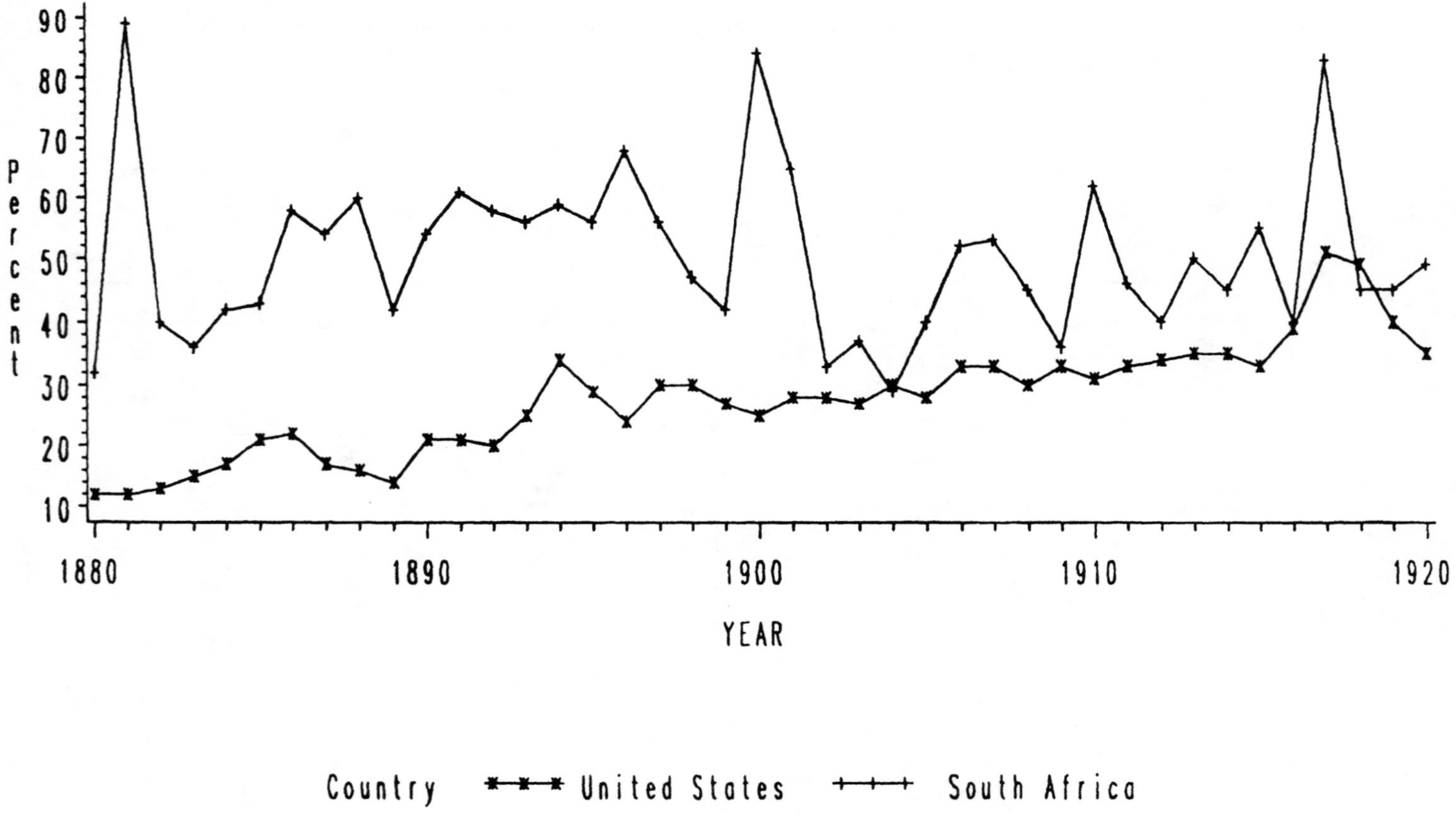

Figure 2.4 Single Adult Emigrants by Continent, 1880–1920

SOURCE: *Bijdragen tot de Algemene Statistiek van Nederland*, 1880–99; and . . . *Nieuw Volgreeks*, 1901–20

Dutch migration was thus a "family affair" to a greater degree than that of any other nationality. Over 80 percent of all immigrants prior to 1880 departed with immediate family members. Two thirds of these were couples with children; half of the remainder were childless couples, and half were single-parent families with children (Table 2.9). The Dutch emigrants had more children than other groups or even families in the Netherlands itself. As a result, Dutch immigrant household heads were older than those from other northern European countries.[30] The average age of the Dutch couples was 38 years for husbands and 36 years for wives.

These findings reveal that Dutch overseas emigration was more of a folk type than that of any other northern European countries. Only in the era of the First World War did labor migration begin. Dutch overseas emigrants were pre-industrial and rural, sustained by traditional clannishness and familism. This also explains why most immigrants in the United States settled near relatives and neighbors rather than strike out on their own. The transatlantic migration "filter" screened out industrial-type movers until the war.

Occupations

The occupations of the emigrants lend further support to the folk argument. According to the national occupational distribution in the Netherlands 1849 census of those gainfully employed, the agricultural sector (including fishing and hunting) included 44 percent, industry 22 percent, trade 6 percent, service 18 percent, and transportation 5 percent.[31] Among emigrants from 1835 through 1880, however, the number of farmers and farm laborers (26 percent) was eighteen points below the national average; day laborers, some of whom also worked in agriculture, comprised another 39 percent (Table 2.10). An additional 21 percent were employed in the pre-industrial crafts and 4 percent in industry, which was equal to the national average. Blue-collar workers thus made up about 80 percent of the Dutch labor force, but they comprised only 65 percent of the emigrant workforce.

Unskilled workers outnumbered skilled craftsmen by a two to one ratio. Three quarters originated in the clay soil regions, whereas skilled craftsmen hailed from both clay and sandy soil areas. Thirty percent of the skilled emigrants were from urban municipalities compared to only 5 percent of the unskilled emigrants. Approximately two thirds of both groups were of middling economic status, but one third of the unskilled were needy and in dire straits, compared to one fifth of the skilled workers. More than one half of both groups were married, with the unskilled surpassing the skilled by 10 points.

In short, the blue collar emigrants consisted of the rural craftsmen and day laborers who were most affected by the sluggish pace of Dutch industrialization. Rural protoindustry did not expand sufficiently to absorb them at home, nor did large-scale industry in the seacoast cities of Rotterdam, Amsterdam, and Haarlem, or the textile centers of Twente and Noord-Brabant. Most of the laborers were traditional farmhands and pre-industrial craft workers for whom America held out greater promise of economic advancement. Their economic status was middling to

Table 2.8 Co-migrating Household Types by Decade, 1820–80

Household Type	1820–29		1830–39		1840–49		1850–59		1860–69		1870–79		Totals	
	Number	%	Number	%	Number	%	Number	%	Number	%	Number	%	Number	%
Solitaries	189	46	305	31	1,861	14	3,195	21	1,814	21	3,829	24	11,193	21
Simple	207	51	541	55	8,490	66	9,110	61	5,210	61	10,198	63	33,756	63
Extended	5	1	16	1	469	4	456	3	336	4	516	3	1,788	3
Multiple	2	0	83	8	1,646	13	1,535	10	796	9	1,178	7	5,240	10
Siblings	6	2	42	4	386	3	744	5	344	4	500	3	2,022	4

Source: Compiled from Robert P. Swierenga, comp., *United States Ship Passenger Manifests: An Alphabetical Listing by Household Heads and Independent Persons*, 2 vols. (Wilmington, DE: Scholarly Resources, 1987).

Table 2.9 Family Type per "Migrant Unit" by Decade, 1820–80

Family Type	1820–29		1830–39		1840–49		1850–59		1860–69		1870–79		Totals	
	Number	%	Number	%	Number	%	Number	%	Number	%	Number	%	Number	%
Couples w/ children	27	55	97	64	1,517	72	1,550	67	943	69	1,687	64	5,821	67
Couples w/o children	10	20	31	20	342	16	416	18	215	16	453	17	1,467	17
Single parent male	8	16	10	20	128	6	183	8	103	7	196	7	628	7
Single parent female	4	8	14	9	110	5	160	7	110	8	317	12	715	8

Source: Central Bureau for Statistics, "Statistiek van den loop der bevolking van Nederland . . . 1880–1920," *Bijdragen tot de Statistiek van Nederland* (The Hague, 1880–1900); *Bijdragen tot de Statistiek van Nederland, Nieuwe Volgreeks* (The Hague, 1901–20).

TABLE 2.10 Occupations by Economic Sector per Period, 1835–80*

	1835–57		1858–68		1869–80		TOTAL	
SECTOR	ROW NUMBER	ROW %	ROW NUMBER	ROW %	ROW NUMBER	ROW %	ROW NUMBER	COL. %
Primary								
Farmers	1,245	44	779	28	813	29	2,837	16
Farm laborers	540	31	465	27	738	42	1,743	10
Total								26
Secondary								
Preindustrial crafts								
building trades	653	43	371	25	484	32	1,508	8
food processors	261	33	295	37	235	30	791	4
metal workers	162	49	76	23	93	28	331	2
wood workers	487	49	234	23	271	23	994	5
clothing trades	148	40	113	30	112	30	373	2
Total								21
Industrial								
textiles	160	60	56	21	49	18	265	2
iron and steel	6	35	5	29	6	35	17	0
engineers	14	37	12	32	12	32	38	0
watch\instrument	134	38	96	27	122	35	352	2
printers	4	16	11	14	11	40	26	0
misc.	14	25	17	30	26	46	26	0
Total								4
Laborers (unspecified)	2,176	31	2,256	32	2,673	38	7,105	39
Tertiary								
clerical	24	19	41	32	64	50	129	1
commercial	310	37	218	26	300	36	828	4
gov't officials	31	15	98	46	82	39	211	1
professionals	148	26	212	38	199	36	559	3
gentlemen, students	44	44	25	25	31	31	100	1
service	29	52	10	18	17	30	56	0
TOTALS								100

* The 2,043 individuals with no occupation, trade, or unemployed are excluded. The categories are those of Charlotte Erickson, "Emigration from the British Isles to the U.S.A. in 1831," *Population Studies* 35 (July 1981): 175–97, Tables 11, 13, 14, 15.

SOURCE: Robert P. Swierenga, comp., *Dutch Emigrants to the United States, South America, South Africa, and Southeast Asia, 1835–1880: An Alphabetical Listing by Household Heads and Independent Persons* (Wilmington, DE: 1983). This file is missing 2,933 emigrants in the years 1835–46 and 1877–80. See discussion of sources in Chapter 12.

poor, but few were in dire want. In this respect, the Dutch are akin to the English, who according to Charlotte Erickson, "were probably not people expelled by need or absolute hardship, but people able to make rational and conscious choices."[32] Netherlanders were pulled away by the American "magnet" more than they were pushed away by any Dutch "devils."

White-collar workers—professionals, business executives, clerks, government officials—together comprised only 10 percent of all emigrant households. Almost one half of these white-collar emigrants came from Amsterdam and neighboring cities of Randstad Holland. In contrast to this, Zeeland contributed one third (34 percent) of the farmers and day laborers, and Gelderland more than one-fourth (31 percent) of the farmers and service personnel (26 percent) and one fourth (28 percent) of the village craftsmen. Thus, the lack of adequate job opportunities prompted emigration to a greater extent from the rural villages and farms than from the large urban centers.

The lack of occupational diversity and job specialization among the Dutch emigrants is remarkable and clearly reflected a pre-industrial labor force. Although there were 163 specific occupations represented among the emigrants in the period from 1835 through 1880, none of the new industrial jobs was included among the top twenty occupations. The three most common—day laborer, farmer, and farmhand—accounted for nearly 60 percent of the adult male workforce (Table 2.11). Almost nine out of ten (86 percent) of the emigrant males worked in fewer than twenty occupations. Apart from the top three, only carpenters and merchants accounted for more than 3 percent. Merchants, clergymen, government officials, and teachers were the only non-blue-collar occupations among the top twenty. Nor

TABLE 2.11 Twenty Most Common Occupations, Male Emigrants, 20+, 1835–80

RANK	OCCUPATION	NUMBER	CUMULATIVE PERCENTAGE	RANK 1835–57	RANK 1858–68	RANK 1869–80
1	Laborer	5,712	36	1	1	1
2	Farmer	2,668	53	2	2	2
3	Carpenter	880	58	3	4	4
4	Farmhand	851	63	4	3	4
5	Merchant	580	67	5	5	5
6	Tailor	356	69	6	9.5	7
7	Shoemaker	343	71	7	11	8
8	Sailor	287	73	11	8	6
9	Baker	275	75	9	12	9
10	Blacksmith	257	77	10	14	10
11	Weaver	234	78	8	13	18
12	Soldier	200	79	11	5	17
13	Clergyman	198	80	14	9.5	13.5
14	Painter	198	81	12	16	11
15	Mason	175	82	13	18	13.5
16	Gov't official	166	83	21	7	12
17	Teacher	154	84	15	15	15
18	Miller	115	85	16	21.5	19
19	Clerk	101	86	23	17	16
20	Wagonmaker	88	86	18	19	20

SOURCE: Robert P. Swierenga, comp., *Dutch Emigrants to the United States, South America, South Africa, and Southeast Asia, 1835–1880: An Alphabetical Listing by Household Heads and Independent Persons* (Wilmington, DE: 1983). This file is missing 2,933 emigrants in the years 1835–46 and 1877–80. See discussion of sources in Chapter 12.

does the pattern change substantially over time. The occupational rankings remain virtually the same in the three major periods of emigration.

Only when the three major soil regions are differentiated is it possible to discern the economic forces at work in the rural Netherlands. Over half (57 percent) of all emigrants originated in the clay soil area, a third (32 percent) hailed from the thin sandy soils, and only one tenth (11 percent) came from dairy regions (Table 2.12). The dairy farms were small, single-family operations. Dairy farmers enjoyed stable prices and technology had little impact, so the propensity to emigrate was almost nil. Agriculturalists in the inland sandy regions also had less pressure to emigrate, because land reclamation in the nineteenth century and improved soil productivity (due to the introduction of artificial fertilizers) allowed several generations of farmers to keep their married sons at home by subdividing their farms.

In contrast, the sea clay regions along the North Sea coast of Zeeland, Groningen, and Friesland led in the development of commercial farming, cattle breeding, and participation in international markets. Agriculture was highly specialized and the farm owners were more entrepreneurial-minded in the coastal areas than elsewhere. The clay soil farms were especially large and prosperous by Dutch standards. They employed numerous farm workers who comprised a landless proletariat. Formerly the laborers were part of a patriarchal and mutually dependent, communal society. But with the introduction of capital economics in the eighteenth century, farmers sought higher profits by changing from stock raising to grain farming, by introducing scientific agricultural practices, by consolidating ancient holdings, and by cutting the workforce and reducing farm workers to the status of independent day laborers.

TABLE 2.12 Occupational Class by Economic Region, Household Heads and Single Adults, 1835–80

	Economic Regions							
	Clay Area		Sandy Area		Dairy Area		Row Totals	
Occupation Class*	Number	%	Number	%	Number	%	Number	%
High white collar†	312	42	251	34	176	24	739	4
Low white collar‡	524	44	286	24	370	31	1,180	6
Farmer	679	24	1,828	66	278	10	2,785	15
Farm laborer	1,117	82	223	16	27	2	1,367	8
Skilled\semiskilled	1,989	44	1,711	38	775	17	4,475	25
Unskilled	5,893	76	1,513	20	337	4	7,743	42
Column totals	10,514	57	5,812	32	1,963	11	18,289	100

* The occupational social class categories follow the codebook of Lynn Hollen Lees, "Patterns of Lower-Class Life and Irish Slum Communities in Nineteenth-Century London," in Stephen Thernstrom and Richard Sennett, eds., *Nineteenth-Century Cities: Essays in the New Urban History* (New Haven: Yale University Press, 1969), 359–85.

† Includes professionals, subprofessionals, owner-entrepreneurs, submanagerials, gentlemen, and students.

‡ Includes clericals, civil service employees, merchants, shopkeepers, and peddlers.

SOURCE: Robert P. Swierenga, comp., *Dutch Emigrants to the United States, South America, South Africa, and Southeast Asia, 1835–1880: An Alphabetical Listing by Household Heads and Independent Persons* (Wilmington, DE: 1983). This file is missing 2,933 emigrants in the years 1835–46 and 1877–80. See discussion of sources in Chapter 12.

The laborers, who had formerly been members of the farmer's family group, became strangers to be hired as needed during peak seasons of planting and harvesting. The workers thus became especially vulnerable to periodic food crises. This occurred in 1846–47 when rising potato and grain prices brought hunger to workers and windfall profits to the farmers.[33] These distressed workers, forever immortalized in Vincent van Gogh's painting *The Potato Eaters*, were the prime candidates for overseas migration. As Table 2.12 shows, 82 percent of all emigrant farm laborers originated in the clay soil regions, compared to only 24 percent among farmers. In sharp contrast, 66 percent of the farmer emigrants tilled sandy soil, compared to only 16 percent of the emigrant farm laborers. Over three quarters of all emigrant unskilled laborers also left sea clay areas, where many had worked in agriculture or related industries as well.

Farmers and farm laborers had contrasting time-specific emigration rates (Table 2.13). Farmers left mainly in the earliest period 1835–57; farm workers and day laborers began to emigrate heavily in the 1870s. This coincided with the Dutch agricultural crisis and the opening for homesteading of the last agricultural frontier in the American West. The remarkable difference in emigration rates and timing between farmers and laborers reinforces the point that the soil-rich "low" Netherlands, where farmers were mechanizing rapidly, needed fewer hired hands, whereas farmer's sons could still find a small plot in the sandy soils of the "high" Netherlands.

Demographic differences between farmers and laborers reflected their life situations. Farmers who chose to emigrate, often for long-term familial goals, were considerably older than farmhands (three quarters of farmers were above 30 years, compared to only one quarter of farmhands). Over one half of the farmers were married, compared to less than one fifth of the laborers; and farmers had more

TABLE 2.13 Occupational Class by Emigration Periods, Household Heads and Single Adults, 1835–80

Occupational Class*	Emigration Periods: 1835–37 Number	%	1858–68 Number	%	1869–80 Number	%	Row Totals Number	%
High white collar†	198	27	293	39	251	34	742	4
Low white collar‡	395	33	330	28	462	39	1,187	6
Farmer	1,236	44	768	27	792	28	2,796	15
Farm laborer	399	29	403	29	565	41	1,367	8
Skilled\semiskilled	1,918	43	1,211	27	1,361	30	4,490	25
Unskilled	2,446	32	2,388	31	2,918	38	7,752	42
Column totals	6,592	36	5,393	29	6,349	35	18,334	100

* The occupational social class categories follow the codebook of Lees, "Patterns of Lower-Class Life," 359–85.
† Includes professionals, subprofessionals, owner-entrepreneurs, submanagerials, gentlemen, and students.
‡ Includes clericals, civil service employees, merchants, shopkeepers, and peddlers.
SOURCE: Robert P. Swierenga, comp., *Dutch Emigrants to the United States, South America, South Africa, and Southeast Asia, 1835–1880: An Alphabetical Listing by Household Heads and Independent Persons* (Wilmington, DE: 1983). This file is missing 2,933 emigrants in the years 1835–46 and 1877–80. See discussion of sources in Chapter 12.

children. Among farm laborers, 88 percent had no children, compared to 41 percent of the farmers.

In the period 1835–57, 92 percent of the farm laborers were single. By the 1870s this figure dropped only slightly to 85 percent.[34] Unlike the pattern among industrial migrants, there was no shift over time from married to single farm laborers. Singles always predominated among the emigrant rural laborers. In terms of economic status, 25 percent of the farmers were well-to-do and only 8 percent were needy. Among farm workers 21 percent were needy (Table 2.14). Quite obviously, long-term economic shifts, coupled with periodic crop failures, cast adrift the many small renters and farm laborers from the most commercialized agricultural regions.

White-collar emigrants were most underrepresented. They included about 40 percent of the gainfully employed in the home country but made up only 10 percent of all emigrant household heads. Of these, the low white-collar group (teachers, clerks, civil servants, etc.) outnumbered by two to one the high white-collar professionals and managers. More than half of the professionals migrated to the Dutch colonies rather than to the United States (Table 2.15). Six out of ten were single. Some of these were not bonafide emigrants but civil administrators and military and church personnel fulfilling a tour of duty in one of the Dutch colonies.[35] Nearly half were urban in origin, primarily from Amsterdam, Rotterdam, and The Hague.

The occupational data before 1880 thus show that developments in agriculture and rural industry, coupled with demographic and social changes, provide the setting for overseas emigration. A potato crisis and religious conflict instigated widespread emigration in the 1840s, and the great agricultural depression of the 1880s provided the final impetus for rural mass migration. Blue-collar and agricultural workers supplied the majority of emigrants, with farmers from the poorer sandy soil regions following behind.

TABLE 2.14 Occupational Class by Social Class, Household Heads and Single Adults, 1835–80

	Social Class					
	Well-to-do		Middling		Needy	
Occupational Class*	Number	%	Number	%	Number	%
High white collar†	408	57	273	38	38	5
Low white collar‡	285	25	721	64	121	11
Farmer	668	25	1,780	67	198	8
Farm laborer	38	3	1,012	76	283	21
Skilled\semiskilled	474	11	3,017	70	793	19
Unskilled	93	1	5,014	65	2,561	33
Column totals	1,966	11	11,817	67	3,994	22

* The occupational social class categories follow the codebook of Lees, "Patterns of Lower-Class Life," 359–85.

† Includes professionals, subprofessionals, owner-entrepreneurs, submanagerials, gentlemen, and students.

‡ Includes clericals, civil service employees, merchants, shopkeepers, and peddlers.

Source: Robert P. Swierenga, comp., *Dutch Emigrants to the United States, South America, South Africa, and Southeast Asia, 1835–1880: An Alphabetical Listing by Household Heads and Independent Persons* (Wilmington, DE: 1983). This file is missing 2,933 emigrants in the years 1835–46 and 1877–80. See discussion of sources in Chapter 12.

Table 2.15 Occupational Class by Continental Destination, 1835–80

Occupational Class*	U.S. Number	U.S. %	Non-U.S. Number	Non-U.S. %
High white collar†	361	50	365	50
Low white collar‡	886	77	271	23
Farmer	2,630	98	67	2
Farm laborer	1,324	98	23	2
Skilled\semiskilled	3,869	89	474	11
Unskilled	7,355	97	241	3
Column totals	16,425	92	1,441	8

* The occupational social class categories follow the codebook of Lees, "Patterns of Lower-Class Life," 359–85.
† Includes professionals, subprofessionals, owner-entrepreneurs, submanagerials, gentlemen, and students.
‡ Includes clericals, civil service employees, merchants, shopkeepers, and peddlers.
Source: Robert P. Swierenga, comp., *Dutch Emigrants to the United States, South America, South Africa, and Southeast Asia, 1835–1880: An Alphabetical Listing by Household Heads and Independent Persons* (Wilmington, DE: 1983). This file is missing 2,933 emigrants in the years 1835–46 and 1877–80. See discussion of sources in Chapter 12.

The occupations of the emigrants after 1900 reflect the new industrial economy. The proportion employed in agriculture and industry decreased while those in the service sector increased (Table 2.16). The percent in farming dropped from 17 to 9 after 1915. Farmers, plus fishermen, miners, and peat diggers, totaled only 16 percent of all working emigrants in the period 1901–20, whereas the extractive sector counted 29 percent of the total Dutch labor force. Thus, primary sector emigrants were fully 45 percent below their proportion of the national Dutch workforce in these years.

In the industrial sector, which includes manufacturing, construction, and common laborers, more than two thirds of the emigrants worked in manufacturing, led by clothing, food processing, and luxury goods such as pottery and precious stones. While manufacturing jobs held steady over the period at 25 percent of the emigrant workforce, the secondary sector generally declined because of sharp drops in construction workers (from 9 to 4 percent between 1905–09 and 1919–20) and day laborers (from 9 to 2 percent between the same time periods). Emigrants employed in the secondary sector were overrepresented by 20 percent, compared to the overall Dutch workforce.

The service sector of commerce, transport, social services, the professions, and government employees became dominant among emigrants, rising by one third (from 42 to 56 percent) between 1901–05 and 1919–20. This large increase was due to a 67 percent rise in the professional category (12 to 20 percent) and a 50 percent rise in commerce (8 to 12 percent). Compared to the entire Dutch labor force, the emigrants in the tertiary sector were again overrepresented by 20 percent, as were those employed in the secondary sector.

The emigrant labor force in the years 1900–20 was 83 percent male, compared to a rate of 77 percent in the entire Dutch working population. In the primary and secondary sectors, 94 percent of the emigrants were male. Females were concentrated

TABLE 2.16 Emigrant Occupations by Economic Sector per Period, 1901–20 (in percent) and Overall Dutch Labor Force

ECONOMIC SECTOR	1901–1904	1905–1909	1910–1914	1915–1918	1919–1920	TOTAL 1901–1920	OVERALL LABOR FORCE 1899–1920
Primary							
1. Agriculture	17	15	15	9	10	14	27
2. Fish/Mining	1	2	2	1	2	2	2
TOTALS 1–2	18	17	17	10	12	16	29
Secondary							
3. Textile	3	3	3	1	1	3	3
4. Apparel	6	6	8	10	9	7	5
5. Wood	2	1	1	1	1	1	2
6. Metals	2	3	1	3	3	2	3
7. Food	6	6	6	4	4	5	4
8. Luxury	7	5	4	3	5	5	3
9. Other	1	1	2	2	2	2	4
TOTALS	27	25	25	24	25	25	24
Construction							
10. Construction	7	9	8	5	4	7	8
Laborer							
11. Laborer	6	9	6	3	2	6	—
TOTALS 3–11	40	43	39	33	31	38	32
Tertiary							
12. Commerce	8	8	8	9	12	9	12
13. Transport	7	7	8	8	10	8	7
14. Service	11	10	9	7	8	9	13
15. Professional	12	12	14	22	20	15	4
16. Government	4	3	5	11	6	5	2
TOTALS 12–16	42	40	44	57	56	46	38
TOTALS	36,574	58,064	69,398	20,520	39,038	223,594	

SOURCE: The Dutch labor force structure was computed from detailed tables in Central Bureau for Statistics, *13e Algemene volkstelling, 31 mei 1960, Deel 10 Beroeps-bevolking, C. Vergelijking van de uitkomsten van de beroepstellingen 1849–1960* (Hilversum, 1966), 28–39.

in the service sector, of which one fourth (27 percent) were female, primarily as domestics, teachers, and nurses. The occupational structure of the emigrants after 1900 thus mirrors the emerging industrial economy; emigrants in the agricultural sector were underrepresented while those in the manufacturing and service sectors were overrepresented.

Socioeconomic Status

Statistics on socioeconomic status also show a migration of upwardly mobile persons. In the Netherlands emigration records local officials classified each departing family or single adult as either well-to-do (*welgestelden*), less prosperous or middling (*minegegoeden*), or needy (*behoeftigen*), which denoted a family receiving some type of public dole. The highest proportion of the middling class originated in the northern provinces of Groningen (80 percent), Drenthe (72 percent), Overijssel (70 percent), and Friesland (69 percent)(Table 2.17). Zeeland had the greatest incidence of emigration by the needy; over one-third of all emigrant households, more than 1,400 in all, were classed as needy, whereas only 4 percent were well-to-do. Gelderland, another soil-poor province in the east, had the second highest number of needy at 20 percent. In contrast, the urban provinces of Noord-Holland, Zuid-Holland, and Utrecht had the most wealthy emigrants, 24 percent, 11 percent, and 29 percent, respectively. The fact that more needy families than wealthy ones also left these urban provinces, however, shows that poverty propelled urban as well as rural folk to emigrate.

After the industrial revolution in the Netherlands, the socioeconomic status of the emigrants improved markedly. Compared to the years before 1880, the emigration thereafter included one third more wealthy persons (17 versus 13 percent) one tenth more people of middling status (72 versus 65 percent), and only one half as many poor (11 versus 22 percent)(Table 2.17). The proportion of wealthy emigrants rose markedly during the World War, reaching a high point of 33 percent in 1917, which was nearly double the norm. Conversely, far fewer poor people emigrated during the war, and slightly fewer of middling status (Table 2.18).

TABLE 2.17 Emigrant Socioeconomic Status by Province, 1835–1920 (in percent)

	WELL-TO-DO				MIDDLING				POOR			
	1835–80		1880–1920		1835–80		1880–1920		1835–80		1880–1920	
PROVINCE	%	RANK	%	RANK	%	RANK	%	RANK	%	RANK	%	RANK
DR	15	6	4	11	72	2	81	3	13	9.5	16	5
FR	10	7.5	6	10	68	4	80	4	21	5.5	14	6
GE	17	5	19	2	62	9	59	10	21	5.5	21	4
GR	6	10	7	8	80	1	81	2	13	9.5	11	9
LI	18	4	14	5	65	6	74	6	17	8	12	8
NB	9	9	17	4	63	7.5	60	8	19	7	23	2
NH	24	2	10	7	51	10	86	1	25	3	4	11
OV	19	3	6	9	69	3	72	7	12	11	23	3
UT	30	1	17	3	40	11	60	9	30	2	23	1
ZH	4	11	36	1	63	7.5	57	11	33	1	7	10
ZE	10	7.5	10	6	66	5	78	5	24	4	12	7
TOTALS	13		17		65		72		22		11	

SOURCE: Robert P. Swierenga, comp., *Dutch Emigrants to the United States, South America, South Africa, and Southeast Asia, 1835–1880: An Alphabetical Listing by Household Heads and Independent Persons* (Wilmington, DE: 1983). Central Bureau for Statistics, *Bijdragen tot de Statistiek van Nederland*, 1881–1900; *Bijdragen ..., Nieuwe Volgreeks*, 1901–20.

TABLE 2.18 Emigrant Socioeconomic Status by Time Periods, 1835–1920 (in percent)

TIME PERIODS	WELL-TO-DO	MIDDLING	NEEDY
1835–57	12	64	24
1858–65	21	50	29
1866–80	12	69	19
TOTALS 1835–80	13	65	22
1881–1900	NA	NA	NA
1901–04	16	71	13
1905–09	16	71	12
1910–14	16	72	12
1915–18	26	67	7
1919–20	17	75	8
TOTALS 1881–1920	17	72	11
TOTALS 1835–1920	17	71	12

SOURCE: Robert P. Swierenga, comp., *Dutch Emigrants to the United States, South America, South Africa, and Southeast Asia, 1835–1880: An Alphabetical Listing by Household Heads and Independent Persons* (Wilmington, DE: 1983). Central Bureau for Statistics, *Bijdragen tot de Statistiek van Nederland*, 1881–1900; *Bijdragen . . . , Nieuwe Volgreeks*, 1901–20.

Zuid-Holland, including the port city of Rotterdam and the government center of The Hague, had the highest level of wealthy emigrants in the period 1901–20 at 36 percent. The province of Gelderland, which boasted the cities of Nijmegen and Arnhem, was second with 19 percent well-to-do emigrants. The urban province of Noord-Holland, including the largest city, Amsterdam, had the highest percentage of middling emigrants at 86 percent; another 10 percent were wealthy. By contrast, this province also had the fewest poor emigrants with only 4 percent. Four provinces with nearly one-quarter of their emigrants on the public dole were the interior provinces of Utrecht, Overijssel, Gelderland, and Noord-Brabant. These more isolated regions were not as economically healthy as the Randstad, and there was a wider gulf between rich and poor.

Although the published government figures do not differentiate socioeconomic status between U.S.-bound immigrants and those settling in the Dutch colonies, the fact that the war years witnessed a sharp increase in wealthy emigrants and a concomitant rise in the migration stream to the East Indies suggests that the young professionals, servants, and businessmen were seeking opportunities in the Orient.

Rural-Urban Differentials

When the continental destination of the post-1900 emigrants is distinguished by place of origin, big cities had a very different pattern than rural villages. Not only did the proportion of emigrants from cities above 100,000 population increase by 50 percent—from 39 to 58 percent—between 1905 and 1920 (Table 2.19 last

TABLE 2.19 Population Size of Municipality of Origin, by Continental Destination and Time Period (in percent), 1905–20

YEARS	EUROPE	USA	ASIA	SOUTH AMERICA	AFRICA	TOTALS	TOTAL PERCENTAGE
1905–09							
100,000+	70	13	13	3	1	29,864	39
20,000	64	24	7	3	2	9,872	13
5,000	63	31	3	2	1	20,498	27
–5,000	54	40	2	3	1	16,262	21
The Nation	64	25	7	3	1		
1910–14							
100,000+	60	14	20	4	2	36,263	42
50,000	65	20	7	6	1	6,886	8
20,000	58	26	12	3	1	8,759	10
5,000	52	36	7	4	1	19,713	23
–5,000	47	45	3	3	1	14,419	17
The Nation	56	26	13	4	1		
1915–18							
100,000+	53	11	32	3	1	14,811	55
50,000	67	12	16	4	1	2,006	7
20,000	55	17	25	3	1	2,797	10
5,000	54	24	18	3	1	5,260	19
–5,000	56	28	12	2	1	2,287	8
The Nation	55	16	26	3	1		
1919–20							
100,000+	66	7	23	2	1	29,624	58
50,000	75	9	12	3	2	2,656	5
20,000	63	13	21	2	1	4,075	8
5,000	58	24	14	3	1	8,230	6
–5,000	70	20	8	1	1	6,507	13
The Nation	66	12	19	2	1		

SOURCE: Robert P. Swierenga, comp., *Dutch Emigrants to the United States, South America, South Africa, and Southeast Asia, 1835–1880: An Alphabetical Listing by Household Heads and Independent Persons* (Wilmington, DE: 1983). Central Bureau for Statistics, *Bijdragen tot de Statistiek van Nederland*, 1881–1900; *Bijdragen ..., Nieuwe Volgreeks*, 1901–20.

column), but two thirds (66 percent) moved within northern Europe (first column), except during the war years when the Dutch colonies in the East Indies provided a safe haven.

For emigrants to the United States, the more rural the place of origin, the greater the exodus. There was a perfect inverse relationship between population size and emigration. As the population of the municipality decreased, the percentage emigrating to the United States increased. Three times as many emigrants went to North America from villages under 5,000 population than from large cities over 100,000. Conversely, among emigrants to the Dutch East Indies, the larger the population of origin, the greater the emigration. More than twice as many emigrants to the Indies hailed from cities over 100,000 as from villages under 5,000. These geographical differences indicate that rural and small-town Hollanders continued to be more attracted to the United States than were emigrants from the cities above 20,000, who went to European cities or to the Dutch overseas colonies.

When family status is also factored into the urban-rural differential, the picture becomes even sharper. Emigrants from the largest cities (above 100,000 population) consistently included more singles; indeed, they exceeded by 10 points the percent of singles among emigrants from villages below 5,000. Between 40 and 46 percent of all emigrants from the largest cities departed alone, compared to 31 to 34 percent from small towns. Among the single emigrants, males predominated. From the largest cities the proportion of male singles ranged up to 77 percent. But from small towns the proportion of male and female single emigrants was close to 50–50, and female singles dominated among those going to South Africa by a three to one ratio. Unmarried farmer's daughters clearly were attracted to South Africa as maids and prospective wives of the Boers.

Conclusion

Progress in industrialization was minimal in the Netherlands from 1850 until the 1880s, and full-blown "take-off" did not begin until the late 1890s. From then until 1914, annual growth in investment capital exceeded 10 percent, foreign trade expanded greatly, and many industrial sectors such as textiles and later metals led the expansion. The Netherlands after 1900 began to emulate the United Kingdom and Germany, which had industrialized a generation or two earlier. Thus, the Dutch economy only belatedly was integrated into the international economy of the Atlantic world.

The process of industrialization caused a major social structural change in Dutch overseas migration at the turn of the century. Traditional emigration by rural families gave way to urban singles, primarily male. The United States remained the primary destination, but by a very small 6:5 ratio, compared to the 10:1 ratio of the nineteenth century. The Dutch colonies in Asia, and to a much lesser extent colonies in South America and the Dutch culture region of South Africa, became increasingly attractive. Instead of farmers, day laborers, and hand craftsmen, service workers and factory laborers became predominant.

Between 1900 and 1920 a system of labor migration belatedly replaced the normal folk movement that characterized Dutch overseas migration throughout the nineteenth century. The Netherlands had finally "caught up" with England, Ireland, Germany, and the rest of northern Europe in the shift from family to industrial migrants.

Notes

1. Brinley Thomas, *Migration and Economic Growth*, 2d ed. (Cambridge: Cambridge University Press, 1973), 83–183, 286; Pieter R. D. Stokvis, "Dutch Mid-Nineteenth Century Emigration in European Perspective," in *Dutch Immigration to North America*, Herman Ganzevoort and Mark Boekelman eds. (Toronto: Multicultural History Society, 1983), 35–38. For a critique of the push-pull model, see Dudley Baines, *Emigration from Europe, 1815–1930, Studies in Economic History and Social History* (Houndmills, UK. Macmillan Education Ltd, 1991), 13–14.
2. Many scholars note the German influence on early Dutch emigration. Henry S. Lucas, *Netherlanders in America: Dutch Immigration to the United States and Canada* (Ann Arbor: University of Michigan Press, 1955; repr. Grand Rapids: Wm B. Eerdmans, 1989), 37; Jacob van Hinte, *Netherlanders in America: A Study of Emigration and Settlement in the Nineteenth and Twentieth Centuries in the United States of America*, ed. Robert P. Swierenga, chief trans. Adriaan de Wit (Grand Rapids: Baker Book House, 1985), 122.
3. Herbert J. Brinks, "Germans [Graafschap Bentheimers] in the Christian Reformed Church, 1857–1872," *Origins* 9, no. 2 (1991): 36–43; and Brinks, "Ostfrisians in Two Worlds," in *Perspectives on the Christian Reformed Church: Studies in its History, Theology, and Ecumenicity*, eds. Peter De Klerk and Richard R. De Ridder (Grand Rapids: Baker Book House, 1983), 21–34.
4. Lucas, *Netherlanders in America*, 213–17.
5. James W. Oberly, *Sixty Million Acres: American Veterans and the Public Lands Before the Civil War* (Kent, OH: Kent State University Press, 1990); Robert P. Swierenga, *Pioneers and Profits: Land Speculation on the Iowa Frontier* (Ames, IA: Iowa State University Press, 1968), ch. 5.
6. Swierenga, *Pioneers and Profits*, 96.
7. Jonathan R. T. Hughes, "The Commercial Crisis of 1857," in *Papers in Economic History, Part III*, 207–34; Bertus Harry Wabeke, *Dutch Emigration to North America, 1627–1860: A Short History* (New York: Netherlands Information Bureau, 1944), vii.
8. Hille de Vries, *Landbouw en bevolking tijdens de agrarische depressie in Friesland (1878–1895)* (Wageningen: H. Veenman en Zonen, 1971).
9. E. P. Hutchinson, *Legislative History of American Immigration Policy, 1789–1965* (Philadelphia: University of Pennsylvania Press, 1981), 174–94, 368–77; Philip Taylor, *The Distant Magnet: European Emigration to the USA* (New York: Harper & Row, 1971), 250–55. In 1917 the United States government instituted a literacy test, which required adult immigrants to demonstrate the ability to read a passage (usually from the Constitution) in their native language.

10. "Dutch Alarmed at Soaring Emigration," *Los Angeles Times*, 25 Dec. 1979, part IX, p. 4.
11. Frans Buysse, "De Zeeuwse gemeenschap van Holanda, Brazilië (1858–1982). Een antropologische studie over integratie en identiteit," *Bijdragen tot de geschiedenis van West Zeeuws-Vlaanderen* 13 (1984): 1–151; Martin C. Saris, *Emigratie naar Brazilië uit West-Zeeuws Vlaanderen, 1858–1862* (Murray, UT: Saris, 1977). A pathetic picture of the "forgotten" colony today is "the Lost Dutch of Espirito Santo," *The Windmill Herald* (Vancouver, B.C.), 14 March 1977, 10–11, summarizing a larger report in *Holland Herald* by Jan van Bentum.
12. Robert P. Swierenga, "Dutch International Labour Migration to North America in the Nineteenth Century," in Ganzevoort and Boekelman, *Dutch Immigration to North America*, 13, Table 6.
13. Annemieke Galema, *Frisians to America, 1880–1914: With the Baggage of the Fatherland* (Groningen: Regio-Projekt, and Detroit: Wayne State University Press, 1996).
14. John D. Bussink, "Regional Differences in Marital Fertility in the Netherlands in the Second Half of the Nineteenth Century, *Population Studies* 25 (1971): 366–69; William S. Petersen, *Some Factors Influencing Postwar Migration from the Netherlands* (The Hague: Martinus Nijhoff, 1952), 16.
15. Stokvis, "Dutch International Migration, 1815–1910," 43–63; Stokvis, "Nederland en de international migratie, 1815–1960," in *De Nederlandse samenleving sinds 1815*, ed. F.L. van Holthoon (Assen: Van Gorkum, 1980), 71–92. The "North Sea System" of migratory labor in the 19th century is described in Jan Lucassen, *Migrant Labour in Europe 1600–1900* (London: Croom Helm, 1987), 129–71.
16. D. B. Gregg, "E. G. Ravenstein and the 'laws of migration,'" *Journal of Historical Geography* 3 (1977): 41–54, esp. 43.
17. Bo Kronberg, Thomas Nilsson, and Andres A. Svalestuen, eds., *Nordic Population Mobility: Comparative Studies of Selected Parishes in the Nordic Countries, 1850–1900* (Uppsala, Sweden: Universitetsforlaget, 1977).
18. Paul Deprez, "The Low Countries," in *European Demography and Economic Growth*, ed. W. R. Lee (New York: St. Martin's Press, 1979), 265.
19. Kristian Hvidt, *Flight to America: The Social Background of 300,000 Danish Emigrants* (New York: Academic Press, 1975), 84.
20 William S. Petersen, *Population* (New York: Macmillan, 1961), 263.
21 John S. Lindberg, *The Background of Swedish Emigration to the United States: An Economic and Sociological Study in the Dynamics of Migration* (Minneapolis: University of Minnesota Press, 1930), 190–91.
22. The ship manifests seldom designate the relationship to the family head of each individual in the "emigration unit." Fortunately, the functionaries usually followed the standard census procedure of listing the household head first, followed by the wife, children, and sometimes siblings or

parents. To be consistent, the inferred family status of each of the 54,000 Dutch immigrants was determined according to rules adapted from Buffington Clay Miller's analysis of the 1880 federal population census ("A Computerized Method of Determining Family Structure from Mid-Nineteenth Century Census Data" [M.S. thesis, University of Pennsylvania, 1972]). See Theodore Hershberg, "The Philadelphia Social History Project: A Methodological Inquiry" (Ph.D. diss., Stanford University, 1973), 233.

23. Hvidt, *Flight to America*, 93; Wolfgang Kollmann and Peter Marschalk, "German Emigration to the United States," *Perspectives in American History* 7 (1973): 499–554; Mack Walker, *Germany and the Emigration, 1816–1885* (Cambridge, MA: Harvard University Press, 1964), 186.
24. Sten Carlson, "Chronology and Composition of Swedish Emigration to America," in *From Sweden to America: A History of the Migration*, eds. Harald Runblom and Hans Norman (Minneapolis: University of Minnesota Press, 1976), 132.
25. Z. Z. Lyden, ed., *The Story of Grand Rapids* (Grand Rapids, MI: Kregel Publications, 1966), 43.
26. Lindberg, *Background of Swedish Emigration*, 193.
27. Superb studies are Suzanne M. Sinke, "Home is Where You Build It: Dutch Immigrant Women in the United States, 1880–1920 (Ph.D. diss., University of Minnesota, 1993); and "Dutch Immigrant Women in the Late Nineteenth Century: A Comparative Analysis" (M.A. thesis, Kent State University, 1983).
28. Simple family households are married couples with or without children and widowed persons with children; extended family households include three or more generations; and multiple family households contain two or more conjugal family units connected by kinship or marriage. See "Introduction: The History of the Family," in *Household and Family in Past Time*, eds. Peter Laslett and Richard Wall (Cambridge: Cambridge University Press, 1972), 28–32. It is important to emphasize that the family units are not co-residing census households but co-emigrants who may or may not reside together before or after the transatlantic passage.
29. U.S. Bureau of the Census, *Report of the Superintendent of the Census for December 1, 1852; To Which is Appended the Report for December 1, 1851* (Washington, D.C., 1853), 111–19.
30. E. W. Hofstee, "Population Increase in the Netherlands," *Acta Historiae Nederlandica* 3 (1968): 43–125; Petersen, *Population*, 263; Hvidt, *Flight to America*, 89.
31. William Petersen, *Planned Migration: The Social Determinants of the Dutch-Canadian Movement* (Berkeley and Los Angeles, University of California Press, 1955), 22.
32. Charlotte J. Erickson, *Leaving England: Essays on British Emigration in the Nineteenth Century* (Ithaca, NY: Cornell University Press, 1994), 157.
33. J. Haveman, "Social Tensions Between Farmer and Farm Laborer in Northern Holland," *American Journal of Sociology*, 60 (Nov. 1954): 246–54.

34. The specific figures for farm laborers are: 1835–57; 499 singles, 41 families; 1858–68, 411 singles, 54 families; 1869–80, 622 singles, 116 families.
35. Dutch officials in The Hague repeatedly complained about the loose classification of overseas emigrants. Even people who emigrated to countries on the European continent were sometimes included. See for example, *Staatkundig en Staathuishoudkundig Jaarboekje over 1854*, 272; ibid., 1862, 7.

CHAPTER 3

Anatomy of Migration

Frank Thistlethwaite in 1960 encouraged scholars to explore the "true anatomy of migration" by placing the mass of data under a microscope and identifying the "honeycomb of innumerable particular cells."[1] This chapter describes individual cells in one such network of migration, that of Dutch communities linked by the transatlantic flow of migrants in the years 1835 to 1880.

Each area of the Netherlands had its own emigration history.[2] As Thistlethwaite aptly stated: "We must not talk of Wales, but of Portmador or Swansea, not of North or South Italy but of Venetia or Calabria, not of Greece but of Tripolis or Sparta, not even of Lancashire, but of Darwin and Blackburn."[3] Not merely every country, or even every major region of a country, but every locality and village had its own migration experience.[4]

The historic cultural-geographical landscape of the Netherlands, as portrayed in Figure 3.1, reveals a complex patchwork of nearly one hundred regions each with unique characteristics. Ecologically, at the broadest level the sea clay soil provinces of Zeeland, Friesland, and Groningen, supported a different agricultural system than the inland sandy soil provinces of Gelderland, Overijssel, Drenthe, Noord-Brabant, and Limburg. Likewise, the urban, commercially-oriented western provinces of Noord- and Zuid-Holland and Utrecht differed from the rural, isolated interior provinces. Religiously, the Catholic southern provinces of Noord-Brabant and Limburg embodied a culture that conflicted with that in the Protestant north.

Within the various localities the intensity of emigration was affected by many forces, only some of which can be identified, let alone measured. A full explanation would include the historical tradition and conditions relating to religion, education, political power, and the social and economic culture; structural factors of a demographic, economic, or social nature; stimulators such as sharp business cycle changes, agricultural crises, war, and the flow of information; and psychological and sociological factors. Each of these developments prompted some individuals and groups to emigrate more than others.

Swedish scholars, who have made sophisticated scientific analyses of parish emigration patterns in the nineteenth century, isolated several keys to explaining local

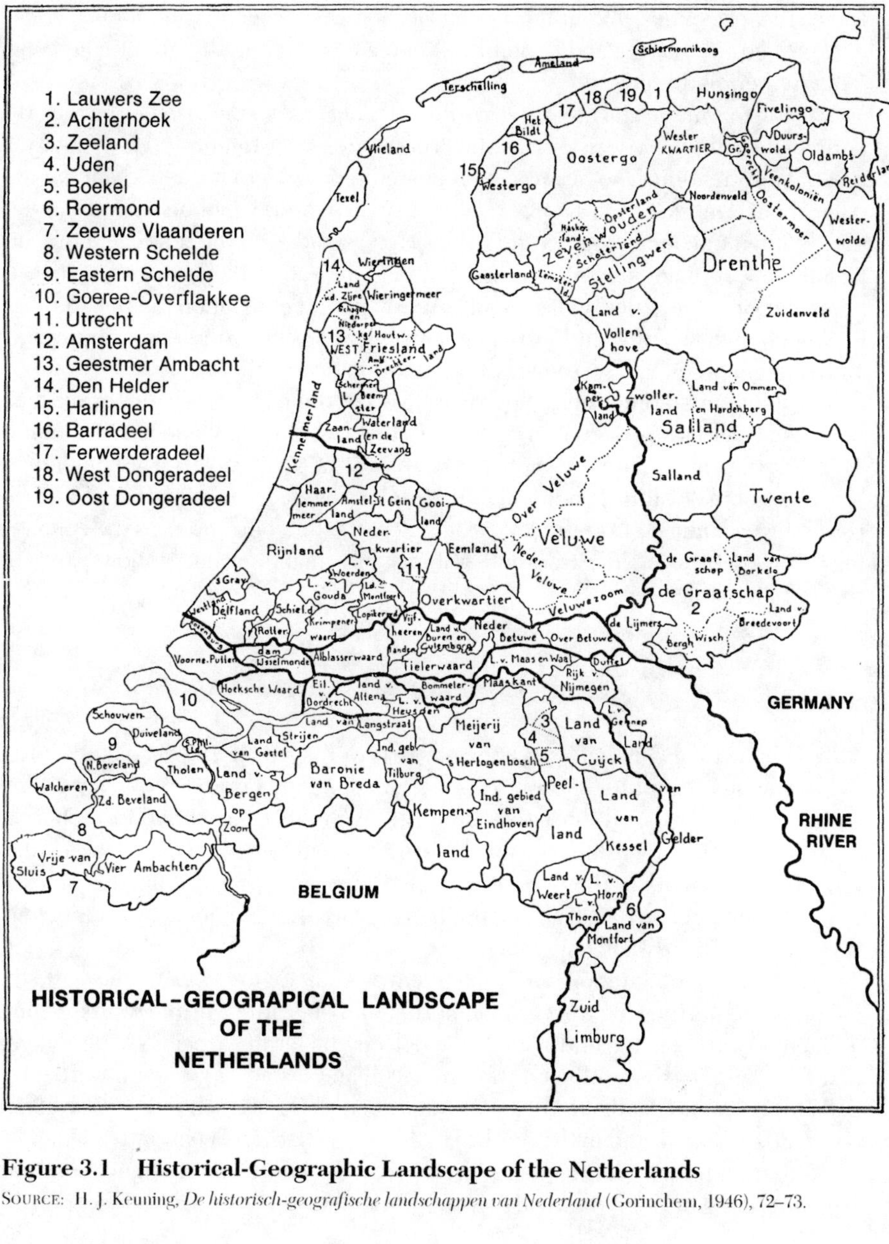

Figure 3.1 Historical-Geographic Landscape of the Netherlands

SOURCE: H. J. Keuning, *De historisch-geografische landschappen van Nederland* (Gorinchem, 1946), 72–73.

variations.[5] Most relate to work opportunities and the amount of information available about American destinations. The extent of industrialization in the parish, or the distance to the nearest urban industrial center, as well as the degree of general mobility between other regions within the country, also affected the opportunity cost of parish inhabitants. A factor of equal if not greater importance was the existence of an emigration tradition, which increased contact and knowledge about America.[6] Excess laborers in a modernizing agricultural economy did not have a choice to move or not, but rather they had a choice between two migrational objectives—to go to America and hopefully obtain a farm or join the urban blue-collar ranks in their native land.[7]

Moving to America involved the greatest risk because of the distance barrier, the permanence of such a decision, the shock of cultural adjustment, and the paucity of reliable information. The best way to reduce the risk was to have firsthand knowledge about America from family, relatives, friends, and neighbors already settled there.[8] Their encouragement, offers of assistance, and even the sending of prepaid tickets were sufficient to entice others to emigrate, rather than stay put or seek an industrial job in the cities. Villages with an early start of emigration thus had the best likelihood of developing and sustaining a strong emigration tradition over decades and even generations. The sooner the emigration began, the stronger the outflow.

But if an emigration tradition is critically important, this raises the prior question: What causes an emigration tradition to begin in one place and not in another? This question again requires microscopic analysis at the local level, although macroanalysis of the historic conditions, structural changes, cyclical simulators, and the psychological mind-sets of the people all affect the outcome. So does the connecting infrastructure, such as transport systems, informal information flows, and the role of religious leaders.

Geography of Migration

Although the total Dutch immigration was relatively small, its impact on the United States was significant for several reasons. The emigrants originated in a very few Netherlands villages. Of the 1,156 administrative units (*gemeenten*) in 1869—the equivalent of U.S. townships—only 134, or 12 percent, provided nearly three quarters of all emigrants in the period from 1820 through 1880; 55 municipalities (5 percent) sent out one half of all emigrants; and a mere 22 municipalities (2 percent) furnished one third of all emigrants.[9]

These major emigration fields are identified in Figure 3.2. In the east, the Gelderse Achterhoek on the German border early became a prime source region, as did the Veluwe; in the north, it was the rich coastal farming regions of Groningen and Friesland; in the southwest, the Zuid-Holland island of Goeree-Overflakkee and the Zeeland islands of West Vlaanderen, Walcheren, Schouwen-Duiveland, and Zuid Beveland; and in the southeast, the Brabantse Peel centered in Uden.

Netherlanders also had a greater presence in the United States than their numbers warranted because they had a strong "America-centeredness." Ninety percent

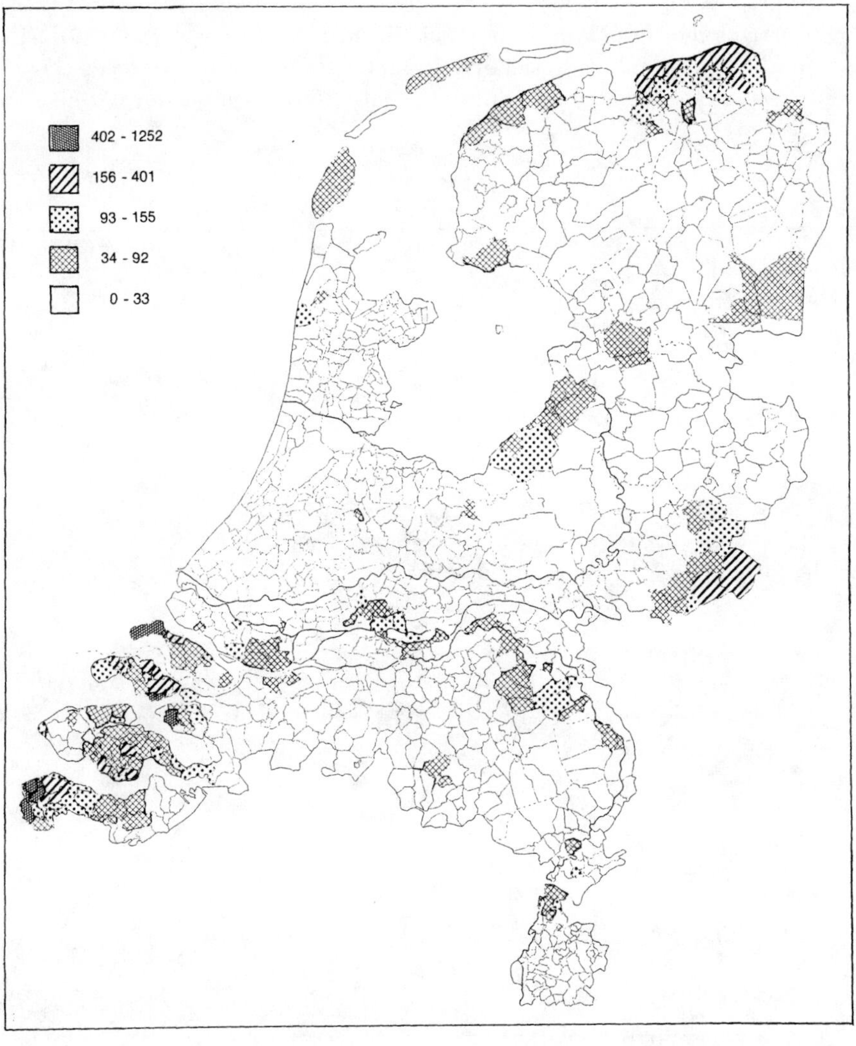

Figure 3.2 Emigration Rate per Municipality, 1835–80, per 1,000 Average Population, 1830–78

SOURCE: R. P. Swierenga, *Dutch Emigrants to the United States, South Africa, South America, and Southeast Asia: An Alphabetical Listing by Household Heads and Independent Persons, 1835–1880* (Scholarly Resources: Wilmington, DE, 1983); *Volkstelling*, 1 January 1830; *Bijdragen tot de Algemene Statistiek van Nederland, 1878, Bevolking, Oppervlakte*, 1, 1–73.

of all Dutch overseas emigrants before the mid-1890s settled in the United States. By the time of the 1870 census, after 60,000 to 70,000 of the "new" immigrants had arrived, 60 percent could be found in only twenty-two counties in seven midwestern and two mid-Atlantic seaboard states (38 percent lived in only forty-six townships and city wards).[10] This funneling pattern, like a megaphone, amplified the Dutch visibility in America.

The primary settlement field was within a fifty-mile radius of the southern Lake Michigan shoreline from Muskegon, Grand Rapids, Holland, and Kalamazoo on the east to Chicago, Milwaukee, Sheboygan, and Green Bay on the west side (Figure 3.3). Secondary settlement areas were in central Iowa, southeastern Minnesota,

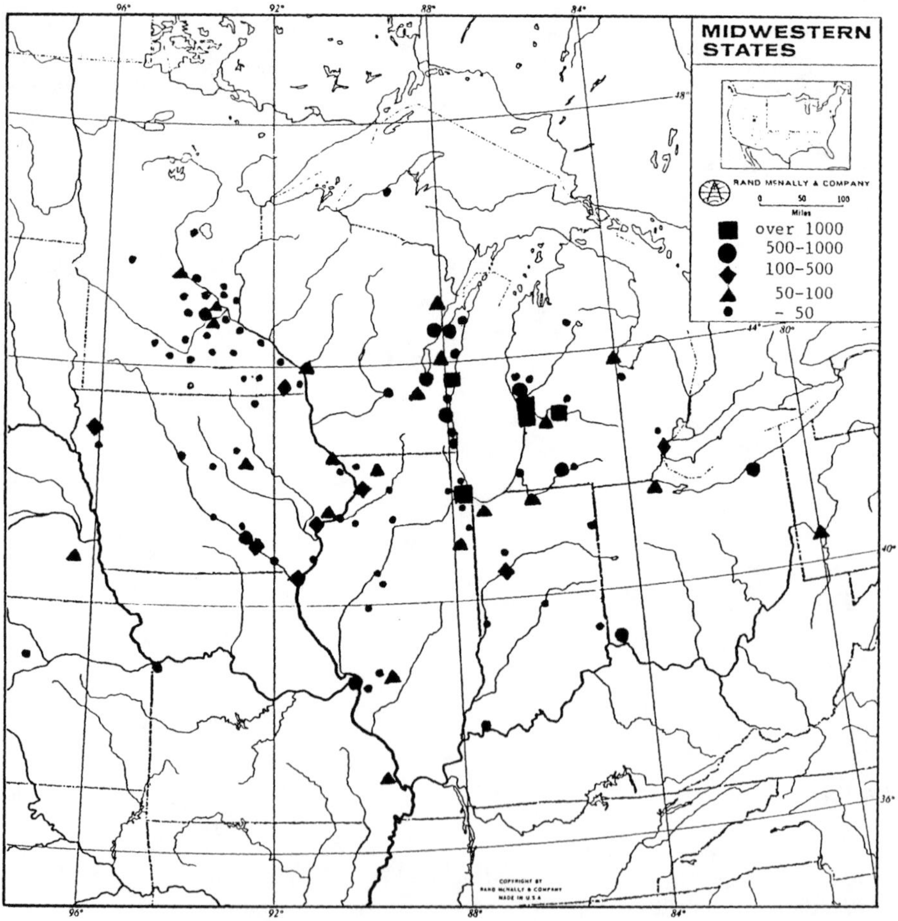

Figure 3.3 Dutch-born in Midwestern States, 1870

SOURCE: Swierenga study data derived from the Federal Manuscript Population Census of 1870

and the New York City region including northern New Jersey (Figure 3.4). Subsequently, the Dutch dispersed themselves over a wider area of the Great Plains and Far West in search of cheap farm land. But few immigrant groups, if any, have clustered more than the Dutch. Thus, despite a relatively low number of overseas emigrants, the Dutch single-mindedness for the United States and their clannish settlement behavior created a choice environment in which to nurture and sustain a strong sense of "Dutchness" for many generations.

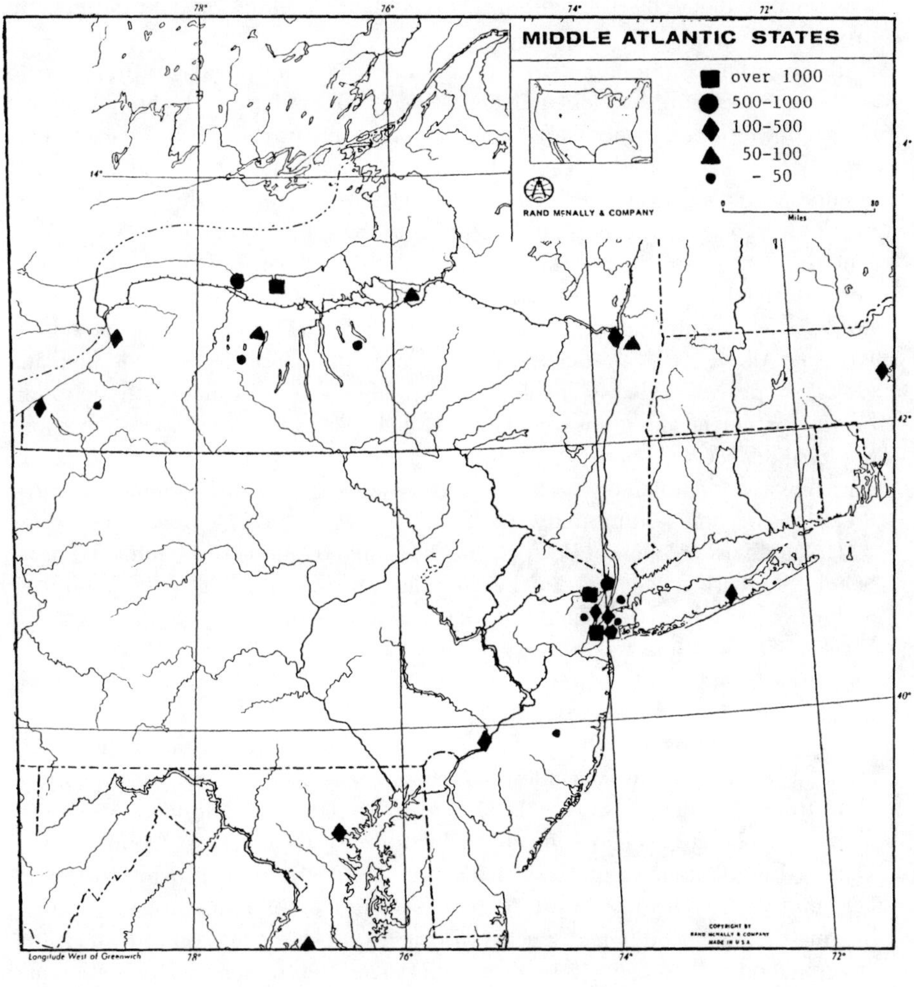

Figure 3.4 Dutch-born in Middle Atlantic States, 1870

SOURCE: Swierenga study data derived from the Federal Manuscript Population Census of 1870

Settlement Behavior

Dutch immigrants carried a traditional familism and localism to America as part of their cultural baggage. Like other European peasants from areas generally isolated from the forces of the Industrial Revolution, Dutch immigrants valued an ordered, traditional society based on kinship, village, and church. When these people emigrated, and this is especially true of the Calvinists, they sought to transplant their village cultures, churches, and kin networks. Most were not innovators seeking to break free of their identity group, but conservatives intending to maintain their culture in a new environment. Group identity and the desire for religious and cultural maintenance dictated settlement in segregated communities on the frontier or in urban neighborhoods.

Because Dutch immigrants from the same Old Country villages preferred to settle together in order to lessen the emotional shock of leaving the homeland and to facilitate the adjustment to a new environment, provincial or local loyalties remained strong in most settlements in the United States, at least until the first generation passed from the scene. In the classic example of this phenomenon, nearly every village and town in half a dozen townships surrounding the largest Dutch colony of Holland in Ottawa County, Michigan, boasted a Dutch place-name derived from the province or town where most of the first settlers originated (Figure 3.5). The central city of Holland, founded in 1847 under the leadership of Dominie Albertus C. Van Raalte, consisted largely of people from Gelderland and Overijssel provinces. New arrivals soon founded villages within a ten-mile radius bearing provincial and municipal names of their places of origin where they spoke the local dialect and perpetuated dress and food customs. The entire settlement was known as "de Kolonie," but it required the passing of the first generation before the colony became a community.[11]

Holland's sister colony of Pella, Iowa, also founded in 1847 by Dominie Henry P. Scholte, similarly had its cultural divisions. Settlers from the large cities of Utrecht and Amsterdam lived in or near the village center, while on the periphery was the "Frisian Neighborhood" northwest of town, the hamlet of Kockengen to the north for people from that village in Utrecht Province, and the Herwijnen neighborhood of those from the village bearing that name in Gelderland Province. Although the entire colony consisted initially of religious Seceders, their provincial differences caused friction for many years, despite a shared religious bond.[12]

In frontier settlements in the 1880s and 1890s, new Dutch immigrants continued to perpetuate such provincial distinctions. In Charles Mix County, South Dakota, for example, a group of Calvinist immigrants from the provinces of Friesland and Overijssel in 1883 established separate communities five miles apart, bearing the names of their respective provinces. Each insisted on its own church congregation and edifice, although they belonged to the same denomination and shared a minister between them.[13]

In American cities and villages that predated Dutch occupancy, the new immigrants likewise clustered in neighborhoods with kin and friends. In Grand Rapids,

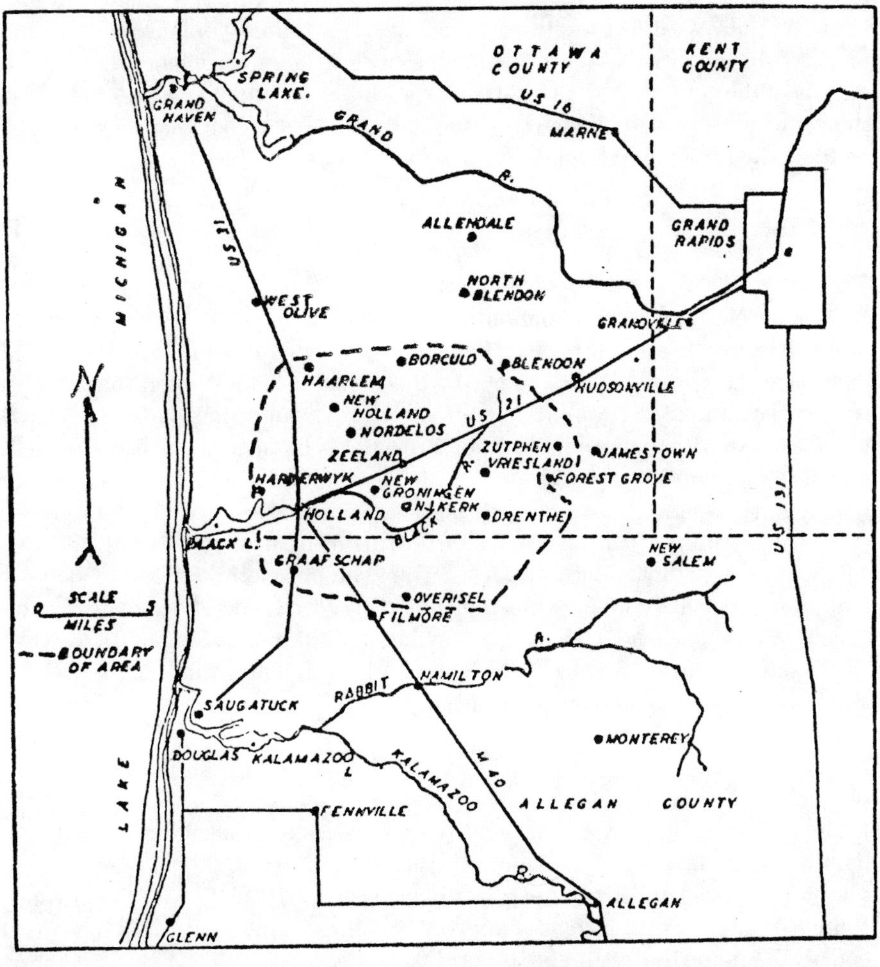

Figure 3.5 Area of Dutch Place Names in Kent, Allegan, and Ottawa Counties, Michigan

SOURCE: Roger Leetsma, "Origin of Dutch Place Names: Kent, Allegan, and Ottawa Counties, Michigan," in *Papers of the Michigan Academy of Sciences, Arts and Letters* 34 (1948), 147–51.

the quintessential Dutch-American large city where 40 percent of the population was of Dutch birth or ancestry in 1900 (the largest population of Dutch in any American city over 25,000), the Dutch isolated themselves not only from the west-side Poles but also from other Dutch. David Vanderstel, in his study of the Dutch in Grand Rapids from 1850 to 1900, identified twelve distinct neighborhoods, each composed mainly of immigrants from certain communities and regions in the Netherlands. As Vanderstel stated: "Even though each neighborhood could easily be characterized as a 'little Holland,' it would be more accurate to identify each residential cluster as a 'little Zeeland,' 'little Groningen,' or 'little Friesland,' thereby affirming the provinciality of the particular settlements."[14] Not only did immigrants from the same province settle together, they often hailed from the same villages. Even later moves within the city were often dictated by these connections; only one fourth of the families that moved within the city left their own neighborhoods. The magnet at the center of each locality was the church where the people could worship in the old way in the Dutch language, and even be served in many instances by pastors called from their home villages in the Old Country.

Migration Streams

By linking Netherlands emigration and U.S. census records, a comprehensive profile has been created for some 55,000 emigrants that identified each family in the village of origin and traced them to their destination in the United States.[15] This reveals the unique geographic migration streams connecting particular Dutch municipalities with their American counterparts. Each province and historical geographical subregion deserves its own detailed description, but only the most salient findings are discussed here at the provincial and regional level.

We begin with the southwest, and then turn to the urban west, the north, the east, and finally the Catholic south. In each region energetic clerics and laymen led the migration, especially among the religious dissenters. The clerics Van Raalte, Scholte, Cornelius Vander Meulen, Siene Bolks, Marten A. Ypma, and H. G. Klyn, all planted colonies in 1846 and 1847. So did lay leaders Jannis Vande Luyster, Worp Van Peyma, Oepke Bonnema, Jan Wabeke, Jan Smallegange, and Pieter De Jong.[16]

Zeeland

Emigration from the province of Zeeland was the heaviest in all of the Netherlands, both in raw numbers (14,300) and per capita (87.8 per 1,000). Zeeland's pace-setting role began already in the catastrophic years of 1846–47, and the province continued to export its citizens at a record rate for seventy years, until the virtual end of emigration during the First World War.[17]

Geographically, Zeeland consisted of three distinct regions: Zeeuws Vlaanderen (Zeeland Flanders) on the Belgian border, and two island clusters: Walcheren-Beveland (Zuid and Noord) lying between the Eastern and Western Schelde rivers, and Schouwen-Duiveland-Tholen lying between the Eastern Schelde and the

Brouwershavenschvat (Figure 3.6). Walcheren-Beveland (Zuid and Noord) had the heaviest emigration, totaling over 5,300 persons in the years 1835–80. Zeeuws-Vlaanderen, south of the Western Schelde, had nearly 5,000 emigrants. The northernmost island group of Schouwen-Duiveland plus the peninsula of Tholen had nearly 3,000 emigrants.

Municipal emigration patterns provide a finer grain. In Walcheren-Beveland, the provincial capital of Middelburg and the municipality of West Kapelle, furnished most of the emigrants in the early years. Borssele on Zuid-Beveland had the heaviest emigration until 1860, but then the stream shifted from the south to the north of the island. In the 1870s the focus shifted again to the eastern municipalities.

In Zeeuws-Vlaanderen, the heaviest emigration field was the northwestern region of Cadzand, Groede, and Oostburg. The municipality of Axel in the east central region was a focal point in the earliest years until 1850, after which emigration ceased. But it continued at a moderate pace after 1860 from the adjacent municipalities to the north—Zaamslag, Hoek, and Terneuzen. Essentially, over three fourths of the emigrants from the Protestant eastern part of Zeeuws-Vlaanderen departed before 1860, while emigrants from the Catholic western part left more steadily over the entire period. From Schouwen-Duiveland-Tholen, Zierikzee was the place of heaviest emigration. Tholen became important only after 1870; 70 percent of all its emigrants left in the 1870s.

The Western Schelde served as a clear demarcation line—emigrants to the south went primarily to New York and Wisconsin and those to the north went to Michigan. Two thirds of the emigrants from Zeeuws Vlaanderen settled in Rochester, Clymer, and Buffalo, New York, and one third settled in southeastern Wisconsin (mainly Oostburg, Sheboygan, Alto, and Milwaukee). Two thirds of all Zeelanders in New York originated in Zeeuws Vlaanderen; one third hailed from only three municipalities—Groede, Zuidzande, and Cadzand. In Wisconsin, 15 percent of the Zeelanders came from one municipality, West Kapelle (Walcheren). Zeelanders from north of the Western Schelde went almost exclusively to Zeeland, Michigan, but no one place of origin dominated. Indeed, sixty-six municipalities contributed at least one emigrant to the Michigan frontier, led by Zierikzee and Goes. Despite the many villages represented, the emigrants shared a common religious bond: most were persecuted Seceders.

The economic and religious history of the region helps to make sense of its emigration patterns. Zeelanders produced madder (rape seed that yielded a red dye needed for coloring cloth) for the English textile market via Rotterdam exporters, but after 1820 French farmers were able to undersell the Dutch.[18] The price fell precipitously to a point that often was below production costs. By 1840 France exported five times as much madder as the Netherlands. Prices of other cash crops—wheat, oats, beans, and peas—similarly declined by one third between 1820 and 1850. The potato disease that struck first in 1846 dealt another harsh blow to an important export article.[19]

Zeeland's sea-clay soils, especially Zeeuws-Vlaanderen and Noord-Beveland, were the premier wheat region in the nation by the 1840s. Farmers specialized in dairying in Walcheren, Schouwen, and Zuid-Beveland. Typically, emigration was

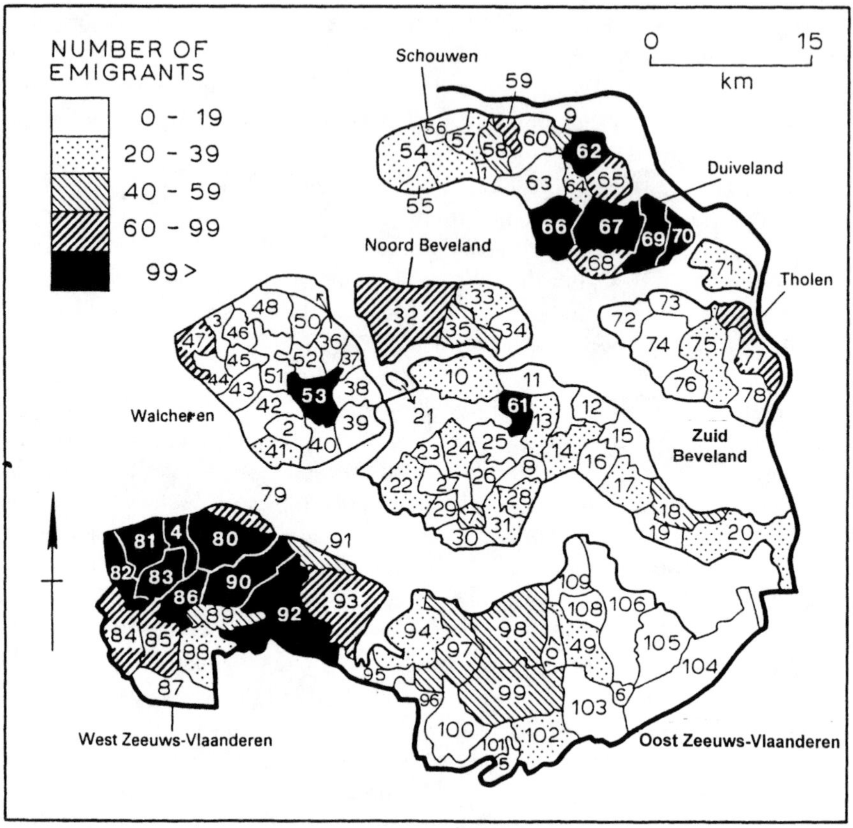

Figure 3.6 Municipalities, Province of Zeeland, 1899

SOURCE: Robert P. Swierenga, Dutch Emigration data file; and Michael Wintle, "Push-factors in Emigration: The Case of the Province of Zeeland in the Nineteenth Century," *Population Studies* 46 (1992): 529

1. Serooskerke (Schouwen)
2. Souberg
3. Domburg
4. Nieuwvliet
5. Overslag
6. Hulst
7. Oudelande
8. 's Gravenpolder
9. Brouwershaven
10. Wolphaartsdijk
11. Kattendijke
12. Wemeldinge
13. Kloetinge
14. Kapelle
15. Yerseke
16. Schore
17. Kruiningen
18. Krabbendijke
19. Waarde
20. Rilland-Bath
21. 's-Heer Arendskerke
22. Borssele
23. 's-Heerenhoek
24. Heinkenszand
25. 's-Heer Abtskerke
26. Nisse
27. Ovezande
28. Hoedekenskerke
29. Driewegen
30. Ellewoutsdijk
31. Baarland
32. Wissekerke
33. Colijnsplaat
34. Kats
35. Kotgene
36. Vrouwenpolder
37. Veere
38. Arnemuiden
39. Nieuw en Sint Joosland
40. Ritthem
41. Vlissingen
42. Koudekerke
43. Biggekerke
44. Zoutelande

45. Meliskerke
46. Aagtekerke
47. Westkapelle
48. Oostkapelle
49. Stoppeldijk
50. Serooskerke (Walcheren)
51. Grijpskerke
52. St. Laurens
53. Middelburg
54. Haamstede
55. Burgh
56. Renesse
57. Noordwelle
58. Ellemeet
59. Elkerzee
60. Duivendijke
61. Goes
62. Zonnemaire
63. Kerkwerve
64. Noordgouwe
65. Drieschor
66. Zierikzee
67. Nieuwerkerk
68. Ouwerkerk
69. Oosterland
70. Bruinisse
71. St. Philipsland
72. Stavenisse
73. St. Annaland
74. St. Maartensdijk
75. Poortvliet
76. Scherpenisse
77. Oud Vossemeer
78. Tholen
79. Breskens
80. Groede
81. Cadzand
82. Retranchement
83. Zuidzande
84. Slius
85. Aardenburg
86. Oostburg
87. Eede
88. St. Kruis
89. Waterlandkerkje
90. Schoondijke
91. Hoofdplaat
92. Ijzendijke
93. Biervliet
94. Hoek
95. Philippine
96. Sas van Gent
97. Terneuzen
98. Zaamslag
99. Axel
100. Westdorpe
101. Zuiddorpe
102. Koewacht
103. St. Janssteen
104. Clinge
105. Graauw
106. Hontinisse
107. Boschkapelle
108. Hengsdijk
109. Ossenisse

heaviest in the grain-growing areas. As prices fell and rents remained high, farmers laid off day laborers. Some villages needed only a third of the workers as previously. In the villages of Westdorpe and Zaamslag in 1849, paupers comprised 20 percent of the population; in Groede they numbered 10 percent.[20]

Conditions improved after 1850, both for farmers and dairymen. Farmers introduced more machines and modernized their operations. Crop prices climbed and land values rose 40 percent by the 1870s. The English cotton textile industry grew so rapidly that it could absorb both the French and Dutch madder production. But after the introduction of synthetic dyes in the early 1870s, madder entirely lost its market within two years. Hence, Zeeland experienced an agricultural depression before the nationwide grain crisis in the 1880s.[21]

Four out of five Zeeland emigrants worked in agriculture at a time when only one half of the province workforce farmed. This was an overwhelmingly rural group. All but 5 percent of the agricultural emigrants were farm laborers rather than farm owners. Skilled artisans and a few professionals made up the remainder. Their expressed reasons for leaving were economic; 85 percent hoped for a better livelihood.

However, the first immigrants in the mid-1840s were strongly influenced by religious motives. Seceders comprised 24 percent of all emigrants before 1849, although only 9 percent of Zeeland emigrants through 1880 were Seceders. Almost half (48 percent) of all Seceder emigrants departed in the 1840s. More than one half expressed the desire for "religious freedom" when they registered to emigrate. They hailed mainly from Tholen, Zuid-Beveland, and Oost Zeeuws-Vlaanderen, where they made up 25 percent of all emigrants. The Seceders formed an emigrant society led by the Reverend Vander Meulen of Goes, "the apostle of Zeeland," and the wealthy farmer Jannis Vande Luyster of Borssele. Van de Luyster sold his farm for $24,000 and paid for the journey to America of his family plus seventy-seven destitute Seceders.[22]

Catholics were greatly underrepresented in the overseas exodus. They had job opportunities in Belgium and Noord-Brabant. Moreover, their clerics discouraged rather than promoted emigration. And the church provided more effective poor relief and pastoral care than did the Protestants.[23] Two thirds of the Catholic emigrants left after 1860. Overall, 9.5 percent of Zeeland emigrants were Catholic, although they comprised 25 percent of the provincial population. Thus, Catholics who slightly outnumbered Seceders among Zeeland emigrants were more reluctant to emigrate until the 1860s. The primary Catholic region was West Zeeuws-Vlaanderen, whose emigrants were 19 percent Catholic, twice the rate in the province as a whole. All came from the Catholic southern municipalities, while the more populous northern villages were Protestant.

Disillusioned Calvinists from Zeeuws-Vlaanderen joined the trek to America. Catholics had gained the dominant position in this region after the breakup of the United Provinces in 1839. Historian J. Was of the village of Waterlandkerkje drew a direct causal link between Catholic encroachment and Protestant emigration. Lamenting the practice of Belgian absentee landlords of importing Catholic tenants for the village farms, Was explained: "It is any wonder that so many of our religion [Calvinists] are forced to go and eke out their existence elsewhere, to which witness the fact that this year [1846] again 170 of them have left the area and moved to the United States of America?"[24]

Zuid-Holland

The province of Zuid-Holland, to the north of Zeeland, includes the seaport of Rotterdam, the government center of The Hague, and such historic cities as Dordrecht, Delft, and Gouda. Farmers specialized in dairying, vegetable cultivation, and flower bulb production. The cities grew in population, jobs, and industry, which lessened the pressure to emigrate overseas.

Emigration from Zuid-Holland numbered only 7,500 persons and was centered in two rural localities: the island of Goeree-Overflakkee, south of the Haringvliet, which was tied economically and culturally to the Zeeland islands; and the river clay regions of the Hoekse Waard and Alblasserwaard, which were wheat-growing areas "between the rivers," the Lek, Waal, and Maas.[25]

The island of Goeree-Overflakkee, centered at Middelharnis, had 4,200 emigrants, fully 56 percent of all emigrants from the entire province. This backward, self-contained island had the highest per capita emigration in the Netherlands; indeed, it was three times higher than anywhere else. The polder village of Ouddorp in the Goeree region had 1,840 emigrants between 1835 and 1880 for a rate of 716 per 1,000 average population from 1849 to 1878. From the village of Goedereede, less than two miles to the east, another 942 persons emigrated, for a rate of

846 per 1,000. These two rates were more than one hundred times the national average of 7.2 per 1,000. Both villages and indeed the entire island suffered an absolute population decline in the second half of the nineteenth century.

The reason for the mass exodus from Goeree-Overflakkee was a combination of demographic and agricultural changes. The population increased sharply after the Napoleonic times because infant mortality dropped, but the thin sandy soil could not sustain the growth. The island was isolated without a bridge to the mainland or rail link to Rotterdam until after 1900. Madder, the main cash crop, became outmoded by artificial dyes, and chickory, another root crushed to a brown powder (in chickory factories) and mixed with coffee and other food to sharpen the taste, fell on hard times when it too was replaced by substitutes. When these cash crops failed, marginal farm workers became unemployed, and many chose to emigrate in order to continue a life in farming. The farm exodus was also hastened by declining land prices and the consolidation of small farms into larger, more efficient fodder, potato, and sugarcane operations.[26]

The Flakkeërs are remarkable for their focused settlement in the Paterson, New Jersey area; 70 percent of the emigrants from the thirteen municipalities on the large island settled in northern New Jersey, where they comprised 97 percent of the Zuid-Hollanders in the Garden State. This was by far the most focused emigration from any of the islands of the southwestern Netherlands.

The Flakkeër emigrants resembled those from Zeeland generally. Most were unskilled farm laborers, with an eye only for America, and noted for religious piety and social conservatism. Only 6 out of 1,265 emigrants did *not* go to the United States, and 75 percent were unskilled, compared to 29 percent of the other Zuid-Holland emigrants. Two thirds emigrated as families, compared to just over half among the others. The motive for emigration was largely economic; families on public relief were 10 points above average.

While Flakkeërs were religious pietists with a tendency toward zealotry, those leaving were not malcontents, but poor, young, unskilled rural laborers seeking jobs in an industrializing urban center. Paterson, known as "silk city," provided skilled jobs in a stable environment.[27] Eleven textile firms in 1860 employed 900 workers, and by 1900 the industry expanded to 175 firms employing over 20,000 workers. The Dutch provided much of the labor for these mills, where they worked alongside British, German, and Swiss emigrants. Immigrants comprised one third of the silk labor force in 1880. The Dutch historian Jacob van Hinte, after a visit to Paterson in 1928, boasted that "our workers in Silk City are tops and quite a number of them had risen to become foremen."[28]

In the polder area between the Lek and the Waal ("between the Rivers"), the early focus of emigration was the Beijerland municipalities of the Hoekse Waard centered in Zwijndrecht and the western Alblasserwaard region centered in Dordrecht. Beijerland was a cash crop region, producing wheat, potatoes, and oats for Rotterdam and Dordrecht markets with seasonal laborers. During the 1840s prices slumped to fifty-year lows and many farmers faced eviction.[29]

In the 1850s and 1860s the migration fields spread to Seceder strongholds in the eastern region of Alblasserwaard (Noordeloos, Heukelum, and Vianen). Before

1850, 36 percent of all emigrants were Seceders, even though they comprised less than 1 percent of the general population of Zuid-Holland. Half of these pious folk expressed a desire for religious freedom as the chief reason for emigrating.

The American destinations of Zuid-Hollanders were diverse and yet clear patterns are evident. The Flakkeërs' route to Paterson has already been noted; northern New Jersey was the destination for 37 percent. Pella attracted 24 percent, one quarter of whom originated in the wheat-growing region of the Hoekse Waard (Klaaswaal and Westmaas) and Vijfheerenlanden (Vianen), from which places almost 90 percent of all emigrants went to Pella. Michigan, with 21 percent, was the third preferred destination, one third of whose emigrants came from Ouddorp, Goedereede, and Noordeloos. Almost one half of the Noordeloos emigrants went to the village of Noordeloos, Michigan.

Most of the remaining Zuid-Holland emigrants settled in South Holland, Illinois, a market gardening colony twenty-five miles south of Chicago. In this Zuid-Holland colony, nearly 40 percent hailed from the dairy region of eastern Alblasserwaard and Vijfheerenlanden (notably the municipalities of Noordeloos, Hardinxveld, Groot Ammers, Giessen Nieuwkerk, and Goudrian). Flakkeërs accounted for another 25 percent. Thus, the pioneer settlers of South Holland were dominated by people from "between the rivers" and from Overflakkee. New York, Wisconsin, Ohio, Minnesota, and other Dutch destinations held little attraction for the clannish Zuid-Hollanders.

In total, 37 percent of Zuid Hollanders went to New Jersey, 24 percent (mainly from the Hoekse Waard) chose the Iowa colony of Pella, 21 percent settled in the Michigan colony of Holland (especially the village of Noordeloos), and 9 percent (also from the area between the rivers) went to South Holland, Illinois. Thus, more than 90 percent of Zuid Hollanders settled in four colonies—Paterson, Noordeloos, Pella, and South Holland.

Noord-Holland

Noord-Holland, the most populous province, contained very few emigrant "hot spots." Only 5,406 persons left for overseas destinations in the period, and fully one third went elsewhere than the United States. Many of these were white-collar workers and skilled craftsmen from Amsterdam and the nearby cities of Haarlem and Zaandam. Among Noord-Holland emigrants, 28 percent were white collar, 34 percent were skilled craftsmen, many in preindustrial trades. Only 18 percent worked in farming and 20 percent were unskilled.

In the years before 1850, emigration was clearly a response to religious forces. Seceders made up 20 percent and Jews 20 percent, although their share of the provincial population in 1849 was less than 1 percent and 6 percent, respectively.[30] After 1850 Seceders and Jews continued to be overrepresented. Catholic emigrants increased their share to over 20 percent by the late 1870s. Since Catholics totaled over 28 percent of the population, however, they continued to be underrepresented. Jews and Catholics cited economic reasons, as did the Reformed. Almost all of the Seceders in the 1840s sought religious freedom.

Three cultural regions contributed the most emigrants: the major city of Amsterdam (42 percent), the rural North Sea islands of Texel and Terschelling, and the northern regions of Geestmerambacht and Den Helder. Many Protestant Amsterdammers were Seceders who followed Dominie Scholte to Pella. One third of Amsterdam emigrants were Jews—three times their proportion of the population—bound primarily for New York City, with secondary destinations in Philadelphia, Boston, Baltimore, New Orleans, Cincinnati, Detroit, and Chicago.[31] Dutch Jews in New York City numbered nearly 20 percent of all Noord-Hollanders in the Empire State.

The sparsely populated islands of Texel and Terschelling sent out 700 emigrants. In the decade 1865–75 these two islands had the highest emigration in the province—Texel's rate was 46 per 1,000 and Terschelling's was 66 per 1,000.[32] This compares with a rate of fewer than 3 for Amsterdam and 6 for Haarlem, which cities barely missed those departing. Texel emigrants showed a proclivity for northern New Jersey, where one third settled. Another fifth went to the village of Noord-Holland in the Michigan colony. Thirty people had accompanied the wealthy capitalist, Paulus Den Bleyker, who himself settled in Kalamazoo, Michigan.[33]

Terschelling had negligible emigration until 1862, but then, from 1862 to 1880, 232 persons emigrated to the United States. They were farmers, laborers, and seamen, primarily from the eastern half of the island. West and East Terschelling were two different worlds at the time. The West had a maritime economy, but the East was agriculturally oriented, centered in the rich sea clay soil of the Terschelling polder. There was very little personal contact between the two populations and virtually no intermarriage between "die van Oost" (those from the East) and "die van West" (those from the West). Changes in agriculture in the East prompted the emigration. Some sacrificed their farms at prices that "stood in no relation to the productivity of that land," according to a municipal official. Several villages, Osterend, Formerend, and Midsland, actually suffered a net population loss because of the emigration overseas. These municipalities lay within the Terschelling polder, where agriculture was becoming modernized.[34] Terschelling emigrants favored the Iowa prairies. Thirteen families settled in German Township in Grundy County in 1865, and seven families went to Washington Township in Butler County between 1865 and 1869.

The rural Geestmerambacht region (lying thirty to forty miles north of Amsterdam) and especially the villages of Schoorl and Zijpe sent emigrants mainly to the suburban Chicago village of Roseland, a market gardening region that became a Seceder colony in the 1840s and 1850s. Pieter De Jong, the schoolmaster of Schoorl, led a group of fourteen families to Roseland in 1849. Only four of the fourteen families were not interrelated.

The distribution of Noord-Hollanders in the United States was 33 percent in Michigan, 19 percent in Illinois, 14 percent in New York, and 11 percent in New Jersey. Half of the Noord-Hollanders in Michigan originated in three municipalities (Texel, Den Helder, and Amsterdam), and half of those in Illinois, mainly in Roseland, came from the villages of Schoorl and Zijpe.

Demographically, Noord-Holland emigrants were the youngest of all Dutch emigrants—one third were in the 25–35 year age group. The average age of family heads and singles dropped steadily from 35.1 years in the early years to 29.8 years after 1875. Two thirds emigrated alone. Those from Amsterdam and Haarlem are readily distinguishable from rural emigrants; three quarters departed as singles, compared to one half among rural folk.

The America-centeredness of Noord-Holland emigrants was low; only 69 percent settled in the United States. Most were from rural municipalities, the polder regions of Haarlemmermeer, Wieringen, Anna Paulowna, and Groet Winkel, and the Geestmerambacht region (Zijpe, Schagen, Sint Maarten, and Warmenhuizen). More than half were on the public dole. Largely unskilled day laborers, these people with their families began emigrating heavily after 1865, and more than 80 percent went to the States in hopes of land and jobs. The proportion of Seceders among these rural families was two times the overall average. From the Geestmerambacht region, fully 39 percent of all emigrating households were Seceders, which was four times the overall rate of 10.8 percent.

Utrecht

Utrecht was the least important emigration area. Only 1,171 persons left by 1880; nearly two thirds were residents of the provincial capital of Utrecht. The remainder were from the eastern dairy area and the southern sandy soil area of diversified agriculture. The one focused migration was a band of Scholte's followers from the city of Utrecht who left in the first decade for Pella.

Utrecht emigrants consisted of two distinct groups: Scholte's religious followers and a later labor migration of singles. Seceders dominated among Utrecht emigrants in the first wave before 1850; they numbered two thirds of all emigrants in those years. In the 1850s Seceders made up 16 percent, but from 1860 to 1880 only five Seceder families emigrated. Thus, 70 percent of all Seceder emigrants departed in the initial years when Scholte's influence was strong. More than half of the Seceders expressed the desire for religious freedom as their primary reason for emigrating.

Half of all Utrecht emigrants settled in Scholte's colony of Pella; 60 percent hailed from the city of Utrecht and the municipality of Kockengen. Utrecht's Seceder congregation was formed in 1835, and Scholte pastored the church from 1837 until he emigrated with many of its members in April 1847. The Kockengen Seceder congregation dates from 1836, and H.G. Klyn served as the first pastor from 1839 until 1845. Klyn emigrated to Zeeland, Michigan in 1849 with 150 families from the congregation he was then serving at Middelburg in Zeeland Province. Understandably, therefore, Holland and Zeeland, Michigan were the secondary destination where 20 percent of Utrecht emigrants settled. Again the Utrecht congregation was the main source. The normal chain migration did not occur with the Utrecht Seceders because hard times in farming and personality conflicts and religious schisms in the Pella church dissuaded many family and friends from following. By the mid-1850s Scholte's leadership had been largely repudiated.[35]

Scholte's Seceder emigration had an economic as well as a religious dimension.

Well-to-do persons advanced funds for poor and needy co-religionists to emigrate with their congregations. For example, H. Y. Vierson of Leeuwarden in Friesland provided nearly $2,000 to a number of poor families for travel expenses and the purchase of Iowa farmland. Scholte's church building at Utrecht was also sold for $2,000, and the net proceeds were deposited with the Utrecht Emigration Association to help needy members come to the United States. Given the ready assistance, it is not surprising that among the Seceder emigrants unskilled laborers and small farmers were overrepresented. Most were middling in economic status, but the number of poor families in the Utrecht emigration exceeded that of all other provinces except Zeeland.

The year of 1860 is the fault line in Utrecht emigration. Seceder families following Scholte gave way to poor urban women and aspiring young men seeking positions in the Dutch East Indies. Before 1860, 80 percent of Utrecht emigrants settled in the United States; after 1860 only 20 percent did so. Nearly one half (47 percent) of all emigrants in the years 1865–75 were classified as "needy" in the records. This was 17 points above the average for all emigrants. The pace of outmigration also gathered speed after 1860, when 443 persons departed from the city of Utrecht compared to only 272 persons before 1860. But the loss of several hundred persons by emigration was inconsequential in a population of 53,000 in 1870.

Occupationally, skilled craftsmen and clerical workers were overrepresented in the post-1860 emigration, the former by 16 points. Unmarried females numbered over one third of all emigrants in the years 1876–80, which was a unique phenomenon in Netherlands emigration in the nineteenth century. Moreover, nearly 80 percent of Utrecht emigrants after 1860 were singles. Fewer families and more singles emigrated from Utrecht than from any other province; only Noord-Hollanders had a similar pattern. Utrecht after 1860 was one of the rare examples of a labor migration, and the destination was the Dutch colonies in Asia, not the farms of the American Midwest.

Friesland

Friesland also had a low emigration rate before 1880, by comparison to Groningen, its sister province on the north coast. Fewer than 4,000 persons emigrated, which was less than half the number from Groningen. The rate per 1,000 average population in Friesland was 13.6, or less than a third the rate of 40.1 in Groningen.

The clay soil wheat region along the North Sea coast had the greatest overseas emigration, particularly in the years after 1865. Almost half (48 percent) of all Frisian emigrants originated in the ten municipalities of the north coast from Harlingen to the Lauwerszee, with Het Bildt and Ferwerderadeel in the center as the major area.[36] The region second in importance was the western half of the province: from Leeuwarden, the provincial capital, westward to Wonseradeel and southward to Stavoren at the Zuiderzee. From this dairy district, 1,340 persons emigrated, or 35 percent of the Frisian total. The third district, with only 17 percent of the emigration (665 persons) was the eastern part, a sandy soil region with a general three-field system of farming.

Chronologically, the earliest emigration field centered in the grain region of the North Sea coastal municipalities from Het Bildt to the Groningen border. In the 1850s and 1860s the heaviest outpouring continued in the northern municipalities, but emigration also spread southwest along the Zuiderzee and into the inland dairy lands. In the 1870s emigration from the interior west central area dried up, but it suddenly exploded along the southeastern border with Overijssel and Drenthe.

The characteristics of the emigration from each of the three major areas differed. In the 1840s nearly 700 persons departed, with one third from the coastal region and one fourth from the sandy soiled east. In the 1850s the proportion from the north coast increased to one half, with one third from the dairy district, and less than an eighth from the sandy east. The emigration fields became more concentrated in the fifties. Three municipalities—Gaasterland, Ferwerderadeel, and Westdongeradeel—accounted for one half of the entire province's emigration.

In the 1860s the emigration field spread inland into the dairy region, but the heaviest outpouring was from the cash grain coastal region from Het Bildt to Kollumerland. In the 1870s there was a sudden exodus of emigrants from Weststellingwerf and Ooststellingwerf on the Drenthe border in the southern sandy soil region. Het Bildt and Ferwerderadeel also had extremely heavy emigration in the 1870s. For the entire period 1835–80, Het Bildt's emigration rate was 53 per 1,000 and that of Ferwerderadeel was 54 per 1,000, which rates far exceeded the provincial average of 14 per 1,000.

The socioeconomic characteristics of emigrants from the three areas differed. The north coast commercial wheat region sent out a greater proportion of farmhands, day laborers, and small farmers: 58 percent were day laborers and 15 percent farmers. The sandy soil area sent out a greater relative proportion of farmers (23 percent) and skilled craftsmen (25 percent) and a lesser number of unskilled workers (40 percent). The dairy district had more of an urban emigration with 48 percent originating in the cities. Thirty percent were skilled emigrants and 19 percent held white-collar positions. Those on the public dole from eastern Friesland totaled only 9 percent, compared to 23 percent from the western dairy area and 25 percent from the northern clay soil area.

Religiously, the highest proportion of emigrating Seceders (33 percent) came from the sandy eastern region; Seceders from the dairy and sand regions numbered 21 and 23 percent, respectively. One in five Seceder families specified religious freedom as their chief motive. The first contingent left in 1847 in a group of forty-nine adults and many children, led by the Reverend Marten A. Ypma of Hallum. In a meeting at Leeuwarden, the provincial capital, Ypma agreed to "go with them as their shepherd and instructor and to live with them where the Lord would lead."[37] Roman Catholics comprised 9 percent of the emigrants from the dairylands, 6 percent from the sandy region, and 5 percent from the coastal wheat lands.

The emigration changed over time from a religious to an economic movement. In the 1840s over one half (53 percent) of all emigrants were Seceders, but in succeeding decades Seceders never numbered more than 20 percent. After a lull during the Civil War years, Frisian emigrants hailed increasingly from the ranks of poorer rural day laborers in the sea clay soil region. By the mid- to late 1870s, two thirds of all Frisian emigrants were common laborers, and more than a quarter were on the public dole. Almost three fourths originated in the sea clay region.

The preferred destination of northern Frisians before 1880 was western Michigan, especially Grand Rapids and Ypma's village of Vriesland in the Holland colony. One half of the northern Frisians settled in Michigan, including 80 percent of the emigrants from Ferwerderadeel, 70 percent from Barradeel, and 60 percent from Kollumerland. The "Frisian Hoek" on the north edge of Pella primarily attracted people from Het Bildt and Westdongeradeel. The remaining north coast emigrants settled in two Wisconsin Frisian colonies—New Amsterdam (La Crosse) and Friesland—and in Lancaster, New York, and New Paris (Goshen), Indiana.

Emigrants from the eastern sandy-soil area of Friesland preferred Pella, where half settled. The remainder went to Friesland (WI); Chicago; and Lancaster (NY). From the dairy area one third of the emigrants were Mennonites from Gasterland, who went to Goshen, Indiana. Another third were Reformed, who settled in western Michigan, and 12 percent went to Pella. Frisians, always more independent-minded, dispersed themselves in America more than other Netherlanders.

The New Amsterdam colony, located a dozen miles north of La Crosse, was founded in 1853 by ninety-two Frisians, led by Oepke H. Bonnema, a wealthy grain dealer and philanthropist from Kimswerd (Municipality of Franekeradeel), and Broer Baakes Haagsma, a schoolteacher from nearby Arum.[38] Bonnema and Haagsma gathered needy friends and led them across the Atlantic to frontier Wisconsin to Holland township. The settlers were not Seceders but members of the national Reformed Church. In New Amsterdam, a quarter century passed before a Dutch Reformed Church was founded in 1873, which became Presbyterian within a decade.[39] This colony, which had a promising beginning but lacked the glue of a church, lost its Dutch character and became Americanized by the second and third generation.

In contrast to the secular village of New Amsterdam in southwestern Wisconsin, the dozen families in Friesland (Columbia County), founded in 1861, immediately formed a Reformed Church and shared a pastor with the Dutch colony of Alto, eighteen miles northeast, founded by Gelderlanders in 1845.[40] Friesland and neighboring Randolph, Wisconsin remain Dutch Calvinist settlements to the present day.

The Frisian settlement in Lancaster, New York, twelve miles east of Buffalo, began in 1849 when Worp Van Peyma, a gentleman farmer and anti-monarchist from Ternaard in Westdongeradeel, led his extended family and friends to democratic America. Although they established prosperous dairy farms on fertile clay soil, the colonists had no commitment to the Reformed religion, and they never founded a church. Without this agency of cultural maintenance, the Dutch language quickly died out and the group assimilated rapidly.[41]

Frisian emigrants from the eastern sandy area, farmers and craftsmen primarily, preferred Pella, Iowa, where more than half settled. Five municipalities—Dantumadeel, Tietjerksteradeel, Achtkarspelen, Smallingerland, and Weststellingwerf—were strongly oriented to Iowa. Only a quarter of the sandy soil Frisians went to

Western Michigan. Clearly, the rich prairie lands of central Iowa had a special appeal for these small farmers and rural laborers. Friesland (WI), Chicago, and Lancaster absorbed most of the remainder.

A unique pattern is evident among emigrants from the adjacent municipalities of Ooststellingwerf and Weststellingwerf. Over 80 percent of emigrants from the former place settled in Michigan and 75 percent from the latter place went to Iowa. The process of chain migration continued to bring family and neighbors of the first settlers after them.

Emigrants from the western dairy area divided evenly between Indiana and Michigan (about 30 percent to each state), with Iowa a distant third at 12 percent. The rest divided between Friesland (WI) and Lancaster. The conservative Mennonites from the village of Balk in Gaasterland, all pacifists who left the fatherland to avoid compulsory military service, had the most focused pattern. Almost 85 percent followed the clerics Ruurd Smit and Ruurd Jacob Siemensma (Symensma) to New Paris, Indiana, which became the nucleus for a small Mennonite colony.[42] Mennonites comprised 54 percent of all Frisians in the Hoosier State. From the adjacent municipality of Humeler Oldephaert in Noordwolde another one third of the emigrants went to New Paris.

Generally speaking, Frisian emigration to the United States was not as concentrated as among other Netherlanders. Most Frisian colonies were small and several lacked the glue of religious institutions to enable them to resist the inevitable process of Americanization.

Groningen

The province of Groningen ranked second (behind Zeeland) in its emigration rate —41 per 1000 average population. More than 8,700 persons emigrated in the years 1830–80. The three cash grain regions of northern Groningen led in the emigration. The Hunsingo area was dominant with 5,900 emigrants (68 percent), the Fivelingo area had 1,000 (12 percent), and the Westerkwartier on the Frisian border had only 800 emigrants (9 percent).

Three fourths of Groninger emigrants before 1880 left in the years after 1865, when the northern Netherlands experienced an agricultural revolution. Farmers mechanized rapidly and adjusted their operations to utilize the new machines more efficiently. Steel plows, threshing machines, steam tractors, combines, hay rakes, reel drills, and other implements offered tremendous advantages to large-scale, cash crop farmers who had to increase their efficiency in order to compete in world markets against cheaper grain from North America, Ukraine, Argentina, and elsewhere. By 1885 Groningen led the nation in horse-drawn threshing machines, steel plows, row seeders, and steam tractors.[43]

The consolidation of farms increased the pressure on land prices, left few openings for new farmers, and threw farmhands out of work. The Reverend Bernardus De Beij, who in 1868 led hundreds of Groningers to Chicago from his Seceder congregation in Middelstum, described well the dismal prospects in the homeland in a letter written from Chicago:

> There is a great number of farmer's sons and daughters in Groningen who possess considerable capital, and who gladly would like to buy a farm in accordance with their available capital. However, that is not possible because all the land is occupied. When a farm comes up for sale there are twenty who would like to buy, but only one can become the owner. The price is driven so high that in order to live himself, he later needs the sweat and blood of day laborers, family, buyers, and tradesmen. Others wait for the death of the grey landowner.[44]

For many agriculturalists there was no alternative but to migrate to Dutch cities or leave for America. Groninger emigrants went almost exclusively (96 percent) to the United States; they were second only to Frisians in their America-centeredness. Virtually all hailed from the countryside. Agricultural workers comprised three quarters (77 percent) of all emigrants, skilled craftsmen totaled 17 percent, and white-collar persons only 6 percent. Eighty percent of the Groningen emigrants were of middling economic status, which was the highest proportion of any province. The national average among all emigrants was 65 percent.

The notable feature of the early emigration from Groningen was that it was spearheaded by Seceders, followers of the fiery preacher of Ulrum, Reverend Hendrik de Cock, who had sparked the Secession of 1834 throughout the northern Netherlands.[45] At a time when Seceders numbered less than 6 percent of the province's population, 70 percent of all Groningen emigrants in the 1840s were Seceders. In the 1850s this dropped to 17 percent, but after the Civil War Seceders again numbered 30 percent. One in five of the Seceder families left primarily to gain religious freedom and the right to found free Christian day schools for their children. Roman Catholics, another religious minority, totaled 13 percent of the Groninger pioneers. Only 14 percent of the emigrants before 1850 were members of the predominant Hervormde Kerk, but thereafter two thirds were Hervormden.

The early emigrants were an older population of financially stable craftsmen and small farmers. One third were craftsmen and a quarter were farmers. Over 80 percent were of middling economic status, and 11 percent were wealthy. A quarter of the early emigrants were subject to the head tax on income, compared to only 7 percent among later emigrants. This was clearly a religious protest movement of comparatively well-off families.

The emigration patterns from the five geographic regions of the province present sharp contrasts. The Hunsingo area along the North Sea coast had the richest, most productive clay soil in the Netherlands. The agricultural revolution struck early here and with great impact on the farm workers who were hired as needed and worked by the season at best. These excess hands emigrated to America in large numbers.

Of Hunsingo emigrants, 58 percent were rural day laborers, and another 26 percent were small farmers and farmhands. Thus, 84 percent were agricultural workers. Half of the Hunsingo emigrants were single adults, who had to delay marriage because they could not obtain steady work or a farm in order to support a wife and family. Almost to the last person, Hunsingo emigrants went to the United States. Religiously, 64 percent were members of the Hervormde Kerk, a very large 29 percent were Seceders, and 7 percent were Catholic. In the province in 1849, the Hervormde Church claimed 81 percent of the population, Catholics 7 percent, and Seceders 6 percent.[46] Thus Seceders were overrepresented almost five-fold and Hervormde Church members were underrepresented by 25 percent.

The preferred destination of Hunsingo emigrants was western Michigan, where two thirds (66 percent) settled. Chicago attracted 17 percent, 4 percent went to Lafayette, Indiana (a Groningen farm community), and 4 percent went to Wisconsin. The Chicago Groningers, who settled near the city center on the near west side, hailed mainly from Uithuizermeeden, Usquert, Middelstum, Eenrum, and Baflo. Emigrants from Leens, Uithuizen, Warffum, Bedum, Adorp, and Ulrum preferred western Michigan. Most Lafayette Groningers came from Kantens, Eenrum, Leens, and Ulrum.

Fivelingo, a rich cash grain area comparable to Hunsingo, spanned the area northeast of the city of Groningen to the seaport of Delfzijl. Its emigration characteristics are similar to those from the Hunsingo except for several notable differences. Again, 55 percent of those departing were rural day laborers and 19 percent were farmhands and small farmers. Together, the farmers and farm workers included 76 percent of all emigrants, compared to 84 percent in the Hunsingo. The difference was that Fivelingo emigrants numbered more skilled craftsmen—21 percent compared to 13 percent in Hunsingo. Unmarried singles comprised 39 percent of Fivelingo emigrants, 10 points less than in Hunsingo. Religiously, emigrants from the two areas had the same proportion of Calvinists—two thirds Hervormde and one third Seceder.

Over 99 percent of Fivelingo emigrants went to the United States. The favored destination for two thirds was western Michigan, especially Grand Rapids. Chicago was preferred by one third. The municipalities of 't Zandt and Stedum were the most important emigration fields. More than one third of 't Zandt emigrants and over one quarter of Stedum emigrants settled in Chicago where they comprised most of the residents in the "Groninger Hoek."

From the third sea-clay region, the Westerkwartier on the Frisian border south of the Lauwerszee, only 766 emigrants left, led by the municipality of Grijpskerk. Emigration began later here than elsewhere in Groningen; only 3 percent left before 1865 and 97 percent from 1865 through 1880. More than half (57 percent) were Seceders. This was the highest percentage of any region of the Netherlands and more than ten times the proportion of Seceders in the province.

The Westerkwartier Seceders were strongly influenced to leave by their fellow dissenters who had emigrated earlier from Hunsingo and Fivelingo. The agricultural revolution also reached the Westerkwartier later and this delayed the onset of the out-migration. Again, two thirds (74 percent) of all emigrants were farmers and farm laborers, with 18 percent skilled craftsmen and 8 percent in white-collar positions. They were slightly poorer than other Groningen emigrants; 22 percent were on the public dole and 71 percent were of middling status, compared to 17 percent and 76 percent, respectively, from Fivelingo and 12 percent and 85 percent, respectively, from Hunsingo.

The United States received 97 percent of Westerkwartier emigrants, led by western Michigan, mainly Grand Rapids, with 68 percent. Iowa gained 15 percent and Chicago 13 percent. Grijpskerk and Zuidhorn emigrants were the most focused—they went almost entirely to western Michigan. Those from Oldehove also favored Michigan, but a few went to Iowa and Chicago. Aduard emigrants went mostly to Chicago.

The Oldambt and Reiderland areas on the German border differed from the sea clay regions. The soil was sandy and less fertile and farms were smaller. Rye was the chief crop and it was produced for local consumption, although some wheat was grown on clay soils to the north but with crop rotation. The pressure to emigrate in the Oldambt was minimal and only 6 percent of the Groningen emigrants originated here. Nearly half of these (44 percent) were skilled craftsmen and 12 percent were in white-collar positions. Thus fewer than half were in farming, which contrasts sharply with the clay area where 75 to 85 percent of the emigrants were in farming.

The Oldambt emigration began in earnest twenty years earlier than elsewhere. Nearly one third of its emigrants through 1880 departed in the 1840s. Religiously, 33 percent were Seceders, 9 percent were Catholic, and 5 percent Jewish. All three groups were overrepresented, the Seceders by six-fold. One in five Seceders expressed a desire for religious liberty; these pious folk had suffered much for the faith. The Oldambt emigration was an exodus of tradesmen more than farmhands, and religious discontent played a major role in instigating the emigration. In economic standing, 78 percent were of middling status, 10 percent wealthy, and 12 percent needy. The United States was the destination of 94 percent, which was only 5 points less than among clay-soil emigrants. Again, Grand Rapids was the primary destination (77 percent), with Chicago the home of 10 percent. The municipalities of Wildervank, Nieuwe Pekela, and Hoogezand were the main places of origin of those bound for Grand Rapids.

The provincial capital, Groningen City, sent out only 487 emigrants, 6 percent of the total, although it held nearly 17 percent of the total provincial population. This was a unique migration, because 42 percent held white-collar positions and 51 percent were craftsmen. Over one half were singles, of whom almost one quarter were women. Thirty-nine percent were wealthy—more than six times the average among all emigrants from the province. And a very high 43 percent did not settle in the United States, compared to 5 percent or less among those from the countryside. Religiously, 71 percent were Hervormde, 16 percent Catholic, 7 percent Seceder, and 6 percent Jewish. Thus, the proportion of Catholic and Jewish emigrants from Groningen City was unusually high, as was the percentage of craftsmen and white-collar workers. The emigration from the city was thus split between Catholic and Reformed tradesmen going to America and Reformed white-collar types seizing job opportunities in the Dutch East Indies, Netherlands Antilles, Surinam and Curaçao, and South Africa. Of the city's emigrants to the United States, half chose western Michigan, a quarter Chicago, and a fifth Buffalo.

Emigration from the province of Groningen was dominated by the exodus of farmers from the clay regions, led by the Hunsingo area. By contrast, Oldambt and the capital city had only minimal emigration and that mainly of craftsmen and white-collar workers, many of whom opted for the Dutch overseas colonies. That so many rural emigrants ended up in Chicago, Grand Rapids, Muskegon, Lafayette, and other urban places, is remarkable. They desired farmland but simply could not afford to buy it, at least not until they had worked for some years. The magnet of the cities was jobs. City folk also needed to be fed, so many Groningers specialized in truck farming on rented land at the periphery of the growing cities.

Drenthe

The three eastern provinces, all sandy soiled, are Drenthe, Overijssel, and Gelderland. Drenthe was the most isolated and least densely populated province. Nevertheless, the province ranked fourth, with an emigration of 1,537 persons through 1880, which was a rate of 15.5 per 1,000 average population—double the national rate. Drenthians are a stand, conservative people who were extremely reluctant to emigrate, but a convergence of religious and economic forces drove them out.[47]

The generally unproductive sandy soils of Drenthe were dominated by small family farms practicing a diversified agriculture.[48] The population was overwhelmingly rural, outside of the small provincial capital of Assen and the few market centers of Emmen, Coevorden, Hoogeveen, and Dalen. A modernization movement, begun in the French period (1795–1813), brought improvements in public education and transportation, which led to greater mobility, and generally integrated Drenthe more with the other provinces.

Throughout the nineteenth century, however, Drenthe had the lowest level of regional income in the Netherlands, and it was the least industrialized province. Conversely, its share of the labor force in agriculture was among the highest (55 percent in 1859), and its productivity in farming was slightly above the national average. During the nineteenth century winter rye accounted for two thirds of the area under crop, with potatoes and, to a lesser extent, buckwheat and oats, taking up the remainder. After 1840 Drenthe farmers took advantage of the increasing British demand for butter and pork and the German demand for hogs, under the new free trading system, to use their rye and potatoes as animal fodder and to export butter and pork. Cattle production rose, and Drenthe became the swine-breeding center of the Netherlands.[49]

Before the new agricultural system took hold fully in the 1850s and 1860s, Drenthe experienced severe hard times in the 1840s. The population, which had only doubled in the previous two hundred years, quadrupled after 1800 within less than a century. After decades of low growth averaging 3.6 percent per year from 1630 to 1805, the population spurted. In the years 1815–30 it grew at 16 percent per year, and in the 1850s growth reached 17.2 percent per year.[50]

The rapid population growth led to an increase in landless farmers who were pushed to the margins of agriculture. When the potato blight struck in 1845 and crops failed for several years, an "acute pauperization" occurred. Only gradually did Drenthe farmers adjust to the new export-based farming system with more labor-intensive, smaller farms. Eventually the marginal workers were reabsorbed into the farming system. Farmland reclamation of the vast heathlands of Drenthe also kept pace with the population growth, so that Drenthians had less economic and demographic pressures to emigrate, except in the brief periods of extreme stress, compared to the commercial farming areas of northern Groningen and Friesland.

Culturally, Drenthians were a "home-bound" people who did "not like to travel," according to local writers.[51] Moreover, they were a hardy lot who could survive crop failures on the thin soils. In the crop failure year of 1817, only 5 percent of the people of Drenthe were on public welfare, compared to 11 percent nationally. Neighboring Friesland had 8 percent of its citizens on the dole. The clannish Drenthians clung to family and friends more than other Hollanders. "The Drenthian is innately a community person, devoted to his own village community and his own soil," concluded H. J. Prakke, a Drenthe native and historian; they were not "emigrants by nature."[52]

Given the traditional peasant values and an improved farming system, it is surprising that as many Drenthians emigrated in the nineteenth century. Their emigration rate ranked fourth, slightly above the neighboring provinces of Overijssel and Friesland. The reason for this seeming incongruity with Drenthe culture and farming life lies in the religious sphere.

The pioneer Drenthe emigrants of the 1840s did not choose to leave the Fatherland; they were *forced* to leave by religious persecution. This is clear from an analysis of the emigrant population. Apart from a few Catholics from the border village of Nieuw-Schoonebeek in 1845, who were doubtless influenced by the earlier German emigration from Hannover, Germany, barely half a mile away, the only Drenthians to emigrate in the first wave of 1846 and 1847 were Seceders. Religious motives clearly were central to the breakdown of the bonds of the village communities.[53]

The Seceder movement in Drenthe began independently in the 1820s, led by a Dwingeloo shopkeeper turned cleric, Fredrick S. Kok, who later joined with Hendrik de Cock of Ulrum, Groningen, the "Father of the Secession."[54] Kok's brother, Walter A. Kok, formerly a farmer, became a dominie and professor in the first seminary "school" of the Seceders which brother Frederick had founded to train ministers. The informal school met in Walter's manse in Ruinerwolde and later in Hoogeveen.

Within a month of De Cock's formal withdrawal from the Hervormde Kerk in 1854, a Seceder congregation sprang up at Smilde in Drenthe, and another in Assen soon followed. In early 1835 Dwingeloo and Hoogeveen had Seceder churches. The Reverend De Cock came from Ulrum in 1835 to pastor the Smilde congregation, which became the focal point for the movement in the southwestern sector of the province. By 1836 there were fourteen Seceder churches in Drenthe, with four more by 1845.

Many Seceders were persecuted by fearful public authorities, especially in the most militant Cocksian center in the southwest, framed by the cities of Assen, Hoogeveen, and Meppel. By contrast, the Zuidwolde in southeastern Drenthe had less conflict with authorities because of its more irenic tradition. This region was under the influence of the Seceder leader, Albertus C. Van Raalte, pastor of the

Seceder congregation of Ommen in Overijssel Province about fifteen miles to the south. Ommen was the trade and cultural center of the provinces of Overijssel and Drenthe and Graafschap Bentheim in Germany because of its annual trade fair, the Ommerbissing.

The Drenthe emigration of 1846–47 stemmed directly from the Secession movement and public opposition to it. The earliest emigration centers were in the farming communities of Sleen, Erm, Emmen, and Noordbarge. Over 5 percent of Sleen's inhabitants emigrated, as did 10 percent of Erm's people. Auction notices in the local newspaper, the *Drentsche Courant*, reveal that substantial farmers led the out-migration, but special arrangements were also made for the poor to leave with the congregation.

The Drenthe Seceders represented a true cross section of the province's social classes. The perceptive comment of a Zweeloo reporter sums it up: "Here, the desire to leave the native country exists exclusively with the Secessionists. It is not limited to any specific class, but rather seems to be the result of a certain religious confession." Some of the auction notices, quoted by Prakke, are worth noting. The Erm farmer Hendrik Lanning's advertisement in the *Drentsche Courant* announced a public sale of "a complete farming estate consisting of 2 horses, 20 cows, 50 sheep, hay straw, furniture, etc." Lanning was a large farmer by Drenthe standards. A second Lanning auction notice offered his farm of 7.5 hectares [18.5 acres] of cultivated land, plus meadow and pasture land and a three-eighths portion in the common mark, or village commons, of Erm. The provincial governor estimated Lanning's wealth at f16,000 ($6,400), which was a very large amount in those days. Others who auctioned their farms and personal property in this way were Klaas Hunderman, Hendrik Stokking, and Klaas Schoenmaker, all of Erm, and Jan Riddering and Johannes Weggemans of Sleen. The stated reason for all these auctions was "because of departure to North America." Lanning, together with Riddering and Weggemans, brought f31,000 ($12,400) in cash to America.[55]

Riddering and Weggemans headed the opposition in Sleen to the liberals who controlled the parish church, led by its German-born pastor Otto Schultz, who had married into a local family. Schultz worked to maintain religious uniformity in the church and community, drawing on the strong aversion of these close-knit peasants to any threats to their unified lifestyle. The Seceders held to the same values, and only the greatest pressures could force them to break publicly with the church and village. Religious enthusiasm was such a force. They felt constrained to break the Drenthian tradition of conformity. Instead of acquiescing in silence—the usual remedy—they completely rejected the authority of the liberal dominie. The French occupation and subsequent chaotic political and ecclesiastical conditions had undermined the authority of the traditional village leaders throughout the Netherlands, and Sleen was no exception. In the end, despite the dissenters' determined challenge to the village values, they were "spewed out." A publicly ostracized minority, shunned by friends, boycotted in their trades and businesses, they felt that they had no other choice.[56]

When Dominie Van Raalte in nearby Ommen organized his group migration of Seceders to North America in the fall of 1846, fifty-seven Drenthe families and eighteen single adults from Sleen, Coevorden, Borger and elsewhere in the Zuidwolde area joined him and even provided leaders for his colony in Holland, Michigan. There they found the religious freedom they so desperately sought. The tensions this religious conflict wrought in Sleen were so great that despite his victory, Dominie Schultz committed suicide and the opposing family clans in the village developed such deep-seated animosity that conflict lasted for generations.

Not only in its inception but subsequently as well, Drenthe emigration had distinct religious patterns. In the initial period of the 1840s Seceders overwhelmingly dominated with 82 percent of the emigration. The early leavers were mainly farmers (53 percent), several of whom owned considerable wealth, as already noted. Another one quarter were poor farm laborers, with village craftsmen of middling wealth comprising the final quarter. The Seceders had strong religious motives for going to the United States; almost 60 percent cited a desire for religious freedom as their primary reason for emigrating. But poverty was also a factor. One in five of the pioneer emigrants before 1850 had been living on the public dole. Over 70 percent of the emigrants of the 1840s departed in family units and 90 percent were of rural origin.

In the 1850s the character of Drenthe emigration changed from religious to economic. Emigration was no longer a mark of deviant behavior but had become acceptable and even commendable. Roman Catholic emigrants from Dalen and Emmen on the southeastern border with Bentheim, Germany played a larger role than Seceders. Twice as many Catholics as orthodox Calvinists departed in the fifties. Instead of the farm family movement of the forties, the Catholic emigrants were mainly single, well-to-do adults holding white-collar, urban jobs. Fully 30 percent of all Drenthe emigrants in the fifties were wealthy, the highest proportion in the Netherlands as a whole. One third held white-collar positions, 38 percent were Catholic, two thirds were single emigrants—again a very high proportion—a quarter of whom were of urban origins, and a third did not go to the United States, compared to only 10 percent of the Seceders. The urban professional emigrants least likely to go to the United States were members of the national Reformed Church, who sought opportunities in the Dutch East Indies, South Africa, and South America. Urban Catholics preferred the United States.

In the third phase of Drenthe emigration, from 1865 through 1880, the composition again changed. Reformed Church members totaled nearly half (47 percent) of the emigrants, Seceders 39 percent, and Catholics only 13 percent. Half were farm workers and one third farmers. Two thirds emigrated as families, 97 percent went to the United States, and 97 percent specified economic reasons as their chief motive for leaving. These were not desperately poor peasants. Three quarters were of middling status, 18 percent were wealthy, and only 10 percent were on the dole. The post-war Seceders mainly followed their co-religionists who had settled in Michigan twenty years earlier. Most hailed from the municipalities of Emmen and Assen, with Nijeveen and Smilde in secondary roles. In the pioneer phase, most Seceders had come from Beilen and Sleen, but after 1850 this movement stopped entirely. A small number of Catholics from Dalen continued to emigrate after 1865, as they had earlier.

Where did the Drenthians settle in America? Almost 90 percent went to the Holland colony in Western Michigan where they carved out of the virgin forest near Lake Michigan a new community named Drenthe. One third of these newcomers, Seceders all, departed before 1850 and founded Drenthe in Michigan. Hard times and the Civil War led to a hiatus until 1865, but in the next fifteen years 55 percent of all Drenthe emigrants followed the pioneers to Michigan in a chain migration.

The Drenthe emigration was very focused. Only eight municipalities provided over three fourths of the Michigan Drenthe newcomers, most notably Emmen, Beilen, Assen, and Sleen. Apart from the 90 percent of Drenthe emigrants who chose Michigan, 5 percent went to Iowa, and 5 percent, mainly Reformed Church members, went to other continents. Fully one half of all Drenthe emigrants through 1880 were Seceders, and 14 percent were Catholics. In the total Drenthe population in 1849, Seceders and Catholics numbered less than 6 percent.[57] Thus, Seceders were overrepresented among the emigrants by nearly 900 percent, and Catholics were overrepresented by 237 percent. More than 16 percent of the Drenthe emigrants cited a desire for religious freedom as their primary motive for leaving, which is a far higher percentage than elsewhere in the Netherlands. Drenthe emigrants also left mainly as families with wives and children; only 38 percent left alone. The average age of the family heads and adult singles was nearly 40 years, which was a higher average than among emigrants from any other province.

The community of Drenthe, Michigan, was a microcosm of village life in the old country.[58] Drenthians lived in the eastern part of the village and Staphorsters (from nearby Overijssel Province) lived in the western part. The two groups argued over naming the village, but Drenthians prevailed. They also argued over the church. At first the community had only one congregation, the Drenthe Reformed Church, organized in 1847. But the Drenthe and Staphorst factions squabbled from the outset. It was a "matter of clannishness," concluded Prakke.[59] Finally in 1857, because of the "assertiveness of the people from Staphorst toward those who had come from the province of Drenthe," in the words of historian Henry Lucas, the Staphorst faction seceded and organized a Presbyterian Church, led by the congregation's pastor, Roelof Smit, who was also expelled for "*promoting factions*."[60] The Drenthians remained with the Reformed Church and had to endure without a pastor until 1861.

Not only did each group have its own church in the village, it also had its own Dutch school and cemetery. Eventually, the church schools gave way to the village public school which was tax-supported, and by the 1880s both congregations had merged into the Christian Reformed Church, the immigrant church of the Dutch Calvinists in North America.

Thus, the clannishness of old Drenthe was carried to new Drenthe.[61] The community of Drenthe was unique among the villages and towns of "de Kolonie" for its stockade mentality; its negative, almost hostile, attitude toward other villages; and its closed, corporate peasant clannishness. The Drenthians clung to community and family even more than other Hollanders.

Prakke's conclusion is apt: "The Drenthian is innately a community person, devoted to his own village community and his own soil. By nature he is neither a dissenter nor an emigrant. Yet, during one period of the history of this region we see Drenthians separate into sectarian groups. . . ." And the minority who rejected the constant pressures of the "preservers of unity," finally emigrated to Michigan where they reestablished a new village community rooted in the soil. By refusing to conform in Drenthe, they suffered complete ostracism. The only out was to move.[62]

Overijssel

Overijssel Province, like Drenthe, had small family farms on sandy soils, but it also boasted a major textile industry in the Twente district on the German border, centered in the cities of Enschede, Almelo, and Deventer. In the years 1835–80, 2,921 persons emigrated from Overijssel for a rate of 12.5 per 1,000 average population, which was less than the rate of Drenthe.

Geographically, Overijssel had three district regions: a large central area, called Salland, of general three-field farming from which two thirds of the emigrants originated; the Twente rye and textile district to the east from which a quarter of the emigrants came; and a small meadow area of dairying along the Zuiderzee (Land van Vollenhove and Kamperland) from which only one sixth of the emigrants came. This prosperous western region included the provincial capital of Zwolle and the harbor town of Kampen.

The locus of emigration was the central farming region from Staphorst at the north, which had the heaviest emigration in the entire province, to Diepenham on the southern border of Gelderland. Emigration began in earnest in the Staphorst vicinity in 1846 among the disgruntled followers of the Seceder leader, Dominie Van Raalte of Ommen. This congregation drew members from the neighboring municipalities of Staphorst, Hardenberg, Den Ham, Hellendoorn, Nieuwleusen, and Avereest. Other followers of Van Raalte lived in the eastern dairylands of Zwolle and Genemuiden, as well as in the south-central farming area of Diepenham and Haaksbergen. In early 1847 Seine Bolks, Van Raalte's understudy at Hellendoorn, led twenty-three families from his congregation to the Michigan colony, where they carved out of the forest a new settlement called Hellendoorn (later Overisel, after the home province).[63]

In the 1847 list of overseas emigrants from Overijssel that Dutch officials forwarded to The Hague, they appended the following remark: "The Reformed are all Seceders, whose departure is ascribed to religious zeal."[64] Fully 29 percent of all Overijssel emigrants were Seceders, although they composed only 1.5 percent of the total population in 1849.[65] Thus, they were overrepresented by twenty-fold. One in five Seceders specified a desire for religious liberty as the chief motive for leaving. This was a family emigration of small farmers, farm workers, and village craftsmen of middling economic status. Almost all accompanied or followed Van Raalte and Bolks to Holland, Michigan.

A lesser emigration center, numbering about 250 persons, was of Roman Catholics from the Twente district. Most of these folk settled in Cleveland and in the Bay City area of eastern Michigan. Catholics from Twente emigrated steadily so that ultimately Catholics totaled 26 percent of Overijssel emigrants, which was only a few points below their proportion in the population. Unlike the Seceder families, Catholics emigrated mostly as single adults. Only 35 percent left with family. They were mainly professionals and craftsmen—tailors, weavers, carpenters, smiths, and bakers.

Chronologically, Overijssel emigration passed through five phases. The pioneer period of the forties was dominated by Seceders, who made up half of all emigrants. In the 1850s the emigration shifted to members of the Hervormde Kerk, who were mainly (57 percent) small farmers of middling status desirous of economic improvement. Only 88 percent went to the United States, compared to 99 percent of the Seceders.

During the 1860s Overijssel emigration changed, as it did elsewhere in the Netherlands in these years. Prosperous white-collar workers—lawyers, preachers, druggists, bookkeepers, surveyors, dealers, and peddlers—now composed a third of the emigrants. But very poor tradesmen and laborers were also common. Twice as many of the sixties emigrants were on the public dole. These were economically driven emigrants, led by the desperately poor and the upwardly mobile.

After 1865 Overijssel emigration began to shift to an industrial type. The proportion of urban emigrants more than doubled to 22 percent and twice as many singles as families emigrated. Forty percent were skilled craftsmen and only 34 percent were farmers. The number of Seceders increased to 18 percent, indicating a second wave chain migration, but Hervormde members were in the majority with 57 percent. After 1875 the shift to industrial-type migration became even more pronounced. Urban emigration continued at 19 percent; one in nine were factory workers and white-collar persons—clerks, teachers, nuns, merchants, doctors—doubled to 21 percent. Those of wealthy status doubled to 40 percent, 60 percent were unmarried, and 62 percent were Reformed. Only 25 percent went to the United States.

Overijssel emigration thus began with traditional Seceder farmers and craftsmen and became more of an urban, white-collar emigration of unmarried persons. Catholics from Twente consistently made up a quarter to a third of the emigration. Apart from the Catholic provinces, this was the highest proportion of Catholic emigration in the Protestant Netherlands.

The focal point of American destinations of Overijssel emigration was western Michigan, especially the village of Overisel. From Staphorst, Den Ham, Hellendoorn, Nieuwleusen, and Zwolle, 92 to 100 percent of all emigrants went to western Michigan. Staphorsters alone numbered 30 percent of the Overijsselers in western Michigan. Over 60 percent of the Michigan Dutch originated in Overijssel. This was not as concentrated an emigration stream as that from Drenthe, where 90 percent went to Michigan, but it exceeded that of all other provinces except the Noord-Brabant and Wisconsin connection discussed below.

Gelderland

The large province of Gelderland ranked second behind Zeeland in total emigrants (12,400) and third in the rate of emigration (32 per 1,000 average population). The province consisted of three distinct regions: the Achterhoek, literally "Backcorner" (or de Graafschap), bounded by the Ijssel River and the German border; the Veluwe on the southeast side of the Zuiderzee; and the Betuwe astride the Rhine River in the south.

The Achterhoek, a region of small, diversified farms, was always the focal point of Gelderland emigration and even of Dutch emigration nationally.[66] People departed earlier and in greater numbers from this borderlands region than from anywhere else. More than 6,300 persons, which was more than half of all Gelderland emigrants, came from the Achterhoek, and particularly from one community, Winterswijk, the seat of municipal government. With 2,200 emigrants—a rate of 289 per 1,000 average population—Winterswijk had the third highest emigration of all Dutch municipalities. This early outflow was clearly influenced by the mass emigration to America from northwest Germany (the Westfalia-Osnabrück region) that began in earnest in the 1830s and early 1840s.[67]

Achterhoek emigrants were people trying to climb the agricultural ladder to farm ownership in America. Small farmers and farmhands comprised the largest occupation group at 38 percent. Skilled craftsmen made up 35 percent, rural day laborers 22 percent, and white-collar persons only 4 percent. Farmers and skilled workers were overrepresented.

Religiously, a relatively high proportion (21 percent) of Achterhoek emigrants were Seceders, compared to 15 percent among all Gelderland emigrants. Both numbers are extremely high, considering the fact that only 1 percent of the Gelderland populace belonged to the Seceder Church in 1849. Indeed, in the 1840s over one half (53 percent) of all emigrants from the province were Seceders. Catholic emigrants, by contrast, were underrepresented; they totaled 38 percent of the provincial population but only 21 percent of the emigrants. National Church adherents numbered 59 percent of the population and also 59 percent of the emigrants.[68]

The center of Seceder strength was in the municipalities of Winterswijk, Aalten, Neede, and Wisch. From these communities the proportion of Seceders among the emigrants in 1844–47 ranged from 40 percent in Wisch, to 22 percent in Aalten and Winterswijk, and 16 percent in Neede. The 182 Seceders who departed from Winterswijk included two thirds of the Seceder congregation there. The Wisch Church was also left nearly empty by the exodus. The Seceder leaders received sanctuary and moral support from their brethren of the Evangelical Church in the Westfalian area of Germany. The Seceder, Lammert Rademaker, a clergyman, and Dirk Meengs, a weaver, led the Achterhoek emigration.[69]

So many farmers and craftsmen sold their houses, furniture, and farms with crops in the field in the 1840s that, according to the *Amsterdamsche Handelsblad*, farm property values declined 25 to 35 percent and the number of tenant farm leases dropped 15 to 20 percent. "If letters from people who have emigrated from this place to North America, continue to report favorable news, as they have till now," said the reporter with alarm, "it is certain that within half a year a third or one half of the inhabitants of Winterswijk will leave."[70]

These sanguine reports came from Alexander Hartgerink, a young Seceder schoolmaster from Neede who had emigrated to America already in 1845, and from several Gelders families in Milwaukee, Wisconsin and Decatur, Illinois. They urged compatriots to come where poor people ate pork and beef three times a day and were liberated from Holland's rigid social distinctions: "The poor here are as good as the rich; no one has to doff his hat to any one, as in Holland."[71]

Another stimulus was the energetic promotion of emigrant agents at Winterswijk, especially Hendrikus Swytinck and a man named Bolwerk who booked Catholics. Swytinck was an agent for the large Rotterdam booking firm of Wambersie & Crooswijk; he earned f10 ($4) for each passenger ticketed. In 1850 after the first emigration wave receded, Swytinck also emigrated with his family.[72]

Apart from the Winterswijk region, where emigration began early and continued unabated, except for a brief hiatus during the American Civil War, Gelderlanders did not begin to emigrate in large numbers until the 1850s. In the early years (1835–49) nearly 1,600 persons emigrated overseas from Winterswijk alone, and only 800 left from the remainder of the province. In the 1850s another 1,300 persons left Winterswijk for overseas places, but these were joined by 2,400 others from elsewhere in the province. This was a threefold increase over the pre-1850 period and demonstrated the spreading emigration fever.

The greatest emigration period was the decade 1865–75 when 6,000 persons departed, one half of the total for the entire period 1835–80. Winterswijk again led with nearly 1,500 persons, but 4,500 emigrants departed from other parts of Gelderland. This was almost double the number in the 1850s and six times the number in the 1840s. After 1865 the center of emigration shifted westward and northward from Winterswijk into adjacent municipalities. The Achterhoekers settled primarily in Dutch colonies in western New York in Monroe County (Ontario, East Williamson, and Palmyra) and in Sheboygan and Alto, Wisconsin.[73]

The Betuwe and Veluwe areas shared equally the remaining half of Gelderland emigrants, numbering 3,150 from the Betuwe and 2,950 from the Veluwe. The Betuwe region included the entire meadowlands between the Rhine and Waal rivers in the vicinity of Nijmegen. This was the most Catholic area of the Netherlands outside of the Catholic provinces of Limburg and Noord-Brabant. Nearly half (45 percent) of all Betuwe emigrants were Catholics. The 9 percent of Seceder emigrants came mainly from the Tiel and Bommelerwaard regions.

The major emigration villages in the Tiel district were Herwijnen, Haaften, and Vuren, all situated along the north bank of the Waal River. In the Bommelerwaard area on the south bank of the Waal, the municipality of Gameren was the most important, followed by Rossum and Kerkwijk. Emigrants from Herwijnen and Vuren were mainly Seceder followers of Scholte who accompanied their leader to Pella, while those from neighboring Haaften were mostly Hervormden who followed Van Raalte to Holland, Michigan. Gameren emigrants divided between Iowa and Michigan, with the Seceders again choosing Pella. Emigrants from the nearby municipalities of Rossum and Kerkwijk, mainly Hervormden, also went to Pella.

The social characteristics of the Betuwe emigrants reveal their more urban character. Twenty-five percent originated in cities, especially Nijmegen. This was the highest level of urban emigrants in the Netherlands outside the Randstad. Over 60 percent of Betuwe emigrants left as singles, which is characteristic of urban origins. More than 12 percent held white-collar positions compared to 5 percent among all other Gelderland emigrants. There were also more unskilled workers at 37 percent, compared to 27 percent elsewhere. The social status of Betuwe emigrants reflected the urban influence, with an above average proportion of wealthy at 27 percent, compared to 14 percent among other Gelderland emigrants. The major period of emigration was the 1850s, with a second lesser peak in the 1865–75 decade. Thus, the Betuwe was the second area to experience heavy emigration, following the initial wave from the Achterhoek.

Except for emigrants from Nijmegen, the destination of Betuwe emigrants was primarily Van Raalte's Holland colony, with Pella a secondary preference. The northern sector, known as Overveluwe, was also oriented heavily toward western Michigan. From Ermelo, Dornspijk, Harderwijk, Oldebroek, and Apeldoorn, half to three quarters of the emigrants went to western Michigan.

The Veluwe was the last region to develop an emigration tradition. Three quarters of all Veluwe emigrants departed after 1860. Some 21 percent were urban, mainly from Arnhem, compared to 25 percent in the Betuwe and only 5 percent in the Achterhoek. Only 41 percent emigrated alone, compared to 60 percent in the Betuwe and 52 percent in the Achterhoek. Nearly 90 percent of Veluwe emigrants were Hervormde, which was twice the proportion of those from the Betuwe and one third higher than the Achterhoek emigrants.[74] There were more needy families at 27 percent, compared to less than 20 percent among the emigrants from the other districts. The Veluwe emigration was led by unskilled laborers (39 percent), as had been true in the Betuwe. Another 35 percent were farmers, as in the Achterhoek group. Nearly one half of the Gelderlanders in Michigan hailed from the northern Veluwe (Overveluwe).[75] From the southern sector, including Putten and Ede, Iowa was the preferred settlement area, with 75 percent and 85 percent, respectively, of the emigrants going to the Hawkeye State.

In sum, the Achterhoek was the center of Gelders emigration with Seceder farmers and craftsmen of middling means leading the way to New York and Wisconsin. The more urban, wealthier Catholic emigrants from the Betuwe were the next to leave in large numbers, and they scattered widely across the northern and central states. They were followed by the poorer, unskilled workers and small cottagers from the Veluwe Hervormde Kerk, most of whom settled in Michigan and Iowa.

The Catholic Provinces

The southern Catholic provinces of Noord-Brabant and Limburg formed a unique cultural region. The area was more Catholic than the northern Netherlands was Protestant. It was more on the periphery of the national economy, more a subsistence economy than a commercial one, and more involved in traditional handicraft or cottage industries such as linens, woolens, and shoemaking, which gave farm families work in the off season. The Catholic provinces had the highest birth rates and greatest intra-provincial mobility and provincial outmigration in the mid-nineteenth century. Given the press of population, it was mandatory here to delay marriage, practice celibacy, and limit the number of children.[76]

Despite the pressures, Catholic Netherlanders were reluctant to emigrate overseas. When urban factory work opened up after 1865 in the southern part of the region, they eagerly seized it and stayed within the country. Those who did leave the motherland were primarily small marginal farmers least involved in commercial agriculture and thus most dependent on home "piece work." When structural changes in the economy took away this source of extra income, while food prices shot up from the potato and rye crises of the 1840s, the marginal farmers decided to go to Catholic settlements in America.

Noord-Brabant

The province of Noord-Brabant is the largest in land area but among the smaller in population density. Hence, even though this province had the highest birth rate in the country at mid-century (34 percent average increase from 1840 to 1864), it also had the lowest population increase per land area.

Total overseas emigration in the years 1835–80 was 3,459 persons, or 8.2 per thousand average population (1830–78). Only the province of Utrecht had a lower rate. This number is deceptive, however. Brabanders were a highly mobile people in terms of intra-provincial moves. One quarter of the population entered or left their municipalities between 1850 and 1865; this was second only to Limburg's 29 percent. Nearly 28,000 of Brabant residents, on average, moved into or out of their municipalities each year between 1850 and 1865. The national average mobility per municipality was 23,760 persons.[77]

Noord-Brabant in the nineteenth century consisted of five agricultural regions and thirteen traditional cultural areas (see Fig. 3.7).[78] The major distinction was between the northwestern alluvial clay-soil area including the valley of the Maas (Meuse) River (regions A, D, and E) where commercial agriculture predominated, and the southeastern diluvial sandy-soil region (region B), which was characterized by subsistence agriculture combined with home industry. The southwest part of the province (region C) was a transitional zone that gradually became integrated into the national market system.

The heavy alluvial soils, which had been created in the seventeenth and eighteenth centuries by poldering, required large capital investments in machinery and horsepower to make commercial wheat and flax production profitable. Land values were high, farms large, population widely dispersed, and few cities developed. The excess farm laborers migrated seasonally to the Ruhr valley of Germany and others resettled in the urbanizing western part of the Netherlands. But there was little overseas emigration to North America, in sharp contrast to the steady emigration from other sea clay soil regions in the western and northern parts of Holland.

The Maas River valley in northeastern Brabant had both specialized dairy areas and commercial wheat areas. Only the latter, in the Maasland region, had significant emigration overseas. Farms were smaller, people more densely packed, and home industry more important in the Maas valley than in the polder region to the west.

In the less productive sandy soil regions of the southern two thirds of Noord-Brabant Province, farmers in the eastern half (region B) continued to follow the traditional three-field system supplementing their income with sheep herding on the heathlands and working in home industries.[79] Farms were small and inefficient, lacking in fertilizer and transportation links to outside markets. Hence, subsistence crops such as rye and buckwheat were overrepresented. The eastern part also had the highest population densities in the province.

Farmers in the southwestern region (C) followed the traditional Flemish three-field system that emphasized livestock rather than sheep raising. The livestock provided meat and milk for export markets as well as manure for intensive cultivation of fodder crops and for bringing higher yields for all crops. This area also was bisected by roads and waterways, especially the Zuid Willems Canal, which had bypassed the southeastern region. All these advantages enabled farmers in the southwest to benefit from the rapid commercialization in agriculture, while in the eastern part of Brabant farmers remained traditional and their land underutilized.

These differing farming patterns created varying incentives for emigration. Prosperous clay soil farmers obviously had little inclination to move, compared to the struggling small farmers on marginal sandy soils. Much of the sandy land was heath and useful only for sheep grazing unless reclaimed and heavily fertilized. Efforts to reclaim the heathland met with only limited success in the mid-nineteenth century due to resistance by small farmers and squatters who valued the heath as a free commons for sheep grazing and as a source of peat fuel, or even for illegal settlement. Since annual population growth was almost 1 percent at the time, agricultural production notably lagged.

The only alternative for these subsistence farmers and cottagers was to engage in "home industry," spinning and weaving in the off season. Textile manufacturing had developed in the Netherlands under the "putting-out" system, and small farmers began working for merchants in the regional cities, such as Tilburg and Helmond. The national government promoted cotton textile exports to the Netherlands East Indies and protected the industry from English competition with high tariffs. But in 1847 England and Holland signed a trade agreement that lowered import duties, and English factory-made cotton yarn quickly replaced Dutch home-made yarn. The Dutch merchants responded by developing steam-powered textile mills and concentrating production in new centers. Between 1850 and 1870, textile production was transformed from a home into a factory industry, and thousands of home weavers who doubled as small farmers lost their much needed supplemental income. Modernization in the textile industry had destroyed another traditional craft and forced the victims to consider emigration overseas.[80]

Emigration from Noord-Brabant was highest in the southeastern region (B and E in Figure 3.7), which had the highest population densities and least developed market economy. Although the commercially oriented and less populated northwestern area had higher population growth rates in the years 1811 to 1850, the southeastern area was least able to absorb more people since it was already

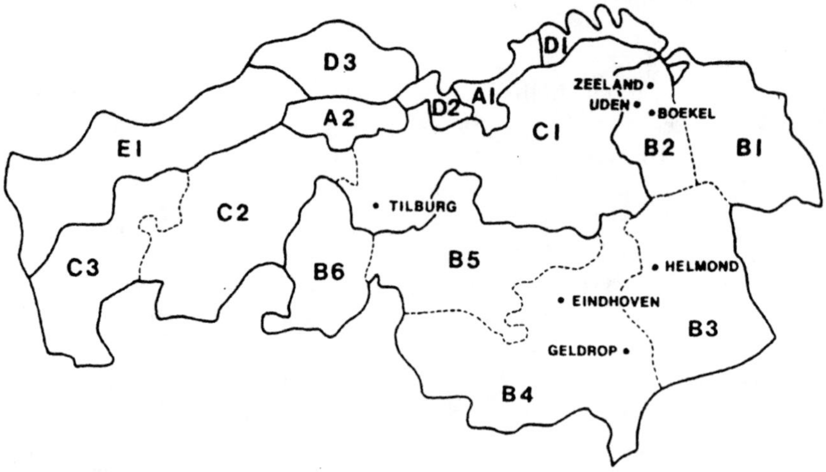

Agricultural System

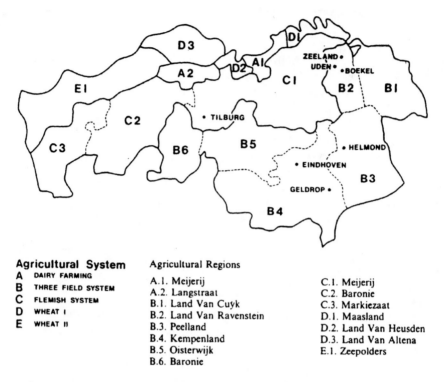

- A DAIRY FARMING
- B THREE FIELD SYSTEM
- C FLEMISH SYSTEM
- D WHEAT I
- E WHEAT II

Agricultural Regions

A.1. Meijerij
A.2. Langstraat
B.1. Land Van Cuyk
B.2. Land Van Ravenstein
B.3. Peelland
B.4. Kempenland
B.5. Oisterwijk
B.6. Baronie
C.1. Meijerij
C.2. Baronie
C.3. Markiezaat
D.1. Maasland
D.2. Land Van Heusden
D.3. Land Van Altena
E.1. Zeepolders

Figure 3.7 Brabantse Peel Region, Province of Noord-Brabant

SOURCE: Annual Report of Agriculture, *Verslag van de Landbouw* (1875), "Grotte der Gronden, Province van Noord-Brabant," 202–03, in Yda Schreuder, *Dutch Catholic Immigrant Settlement in Wisconsin, 1850–1905* (New York: Garland Publishing, 1989), 31.

crowded, and economic opportunities were too limited to absorb new workers (see Table 5.1).[81] Agricultural expansion was minimal, and rural industry faltered by 1852. Yet this was the only part of Brabant that had a net migration surplus, that is, more people entered than left the region.

By 1865 the situation changed markedly. The southern part of Noord-Brabant experienced rapid industrial development, and this created new manufacturing jobs that attracted residents from the northern area where home industry could no longer compete. In 1865 the Peelland (B3) and Oisterwijk (B5) regions, as well as the city of Eindhoven (in B4), had heavy in-migration, whereas the Land of Cuyk (B1), Land of Ravenstein (B2), and Baronie (B6) suffered large losses from out-migration. In short, employment increased in the southern and central parts of Brabant at the expense of rural de-industrialization, which plagued the northeastern area.

Emigration patterns in the province were closely related to this economic shift. In the 1830s and 1840s overseas emigration began in the northeastern region in the Land of Cuyk and Ravenstein (B1, B2), in Maasland (D1), and Oisterwijk (B5). In this region, lying south of Nijmegen, home industries were being undermined by the growing factory production in the southern cities (Eindhoven, Helmond, Geldrop, and Tilburg). Indeed, the decline in rural industry in this region was a more immediate and lasting cause of overseas emigration than the much publicized potato crop failures in the mid-1840s throughout the Netherlands.[82]

In the 1850s the outflow from the northeastern region peaked, and the emigration fields spread westward and southward to the areas of 's Hertogenbosch, the provincial capital, and Tilburg. Three quarters of all emigrants before 1880 departed in the 1850s from De Peel (B3), Oisterwijk (B5), and the Meijerij van 's Hertogenbosch (C1). During the American Civil War, emigration virtually stopped except for white-collar professionals from Breda and 's Hertogenbosch who went to the Dutch East and West Indies.

In the decade after the Civil War, the western part of the province experienced its heaviest emigration. Half of the Breda area (C2, C3) emigrants departed then, as did two thirds of the largely Protestant emigrants from the region on the east side of Dordrecht, the Zeepolders (E1) and the Land of Altena (D3). The Reformed Church was dominant there and Seceder congregations were common. These emigrants were craftsmen and unskilled workers of middling economic status, 58 percent Reformed and 16 percent Seceder, bound for the United States (93 percent) in order to improve their economic fortunes.

Thus, there were only three areas in northeastern Noord-Brabant that consistently experienced overseas emigration: the Land of Cuyk (B1), Land of Ravenstein (B2), and Maasland (D1).[83] The Peel region municipalities of Uden, Zeeland, and Boekel (in C1) also had strong emigration in the early years, 1847–56, particularly a large group migration to Little Chute, Wisconsin, led by Father Theodorus Vanden Broek.

The story of the Peel communities, which was the leading emigration center in northeast Noord-Brabant, exemplifies the impact of structural economic shifts. Between the 1840s and 1870s, the home industries of linen textile goods gave way to factory machine production. Farmers who doubled as part-time weavers and shoemakers lost their much needed supplemental income due to the forces of de-industrialization of the countryside.

The Peel is a peatbog and heathland area that was relatively isolated in the mid-nineteenth century due to the lack of canals and waterways and the physical barriers of dense woods and marshy soil. The three municipalities on the western edge of the Peel bogs were centered around the three governmental and market centers of Uden, Zeeland, and Boekel. Farmers were dispersed in smaller settlements in the region. The area had nearly 10,000 inhabitants in 1849, led by Uden with nearly 6,000. In the village of Uden stood the large parish church. This was truly the central place, since the population was 99 percent Catholic.

A careful analysis of local population records revealed that the emigrants were not townspeople but marginal farmers who had moved to the edges of the boglands and tried to open small farms. Land taxes were lower there, and waste land was available. These poorer parts of the villages, which had higher population growth, were the emigration centers in all three villages. In the years 1848–70, three fourths of the emigrants were small farmers (5 to 10 acres) and farmhands, and one quarter were linen weavers and general laborers. Most left in family groups with large numbers of children. Many had followed infrequent jobs elsewhere in the region and were a sort of floating proletariat who often changed jobs and residences. Stuck in their poverty and facing another agricultural crisis, they decided to emigrate.

The immediate stimulus was the return in 1846 of native son Father Vanden Broek, who had served as a priest to the Menominee Indians at Little Chute, Wisconsin since 1836.[84] In 1846 the federal government relocated the tribe and discharged Vanden Broek. Since the priest had recently bought over 300 acres of land in Little Chute, he decided to return to his homeland and offer aid for Catholic poor to emigrate to Wisconsin. His timing was perfect, and the visit received much publicity in Catholic newspapers and periodicals. By the spring of 1848 the first wave of Brabanders left Rotterdam in three chartered ships. This group became the nucleus of the Dutch Catholic colony in the Fox River Valley south of Green Bay.

Not surprisingly, even among emigrants from the same religious and geographic background, village distinctions were carried to Wisconsin. Two separate settlement clusters were formed from the chain migration—Hollandtown and Little Chute.[85] Uden and Zeeland residents concentrated in Hollandtown (Outagamie County), whereas Boekel residents scattered more widely. The Little Chute colony, in contrast to Hollandtown, represented mostly emigrants from elsewhere in Noord-Brabant. No Uden families and only two Zeeland families lived there. After the Civil War, Catholic Dutch from Limburg Province arrived in the Fox River Valley and these settled further south in yet a third node at De Pere. Some later Brabant emigrants also settled in the De Pere area, but no Limburg emigrants settled in the original Hollandtown and Little Chute colonies.

Wisconsin became the primary locus of Noord-Brabant emigrants not only from the Peel area but from all Catholic centers. More than three quarters (77 percent) of Brabant emigrant families and singles in the years before 1880 settled in Wisconsin. Two thirds of these hailed from only ten municipalities (in descending order of importance): Uden, Boekel, Zeeland, Beugen, Oploo, Gemert, Mill en St. Hubert, Nistelrode, Neunen, and Reek. More than nine of every ten emigrants from all of these villages settled in the Fox River Valley.

Noord-Brabant emigration overseas was much broader than Wisconsin. Indeed, 12 percent went to the Dutch West Indies, Dutch East Indies, Surinam, Brazil, and other South and Central American countries. Brabanders also settled in Catholic urban centers in New York (New York City, Buffalo, and Rochester), Indiana (Evansville, South Bend, and Muncie), Ohio (Cleveland and Cincinnati), Detroit, St. Louis, and New Orleans. One third of the emigrants from St. Oedenrode went to New York and Ohio and all those from Werken went to Illinois.

The minority Protestant emigrants from the western part of Noord-Brabant settled in an entirely different pattern. They joined the two major Calvinist colonies of Holland and Pella. More than 10 percent of all Brabant emigrants were Calvinists who settled in western Michigan. These hailed (in descending order) from

Klundert, Zevenbergen, Oirschot, and Zwalue. Thus, religious forces were determinative in settlement patterns. Catholic Brabanders chose Father Van den Broek's colony in the Fox River Valley, but Calvinists in smaller numbers followed dominies Van Raalte and Scholte.

Structural changes in industry best explain the low rates of Catholic emigration. In the 1840s and 1850s, when traditional rural industry declined and subsistence farming stagnated under the potato and rye crop disasters, rural folk emigrated throughout the northeastern part of the province. But after 1865 when manufacturing developed in the south, rural laborers had an alternative to emigration. Thereafter, only the cottagers in the more isolated northeast area continued to emigrate overseas since their locale was not participating in the new industrial growth.

Limburg

Limburg was an agrarian province characterized by small, inefficient farms of ten acres or less in which the cottage textile industry augmented family incomes. The population grew by 54 percent between 1815 and 1870, and life there was difficult and hard. Struggling Limburgers historically also worked as seasonal laborers in Belgium and Germany. Others moved to the rising industrial city of Maastricht in the extreme south and found employment in coal mining and textile industries. Limburgers had a long tradition as migrant laborers within Europe and overseas utopias held little appeal.[86]

The general cause of Limburg emigration was the potato crisis that severely struck farmers in the sandy soil northern region. Forty percent of the potato crop in the province was lost in 1845, and rye prices climbed sharply when this cereal crop was also hit by a disease in 1847. Compared to the adjacent provinces of Noord-Brabant and Gelderland, however, where potato crop losses were an overwhelming 99 percent and 94 percent, respectively, in 1845, Limburg's loss was mild. Hence, only a relatively few Limburg farmers decided to emigrate to the United States.[87] Most were small farmers and farm laborers, along with a few industrial wage laborers who wished to escape from a depressed agricultural economy in the years 1865–75. However, the economic situation in Limburg was not as bleak as in Noord-Brabant, which may explain why fewer Limburgers emigrated.

Although Limburg emigration was low (1,849 persons emigrated, a rate of 8.7 per 1,000) and began in earnest only after 1860, it is also the most clearly focused. One can draw a line bisecting the province near the center immediately south of Roermond. Emigrants north of the line settled in Wisconsin on the fringe of the Fox River settlement of fellow Catholics from Noord-Brabant. Emigrants south of line, from the region of middle Limburg, went exclusively to Carver County, Minnesota, beginning during the Civil War years.[88] The emigration from middle Limburg was so concentrated in time and place that in one municipality, Montfort, 13 percent of the populace emigrated in one year. Nowhere else in the Netherlands is the regional character of emigration so clearly demonstrated as in the demarkation line in Limburg between Wisconsin and Minnesota destinations. Never did the twain mix.

The earliest emigration, which began in the northeastern region in the years 1847–59 and flowed to Wisconsin, was very small, numbering only 78 persons. No local newspaper was published in this area to provide details about the movement. Since the emigrants primarily joined the Noord-Brabant colony in the Fox River Valley, it would seem that the Brabanders indirectly instigated the Limburg migration and determined the choice of location. But any direct links cannot be proven.[89]

Perhaps the answer lies in the promotional activities of a Netherlands land company, the Amsterdam-based Maatschappij van Grondbezit, which bought large quantities of raw land in Minnesota. The company advertised the advantages of this virgin Minnesota farmland in the Dutch press, and the Limburgers were clearly attracted. The Homestead Act of 1862 provided an additional stimulus for middle Limburgers. The provisions of this act were widely advertised in Limburg newspapers, beginning in early 1863, by the Antwerp emigration agent Adolph Strauss, who worked the local villages intensively.[90] Middle Limburgers undoubtedly also learned about the possibilities in Minnesota from neighboring Germans across the border, who likewise chose Minnesota.

There is no direct evidence that the land company, agent Strauss, or the Germans prompted middle Limburgers to emigrate. It is just as likely that the Limburg migration was self-generated by one or more early emigrants from the region.[91] Jan Willem Meuleners, a well-to-do farmer from Nieuwstadt, had emigrated to Benton Carver, Minnesota, in 1860 with his wife, five children, and a hired hand. The next year a younger brother and his family of four, a brother-in-law, and two other friends from Nieuwstadt followed Meuleners, after receiving letters describing the favorable situation in Minnesota. In 1862, another brother left for Benton Carver, along with many other families from Nieuwstadt and environs. Soon, "bacon letters" from Nieuwstadters in Minnesota began arriving in middle Limburg villages and this stimulated a genuine group migration.[92] In short, with the stimulus of the land companies, emigration agents, and example of the Germans, the America letters from fellow Limburgers created the typical chain migration pattern in middle Limburg that was so common in all of Europe.

Conclusion

This survey shows that Dutch immigration, like European immigration generally, was both region-specific in origin and focused in destination. Each locality had its own pattern of response, or lack of it, to the forces of change that stimulated emigration. The urban-rural dichotomy was particularly salient. The urban emigrants who chose the States settled in inland cities along the Erie Canal, on the Great Lakes, or in the Ohio Valley. Of those entering the States from Noord-Holland, 72 percent settled in New York and northern New Jersey, as did 77 percent of Zuid-Holland emigrants. But the rural-based emigrants immediately headed for midwestern farmsteads and the Dutch colonies there, unless they lacked the money or the energy to continue to their destination.

This rural-to-rural pattern of emigration was concentrated in the north-central states of Michigan, Illinois, Wisconsin, and Iowa. Among the Dutch settling in the Midwest, Limburg and Drenthe led the way, with over 90 percent of their emigrants moving to the Midwest—notably Wisconsin (Limburg) and Michigan (Drenthe). Groningen, Friesland, Overijssel, and Gelderland, all rural provinces, also were high on the list of emigrants bound for the American interior.[93] The question then emerges, to what degree did this urban-rural dichotomy continue to manifest itself in terms of occupational, social class, and cultural variables?

Three main factors instigated an emigration in the several regions of the Netherlands: the religious schism in the Hervormde Kerk, the modernization of agriculture in the sea-clay grain regions, and the decline of cottage industry in the sandy-soil region. Where a migration tradition began early, it continued long and strong. And since moving to America was a risky and permanent venture, the migrants used the information chain of family, friends, and neighbors already there. As a result, strong links were formed between specific Dutch and American localities.

Notes

1. Frank Thistlethwaite, "Migration from Europe Overseas in the Nineteenth and Twentieth Centuries," XIe Congrès International des Sciences Historiques, *Rapports* (Göteburg, Stockholm, Uppsala, 1960), 32–60.
2. Maldwyn Allen Jones, *American Immigration* (Chicago: University of Chicago Press, 1973), 3–4.
3. Thistlethwaite, "Migration from Europe," 34.
4. Scandinavian and German migration studies have confirmed this theory of localism. See Walter D. Kamphoefner, *The Westfalians: From Germany to Missouri* (Princeton: Princeton University Press, 1987); Jon Gjerde, *From Peasants to Farmers: The Migration from Balestrand, Norway, to the Upper Middle West* (Cambridge and New York: Cambridge University Press, 1985); Robert C. Ostergren, *A Community Transplanted: The Trans-Atlantic Experience of a Swedish Immigrant Settlement in the Upper Middle West, 1835–1915* (Madison: University of Wisconsin Press, 1988).
5. Harald Runblom and Hans Norman, eds., *From Sweden to America: A History of the Migration* (Minneapolis: University of Minnesota Press, and Uppsala: University of Uppsala, 1976), 149–64.
6. Ibid., 154–55.
7. Ibid., 163–64.
8. Herbert J. Brinks, *Dutch American Voices: Letters from the United States, 1850–1930* (Ithaca, NY: Cornell University Press, 1995).
9. Robert P. Swierenga, comp., "Netherlands Census, Labor, Land, and Migration Data by Municipality, 1830–1878" (Kent, OH, 1979).

10. Compiled from Robert P. Swierenga, comp., *Dutch Immigrants in U.S. Population Censuses, 1850, 1860, 1870: An Alphabetical Listing by Household Heads and Independent Persons*, 3 vols. (Wilmington, DE: Scholarly Resources, 1987).
11. Roger Leetsma, "Origin of Dutch Place Names: Allegan and Ottawa Counties, Michigan," in *Papers of the Michigan Academy of Sciences, Arts and Letters* 34 (1948): 147–51.
12. See, for example, the pamphlet published in the Netherlands written by the Pella pioneer Sjoerd Aukes Sipma. An English translation with introduction is Robert P. Swierenga, ed., "A Dutch Immigrant's View of Frontier Iowa," *Annals of Iowa*, 3rd. ser. 38 (Fall 1965): 81–118.
13. *75th Anniversary Booklet 1883–1953*, Platte Christian Reformed Church, Platte, SD, 7–9.
14. David G. Vanderstel, "Dutch Immigrant Neighborhood Development in Grand Rapids, 1850–1900," in *The Dutch in America: Immigration, Settlement, and Cultural Change*, ed. Robert P. Swierenga (New Brunswick, NJ: Rutgers University Press, 1985), 125–55, quote 131. This article is based on Vanderstel's primary work, "The Dutch in Grand Rapids, Michigan, 1848–1900: Immigrant Neighborhood and Community Development in a Nineteenth Century City" (Ph.D. diss., Kent State University, 1983), esp. chapters 4 and 5.
15. The source files are Robert P. Swierenga, comp., *Dutch Emigrants to the Unites States, South Africa, South America, and Southeast Asia, 1835–1880: An Alphabetical Listing by Household Heads and Independent Persons* (Wilmington, DE: Scholarly Resources, 1983); Swierenga, *Dutch Immigrants in U.S. Ship Passenger Manifests, 1820–1880: An Alphabetical Listing by Household Heads and Independent Persons*, 2 vols. (Wilmington, DE: Scholarly Resources, 1983); and Swierenga, *Dutch Immigrants in U.S. Population Censuses, 1850, 1860, 1870.*
16. Henry S. Lucas, *Netherlanders in America: Dutch Immigration to the United States and Canada, 1789–1950* (Ann Arbor: University of Michigan Press, 1955; reprinted Grand Rapids, MI: Wm B. Eerdmans, 1989), 279–84.
17. Michael Wintle, "Push-factors in Emigration: The Case of the Province of Zeeland in the Nineteenth Century," *Population Studies* 46 (1992): 523–37; reprinted slightly revised as "Positive and Negative Motivation in Dutch Migration to North America: The Case of the Province of Zeeland in the Nineteenth Century," in *Connecting Cultures: The Netherlands in Five Centuries of Transatlantic Exchange*, eds. Rosemarijn Hoefte and Johanna C. Kardux, (Amsterdam: VU University Press, 1994), 134–53.
18. Madder was an industrial crop harvested by migrant workers and intensively cultivated in a small area along the southwestern coast of the North Sea: Tholen, St. Philipsland, and Schouwen in Zeeland, and Goeree-Overflakkee and Voorne-Putten in the province of Zuid-Holland. Laborers

dug the roots of the plant in the fall months and dried them in special ovens. The industry was labor-intensive and highly capitalized. See Jan Lucassen, *Migrant Labour in Europe, 1600–1900: The Drift to the North Sea* (London: Croom Helm, 1987), 58–60.

19. Lucassen, *Migrant Labour*, 58–59; D.J. Bouman, *Geschiedenis van den Zeeuwsche landbouw-maatschappij, 1843–1943* (Wageningen: H. Veenman & Zonen, 1946), 101–02, 106–07, 114–16, 131–32, 143–44.
20. The proportion of farmland to pasture land in the five regions was Walcheren 2:3, Schouwen-Duiveland-Tholen 8:5, Noord- and Zuid-Beveland 8:3, West Zeeuws-Vlaanderen 5:1, Oost Zeeuws-Vlaanderen 6:1. Bouman, *Geschiedenis*, 110, 120, 138, poverty figures compiled from data in table, 146. Cf. A. Doedens, "'Doch hier is alles rustig'; Zeeuws-Vlaanderen en de belgische opstande, 1830–1831," in *Autbarteit en strijd, elf bijdragen tot de geschiedenis van collectief verzet in de Nederlanden, met name in de eerste helft der negentiende eeuw*, ed. Doedens (Amsterdam, 1981), 101–30, esp. 105, 108.
21. Bouman, *Geschiedenis*, 159–64, 190–200.
22. Jacob Van Hinte, *Netherlanders in America: A Study of Emigration and Settlement in the Ninteenth and Twentieth Centuries in the United States of America* (2 vols., Groningen: Noordhof, 1928), ed. Robert P. Swierenga, chief trans. Adriaan de Wit (Grand Rapids, MI: Baker Book House, 1985), 127–28, 144–48.
23. Wintle, "Push-factors," 140–41; Wintle, *Zeeland and the Churches: Religion and Society in the Province of Zeeland (Netherlands) in the Nineteenth Century* (Middelburg, 1988), 98–101, 183–84.
24. J. Was, "Oorsprong en lotgevallen van het dorp Waterlandkerkje in westelijk Zeeuwsch-Vlaanderen," *Zeeuwsche Volks-almanak* 11 (1846): 69, cited in Wintle, "Push-factors," 26. Wintle, I think, makes too much of the religious tensions between Protestants and Catholics, as well as episodic epidemics, as major causes of the overseas emigration.
25. P. B. Vermey, *De Zuidhollandse eilanden* (Zwolle: De Ervan, 1952), 118–24; B. Boers, *Beschrijving van het eiland Goedereede en Overflakkee* (Sommelsdijk, 1843).
26. A local historian reported: "A cry of distress arises from the region.... Give us another type of crop! Enlarge our crop cycle!" J. van der Waal and F. O. Vervoorn, *Beschrijving van het eiland Goedereede en Overflakkee, zijne wording en zijn voortbestaan tot op heden* [Description of the Island Goedereede and Overflakkee: Its Origin and Existence to the Present] (Sommelsdijk, 1896), 13–29, 64–67, quote on 17.
27. Philip B. Scranton, ed., *Silk City: Studies on the Paterson Silk Industry, 1860–1940* (Newark: New Jersey Historical Society, 1985), 4, 26.
28. Van Hinte, *Netherlanders in America*, 814.
29. C. Baars, *De geschiedenis van de landbouw in de Beijerlanden* (Wageningen: Centrum voor landbouwpublikaties en landbouwdocumentatie, 1973), 211–17.

30. J. A. de Kok, *Nederland op de breuklijn Rome-Reformatie* (Assen: Van Gorcum, 1964), 294.
31. In 1809 88 percent of Amsterdam Jews were "Germanic" (Ashkenazic) and 12 percent were "Portugese" (Sephardic). De Kok, *Nederland op de breuklijn Rome-Reformatie*, 325. On the settlement in the United States, see Robert P. Swierenga, *The Forerunners: Dutch Jewry in the North American Diaspora* (Detroit: Wayne State University Press, 1994).
32. Between 1850 and 1880 484 persons emigrated from Texel and 285 from eastern Terschelling.
33. Lucas, *Netherlanders in America*, 280.
34. G. Smit, *The Agrarisch-maritieme struktuur van Terschelling omstreeks het midden van de negentiende eeuw* (Groningen: Miedema, 1971), 180–204, esp. 204.
35. Van Hinte, *Netherlanders in America*, 288–90, 362–65; Lucas, *Netherlanders in America*, 190–93; Robert P. Swierenga, "The Ethnic Voter and the First Lincoln Election," *Civil War History* 11 (March 1965):39–43.
36. Annemieke Galema, *Frisians to America: With the Baggage of the Fatherland* (Groningen: REGIO-Projekt, and Detroit: Wayne State University Press, 1996).
37. Van Hinte, *Netherlanders in America*, 149; Jelle Ypma, *Ds. Marten Annes Ypma 1810–1863, Van Minnertsga (Friesland) naar Vriesland (Michigan)* (Leeuwarden: Friesch Dagblad, 1986), 21–41.
38. Lucas, *Netherlanders in America*, 210–12.
39. Peter N. VandenBerge, *Historical Directory of the Reformed Church in America* (Grand Rapids, MI: Wm. B. Eerdmans, 1978), 309. The congregation never secured a minister.
40. Lucas, *Netherlanders in America*, 204–05.
41. Ibid., 246–47.
42. Ibid., 247–49.
43. J. M. G. Van Der Poel, *Honderd jaar landbouwmechanisatie in Nederland* (Wageningen: Vereniging voor Landbouwgeschiedenis, 1983), 139–208.
44. *Provinciaal Groninger Courant*, 13 Feb. 1869.
45. There is no biography in English. For a brief account see Marian M. Schoolland, *De Kolonie* (Grand Rapids: Board of Publications of the Christian Reformed Church, 1973–1974), 78–83. De Cock's role in the schism is recounted in H. Bouwman, *De crisis der jeugd: eenige blazijden uit de geschiedenis van de kerken der Afscheiding*, ed. Cornelis Smits (Kampen: J.H. Kok, 1976); J. Wesseling, *De Afscheiding van 1834 in Groningerland*, 3 vols. (Groningen: Vuurbaak, 1973–1978), 1:117–19; 3:137–58, passim.
46. De Kok, *Nederland op de breuklijn Rome-Reformatie*, 292–93. The core Hunsingo emigration fields were the municipalities of Uithuizermeeden, Uithuizen, Usquert, Baflo, Kantens, Eenrum, Kloosterburen, Leens, and Ulrum.
47. K. van der Kleij, *Het Drentse volkskarakter zoals zich dit in de loop der tijden heeft gevormde* (Herloo: Kinheim, 1946), 37–39, 65–68, passim.

48. A superb survey of Drenthe farming developments is Jan Bieleman, *Boeren of het Drentse zand, 1600–1910: Een nieuw visie op de "oude" landbouw* [A. A. G. *Bijdragen*, Vol. 29, 1987] (Wageningen: Afdeling Agrarische Geschiedenis Landbouw-Universiteit, 1987).
49. Bieleman, *Boeren*, 684–85.
50. Ibid., 71–72.
51. H. J. Prakke, *Drenthe in Michigan* (Grand Rapids, MI: Wm. B. Eerdmans, 1983), 1–2, 72–73, 30. I have relied heavily on Prakke for the cultural and religious characteristics of Drentians.
52. Ibid., 72, 13.
53. Ibid., 9–11.
54. Ibid., 15–24.
55. Ibid., 38, 52.
56. Ibid., 37–44, 68–71, quote on 46.
57. De Kok, *Nederland op de breuklijn Rome-Reformatie*, 296–97.
58. Prakke, *Drenthe*, 55–59; Lucas, *Netherlanders in America*, 138–40.
59. Prakke, *Drenthe*, 56.
60. Lucas, *Netherlanders in America*, 512.
61. Prakke, *Drenthe*, 57–59.
62. Ibid., 72, following the Drenthe folklore historian K. van der Kleij, *Drentse Volkskarakter*.
63. Suzanne M. Sinke, "Overisel, Michigan: An American Immigrant Community in the Late Nineteenth Century" (B.A. Honors thesis, University of Northern Colorado, 1980), ably describes the origin and development of this Seceder village.
64. *Overijssel Provinciaal Verslag*, 1987, 15.
65. De Kok, *Nederland op de breuklijn Rome-Reformatie*, 296.
66. G. H. Ligterink, *De landverhuizers: Emigratie naar Noord-Amerika uit het Gelders-Westfaalse grensgebied tussen de jaren 1830–1850* (Zutphen: De Walburg Pers, 1981); Verena de Bont, "Ik druk voor het laatst uw hand in het oude vaderland: Emigratie uit de Gelderse Achterhoek naar Noord Amerika in de period 1847–1877 (Ph.D. diss., University of Tilburg, 1983); Liesbeth Hoogkamp, "Wisch-Scenario 1830–1850: Verslag van een onderzoek naar de sociaal-economische omstandigheden, de Afscheiding en de landverhuizing in de gemeente Wisch tussen 1830 en 1850" (Ph.D. diss., University of Utrecht, 1982). A sentimental, fictionalized account of Achterhoek immigrants is H. W. Heuvel, "Achterhoeksche Menschen in Amerika," *Vragen van der Dag* 38 (1923): 266–82, 381–93. Since the Protestant separation of 1559, this region was under the strong Catholic influence of the bishopric of Munster. The Catholic enclaves of Groenlo and Lichtenvoorde reflect that tradition. See G. J. H. Krosenbrink, *De Achterhoek in grootvaders tijd* (The Hague: Kruseman, 1975), 19–24.
67. Kamphoefner, *Westfalians*, describes this emigration in excellent detail. For the German influence on the Dutch, see Prakke, *Drenthe*, 25; Van Hinte, *Netherlanders in America*, 39, 122; Ligterink, *Landverhuizers*,

109–10, 33–34; De Bont, "Emigratie uit de Gelderse Achterhoek," 21, 97; Hoogkamp, "Wisch-Scenario," 88; J. Stellingwerff, ed., *Amsterdamse emigranten: onbekende brieven uit de prairie van Iowa, 1846–1873* (Amsterdam: Buijten and Schipperheijn, 1975), 41; Hermanus Strabbing's "Ervaringen," *De Grondwet*, 14 Nov. 1911, reprinted Henry S. Lucas, ed., *Dutch Immigrant Memoirs and Related Writings*, 2 vols. (Assen: Van Gorcum, 1955; rev. ed., Grand Rapids MI: Wm. B. Eerdmans, 1997), 1:254–55.

68. De Kok, *Nederland op de breuklijn Rome-Reformatie*, 296.
69. Ibid., 31, 25–26.
70. Lucas, *Netherlanders in America*, 62.
71. Letter of A. Hartgerink, Toledo, OH, 3 May 1846, quoted in Van Hinte, *Netherlanders in America*, 122–23; Letters of A. Hallerdijk, Milwaukee, 1845, and J.A. Buekendorst, Decatur, IL, 16 June 1845, both quoted in Lucas, *Netherlanders in America*, 61–62.
72. Ligterink, *Landverhuizers*, 28–30; Lucas, *Netherlanders in America*, 67.
73. Willem Wilterdink, *Winterswijkse pioniers in Amerika* (Winterswijk: Vereniging "Het Museum," 1990). The Winterswijk emigration field spread into the municipalities of Dinxperlo, Wisch, Doetinchem, and Zelhem to the west, and Neede, Zutphen, and Borculo to the north.
74. The best study of religious life is H. K. Roessingh, *Het Veluwse kerkvolk geteld: De uitkomsten van de godsdienststelling van 1809 in sociaal-historisch perspectief* (Zutphen: De Walburg Press, 1978).
75. From Ermelo, Dornspijk, Harderwijk, Oldebroek, and Apeldoorn from one half to three quarters of the emigrants through the year 1880 went to western Michigan.
76. Yda Schreuder, *Dutch Catholic Immigrant Settlement in Wisconsin, 1850–1905* (New York and London: Garland Publishing, 1989), 10–13, 25–26. Catholics numbered 88 percent in Noord Brabant and 97 percent in Limburg, whereas Protestants totaled less than 75 percent elsewhere and in several provinces (Utrecht, Gelderland, and Overijssel) less than 65 percent. See Kok, *Nederland op de breuklijn Rome-Reformatie*, 295–97.
77. Swierenga, comp., "Dutch Census, Labor, Land, and Migration Data by Municipality, 1830–1878."
78. Schreuder, *Dutch Catholic Immigrant Settlement*, 16–25.
79. B. H. Slichter van Bath, *De agrarische geschiedenis van West Europe, 500 A.D.–1850* (Utrecht, 1962), describes the three-field system of agriculture common in western Europe for centuries.
80. Schreuder, *Dutch Catholic Immigrant Settlement*, 26–33.
81. Ibid., 33–34.
82. Schreuder, ibid., 14–16, argues cogently that, while the potato disease and resulting high food prices directly led to emigration in the sea-clay provinces of Zeeland, Groningen, and Friesland, the causal link is missing in Noord-Brabant. Areas with declining home industries had high emigration, but not the potato farming regions.

83. This and the next four paragraphs rely on ibid., 79–81.
84. Frans H. Doppen, "Theodore J. van den Broek, Missionary and Emigration Leader: The History of the Dutch Catholic Settlement at Little Chute, Wisconsin," *The Catholic Historian* 3 (Fall/Winter 1983): 202–25. Jesuit and Crosier Fathers from Noord-Brabant had long been active in missionary work among the American Indians in Missouri, Wisconsin, and elsewhere. See Henry A. V. M. van Stekelenburg, *Landverhuizing als regionaal verschijnsel van Noord-Brabant naar Noord-Amerika: 1820–1880* (Tilburg: Stichting Zuidelijk Historisch Contact, 1991), 37–81; Van Stekelenburg, *"Hier is alles vooruitgang: Landverhuizing van Noord-Brabant naar Noord-Amerika* 1880–1940 (Tilburg: Stichting Zuidelijk Historisch Contact, 1996); and Van Stekelenburg, "Dutch Roman Catholics in the United States," in *Dutch in America*, ed. Swierenga, 64–77.
85. Schreuder, *Dutch Catholic Immigrant Settlement*, 81–92.
86. Lucassen, *Migrant Labour in Europe*, 188.
87. A detailed study of Limburg emigration is A. J. M. Koeweiden-Wijdeven, *Vergeten emigranten: landverhuizing van noord en midden-Limburg naar Noord Amerika in de jaren 1847–1877* (Venlo, May 1982). The four major emigration regions, moving from north to south, were northeast Limburg with an emigration rate of 10 per thousand inhabitants, northwest Limburg centering around Montfort with 27 per thousand, middle Limburg centering around Nieuwstadt to the south with the highest rate of 39 per thousand, and the southern region of the province, which had virtually no overseas emigration. Only six municipalities had an emigration of more than 45 per thousand, placing them in the top quartile (Meerlo in the northeast, Montfort in the north central area; and Borne, Roosteren, Nieuwstadt, and Limbricht in lower middle Limburg).
88. Limburgers in Minnesota originated primarily in Nieuwstadt (12.1 percent), Echt (14.9 percent), Sittard (14.2 percent), Born (11.3 percent), Limbricht (9.2 percent), Roosteren and Susteren (each 7.8 percent), and Obbricht (3.5 percent). Together, these eight municipalities accounted for 80 percent of all Limburgers in Minnesota. Also, almost every emigrant from these localities chose Minnesota rather than Wisconsin.
89. Koeweiden-Wijdeven, *Vergeten emigranten*, 21–22.
90. Ibid., 42–43, 68.
91. This is Koeweiden-Wijdeven's reasonable opinion in ibid., 42–44, 68–69.
92. Ibid., 76, 44–45.
93. Swierenga and Harry S. Stout, "Socio-Economic Patterns of Migration in the Netherlands in the Nineteenth Century," in *Research in Economic History: An Annual Compilation of Research*, vol. 1, ed., Paul Uselding (Greenwich, CT: JAI Press, 1976), 303–04.

CHAPTER 4

Journey Across

DUTCH EMIGRANTS THOUGHT long and hard before deciding to go to America, and once the decision was made they were just as deliberate about planning the journey across the ocean and selecting the place of settlement. They had time to plan their journey to America because they were not forced like the Irish to flee from famine, or like the Germans to run from revolution, or like the Russian Jews to escape persecution.

The key questions were: what port city was most conveniently located, taking account of fares and the quality of service offered by the various shipping companies? What was the most favorable time of year to sail, considering weather conditions and also the prospects for finding work upon arrival? Was it advantageous to travel in large groups, which offered greater security but also the inevitable delays and loss of control over travel arrangements? What shipping companies had the best reputation for reliability, cleanliness, and service?

The answers to these and many similar questions about immigrant traffic can be found in official records and reports, personal travel diaries, and in letters sent back to family and friends about the journey across. The letters and diaries portray individual experiences and reveal the pathos of leaving, the routine of the ocean passage, and the exhilaration of arrival in the land of promise. But the personal experiences of the few whose accounts have survived may not be typical. Hence, it is necessary to consult shipping company passenger manifests, which formed the basis of United States customs reports and immigration statistics.

Ship Passenger Law of 1819

The U.S. ship passenger lists, which begin in 1820, contain biographical information on 25 million persons who entered the United States in the following one hundred years. Among this number were 200,000 Dutch nationals who sailed into U.S. ports between 1820 and 1920. This chapter is based upon the 55,000 Dutch who arrived through the year 1880. Exploring the social characteristics and travel patterns of this large group reveals some of the dynamics of international migration. The passenger lists also provide the only age-specific data on all Dutch emigrants, since the Netherlands emigration lists only provide the age of the head of the household or single persons.

A congressional law of 1819 first required ship captains to submit to American customs officials sworn manifests of arriving passengers (see Figure 12.2 on page 317).[1] The law, which took effect January 1, 1820, called for the reporting of such personal information as name, age, sex, occupation, country of last residence, and country or place of intended destination. Congress in 1855 added a question on shipboard accommodations—whether cabin, second class, steerage, etc.—and in 1882 and 1893 the lawmakers added questions on family relationships, marital status, literacy, financial resources, ticketing details, whether a temporary or permanent immigrant, the specific place of origin, and the "zone" or city of destination.

That the U.S. immigration laws prior to 1882 did not ask immigrants to report their specific communities of origin and destination is the most serious deficiency for those desiring to understand the localistic tendencies and geographical selectivity of emigration.[2] Without this information, the place of origin of emigrants cannot be known directly. There is an acceptable indirect method, however, in the case of European nations such as the Netherlands, which compiled annual lists of overseas emigrants from each local community. The Dutch emigration records begin in the mid-1830s, and they have been linked with the ship passenger manifests containing Dutch nationals during the period 1835–80. After 1880, the Netherlands emigration lists are too incomplete to warrant general linkage efforts, except for the several provinces with good data.

Ships and Ports of Embarkation

The immigrant trade was clearly tied to the normal lines of transatlantic commerce. The early vessels were mainly freighters that carried raw American produce such as cotton to Europe and on the return trip "human freight" provided a paying ballast. Since Liverpool's Waterloo Docks was the leading European freight port, and New York City controlled the cotton trade, ships from these ports could offer immigrants the cheapest fares. The Irish particularly took advantage of these bargains. Ports with more frequent departures also lessened the problem of costly waiting time in harbor cities.

Dutch immigrants in the period 1820–80 traveled on more than two thousand different ships. But in the 1860s, as the packet steamers came to replace the often irregular sailing vessels, the Dutch, like the other Europeans, increasingly took passage on relatively fewer, specially designed immigrant ships that shuttled between Europe and America on regular schedules.[3]

In the early years, before the onset of the Great Migration in the mid-1840s, Dutch nationals traveled singly or as single families. Of 500 ship crossings with Dutch nationals aboard in the years 1820–44, 62 percent had fewer than 10 Dutch passengers and only one vessel carried more than 100 Dutch.[4] After the mass emigration began in the mid-1840s, however, more than one half of the Dutch crossed in groups of 10 or more. In 1846–47, several Seceder congregations emigrated in very large groups of up to 400. But the leaders divided the travelers into smaller contingents of 100 to 150 because of the limited carrying capacity of the sailing vessels. There was also the practical consideration that smaller groups were easier to manage and to ensure adequate travel accommodations. Thus, the picture of Dutch emigration is clearly that of a constant trickle rather than a flood. Apart from the years 1846 and 1847, passage in large groups was the exception rather than the rule.

Dutch, English, Belgian, French, and German shipping companies dominated the northern European passenger trade in the mid-nineteenth century. Prior to the 1840s the ports of Amsterdam and Le Havre vied for dominance over the Dutch emigrant traffic, with Bremen gaining ground in the 1830s. Amsterdam's early preeminence stemmed from its direct link to the North Sea at Den Helder via the North Holland Canal constructed in 1819–24. But the waterway was woefully inadequate and Amsterdam shipping was handicapped until 1895 when the North Sea Canal was cut through to the sea at nearby Ijmuiden. Bremen was seriously disadvantaged at first by its inland location on the Weser River thirty-three miles from the North Sea, until the commodious new port of Bremerhaven was completed in 1830. The timing coincided with the onset of mass emigration, and Bremerhaven quickly became the premier transatlantic port serving northern Europe with four or more regular weekly departures. It even attracted trade from the Rhineland and southern Germany. Even some Dutch emigrants in the 1840s sailed from Rotterdam to Bremerhaven, where they took passage to New York. Hamburg shippers responded in the 1840s to the challenge from Bremerhaven by also offering regular transatlantic sailings, and in 1847 they founded the Hamburg-America Line.[5]

After 1840 Rotterdam supplanted Amsterdam and became the preferred port for Dutch emigrants. In 1830 Rotterdam city fathers cut a canal across the island of Voorne to the navigable Haringvliet, which provided direct access to the North Sea. In the 1840s, 62 percent of Dutch emigrants embarked at Rotterdam; only 15 percent sailed from Amsterdam (Table 4.1). But the Voorne canal proved inadequate in the 1860s, and Rotterdam became a mere transit port for emigrants to reach England, Antwerp, or Bremen. In the 1860s Liverpool and London carried 4,200 Dutch, compared to only 1,600 at Rotterdam. Rotterdam city leaders then constructed the New Waterway directly to the sea at Hoek van Holland, which enabled Rotterdam to recover its salient position.

The Dutch government helped by creating in 1861 an oversight agency, the Commission for the Supervision of the Transit and Transport of Emigrants [Commissie voor toezicht op de doortogt en het vervoer van landverhuizers]. The major shipping companies also worked with a will to recapture the carrying trade. The firm of Wambersie, one of the major emigrant agencies and shipping companies, in 1871 helped establish the Netherlands-American Steamship Company (N.A.S.M.). In 1873 this forerunner of the Holland-America Line began regular passenger and freight service, and by 1890 it had 2,000 agents throughout the Netherlands

TABLE 4.1 Ports of Embarkation by Decade, Dutch Immigrants, 1820–80

	1820–29		1830–39		1840–49		1850–59		1860–69		1870–80		TOTAL 1820–80	
PORT	NUMBER	%	NUMBER	%	NUMBER	%	NUMBER	%	NUMBER	%	NUMBER	%	NUMBER	%
Netherlands														
Amsterdam	179	42	328	33	1,897	15	842	6	57	1	1	0	3,304	6.1
Rotterdam	13	3	85	9	7,964	62	7,138	48	1,585	19	8,475	52	25,260	46.7
Nieuwdiep	0	0	0	0	119	1	1	0	0	0	0	0	120	0.2
England														
Liverpool	34	8	36	4	165	1	2,200	15	2,217	26	5,380	33	10,032	18.5
London	7	2	33	3	348	3	337	2	2,038	24	244	2	300	75.6
Glasgow	0	0	0	0	0	0	3	0	539	6	457	3	999	1.9
Other Atlantic														
Antwerp	39	9	21	2	951	7	2,526	17	1,286	15	1,361	8	6,184	11.4
Le Havre	94	22	286	29	872	7	1,651	11	175	2	63	0	3,141	5.8
Other	2	0	1	2	294	2	0	0	4	0	18	1	319	0.6
North Sea/Baltic														
Bremen	1	0	130	13	286	2	211	2	484	6	163	1	1,275	2.4
Hamburg	5	1	9	1	4	0	51	0	90	1	47	0	206	0.4
Other	0	0	0	0	0	0	0	0	13	0	0	0	14	0.0
Mediterranean	3	0	3	0	2	0	0	0	0	0	0	0	8	0.0
Latin America	40	9	47	5	23	0	47	0	37	0	46	0	240	0.4
East Indies/Africa	2	0	1	0	0	0	1	0	5	0	2	0	11	0.0
United States	2	0	3	0	2	0	0	0	0	0	0	0	7	0.0
British North America	2	0	0	0	2	0	0	0	3	0	9	0	16	0.0

SOURCE: Data file: Dutch Immigrants in U.S. Ship Passenger Manifests, 1820–80

recruiting emigrants and offering free lodging in Rotterdam.[6] In the 1870s, therefore, Rotterdam regained its lead, shipping 8,500 Dutch emigrants (52 percent) compared to 5,400 through Liverpool, which had by then totally eclipsed London.[7]

Liverpool gained a larger share of the Dutch traffic only because of their lower fares. Poorer emigrants were willing to tolerate the inconveniences of transshipping via England in order to garner the savings on the transoceanic ticket. More than twice as many day laborers traveled through Liverpool as went directly to America from Rotterdam.

The more southerly ports of Le Havre and Antwerp tried to compete for the Dutch traffic with Rotterdam and Liverpool, but they met with minimal success. Le Havre was too distant and primarily served the Paris region and industrial centers of the lower Seine River valley. Nearby Antwerp fared better; in the 1850s it attracted nearly one fifth (17 percent) of all Dutch immigrants. The construction in 1859 of a canal between the Meuse and the Scheldt rivers better enabled Antwerp to tap its hinterland.[8]

For the entire sixty-year period, 25,000 Dutch crossed to America out of Rotterdam, 10,000 passed through Liverpool, 6,200 used Antwerp, and about 3,000 each embarked from Amsterdam, Le Havre, and London. In percentages, 47 percent sailed from Rotterdam; 18 percent transshipped from Liverpool; 11 percent used Antwerp; and Amsterdam, London, and Le Havre each shared approximately 6 percent (Table 4.1).

Proximity, price, scheduling, comfort and familiarity, and the activity of shipping company agents were all factors in the selection of a port of embarkation and a particular vessel of passage.[9] The Dutch transportation network of canal boats and later of railroads funneled people into the port cities of Rotterdam and Amsterdam and made them easily accessible to emigrants. Limburgers, Noord-Brabanters, and Zeelanders from the south of the Netherlands, by the same token, traveled to nearby Antwerp or more distant Le Havre. More than three-quarters of the Limburg emigrants in the years before 1860 departed from Belgian and French ports, as did 23 percent of the Brabanters and 19 percent of the Zeelanders (Table 4.2). Conversely, emigrants from Friesland and Overijssel had the highest proportion (14 percent and 12 percent, respectively) who transshipped via English ports.

During the 1860s, as was noted above, Liverpool's share of the Dutch emigrants increased dramatically, and Rotterdam's share slipped. For emigrants from five provinces—Noord-Holland, Noord-Brabant, Drenthe, Gelderland, and Overijssel—the proportion embarking from British ports increased from below 10 percent before 1860 to 40–55 percent thereafter. The three provinces lying farthest inland and hence at the greatest distance from England showed the sharpest increase. The proportion of emigrants from Drenthe using Liverpool and London increased from zero before 1860 to 41 percent after 1860. Comparable percentages for Gelderlanders and Brabanters are 3 to 52 and 7 to 55.

In the other provinces, the shift to English ports was more modest, rising from below 5 percent before 1860 to 30 percent afterward. Nearly one-third of the Zeelanders and one-half of the Limburgers also continued to use nearby Antwerp. The Dutch ports after 1860 snared at least one-half of the emigrants only from the

TABLE 4.2 National Ports of Embarkation by Province of Origin, Pre- and Post-1860 (in percent)

	National Ports of Embarkation							
	Dutch		British		Belgian-French		German	
Periods	35–60	61–80	35–60	61–80	35–60	61–80	35–60	61–80
Western provinces								
Noord-Holland	84	51	9	44	7	1	0	4
Utrecht	89	61	2	26	10	9	0	4
Zuid-Holland	86	67	4	29	9	3	0	1
Northern provinces								
Drenthe	94	56	0	41	4	0	2	3
Friesland	72	63	14	25	12	2	2	0
Groningen	87	48	9	44	4	1	1	8
Eastern provinces								
Gelderland	84	32	3	52	13	12	0	5
Overijssel	80	52	12	44	6	2	4	2
Southern provinces								
Limburg	24	32	0	22	76	45	0	1
Noord-Brabant	70	29	7	55	23	11	1	5
Zeeland	72	44	9	25	19	31	1	0

SOURCE: Data file: Dutch Immigrants in U.S. Ship Passenger Manifests, 1820–80

western provinces and the inland provinces of Overijssel and Drenthe that either bordered the Ijsselmeer or had ready water access to it.

Liverpool and London, though more inconvenient, gained a larger share of the Dutch traffic only because of their lower fares. To reach the English harbors, Dutch emigrants had first to cross the English Channel to Hull and then take the train to London or, more commonly, to traverse England by "fast train" directly to Liverpool. Going via England added a week or more to the total voyage, in addition to the extra overland travel costs and the language problems with Englishmen. Father Theodore Vanden Broek of Little Chute, Wisconsin, wrote his compatriots in Noord-Brabant in 1847: "I would not advise anyone to go by way of England; because in addition to the freight being higher, a person has a great deal of trouble with the English officials. So it is much better to leave by ship directly from Rotterdam or from Amsterdam, or even by way of Le Havre by steamer to New York."[10] Le Havre offered ocean steamers already in 1847.

The poorer emigrants, it appears, were more willing to tolerate the inconveniences of transshipping via England in order to obtain the cost savings on the transoceanic ticket. This is indicated by the occupations of the emigrants using the various ports. Sixty percent of the unskilled emigrants sailed from British ports, which was more than twice the rate for craftsmen and white-collar persons, and four times the rate of farmers (Table 4.3). British ports were used by 32 percent of white-collar emigrants, 28 percent of craftsmen, 14 percent of farmers, and a whopping 60 percent of unskilled workers. Dutch ports were utilized by 58 percent of farmers, 50 percent of craftsmen, 42 percent of the white-collar group, but only 27 percent of the unskilled. Belgian ports served more Dutch farmers and craftsmen than unskilled workers, as did French and German ports to a lesser extent. Indirect evidence also shows that the proportion of emigrants who were subject to the Dutch head tax (*hoofdelijke omslag*),[11] which was based on income, was lowest among the Dutch departing from British ports and higher among those leaving from Dutch ports.

Inferences drawn from these findings are just that. The port of preference was clearly the nearest port city—Rotterdam—unless cost considerations gave the edge to more distant, usually foreign ports. In the latter case, those emigrants for whom cost was an overriding factor would be attracted. This usually meant going to Liverpool, but it also sent emigrants to Antwerp, Le Havre, Bremen, and Hamburg.

Immigrant Agents

Emigrant agents also had a hand in the shipping flow. The major immigrant agency and ship broker in the Netherlands in the middle decades of the nineteenth century was the Rotterdam firm of Wambersie, founded in 1838 by Johan Wambersie (1806–74).[12] Wambersie was ideally suited to capture the immigrant transport market because he knew the English language and the American scene at first hand, having been born of Dutch parents at Savannah, Georgia. He returned to the Netherlands by the time of his marriage at Rotterdam in 1833 and spent the next fifty years in the shipping business. Wambersie's partner in the 1840s was a fellow Rotterdammer, Hendrikus W. C. Crooswijk, but by the mid-fifties, Wambersie's son August replaced Crooswijk as the junior partner. In 1847 the Rotterdam firm offered to bring emigrants to New York "as cheaply as possible—in fact, for 30 guilders each."[13] Transatlantic ticket prices in 1846–50 ranged from 30 to 45 guilders ($12 to $18) per person, with an additional sum of 35 guilders ($14) for provisions aboard ship.[14]

The Seceder emigrant groups of 1846 and 1847 especially used the services of Wambersie and Crooswijk of Rotterdam. Hendrik Scholte's Amsterdam emigrants signed with them, and Albertus van Raalte's associate, the Reverend Cornelius Vander Meulen, wrote from Michigan: "I recommend the office of Wambersie and Crooswijk in Rotterdam."[15] Another Seceder clerical leader, the Reverend Gerrit Baay of Appeldoorn in Gelderland, who hired the firm to transport his congregation to Wisconsin, reported that "we cannot complain ... but we certainly could have saved f50 if we had chosen to sail from Amsterdam." Baay continued, "I would advise ... to make use of the services of H.H. Wehlburg and Breuker on the outskirts of Amsterdam."[16] Amsterdam ticket prices were considerably cheaper than those from Rotterdam, but sailings were less regular. Wambersie also did extensive business in the northern province of Groningen; he had an agent at Uithuizen in the center of the main emigration region.[17]

TABLE 4.3 Occupational Status by Ports of Embarkation, 1820–80

	PORT OF EMBARKATION												
	DUTCH		ENGLISH		BELGIAN		FRENCH		GERMAN		OTHER		TOTAL
OCCUPATION	NUMBER	%	NUMBER	%	NUMBER	%	NUMBER	%	NUMBER	%	NUMBER	%	NUMBER
White collar	934	42	706	32	159	7	110	5	146	7	173	8	2,228
	(10)		(11)		(7)		(9)		(23)		(58)		(11)
Farming	4,625	58	1,108	14	1,101	14	930	12	234	3	14	0	8,012
	(47)		(17)		(46)		(73)		(37)		(5)		(38)
Craftsmen	2,114	50	1,162	28	557	14	128	3	141	3	100	2	4,222
	(22)		(18)		(24)		(10)		(22)		(33)		(20)
Unskilled	1,342	27	3,015	60	466	9	76	2	84	2	9	0	4,992
	(14)		(46)		(20)		(6)		(13)		(3)		(24)
Adults not employed	746	49	621	41	91	6	31	2	25	2	3	0	1,517
	(8)		(9)		(4)		(2)		(4)		(0)		(7)
TOTALS	9,761	46	6,612	32	2,394	11	1,275	6	630	3	299	1	20,971

SOURCE: Data file: Dutch Immigrants in U.S. Ship Passenger Manifests, 1820–80

Wambersie faced stiff competition in the north from the firm of Prins & Zwanenburg, "expediteurs van landverhuizers" based in the city of Groningen, who in April 1867 opened a shipping office for emigrants and freight cargo to North America. Anne Zwanenburg staffed the headquarters office in the Frisian port of Harlingen, and senior partner Arend Martens Prins became resident agent in the head office at Groningen city. Prins and another partner, S. M. Kimm, had previously been major emigrant recruiters in the province of Groningen. The new firm also had agents throughout the province, particularly at Veendam. They also drew German emigrants away from Bremerhaven.[18] In March 1872, according to a report in the *Nieuwe Groninger Courant*, Prins & Zwanenburg ticketed a group of 160 emigrants to North America from the Middelstum area.[19] Prins & Zwanenburg also operated in Noord-Holland Province, where they were served by their resident agent, Koppe & Van den Ende. The firm dealt with the Koninklijke Nederlandsche Stoomboot-Maatschappij (Royal Dutch Steamship Company) of Amsterdam.[20]

In addition to its network of ticketing agents throughout the Netherlands and northern Europe, Prins & Zwanenburg placed partners and representatives among the Dutch settlements in the United States to sell prepaid tickets and to serve as immigration agents for American railroad companies such as the Erie, Nickel Plate, and Milwaukee Road. Martin W. Prins, Jr., son of the senior partner, migrated to Chicago, and his partner Theodore F. Koch settled in St. Paul. The American associates borrowed capital from Prins & Zwanenburg and Dutch banking houses to export Frisian-Holstein cattle to the United States and to invest in frontier lands in Minnesota, Texas, and elsewhere. The firm printed glossy brochures and advertised their services and lands regularly in local newspapers such as *Het Weekblad voor het Kanton Bergum*. A broadside by Mr. J. Wijkstra, their agent in the Frisian village of Ee, for example, touted in glowing terms the lands of the Northern Pacific Railway, complete with a huge map detailing the cities and villages.[21] The extensive activities of Prins & Zwanenburg in the Netherlands and on the American frontier are only dimly perceived and merit a detailed investigation.

Other Dutch immigration firms were Hudig & Blokhuizen, Van Dam & Sweer, Cornelius Balquere & Son, and De Kuipers, all of Rotterdam; and at Amsterdam Wehlburg & Breuker and Ponselet & Zonen. Van Raalte's group, who sailed on the *Southerner* in September 1846, hired the Rotterdam firm of Hudig & Blokhuizen. Ponselet served as agent for the Reverend Pieter Zonne's Seceder group from Overijssel in May 1847, which was booked on the Amsterdam bark *Snelheid*.[22]

The emigration companies in the port cities of Rotterdam and Amsterdam, and even Harlingen, not only stationed agents in interior cities but advertised widely in newspapers throughout the Netherlands. They had to work hard to compete for the lucrative trade with foreign agencies from Antwerp and elsewhere that operated alongside the Dutch houses. The house of Oolgaardt and Bruinier, which represented two Liverpool steamship companies, operated in the province of Noord-Holland.[23] In the province of Limburg, the Antwerp expediter and ship broker, Adolph Strauss and his son Henri were very active, placing resident agents at Sittard, Nieuwstadt, and three other cities. Steinman & Company, also of Antwerp,

Koninklijke Nederlandsche Stoomboot-Maatschappij.

DIRECTE LIJN

Amsterdam. — New-York.

PRINS & ZWANENBURG,
GENERAAL-AGENTEN
VOOR HET
PASSAGE-DEPARTEMENT
AMSTERDAM,
Prins Hendrikkade 161.
Rotterdam, Boompjes 118.
Groningen, Bloemstraat.
Harlingen, Droogstraat.
Hamburg, St. Annen 7.

TELEGRAM-ADRES:
Voor Amsterdam: PRINS ZWANENBURG.
" Groningen: } PRINS.
" Harlingen: }
" Hamburg: } ZWANENBURG.
" Rotterdam: }

Amsterdam, den 21. Mai 1882

Herrn G. Tapkorn, Essen i/Oldenb.

Figure 4.1 Letterhead of Prins & Zwanenburg, Emigrant Shipping Agent for the Koninklijke Nederlandsche Stoomboot-Maatschappij, Amsterdam

SOURCE: Grouwstra Letter Collection, National Archives, Leeuwarden, courtesy of Annemieke Galema.

likewise had an agent at Sittard. P. A. Van Es & Company of Rotterdam stationed a representative at Nieuwstadt, and Wambersie and Son of Rotterdam located their man in Limbricht.

Strauss and Steinman advertised weekly in the regional Limburg newspaper, *Mercurius*. Strauss's ads in 1862 and 1863 cleverly included the text of the new American Homestead Law, which appealed to small Limburg farmers. The ads also stressed that there were regular sailings each Saturday by steamboat directly from Antwerp to New York, as well as twice a month sailings on a large and speedy three-mast schooner with clean, first class accommodations. Not only was the trip shorter than going across England, but the fares on the schooner were 20–25 francs per person cheaper than other shipping companies that went from English ports.

Most middle Limburgers who emigrated to Minnesota in the years 1860 to 1866 found Strauss's services irresistible. For poorer emigrants the discount was significant because transatlantic tickets cost from one to three times the average monthly wage of a laborer or craftsman. Although the advertisements designated New York as the port of arrival, several "America letters" from middle Limburgers in Minnesota state that sometimes Strauss's ships landed at Quebec instead of New York, and then the Limburg immigrants went inland via Montreal and the Great Lakes to St. Paul, Minnesota.[24]

Ports of Arrival

The preferred port of arrival in North America for the Dutch immigrants was always New York City, but it did not really dominate the traffic until the opening in 1855 of the Castle Garden reception center on the tip of Manhattan Island. In the previous decades Philadelphia, Baltimore, New Orleans, and even Boston, together managed to lure a third of the Dutch emigrants (Table 4.4). In the 1820s, Philadelphia welcomed one-fifth of the Dutch, but in the 1830s and 1840s New Orleans and Baltimore cut into Philadelphia's share, and New York upped its share from two thirds to nearly four fifths. Boston hosted only 5 percent of the Dutch in the 1830s and 2 percent overall.

Several thousand Dutch immigrants landed at Quebec and then went inland via the St. Lawrence River and Great Lakes system. After 1860 most took the train through Montreal over Windsor to Detroit. Many went on to Grand Rapids, but those heading farther west boarded a steamer bound for Chicago, Sheboygan, Green Bay, St. Paul, or some other port on Lake Michigan or Lake Superior.[25] The Netherlands emigration lists occasionally refer in the "Remarks" column to persons who landed at Quebec and then entered the United States at one of the Great Lakes ports. In 1848, a "Mr. Bosdyke," a gentleman of rank, came from Amsterdam by way of Canada. Other emigrants from the German border district of Graafschap Bentheim, who often accompanied Dutch emigrants, left from Bremerhaven in 1848 by sailboat on a voyage to Quebec and from there they went by steamboat to Buffalo. In 1886 eighteen Amsterdam families, comprising forty-eight persons, departed for Holland, Michigan "via Quebec."[26]

Table 4.4 Ports of Arrival by Decade, 1820–80

Port	1820–29		1830–39		1840–49		1850–59		1860–69		1870–80		Totals 1820–80	
	Number	%	Number	%	Number	%	Number	%	Number	%	Number	%	Number	%
New York	273	65	618	63	10,122	78	14,042	93	8,066	95	15,237	94	48,358	89
Baltimore	0	0	45	5	1,538	12	226	2	173	2	301	2	2,283	4
New Orleans	29	7	94	10	879	7	574	4	36	0	55	0	1,667	3
Boston	18	4	51	5	229	2	162	1	213	2	257	2	930	2
Philadelphia	85	20	170	17	163	1	48	0	8	0	416	3	890	2
Other Atlantic and Gulf ports	18	4	3	0	2	0	0	0	38	0	0	0	61	0

Source: Data file: Dutch Immigrants in U.S. Ship Passenger Manifests, 1820–80

Between 1850 and 1880, almost 95 percent of the registered Dutch immigrants arrived at New York. This compares to 66 percent for all immigrants at mid-century. No other port could rival its reception facilities. Castle Garden was so commodious, well-run, and protective of the new arrivals that its fame spread throughout Europe. The *New York Times* in 1874 asserted somewhat boastfully that "Castle Garden is now so well known in Europe that few emigrants can be induced to sail for any other destination. Their friends in this country write to those who are intending to emigrate to come to Castle Garden where they will be safe, and if out of money, they can remain until it is sent to them."[27] By 1888, 76 percent of the total immigration to the United States came via Castle Garden, and after Ellis Island opened in 1892, New York's share surpassed 95 percent.

The Empire City was less "foreign" to the Dutch than other ports because of its Netherlandic origins and culture. Dutch immigrant aid societies welcomed the newcomers. In early 1847 leaders of the Dutch Reformed Church of America (RCA), particularly the Reverend Thomas De Witt of New York City, formed the "Netherlands Society for the Protection of the Emigrants from Holland." Pieter I. G. Hodenpijl, himself an immigrant in 1840 and professor of modern languages at the RCA college of Rutgers in New Brunswick, New Jersey, from 1843 to 1846, served as the "general agent" of the "True Netherlands Society" (as it was popularly known) until 1854. Hodenpijl met all Dutch immigrants at the docks and directed them to several rooming houses near the harbor run by Dutch proprietors, notably Albert's Hollandsche Logement at No. 26 West Street on the North River and the Company for Dutch Emigrants at 157 Cedar Street.[28] Unfortunately, Hodenpijl incurred the mistrust of the immigrants when he became involved as agent for Dutch-American land speculators in western Michigan.[29]

In the years 1870–84 the Reverend A. H. Bechthold, pastor of the Holland Reformed Church of New York, and his son met each Dutch immigrant ship and helped their compatriots during their stay in the city.[30] Until 1881, the usual Dutch stopping place was the Holland Hotel at 3 Battery Place near Castle Garden, kept by a Mr. Rolffs. When it closed in 1881, the Dutch immigrants were directed to the German Immigration House sponsored by the Lutheran Mission Society. The cost was $l per day per person.[31]

The city itself was also ideally situated geographically and had adequate inland transport to enable the Dutch to reach their ultimate destinations in the Great Lakes region. Most Dutch viewed the city not as the final destination but merely the port of entry. The census of 1850 registered fewer than 600 Dutch-born in New York and Brooklyn, the 1860 census numbered 1,400, and in 1870 the count of Dutch-born was up modestly to 1,700. As many as a third of these were Dutch Jews, primarily from Amsterdam.[32]

There are several reasons why so few Dutch remained in New York City (or any eastern port city). Most important, the rural Dutch found the bustling city a threatening and strange environment, teaming with "sharks" and "runners," some of whom were even Dutch-speaking "friends" who tried to swindle the new arrivals. As Dominie Baay, one of the 1847 Seceder leaders, warned in a letter to the homeland: "trust no one," including countrymen who speak Dutch, and get out of the city as soon as possible. Since the Hudson River steamship leaves for Albany daily at 6 P.M., Baay recommended transferring baggage from the ocean vessel to the steamship on the day of arrival and proceeding directly to Albany, where there were helpful and trusted Dutch-speaking clerics, notably Isaac N. Wyckoff. Similarly, Baay warned about stopping in Buffalo and urged his followers to board the lake steamer for Milwaukee without delay. Another Seceder, J. Berkhout, reported in a letter to the Netherlands in 1848: "New York is in many places a danger for pedestrians because of the masses of carts and wagons and the din of the people going back and forth. I said big, busy, dangerous, also dirty, but gracefully-built New York."[33]

There was also the danger of spiritual pollution. As the Reverend Baay explained: "The religious condition of those living in the [eastern seaboard] cities leaves much to be desired—a reason why, in general, people wish to be where the Dutch are congregated more together," that is, in the Midwest. One family who stayed in the city temporarily expressed this sentiment clearly in a letter to the Netherlands: "We are located here *as a lonely sparrow on the roof* (italics mine) destitute of public worship and of His people. The way for me is narrow and fearful. . . . There are Reformed Churches here but they are all English [speaking]."[34]

Since nine out of ten of all Dutch immigrants entered the United States via New York City, the statistics for this port provide the norm, and any differences with other places of entry are minor and not statistically significant. Only ships from Germany deviated from the norm. Of the Dutch from German ports, 66 percent arrived at New York; Baltimore attracted 23 percent and New Orleans 12 percent (Table 4.5). Ships from French ports with Dutch aboard also showed a tendency to use New Orleans (10 percent) as the alternative to New York.

People from the individual Dutch provinces also varied in the proportion to which they arrived at New York harbor. This was a result of their differing ultimate destinations and their imperfect knowledge of the American internal transportation system. In the pioneering phase of the 1840s and 1850s, the proportion of immigrants using New York ranged from 100 percent by settlers from Groningen and Limburg to a low of 54 percent by settlers from Utrecht Province (Table 4.6). These Utrechters were mainly the followers of the Reverend Hendrik Scholte who were bound for east-central Iowa via the Ohio and Mississippi river systems. Thirty-seven percent of Scholte's followers from Utrecht landed at Baltimore, and another 8 percent entered via New Orleans. Seceders from other provinces—Friesland, Drenthe, Gelderland, Overijssel, and Zuid Holland—also used Baltimore and New Orleans to some extent (12–16 percent). But after 1860, New York City had a virtual monopoly, except among Gelderlanders, of whom 7 percent used Halifax, 5 percent Baltimore, and 2 percent Boston. Even Utrecht immigrants switched to New York after 1860, with 96 percent disembarking there, compared to only 54 percent before the Civil War. The railroad link from New York to Chicago and west was now complete and clearly provided the cheapest and easiest access into the midwest region where the Dutch settlements were concentrated.

Transatlantic fares were relatively cheap at the time of the Great Migration, and they became even cheaper after the Civil War.[35] Fares varied, of course, with

TABLE 4.5 Ports of Embarkation by Ports of Arrival, 1820–80

Ports of Embarkation	Ports of Arrival: Baltimore Number	Baltimore %	Boston Number	Boston %	New Orleans Number	New Orleans %	New York Number	New York %	Philadelphia Number	Philadelphia %	Totals Number
Dutch	1,674	6	392	1	744	3	25,621	89	319	1	28,750
		(73)		(42)		(44)		(53)		(36)	(53)
British	249	2	405	3	196	1	13,206	93	128	1	14,184
		(11)		(44)		(12)		(27)		(14)	(26)
Belgian	0	0	58	1	191	3	5,861	91	329	5	6,439
		(0)		(6)		(11)		(12)		(37)	(12)
French	2	0	0	0	327	10	2,795	87	95	3	3,219
		(0)		(0)		(19)		(6)		(11)	(6)
German	341	23	1	0	171	11	977	66	2	0	1,492
		(15)		(0)		(10)		(2)		(0)	(3)
Other	32	7	68	16	79	18	231	53	26	6	436
		(1)		(7)		(5)		(0)		(3)	(1)
Totals	2,298	4	924	2	1,708	3	48,691	89	899	2	54,520

SOURCE: Data file: Dutch Immigrants in U.S. Ship Passenger Manifests, 1820–80

TABLE 4.6 U.S. Ports of Arrival by Province of Origin, Pre- and Post-1860 (in percent)

	New York		Baltimore		New Orleans		Boston		Philadelphia		Halifax	
Periods	1835–60	1861–80	1835–60	1861–80	1835–60	1861–80	1835–60	1861–80	1835–60	1861–80	1835–60	1861–80
Western provinces												
Noord-Holland	95	93	2	3	3	0	1	1	1	0	—	3
Utrecht	54	96	37	4	8	0	2	0	0	0	—	0
Zuid-Holland	90	99	4	0	6	0	0	1	1	0	—	1
Northern provinces												
Drenthe	86	94	12	3	2	0	0	3	0	0	—	0
Friesland	82	98	4	0	12	0	0	1	1	0	—	0
Groningen	100	98	0	2	0	0	0	0	0	0	—	0
Eastern provinces												
Gelderland	85	85	5	5	7	0	1	2	2	0	—	7
Overijssel	87	97	5	1	7	1	1	1	2	0	—	0
Southern provinces												
Limburg	100	100	0	0	0	0	0	0	0	0	—	0
Noord-Brabant	92	99	1	0	2	0	7	2	0	0	—	0
Zeeland	94	95	4	0	1	0	1	1	0	3	—	1

SOURCE: Data file: Dutch Immigrants in U.S. Ship Passenger Manifests, 1820–80

demand, season of the year, and destination (New York was cheapest and New Orleans most expensive because the trip there was ten to twenty days longer). In the 1840s Rotterdam to New York fares averaged $14 (35 guilders) for a third-class ticket in steerage, the infamous "between decks" (*tussendeks*). Fares were comparable at other Continental ports, although Liverpool was the lowest at $12. But the fare from Rotterdam to Liverpool was $4, and the trip by ship and rail took seven to ten more days. In addition, emigrants had to provide their own food during the long voyage (about $8 per person), plus the transport and lodging costs to reach their European departure port, where occasional delays in sailings might add to the expense. It took three to four days, for example, to reach Rotterdam from Groningen and the fare was $1.25. Once in Rotterdam, shipping companies allowed ticketed passengers to live free on the ship until sailing.

Upon arrival in New York or another east coast port the newcomers faced the inland trip to the upper Midwest that took up to three months before the completion of the rail line to Chicago in 1852 and westward across the Mississippi River in 1856. Thereafter, the emigrant train from New York to Chicago covered the thousand miles in five days for a third-class fare of $5 ($16 first class and $9.50 second class). Before 1852 the Dutch immigrants took the Hudson River steamer to Albany for a fare of only 25 cents, and then the Erie Canal to Buffalo for a fare of $7–8. At Buffalo they boarded a Lake Erie steamer to Detroit for $4 and then took another steamer for an additional $5–6 to traverse Lakes Huron and Michigan via the Mackinaw Straits to Chicago, Milwaukee, or Sheboygan. By the early 1850s the hassles of all these ship transfers ended with the completion of the rail link to Chicago. Thus, by the mid-1850s the total cost of emigrating from the Netherlands to Chicago was about $20 per person plus food costs of another $10. This was within the means of all but the poor, who were often assisted by relatives, wealthy patrons, and fellow church members.

Crossing the Atlantic Ocean made an indelible impression on every emigrant, and all had a ready story to tell to any and all who would listen. Most were landlubbers who had never been at sea and were haunted by its mysterious powers and changing moods. Apart from the extreme grief of leave taking at the departure docks, however, the voyage was a pleasant holiday for most travelers who enjoyed calm seas, favorable winds, and a clean, well-run ship with adequate food. Meals improved greatly after new regulations in the 1850s made ship owners responsible for providing food supplies and preparing meals. Sunday worship services were observed whenever possible. But stormy seas, accidents, and in the early years a frequent lack of wholesome food, coupled with shipboard epidemics, caused exceeding pain and loss for others. Then seasickness, groans and cries of fright in storms, and burials at sea became all to commonplace. Since the difficult crossing was more vivid and memorable than the uneventful passage, immigrant letters, diaries, and memoirs often stressed the unpleasant experiences. But for most, the voyage was merely eventful, or at worst a boring routine, sandwiched between the melodramatic departure and exciting first glimpse of America. The fear of the unknown future in the United States weighed more heavily than the crossing itself.[36]

Chroniclers and popular historians have made much of the fatalities at sea due to epidemics and accidents.[37] Especially in the earlier days of sailing vessels and longer voyages, and during periods of famine as in the mid-1810s and the mid-1840s, the death rate occasionally soared. From the American Revolution until the close of the Napoleonic wars, European immigration was minimal, perhaps only 3,000–4,000 per year, and travel conditions, while spartan, were not overcrowded. But after peace came to Europe in 1815 and a great famine struck in the next year, emigration gained momentum. In 1817 over 22,000 European immigrants reached American ports. To take advantage of the new business, avaricious ship owners began overcrowding their cargo holds and steerage decks with human cargo. Improper food and poor hygiene resulted in thousands of deaths from typhus or "ship-fever," cholera, and smallpox. Mortality rates on passage averaged 9 percent and on some ships soared as high as 30 percent. Of 1,000 immigrants on the ship *April* from Amsterdam to Philadelphia in 1817, 470 died of sickness.[38] The United States Congress moved quickly in 1819 to rectify these horrendous facts by enacting the first of many regulatory acts to improve shipboard conditions. Although health problems were not wholly ameliorated until the advent of steamers built especially for passengers in the 1850s and 1860s, the death rate at sea dropped sharply.

There are unfortunately few systematic estimates of immigrant mortality on the Atlantic in the nineteenth century, although the ship passenger manifests always recorded deaths at sea. Beginning in 1853, the U.S. congressional reports occasionally included such statistics. These document a steady decline in deaths at sea: 8.0 per thousand in 1853, 6.3 in 1854, 2.1 in 1855, 2.1 in 1856, 1.6 in 1857, 1.3 in 1859, and only .5 in 1893.[39] The only systematic study of the passenger lists, a 9.3 percent random sample (276,000 passengers) for the years 1836–53, showed a loss rate of 13.2 per thousand, which is considerably higher than death rates on land in these years. The years from 1846 through 1849 were the worst, coinciding with the famine migration. Ships from Rotterdam (for unknown reasons) had losses in these years about 1 percent higher than the average for all ships from Europe.[40]

Sailing vessels, whose average length of voyages was six weeks in the 1860s and 1870s, had mortality rates over ten times greater than steamships, which crossed the Atlantic in two weeks. In 1867 steamship crossings averaged 1.0 death per thousand passengers, compared to 11.7 per thousand for sailing vessels. In 1872 the numbers under steam and sail were .3 and 5.4 per thousand, respectively. Ships leaving from the same port but owned by different companies also had differing mortality rates. This was even true among steamship companies. In 1870 official returns on emigrants from the United Kingdom landing at New York revealed that the Inman and Cunard steamship lines had the lowest mortality rates (.5 and .4 per thousand, respectively), and the National and Anchor lines had the highest death rates (1.0 and .7 per thousand, respectively). Thus, the Inman and Cunard lines had only half the death rate of the National and Anchor ships.[41]

The number of Dutch who died at sea was lower than the average for all groups.[42] In the years 1820–80, of the nearly 55,000 persons crossing, mostly in steerage, only 507 died, for a rate of 9 per thousand (Table 4.7). The rates were slightly

TABLE 4.7 Deaths at Sea, by Family Status, Age, and Decade, 1820–80

STATUS AND AGE GROUP	NUMBER	PERCENTAGE	
Husband	76	15	
Wife	47	9	
Infants (below age 1)	91	18	
Children (age 1–13)	251	50	
Other adults (age 14+)	42	8	
TOTALS	507	100	
DEATHS BY DECADE	**NUMBER**	**PERCENTAGE**	**RATE PER 1,000**
1820–1829	0	0	0
1830–1839	1	0	0
1840–1849	147	29	11
1850–1859	206	41	14
1860–1869	103	20	10
1870–1880	50	10	3
ALL YEARS	507	10	9

SOURCE: Data file; Dutch Immigrants in U.S. Ship Passenger Manifests, 1820–80

higher from the 1840s through the 1860s, but they were much lower in the 1870s (3 per thousand) when mortality at sea dropped to one-fourth of its previous levels. Two-thirds of the deaths were children, usually infants under one year. On the other hand, 19 infants were reported born on board ship and survived the voyage. Many other births doubtless went unrecorded in the ship manifests. One quarter of the deaths en route were husbands or wives, which was a far more serious blow to the family than the loss of an infant or child. The low death rate was a result of the relatively good health of the Dutch emigrants and their proverbial cleanliness. Few Dutch immigrants were in dire poverty or in advanced stages of starvation, as were German emigrants in the 1810s–30s, many of whom sailed from Rotterdam, or the "famine Irish" in the 1840s.

Emigrants also died en route after arriving in the United States, especially before rail travel became commonplace. Of 900 Dutch immigrants whom Scholte shepherded to his Iowa colony in 1847, 20 (half of them children) died at sea, and 4 succumbed during inland travel in America. But 126 died within the first six months after arrival, many in St. Louis, due to disease brought on by poor living conditions.[43] Arriving in America in a weakened state, due to generally poor provisions and conditions aboard ship, immigrants also faced the notorious accommodations of Erie canalboats and the hazards of Great Lake steamers and Mississippi River paddleboats. One lake steamer, the ill-fated *Phoenix*, with about 150 Dutch immigrants aboard, caught fire and burned to the waterline one wintry night within sight of the Sheboygan, Wisconsin, harbor, which was their final destination. Their relatives and friends on shore watched helplessly while about 125 of their compatriots were burned to death or perished in the icy waters. Most hailed from the

Winterswijk area of Gelderland province.[44] Despite this tragedy, the Hollanders always recalled the lake steamboats from Buffalo with pleasure, in sharp contrast to the Erie canalboats. The Hudson River steamboats, such as the *I. Newton*, were also praised as splendid "floating palaces."[45]

The reputation of the Erie canalboats could hardly have been worse. The "wretched" barges were unheated, overcrowded, and moved at a snail's pace. Worse yet, the crews were uncaring. The 346-mile trip from Albany to Buffalo took up to two weeks and "was an experience full of hardship," reported Sietze Bos who voiced the sentiments of many.[46] One Dutch traveler experienced "much trouble and suffering" on the canal, and another reported a "miserable trip." Albertus G. Van Hees, who traveled the canal in early November 1847, wrote: "We suffered great hardships. It was quite cold and there was no heat on board the boat and it was impossible to get warm food or drink." Van Hees's mother suffered a heart attack on the boat but survived.[47] Summer travel created the reverse problem of heat. When Rev. Cornelius Vander Meulen and his group of Zeelanders traversed the canal in July 1847, he wrote: "On the barge it was stifling hot and one had no room to sit down, there were no cooked meals and very little or no hot drinks." Three of Vander Meulen's parishioners died on the boat, and one more died shortly after reaching Buffalo.[48] Roelof Brinks took sick en route and had to remain in Buffalo hospitalized for four months. J. D. Werkman reported being "packed like herring in a vat," an apt metaphor his Dutch readers could appreciate. Some escaped the crush of people on the boat by walking the canal path. As Hermannus Strabbing noted: "We scarcely had any room to sit. To lie down, rest, or sleep was out of the question. Our protests availed nothing. The crew acted as if it could not understand us, with which we had to be satisfied."[49]

To lessen the hardships, the Dutch emigrants were careful to take ocean passage during the most healthful time of the year, in the late spring and early summer. Over the sixty-year period, almost one half (47.1 percent) of all crossings occurred in April, May, and June, before the summer epidemics broke out, but after the dangerous winter storms on the North Atlantic (see Table 4.8). The Dutch emigrants had not always planned so carefully. In the early decades they traveled in some of the worst months. In the 1820s, July, October, and November were the major months of arrival, which meant the newcomers bore the brunt of the summer heat or arrived too late in the year to establish themselves in jobs and homes before winter set in. In the 1830s, the three most popular months were June, August, and December, which had similar disadvantages. Dominie Van Raalte and his group of 109 arrived in New York on November 7, 1846, and sailed immediately to Albany and then proceeded by train to Buffalo, where they caught the last steamer of the winter for Detroit. Here they were stuck until spring, but the captain of their lake steamer hired the men to work in his shipbuilding shop. Hundreds of followers in later ships, who arrived in New York in late November and December, were not as fortunate. They had to winter in New York City, Albany, and Buffalo, where they endured considerable hardship from lack of money and jobs were difficult to find. A few of the hardier souls actually walked from Buffalo to Detroit in mid-February crossing the Detroit River over ice floes.[50]

Table 4.8 Month of Arrival by Decade, 1820–80

Month	1820–29		1830–39		1840–49		1850–59		1860–69		1870–79		1870–80	
	Number	%	Number	%	Number	%	Number	%	Number	%	Number	%	Number	%
Jan	17	4	41	4	583	4	456	3	343	4	281	2	1,721	3
Feb	7	2	20	2	40	0	357	2	155	2	372	2	951	2
Mar	20	5	19	2	152	1	165	1	330	4	1,643	10	23,229	4
1st quarter	44	10	80	8	775	6	978	6	828	10	2,296	14	5,001	9
Apr	33	8	15	1	842	7	952	6	693	8	3,253	20	5,788	11
May	26	6	63	6	2,017	16	2,864	19	1,677	20	3,377	21	10,024	18
June	42	10	260	26	3,135	24	2,936	20	1,908	22	1,452	9	9,733	18
2nd quarter	101	24	338	34	5,994	46	6,752	45	4,278	50	8,082	50	25,545	47
July	82	19	92	9	1,884	15	1,494	10	690	8	1,117	7	5,359	10
Aug	21	5	244	25	1,085	8	1,128	8	389	4	1,229	8	4,096	8
Sept	34	8	43	4	1,063	8	1,673	11	722	8	1,231	8	4,766	9
3rd quarter	137	32	379	39	4,032	31	4,295	29	1,801	21	3,577	22	14,221	26
Oct	74	18	35	4	871	7	1,652	11	602	7	854	5	4,088	8
Nov	43	10	48	5	595	5	740	5	690	8	887	5	3,003	6
Dec	24	6	101	10	666	5	635	4	335	4	570	4	2,331	4
4th quarter	141	33	184	19	2,132	16	3,027	20	1,627	19	2,311	14	9,422	17
Decade Totals	423	0	981	2	12,933	24	15,052	28	8,534	16	16,266	30	54,189	

Source: Data file: Dutch Immigrants in U.S. Ship Passenger Manifests, 1820–80. *Note*: Monthly percentages do not add up to quarterly percentages because of rounding.

The problems encountered by the 1846 emigrants because of their winter passage prompted them to urge the Secessionist leaders in the Netherlands to send the next year's contingent of colonists much earlier in the year, preferably in the second quarter. They must not leave in the fall, an "unpropitious season," as did the first group, "at the season of the year when they must remain in the city at expense and thus expend the means to carry them into the interior." Mr. Mensink, one of the men in Van Raalte's first contingent, wrote in late December 1846 from Albany to "fellow believers in the Netherlands": "It is winter now and then Americans do not want to work; they earn too much in the summer that it is not necessary. [We do not] advise anyone to come in the latter part of the year, not later than August." The "Knickerbocker Hollanders," New Yorkers of Dutch descent, likewise advised the immigrants to avoid winter arrivals.[51] Those colonists who planned to reach the Upper Mississippi Valley via New Orleans, which was the cheapest way, were particularly advised to leave even earlier, in late February, so as not to arrive in the summer heat when epidemics and fevers raged.[52] Coming from a moderate northern European climate, the Dutch could not tolerate the humid, summer heat of the American South.

The emigrants of 1847 and subsequent years generally followed this sound advice. Those who did not sometimes paid a high price. Andreas N. Wormser left the Netherlands in late July 1848 and by the time the family traversed the United States from New York to Pella, Iowa, during October, two daughters contracted scarlet fever and died within three weeks of their arrival.[53] In the decades of the 1840s, 1850s, and 1860s, 40 percent or more of the Dutch immigrants to North America arrived in May and June. Only in the 1870s, when faster steamers had replaced sailing vessels, did the prime arrival time move ahead slightly, to April and May, rather than May and June.

Conclusion

In conclusion, most Dutch immigrants used the convenient Rotterdam–New York route, although poorer people had to endure the longer but cheaper passage through Liverpool. These unfortunates faced the language barrier with English crews, whereas those taking Dutch-manned vessels from Rotterdam found the strain eased of the long voyage across a fearful sea. Antwerp, and to a lesser extent Le Havre, attracted fellow Flemish immigrants from the southern Netherlands, especially in the middle decades.

As for the crossing itself, the danger of death was real but exaggerated in the case of the Dutch. Out of more than 55,000 immigrant crossings to North America, less than 1 in 100 died on the sea in the period 1820–80, and two thirds of those were children and infants. The Dutch immigrants were healthier, they took more concern for cleanliness, as did the Dutch shippers, and they were careful to depart in the healthiest time of the year, the spring. The Dutch, it is clear, planned their transoceanic journey as carefully as they made the decision to migrate in the first place and to choose their ultimate destinations.

Notes

1. The pertinent section of the Act of March 2, 1819 (3 Stat. 489) is reprinted in E. P. Hutchinson, "Notes on Immigration Statistics of the United States," *Journal of the American Statistical Association* 53 (Dec. 1958): 1016. This act and subsequent laws pertaining to immigrant passengers are conveniently summarized in William J. Bromwell, *History of Immigration to the United States* (New York, 1956; repr. New York: Arno Press, 1969), 206–55; and E. P. Hutchinson, *Legislative History of American Immigration Policy, 1789–1965* (Philadelphia: University of Pennsylvania Press, 1981), esp. 20–47, 534–40.
2. Act of August 2, 1882 (22 Stat. 189) and Act of March 3, 1893 (27 Stat. 569); Hutchinson, "Notes on Immigration Statistics," 1017–19.
3. Edwin C. Guillet, *The Great Migration: The Atlantic Crossing by Sailing-ship Since 1770* (Toronto: Thomas Nelson and Sons, 1937); Richard Armstrong, *The Merchantmen* (London: Ernest Benn, 1969), 71–79; Conway B. Sonne, *Saints on the Seas: A Maritime History of Mormon Migration, 1830–1890* (Salt Lake City, UT: University of Utah Press, 1983), ch. 3–4, 6–7; Benjamin W. Labaree, *The Atlantic World of Robert G. Albion* (Middletown, CN: Wesleyan University Press, 1975), 110–43, 228–34; Robert G. Albion, *The Rise of New York Port [1815–1860]* (New York: Charles Schribner's Sons, 1939); Frank C. Bowen, *A Century of Atlantic Travel: 1830–1930* (Boston: Little, Brown, 1939).
4. This was the *XYZ* from Bremen to New York, which arrived on August 2, 1832, with 116 Dutch nationals.
5. N. J. G. Pounds, *An Historical Geography of Europe, 1500–1840* (Cambridge: Cambridge University Press, 1979), 362–63; Cees Zevenbergen, *Toen zij uit Rotterdam: Emigratie van Rotterdam door de eeuwen heen* (Zwolle: Wanders, 1990), 28–36; L. A. van der Valk, "Landverhuizersvervoer via Rotterdam in de negentiende eeuw" *Economisch en Sociaal Historisch Jaarboek* 39 (1976): 148–71; Jan Hospers "Autobiography," in *Amsterdamse emigranten. Onbekende brieven uit de prairie van Iowa*, J. Stellingwerff (Amsterdam: Buijten and Schipperheijn, 1975), 233–34. See also Frank Broeze, "Connecting the Netherlands and the Americas: Ocean Transport and Port/Airport Rivalry," in *Connecting Cultures: The Netherlands in Five Centuries of Transatlantic Exchange*, eds. Rosemarijn Hoefte and Johanna C. Kardux (Amsterdam: VU University Press, 1994): 77–99, esp. 79–80.
6. Pounds, *Historical Geography*, 362–63; Jacob van Hinte, *Nederlanders in Amerika. Een studie over landverhuizers en volksplanters in de 19e en 20ste eeuw in de Vereenigde Staten van Amerika* (2 vols., Groningen: P. Noordhoff, 1928), published in English translation as *Netherlanders in America: A Study of Emigration and Settlement in the Nineteenth and Twentieth Centuries in the United States of America*, ed. Robert P.

Swierenga, chief trans. Adriaan de Wit (Grand Rapids: Baker Book House, 1985), 603.

7. For the story of Liverpool shipping developments see Francis E. Hyde, *Liverpool and the Mersey: An Economic History of a Port, 1700–1970* (Newton Abbot, England: David & Charles, 1971), and the same author's *Cunard and the North Atlantic: A History of Shipping and Financial Management* (Atlantic Highlands, NJ: Humanities Press, 1975).

8. Pounds, *Historical Geography*, 363. J. Everaert argues, on the contrary, that Antwerp rivaled Rotterdam as an emigrant port before 1860. Antwerp harbor merchants promoted the emigrant traffic from 1837 onward, and the completion of the Cologne-Antwerp railroad—the "Iron Rhine"—in 1843 reduced inland travel costs by 30 percent and enabled Antwerp to tap the Rhineland, South Germany, Switzerland, and the Tirol. In 1843 Antwerp established an emigration office with an ombudsman to resolve disputes with emigrant agents. All this, says Everaert, enabled Antwerp successfully to compete for the emigrant traffic. Between 1843 and 1859, Antwerp averaged 10,000 emigrants per year. See J. Everaert, "Antwerpen als emigratiehaven: De overzeese landverhuizing naar Amerika (1830–1914)," *Mededelingen* (Marina-Academie, Antwerp) 26 (1980–1982): 55–67, esp. 56.

9. A very readable pictorial history of Dutch immigrant shipping is Zevenbergen, *Toen zij uit Rotterdam*. Pieter R. D. Stokvis, *De Nederlandse trek naar Amerika, 1846–1847* (Leiden: Universitaire Pers, 1977), 162–82, discusses the shipping agents. See also James M. Cameron, "The Role of Shipping from Scottish Ports in Emigration to the Canadas, 1815–1855," in *Canadian Papers in Rural History* (ed. D. A. Akenson) 2 (1980), 135–54; and Sonne, *Saints on the Seas*.

10. T. Vanden Broek, *Journey*, 24; Noord-Holland Province Emigration List, 1856; Arnold Verstegen, "Letters from Little Chute, Wisconsin [1850–1871]," in *Dutch Immigrant Memoirs and Related Writings*, 2 vols., Henry S. Lucas ed. (Assen: Van Gorkum 1955; repr. Grand Rapids: Wm. B. Eerdmans, 1997), 2:165–66. Many immigrant letters and memoirs record the inconveniences of the Hull-Liverpool route. See, for example, Henry S. Lucas, ed., "Memoir of John Vogel, Immigrant and Pioneer," trans. B. G. Oosterbaan, *Michigan History* 30 (July–September 1946): 548, 555. There is at least one instance of a group of Dutch immigrants led by Jan Hospers who in May of 1849 sailed first from Rotterdam to Bremerhaven, where they took passage for New York on the Russian vessel *Francisco*. Ten persons died en route, including three of Hospers' ten children, which suggests that shipping indirectly over Bremen also had its problems. Jan Hospers's travel account is *Amsterdamse emigranten*, 231–37.

11. The municipal head tax was a graduated tax based on property values and income; lower income groups were exempt. See W. Meijer, J. W. B. van Overhage, and P. de Wolff, "De financien van de Nederlandse provincies in de period 1850–1914," *Economisch en Sociaal Historische Jaarboek* 33

(1970): 27–67; D. Damsma and L. Noordegraaf, "Standen en klassen in een Zuidhollands dorp," *Tijdschrift voor Sociale Geschiedenis* 3 (1977): 243–69.

12. The initial partners were Jan Hudig (1806–57) and Cornelius Gerbrand Blokhuizen (1773–1857). Both were ship owners and overseas traders as well as brokers. Hudig was a chartering broker and officer in the Royal Navy. Blokhuizen was fluent in English since his family had long belonged to the English Reformed Church in Rotterdam. This information again comes from the Rotterdam Population Registers, courtesy of archivist Schoone. Cf. Maureen Callahan, "The Harbor Barons: Political and Commercial Elites and the Development of the Port of Rotterdam," (Ph.D. diss., Princeton University, 1981).
13. Crooswijk was born in Rotterdam in 1806 and died in Bonn, Germany, in 1859. The biographical data is from Rotterdam Population Registers. In the 1850s the office of Wambersie & Son was located on the "Boompjes," according to the Rotterdam City Directory of 1859. I am indebted for this information to F. A. M. Schoone, deputy archivist in Rotterdam.
14. G. H. Ligterink, *De landverhuizers: Emigratie naar Noord-Amerika uit het Gelders-Westfaalse grensgebied tussen de jaaren 1830–1850* (Zutphen: De Walburg Press, 1981), 28–30; Lucas, *Netherlanders in America*, 67.
15. Jan Hospers, "Autobiography," in *Amsterdamse emigranten*, 71, 129, 233; Van der Valk, "Landverhuizersvervoer," 156–58; C. Vander Meulen, *Aan al myne geliefde vrienden in Nederland* (Goes, 1847), 8, typescript, English translation by John J. Dahm, Sr., Heritage Hall Archives, Calvin College, Grand Rapids, MI.
16. Letter, Gerrit Baay (Town Alto, WI) to friends in the Netherlands, 4 January 1849, English-language typescript by E. R. Post and D. F. Van Vliet, Calvin College Archives.
17. Groningen *Provinciaal Verslag* (1867), 535.
18. See advertisement in *Provinciale Groninger Courant*, 8 May 1867; Prins & Zwanenburg, Groningen, to the Mayor and Alderman of Groningen, 23 July 1868; ibid., 21 April 1870, Gemeentearchief Groningen; Groningen *Provinciaal Verslag*, 1867, 20; 1869, 11; 1870, 9; 1872, 28. I am indebted to Annemieke Galema for information about this firm in the municipal archives of Groningen.
19. Cited in Jan A. Niemeyer, *Kroniek van het geslacht Niemeyer* (Groningen 1971), 52–53.
20. Noord-Holland *Provinciaal Verslag* (1869), 78–79.
21. Robert Schoone-Jongen, "From Expensive Land to Cheap Land: Theodore F. Koch, Colonizer," *Minnesota History* 53 (Summer 1993): 214–24; Annemieke Galema, "'Now I Will Write You Something About America ...': Dutch Migrants' Views of the United States Around the Turn of the Century," in *Images of the Nation: Different Meanings of Dutchness, 1870–1940*, eds. Annemieke Galema, Barbara Henkes, and Henk te Velde (Amsterdam and Atlanta: Rodolpi, 1993), 113–14.

22. Letter, A. C. van Raalte (Arnhem) to Groen G. van Prinsterer (Den Hague), 21 September 1846, in Lucas, *Dutch Immigrant Memoirs*, 1:23; "Hendrik van Eyck's Diary," in ibid., 1:470; Van der Valk, "Landverhuizersvervoer," 157.
23. Noord-Holland *Provinciale Verslag* (1869), 79. The firms were the Liverpool-New York and Philadelphia Steamship Company and the Montreal Ocean Steamship Company.
24. A. M. Koeweiden-Wijdeveen, *Vergeten emigranten, landverhuizing van noord- en midden-Limburg naar Noord Amerika in de jaren 1847–1877* (Venlo, 1982), 63–64, 47–48; "Vergeten emigranten," *Spiegel Historiael* 19 (1984): 122–24.
25. There are no official statistics prior to 1900 of arrivals of Dutch nationals at the Canadian ports of Quebec and Montreal. The Quebec ship passenger lists of the Montreal Ocean Steamship Company are generally complete from 1865, and I have identified 1,828 possible Dutch nationals in the column labeled "Aliens" or "Foreigners" in the years 1865–80. Microfilm Reel Nos. C4520–C4530, Public Archives of Canada, Ottawa. See also Koeweiden-Wijdeveen, *Vergeten emigranten*, 47–48, citing the Netherlands newspaper, *Mercurius*, 22 Nov. 1862, which published Joseph Scheper's description of his voyage from Antwerp via Quebec to St. Paul, MN. Joan Magee, *A Dutch Heritage: 200 Years of Dutch Presence in the Windsor-Detroit Border Region* (Windsor, 1983), 39–40, recounts the trip of the Evert Wonnink family in 1862 from Geesteren (Netherlands) to Grand Rapids, Michigan. The *Cleveland Leader*, 22 Sept. 1870, reported the official statistics; during the year ending 30 June 1820, 40,403 immigrants passed from Canada into the United States. Many were British, coming via the St. Lawrence River.
26. *Dutch Immigrant Memoirs*, 2:510, 105; Noord-Holland Province Emigration List, 1866.
27. Philip Taylor, *The Distant Magnet: European Emigration to the USA* (New York: Harper & Row, 1971), 126; the quote is in Maldwyn Jones, *Destination America* (New York: Holt, Rinehart & Winston, 1976), 52–53.
28. G. Baay, "Dear Friends Back Home . . . ," *Delta* (September 1959): 26–35, esp. 28. This is an English-language translation of Baay's letter from Alto, Wisconsin, to "My Dear Friends in Holland," 4 Jan. 1849.
29. Van Hinte, *Netherlanders in American*, 303–04; Robert P. Swierenga, ed., "A Dutch Carpenter's 'America Letter' From New York in 1849," *New York History* 72 (October 1991): 433–34. Dirk Van Bochove, the letter writer, alerted his family and friends about the land schemers. "These fellows are in cahoots with the most wily bad office of Hodenpijl established here in N.Y., against which I can not warn you enough."
30. Vander Meulen, *Geliefde vrienden*, 8. The Holland Reformed Church at the time was located at 279 West 11th Street, New York City.
31. Lucas, *Netherlanders in America*, 234.

32. These figures are derived from a compilation of the Dutch-born persons recorded in the manuscript population censuses. See Robert P. Swierenga, comp., *Dutch Households in U.S. Population Censuses, 1850, 1860, 1870: An Alphabetical Listing by Family Heads*, 3 vols. (Wilmington, DE: Scholarly Resources, 1987).
33. Baay, "Dear Friends Back Home," 28–29; Jan Berkhout, *Brief uit Noord Amerika* (Amsterdam, 1849), 8, typescript, English translation by John J. Dahm, Sr., Heritage Hall Archives, Calvin College.
34. Baay, "Dear Friends Back Home," 29; Letter of J. Benjaminse-Jansen, 26 Nov. 1847, in Vander Meulen, *Geliefde vrienden*, 12–13.
35. Information on transportation fares is widely scattered and very diverse. The best sources are M. D. Teenstra, *Mentor: de getrouwe leidsman en raadgever voor landverhuizers, die naar Noord-Amerika willen vertrokken* (Groningen, 1855), 30–45, 56–70; Bertus Harry Wabeke, *Dutch Emigration to North America, 1624–1860* (New York: Netherlands Information Bureau, 1944), 107–09. See also *Dutch Immigrant Memoirs*, 1:194ff, 306ff, 2:91ff, 165ff, 436; *Amsterdamse emigranten*, 66–69; Vanden Broek, *Journey*, 24.
36. For Dutch accounts of the Atlantic ocean crossing, see Henry S. Lucas, ed., "Reminiscences of Arend Jan Brusse on Early Dutch Settlement in Milwaukee," *Wisconsin Magazine of History* 30 (Sept. 1946): 86–87; Johannes Remeeus, "The Journey of an Immigrant Family from the Netherlands to Milwaukee in 1854," ibid., 29 (Dec. 1945): 201–23; and Jan W. Bosman, "Ervaringen van Jan W. Bosman," *De Grondwet*, 12 Feb. 1912. Bosman's account is reprinted in English translation in *Dutch Immigrant Memoirs*, 2:82–91. Herbert J. Brinks, "Crossing the Atlantic," *Origins* 2, No. 1 (1984): 2–5, recounts the fears immigrants expressed in their letters. For an extensive collection of immigrant travel memoirs, see Herbert J. Brinks, "Ocean Voyage Accounts, 1856–1920," *Origins* 8 , No. 1 (1990): 2–32.
37. The only comprehensive survey of the literature, as well as a limited analysis of the data on this neglected subject, is Raymond C. Cohn, "Mortality on Immigrant Voyages to New York, 1836–1853," *Journal of Economic History* 44 (June 1984): 289–300. See also Frederick Kapp, *Immigration and the Commissioners of Emigration of the State of New York* (New York: Nation Press, 1870; repr. New York: Arno Press, 1969), 20–27; Van Hinte, *Netherlanders in America*, 105–07.
38. Kapp, *Immigration*, 27, 22; Robert P. Swierenga and Henry Lammers, "'Odyssey of Woe': The Journey of the Immigrant Ship *April* from Amsterdam to New Castle, 1817–1818," *Pennsylvania Magazine of History and Biography* 118 (Oct. 1994): 303–23; Swierenga, ed., and Lammers, trans., "Captain De Groot's Account of the Tragic Voyage of the *April*, Amsterdam to New Castle, 1817–1818," *The Palatine Immigrant* 18 (Mar. 1993): 82–91.
39. U.S. Congress, Senate, *Report of the Select Committee on the Sickness*

and Mortality on Board Emigrant Ships, 83rd Congress, 1st Session, Senate Reports (No. 386), 1854. "Letter from the Secretary of State transmitting the Annual Report of Passengers arriving in the United States," in Secretary of State Reports, 35th Congress, 1st Session, *Senate Executive Document* No. 32, 32; 36th Congress, 1st Session, *House Executive Document* No. 29, 32-33; U.S. Secretary of the Treasury, "Immigration and Passenger Movement at Ports of the United States during the Year Ending June 30, 1893," 53rd Congress, 2nd Session, *House Executive Document* No. 6, part 2 (Serial Set 3222), 9.

The reported death rates may greatly understate the case, particularly after 1855. Section 14 of the 1855 congressional act to regulate the immigrant traffic gave ship captains a financial disincentive for reporting deaths at sea. It required captains to pay the port collector $10 for every passenger above 8 years of age who died en route of "natural disease," the money to be used to care for sick and indigent immigrants after their arrival (U.S. *Statutes at Large* X [1855], 715, "An Act to Regulate the Carriage of Passengers in Steamships and Other Vessels," 3 March 1855). New York City also had a quarantine policy for immigrants who arrived with communicable diseases, which gave captains a reason to underreport shipboard epidemics and deaths, if nothing else to protect the reputation of their ship. Since the official statistics rested on the collectors' quarterly reports, when collectors became overwhelmed with a flood of immigrants, they or their untrained and unsupervised clerks and assistants might overlook the deaths listed on the ship manifests. New Orleans collectors in the years 1820–1860 reported only 1,100 deaths or less than 1 per 500 arriving passengers. See Frederick M. Spletstoser, "Back Door to the Land of Plenty: New Orleans as an Immigrant Port, 1820–1860" (Ph.D. diss., Louisiana State University, 1979), 33–39.

40. Cohn, "Mortality on Immigrant Voyages," 292–98. Cohn computes the *monthly* death rate at sea (based on an average 44-day voyage) of 9.3 per 1,000, which compares with mortality rates in Germany and Scandinavia in this period of 1.5 to 2.5 per 1,000 (294–95).
41. Peter C. Marzio, ed., *A Nation of Nations: The People Who Came Through America as Seen Through Objects and Documents Exhibited at the Smithsonian Institution* (New York: Harper & Row, 1976), 126. See also Kapp, *Immigration*, 38.
42. Derived from Robert P. Swierenga, comp., *Dutch Immigrants in U.S. Ship Manifests, 1820–1880: An Alphabetical Listing by Household Head and Independent Persons*, 2 vols. (Wilmington, DE: Scholarly Resources, 1983).
43. Letter C. M. Budde (neè Stomp) (Burlington, Iowa), Summer 1847, to Mr. and Mrs. Wormser-Van der Veen and their children (Amsterdam), in *Amsterdamse emigranten*, 80; G. A. Stout, *Souvenir History of Pella, Iowa* . . . (Pella: Booster Press, 1922), 47; K. Van Stigt, Elisabeth Kempkes, trans., *History of Pella, Iowa and Vicinity* (Pella, 1897), typescript, 48.

44. Herbert J. Brinks, with Martin Dekker and Roger Voskuil, "The Burning of the Phoenix, November 21, 1847," *Origins* 2, no. 2 (1984): 16–23; John H. Izenbaard, "Shattered Dreams: The Burning of the *Phoenix*," *Inland Seas* 30 (Fall 1974): 159–67. An older but still useful account is William O. Van Eyck, "The Story of the Propeller *Phoenix*," *Wisconsin Magazine of History* 7 (Mar. 1924): 281–300.
45. *Dutch Immigrant Memoirs*, 1:256; Lucas, *Netherlanders in America*, 208, 484; Baay, "Dear Friends Back Home," 28.
46. *Dutch Immigrant Memoirs*, 1:309.
47. Ibid., 1:116, 241, 230.
48. Van der Meulen, *Geliefde vrienden*, 3, 9.
49. *Dutch Immigrant Memoirs*, 1:233, 142, 116, 91, 255. A graphic account of the rigors of Erie Canal travel in 1848 is in Berkhout, *Brief van Noord Amerika*. See also Baay, "Dear Friends Back Home," 28.
50. Lucas, *Netherlanders in America*, 70–72, 91.
51. *Dutch Immigrant Memoirs*, 1:39; M. Mensink (Albany, New York) to Fellow Believers in the Netherlands (Amsterdam), 30 Dec. 1846, in *Amsterdamse emigranten*, 68–70.
52. "Letter from Hendrik Berendregt to H. P. Scholte," reprinted in translation in Jacob Van Der Zee, *The Hollanders of Iowa* (Iowa City: State Historical Society of Iowa, 1912), 339–48, esp. 346. See also Isaac Overkamp (Pella, Iowa) to Jan Hospers (Hoog Blokland, Netherlands), 27 Oct. 1847, and H. Hospers (Pella) to Jan Hospers (Hoog Blokland), March 1848, both in *Amsterdamse emigranten*, 118–20, 127–30; *Dutch Immigrant Memoirs*, 1:39.
53. Letters D. A. Budde (Burlington, Iowa) to J. A. Wormser (Amsterdam), 6–9 Nov. 1848, in *Amsterdamse emigranten*, 158–66.

PART II

RELIGION

CHAPTER 5

Religion and Immigration Behavior

ECONOMICS EXPLAINS THE "why" of immigration but religion largely determines the "how" of immigration and its effects. Although most immigrants left their homelands in the hope of economic betterment, religious institutions facilitated the move, guided the newcomers to specific destinations, and shaped their adjustment in the new land. Religion was the very "bone and sinew" of immigrant group consciousness and the "focal point" of their life.[1] One of the first scholars to recognize this was Oscar Handlin, who wrote in *The Uprooted* (1951) that "the very process of adjusting immigrant ideas to the conditions of the United States made religion paramount as a way of life."[2] A few years later, Henry Lucas, in a masterly study of Dutch immigration, observed that "for years religion determined the pattern of Dutch settlement in America."[3]

Churches as Immigration Agencies

The church community was a "shelter in the time of storm," a provider of benevolent and charitable services, an employment agency, and the center of social and cultural life. The newcomers embraced it with a fervor unknown even in the Old country. Nativist attacks forced ethnoreligious groups to close ranks, and even internal conflicts between Americanizers and anti-Americanizers served to define the boundaries of the community.[4] In turn, the communities were shaped by the interaction of successive waves of immigrant groups, each with its unique religious heritage.

Religious communities and their leaders played crucial roles in the decision to emigrate and in determining the ultimate destination. Churches created immigration organizations, clerical and lay leaders promoted and participated in it, and church communities created a supportive emotional and psychological environment in the sending and receiving areas. Religious faith offered stability and helped resolve tensions due to the common feeling of loss, rootlessness, and social disruption that most immigrants experienced.

Church aid societies commonly helped members to migrate overseas. In the 1840s, for example, Dutch Reformed clerics and lay patrons formed organizations such as the Arnhem and Utrecht-based Christian Associations for Emigration to North America. At least a dozen clerics themselves emigrated with some or all of their congregations.[5] Dutch Catholics were somewhat less organized, and the church hierarchy opposed overseas emigration, but several mission-minded priests founded emigration societies such as the Nederlandsche Katholijke Kolonies and the U.S.-based Catholic Colonization Society. American priests organized the latter in 1911 to prevent the dispersion of co-religionists.[6]

American churchmen with ethnic roots also assisted immigrants. At the outset of the Dutch Calvinist migration in the mid-1840s, the Reverend Isaac N. Wyckoff of the (Old) Dutch Reformed Church of Albany, New York, formed the Protestant Evangelical Holland Emigration Society, which became the model for a similar New York City organization Subsequently, Reformed immigrant congregations in the Midwest established common revolving loan funds, derived from annual levies on the entire membership, to provide passage money for eligible relatives who were chosen by lot. The sponsored family pledged to settle in one of the participating church colonies and to repay the loan with a small interest charge as soon as possible.[7] Dutch churches and synagogues also established benevolent and burial societies, health and accident funds, and insurance cooperatives, all mandated by the law of charity.

Not only did churches directly promote and fund immigration, but they created ethnic colonies where religion gave "form and substance" to community life. Religious solidarity provided an even stronger bond than ethnic identity alone and ensured the long-term success of nearly all church-centered colonies. Dutch Calvinists especially, it was said, "stick together not primarily on the bases of ethnicity or nationalism but on the basis of their religion."[8] Consequently, the Dutch Reformed were indifferent to their Catholic, Jewish, or secularist countrymen even when they lived in close proximity in the cities.[9]

While immigrant religion ensured cultural maintenance, it also led to conflict both within and without. Churches with hierarchical ecclesiastical structures such as the Roman Catholic Church had to deal with lay challenges to clerical authority.[10] Every immigrant settlement also faced new conflicts stemming from the internal pressures of Americanization and external intergroup rivalries and conflicts with the dominant Anglo-Protestant host society.[11]

Some ethnoreligious communities were racked with theological controversies carried from the Old Country as part of their cultural baggage. Recent studies of Dutch Reformed and Norwegian Lutheran schisms illustrate the divisive nature of such an inheritance. But internecine theological disputes were also a form of "ritual conflict," incomprehensible to outsiders, that helped maintain cultural walls against the wider American community. Commenting on one such Dutch colony in Amsterdam, Montana, Rob Kroes remarked: "In their attempts at reaffirming the boundary in strict and unambiguous terms, they did not shrink from cutting into their own flesh." "Honest wars" of religion thus worked both ways, creating factions within the camp based on common bonds of discourse that simultaneously walled them off from the society.[12]

Religion thus provided continuity for the immigrants by bridging the Old and New Worlds, which made gradual adjustment to American culture possible and even bearable. At the same time, every group had battles between conservative "slow Americanizers" and liberal "fast Americanizers." Indeed, much of the theological conflict was a reflection of this process of assimilation. The traditional forces believed that "language saves faith" and "in isolation is our strength." Liberals advocated rapid language changeover and the desirability of becoming "good Americans" in every respect.[13]

Multiethnic religious groups struggled with endemic nationality conflicts such as, for example, the Sephardic versus Ashkenazic Jews in the early nineteenth century and the German versus East European Jews later in the century. Other classic battles were the Irish and German struggles in American Catholicism and later the East and South European challenge to the more assimilated northern European Catholics.[14]

While a few immigrants were secularists, for the vast majority religion and ethnicity were so closely intertwined as to be indistinguishable.[15] As Jay Dolan noted in his book, *The Immigrant Church*:

> In New York Irish and German parishes were located within walking distance of one another, but they were as distinctive as German beer and Irish whiskey. They reinforced the ethnic differences of the people and enabled neighbors to build cultural barriers among themselves. As the center of their religious life the neighborhood parish exhibited the piety of the people, and the differences in piety proved to be more striking than the similarities of the urban environment.[16]

Religion or National Identity

If religion strongly influenced the process of migration and subsequent adjustment to American life, it is necessary to differentiate the effects of religion per se from the equally powerful forces of national identity. For immigrants from countries dominated by one religion, such as Irish, Italian, French, or Czech Catholics, nationality and religion were interwoven. Which beliefs and practices arose from religious identity and which from national identity? Was the puritanical streak among Irish Catholics in America a product of traditional Irish rural life, or religious defense against American Protestantism, or both? Did Dutch Calvinists in America seemingly revel in theological disputes and schisms because they were Dutch or because they were Calvinists?

One possible way to address this issue is to study immigrants from countries such as the Netherlands and Germany where religions were regionally segmented and to compare the immigrant behavior of the religious subgroups. Dutch emigration in the nineteenth century affords such a case. Reformed and Catholic emigrants have been identified and traced from their communities of origin to their communities of destination in the United States. The tracing was done by linking the official emigration records compiled by Dutch government officials with U.S. population census records of Dutch-born nationals in 1850, 1860, and 1870.[17] The linked file permits comparisons between Catholics and Protestants within the same nationality group, which reveal the role of religion, as distinct from nationality (or ethnicity), in shaping the total immigration experience.

Religious Forces in Emigration

The emigration began in the mid-1840s in conjunction with a widespread agricultural crisis caused primarily by the failure of the potato crop. The food problem followed a decade of religious dissension within the privileged Hervormde (Reformed) Church, which had been accompanied by police suppression of Seceders. The religious persecution strengthened the emigration mentality already strong among rural peasants who had long suffered from poverty, land hunger, and a pinched future.[18] Cheap lands in America provided an irresistible lure.

The religious factors in Dutch emigration are evident both in the Old Country and in the New. At home, Catholics were more reluctant than Protestants to

TABLE 5.1 Emigration by Religion, 1831–80

	Periods of Emigration						
	1831–57		1858–68		1869–80		Total
Religion	Number	%	Number	%	Number	%	Number
Reformed*	12,180 (47%)	32	11,617 (66%)	31	13,813 (68%)	37	37,610 (59%)
Seceders†	7,569 (29%)	56	1,915 (11%)	17	3,072 (15%)	27	12,556 (20%)
Catholic‡	4,635 (18%)	43	3,261 (19%)	31	2,823 (14%)	26	11,367 (18%)
Jewish	321 (1%)	55	130 (1%)	22	129 (1%)	22	580 (1%)
Protestant§	534 (2%)	32	568 (3%)	35	539 (3%)	33	1638 (3%)
Totals¶	25,885		17,491		20,376		63,751

* Includes Nederduits Hervormd 476, Waals Hervormd 55, Presbyterian Hervormd 4, and English Hervormd 5.

† Includes Christelijk Afgeschieden 7,318, Gereformeerd 2,680, Hervormd Afgeschieden 452, Christelijk Gereformeerd 2,075, and Gereformeerd under het Kruis 31.

‡ Includes Oud Katholiek 9.

§ Includes Lutheren and Hersteld Lutheren 448, Doopsgezinden (Mennonites) 513, "Protestant" 616, and other Protestant 61.

¶ Excludes none 26, Moslem 1, and N.A. 608.

SOURCE: Robert P. Swierenga, comp., *Dutch Emigrants to the United States, South Africa, South America, and Southeast Asia, 1835–1880: An Alphabetical Listing by Household Heads and Independent Persons* ((Wilmington DE: Scholarly Resources, 1983); augmented for the years 1831–47 with data from the Department of Binnenlandsche Zaken report in "Staat van landverhuizers 1831–1847," *Nederlandsche Staatscourant*, 5 September 1848, 2.

emigrate and fewer did so. In America, Catholics settled in cities mainly and assimilated more rapidly than Protestants. Catholics were less prone to emigrate overseas because of cultural and clerical pressures against it, as well as regional differences.[19] One of the earliest brochures to warn against emigration came in 1846 from the pen of a "Catholic citizen." The pamphlet's inflammatory title is sufficient to indicate the strident nature of the text: *Think Before you Start! A cordial word to my Countrymen concerning the illness in our Fatherland called "Emigration."* The desire to emigrate, said the writer, is a "strange disease" that afflicts "a blind crowd," who in the mistaken hope of getting away from "cares and troubles" will instead find a hard, lonely, and despised life in the United States.[20]

Catholics comprised 38 percent of the Dutch population in 1849 but made up only 18 percent of the total emigrants in the years through 1880 (see Table 5.1). Hence, to match their share of the population, more than twice as many Catholics should have emigrated. Seceders, on the other hand, were heavily overrepresented, particularly in the first wave that followed the bitter government repression of the 1830s. Seceders comprised 57 percent of all Dutch emigrants in the years 1845 to 1849; yet they formed only 1.3 percent of the total population in 1849. The new liberal constitution of 1848, which granted complete religious freedom, sharply reduced the Seceder propensity to emigrate. Nevertheless, Seceders numbered 20 percent of the emigrants (1831–80), but they claimed only 3 percent of the Dutch populace in 1869 (Table 5.1). Thus, more than six times as many Seceders departed the fatherland as their share of the total population. Hervormde church emigrants at 59 percent equaled their 55 percent religious share of the populace in 1849.

Protestant–Catholic Differences

As Figure 5.1 shows, Calvinists overshot and Catholics undershot their proportion of the population in every province except Drenthe, which had little emigration. Notably, Catholic emigrants were heavily underrepresented in the populous urban provinces (Noord-Holland, Zuid-Holland, and Utrecht), which indicates that urban Catholics were less likely to emigrate than rural ones. In the traditional Catholic provinces of Noord-Brabant and Limburg, Catholic emigrants fairly matched their share of the population. Catholics clearly were less willing than Calvinists to leave the fatherland.

This Catholic and Seceder disparity in emigration raises the question of causation. Both were religious minorities and traditional culture groups with a strong sense of localism and large families. Yet Catholics were far more reluctant to emigrate. What factor(s) might explain this pattern?[21] The key is leadership. Seceder ministers organized and led the emigration, while Catholic clerics generally resisted emigration because it threatened to disrupt religious supervision and instruction and might lead to the loss of social control. Only a few Catholics priests, notably Father Theodore van den Broek, actively recruited emigrants, and this was done under the cloak of promoting missionary enterprise. Van den Broek had already

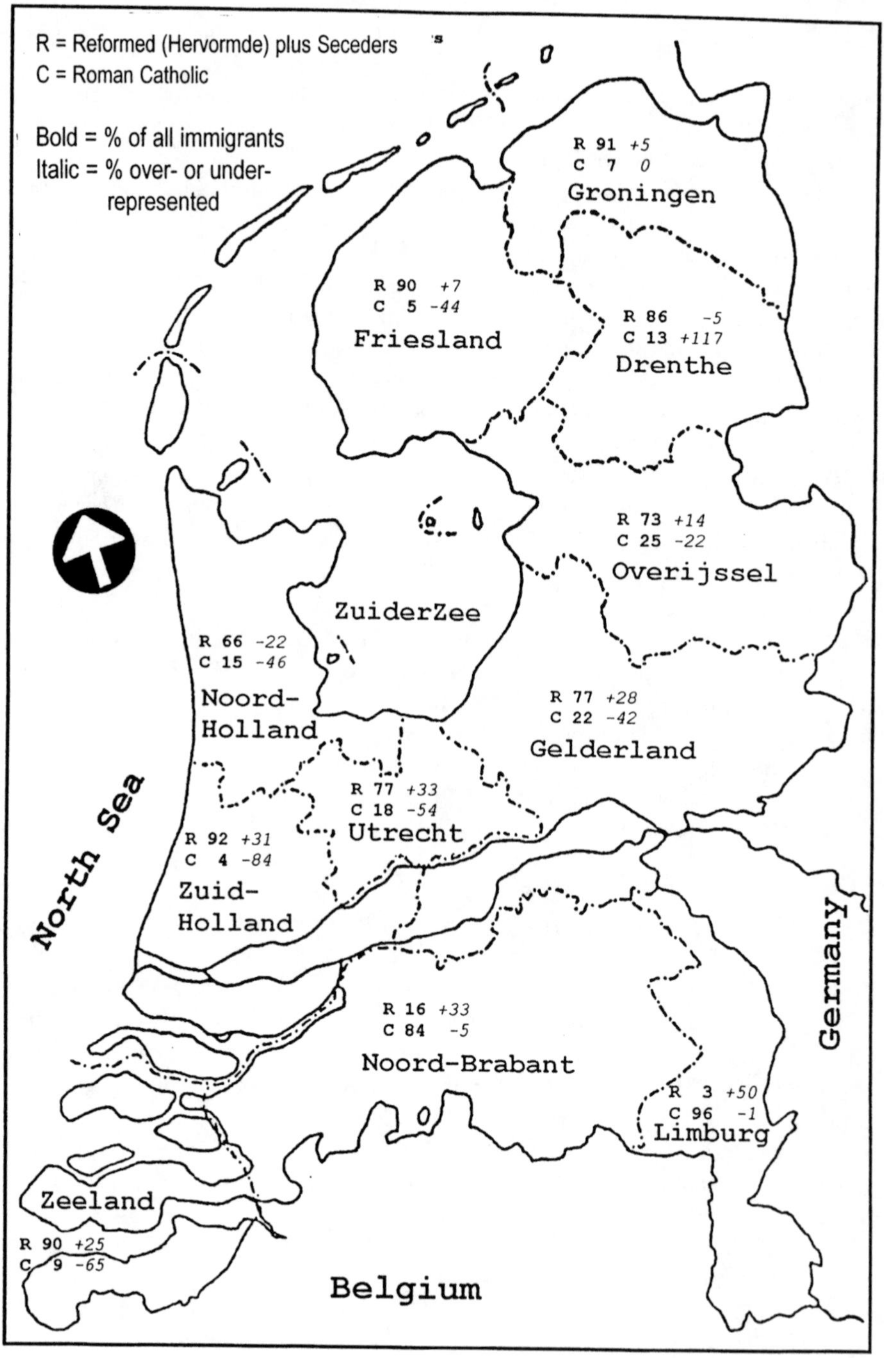

Figure 5.1 Emigration Percentages by Religion by Province: Reformed and Roman Catholics, 1835–80, per 1849 Census

SOURCE: Swierenga data, Table 5.1; and 1849 Census (*Volkstelling*) of the Netherlands

established a mission outpost among the Menominee Indians near Green Bay, Wisconsin, and he sought to build a Christian community there.

Vanden Broek was well aware of the risks to the faith. In an 1847 emigration pamphlet, he warned that in America the numerous Protestant sects may fight each other, but they "stand side by side against the Catholics;... so it is desirable that all Catholic immigrants remain together and choose no other places except where they find their spiritual leaders."[22] Some 500 Catholics responded to Van den Broek's appeals, and in the following decades another 1,000–1,500 persons followed. By 1880 there were at least three Dutch parishes in northern Wisconsin—Green Bay, Little Chute, and De Pere. But this was only a fraction of the more than 10,000 Dutch Catholic immigrants in these years, who scattered widely.[23]

The cultural and institutional forces discouraging Catholic emigration were reinforced by economic developments. The Catholic Netherlands was in the upland, sandy-soil region where traditional small-scale farming remained the norm. The introduction of commercial fertilizers and land reclamation projects in this region enabled fathers to subdivide their farms among their sons or to open new ones on reclaimed lands. By contrast, in the diluvial, sea-clay regions of the Protestant north and southwest, a different farming pattern developed. There the cash grain farmers mechanized their operations, consolidated their holdings in the quest for efficient large-scale production, and cut their labor costs by laying off farm workers. These excess laborers had few alternatives but to leave farming and move to the large cities or emigrate to America where cheap land beckoned.

Another economic factor in the low Catholic emigration rate was that Catholic farmers were heavily engaged in the home production of textiles as part of the textile industry in the region.[24] Home industry augmented farm income and provided a greater measure of stability against fluctuating food prices. After 1865, when the textile industry modernized by shifting production from farm cottages to urban factory centers such as Eindhoven and Tilburg, sons and daughters of farmers could go to the nearby towns and cities for work and still remain within a predominantly Catholic culture. Many Catholics also found temporary work in nearby Germany and Belgium. Catholic peasants thus had more attractive economic alternatives than did Protestant farm workers in the north and west.

In brief, the emerging industrial growth in the textile centers of Limburg and southeastern Noord-Brabant after 1850 served as urban magnets to attract families and single workers from the surrounding rural areas. The only major emigration from Noord-Brabant, therefore, originated in the northeastern part of the province that was farthest removed from the new textile factories.

The timing of Protestant and Catholic emigration also differed (see Table 5.1). Both Catholic and Seceder emigration was heavier in the first wave from 1846 through 1857 and fell off in the next decades. Seceders began to depart in large numbers in 1846, one year earlier than did the Catholics, and over 4,900 Seceders left by 1849. Once the Catholic outflow started in earnest in 1847, they too departed steadily, with the heaviest movement in 1850–54 and 1865–70, mainly originating in the provinces of Noord-Brabant and Gelderland. In the interim years of 1857 to 1865, the adjoining province of Limburg first began contributing emigrants, sending out more than half of all Catholic emigrants during the Civil War era. In the postbellum years (1865–80), the overall Catholic proportion of the emigration declined to about 14 percent. Improved economic conditions at home and job opportunities across the border in Germany dampened the enthusiasm to emigrate. Thus, Catholic emigration was more important before 1865 than in the postwar decade.[25]

On a minor note, a higher proportion of Catholic emigrants settled in the United States than did the majority of Protestants, many of whom—all non-Seceders—went to Dutch colonies in Southeast Asia and South America, or to South Africa. The Seceders, however, had the highest proportion settling in the United States—almost 99 percent, compared to 90 percent of the Catholic emigrants and 89 percent of the Reformed. Seceders and Catholics, the former a new religious minority and the latter a traditional minority, had suffered sufficiently as second-class citizens to dissuade them from emigrating *within* the empire, if equal opportunities beckoned elsewhere.

Contrasting Settlement Patterns

The settlement behavior of Dutch Protestants and Catholics in the United States likewise diverged.[26] Catholics established very few colonies, in contrast to the Calvinists, especially the Seceders, who formed ethnic enclaves wherever they settled, whether in rural areas or major cities. More than one third of Catholic emigrants settled in cities and towns with a population more than 5,000, compared to only one quarter of Seceders. Thus, Catholics and Calvinists in America distanced themselves from one another.

The only lasting Dutch Catholic colonies of the mid-nineteenth century were in the Green Bay area, at Little Chute, De Pere, and Hollandtown.[27] Most immigrants went to the larger cities along the established transportation routes to the Midwest: Cincinnati and Saint Louis from the South, and from the East Coast Rochester, Buffalo, Cleveland, Detroit, Grand Rapids, Chicago, and Milwaukee. All these places were Catholic centers with churches, schools, and social institutional in place. As a result, Dutch Catholics readily worshiped and intermarried with Catholics of other nationalities, especially Germans, Belgians, and Irish. As historian Henry Lucas explained: "The common bond of faith made it possible for them to live happily with people who were not Dutch. . . . Dutch Catholics did not tend so markedly to settle in Dutch communities, but scattered, were speedily assimilated, and so left few distinctive traces."[28]

Cincinnati, Chicago, and Grand Rapids were notable exceptions. Dutch Catholics in Cincinnati, 400 strong, had by 1854 established their own parish with a Dutch-speaking priest, Father Johannes vande Luijtelaar. In Chicago's Kensington district on the far south side, Saint Willebrord, the only Dutch parish in the city, was organized in the early 1890s and totaled 200 souls in the era of World War I, when a Dutch-born cleric, Father J. A. Van Heertum, pastored the parish. Saint Joseph's parish on the near southwest side of Grand Rapids was founded in 1887 to serve some 70 Dutch families in the Furniture City. A Dutch-speaking priest, Henry Frenken, from 's Hertogenbosch served this parish from 1887 to 1906, and the church grew to 120 families by 1915. Dutch-language services ceased in 1906, however, when Father Frenken returned to the Netherlands, and the parish gradually lost its ethnic solidarity.[29]

These Dutch Catholic urban churches were three of only twenty-five congregations nationwide that were primarily Dutch, but they had no mutual connections and all were short-lived. Even the concentrated Fox River Valley Catholic settlements failed to maintain a Dutch ethnic flavor after World War I, except for the small villages of Little Chute and Hollandtown, which still celebrate their annual *Schut* (shooting) festival, which is of Brabantine origin.

By contrast, there were 500 Dutch Calvinist congregations in the 1920s and most continue to the present day. "What held the colonists together," according to Jacob van Hinte, "was the powerful bond of religion—a bond that showed itself to be stronger, in many aspects, than the one of ethnic identity." Thus, "it was the power of religious conviction," Van Hinte continued, "that must be credited for the success of nearly all of these colonies and that made them into the foci of the Dutch presence in America."[30] In short, as Lucas succinctly summarized the matter, "religion encouraged dispersal" for Dutch Catholics because the Catholic churches were everywhere, but religion cemented together Dutch Calvinists.[31] Calvinists, especially Seceders, in contrast to Catholics, preferred settling in isolated rural colonies or forming Dutch neighborhoods in major cities where they could preserve their faith. As of 1870, more than three fourths of the Protestants lived in colonies, whereas less than a third of the Catholics did so.[32]

In general, both groups favored the Midwest. Protestants were concentrated in the states of Michigan, Wisconsin, and Iowa, and Catholics preferred Wisconsin, Minnesota, and Missouri (Table 5.2). According to Table 5.3, 64 percent of Protestants settled in the Great Lakes region, 15 percent went west of the Mississippi River, and 22 percent stayed in the East. Of the Catholics 56 percent could be found in the Great Lakes region, 28 percent were west of the Mississippi River, and 15 percent in the East. The primary settlements dotted the shoreline of Lake Michigan and the Mississippi River and its tributaries. In the East the central regions were in New York City, northern New Jersey, and the cities along the Erie Canal–Great Lakes water route.[33]

In terms of the types of settlements, Protestant and Catholic Dutch both favored rural communities, but the Seceders, who had the highest rate of family migration, were most rural (73 percent). Catholics were next in selecting rural locations (65 percent), and the Reformed members were the least rural (59 percent). Catholics and Reformed had the highest propensity to settle in large cities (over 25,000) at 17 percent, whereas only 9 percent of Seceders resided in large cities.

The reasons for these settlement patterns are many. Leading individuals often directed immigrants to particular places for their own economic, religious, or cultural reasons. Dutch Catholics, for example, went to the Green Bay area because a Dutch priest had begun an Indian mission station there. Seceders followed their "dominies" to sparsely settled regions in order to establish homogeneous colonies.

TABLE 5.2 **Religion by State: Dutch Immigrants and Their Children, 1850, 1860, 1870**

	PROTESTANT					CATHOLIC				
	1850	1860	1870	1850–70		1850	1860	1870	1850–70	
STATE	NUMBER	NUMBER	NUMBER	NUMBER	%	NUMBER	NUMBER	NUMBER	NUMBER	%
IL	204	884	2,881	3,969	94	0	0	239	239	6
IN	28	382	745	1,155	74	0	181	227	408	26
IA	1,053	3,372	5,598	10,023	93	68	237	473	778	7
KA	0	0	22	22	100	0	0	0	0	0
MI	3,325	8,882	17,278	29,485	98	42	221	342	605	2
MN	0	224	551	775	28	0	392	1,622	2,014	72
MO	0	30	78	108	4	202	849	1,515	2,566	96
NE	0	0	110	110	0	0	0	0	0	0
NJ	312	1,311	3,833	5,456	97	0	64	79	143	3
NY	1,281	3,956	5,567	10,804	61	1,473	3,530	1,889	6,892	39
OH	81	580	787	1,448	28	283	1,378	2,137	3,798	73
WI	904	3,966	5,730	10,600	57	163	2,904	4,274	7,941	43
TOTALS	7,188	23,587	43,180	73,955	74	2,831	9,756	12,797	25,384	26

SOURCE: Compiled from Robert P. Swierenga, comp., *Dutch Households in U.S. Population Censuses, 1850, 1860, 1870: An Alphabetical Listing by Family Heads* (Wilmington, DE: Scholarly Resources, 1987).

TABLE 5.3 Religion by Geographic Region: Protestant and Catholic Dutch, 1870

	GREAT LAKES		MIDWEST		EAST	
RELIGION	NUMBER	%	NUMBER	%	NUMBER	%
Protestant	27,421	64	6,359	14	9,400	22
Catholic	7,219	56	3,610	28	1,968	15

SOURCE: Compiled from Robert P. Swierenga, comp., *Dutch Households in U.S. Population Censuses, 1850, 1860, 1870: An Alphabetical Listing by Family Heads* (Wilmington, Del. Scholarly Resources, 1987).
NOTE: See note 33 for description of the method for determining religion.
Great Lakes=Illinois, Indiana, Michigan, Ohio, Wisconsin. Midwest=Iowa, Kansas, Missouri, Minnesota, Nebraska. East=New Jersey, New York

The Reformed sometimes sought out descendants of the old colonial Dutch in New York and New Jersey, or they settled in Michigan among the old Dutch who had followed the frontier westward.

Given the historic Protestant-Catholic division in the Netherlands, it was to be expected that Protestants deliberately avoided Catholic-dominated areas such as northern Wisconsin and cities like Cincinnati and Saint Louis. But apart from the religious consideration, most Dutch avoided hot climates and open prairies (both unknown in the Netherlands). The major exception was the Pella, Iowa, colony of the maverick Seceder cleric, Hendrik P. Scholte, who led some nine hundred followers to the rolling prairies. Once the settlers adapted to the new environment, their sons and daughters in the 1870s and 1880s founded many other prairie settlements. The Dutch pioneers usually located near major waterways and markets, and they initially desired areas such as the forest lands of Michigan and Wisconsin that had exploitable natural resources for the cash-hungry settlers.

Assimilation or Not

The geographical and institutional differences had a significant impact on marital assimilation. Already in the first immigrant cohort (1840–70), Dutch Catholics had a higher intermarriage rate than did Protestants. The difference became apparent only a few years after immigration began. In 1850, 32 percent of married Dutch-born Catholics had non-Dutch spouses, compared to only 5 percent among Protestant Dutch. By 1870 the Catholic "outmarriage" rate (i.e., those with non-Dutch spouses) had risen to 46 percent, whereas only 13 percent of Protestants had non-Dutch spouses. The Dutch Catholics in the United States were thus four to five times as likely as Protestants to have non-Dutch spouses (in order—German, Belgian, Irish, and French).

An even more dramatic picture of Catholic internationality marriages emerges when the 1870 census figures are differentiated by couples who married before or after immigration. Those marrying in the U.S. were mainly children of Dutch parents who were minors at the time of immigration. Among Protestants, 10 percent of the already married immigrants had outmarried by 1870, compared to 24 percent of those marrying in the United States. But among Catholics, 37 percent of first-generation couples married non-Dutch spouses and an overwhelming 70 percent of their unmarried children selected non-Dutch spouses. Clearly, the less isolated Catholic communities and the international nature of the Roman church broke down the ethnic identity of Dutch Catholics more rapidly than it did for Protestants.

The explanation for the high Catholic outmarriage rate was the "mixed parish." For example, between 1875 and 1900 in the Diocese of Green Bay, in which all the parishes were of mixed nationality, ten out of fifty-eight parishes included a substantial number of Dutch. Four of these ten Dutch parishes were mixed English and German; two included English, German, and French; one was English, German, and Bohemian; one was simply Dutch and Flemish; and two were Dutch and German.[34]

These mixed parishes, created out of needful compromise in developing regions, were plagued with problems of language, customs, worship liturgies, and weak institutional loyalties. Most evolved into single-nationality or territorial parishes. The immigrant groups, except those that resided in transplanted colonies, experienced a series of transformations. First, they worshiped in an "alien" parish or became part of a mixed congregation; then when their numbers multiplied they established their own parish. Over time, however, unless the congregation was nourished by a steady stream of new immigrants from the mother country, it reverted again to a mixed parish. The U.S. immigration restriction laws following World War I often caused such a reversion.

For millions of immigrant Catholics the nationality parish and parochial school were surrogate associations for the communal village they left behind. Ethnoreligious institutions relieved their emotional stress, protected them from the dominant Protestant world, and facilitated their transition to American life. As James Olson aptly noted: "Church newspapers, parish sodalities and confraternities, parochial schools, emigrant aid and mutual benefit societies, and religious associations dedicated to particular shrines and patron saints reconstructed the community that had died." In the decades before World War I, more than 80 percent of the children of East European immigrants attended parish schools taught in native languages. Churches, schools, and societies provided cultural continuity and became the social and emotional center of the neighborhood. In the minds of most inhabitants, the parish and neighborhood melded together.[35]

However, a strong ethnic parish could retard but not prevent the slow movement toward a "Roman Catholic melting pot." Language was the first to go, even though its maintenance was the major function of the nationality parish. Then the immigrant press declined. Culturally, the patriarchal family and hierarchical church governance weakened, and even national loyalties disappeared through intermarriage.[36]

The role of religion in promoting or retarding assimilation depended on modes of settlement, church institutional structures, and theological traditions. Transplanted churches and nationality parishes ensured the survival of European languages and cultures for three or more generations. Protestants, such as Dutch Calvinists, German Missouri Synod Lutherans, and Norwegian Haugean Lutherans, tended to establish homogeneous rural colonies more than did Roman Catholics, and the Protestant ethnics preserved their cultural ways longer. To what extent this was an artifact of settlement patterns rather than ecclesiastical structures is not always clear. William Petersen attributed the "imperfect integration" into American society of the Dutch Protestant colonies in Michigan and Wisconsin after more than one hundred years to the "efforts of the Orthodox Calvinist ministers to keep their flocks together," whereas Roman Catholics assimilated rapidly "principally because there was no separate Dutch Catholic Church." Lucas noted that "Reformed principles" gave the Calvinists their conception of life and "helped them to organize their social and economic activities.[37]

A group that assimilated even faster than Dutch Catholics were Dutch Protestants who settled away from the colonies and joined Presbyterian and other English-speaking churches. These persons deliberately chose the "fast track" to acculturation and quickly jettisoned their Dutchness. German Forty-Eighters, the so-called secular-club liberals, followed the same path. They consciously abandoned German culture in favor of the American democratic system. Wherever the Forty-Eighter influence was greatest, they promoted rapid assimilation. By contrast the so-called church Germans, who were less cosmopolitan in their mental outlook and religiously conservative, formed "language islands" throughout the United States centered on church and creed. Lutherans clung to their various synods (Missouri, Wisconsin, etc.) and Catholics to their dioceses, priests, and bishops.[38]

Theological tenets also influenced the rate of assimilation. Churches with a prophetic (or pietistic) theology that stressed individual conversion and a life of benevolence ("good works") made it easier for members to shake off old cultural patterns and adopt new ones. The converts personally appropriated their faith and enlisted in the social reform crusades of the Second Great Awakening, eventually appropriating the American individualistic success ethic. Churches with an orthodox theology or priestly hierarchy, on the other hand, stressed cultural maintenance and were therefore inherently countercultural and even anti-American.[39]

Dutch Calvinists even had a theological rationale for cultural separation, the doctrine of the *antithesis*, which held that believers' religious value systems were squarely opposed to those of unbelievers. The power of resistance to Americanization inherent in this key doctrine of Calvinist orthodoxy proved to be the pioneers' most valuable asset. As Adriaan J. Barnouw remarked: "For, thanks to that same power, they were able to withstand the trials and hardships of the life that awaited the first settlers in the forests of Michigan and the prairies of Iowa. Calvinism, thanks to the fervor with which it inspires the faithful, is a great builder of colonies." A tight theological and ecclesiastical system certainly slowed the process of assimilation and sustained a secure fortress mentality. As Barnouw observed: "The stubbornest resistance to Americanization is offered by the most orthodox believers."[40] Religious faith and theology, in short, were crucial to the existence of ethnic enclaves, led to resistance against nearby "out-groups," and strengthened commitments to the church community. The immigrant church also cushioned the shock for newcomers on a personal level and facilitated their gradual adjustment to the new society.[41]

Conclusion

The thrust of current immigration research is that religious affiliation significantly influenced the entire resettlement process—the decision to emigrate, the direction of the emigrant stream, and the subsequent adjustment and adaptation in the new homeland. But religious forces operated within a common context. Economic forces primarily spurred emigration among lower and middle classes in all religious communities, although with greater or lesser intensity. Immigrants of all religious affiliations overwhelmingly chose the United States as their destination, but dissenting religious minorities were the most America-centered because of the proffered freedoms. All immigrants relied on family resources and information networks in the first instance and created family migration chains.

Catholic and Jewish immigrants experienced a greater uprooting than did Protestants, and they assimilated more readily. The international character of Catholicism weakened national identities and ethnic feelings at the same time that Protestants transplanted their church-centered colonies and maintained their language and institutional life. Protestants even carved out new daughter colonies when expansion became necessary after the mother colony reached saturation.[42] Religion was truly the "bone and sinew" of immigrant group life and determined its form and character.

Notes

1. Randall M. Miller, "Introduction," in *Immigrants and Religion in Urban America*, eds. Randall M. Miller and Thomas D. Marzik (Philadelphia: Temple University Press, 1977), xv; and John Bodnar, *The Transplanted: A History of Immigrants in Urban America* (Bloomington: Indiana University Press, 1985), 144–68.
2. Oscar Handlin, *The Uprooted* (New York: Grosset and Dunlap, 1951), 117. Sociologists and psychologists of the postwar decades assumed that faith was irrelevant to the successful adjustment of immigrants. See, for example, Abraham A. Weinberg, *Psychosociology of the Immigrant: An Investigation into the Problems of Adjustment of Jewish Immigrants into Palestine Based on Replies to an Enquiry among Immigrants from Holland* (Jerusalem: Israel Institute of Folklore and Ethnology, 1949), 20, and L. J. Menges, *Geschiktheid voor emigratie: een onderzoek naar enkele psychologische aspecten der emigrabiliteit* (The Hague: Staatsdrukkerij-en Uitgeverijbedrijf, 1959), 104.
3. Henry S. Lucas, *Netherlanders in America: Dutch Immigration to the United States and Canada, 1789–1950* (Ann Arbor: University of Michigan Press, 1955; repr. Grand Rapids, MI: Wm. B. Eerdmans, 1989), 473.

4. James D. Bratt, *Dutch Calvinism in Modern America: A History of a Conservative Subculture* (Grand Rapids, MI: Wm. B. Eerdmans, 1984); Lawrence J. Taylor, *Dutchmen on the Bay: The Ethnohistory of a Contractual Community* (Philadelphia: University of Pennsylvania Press, 1983); Andrew T. Kopan, "Greek Survival in Chicago: The Role of Ethnic Education 1890–1980," in *Ethnic Chicago*, eds. Peter d'A Jones and Melvin G. Holli (Grand Rapids, MI: Wm. B. Eerdmans, 1981), 95.
5. Lucas, *Netherlanders in America*, chaps. 3–5. An example in the 1700s was the practice of Jewish synagogues in Amsterdam and The Hague to provide grants for paupers in their communities to emigrate to America. See Bertram Wallace Korn, *The Early Jews of New Orleans* (Waltham, MA: American Jewish Historical Society, 1969), 13.
6. J. Stellingwerff, *Amsterdamse emigranten: onbekende brieven uit de prairie van Iowa, 1846–1873* (Amsterdam: Buijten & Schipperheijn, 1975), 15; Jacob van Hinte, *Netherlanders in America: A Study of Emigration and Settlement in the Nineteenth and Twentieth Centuries in the United States of America*, Robert P. Swierenga, general ed., Adriaan de Wit, chief trans. (Grand Rapids, MI: Baker Book House, 1985), 729–30; Mary Gilbert Kelly, *Catholic Immigrant Colonization Projects in the United States, 1815–1860* (New York: United States Catholic Historical Society, 1939).
7. Van Hinte, *Netherlanders in America*, 131, 390.
8. Lucas, *Netherlanders in America*, 473, 579, 315.
9. An example of this is Bastiaan Broere, a devout Calvinist in West Sayville, Long Island, who deliberately avoided any contact with two neighboring Dutch families because "they would offend us with their ungodly language." Van Hinte, *Netherlanders in America*, 315.
10. Dennis J. Clark, "The Irish Catholics: A Postponed Perspective" in *Immigrants and Religion*, 48–68; Henry B. Leonard, "Ethnic Conflict and Episcopal Power: The Diocese of Cleveland, 1847–1870," *Catholic Historical Review* 62 (July 1976): 388–407; Timothy L. Smith, "Lay Initiative in the Religious Life of American Immigrants, 1880–1950," in *Anonymous Americans: Explorations in Nineteenth Century Social History*, ed. Tamara K. Hareven (Englewood Cliffs, NJ: Prentice-Hall, 1971), 214–49; and Jay P. Dolan, *The Immigrant Church: New York's Irish and German Catholics, 1815–1865* (Baltimore: Johns Hopkins University Press, 1975), 14.
11. Clark, "Irish Catholics"; Rudolph J. Vecoli, "Prelates and Peasants: Italian Immigrants and the Catholic Church," *Journal of Social History* 2 (Spring 1969): 228–51; Jed Dannenbaum, "Immigrants and Temperance: Ethnocultural Conflict in Cincinnati, 1845–1860," *Ohio History* 87 (Spring 1978): 125–39; and Nora Faires, "The Evolution of Ethnicity: The German Community in Pittsburgh and Allegheny City, Pennsylvania, 1845–1885" (Ph.D. diss., University of Pittsburgh, 1981). Faires argues for a dynamic concept of ethnicity, which suggests that churches played a greater role among immigrants in America than they did in the homeland (pp. 66–68). See also Sylvia June Alexander, "The Immigrant Church and

Community: The Formation of Pittsburgh's Slovak Religious Institutions, 1870–1914" (Ph.D. diss., University of Pittsburgh, 1980), 11.

12. Rob Kroes, *The Persistence of Ethnicity: Dutch Calvinist Pioneers in Amsterdam, Montana* (Urbana and Chicago: University of Illinois Press, 1992), 101–03; Taylor, *Dutchmen on the Bay*, 141, 152, 160. See also Bratt, *Dutch Calvinism*; Jon Gjerde, "Conflict and Community: A Case Study of the Immigrant Church in the United States," *Journal of Social History* 19 (Summer 1986): 681–92; and Dolores Ann Liptak, *European Immigrants and the Catholic Church in Connecticut* (New York: Center for Migration Studies, 1987).
13. Miller, "Introduction," viii; Andrew M. Greeley, *The Catholic Experience* (New York: Doubleday, 1967), 22–23; James S. Olson, *Catholic Immigrants in America* (Chicago: Nelson Hall, 1987), 186; Jay P. Dolan, "Philadelphia and the German Catholic Community," in *Immigrants and Religion*, 71.
14. Clark, "Irish Catholics;" Dolan, "German Catholic Community;" Olson, *Catholic Immigrants*, 101–25.
15. Harry S. Stout, "Ethnicity: The Vital Center of Religion in America," *Ethnicity* 2 (April 1975): 204–24; Martin E. Marty, "Ethnicity: The Skeleton of Religion in America," *Church History* 41 (March 1972): 5–21; William J. Galush, "Faith and Fatherland: Dimensions of Polish-American Ethnoreligion, 1875–1975," in Miller and Marzik, *Immigrants and Religion*, 84–102; Timothy L. Smith, "Religion and Ethnicity in America," *American Historical Review* 83 (December 1978): 1155–85, esp. 1181; and James D. Bratt, "Religion and Ethnicity in America: A Critique of Timothy L. Smith," *Fides et Historia* 12 (Spring 1980): 8–17.
16. Dolan, *Immigrant Church*, 44.
17. Robert P. Swierenga, comp., *Dutch Emigrants to the United States, South Africa, South America, and Southeast Asia, 1835–1880: An Alphabetical Listing by Household Heads and Independent Persons* (Wilmington, DE: Scholarly Resources, 1983); Swierenga, comp., *Dutch Households in U.S. Population Censuses, 1850, 1860, 1870: An Alphabetical Listing by Family Heads*, 3 vols. (Wilmington, DE: Scholarly Resources, 1987).
18. Robert P. Swierenga, "Dutch Immigration Patterns in the Nineteenth and Twentieth Centuries," in *The Dutch in America: Immigration, Settlement, and Cultural Change*, ed. Robert P. Swierenga (New Brunswick, NJ: Rutgers University Press, 1985), 27–32; Robert P. Swierenga, "Local-Cosmopolitan Theory and Immigrant Religion: The Social Bases of the Antebellum Dutch Reformed Schism," *Journal of Social History* 14 (Fall 1980): 113–35.
19. H. Blink, "Immigratie in Amerika en emigratie uit Europe in verband met de economische toestanden," *Vragen Van Den Dag*, 30 (1910): 630; Henry van Stekelenburg, *Landverhuizing als regional verschijnsel: Van Noord-Brabant naar Noord-Amerika* (Tilburg: Stichting Zuidelijk Historisch Contact, 1991), 1–6, 267. Lucas, *Netherlanders in America*, 213, contests this point unconvincingly and also greatly overestimates Catholic emigration.

20. *Verzint eer gij begint! Een hartelijk woord aan mijne landgenooten, over de in ons vaderland heerschende ziekte ganaamd: landverhuizing* ('s Hertogenbosch, 1846).
21. Roman Catholic emigration is described in greater detail in Robert P. Swierenga and Yda Schreuder, "Catholic and Protestant Emigration from the Netherlands in the 19th Century: A Comparative Social Structural Analysis," *Tijdschrift voor Economische en Sociale Geografie* 74 (1983): 25–40.
22. Henry S. Lucas, "De Reize naar Noord-Amerika van Theodorus J. van den Broek, O.P.," *Nederlandsch Archief voor Kerkgeschiedenis* 41 (1955): 96–123, quote 115. An English translation by E. R. Post and D. F. Van Vliet, titled "The Journey to North America of Theodorus J. van den Broek, O.P.," is in the Heritage Hall Archives, Calvin College; quote is on p. 25. Calvinist leaders likewise avoided Catholic regions. Van Raalte, the clerical founder of the Michigan colony, changed his original plan to settle in Wisconsin after he learned that the state was inhabited largely by "the mixed multitude from Europe," especially Germans. See A. C. Van Raalte, *Holland in Amerika, of, de Hollandsche Kolonisatie in den Staat Michigan* (1847), English trans. G. Vander Ziel, *Holland in America, or, The Holland Colonization in the State of Michigan* (1977), Calvin College Archives.
23. Lucas, *Netherlanders in America*, 223–25.
24. Yda Schreuder, *Dutch Catholic Immigrant Settlement in Wisconsin, 1850–1905* (New York and London: Garland, 1990); idem, "Emigration and the Decline of Traditional Industries in Mid-Nineteenth Century Europe," *Immigration History Newsletter* 17 (May 1985): 8–10; idem, "Dutch Catholic Emigration in the Mid-Nineteenth Century: Noord-Brabant, 1847–1871," *Journal of Historical Geography* 11 (1985): 48–69.
25. Yda Schreuder and Robert P. Swierenga, "Catholic Emigration from the Southern Provinces of the Netherlands in the Nineteenth Century," Working Paper No. 27, Netherlands Interuniversity Demographic Institute (Voorburg, 1982), 15–17, 46. The tabular data reported in the above article is for household units. The figures in this chapter are individual-level data.
26. Henry A. V. M. van Stekelenburg, *Landverhuizing als regionaal verschijnsel*, 259, 275; idem, "Rooms Katholieke landverhuizers naar de Vereenigde Staten," *Spiegel Historiael* 12 (1977): 681–89; Lucas, *Netherlanders in America*, 213–25, 444–59; Van Hinte, *Netherlanders in America*, 555–557; Irene Hecht, "Kinship and Migration: The Making of an Oregon Isolate Community," *Journal of Interdisciplinary History* 8 (Summer 1977): 45–67.
27. Family networks in the founding of Little Chute are documented in Yda Schreuder, *Dutch Catholic Immigrant Settlement*, 81–92. For the role of the Dominican Order at Amsterdam in this settlement, see Kelly, *Catholic Immigrant Colonization Projects*, 183–85, 270–72; Frans H. Doppen,

"Theodore J. van den Broek: Missionary and Emigration Leader: The History of the Dutch Catholic Settlement at Little Chute, Wisconsin," *U.S. Catholic Historian* 3 (1983): 202–25; Van Stekelenburg, *Landverhuizing*, 82–110.

28. Lucas, *Netherlanders in America*, 214. See also Van Stekelenburg, *Landverhuizing*, 229–31.
29. Van Hinte, *Netherlanders*, 856–57. The information on St. Joseph's Parish was provided by Dr. Dennis W. Morrow of the Grand Rapids Diocesan Archives.
30. Van Hinte, *Netherlanders in America*, 579.
31. Lucas, *Netherlanders in America*, 459. For details see 492–506.
32. This estimate is derived from Swierenga, *Dutch Households in U.S. Population Censuses*.
33. The religious variable in tables 5.1, 5.2, and 5.3 is determined by classifying each township and city ward in the United States census file by the "primary religious orientation" of its Dutch immigrant population according to one of five categories: Protestant, Catholic, Jewish, mixed, and unknown. The designation is based on several factors. The most reliable is the religion in the Netherlands of all families and individuals in the United States Census that were linked with the Netherlands emigration records. Secondary evidence was the family and given names common in the locality, the presence of ministers or priests, the nationality of marriage partners, occupation, and other social and cultural clues. The tables only include the first two categories, Protestant and Catholic.
34. Olson, *Catholic Immigrants*, 105.
35. Ibid., 113–15, 117, 125.
36. Ibid., 185–193, 203, 215–17. However, as late as the 1960s survey data showed that ethnicity was yet the strongest factor in differential church attendance rates and support for parochial schools among Catholics. See Harold J. Abramson, "Ethnic Diversity Within Catholicism: Comparative Analyses of Contemporary and Historical Religion," *Journal of Social History* 4 (Summer 1971): 354–88, esp. 360–61.
37. William S. Petersen, *Some Factors Influencing Postwar Emigration from the Netherlands* (The Hague: Martinus Nijhoff, 1952), 65–66; Lucas, *Netherlanders in America*, 473.
38. Günther Moltmann, "German Emigration to the United States During the First Half of the Nineteenth Century as a Social Protest Movement," in *Germany and America: Essays on Problems of International Relations and Immigration*, Hans L. Trefousse, ed. (New York: Brooklyn College Press, 1980), 104–36, esp. 126–27; Frederick Luebke, "The Immigrant Condition as a Factor Contributing to the Conservatism of the Lutheran Church —Missouri Synod," *Concordia Historical Institute Quarterly* 38 (April 1965): 19–28; and Jon Gjerde, *From Peasants to Farmers: The Migration from Balestrand, Norway, to the Upper Middle West* (Cambridge: Cambridge University Press, 1985), 157, 160–65.

39. J. J. Mol develops this intriguing line of argument in "Churches and Immigrants (A Sociological Study of the Mutual Effect of Religion and Immigrant Adjustment)," *R.E.M.P. Bulletin.* [Research Group for European Migration Problems] 9 (May 1961): 11–15. Mol (pp. 54–55) also cites S. N. Eisenstadt, *The Absorption of Immigrants* (Glencoe, IL: Free Press, 1955), 217–18, who notes that in the founding of Israel (1945–48) the majority, who were strongly Zionist-oriented immigrants, assimilated more rapidly than the minority of secularists who emigrated for economic reasons. The Zionists readily discarded their former cultural traditions in favor of Zionist ideals and goals.
40. A. J. Barnouw, "Dutch Americans," in Frances J. Brown and Joseph Slabey Roucek, eds., *Our Racial and National Minorities: Their History, Contributions, and Present Problems* (New York: Prentice-Hall, 1937), 143–44. Cf. Mol, "Churches and Immigrants," 11, for whom I am indebted for the Barnouw article.
41. Mol, "Churches and Immigrants," 17.
42. This is also the conclusion of a study of the differential process of assimilation of Dutch Calvinists and Catholics in Canada in the twentieth century. See Joe Graumans, "The Role of Ethno-Religious Organizations in the Assimilation Process of Dutch Christian Reformed and Catholic Immigrants in South Western Ontario" (M.A. thesis, University of Windsor, 1973). Graumans found that "Calvinists build their own Church and Church-related organizational structures in Canada, whereas the Catholics join existing Canadian Catholic organizations" (ii). Unfortunately, Graumans did not investigate intermarriage rates by nativity or ethnicity between the two populations. He did, however, find that 88 percent of the Calvinists and 77 percent of Catholics preferred a marriage partner of the same religion for their children, so we can assume that the Calvinists would marry Dutch Reformed while the Catholics, as a minority group, would be unlikely to do so (71).

CHAPTER 6

Social Factors in the 1857 Dutch Reformed Schism

THE SLAVERY CRISIS in the United States divided almost every major denomination in the middle years of the nineteenth century. But ethnic churches were mainly concentrated in the North, and therefore were relatively unaffected by the slavery debate and Confederate secession.[1] For these hyphenated bodies with their enduring ties to the Old Country, historic theological and cultural conflicts rather than moralistic politics caused most internal dissension. Old World religious disputes and traditions—especially the Free Church movements in the Swiss, Lutheran, Scandinavian, Scottish, and Dutch churches[2]—inevitably affected the American daughter denominations, if for no other reason than that new immigrants constantly arrived, carrying the intellectual controversies along with their cultural baggage. This forced the settlers to choose between two conflicting orientations—the Fatherland with its establishmentarian basis or the adopted land of voluntary denominations to which they were increasingly acculturated.[3] Religious pluralism in America made the choice all the more difficult because of the absence of any governmental restraints on schismatics.[4]

Scholars have explained ecclesiastical divisions from differing perspectives—theological-institutional, economic class conflict, ethnic rivalries, and simple nationalism. Sidney Ahlstrom in his *Religious History of the American People* identifies five major types of ecclesiastical accommodation, based upon Old Country institutional affiliations—nominal secularists, national church loyalists, disciplined or "incipient sectarian" Free Church adherents, and pietistic dissenters.[5] Ahlstrom's categories are helpful but many groups, including the two Dutch Reformed denominations—the Reformed Church in America and the Christian Reformed Church—are not so readily classified. Other scholars have sought to understand church splits as a product of alternative "social bases."[6] They point out that religious and ideological conflicts are primarily rooted in different membership reference groups. For example, Robert Doherty offered a class conflict explanation of the Presbyterian schism of 1837–38 in Philadelphia, in which New School revivalists attracted the rising middle- and upper-class sectors of the populace, while the "disinherited ones" remained faithful to the conservative Old Schoolers.[7]

As a counter to Doherty's economic framework, Ira Harkavy has argued that "ethnicity was the primary cleavage separating the two schools." The New School group, according to Harkavy, consisted of English, Welsh, and New England elements, and the Old Schoolers were Scottish and Scotch-Irish Ulsterites for whom the English Puritans were a negative reference group. "Quite simply," says Harkavy, "each ethnic group's past experience predisposed its members to accept and espouse a certain kind of world view" that led to conflicts over values and life styles.[8] In this framework it is likely that disputes would flare up during periods of accelerated social change and dislocation. The mid-nineteenth century in the Atlantic community was a time of transition from a small-scale rural and commercial economy to a large-scale industrial one. Modernizing forces such as migration to urban centers or long-distance moves overseas, social mobility and dislocations, cultural heterogeneity, and other facets of rapid economic change created a social environment primed for religious conflict and schism.

The reference group approach of Doherty and Harkavy is a useful starting point for analyzing the schism of 1857 among Dutch Calvinists in the United States. Since the Dutch separation involved immigrants from the same ethnic, nationality, and religious background, however, an explanation centering on economic or ethnic group membership is inappropriate. The Dutch Reformed division is more complex and derives from historical cultural and lifestyle differences in the Mother Country that can best be understood in terms of Robert K. Merton's local-cosmopolitan theory.[9] According to this theory, localism and cosmopolitanism are alternate nodal points of reference group orientation and of social interaction. Basically, the local versus extralocal distinction may be conceptualized as a measure of the individual's primary point of orientation toward the world around him: one that fixes identity with reference to one's immediate family and church or to broader impersonal values and perspectives. Stated another way, the local-cosmopolitan concept refers to the alternative symbolic bridges between self and society—bridges constructed either with reference to the world of immediate face-to-face relationships or to the broader world "out there" conveyed through urbanization, mass media, and mass public education. Such a distinction only becomes meaningful in a pluralistic culture where people can choose from the marketplace of worldviews.[10]

In transitional societies such as the Netherlands in the second half of the nineteenth century, the orientational polarity increased between localistic, traditional cultural patterns and cosmopolitan, societal-wide lifestyles and value commitments. As the scale of social integration and differentiation increased, due to the rise of efficient bureaucracies, new waterways and railroads, and a more open economy, individuals had wider reference group options. Traditionalists, however, continued to cling to their limited, personalized "small worlds" of family, village, and parish. Their social location in society was such that local primary groups were determinative in shaping their worldview. Moreover, the economic, social, and religious dislocations in the Netherlands, resulting from the Napoleonic wars (1802–13) and the Belgian War of Independence (1830–39) coupled with the transoceanic migration to the Michigan wilderness of thousands of dissident Dutchmen, created a social environment in which further religious conflict could be expected.

This chapter, then, applies Mertonian theories of social group behavior in an attempt to explain the mid-nineteenth century religious conflict among Dutch Protestant immigrants in the Midwest. The methodology is a comparative statistical analysis of the Old World behavioral traits of a sample of one thousand member families of the Reformed Church in America and one thousand member families who joined the 1857 secessionist group, the Christian Reformed Church. It is argued that a greater proportion of adherents of the Reformed Church in America were cosmopolitan in their geographic and social origins and that the Christian Reformed secessionists hailed from more localistic and traditional regions of the Netherlands.

Religious Antecedents to Emigration

The roots of the Reformed Church in America run deeply into the American past.[11] It was founded in the New Netherlands colony in 1628 under the jurisdiction of the Classis of Amsterdam of the Netherlands Hervormde Kerk. In 1792 in response to the changed political climate of the revolutionary era, it declared ecclesiastical independence from Amsterdam and adopted its first denominational constitution. The denomination numbered 116 churches and 40 ministers in 1791 and was heavily concentrated in New York State and northern New Jersey. During the next fifty years, the Reformed Church became increasingly Americanized and grew steadily, until it totaled 274 churches and 33,000 communicants by 1845.[12] The final Dutch-language service was held in 1844, only two years before the beginning of the great Dutch migration of the nineteenth century. The process of Americanization had been hastened by the Dutch tendency for Anglo-conformity, the affinity of the Reformed religion with the "Puritan legacy," and the very low rate of Dutch immigration in the post-Napoleonic decades. Until the mid-1840s, immigration averaged only 100–200 persons a year. Such a small influx was obviously insufficient to slow the pace of assimilation of the old Dutch.

While the Reformed Church in America was undergoing change, an upheaval occurred in the mother church in the Netherlands that had major repercussions in the United States. In 1834 a largely rural, pietist group, led by a few university professors and their students, separated themselves from the Hervormde Kerk over issues of theological liberalism and church polity.[13] The confessional revolt (known as the *Afscheiding*) spread quickly throughout the countryside among conservative Calvinists, who believed that the leaders of the Hervormde Kerk were indifferent to historic Reformed orthodoxy. The Seceders also rejected King Willem I's structural reorganization of the national Hervormde Kerk in 1816, which had abolished the historic localistic form of church government and replaced it with a centralized structure in which the monarch appointed all key officials. Within a decade the Seceders numbered over forty thousand adherents throughout the Protestant northern and western provinces of the Netherlands.[14]

Dutch authorities at first tried to check the Secession movement by levying stiff fines on dissenting clerics and banning worship services. Some employers refused to hire Seceders. Such harassment created an emigration mentality and when the potato blight struck in 1845 and 1846, entire congregations of Seceders departed en masse for North America. The "Groote Trek" was led by a half-dozen Seceder clergymen, notably Albertus Van Raalte and Hendrik Scholte, who directed many hundreds of their followers to Holland, Michigan, and Pella, Iowa, respectively. Other thousands of Seceders soon followed (Table 6.1). In the years from 1846 through 1850, 80 of every 1,000 Seceders departed the Fatherland, compared to only 4 per 1,000 among Hervormde Kerk adherents.[15] These people had a remarkable impact on the American Reformed community, especially when one considers the fact that they comprised only a minor part (20 percent) of the much larger migration from the Netherlands in the last half of the nineteenth century (see Table 5.1 in Chapter 5).[16]

Migration patterns also differed markedly between Hervormde Kerk and Seceder groups. Fully 60 percent of the Seceders left in the early years before 1857, whereas Hervormde Kerk emigrants departed at a steadier pace over the entire period. The intense and focused migration of the minority Seceders, therefore, gave them a strong presence in the Midwest that was disproportionate to their numbers. Hervormde Kerk emigrants outnumbered Seceders in every year except 1845, 1846, and 1847, which were the peak years of Seceder migration (Table 6.2). In those few years Seceders totaled 57 percent of all overseas emigrants. The year 1847 saw 3,200 Seceders emigrate, or 79 percent of all emigrants.

Geographically, there was little difference in province of origin (Table 6.3). Most of the Reformed emigrants came from the same four provinces—Zeeland, Gelderland, Zuid-Holland, and Groningen. But the Separatist proportion differed. Over one half of the Drenthe emigrants were Separatists, one third from Overijssel and Groningen, one quarter from Friesland and Utrecht, and one fifth from Noord-Holland and Gelderland. Economically about two thirds of both groups were middle class, but the Seceders boasted more well-to-do and the Hervormde Kerk emigrants had proportionally more poor people (Table 6.4). The religious persecution had obviously not driven all Seceders into poverty. In short, the Dutch migration was a rural, family movement of farmers, workmen, and day laborers, led by a few professionals, merchants, and skilled craftsmen. It was not unlike the contemporary outflow from the other northern European nations.

Union and Separation

Once settled in the United States, the Dutch emigrants staked out a tangled religious path. The key ecclesiastical events were the union of 1850 with the Reformed Church in America and the separation of 1857.[17] Initially in 1848, the Dutch Seceder congregations in western Michigan led by Van Raalte had created an independent church organization, known as Classis Holland, but within two years the Classis merged with the Reformed Church in America, centered in New York and New Jersey. This union of 1850 was a natural outgrowth of strengthening ties that developed even prior to emigration between the Seceder leaders and the old

TABLE 6.1 Separatist Emigrants by Denomination, 1835–80

YEAR	CHRISTELIJK AFSCHEIDING	GEREFORMEERD*	HERVORMD AFSCHEIDING	CHRISTELIJK GEREFORMEERD	TOTAL
1835		6			6
1836		3			3
1837		1			1
1838		—			—
1839		5			5
1840		—			—
1841		7			7
1842		5			5
1843	2	5			5
1844	15	50			65
1845	56	160			216
1846	341	605	11		957
1847	1,899	1,318	—	6	3,223
1848	499	188	92		779
1849	583	108			691
1850	42	28	7		77
1851	88	26	4		118
1852	57	3	—		60
1853	105	—	47		152
1854	250	24	128		402
1855	254	—	88		342
1856	251	—	60		311
1857	84	43	15		142
1858	28	—			28
1859	11	—			11
1860	9	—			9
1861	30	7			37
1862	21	—			21
1863	8	—			8
1864	46	—			46
1865	167	—			167
1866	271	2			273
1867	793	34			827
1868	488	—			488
1869	459	—		46	505
1870	142	3		46	191
1871	44	35		200	279
1872	65	14		463	542
1873	93			543	636
1874	79			49	128
1875	32			20	52
1876	1			21	22
1877	5			5	10
1878	—			7	7
1879	—			61	61
1880	—	31		608	639
1835–80	7,318	2,711	452	2,075	12,556

* Includes 5 Waals and English Gereformeerd, 31 Gereformeerd under het Kruis (1880).
In the years 1876–80 the data are incomplete.
SOURCE: Robert P. Swierenga, comp., *Dutch Emigrants to the United States, South Africa, South America, and Southeast Asia, 1835–1880: An Alphabetical Listing by Household Heads and Independent Persons* (Wilmington Del. Scholarly Resources, 1983); augmented for the years 1831–47 with data from the Department of Binnenlandsche Zaken report in "Staat van landverhuizers 1831–1847," *Nederlandsche Staatscourant*, 5 September 1848, 2.

TABLE 6.2 Emigration by Year, Hervormde Kerk and Separatist, 1835–57

	Hervormde Kerk*		Separatist†		Total
Year	Number	%	Number	%	Number
1835–44	152	61	99	39	251
1845	210	49	216	51	426
1846	349	27	957	73	1,306
1847	835	21	3,223	79	4,058
1848	837	52	779	48	1,616
1849	1,006	59	691	41	1,697
1850	333	81	77	19	410
1851	565	83	118	17	683
1852	764	93	60	7	824
1853	801	84	152	16	953
1854	2,457	86	402	14	2,859
1855	1,376	80	342	20	1,718
1856	1,300	81	311	19	1,611
1857	1,191	89	142	11	1,333
Totals	12,176	62	7,569	38	19,745

* Includes Nederduits Hervormd 285, Presbyterian Hervormd 3, Waals Hervormd 13, and English Hervormd 4.

† Includes Christelijk Afgescheiden 4,526, Gereformeerde 2,580, Hervormde Afgescheiden 452, Christelijk Gereformeerd 6, Waals Gereformeerd 4, and English Gereformeerd 1.

Source: Robert P. Swierenga, comp., *Dutch Emigrants to the United States, South Africa, South America, and Southeast Asia, 1835–1880: An Alphabetical Listing by Household Heads and Independent Persons* (Wilmington DE: Scholarly Resources, 1983); augmented for the years 1831–47 with data from the Department of Binnenlandsche Zaken report in "Staat van landverhuizers 1831–1847," *Nederlandsche Staatscourant*, 5 September 1848, 2.

colonial Dutch.[18] Most important was the assistance that the old Dutch gave the immigrants who arrived at New York harbor. They met the newcomers at customs; provided temporary lodging; gave food, clothing, and money to the destitute; and even loaned several thousand dollars to purchase land. Needless to say, these acts of kindness engendered much goodwill among the first contingents of Dutch dissenters during their "time of troubles."

But all was not harmonious, especially among some of the Michigan colonists. Their tradition of separatism and suspicion of autocratic synods made them wary, as did the syncretistic nature of the host culture. Within two years of the 1850 merger, one cleric and two thirds of his congregation in the settlement of Drenthe, Michigan, seceded from Classis Holland.[19] The subsequent arrival of new colonists further complicated the situation. Those who came directly from the Netherlands, such as the congregation of Dominie Koene Vanden Bosch in 1856, could not appreciate the crucial help from the East in the early days. Vanden Bosch decried the Seceders' union with the Reformed Church in America as "a welcoming of the Assyrian and begging bread of the Egyptians."[20] Other emigrants who had temporarily remained in the East among Reformed communities brought reports of purported "irregularities" in the churches. For example, some ministers and elders held membership in "secret societies" (masonic lodges), churches practiced "open"

TABLE 6.3 Emigration by Religion by Province, 1835–80

PROVINCE	NH		SE		RC		NI		OP		TOTAL.*
	NUMBER	%	NUMBER	%	NUMBER	%	NUMBER	%	NUMBER	%	NUMBER
DR	436	29	885	58	192	13	1	0	18	1	1,532
	(1)		(7)		(2)		(0)		(1)		(2)
FR	2,526	66	953	25	156	418		—	194	5	3,847
	(7)		(8)		(1)		(3)		(12)		(6)
GE	7,736	62	2,136	17	2,478	20	20	—	88	1	12,458
	(21)		(19)		(23)		(3)		(5)		(20)
GR	5,048	58	2,998	34	527	6	40	—	86	1	8,699
	(14)		(26)		(5)		(7)		(5)		(14)
LI	23	1	1	1	1,891	98	4	—	8	—	1,927
	(0)		(0)		(18)		(1)		(0)		(3)
NB	327	10	152	5	2,708	85	2	—	8	—	3,197
	(1)		(1)		(25)		(0)		(0)		(5)
NH	2,017	46	574	13	588	13	393	9	837	19	4,409
	(5)		(5)		(5)		(68)		(51)		(7)
OV	1,137	39	1,094	37	581	20	14	—	94	3	2,920
	(3)		(10)		(5)		(2)		(6)		(5)
UT	660	56	283	24	134	11	5	—	87	7	1,169
	(2)		(2)		(1)		(0)		(5)		(2)
ZE	11,490	80	1,491	10	1,41	9	2	—	58	—	14,282
	(31)		(13)		(12)		(0)		(4)		(23)
ZH	6,201	82	826	11	251	3	81	1	165	2	7,524
	(16)		(7)		(2)		(14)		(10)		(12)

Legend: NH Nederlands Hervormd; SE Separatist; RC Rooms Katholiek, NI Nederlands Israelite, OP Other Protestant

* Excludes 608 missing, 26 none, and 1 Moslem. Data incomplete in years 1831–47, primarily of Separatists and Catholics.

SOURCE: Robert P. Swierenga, comp., *Dutch Emigrants to the United States, South Africa, South America, and Southeast Asia, 1835–1880: An Alphabetical Listing by Household Heads and Independent Persons* (Wilmington, DE. Scholarly Resources, 1983).

TABLE 6.4 Religious Affiliation by Social Class, 1835–80

RELIGIOUS GROUPS	DUTCH SOCIAL CLASS					
	WELL-TO-DO		MIDDLING		POOR	
	NUMBER	%	NUMBER	%	NUMBER	%
Hervormde Kerk	1,416	11	8,107	64	3,085	25
1834 Separatist	382	14	1,902	69	468	17
Roman Catholic	556	14	2,666	67	751	19
Jewish	27	10	164	61	78	29

SOURCE: Robert P. Swierenga, comp., *Dutch Emigrants to the United States, South Africa, South America, and Southeast Asia, 1835–1880: An Alphabetical Listing by Household Heads and Independent Persons* (Wilmington Del. Scholarly Resources, 1983); augmented for the years 1831–47 with data from the Department of Binnenlandsche Zaken report in "Staat van landverhuizers 1831–1847," *Nederlandsche Staatscourant*, 5 September 1848, 2.

(e.g. unregulated) communion, used choirs in worship services, and sang "man-made" hymns rather than psalms; one elder's nine children were not baptized; some ministers rejected the doctrine of election, and so forth. A layman, Gysbert Haan, was one of those who lived for a time in Albany and Rochester and then in 1850 resettled in western Michigan where he related the objectionable practices he had observed or learned from others. More than any other individual, Haan's polemics "fed the fires of discontent."[21]

The end result of the constant vexation was yet another secession and the creation of the True Dutch Reformed (later Christian Reformed) Church. Four congregations decided by majority vote to withdraw from the Reformed Church in America and "return" to an independent status. A fifth church joined them shortly. Altogether, the 1857 Secession involved 250 communicant members, or 10 percent of the membership of Classis Holland.[22]

When the dissenting churches formally organized a new denomination later in 1857, Koene Vanden Bosch was the only ordained minister among the five charter congregations. The remainder were led by lay elders. Vanden Bosch remained the sole cleric of the Christian Reformed Church for its first six years. So difficult were these early years that in 1863 the leaders seriously considered disbanding.[23] But primarily through effective lay leadership, the struggling Seceders survived, and after the Civil War when the flow of Dutch immigrants resumed, dissenting congregations sprang up throughout the Midwest and even in the East.

There were also continuing defections from the Reformed Church in America. By 1880 the new denomination had 12,300 baptized and communicant members. In virtually every Dutch Protestant settlement, one could find church buildings of both denominations existing side by side or facing each other across Main Street. In the thirty years from 1873 to 1900, the Christian Reformed Church grew 800-fold, compared to a 100-fold increase in the immigrant congregations of the Reformed Church of America (Table 6.5).

Who Seceded and Why

The causes of the 1857 schism are historical, theological, cultural, and idiosyncratic. They have been much debated and there is little need to rehearse them. Rather than asking the "why" question, it seems useful to pose a prior question: *which* Dutch Calvinist immigrants living in southwestern Michigan took part in the schism in 1857? Were the Seceders of 1857 a remnant of the Free Church movement in the Netherlands stemming from the 1834 Secession? Knowing who seceded may explain some of the dynamics of the movement at its inception and enhance our understanding of Dutch religious culture at mid-century.

Scholars have suggested several common socioeconomic characteristics of the 1857 Seceders. The Netherlands historian, Jacob van Hinte, who wrote the first scholarly history of the Dutch in America (1928), contended that many had not been part of the initial 1846–47 contingent that had endured hardship together and learned to appreciate help from their Dutch-American brethren in the East.[24]

TABLE 6.5 Reformed and Christian Reformed Church Growth Rates, 1873–99

DENOMINATION	1873–1875	1875–1881	1881–1884	1884–1887	1887–1890	1890–1893	1893–1896	1896–1899
Reformed*								
Periodic rate	3	4	3	6	2	10	7	4
Cumulative rate	3	7	10	17	19	31	40	45
Reformed (immigrant classes only)†								
Periodic rate	18	3	3	20	14	14	6	2
Cumulative rate	18	22	25	50	70	94	106	111
Christian Reformed‡								
Periodic rate	41	52	66	31	28	28	11	9
Cumulative rate	41	116	257	367	496	664	748	831

* Based on number of families, communicant and noncommunicant.
† Includes Wisconsin, Grand River, Holland, Illinois, Iowa, and Dakota Classes.
‡ Based on number of souls, communicants and baptized members, including children.
SOURCE: Reformed Church in America Acts and Proceedings, 1873–99; Christian Reformed Church *Jaarboeken*, 1875, 1881–99; *De Wachter*, 19 September 1973.

Van Hinte is undoubtedly correct. Only 52 (22 percent) of the 242 known charter members of the Christian Reformed Church can be found among the 1846–47 group of colonists. Sixty-four others emigrated in 1848 and 1849. However, the fact that the colony's population increased from 1,700 in 1847 to 6,000 in 1857 indicates that not only the dissenters, but many settlers had not experienced the early struggles.

A more complex theory is that of Henry Beets, the first historian of the Christian Reformed Church. Beets reported that "it was said in the Netherlands at the time that Groningers went to the seceders [Christian Reformed Church] while the Frisians, Zeelanders, Overiselers, and Hollanders [Noord- and Zuid-Holland] went to the Reformed Church."[25] Van Hinte adds a variation to this provincial scheme by insisting that the Seceders of 1857 were, in the main, members of the rural and conservative Northern party in the Netherlands, whereas the more broad-minded Southern party of Van Raalte remained with the Reformed Church in the East. Van Hinte also asserts that the Christian Reformed founders in western Michigan were poorer and were largely city dwellers, that is, from Grand Rapids.[26] To this latter point there was disagreement from sociologist Henry Ryskamp, who contended that over half of the seceding families in the Grand Rapids area lived in the country, not in the city, and that the "urban-rural distribution of the Reformed Church, if not at that time, after 1857 was about the same as that of the Seceding Church."[27]

The ideas of Beets and Van Hinte can be clarified by comparing American church membership lists with the Dutch emigration lists, which tell for each family the place of last residence, occupation, social class, denominational affiliation, and year of departure. By comparing available church records against emigration lists,

I have assembled a background profile of 2,329 Dutch immigrant family heads and single adults (8,716 persons) in the years through 1880. Of these, 1,177 family heads and singles belonged to immigrant congregations of the RCA and 1,152 were affiliated with the Christian Reformed Church. This is a sufficient sample for a comparative analysis of the membership of the two denominations, although it is not without some deficiencies, because Dutch emigration lists are incomplete before 1848.[28] Since the 1857 secession is the key event in the history of the Reformed churches in America, I will focus especially on that seminal period. The pre-1857 group in the sample totals 1,048 heads of households and single adults, 723 (69 percent) in the Reformed Church in America and 325 (31 percent) in the Christian Reformed Church.

The major questions are: Who seceded in 1857 and who did not? Were Seceders any different from non-Seceders? Did they vary in religious, social, and economic backgrounds in the Old Country? If so, which characteristics are significant and which are not?

The results are as follows. First, 31 percent (176) of 565 Seceders of 1834 in Michigan seceded again in 1857 (Table 6.6). Another 34 (6 percent) joined the Christian Reformed Church in the years following. If "the word *secession* rang like a 'magic word' in their ears and minds," as Van Hinte believed, it is remarkable that only one third were twice seceders.[29] More than two thirds (69 percent) of the Netherlandic Seceders remained with Van Raalte and accepted union with the Reformed Church in America. Thus, Classis Holland was more of an Afscheiding stronghold than was the upstart church. Nevertheless, the defection of this large minority testifies to the independent spirit and antisynodical feelings that characterized the 1834 Seceders.

TABLE 6.6 Netherlands and U.S. Denominational Affiliation Compared, Pre- and Post-1857 Immigrants, Household Heads and Single Adults

	1835–56				1857–80			
Netherlands Affiliation	Reformed		Christian Reformed*		Reformed		Christian Reformed	
	Number	%	Number	%	Number	%	Number	%
Hervormde Kerk	334 46%	69	149 46%	31	348 80%	44	436 61%	56
1843 Separatist	389 54%	69	176 54%	31	86 20%	23	281 39%	77

* Excludes 58 Hervormde Kerk members and 34, 1834 Separatists who affiliated after 1856.

SOURCE: Robert P. Swierenga, comp., *Dutch Emigrants to the United States, South Africa, South America, and Southeast Asia, 1835–1880: An Alphabetical Listing by Household Heads and Independent Persons* (Wilmington DE: Scholarly Resources, 1983); augmented for the years 1831–47 with data from the Department of Binnenlandsche Zaken report in "Staat van landverhuizers 1831–1847," *Nederlandsche Staatscourant*, No. 210, 5 September 1848, 2. Church membership lists were compiled from archival records and anniversary booklets in the Calvin College Archives; The Joint Archives, Hope College; Herrick Public Library, Holland; Western Theological Seminary, Holland; and New Brunswick Theological Seminary, New Jersey. Church membership lists are extant for fewer than a dozen congregations prior to 1870.

Second, the 483 Hervormde immigrants divided in exactly the same proportion as did the Afgescheidenen—31 percent joined the Christian Reformed Church and 69 percent remained with the Reformed Church in America (Table 6.6). Thus, the rival American churches had the same proportional membership composition in terms of Netherlands denominational background. Of 723 members of Classis Holland, 46 percent were Hervormden and 54 percent were Afgescheidenen. Of 325 members of the infant Christian Reformed Church in 1857, the proportions were also 46 percent Hervormden and 54 percent Afgescheidenen. There is no statistical correlation between religious affiliation before and after migration, and the Afgescheidenen of 1834 were no more inclined to secede again in 1857 than were the Hervormden. Religious affiliation in the Netherlands, per se, has no predictive value whatever in these early years in indicating which Dutch Reformed denomination the immigrants would join.

Third, 46 percent of the pre-1857 immigrants in both Michigan Dutch Reformed classes belonged to the Hervormde Kerk. That nearly one half of the members of Classis Holland were Hervormden is a fact often overlooked and seldom acknowledged. It is assumed that because the dominies were all Afgescheidenen, and they came with large contingents of their congregations, that therefore the churches were comprised almost entirely of the same people. This was the case the first year or two, but quickly changed with continuing immigration.

Even more remarkable is the fact that nearly one half of the charter members of the Christian Reformed Church in 1857 were Hervormden. It is assumed that the infant CRCNA was the church of the "true brothers," the twice-seceders. So how is it that 149 (46 percent) of the founding families and singles were Hervormden? Who were these Hervormden seceders? Their places of origin were widely scattered. No municipality contributed more than five families except Staphorst with nineteen, but two-thirds came from the provinces of Overijssel, Zeeland, and Zuid-Holland. Nearly three-quarters emigrated between 1850 and 1856 and were not part of the initial Afscheiding migration. Economic reasons prompted their leaving; none stated religious reasons, as did many Afgescheidenen. The Grand Rapids congregation had the highest number (42), followed by Graafschap (26) and Drenthe (23).

A possible explanation for the large number of Hervormde Kerk immigrants joining the 1857 secession in America is that they were secret sympathizers of the Afscheiding who lacked the courage or opportunity to defect in the home villages. To be a Seceder meant opening oneself to rejection by family, ostracism by the community, and economic boycotts and blacklists. In America, there was much less social stigma in identifying with the Christian Reformed Church. Other Hervormden may have chosen this body because it was less Americanized and therefore more comfortably Dutch. Some had little choice. In the homeland they may have lived in villages with no Afscheiding church. Or as immigrants they settled in places such as Grand Rapids, Graafschap, and Drenthe, which had no viable Reformed Church nearby once the majority decided to secede. Perhaps some Hervormd members simply "went along to get along."

The members of the rival American churches also had similar socioeconomic backgrounds, but the Reformed Church in America had more of *de fijnen* (Table 6.7). Local government officials in the Netherlands classified each departing family economically into three categories: well-to-do, middling, and needy. Before 1857 about two thirds of members of both churches were of middling status; after 1857 the percentages increased to three quarters, with the Christian Reformed Church exceeding the Reformed Church by about 5 points. The Reformed Church had more well-to-do members, 16 percent compared to 12 percent before 1857. The gap widened thereafter and the Reformed Church had twice as many wealthy as did the Christian Reformed Church (13 to 7 percent). The proportion of poor was the same in both churches, between 17 and 20 percent. Also, their general wealth holdings were similar; nearly the same proportion (42 and 40 percent) of pre-1857 immigrants in both denominations owned sufficient property in the Netherlands to be subject to municipal income taxes (Table 6.8). Occupationally, the Christian Reformed Church included a slightly higher proportion of farmers and day laborers and fewer professional and business people than did the Reformed Church, but the differences were fewer than 10 percentage points (Table 6.9). In age and family characteristics, the immigrant households in both denominations were virtually identical.[30]

Place of origin, which is a proxy for historic cultural and religious differences, reveals some contrasts. As Table 6.10 and Figure 6.1 show, Christian Reformed Church members before 1857 came mainly from the provinces of Zeeland (25 percent), Overijssel (15 percent), Zuid-Holland (14 percent), Drenthe (12 percent), and Groningen (11 percent). RCA families came largely from: Zeeland (23 percent), Gelderland (18 percent), Zuid-Holland (15 percent), Groningen (12 percent), and Overijssel (10 percent). The Christian Reformed Church had

Table 6.7 Netherlands Social Classes by U.S. Denominational Affiliation, Pre- and Post-1857 Immigrants, Household Heads and Single Adults

	1835–56				1857–80			
	U.S. Denomination*				U.S. Denomination			
	Reformed		Christian Reformed		Reformed		Christian Reformed	
Socioeconomic Class	Number	%	Number	%	Number	%	Number	%
Well-to-do	101	16	50	12	56	13	54	7
Middling	409	64	277	68	311	70	540	74
Poor	129	20	74	19	74	17	132	18

* Totals include those affiliating after 1857.

Source: Robert P. Swierenga, comp., *Dutch Emigrants to the United States, South Africa, South America, and Southeast Asia, 1835–1880: An Alphabetical Listing by Household Heads and Independent Persons* (Wilmington DE: Scholarly Resources, 1983); augmented for the years 1831–47 with data from the Department of Binnenlandsche Zaken report in "Staat van landverhuizers 1831–1847," *Nederlandsche Staatscourant*, No. 210, 5 September 1848, 2. Church membership lists were compiled from archival records and anniversary booklets in the Calvin College Archives; The Joint Archives, Hope College; Herrick Public Library, Holland; Western Theological Seminary, Holland; and New Brunswick Theological Seminary, New Jersey. Church membership lists are extant for fewer than a dozen congregations prior to 1870.

TABLE 6.8 Netherlands Income Tax Assessment by U.S. Denominational Affiliation, Pre- and Post-1857 Immigrants, Household Heads and Single Adults

	1835–56				1857–80			
	Reformed		Christian Reformed		Reformed		Christian Reformed	
Income Tax Assessment	Number	%	Number	%	Number	%	Number	%
Yes	274	42	151	40	115	26	184	29
No	385	58	226	60	319	74	455	71

SOURCE: Robert P. Swierenga, comp., *Dutch Emigrants to the United States, South Africa, South America, and Southeast Asia, 1835–1880: An Alphabetical Listing by Household Heads and Independent Persons* (Wilmington DE: Scholarly Resources, 1983); augmented for the years 1831–47 with data from the Department of Binnenlandsche Zaken report in "Staat van landverhuizers 1831–1847," *Nederlandsche Staatscourant*, No. 210, 5 September 1848, 2. Church membership lists were compiled from archival records and anniversary booklets in the Calvin College Archives; The Joint Archives, Hope College; Herrick Public Library, Holland; Western Theological Seminary, Holland; and New Brunswick Theological Seminary, New Jersey. Church membership lists are extant for fewer than a dozen congregations prior to 1870.

TABLE 6.9 Netherlands Occupational Classification by U.S. Denominational Affiliation, Pre- and Post-1857 Immigrants, Household Heads and Single Adults

	1835–56				1857–80			
	Reformed		Christian Reformed		Reformed		Christian Reformed	
Occupational Classification	Number	%	Number	%	Number	%	Number	%
White Collar/ Professional	18	3	5	1	6	1	12	2
Manager/broker	37	6	17	4	18	4	29	4
Farmer	148	22	103	26	74	17	89	13
Skilled Worker	181	27	88	22	87	20	121	17
Unskilled & Farm Laborer	280	42	185	46	247	57	456	64
Totals	664	99	398	99	432	99	707	100

SOURCE: Robert P. Swierenga, comp., *Dutch Emigrants to the United States, South Africa, South America, and Southeast Asia, 1835–1880: An Alphabetical Listing by Household Heads and Independent Persons* (Wilmington Del. Scholarly Resources, 1983); augmented for the years 1831–47 with data from the Department of Binnenlandsche Zaken report in "Staat van landverhuizers 1831–1847," *Nederlandsche Staatscourant*, no. 210, 5 September 1848, 2. Church membership lists were compiled from archival records and anniversary booklets in the Calvin College Archives; The Joint Archives, Hope College; Herrick Public Library, Holland; Western Theological Seminary, Holland; and New Brunswick Theological Seminary, New Jersey. Church membership lists are extant for fewer than a dozen congregations prior to 1870.

proportionally three times as many members from Drenthe as did the Reformed Church, and 50 percent more from Overijssel. In contrast, the Reformed Church had proportionally twice as many from Gelderland. Immigrants from Zeeland, Zuid- and Noord-Holland, Groningen, Friesland, Utrecht, and Noord-Brabant divided equally between both American denominations.

Municipality data give a finer-grained picture, but the geographical source areas of the immigrants are wide and thinly distributed. Municipalities providing 1.5 percent (5) or more Christian Reformed members in the years before 1857 were Coevorden, Emmen, and Smilde (DR); Winterswijk (GE); Leens and Ulrum (GR); Staphorst (OV); Baarland, Borssele, Zaamslag, and Zierikzee (ZE); and Zuid-Beijerland, Hardinxveld, and Strijen (ZH). Municipalities that contributed 1.5 percent (11) or more families to the Reformed Church before 1857 were Beilen (DR); Herwijnen, Vuren, and Winterswijk (GE); Leens and Ulrum (GR); Hellendoorn (OV); and Oudorp (ZH). Leens, Ulrum, Oudorp, and Winterswijk were bases for both American denominations. Staphorst and Leens were the Christian Reformed hotbeds; and Winterswijk, Hellendoorn, and Ulrum were the prime Reformed Church source areas.

Differences by subregion are also evident. In Zeeland, for example, which is composed of three groups of island "fingers" in the Rhine delta, immigrants from the islands closest to Rotterdam (Schouwen-Duiveland-Tholen) were more likely by two-to-one to join the Christian Reformed Church. Among those from the middle island group of Walcheren-Zuid Beveland, the ratio was nearly one-to-one. But among immigrants from Zeeuws-Vlaanderen along the Belgian border, the RCA attracted six families for every four who joined the CRC. Gelderland, which

TABLE 6.10 Netherlands Province of Last Residence by U.S. Denominational Affiliation, Pre- and Post-1857 Immigrants, Household Heads and Single Persons, 1835–80

	1835–56				1857–80			
	Reformed		Christian Reformed*		Reformed		Christian Reformed	
Province	Number	%	Number	%	Number	%	Number	%
Drenthe	33	4	41	12	6	1	56	8
Friesland	68	9	22	7	30	7	65	9
Gelderland	130	18	25	8	104	23	88	12
Groningen	87	12	36	11	107	24	269	37
Noord-Brabant	10	1	9	3	7	2	7	1
Noord-Holland	34	5	14	4	31	7	30	4
Overijssel	77	10	49	15	20	4	39	5
Utrecht	18	2	4	1	3	1	2	0
Zeeland	170	23	82	25	67	15	94	13
Zuid-Holland	109	15	45	14	69	15	78	11
Totals	736	99	327	100	444	99	728	100

* Totals exclude 94 affiliating after 1857.

SOURCE: Robert P. Swierenga, comp., *Dutch Emigrants to the United States, South Africa, South America, and Southeast Asia, 1835–1880: An Alphabetical Listing by Household Heads and Independent Persons* (Wilmington Del. Scholarly Resources, 1983); augmented for the years 1831–47 with data from the Department of Binnenlandsche Zaken report in "Staat van landverhuizers 1831–1847," *Nederlandsche Staatscourant*, No. 210, 5 September 1848, 2. Church membership lists were compiled from archival records and anniversary booklets in the Calvin College Archives; The Joint Archives, Hope College; Herrick Public Library, Holland; Western Theological Seminary, Holland; and New Brunswick Theological Seminary, New Jersey. Church membership lists are extant for fewer than a dozen congregations prior to 1870.

Figure 6.1 Netherlands Regions of Last Residence, U.S. Reformed Church and Christian Reformed Church Members, 1835–80

SOURCE: Swierenga study data.

similarly comprised three distinct regions—the Achterhoek, Veluwe, and Betuwe —the conservative Veluwe area near the Zuiderzee and the very similar neighboring province of Overijssel provided more members for the Christian Reformed Church than did the more liberal Achterhoek area on the German border and the more urban Betuwe region that lay astride the Rhine. Christian Reformed immigrants from Groningen were concentrated in the northernmost region, particularly Ulrum and Leens. Reformed Church immigrants originated in twenty-nine municipalities throughout the province; Christian Reformed members came from sixteen municipalities.

1857–80 Period

In the post-schism period, the pattern changed dramatically and Van Hinte's image of bell-ringing Seceders in the Christian Reformed Church is more to the point. The proportion of 1834 Seceders in both American denominations declined from 54 percent before 1857; the Reformed Church had only 20 percent Seceders and the Christian Reformed Church had 39 percent. More than three quarters (77 percent) of Seceder immigrants in the years 1857–80 joined the Christian Reformed Church, either immediately upon arrival or after affiliating for a time with the Reformed Church in America (Table 6.6). Thus, the proportion of 1834 Seceder immigrants in the Christian Reformed Church was twice as high as in the Reformed Church. But Hervormden comprised the majority in both churches—80 percent in the Reformed Church and 61 percent in the Christian Reformed Church. More than one half (56 percent) of Hervormde immigrants joined the Christian Reformed Church after 1857. The infant church had positioned itself as the ostensible preserver of the Dutch Reformed heritage.

The Seceder influx in the Christian Reformed Church in the twenty-five years after 1857 brought a marked shift northward in its regional roots. Nearly one half originated in the three northern provinces, whereas before 1857 less than one third did so (Table 6.10). If Overijssel and the Gelderse Veluwe are added, the northern Netherlands contingent in the Christian Reformed Church rises to two thirds.

Among immigrant families in the Reformed Church in America, there is also a northward shift after 1857, but the southern and western areas of the Netherlands furnished 40 percent of the members. Thus, the post-1857 migration from the northern Netherlands fixed the unique and enduring character of the Christian Reformed Church that had been presaged by the early immigration.

Conclusion

The Christian Reformed Church became an Afscheiding outpost in America, as Beets, Van Hinte, and Brinks recognized, but it did not begin as one. In 1857 the junior denomination was no more or less Afscheiding in membership than was the Reformed Church. And over time, however, the number of Hervormden increased in both churches until they became the majority. Despite the similarities in religious background, the rival bodies did have differing social and geographical bases. The Christian Reformed Church increasingly reflected the orthodox mentality of the northern Netherlands and the piety of northern Zeeland, while the Reformed Church bore the more congenial marks of the eastern and central heartland.[31]

The Michigan Seceders of 1857 thus reflected the traditional, localistic regions of the Netherlands more than did the Reformed Church, and their values and customs remained strong for a longer time. Immigrant members of the Reformed Church in America accommodated themselves theologically, ecclesiastically, and culturally to their new environment, whereas the Christian Reformed Church continued to look to the Mother Country for leadership and direction.[32] Its members had not immigrated to create a new culture but to enjoy a better living within a transplanted community where they could continue life as they had known and valued it in the Old Country. The Seceders of 1857 truly remained an immigrant church until after the First World War. This small denomination, says Ahlstrom, "has become perhaps the countrys most solid and dignified bastion of conservative Reformed doctrine and church discipline."[33]

The schism of 1857 in the American Dutch Reformed churches, then, was largely an expression of Old World regional and cultural differences. Immigrants from localistic communities emphasized traditional values and lifestyles and resisted assimilation in America. Immigrants with more cosmopolitan origins disliked religious isolation and preferred a church oriented toward the larger American scene. Regionalism emerges as the most salient variable in explaining socio-religious differences among Dutch immigrant groups. The extent to which similar regional forces affected other ethnoreligious groups appears to be the best starting point in assessing cultural variations in the New World environment.

Notes

For this chapter I wish to acknowledge the assistance of John W Beardslee III, James D. Bratt, Herbert J. Brinks, Elton J. Bruins, Conrad Bult, John Drukker, Ralph Haan, Norman Kansfeld, Harry S. Stout, and Y. C. Spyksma. Needless to add, none bears any responsibility for my interpretation.

1. Sydney E. Ahlstrom, *A Religious History of the American People* (New Haven, 1972), 659–69. Cf. Winthrop S. Hudson, *Religion in America* (New York, 1965), 201–03; William Warren Sweet, *The Story of Religion in America* (New York, 1950), 312–17.
2. D. H. Kromminga, *The Christian Reformed Tradition from the Reformation to the Present* (Grand Rapids, 1943), 88. The Free Churches, following the radical tradition of the Protestant Reformation, rejected the union of church and state (Constantinianism). They are known by Ernst

Troeltsch's term "sectarian Protestantism." See Franklin H. Littell, *The Origins of Sectarian Protestantism: A Study of the Anabaptist View of the Church* (New York, 1964).

3. Ahlstrom, *Religious History*, 751.
4. Sweet, *Story of Religion*, 885. Citing the Evangelical Mission Covenant Church of America, which originated in a lay movement within the Swedish State Church, Sweet says: "The complete religious freedom in the United States helps to account also for other like schisms from transplanted European churches."
5. Ahlstrom, *Religious History*, 752–60.
6. Harry S. Stout and Robert Taylor, "Sociology, Religion, and Historians Revisited: Towards an Historical Sociology of Religion," *Historical Methods Newsletter* 8 (Dec. 1974): 29–38; cf. Robert W. Doherty, "Sociology, Religion, and Historians," ibid. 6 (Sept. 1973): 161–69.
7. Robert W. Doherty, "Social Bases for the Presbyterian Schism of 1837–1838: The Philadelphia Case," *Journal of Social History* 2 (Fall 1968): 69–79.
8. Ira Harkavy, "Reference Group Theory and Advanced Capitalist Societies: The Antebellum Presbyterian Schism in Philadelphia," paper presented to the Social Science History Association meetings, Ann Arbor, 1977, quote p. 14. Cf. Andrew Greeley, *The Denominational Society: A Sociological Approach to Religion in America* (Glenview, IL 1972), 108–26; and H. Richard Niebuhr, *The Social Bases of Denominationalism* (Cleveland, 1957), 106–11.
9. A reference group is any group that serves as a relatively powerful source or continuing basis of significant thoughts and actions. Such a group may have positive or negative orientations toward both membership and nonmembership groups. Robert K. Merton, "Patterns of Influence: Local and Cosmopolitan Influentials," in Merton, *Social Theory and Social Structure* (Glencoe, IL 1949), 387–420. I used Samuel P. Hays's adaptation of Merton's typology in "Political Parties and the Community-Society Continuum," in William Nisbet Chambers and Walter Dean Burnham eds., *The American Party Systems: Stages of Political Development* (New York, 1967), 151–86, esp. 154–55; and W. Clark Roof, "The Local-Cosmopolitan Orientation and Traditional Religious Commitment," *Sociological Analysis* 33 (Spring 1972): 1–15.
10. I am indebted to Harry Stout for helping to clarify this theoretical discussion.
11. See Gerald F. De Jong, *The Dutch in America 1609–1974* (Boston, 1975), chaps. 6, 11.
12. Board of Publication of the Reformed Church in America, *Centennial Discourses: A Series of Sermons Delivered in 1876*… (2d ed., New York, 1877), 530; *Acts and Proceedings of the Reformed Protestant Dutch Church*, 1845, 462; De Jong, *Dutch in America*, 138–47, 259. A quaint early history still useful is David D. Demarest, *History and Characteristics of the Reformed Protestant Dutch Church* (New York, 1856), esp. chaps. 4–5.

13. Gerrit J. tenZythoff, *Sources of the Secession: The Netherlands Hervormde Kerk on the Eve of the Dutch Immigration to the Midwest* (Grand Rapids, MI: Wm. B. Eerdmans, 1987); Lubbertus Oostendorp, *H.P. Scholte: Leader of the Secession of 1834 and Founder of Pella* (Franeker, 1964), Part 1; D. H. Kromminga, *Christian Reformed Tradition*, 79–98; Robert P. Swierenga and Elton J. Bruins, *Family Quarrels in Dutch Reformed Churches in the Nineteenth Century* (Grand Rapids MI: Wm. B. Eerdmans, 1999), "1834—Netherlands Church Secession and the Dutch Emigration," paper presented at Pillar Christian Reformed Church, Holland, Michigan, March 5, 1997.
14. Peter R. D. Stokvis, *De Nederlandse trek naar Amerika, 1846–1847* (Leiden, 1977), 53–55.
15. Figures computed from data on Dutch church affiliation in 1850 in Stokvis, *Nederlandse trek naar Amerika*, Table 6, 54.
16. Lucas estimates that in 1856 there were over 10,000 Seceders in the United States, compared to only 4,000 remaining in the Protestant provinces of the Netherlands. Lucas, *Netherlanders in America: Dutch Immigration to the United States and Canada, 1789–1950* (Ann Arbor: University of Michigan Press, 1955; repr. Grand Rapids: Wm. B. Eerdmans, 1989), 68, 472. That Lucas substantially overestimated the Seceder emigration is confirmed by Table 5.1. Pieter R. D. Stokvis reaches the same conclusion, "The Dutch American Trek, 1846–1847: A Reinterpretation," *Immigration History Newsletter* 8 (Nov. 1976): 4; and Stokvis, *Nederlandse trek naar Amerika*, 36–37.
17. Swierenga and Bruins, *Family Quarrels*; John Kromminga, *The Christian Reformed Church: A Study in Orthodoxy* (Grand Rapids, 1949), 23–39; D. H. Kromminga, *Christian Reformed Tradition*, 98–116; Albert Hyma, *Albertus C. Van Raalte and His Dutch Settlements in the United States* (Grand Rapids, 1947), 193–238; Lucas, *Netherlanders in America*, 506–15; Van Koevering, *Legends of the Dutch: The Story of a Mass Movement of Nineteenth Century Pilgrims* (Zeeland, Mich.: 1960), 487–598; *Minutes Classis Holland 1848–1858* (Grand Rapids, 1950); "Minutes, Christian Reformed Church 1857–1880" (mimeo, Grand Rapids, 1937), Calvin College Archives, Grand Rapids, MI.
18. William O. Van Eyck, *Landmarks of the Reformed Fathers or What Dr. Van Raalte's People Believed* (Grand Rapids, 1923), chap. 25 and passim; Herman D. Praamsma, "The Historical Roots of the Union of 1850," unpublished paper, Heritage Hall Archives, Calvin College; Van Koevering, *Legends of the Dutch*, 506–20.
19. The cleric Roelof Smit affiliated his congregation with the Associate Reformed (formerly Scottish) denomination. Hendrik J. Prakke, *Drenthe in Michigan* (Assen, 1948); Roelof Diephuis, "Reminder of Rev. Roelof Smit and His Life," *Missionary Monthly* 13 (Mar. 1941), typescript translation by Peter H. Bouma in Herrick Library, Holland, Michigan; and four articles in Henry S. Lucas, ed., *Dutch Immigrant Memoirs and Related*

Writings, 2 vols. (Assen, 1955; rev. ed., Grand Rapids, 1997), 1:253–71; *Seventy-fifth Anniversary of the Drenthe Christian Reformed Church 1882–1957*, 7–9, in Calvin College Archives.

20. Centennial Booklet, *Noordeloos Christian Reformed Church, 1857*, 11, in Calvin College Archives.
21. D. H. Kromminga, *Christian Reformed Tradition*, 107–11; John Kromminga, *Christian Reformed Church*, 32–33; Fred E. Velders, "The Reformed Heritage and Historical Background Leading to the Founding of the Christian Reformed Church" (B.D. thesis, California Baptist Theological Seminary, 1953), 64–77. Gysbert Haans account is his *Voice of One Slandered* (1871), typescript English translation by William K. Reinsma, Calvin College Archives; R. John Hager, "Gysbert Haan, A Study in Alienation," *Reformed Journal* 13 (Nov. 1963): 7–10; 13 (Dec. 1963): 12–15; 14 (Jan. 1964): 15–18; Peter Plug, "Gysbert Haan and the Secession of 1857," unpublished manuscript, Calvin College Archives. Forceful apologists for the Reformed Church in America of the events of 1850 and 1857 are Van Eyck, *Landmarks of the Reformed Fathers*; N.W. Dosker, *De Hollandsche Gereformeerde Kerk in Amerika* (Nijmegen, 1888), and Henry E. Dosker, *Levensschets van Dr. A. C. Van Raalte* (Nijkerk, 1893), 240–76.
22. The Christian Reformed Church in 1857 began with 150 families, 250 communicants, and 750 individuals. The Spring Street Church had 50 families; Graafschap 113 communicants; Vriesland 9 families; Noordeloos 18 or 19 members; and Polkton about 20 members. D. H. Kromminga, *Christian Reformed Tradition*, 120; Beets, *Christian Reformed Church*, 71–72; Coopersville Reformed Church, *Nineteenth Anniversary Historical Booklet and Directory, 1854–1944*, 1–2.
23. Henry Zwaanstra, *Reformed Thought and Experience in a New World: A Study of the Christian Reformed Church and Its American Environment, 1890–1918* (Kampen, 1973), 6.
24. Jacob van Hinte, *Netherlanders in America: A Study of Emigration and Settlement in the United States of America in the Nineteenth and Twentieth Centuries*, ed. Robert P Swierenga, Adriaan de Wit, trans. (Grand Rapids: Baker Book House, 1985), 366–60; cf. Henry Ryskamp, "The Dutch in Western Michigan" (Ph.D. diss., University of Michigan, Ann Arbor, 1936), 29–30.
25. Quoted in Ryskamp, "Dutch in Western Michigan," 32. The time period that Beets had in mind is not stated, but he may have intended the years after 1880.
26. Van Hinte, *Nederlanders in America*, 1:391–94.
27. Ryskamp, "Dutch in Western Michigan," 29.
28. An earlier version of this analysis is my article, "Local-Cosmopolitan Theory and Immigrant Religion: The Social Bases of the Antebellum Dutch Reformed Schism," *Journal of Social History* 14 (Fall 1980): 113–35. In the key years of the congregational migration, 1845–1847, 21 percent of the emigrants are not included in the Dutch emigration lists. Van Raalte's

entire Velp-Arnhem congregation of 1834 Seceders is missing from this study sample. The Seceder impact on the Reformed Church in America is thus underestimated.

29. Van Hinte, *Netherlanders in America*, 281.
30. Both averaged 38 years at the time of resettlement and the number of children per family was 3.6 for those affiliating with the Reformed Church and 3.5 for those joining the 1857 Seceder Church. The respective percentages of immigrant "units" or households with a mate was 65 and 72, the percentage of units with children was 61 and 66, and the percentage of male-headed units was 96 and 98.
31. In a behavioral study of Americanization among evangelical and conservative clerical factions in the Dutch and German Reformed churches in late colonial America, Johannes Jacob Mol concluded that different theological orientations rather than behavioral factors accounted for varying rates of assimilation. It is argued here, however, that localism-cosmopolitanism is a surrogate for such theological and religious differences. See Mol, "Theology and Americanization: The Effects of Pietism and Orthodoxy on Adjustment to a New Culture" (Ph.D. diss., Columbia University, 1960).
32. Brinks, "Voices from Our Immigrant Past"; Paul Honigscheim, "Religion and Assimilation of the Dutch in Michigan," *Michigan Historical Magazine* 26 (Winter 1942): 54–66.
33. Ahlstrom, *Religious History*, 755.

CHAPTER 7

Dutch Jewish Immigration and Religious Life

BETWEEN 1800 AND 1880 approximately 6,500 Dutch Jews emigrated to the United States.[1] Although they numbered less than one tenth of all Dutch immigrants and were a mere fraction of all Jews in America in these years, the Dutch helped build American Jewry and did so with a nationalistic flair. It is well known that Dutch Calvinists, and to a lesser extent Catholics, transplanted their communities and churches. So did Dutch Jews. They too emigrated in families, brought special work skills and religious values, and founded Dutch synagogues led by Dutch lay rabbis.[2]

Several facts stand out in the Jewish emigration. The Jews were greatly overrepresented; they made up less than 2 percent of the Dutch population but nearly 10 percent of all emigrants. Second, they were an overwhelmingly urban-to-urban migration in an otherwise mostly rural-to-rural migration. Moreover, Jews were the first Dutch immigrants of the nineteenth century; they began emigrating in substantial numbers during the Napoleonic wars, several decades before the Calvinists and Catholics departed en masse in the 1840s. The Jews were also unique in that many used England as a staging area, while all other Dutch immigrants went directly to the United States. The Tenter Ground in the Spitalfields district of East London was a virtual Dutch Jewish ghetto in the early nineteenth century, formed by decades of cross-Channel business ties and commercial ventures.[3] In London the Dutch Jews learned English, married and began families, and worked in commerce or the crafts. The full extent of Jewish two-stage emigration via England and the rate of intermarriage there is unknown, but in 1850 13 percent of all Dutch Jewish couples in America had English-born spouses, and 5 percent of all Dutch Jewish children were born in England. By 1870 12 percent of the children were English-born, and 10 percent of Dutch Jews had English spouses.[4]

Like their countrymen, Dutch Jews demonstrated the salience of national identity among immigrants and the strong forces for ethnic religious and cultural institutions. In three American cities the Dutch founded Netherlandic synagogues based on the Orthodox Amsterdam rite (*minhag*) as soon as they had sufficient numbers. These were Bnai Israel of New York (1847–c.1902), Bnai Israel of Philadelphia (1852–79), and Beth Eil of Boston (1859–80).

Where they were unable to form an ethnic synagogue, Dutch Jews joined English, German, and Polish congregations, a number of which were led by Dutch-born rabbis. The most famous were Samuel Myer Isaacs of Shaaray Tefila in New York and Jacob Voorsanger of Temple Emanu-El in San Francisco. Even though the primary motive was economic, religious forces shaped the Dutch Jewish immigration and settlement. They migrated within the confines of the synagogue and its life. Most moved from the Amsterdam ghetto on the Old Side of the Amstel River,[5] or from such lesser urban centers as Rotterdam and The Hague, to the Jewish neighborhoods of New York, Philadelphia, Baltimore, Boston, and Chicago. There they purchased cemeteries to bury their dead in consecrated ground, founded charitable and mutual aid societies to fulfill the law of love, and established Hebrew schools to train youth in the faith. Although few letters are known to survive, Jews like other Dutch sent a steady stream of correspondence home urging family and friends to join them. In all this Jews were little different from Calvinists and Catholics.

Like Dutch Catholics, Jews were a small minority within an international religious community that did not value their Dutchness. As a result, they were assimilated into American Judaism more rapidly than the majority of Dutch Protestant immigrants who planted numerous colonies and ethnic churches. The migration behavior of Dutch Jews resembled that of the Catholics more than the Calvinists. Nevertheless, the Jews tried to maintain their Dutchness by living in close proximity, planting Netherlandic synagogues, and marrying fellow Hollanders. As late as 1870 more than half (56 percent) still had Dutch spouses, and several hundred families worshiped in Dutch synagogues led by Dutch-born rabbis. But it was a losing effort. Between 1840 and 1870 Dutch Jewish homogeneity and orthodoxy gave way to the heterogeneity and heterodoxy that characterizes modern American Jewry.[6] In two generations, or at most three, the Dutch, like English, Polish, and even German Jews, lost their national identity and were assimilated into the greater Jewish-American community.

Jewish Migration

Dutch Jews began emigrating during the Napoleonic occupation of the Netherlands, whereas their German and Polish co-religionists did not depart until after Napoleon's defeat and the restored German monarchy abolished liberal reforms. Several factors were involved in the early Dutch exodus.[7] First and primary was the economic damage caused by the war between France and England. Dutch merchants with their long-standing ties to England suffered severely from wartime disruptions in international trade due to the naval blockades and trade embargoes. By 1805 82 percent of Amsterdam Jews were on the public dole, and the wealthier ones found it difficult to fulfill their religious duty to care for the Jewish poor. Migration to England offered a ready alternative to economic ruin and bankruptcy.

Second, before Napoleon's conquest of the Netherlands the House of Orange had granted Dutch Jews full civil rights in the constitution of 1796. Thus, while

German Jews welcomed the French ideals of equality, liberty, and fraternity, Dutch Jews were concerned about *losing* their freedoms. When Napoleon in 1810 annexed the Netherlands to the French empire and placed his brother Louis on the Dutch throne, the Bonapartes imposed a series of intrusive economic, political, and religious "reforms" and created a new centralized bureaucracy. In 1811 all Netherlanders had to register with the authorities and provide such data as name, occupation, rental value of their home, and a list of those residing in their households. This was a prelude to imposing new taxes and quartering French troops in homes. After 1815 the new monarch Willem I implemented a Dutchification program that further increased government demands. This bureaucratization, coupled with economic dislocations, prompted hundreds of Jewish families to leave.

Between 1800 and 1830 about 750 Dutch Jews emigrated to the United States, and an untold number went to England. All but five or six families were Ashkenazi, who comprised nearly 95 percent of the Dutch Jewish population in these years. Sephardi prospered more and had less need to emigrate; those who did were more geographically concentrated than Jews generally. Three fourths of Dutch Jewish immigrants in the United States in 1830 lived in only four cities: New York, Philadelphia, Baltimore, and New Orleans. They comprised 43 percent of the Jewish population in Baltimore and New Orleans, 23 percent in Philadelphia, and 10 percent in New York.[8] By 1850, after the large German-Polish influx, the Dutch made up less than 3 percent of American Jewry, even though their numbers had tripled since 1830. Dutch Jews remained concentrated, four cities accounting for 91 percent of them in 1850, but Boston replaced New Orleans in the top four. In 1860 76 percent of Dutch-American Jews lived in these four East Coast cities, and in 1870, 73 percent (Table 7.1).

Occupational Profile

The occupational profile of the Dutch mirrored that of American Jews generally. Most were self-employed shopkeepers, peddlers, brokers, and traders, but over time the proportion of merchants declined and craftsmen increased, especially in the clothing and tobacco trades. In the early decades more than four fifths were shopkeepers and brokers, but this proportion declined by 1870 to less than one half (Table 7.2), while craftsmen increased from one tenth to one third. Including service and unskilled workers, half the Dutch Jews in 1870 were wage earners. The proportion of professionals was always small, declining from 6 to 3 percent between 1830 and 1870.

The shift in the Dutch Jewish immigrant population over the four decades from shopkeeping and peddling to sweatshop labor reflects broader changes in the Netherlands economy at mid-century, especially the emergence of the cigar and clothing industries. These new consumer industries provided steady, if toilsome, work for the urban working poor, which allowed many to move into the lower middle class in a generation or two.

United States tariff policy stimulated the immigration of Dutch cigarmakers and

TABLE 7.1 Geographical Distribution by City, Dutch Jewish Households: 1850, 1860 and 1870 Censuses

CITY	1850	1860	1870
Albany	14	10	7
Baltimore	103	149	121
Boston	62	269	374
Buffalo	17	20	37
Chicago	0	39	195
Cincinnati	12	74	97
Cleveland	4	27	27
Detroit	0	49	103
Milwaukee	0	20	14
New Orleans	0	98	33
New York (including Brooklyn)	429	835	1,871
Newark	5	40	54
Philadelphia	171	399	406
Pittsburgh	0	0	115
Rochester	0	24	23
San Francisco	0	41	65
St. Louis	13	26	85
Toledo	0	0	34
Troy	0	18	23
Other	8	39	139
TOTALS	838	2,177	3,823

SOURCE: Swierenga, *Dutch Households in U.S. Population Censuses, 1850, 1860, 1870.*

TABLE 7.2 Occupational Groups, Dutch Jews in the United States: 1830, 1850, 1860, 1870 Censuses

OCCUPATIONAL GROUP	1830		1850		1860		1870	
	NUMBER	%	NUMBER	%	NUMBER	%	NUMBER	%
Tradesmen, merchants	52	84	148	63	318	55	527	47
Craftsmen	6	10	64	27	174	30	410	36
Laborers	4	6	10	4	19	3	31	3
Professionals	0	0	12	5	69	12	156	14
TOTALS	62	100	234	99	580	100	1,124	100

SOURCE: Swierenga, *Dutch Households in U.S. Population Censuses, 1850, 1860, 1870*; Rosenwaike, *Edge of Greatness*, 140–54.

diamond craftsmen. In the 1850s Congress gave the developing tobacco industry tariff protection, prompting Dutch cigarmakers from Amsterdam and Rotterdam to shift their operations to New York City, Philadelphia, Boston, and other eastern centers. In no city were cigarmakers as dominant among Dutch Jews as in New York. Between 1850 and 1860 the number of Jewish Hollanders making their living in the cigar sweatshops increased from 10 to 44, and by 1870 there were 136 cigarmakers as well as 21 strippers, tobacconists, and other workers with the weed. In 20 years cigarmakers as a proportion of employed Dutch Jews in New York rose from 7 to 25 percent.[9]

The concentration of lower-class Dutch immigrants in the cigar industry is clearly exemplified in the family of Samuel Gompers, the famed American labor leader and founder of the American Federation of Labor. Gompers is the quintessential Dutch-Ashkenazi Jewish immigrant of the second half of the nineteenth century. The Gompers family had lived in Amsterdam for generations. Samuel's grandfather and namesake, Samuel Moses Gompers, was an import-export merchant who traveled five or six times a year between Amsterdam and London. The Dutch economy at the time was closely tied to that of England, providing mainly foodstuffs in exchange for manufactured goods.[10]

The Gompers family fortunes had shrunk to a level of genteel poverty by the 1840s, and in 1845 Samuel Moses decided to join relatives in the Spitalfields district of London. His oldest son, Solomon, soon married there and took up cigarmaking, as did Solomon's first-born son, Samuel. Young Gompers grew up in the mixed Dutch and English culture of the East End ghetto, speaking a smattering of Dutch at home, learning Hebrew in the Jews Free School, and picking up English on the streets. In 1863, when Samuel was 13 years old, his father decided to migrate to New York, where many friends had gone and where a brother-in-law had settled six months before. The family settled in a little four-room flat in a tenement on Houston Street, among the "Holland Dutchmen," as Samuel put it in his autobiography.[11] Here Samuel and his father resumed cigarmaking. Within ten years, by the mid-1870s, Samuel had became a labor leader who went on to great fame.

While tobacco employed more Dutch, they made the greatest impact on the diamond industry, first in Boston and then New York. For hundreds of years Jewish firms in Amsterdam and London had dominated the international diamond trade. Dutch craftsmen were therefore in a solid position to introduce diamond cutting and polishing into the United States, and they came to dominate the gem trade in the early twentieth century.[12] As in the tobacco industry, Amsterdam diamond houses shifted their operations to America in response to international trade pressures and U.S. protective tariffs. In the 1860s the Dutch diamond industry was depressed, prompting a few cutters and polishers to move to America, where they opened shops first in Boston and Detroit and then primarily in New York. Adam Keizer, an Amsterdam diamond cutter who emigrated in 1853, is reported to have established in Boston in the early 1870s the first diamond cutting and polishing operation in the United States, manned entirely by craftsmen recruited from Amsterdam.

In the 1890s New York supplanted Boston as the diamond center because of its stronger ties to London and Amsterdam importers. When the highly protective

McKinley Tariff of 1890 and Wilson-Gorman Tariff of 1894 imposed prohibitive import taxes on polished or set stones, several Amsterdam firms quickly opened branch factories in New York and offered high wages to Dutch and Belgian craftsmen. By 1894 150 Amsterdam diamond craftsmen had already migrated to New York, and the Dutch came to dominate the industry, which was centered at Nassau Street's jewelry row.

The Dutch diamond workers were slow to assimilate. These elite craftsmen maintained constant contact with the mother country and lived and worked in small enclaves where Dutch was spoken almost exclusively. They were a "typical Dutch colony," says Jacob van Hinte, who held on to their language and customs. They even influenced the American language by introducing the Dutch technical terms of their industry, such as "skive" (adapted from the Dutch *schijf*) for the polishing wheel, *doppen*, a device to hold the diamond on the wheel, and *tangen*, a special pliers. This was not the case in the Grand Rapids furniture industry or the Paterson silk industry, both Dutch dominated.

Religious and Cultural Life

All of the pioneer Jewish congregations in colonial America followed the Sephardic worship ritual, but Ashkenazi immigrants arrived in increasing numbers after the mid-eighteenth century. They outnumbered Sephardi by the early nineteenth century, although the mother synagogues such as Shearith Israel of New York and Mikveh Israel of Philadelphia continued to follow the Sephardic rites.[13]

The early Dutch Jews joined the Sephardic synagogues in New York and Philadelphia, and when the Germans and Poles began seceding in the 1820s and 1830s, most Dutch remained with the mother congregations, which were increasingly dominated by the cultured English Jews. A Dutch minority, however, led in the founding of rival Ashkenazic congregations, such as Bnai Jeshurun (Sons of Israel) and Shaaray Tefila (Gates of Prayer) in New York, Rodeph Shalom (Seekers of Peace) in Philadelphia, and the Baltimore Hebrew Congregation. Indeed, the Dutch provided spiritual leadership for the first Ashkenazic congregations in America until the 1840s, when Germans became dominant everywhere.

No Dutch Jewish cleric in America attained greater prominence in the nineteenth century than Samuel Myer Isaacs (1804–78) of Leeuwarden, who first served Bnai Jeshurun and then Shaaray Tefila in New York. Isaacs father, Meyer, a prominent merchant-banker, fled Holland for the Spitalfields of London in 1814 because he was financially ruined by the French conquest.[14] Meyer Isaacs entered the rabbinate in London and four of his five sons also became rabbis, including Samuel who was young enough to learn to speak English without a Dutch accent. This ability later earned him many speaking engagements in America, where sermons and public addresses in English were much preferred to the customary Yiddish or German tongue.

Samuel attended public school, but as a member of an Orthodox family he also studied Hebrew, the Talmud, and Jewish history in the synagogue school and under the tutelage of his father. After completing his education, Samuel taught Hebrew for a time at the Jewish Orphanage of London and then in the 1830s became principal of a Jewish day school. This position enabled him to become well-connected in the wider Jewish community. He developed a lifelong friendship with the famed Anglo-Jewish banker Sir Moses Montefiore, who shared his devotion to Palestine. Isaacs also became acquainted with Solomon Hirschell, the Chief Rabbi of the Great Synagogue of London, and the leading rabbi in the entire British Empire.

The year 1839 marked the major turning point for the 35-year old Hebrew educator. He was married in the Great Synagogue by Rabbi Hirschell himself, and shortly before this he had decided to emigrate to America with his bride in response to a call from the new Ashkenazic congregation Bnai Jeshurun, an offshoot of Shearith Israel, to be its first preacher and cantor. Isaacs's unique ability to preach in perfect English was a major factor in his appointment, but he also sent splendid recommendations. A few days after his wedding, Isaacs and his new wife, Jane Symmons of London, took their "honeymoon" trip to New York aboard the brig *Emery*, arriving on 10 September 1839, after a lengthy two-month voyage on stormy seas.[15]

Isaacs's title was *hazan* (reader), which signified the chief religious leader, but he was always addressed as rabbi, even though he lacked ordination. American Judaism was not particular about titles in the nineteenth century. As reader (cantor) Isaacs led the services and conducted weddings and funerals. The cantor was recognized by the Gentile community as the "minister" of the congregation. Isaacs introduced regular preaching in the vernacular language, following the model of Protestant ministers, which practice was just entering the synagogue at this time. Isaacs had likely borrowed this innovation from the Great Synagogue of London, which had begun English-language preaching twenty years earlier.[16] This made him very much in demand as a speaker. During his lengthy career he preached sermons in English at the dedication services of 47 synagogues all over the eastern United States and as far west as Chicago.

The Reverend Isaacs ministered at Bnai Jeshurun for five years until a schism in 1844 rent the congregation due to ethnic rivalries. Isaacs and at least twelve other Dutch Jewish families, in addition to a number of English families, withdrew from the increasingly German synagogue, and formed a new congregation, Shaaray Tefila, which he led successfully for thirty-three years.[17] Such splintering over Old World nationality differences was endemic in America among both Jews and Christians. By 1860 New York had 27 synagogues and each nationality or subregional group worshiped according to their customary ritual.

From the outset the Dutch *hazan* promoted Orthodoxy against the rising wave of Reform Judaism which, he lamented, came "from the fertile fields of Germany, where everything grows fast, although not always wholesome." What is at issue, he warned, is that Jews are "assimilating our system to that of Christianity. . . . Shame on those Rabbis who have A.D. in their thoughts." Among other worship practices, Reform Judaism introduced mixed choirs and instrumental music, integrated seating, conducted prayers in English, abolished head coverings, and called men up to the Torah, and confirmed young women as well as young men. Reform congregations also were lax in enforcing religious discipline. In 1857 Isaacs founded and edited for two decades one of the first English-language Jewish periodicals, *The Jewish Messenger*, as a publication to defend Orthodoxy against Reform and to promote Jewish charities, day schools, orphan asylums, and the creation of a national board to present a united front for American Jewry.[18]

Isaacs also led a movement to enforce Sabbath observance and to exclude nonobserving Jews from synagogue membership, but the majority of his congregation favored benign tolerance and he had to refrain. Honoring the Sabbath was difficult for Jewish retail merchants because Saturday was the major American shopping day, and state and local Sunday-closing laws often kept Jewish businesses closed on that day as well, until they won legal exemptions.[19] Isaacs lamented: "In the days of yore, violators were ... publicly stoned to death, ... but now we court their society, give them the first honors in the synagogue, [and] call them up to hear the law recited which anathematizes the Sabbath-violator.... We behold the hands of sacrilege destroying the ten commandments." There is no place, he thundered, for a "doctrine of the *minimum* God, the *maximum* man." Taking a cue from abolitionist polemical writers, Reverend Isaacs expressed his views in a powerful essay, "The Synagogue As It Was, As It Is, As It Should Be."[20] Historian Hyman Grinstein observed that Isaacs was "without doubt the most ardent exponent of Sabbath observance in New York City prior to the Civil War."[21]

Isaacs's larger goal was to safeguard the rank and file of American Jewry from Reform. "My object is ... to prove, from facts, that our system of worship, apart from its *temporalities*, is the best of all systems; and to adduce evidence that adding or diminishing, abrogating, or altering our form of prayers, handed down to us from the Men of the Great Synod,... at the will or caprice of men, who, however well-intentioned, are yet tinctured with the spirit of the age and are not capable of judging correctly or dispassionately—that reforms so instituted—will lead to inevitable ruin in our polity, and tend to unfetter the chain by which we have ever been riveted in union and in love...."[22] Clarion calls such as this put Isaacs at the forefront of the defense of Orthodoxy in New York and throughout the country. Like the clerics of the Dutch Calvinist midwestern colonies, Rabbi Isaacs was a fiery champion of the old ways in religion.

Shaaray Tefila prospered under Rabbi Isaacs. While the liturgy, ritual, and physical arrangement of seating all conformed to the requirements of Orthodoxy, worship services were tempered by such "Protestantizing" practices as regular preaching from English-language Scriptures. Also, Isaacs's expanded role as reader of the congregation was more akin to an Episcopal priest than a traditional cantor. The appreciative congregation increased their rabbi's salary regularly from $1,200 in 1845 to $3,500 by the end of his tenure in the 1870s.

In the 1860s the uptown movement of Jews directly affected the synagogue. Orthodox Jews who lived uptown would not ride on the Sabbath, so they transferred to nearby synagogues. In the face of declining membership and a growing indebtedness, Shaaray Tefila in 1869 was forced to relocate uptown. Barnett L. Solomon, another Hollander, was president during this relocation. Because of the "flourishing condition" of the congregation, their hazan's workload was so heavy that the trustees in 1865 hired an assistant "to conduct the service according to the ancient liturgy with the accepted tunes, leaving the duties of Preacher more especially to the veteran of the New York pulpit."[23]

Besides preaching and writing, Isaacs helped transform unorganized New York Jewry into a more coherent, articulate, and respectable community. But it was a splintering community with a growing secularization among the young. Isaacs recognized the problem and a few years before his death, in hopes of saving historic Judaism, he reluctantly agreed to support a radical plan proposed by another Orthodox rabbi to prepare a liberalized and simplified Ashkenazic worship rite (*minhag*) acceptable to all American synagogues. The time for nationality synagogues with distinctive rites had passed, Isaacs declared: "Portuguese and German, Polish and Hollander, in connection with the manner of worshipping Israel's God, are names that should, long ere this, have been erased from our nomenclature.... The badge we all should have proudly worn is that of 'American Jews'; ... signifying that the circumstances which had given origin to marked differences in ritual had ceased to exist, and that the necessity for reconstructing another, perfectly uniform, and more conformable to our changed condition, had arrived."[24] But the plan was stillborn; it pleased neither the Orthodox nor the Reform advocates.

In addition to his ministerial and journalistic work, Isaacs promoted the customary Jewish tenets of charity, Palestinian relief, and religious education. His motto was "not to touch the worship, but to improve the worshippers." Editorials in the *Messenger* advocated the founding of Hebrew orphanages by harping on the disgraceful case of a Jewish orphan placed in a Christian institution and converted there, all because no Jewish asylum existed. The Hebrew Benevolent Society of New York was smitten by this charge and established the Hebrew Orphan Asylum in 1859. Subsequently, Isaacs worked assiduously to combine all Jewish charities in the city by organizing the United Hebrew Charities in 1873. He also helped establish Mount Sinai Hospital in 1852 and served as its first vice-president.[25]

Internationally, Isaacs crusaded for Palestinian relief and as early as 1849 he began long-term fund raising efforts. In 1853 he became treasurer of the North American Relief Society for Indigent Jews in Palestine, a position he held for many years. When news came of a massive famine in Palestine in 1853–54, Isaacs was the "first to take action; the other ministers followed his lead." He mounted the first national campaign in the United States for the relief of Jews overseas. Rabbi Isaacs's exceptional efforts earned him the accolade of "champion of charitable institutions."[26]

Isaacs also promoted Jewish education, decrying the fact that Jewish children sat under Gentile teachers in the public schools. In 1842 he converted his congregation's afternoon school into an all-day English and Hebrew school, called the New York Talmud Torah and Hebrew Institute, with the Dutch-born Henry Goldsmith as teacher of Hebrew. It was the predecessor of the Hebrew Free School that flourished for many decades. Isaacs also began a Hebrew high school and taught Hebrew there himself.[27] The Dutch rabbi particularly decried the lack of Hebrew seminaries and colleges to provide educated leaders: "Jewish children are hungering for religious food ... and there is none to supply the desideratum; and this in free and happy America! Where are our collegiate establishments? Where our theological institutes?" In 1867 Isaacs helped establish Maimonides College of Philadelphia, the first theological seminary for Jews in the United States.[28]

Besides his religious activities, Isaacs also involved himself in "political" issues, especially efforts to defend Jews worldwide against anti-Semitic outbursts and to unify Judaism in America. The international crusade prompted by the Damascus Affair of 1840, which aimed to rescue a number of Jews imprisoned in Syria, is sometimes considered the beginning of modern Jewish history because it aroused a latent national consciousness and identity. Isaacs and Henry Hart, another Hollander at Bnai Jeshurun, served on a seven-member committee of correspondence to coordinate a petition drive calling on the American government to intervene. Isaacs also joined the Jewish protest chorus against the Papacy in the famous Montara affair of 1858–59, which involved the supposed "child stealing" and baptism of a Jewish child by Italian Catholics. Isaacs chaired a combined committee of all twelve synagogues in New York City, which sponsored a mass meeting of 2,000 persons, both Jews and Protestants, to petition the American president to intervene with the Vatican. When this effort proved unsuccessful, Isaacs led in founding the Board of Delegates of American Israelites, which grew into a national organization of all Orthodox congregations to safeguard Jewish civil and religious rights at home and abroad.[29]

In the 1850s Isaacs endeared himself to the Northern public by using the pages of *The Jewish Messenger* ardently to advocate the antislavery movement, even at the expense of losing his Southern readership. "We want subscribers," he editorialized, "for without them we cannot publish a paper, and Judaism needs an organ; but we want much more truth and loyalty." Isaacs was well acquainted with prominent antislavery leaders, such as Professor Calvin E. Stowe, husband of Harriet Beecher Stowe and a prominent philo-Semite, and in 1856 Isaacs campaigned for the antislavery candidate, John C. Frèmont. But Isaacs refrained from preaching antislavery sermons, not wanting to bring "politics into the pulpit." During the Civil War he strongly defended the Union cause "with or without slavery," and after President Lincoln's assassination he was one of two clerics selected to give prayers at the public memorial services in Union Square.[30]

This son of Friesland, whose family fled the oppression of Napoleon, cut a wide swath within American Judaism. He placed pulpit, pen, and podium in the service of Orthodoxy and valiantly fought against the forces of secularism and liberalism that were rotting the roots of the Jewish faith in the rising age of unbelief. At his death colleagues called him the "Father of the American clergy." His funeral service at Temple Shaaray Tefila in 1878 was the largest Jewish funeral of the century. Every synagogue and Jewish organization in the country sent representatives. Isaacs was a religious leader of major influence, a renowned journalist, and a mover and shaker in Jewish affairs. But he was most honored for his defense of Orthodoxy. Colleagues eulogized him as "a faithful proponent" of Judaism who "lamented the increasing defection amidst our ranks; the prevailing disloyalty to the siniatic covenant." An eminent Christian clergyman, in a glowing tribute sent to Isaacs's sons, described their father as "a bulwark of strength against the infidelity and godlessness that are growing upon us in this great city. His firm devotion to God's holy word brought him into direct and cordial sympathy with us Christians. . . . May his mantle rest on his children. Your father's death is a public calamity. Who shall fill his place? Our city could better spare millions of its money than one such resolute watchman and soldier in its moral defense."[31]

Isaacs's tenure at Shaaray Tefila marked the high point of Orthodoxy in New York Judaism. Ironically, within two years of his death, the congregation began going over to Reform, led by the new rabbi who unkindly called his predecessor "rigidly, obstinately Orthodox." The conservative Dutch contingent resigned in the face of this revolution, along with their English and Polish compatriots. Most of the German Jews, who tended toward Reform, remained. Thus, the end of Dutch leadership marked a crucial turning point in the history of the Shaaray Tefila congregation.[32] More broadly it signaled the waning influence in American Jewish life of the traditional British-Dutch-Polish amalgam, which had succumbed to the overwhelming numbers of German immigrants.

Dutch Synagogues

In the 1840s the pace of Dutch Jewish immigration increased and the newcomers demanded their own ethnic synagogues. In New York City, Philadelphia, and Boston, they founded Netherlandic congregations based on the Amsterdam *minhag* (rite). These synagogues were located in the centers of Dutch Jewish settlements and attracted the more traditional immigrants who wished to remain closely knit, aloof from other nationalities, and linked together by in-group marriages. Such congregations slowed the process of assimilation for several generations, but all succumbed to religious apathy and secularism, or to the unitive forces of American Judaism. By 1905 there was no regular worship following the Amsterdam *minhag* anywhere in the United States, but Dutch cemeteries and mutual aid and charitable societies continued for many generations; some are still hanging on by a thread today.

Bnai Israel of New York, 1847–c.1902

The biggest and longest-lived Dutch synagogue was Bnai Israel of New York, led by Simon Cohen Noot of Amsterdam, the second most important Dutch cleric and educator in America at mid-century. Reverend Noot played a crucial part in establishing Dutch congregations and Hebrew all-day schools in New York, Philadelphia, and Boston.[33] He was born in 1810 and obtained an excellent Hebrew education before he emigrated in 1843. Like Isaacs, Noot was not ordained, but that did not discourage the new Polish-Dutch congregation in Philadelphia, Beth Israel, from calling him as their cantor. Noot accepted. Four years later, in 1847, he left Philadelphia for New York to serve the newly formed "Netherdutch" congregation Bnai Israel, which he led until 1854. Membership in the Dutch synagogue doubled under Noot's capable leadership, reaching at least 60 families, or 60 percent of the 100 Dutch families in New York at mid-century.

The Dutch synagogue followed the orthodox Amsterdam *minhag* and was located initially in a commodious building on Chrystie Street in the Dutch neighborhood.[34] Bnai Israel did not publish the customary 25-year anniversary book and very little is known of the history of the congregation. The poor, struggling group purchased two cemeteries and established several burial and mutual aid societies, the most famous being the Netherland Israelitisch Sick Fund, formed in 1859, which continues to the present day, although the average age of the board members is over 80.[35]

A major accomplishment of Bnai Israel under the Reverend Noot was to establish a successful Hebrew school in New York in 1847. The young congregation from the outset took on the "sacred cause of Education," and Noot served as principal and Hebrew teacher of the school that evolved in 1852 into the Green Street Hebrew School of Bnai Jeshurun Synagogue.[36]

Since Noot's primary interest was education, he left New York in 1854 to help the Dutch-Polish congregation of Boston (Ohabei Shalom) establish a Hebrew day school. Bnai Israel continued for another half century under a long line of readers, notably the Reverend M. R. De Leeuw (1855–67) and Simon Noot's son, Isaac C. Noot (1867–c.85), who led the congregation in the joyous celebration of its twenty-fifth anniversary in 1872. By then Noot lectured in English, but otherwise Bnai Israel remained true to its Orthodox heritage until it disbanded around 1902.

Bnai Israel of Philadelphia, 1852–79

The first Dutch Jews arrived in Philadelphia between 1790 and 1815.[37] Unlike the New York Dutch, they came directly from Amsterdam, except for several families who lived briefly in London. The most prominent Dutch families joined the prestigious pioneer Sephardic synagogue, Mikveh Israel, of which at least a quarter of the members were of Dutch ancestry throughout the nineteenth century. Others affiliated with Rodeph Shalom, the first Ashkenazic synagogue in North America, founded in 1795.[38] About 40 percent of the members of Rodeph Shalom were Dutch in 1810, and its worship ritual followed both "German and Dutch rules," which was clearly a compromise.

By the 1840s German immigrants far outnumbered the Dutch at Rodeph Shalom. The Dutch minority remained the financial mainstay and held leadership positions until 1847, when the synagogue relocated to North Philadelphia, far from the Dutch neighborhood. This move prompted the Dutch to found their own congregation in South Philadelphia, named Bnai Israel (the same name as the sister New York congregation). Laymen took the lead in this venture until Reverend Simon Noot came in 1855, after establishing a Hebrew school in Boston.[39]

Noot served the congregation well for seven years, and with strenuous efforts the congregation in 1857 dedicated its own building in the heart of the Dutch Jewish neighborhood. Henry De Boer, a clothing dealer and dry goods jobber, presided over the governing board for many years. As in New York, the Philadelphia congregation founded a Hebrew school and promoted the Jewish Foster Home. Perhaps for geographical reasons, the Philadelphia Dutch congregation was more isolated than the New York congregation.[40]

After Reverend Noot's return to Boston in 1862, where he became cantor of Ohabei Shalom, the Philadelphia Dutch had to accept a German-born cleric for the next 12 years, until a young immigrant from Amsterdam named Jacob Voorsanger (1852–1908) arrived in 1873. Voorsanger had no rabbinical training, but he cultivated his considerable natural gifts of leadership and was appointed cantor in 1874 at the young age of 22.[41] He served the dying Philadelphia congregation for only three years and was its last cantor. New immigration had ceased, and the old members were relocating to more prestigious uptown districts.

Voorsanger subsequently led congregations in Washington, D.C., Providence, and Houston, and finally rose to the pinnacle of renown as senior rabbi of Temple Emanu-El, the leading congregation of San Francisco and the most influential west of the Rocky Mountains. Voorsanger founded and edited the Anglo-Jewish weekly *Emanu-El*, lectured regularly in Semitics at the University of California, Berkeley, and helped found the California Red Cross. After leaving Philadelphia Voorsanger gradually shifted from Orthodox cantor to Reform rabbi.[42] His transformation was complete by 1895, when Isaac Mayer Wise of Hebrew Union College, the leading Reform rabbi in America, arranged for the college to award Voorsanger an honorary degree of Bachelor of Theology. Eight years later, in 1903, the college bestowed on him a second honorary degree, Doctor of Divinity. Only Reverend Samuel Isaacs of New York held a brighter candle among American Jewry. Isaacs, the traditionalist defender of Orthodoxy, represented the early immigrants, and Voorsanger, the modernist Western leader of Reform, the latecomers.[43]

Beth Eil of Boston, 1859–80s

Boston was the third city with a Dutch synagogue. The Dutch community took shape there after 1840, at the time the greater Jewish settlement began.[44] There were 60 Dutch families by 1860 and 100 in 1870, making them only 5 percent of all Jews in Boston. Most came directly from Holland, but a few had lived in London or some other American city for several years. Dutch Jews initially joined the only synagogue, Ohabei Shalom, which was largely Polish and Dutch. In the 1850s three Dutch in succession served as synagogue presidents, and Reverend Simon Noot filled the pulpit from 1862 to 1867.

But new Dutch immigrants in the 1850s desired a homogeneous congregation, and in 1859 about 36 men seceded and formed a pure Dutch congregation named Beth Eil (House of God). The spiritual leader and driving force was a young peddler, Mark (Markus Jacob) Hamburger, who emigrated from Amsterdam in 1857. Under thirty years of age at the outset and lacking theological training and ordination, Hamburger nevertheless enjoyed a long and active career in Boston as a Hebrew clergyman. His monument in the Hollanders' burial ground is a large stone pulpit, which speaks volumes about his ability.[45]

According to a local chronicler, the Boston Dutch were a close-knit group who remained somewhat aloof from other Jews. They had their own cemeteries and mutual aid society, the *Hollandsche Chevra*. But growth was restricted because few fresh Dutch immigrants came to Boston after the Civil War. The body did experience a brief resurgence in the 1870s when its membership of seventy was augmented by dissatisfied conservatives from Congregation Ohabei Shalom, which was moving toward moderate Reform. In September 1875 the Dutch consecrated a new synagogue at Gloucester Place, and Cantor Hamburger sang the service before a "large assemblage." The Reverend Isaac Noot, former Hebrew teacher at the Free School, returned from New York to deliver the sermon. Despite the revival, declining membership forced the congregation to give up its synagogue sometime in the 1880s. All that remained in the mid-twentieth century was the Hollandsche Chevra and Netherlands Cemetery Corporation, which provided sick benefits and burial in consecrated ground.[46]

Dutch Jews Elsewhere

In Baltimore, New Orleans, Buffalo, Detroit, Chicago, Pittsburgh, and elsewhere, Dutch Jews primarily joined Orthodox German synagogues.[47] At the Baltimore Hebrew Congregation, founded in 1829, Dutchmen comprised one third of the charter members and four of the five petitioners for the first charter. Other Dutch, who resided in the Fells Point district, affiliated with the Hebrew Friendship Congregation, Oheb Israel, founded in 1847. Of the 27 charter members of New Orleans' Touro Synagogue in 1847, four were Dutch, including Manis Jacobs of Amsterdam, the leader of the congregation and a prominent slave trader, real estate investor, and philanthropist. At his funeral Jacobs was eulogized as the "Rabbi of New Orleans."[48] Pittsburgh's 100 Dutch Jews, who made up 10 percent of the city's Jewish population in 1870, were members of the German congregation Rodef Shalom, but when it went over to Reform in 1863, the Dutch withdrew and joined with Poles and Lithuanians in a new Orthodox congregation Etz Hayyim (Tree of Life).[49] In Buffalo the Dutch joined the Polish-dominated Beth El Congregation, founded in 1847. A leading clothing merchant, Nathan Boasberg of Amsterdam, was a charter member and later secretary. Boasberg's father-in-law, Emanuel Van Baalen, led a group of Germans to secede in 1851 and establish Beth Zion, which in the 1860s became the first Reform congregation in Buffalo.[50]

Conclusion

Dutch Jewish emigration was caused by economic forces, but a commitment to Judaism strongly influenced where Dutch Jews settled. The Anglo-French wars and Napoleonic conquest of the Netherlands caused Jewish merchants great hardship, and lagging industrial development further depressed the Jews and forced them onto public relief rolls. Emigration was a very rational response to their straitened situation.

Given their religious Orthodoxy and cultural traditionalism, the Dutch migrated to neighborhoods of their kin in American cities where they preferred, if possible, the pure Amsterdam *minhag* in synagogues led by Dutch cantors. Where Dutch congregations were not feasible, the migrants joined English, Polish, and German ones. The early immigrants felt a natural affinity to the English because Amsterdam and London Jewish centers had strong commercial links, and their synagogues shared nearly identical rituals and liturgies.

The Dutch Jews Americanized more rapidly than the Germans. The Dutch had fewer language problems since many had learned English during a sojourn in London. Most Dutch Jews also spoke Yiddish, the international Jewish language, whereas the German Jews had become Germanized in the Old Country. As the dominant Jewish group in America in the nineteenth century, they continued to use German in worship and at home. While the Dutch, even in their synagogues, readily gave up Yiddish, which as a "mongrel tongue" had little respect in America, the Germans clung to their native German tongue. German remained a respectable language in the eastern cities among both Jews and Gentiles.[51]

With Americanization came religious apostasy, or at least a rejection of Orthodoxy with its inconvenient dietary laws, closed shops on Saturday, the biggest shopping day of the week, and condemnation by the community for marrying a Gentile. The rejection of Orthodoxy began at mid-century, and by the end of the century most Dutch had espoused Reform Judaism. A Dutch immigrant, Emanuel Goudsmit, writing from New York in 1848, was appalled at the "terrible" laxity of his co-religionists: "It is either Koggel [pudding] . . . with barley soup and 3-year old wormy smoked beef [a kosher food dish] or else ham and oysters." This was Goudsmit's colorful way of describing the religious declension.[52]

Within two generations the Dutch Jews had lost first their Dutchness and then their Orthodoxy. They were absorbed into broader American Judaism, which in turn had accommodated itself to Protestant voluntarism and denominationalism by espousing German Reform.

Notes

1. Robert P. Swierenga, *The Forerunners: Dutch Jewry in the North American Diaspora* (Detroit: Wayne State University Press, 1994). The figure of 6,500 is computed from the U.S. federal population census manuscripts, 1800–80, using the estimation method of Pieter R. D. Stokvis: immigration equals the sum of the decadal increase in Dutch-born Jews plus the estimated number of deaths and remigrants. See Stokvis, "Dutch International Migration, 1815–1910," in *The Dutch in America: Immigration, Settlement, and Cultural Change*, ed. Robert P. Swierenga (New Brunswick, N.J.: Rutgers University Press, 1985), 56–60, esp. Table 2.6.
2. Swierenga, *Forerunners*, chap. 1. The story of Dutch Jews in the United

States suffers from a lack of primary sources. Very few immigrant letters are known, no records survive from the three Netherlandic congregations, and there are no Dutch-language periodicals, newspapers, or pamphlets. Federal census records, synagogue histories, and souvenir booklets and histories are the major sources. See the bibliography in ibid., 403–19.

3. L. P. Gartner, *The Jewish Immigrant in England, 1820–1914* (Detroit: Wayne State University Press, 1960), 17, 33.
4. The exact figures are: 1850 census, of 157 Dutch couples, 20 (13 percent) had English spouses and 23 (15 percent) had German spouses; 1860 census, of 385 couples, 40 (10 percent) had English spouses and 70 (18 percent) German spouses; 1870 census, 668 couples, 72 (11 percent) had English spouses and 131 (20 percent) had German spouses. Compiled from Swierenga, *Dutch Households in U.S. Population Censuses, 1850, 1860, 1870: An Alphabetical Listing by Household Heads* (Wilmington, Del.: Scholarly Resources, 1987).
5. Herman Diederiks, "Residential Patterns: A Jewish Ghetto in Amsterdam around 1800," unpublished paper, University of Leiden.
6. I. Harold Sharfman, *The First Rabbi: Origins of Conflict Between Orthodox and Reform: Jewish Polemic Warfare in pre-Civil War America* (Malibu, Calif.: Pangloss Press, 1988), xxi.
7. On Netherlands Jewry, see Jozeph Michman, "Historiography of the Jews in the Netherlands," in *Dutch Jewish History: Proceedings of the Symposium on the History of the Jews in the Netherlands November 28—December 3, 1982, Tel-Aviv—Jerusalem*, Jozeph Michman and Tirtsah Levie, eds. (Jerusalem: 1984), 7–29; Robert Cohen, "Boekman's Legacy: Historical Demography of the Jews in the Netherlands," ibid, 519–40; H. Daalder, "Dutch Jews in a Segmented Society?" *Acta Historiae Neerlandica* 8 (1978): 175–94; H. Beem, *De Joden van Leeuwarden* (Assen: Van Gorcum, 1974), 89–92, 114–17. For the Jewish population in the Netherlands, see J. A. de Kok, *Nederland op de breuklijn Rome-Reformatie* (Assen: Van Gorcum, 1964), 292–95; and Committee for the Demography of the Jews, "Dutch Jewry: A Demographic Analysis," *Jewish Journal of Sociology* 3 (Dec. 1961): 195–242.
8. Ira Rosenwaike, *On the Edge of Greatness: A Portrait of American Jewry in the Early National Period* (Cincinnati: American Jewish Archives, 1985), Table 7, 39, Appendix B, 140–64. The figures are adjusted upward slightly to include other known Dutch.
9. Compiled from Swierenga, *Dutch Households in U.S. Population Censuses, 1850, 1860, 1870.*
10. Samuel Gompers, *Seventy Years of Life and Labor: An Autobiography* (New York: E.P. Dutton, 1920), 2–24; Stuart B. Kaufman, ed., *The Samuel Gompers Papers. Volume 1, The Making of a Union Leader, 1850–86* (Urbana and Chicago: University of Illinois Press, 1985), 2–4.
11. Gompers, *Seventy Years*, 24.
12. This and the next two paragraphs rely on Jacob Van Hinte, *Netherlanders*

in America: A Study of Emigration and Settlement in the Nineteenth and Twentieth Centuries in the United States of America, Robert P. Swierenga, gen. ed., Adriaan de Wit chief trans. (Grand Rapids: Baker Book House, 1985), 615, 835–39, 1007.

13. The standard works are Edwin Wolf II and Maxwell Whiteman, *The History of the Jews of Philadelphia from Colonial Times to the Age of Jackson* (Philadelphia: Jewish Publication Society of America, 1956); Henry Samuel Morais, *The Jews of Philadelphia: Their History from the Earliest Settlements to the Present Time* (Philadelphia: Levytype Company, 1894); Hyman G. Grinstein, *The Rise of the Jewish Community of New York, 1654–1860* (Philadelphia: Jewish Publication Society of America, 1946); Isaac M. Fein, *The Making of an American Jewish Community: The History of Baltimore Jewry from 1773 to 1920* (Philadelphia: Jewish Publication Society of America, 1971); Alfred Ehrenfried, *A Chronicle of Boston Jewry: From the Colonial Settlement to 1900* (Boston: privately printed, 1963). Excellent synagogue histories are Edward Davis, *The History of Rodeph Shalom Congregation, Philadelphia, 1802–1926* (Philadelphia: Rodeph Shalom Congregation, 1926); Simon Cohen, *Shaaray Tefila: A History of Its Hundred Years 1845–1945* (New York: Greenburg, 1945); Israel Goldstein, *A Century of Judaism in New York, Bnai Jeshurun 1825–1925: New York's Oldest Ashkenazic Congregation* (New York: Congregation B'nai Jeshurun, 1930); Adolf Guttmacher, *A History of Baltimore Hebrew Congregation, 1830–1905* (Baltimore: Lord Baltimore Press, 1905).

14. Swierenga, *Forerunners*, 74–87; E. Yechiel Simon, "Samuel Myer Isaacs: A 19th Century Jewish Minister in New York City" (Ph.D. diss., Yeshiva University, 1978); Charles Rezsickoff, "Samuel Myer Isaacs," *Universal Jewish Encyclopedia*, 10 vols. (New York, 1948), 5:594; *Jewish Encyclopedia* (New York and London, 1901), 6:635; Davis, *Emergence of Conservative Judaism*, 340–42. Samuel M. Isaacs was born on 4 Jan. 1804; his mother was Rebecca Samuels, daughter of Jacob Symmons of London. Davis and all other Jewish historians erroneously describe Isaacs as an Englishman or English-born. Meyer Isaacs fell into debt after 1805, and by 1810 he had borrowed f6,300 from family and friends. He fled to England leaving behind his property and debts; see mortgage documents in Gemeentearchief, Leeuwarden: 31 Aug., 12 Nov. 1807; 25 July, 11 Aug. 1810 (Hypotheek 173/83 and 173/91). The Isaacs family belonged to the Leeuwarden Synagogue, whose 600 seats made it the largest in the Netherlands outside the Randstad.

15. Goldstein, *Century of Judaism in New York*, 76, 80–81, 92–93. An incomplete, but useful, genealogical tree of Samuel M. and Jane Isaacs is in Malcolm H. Stern, comp., *First American Jewish Families, 600 Genealogies, 1654–1977* (Cincinnati: American Jewish Archives, 1978), 110.

16. Lance J. Sussman, "Isaac Leeser and the Protestantization of American Judaism," *American Jewish Archives* 38 (Apr. 1986): 8–10; "Preaching," *Encyclopaedia Judaica* 13:1002–7.

17. Cohen, *Shaaray Tefila*, 22–25. This sorry affair is fully documented in *The Occident* 3 (1845):255–60, 300–05, 357, 408–15, 478–80.
18. Grinstein, *Jewish Community of New York*, 216–17, 366–67.
19. Davis, *Emergence of Conservative Judaism*, 134–38, 340; *The Occident* 5 (1847):382–94.
20. Cohen, *Shaaray Tefila*, 9; Grinstein, *Jewish Community of New York*, 340; *The Occident* 2 (1844):150–53, 167, 283–96, 542; 3 (1845):87–93; 4 (1847):537–43.
21. *The Occident* 4 (1847):542, 239; Cohen, *Shaaray Tefila*, 9; Grinstein, *Jewish Community of New York*, 340, 342.
22. *The Occident* 2 (1844):284.
23. Ibid., 26 (1868):93; Cohen, *Shaaray Tefila*, 18–26. In 1850 Samuel Myer Isaacs and his wife Jane lived with their four children at 669 Houston Street between De Paw Place (Thompson Street) and Laurens Street in Ward 15. By 1860 the family, then with five children, had moved into a bigger house at 649 Houston, and by 1870 they moved a final time to the fashionable Uptown district, at 145 West 46th Street near Broadway. In the 1870 census, Samuel reported the value of his home at $30,000. In 1869 the Shaaray Tefila congregation also moved uptown to their 44th Street Synagogue at Sixth Avenue (Ward 22). Simon, "Samuel Myer Isaacs," 7–9; Swierenga, *Dutch Households in U. S. Population Censuses, 1850, 1860, 1870*, 1:484–85; Cohen, *Shaaray Tefila*, 22–25; Goldstein, *Century of Judaism in New York*, 63–96.
24. Davis, *Emergence of Conservative Judaism*, 162–65.
25. *The Jewish Messenger*, 31 May 1878; Grinstein, *Jewish Community of New York*, 160–61, 436; Davis, *Emergence of Conservative Judaism*, 60–64, 70, 78, 129–30.
26. Grinstein, *Jewish Community of New York*, 446–47; *The Occident* 10 (1852):170, 263; 11 (1854):503–04; 18 (1860):202–03.
27. *The Occident* 1 (1843):470–73; 23 (1865):190, 238; Cohen, *Shaaray Tefila*, 2; Grinstein, *Jewish Community of New York*, 231–34, 244–45; "Samuel Myer Isaacs," *Jewish Encyclopedia*, 6:635; Davis, *Emergence of Conservative Judaism*, 38. The classic article on Jews in public schools is Lloyd P. Gartner, "Temples of Liberty Unpolluted: American Jews and Public Schools, 1840–1875," in *A Bicentennial Festschrift for Jacob Rader Marcus*, ed. Bertram Wallace Korn (Waltham, MA: American Jewish Historical Society, 1976), 157–89. See also Isaac Leeser, "The Jews of the United States—1848," *American Jewish Archives* 7 (Jan. 1955):82–84; Alvin Irwin Schiff, *The Jewish Day School in America* (New York: Jewish Education Committee Press, 1966), 22–23.
28. *The Occident* 7 (1849):137–39; Simon, "Samuel Myer Isaacs," 107, 131–32.
29. Grinstein, *Jewish Community of New York*, 217, 430–35; *The Occident* 17 (1859):83, 86–7, 193–94, 218–20.
30. *The Occident* 3 (1845):526; 4 (1847):224; Davis, *Emergence of Conservative Judaism*, 110–11.

31. Obituary in *New York World*, 21 May 1878; *The Jewish Messenger*, 31 May 1878.
32. Cohen, *Shaaray Tefila*, 28–35; *The Jewish Messenger*, 31 May 1878.
33. Swierenga, *Forerunners*, 89–92, 131–32, 168–69. See also Grinstein, *Jewish Community of New York*, 283, 485–88, 546–47; Ehrenfried, *Chronicle of Boston Jewry*, 356–57; Morais, *Jews of Philadelphia*, 108; *The Occident*, 1 (1843):60, 357; 2 (1844):107; 5 (1847):206–07, 560; 7 (1849):614; 8 (1850):575; 10 (1853):506; 12 (1854):469; 14 (1856):309, 453; 15 (1857):240; 18 (1861):280; 20 (1862):328–29, 381–82.
34. Swierenga, *Forerunners*, 87–97.
35. *The Occident* 5 (1847):370; 18 (1860):124; 22 (1865):177–80; Joël Cahen, "Een eigen ziekenfonds voor joden in New York," *Nieuwe Israelietisch Weekblad*, 15 Nov. 1985, Jubilee number, 145–46; Grinstein, *Jewish Community of New York*, 322, 491–92, 570, 585.
36. *The Occident* 5 (1847):317, 370; 10 (1852):158–160; 10 (1853):573; 11 (1853):232–33, 465; 12 (1854):115, 165–66; Grinstein, *Jewish Community of New York*, 115–19.
37. Swierenga, *Forerunners*, 118–29.
38. Compiled from the list of families of Mikveh Israel in Morais, *Jews of Philadelphia*, 68.
39. Morais, *Jews of Philadelphia*, 70–72, 108; Davis, *Rodeph Shalom*, 23–27, 55–62, 152–57; Wolf and Whiteman, *Jews of Philadelphia*, 226–27, 231, 249–52, 439, 493–94; *The Occident* 11 (1853):326.
40. Swierenga, *Forerunners*, 129–35.
41. Ibid., 134–35, 303–09. There is considerable confusion in the literature about Voorsanger's education and ancestry. See Kenneth C. Zwerin and Norton B. Stern, "Jacob Voorsanger: From Cantor to Rabbi," *Western States Jewish Historical Quarterly* 15 (April 1983): 195–201. Voorsanger vaguely claimed to have received his "Jewish education" in Amsterdam. See obituary in *The American Hebrew and Jewish Messenger* 82 (1 May 1908), 660. Voorsanger's brother, A. W. Voorsanger, in his book *Western Jewry: An Account of the Achievements of the Jews and Judaism in California Including Eulogies and Biographies* (San Francisco: Emanu-El, 1916), 157, stated that Jacob earned his rabbinate degree at the Jewish Theological Seminary of Amsterdam. This repeats a brief biography of Voorsanger in *The American Jewish Year Book 5664* (Philadelphia, 1903), 104. Zwerin and Stern, however, after a thorough search of the archives of the Jewish Theological Seminary, which are housed in the Municipal Archives of Amsterdam, can find no record of a student named Jacob Voorsanger, nor were there any rabbinic examinations at the Seminary in 1871 or 1872, when Jacob would have graduated (195–96). A. W. Voorsanger also stated that his grandfather and great-grandfather on both his father's and mother's side were "well-known rabbis in Germany," but Zwerin and Stern are unable to document this assertion in the Municipal Archives of Amsterdam (196).
42. Voorsanger's religious views are described cogently by Marc Lee Raphael,

"Rabbi Jacob Voorsanger of San Francisco on Jews and Judaism: The Implications of the Pittsburgh Platform," *American Jewish Historical Quarterly* 63 (Dec. 1973):185–203. Voorsanger's illustrious career at Emanu-El Temple of San Francisco is described in detail in Fred Rosenbaum, *Architects of Reform: Congregational and Community Leadership, Emanu-El of San Francisco, 1849–1980* (Berkeley: Western Jewish History Center, 1980), 43–69.

43. Zwerin and Stern, "Jacob Voorsanger," 200.
44. Swierenga, *Forerunners*, 164–87; Ehrenfried, *Chronicle of Boston Jewry*, 339–70.
45. Ibid., 427–29; Federal population census manuscripts, 1860, 1870.
46. Ehrenfried, *Chronicle of Boston Jewry*, 428–29, 472–73.
47. Swierenga, *Forerunners*, chaps. 6, 7, 8, 9.
48. Bertram Wallace Korn, *The Early Jews of New Orleans* (Waltham, MA: American Jewish Historical Society, 1979), 196–202.
49. Jacob S. Feldman, "The Early Migration and Settlement of Jews in Pittsburgh, 1754–1894" (typescript, 1959, Hebrew Union College Library, Cincinnati), 43–48, 80–83.
50. Selig Adler and Thomas E. Connolly, *From Ararat to Suburbia: The History of the Jewish Community of Buffalo* (Philadelphia: Jewish Publication Society of America, 1960), 56–58.
51. Grinstein, *Jewish Community of New York*, 170, 207–09.
52. Joël Cahen, director of the Jewish Historical Museum of Amsterdam, where Goudsmit's letter is archived, published large portions in the *Nieuwe Israelietisch Weekblad*, 15 Nov. 1985, Jubilee number, 145–46. Dr. Adriaan de Wit, Professor Emeritus of Romance Languages, Kent State University, translated the letter, and his colleague, Dr. Herbert Hochhauser, Professor Emeritus of German Languages and an authority on Judaica, explained the meaning of the numerous Yiddish words.

CHAPTER 8

Religious Localism—Chicago, Cleveland, and Rural Indiana

THE CRUCIAL DISTINCTION among Dutch immigrants was the historic fault line between dominant Protestants and the minority Catholics. The Dutch Reformed, whether living in booming cities like Chicago and Cleveland or planting farming communities throughout the Midwest, maintained an ethnoreligious identity because they segregated themselves and formed culture islands. Dutch Catholics, by comparison, joined multiethnic Catholic parishes, which hastened their assimilation into American Catholicism, mainly the German wing. Calvinists, by contrast, ghettoized themselves in Dutch-speaking congregations and schools. Despite their cultural cohesiveness, however, the Calvinists divided institutionally into rival denominations, with one church favoring a faster pace of assimilation by sending their children to the public schools, and the other establishing separate Reformed elementary and secondary schools.

The cultural persistence of Dutch Calvinist communities for 150 years defies many assumptions of assimilationist theory. By all expectations, as a small Protestant ethnic group they should have rapidly assimilated, intermarried, and melded into the broader Yankee society. Outwardly, the Dutch were integrated into economic and political life, and they promptly became naturalized citizens. To the non-Dutch they appeared by the second generation to be typical middle-class neighbors, living in neat bungalows in town or in white farmhouses in the country. They were indistinguishable in dress and speech, in the workplace, and in the voting booth. Only the occasional miniature windmill on the front lawn marked a residence as Dutch.

But secondary associations and even language are not the prime markers of ethnicity. One must look to primary associations—the worshiping community, schooling, home life, marriage patterns, and recreation. In these areas the Calvinists built an institutional fortress and demonstrated their religious solidarity. This chapter will describe the cultural localism of the Dutch in Chicago and Cleveland and in the rural Indiana enclaves of Lafayette, Goshen, Munster-Highland, and De Motte.

Urban Dutch of Chicago

By 1900 greater Chicago had 20,000 Dutch and was second only to Grand Rapids as a Dutch center (Table 8.1).[1] The typical residential pattern was to cluster around their churches and schools, thereby to ensure survival as a self-conscious ethnic group in a diverse and threatening environment. The major settlements were in Roseland and South Holland on the far south side, and in the city proper on the Old West Side and in Englewood, its offshoot on the near south side. Roseland and South Holland were stable, homogeneous farm communities that remained intact for more than one hundred years, but the mobile West Siders relocated almost every generation and survived against all odds only because of their staunch Calvinism. As one of the few Dutch Reformed communities in a major metropolis, the West Siders experienced the full force of modernization on their families and institutions.[2]

A Dutch Reformed presence remains today in Chicago because of their religious values and traditional ethnic clannishness. "In large part," Amry Vandenbosch perceptively wrote in 1927, this is "due to their attachment to the church, as well as to their strong race [i. e., nationality] consciousness."[3] The West Side Dutch were primarily farm laborers from the northern province of Groningen. As rural folk they brought a strong sense of localism and loyalty to family and friends. They were "tribal" in their fierce in-group loyalties, behavior of exclusiveness, and the transplanting of Old Country institutions and the Dutch language and culture. But above all they were Calvinists of the old school, dating back to the Synod of Dordrecht (1618–19).

Furthermore, these Groningers were products of the Secession of 1834 against the Netherlands national church (Hervormde Kerk), for which they had suffered persecution, expulsion, and social opprobrium. Later immigrants, though fewer in number, supported the broader neo-Calvinist revival in the Netherlands of 1886, led by the theologian and statesman Abraham Kuyper (1837–1920). This reform movement, known as the *Doleantie* (1875–1920), sought to preserve orthodoxy

TABLE 8.1 Dutch in Chicago (Cook County), 1850–1930

	FOREIGN-BORN		NATIVE-BORN*		
YEAR	NUMBER	%	NUMBER	%	TOTAL
1850	92	93	7	7	99
1860	275	69	124	31	399
1870	1,427	68	668	32	2,095
1880	3,112	49	3,188	51	6,300
1900	9,196	47	10,555	53	19,751
1930	11,970	34	22,817	66	34,787

* Foreign or mixed parentage.
SOURCE: Robert P. Swierenga, comp., "Dutch in Chicago, 1850–1900," derived from Federal Manuscript Population censuses, 1850–1900; Bureau of the Census, *Census of the United States* 1930, Vol. III, Part I *Population* (Washington, 1932), 637, 641.

against the forces of modernism by building an institutional infrastructure of Calvinist schools capped by the Free University of Amsterdam, a Calvinist political party, national newspaper, and Calvinist labor union. Most Chicago Groningers had been nourished in the conventicles and Seceder churches that followed Hendrik de Cock of Ulrum, the father of the 1834 Secession. They were Cocksians more than Kuyperians; pietist confessionalists and not neo-Calvinist triumphalists. In James Bratt's words, they were "vigilant for orthodoxy among themselves and content to let the rest of the world go."[4]

Fearing worldliness and believing the "antithesis" between the church and "the world," they formed themselves into closed communities even as they lived cheek by jowl with Jews and Catholics. In Vandenbosch's mixed metaphor, they were a "handful of Hollanders in a sea of Jews, with whom the Dutch do not mix."[5] Their conservative brand of Calvinism aimed to preserve purity in the home, church, and school; it did not extend to transforming every sphere of life. The Chicago Groningers contended with the culture rather than challenged it. As these predominantly Seceder pietists sorted themselves out theologically in Chicago under the influence of their parsonage-trained "dominies," they divided into revivalist and confessionalist camps (Table 8.2).

The dominant leader was Bernardus De Bey, a Seceder pastor in Middelstum, Groningen, who emigrated with many of his parishioners to lead the First Reformed Church of Chicago for twenty-three years (1868–91).[6] De Bey pulled his Chicago congregation away from the traditional defensive confessionalism of the Secession and toward an optimistic American-style revivalism. De Bey viewed immigration as a chance to jettison Dutch theologizing for American ecumenism, and he deliberately emulated local preaching styles and adopted the "spiritual rhythms of American evangelism—conversion, backsliding, and renewal."[7] De Bey

TABLE 8.2 Four Mentalities of Chicago's Dutch-American Community

	SECEDERS/PIETISTS	NEO-CALVINISTS/KUYPERIANS
	Reformed Church "West"	Positive Calvinists
Outgoing	*Christian Intelligencer*	*American Daily Standard*
Optimistic	Bernardus De Bey	J. Clover Monsma
	Peter Moerdyke	Ralph Dekker (layman)
	M. E. Broekstra	
	Confessionalists	Antithetical Calvinists
Defensive	*De Wachter*	*Onze Toekomst*
Isolation	H. Douwstra	John Van Lonkhuyzen
	Frank Welandt	William Heyns
	H. J. Mokma	Evert Breen
	John O. Vos	Cornelius De Leeuw
	Benjamin Essenburg	Sjoerd S. Vander Heide
	Herman Bell	Jacob Manni

SOURCE: Adapted from Bratt, *Dutch Calvinism in Modern America*, 47.

managed to hold the factions in his congregation together by the force of his strong personality and by continuing to preach in the Dutch language. Immediately after he retired, however, the most acculturated members transferred to the new English-language Trinity Reformed Church (1891), pastored by Peter Moerdyke. De Bey's successors, especially M. E. Broekstra, continued to pull First Reformed Church toward American evangelicalism. By contrast, the First Christian Reformed Church of Chicago, the product of a schism in 1857 in western Michigan, remained introverted and committed to confessional orthodoxy.[8]

During the Progressive era neo-Calvinists made their move, largely under the influence of four successive Kuyperian pastors and their contemporaries at First Christian Reformed Church (and its daughter, the Douglas Park Christian Reformed Church)—namely the Reverends William Heyns (1900–02), Evert Breen (1903–09), Sjoerd S. Vander Heide (1909–18), and John Van Lonkhuyzen (1918–28) at First CRC, and Cornelius De Leeuw (1905–10) and Jacob Manni (1910–16) at Douglas Park CRC. Heyns became professor of Old Testament at Calvin Theological Seminary, the sole seminary of the CRC in Grand Rapids; Breen became editor of various church journals, notably *De Calvinist*; while Van Lonkhuyzen, a friend and follower of Abraham Kuyper, edited Chicago's only Dutch-language newspaper, *Onze Toekomst* (3,500 circulation in 1922) from 1918 to 1928.[9] Dr. Van Lonkhuyzen, a graduate of the Free University of Amsterdam, also promoted Christian secondary education at the newly established Chicago Christian High School (1916), which lay leader James De Boer had spearheaded. However, the next pastor of First CRC, Benjamin Essenburg, who served for seventeen years until 1945, reconfirmed the pietist mentality.

Douglas Park CRC, founded in 1899, similarly aligned itself with the confessionalists, but antithetical neo-Calvinists also made inroads in the Progressive era in this more affluent congregation under dominies De Leeuw and Manni. Klaas Schoolland's call to construct a holy Dutch community as a bulwark against the world resonated among them: "In our *isolation* and in our *independent action* lie our strength and our prospects for the future."[10]

While the boundaries between the Seceders of 1834 and the Kuyperians of 1886 sometimes blurred on the West Side, one mindset had little appeal—that of the cosmopolitan, positivist Calvinists, led by Grand Rapids theologians B. K. Kuyper and Henry Beets. The Groningers seemed to have no vision to transform Chicago into a Christian commonwealth. Few attended Chicago Christian High School or the Kuyperian stronghold of Calvin College, the denominational undergraduate school in Grand Rapids to train pastors and teachers, and few read the triumphalist periodicals, including the short-lived *American Daily Standard*, launched in 1920 by Englewood CRC minister J. Clover Monsma.[11]

The West Side of Chicago was always the most congested and ethnically mixed; it was the quintessential working-class district.[12] Such neighborhoods are always in flux and pass through the natural cycle of growth, maturity, deterioration, and eventual abandonment. The Dutch community fits this classic pattern; it began near the city center and then relocated five times toward the suburbs, due to the encroachment of noisome factories and ethnic groups considered to be uncouth. In each cycle of "Dutch flight" they bought or built new churches, homes, schools, stores, and shops.

The original settlement took shape in the 1840s and 1850s in the region immediately west of the Chicago River. In 1848 several families of Hervormde Kerk background and one Seceder family organized an independent congregation, which five years later joined the Reformed Church in America (RCA) after the Reverend Albertus C. Van Raalte, founder of the Holland, Michigan, colony, came at their request to help them affiliate. Early growth was slow because the congregation had no pastor for its first six years and most of the immigrants were "indifferent" in religious matters.[13]

This church, which became First Reformed, worshiped in rented quarters on Randolph Street immediately west of the Chicago River until 1856 (#1, Figure 8.1), when they erected their own church building a mile south on Foster Street (renamed Law Street in 1881) near Desplaines and Harrison streets (#2). The first pastor (1859–61) was the Reverend Cornelius Vander Meulen, founder of the Zeeland, Michigan, colony, who had a missionary heart and rounded up the scattered Hollanders. He also copied the American practice of opening a Sunday school.[14]

A weak Dutch community formed around Harrison and Halsted streets (in the area later made famous by Jane Addams's Hull House) when the Groninger families of Nicholas (Harm) Ronda, Cornelius Bos, Peter Kooi, and John Evenhouse arrived in 1853 and 1854. In 1867 the settlement experienced its first religious schism. Fifteen mostly Groninger families (seventy-five persons) from First Reformed, led by dissident elder Gerrit Vastenhouw, seceded to form the True Holland Reformed Church (later First CRC). These traditionalists built a small frame church three blocks west of First Reformed on Gurley Street between Miller and Sholto (#5, Figure 8.1).[15] Two years later First Reformed, led by the energetic De Bey, built their new edifice three blocks west of First CRC at Harrison and May streets (#3, Figure 8.1).

De Bey served First Reformed during its flowering period, while the upstart CRC went through seven pastorates and vacancies.[16] De Bey was a strong person mentally and physically, with great leadership abilities and vision. He dabbled in Chicago real estate and made his parsonage the headquarters for resettling Dutch immigrants in the city, some of whom he provided with small business loans.[17] For twenty years De Bey also wrote a series of letters for the *Provinciale Groninger Courant*, the major newspaper of the province, in which he urged those with "an iron will and a pair of good hands" to come to Chicago where laborers were urgently needed, especially after the Chicago Fire of 1871 (shaded area on Figure 8.1).[18] Those who work with their heads—clerks, bookkeepers, small merchants, teachers, and gentlemen—should stay at home, De Bey warned. "Our new Hollanders are cutters of wood and drawers of water. They perform the roughest and heaviest labors."[19] Only farm hands, day laborers, craftsmen, and maids need apply. The dominie thus became the most influential link between the Old and New Worlds for the Chicago Dutch.

The steady arrival of hundreds of Groninger farm families boosted the memberships of both Chicago congregations. First RCA reached 1,000 adherents by

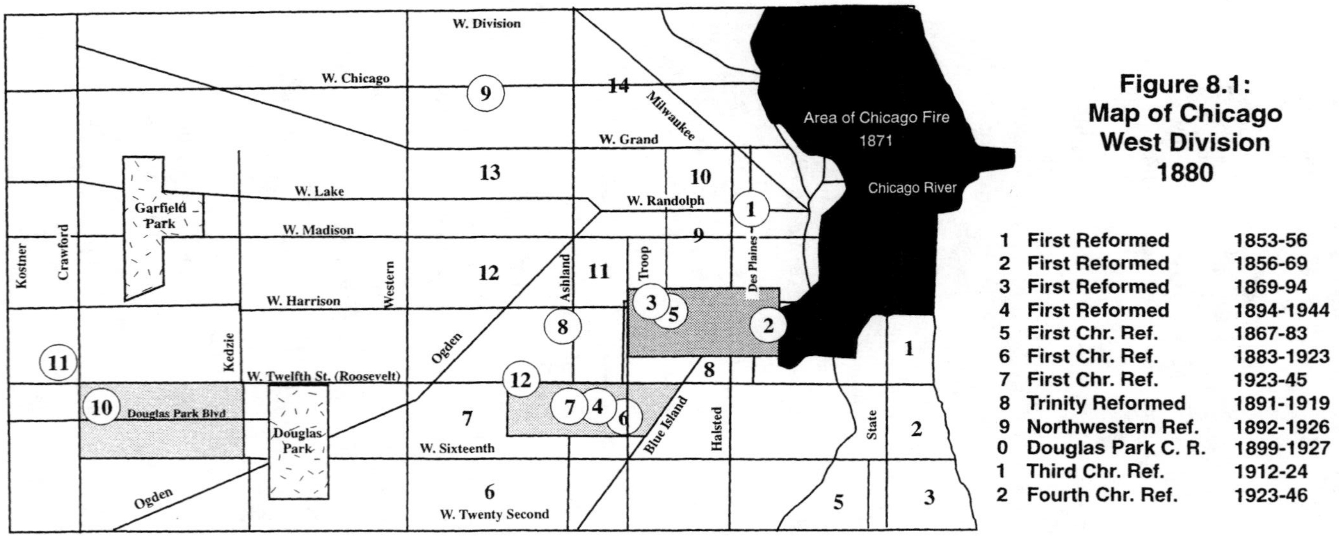

Figure 8.1 Map of Chicago, West Division, 1880

SOURCE: Created by Graphics Department, Kent State University, and modified by the Computer & Information Technology Department, Hope College.

1875 and 1,200 at its high point in 1884 before birthing daughter congregations in Englewood and farther west. First CRC grew to 1,000 adherents by 1886 and 1,200 in 1895; it too mothered congregations in Englewood and Douglas Park.

After the great fire, the Dutch community moved to the renowned Ashland Avenue area a mile to the southwest, where housing was more readily available for the rush of new immigrants. In 1883 First CRC purchased from the Presbyterians a spacious building on 14th Street east of Ashland Avenue, between Troop and Loomis streets (#6, Figure 8.1).

In 1891 young families desiring English-language worship left First Reformed without its blessing and organized Trinity RCA on the north fringe of the Ashland neighborhood (#8, Figure 8.1). The founders insisted that their action would stem the loss of many "choice young friends and families" who felt "compelled to find homes in other denominations," mainly Presbyterian and Episcopalian. "Father must live too," countered De Bey, who had long resisted the language change and secession. In 1893 other members of First RCA living on the far north side transferred to the Dutch-language Northwestern RCA on Superior Avenue (#9, Figure 8.1), which congregation of 240 parishioners had that year left its Presbyterian affiliation and joined the RCA.[20] In 1894 First RCA with its 500 families also relocated into the heart of its changing parochial territory. They sold their Harrison Street building and parsonage and built a new church to seat 1,000 on Hastings Street (13th Place) near Ashland Avenue only a few blocks west of First CRC (#4, Figure 8.1). Here they worshiped until 1944.

Immigrants continued to arrive from the Netherlands in the 1890s, sometimes in groups of seventy-five to one hundred, and the Christian Reformed congregation gathered them in by offering genuine Dutch *gezelligheid* (sociability).[21] Worship services at both mother churches were in Dutch until the 1920s, but First RCA in 1890 began English-language Sunday school and catechism classes and young peoples societies, which turned away new families with children.[22] First CRC held to the Dutch entirely, and the congregation in 1893 also launched Ebenezer Christian School, which began with three hundred pupils. The day school, built at 15th and Ashland Avenue in 1906, stood one block from the church. Hence, the newcomers found the Christian Reformed congregation more congenial than the Reformed body.

A lesser factor in rapid CRC growth was the decision in 1882 of the Netherlands Seceder denomination to direct its numerous immigrating members into the CRC. The Dutch church did so because the national synod of the Reformed Church in America, dominated by its old New York–New Jersey wing, had refused for many years to ban Masonic lodge brothers. The Netherlandic decision stunted the growth of First Reformed of Chicago, as it did all RCA congregations in the Midwest, despite the fact that all refused to accept lodge members.[23]

By 1923 First CRC surpassed 1,200 members and outgrew its "Old Fourteenth Street Church," as the edifice was affectionately called. The congregation bought from the Lutherans a beautiful church a stone's throw from First RCA on the very visible corner of Ashland Avenue and Hastings Street (#7, Figure 8.1). This served the body well until 1946.[24]

From the 1880s to the 1920s Ashland Avenue was the heart of the *Groninger Hoek* (Corner). Henry Stob, a native son, described it in his "Recollections" as a blue-collar neighborhood mixed with Jews and Irish and Polish Catholics. The Hollanders, said Stob, "spoke Dutch at home, worked hard, and harbored intense loyalties to their Dutch churches."[25] While rubbing elbows with outsiders on the street and on the job, they lived their lives from the cradle to the grave within the cocoon of their families, churches, Christian schools, social organizations, and Dutch shopkeepers and professionals.

As consumers, the Dutch also controlled their own economic destiny. They willingly patronized Dutch merchants and craftsmen, took their savings to Dutch banks, bought homes through Dutch realtors, drew up their wills with Dutch attorneys, went to Dutch doctors and dentists with their hurts, and patronized fellow merchants and craftsmen. For employment, as Stob recalled, "some heads of families in the community worked in shops and factories, others held office jobs, and a number ran their own businesses." The Dutch preferred to work for themselves, hiring relatives and fellow church members as needed. But some craftsmen worked in factories, notably Roselanders at the Pullman Car Works and West Siders at the Western Electric Hawthorne Plant in Cicero. South Siders were concentrated in carpentry and masonry work, while West Siders loved to work with horses and found their niche hauling ash, garbage, and general freight, or peddling ice and coal, produce, or milk. They were an industrious and thrifty lot, and few were rich. Novelist Peter De Vries captured their character best in his renowned autobiographical novel, *The Blood of the Lamb*, about growing up Dutch on the old West Side in the 1920s. De Vries recites this street rhyme: "Oh, the Irish and the Dutch, Don't amount to very much."[26] But they were on the way up.

The Dutch saw "gold" in cinders (the residue of coal-fired boilers and trash and waste incineration) and later in garbage, after the city banned burning it. Both byproducts had to be hauled away regularly and often, and the industry was immune from the periodic economic depressions. The West Siders lived near the major source area in the city center, and they willingly exchanged Dutch dirt under the fingernails for Chicago soot, grime, and ash. As it happened, the Dutch virtually monopolized the Chicago garbage collection business. Over the years there were more than 350 Dutch companies ranging from one-man operations to large outfits with dozens of drivers and helpers. The owners were often related to one another, they attended the same churches, and they relied on informal understandings and agreements to control contracts and keep out interlopers. Critics aptly called them the "Dutch Mafia." When in the 1970s many sold their businesses to the garbage conglomerates, Waste Management and Browning Ferris Industries, many of them became instant millionaires.[27]

The more affluent Dutch moved into newer neighborhoods with more open spaces and larger lots: in Englewood seven miles south in the 1880s, in Douglas Park–Lawndale on the "Far West Side" (#10, Figure 8.1), three to four miles west in the 1890s, and in Summit five miles southwest after 1900. The Far West Side churches were the English-speaking Trinity RCA (#8, Figure 8.1), Douglas Park CRC (#10), Third CRC (#11) founded in 1912, and the English-speaking Fourth

CRC (#12) founded in 1923. A second Christian school, Timothy, was established in 1910 on Tripp Avenue near Douglas Park CRC. This area of tree-lined streets, boulevards, and parks between Kedzie and Cicero avenues was the third Calvinist enclave. New home prices in the mid-1870s, which ranged from $3,000 to $8,000, testify to the rising status of the Dutch.

Before World War I, the fourth Dutch hub took shape in the nexus of Cicero, Berwyn, and Oak Park, the suburbs immediately west of the city and two to three miles from Douglas Park–Lawndale (Figure 8.2). A large migration of southern blacks to the Old West Side had set off massive white flight after incidents of harassment as children walked to and from school. The Dutch joined the exodus and by 1935 one RCA and three CRC churches and Timothy Christian School had been relocated in Cicero.[28] By the 1940s the mother churches at Ashland Avenue were no longer viable. The remnants at First RCA and First CRC sold their buildings to black congregations in 1944 and 1945 and built new churches in Berwyn. Ebenezer School was also closed in 1945. The remaining families moved west one after another in rapid succession, leaving behind only a handful of elderly folks.

In the 1960s the West Siders pulled up stakes yet again in the face of incursions by Italians, Poles, and African-Americans. They bought homes more than ten miles farther west in Elmhurst and environs, where in the 1970s three of the Cicero area churches relocated, as did the Timothy Christian grade and high schools (Figure 8.2). This was the second relocation for Timothy Christian School. (There was a similar white flight out of Englewood and Roseland in the 1950s and 1960s into southern Cook County and northern Indiana.)

"Westward Ho!" seemed to be the motto of the Groningers until they had entirely deserted Chicago for the upscale and nonintegrated suburbs. The path of least resistance flowed westward along the commercial and streetcar artery of 12th Street (renamed Roosevelt Road after President Theodore Roosevelt), because major trunk railroad lines and industrial districts hedged them in to the south and north. Later, the Eisenhower (formerly Congress) Expressway channeled the Dutch into the far western suburbs. Whether within the city or beyond its borders, the Dutch Calvinists clustered around their churches and schools in order to preserve an ethnoreligious solidarity.

Several hundred Groningers who wished to continue in agriculture formed small truck farming colonies on rented land on the outskirts—in the Chicago Sanitary District in the 1860s; Summit (Archer Avenue) in the 1870s; Evergreen Park, Oak Lawn, and Mt. Greenwood after 1900; and Western Springs and Des Plaines in the 1920s (Figure 8.2). As late as 1932, 16 percent of the families of the Second Cicero CRC (an urban suburb) were farmers who lived up to 25 miles west and commuted by automobile. Few were able to buy their land; most eventually were forced to retire or farm elsewhere when their land was carved into housing subdivisions.

The cultural life of the Dutch Reformed centered around their churches, which shaped their core beliefs and values.[29] The churches and their numerous programs kept them busy, including men's and women's societies and their feeder groups for young people, ladies' sewing circles, choirs and bands, mission clubs, holiday fests and church picnics, men's softball and bowling, and many similar activities.

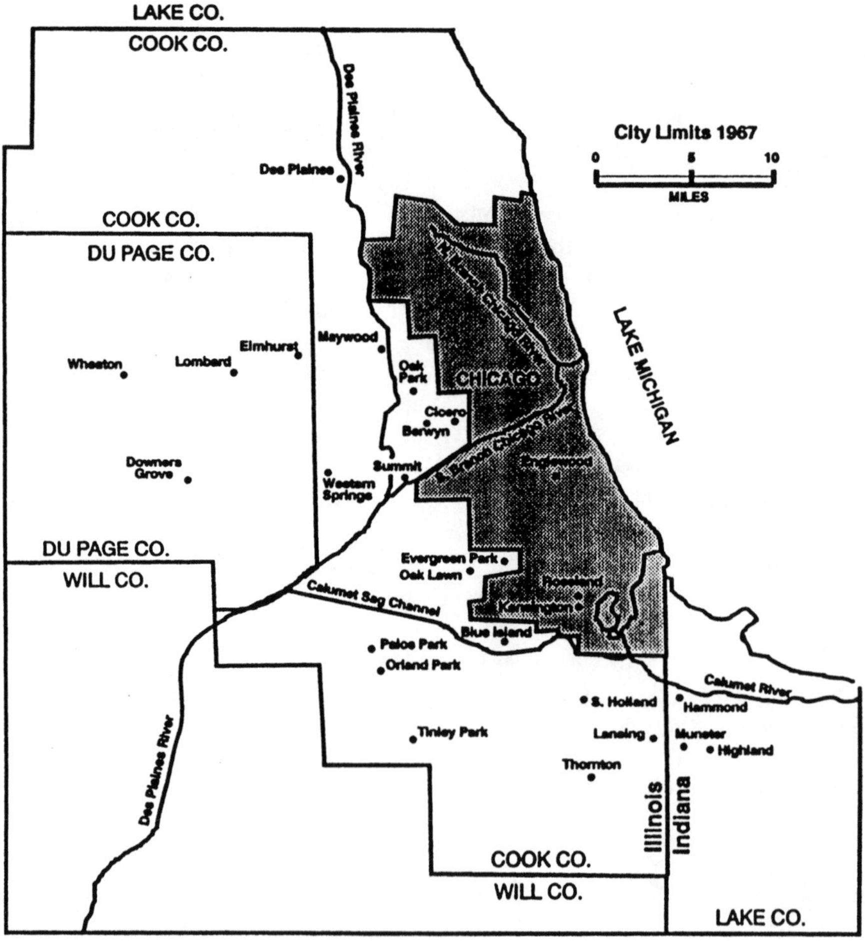

Figure 8.2 Map of Chicago and Environs

SOURCE: Created by Graphics Department, Kent State University.

Augmenting the churches were mutual aid societies, Christian schools, and social clubs. The benevolent societies were dictated by economic necessity in a society with few government "safety nets" and by the religious obligation of doing good to those within the "household of faith." The secular social clubs formed by the professional and business elite appeared only after the immigrants had gained an economic foothold and wished to boast to the Americans of their Dutch heritage. Hence, this was actually a mark of their rapid assimilation.

The oldest and most successful mutual aid agency was the "Zelf Hulp" Burial Fund Society, founded in 1879 by West Siders. By 1913 it had 14,000 members and had paid out about $150,000 in death benefits. It continued for one hundred years until the 1970s, when the need ended for such an ethnic organization.[30] Similar groups were the Roseland Mutual Aid Society (1884), Eendracht Maakt Macht [Union is Strength] (1884), Excelsior Society (1897), Hulp en Nood (1913), Vriendschap en Trouw [Friendship and Loyalty](1910) of Englewood, and the Flemish Society (1905).[31] The Excelsior Society, which primarily served the Ashland Avenue Groninger Hoek, staged annual July 4th picnics featuring the Christian Reformed Church bands Harmonie (First CRC) and Excelsior (Douglas Park CRC). In 1911 it launched a city-wide campaign to establish the Holland Home for the Aged, which opened in Roseland in 1914. This was its major accomplishment.[32]

Ethnic pride, rather than acts of mercy, was the hallmark of the social clubs.[33] They celebrated Dutch royal birthdays and national holidays, especially Sinterklaas (St. Nicholas) Day on December 5. The William of Orange Society (1890) touted their namesake's feats and importance. The Holland Society of Chicago (1895) staged its annual dinner on William's birthday (April 16) and toasted the defeat of the Spanish Duke of Alva and victory for the South African Boers.

The Chicago Section of the General Dutch League (1897) took on more practical projects—the establishment of a Dutch chair at the University of Chicago, a Queen Wilhelmina Library of Dutch-language books, and the annual birthday celebrations of the Queen and, after 1909, Princess Juliana.[34] "The Queen's birthday is for our Dutch people, a day of national rejoicing," declared the editor of the Dutch-language Chicago newspaper *Onze Toekomst* in 1909. "It is a pity that we have been unable so far to make of this day a General Netherlands Day. It could be celebrated by all Netherlanders irrespective of political and religious affiliation. The time for it has come now." Until well into the 1920s, Chicagoland remembered the Queen's day of April 30th with speeches and music amidst unfurled Dutch and American flags.[35] The Chicago World's Fair of 1893 (the Columbian Exhibition) and the World Exposition of 1933 provided other opportunities to showcase Dutch ideals and culture, and the societies took full advantage.

Paradoxically, members of the elitist secular clubs were the most Americanized of the Hollanders. A few even traced their lineage to colonial New Netherlands. They wanted to be "good Americans" and sneered at the pietistic Hollanders who resisted assimilation by ghettoizing themselves and founding Christian day schools. "There are too many Americanizing forces at work for us to remain Dutch," pontificated Peter Moerdyke, pastor of Chicago's first English-speaking Reformed church (Trinity RCA) in 1891. "One might easier hope to withstand the mighty current of the Niagara than to prevent the Americanization of the Dutch people." When the CRC folk attempted to do just that by establishing Christian schools in the face of the rampant Darwinism in the public schools, prominent attorney Henry Vander Ploeg of First RCA chided them for their parochialism and closed-mindedness. "They wish to continue to measure and to judge things by the standard of the home they have left, and not of the home they find. So extreme is this obstinate adherence to Dutch customs and usages," Vander Ploeg continued, "that our worthy Holland people establish Dutch parochial [sic] schools in many places and would, if they could, establish exclusive small Dutch villages or settlements, even in our large metropolitan cities."[36]

The Chicago press approvingly printed a full résumé of the "old timer's" speech, but the resistant ethnics lashed out angrily at Vander Ploeg's "foul imputations," "crude attacks," and "invective against everything Dutch, and everything precious."[37] The truth that Vander Ploeg missed was that Christian Reformed members did indeed succeed in damming the cultural forces for several generations.

The CRC did it by channeling the social life of its children into an exclusively ethnoreligious track. CRC youth attended the Dutch Christian schools from first through twelfth grades, while RCA youth attended public schools, although a minority also went to the Dutch schools. Outside of school, CRC high schoolers later had their Young Calvinist League and junior high youth had the Calvinist Cadet Corp for boys and Calvinette Club for girls. RCA youth, by contrast, organized church Boy Scout and Girl Scout troops and high schoolers had Christian Endeavor on Sunday evenings. These names speak volumes. The CRC stressed Dutch Calvinist roots while the RCA "endeavored" to be simply Christian, whether in scouting or youth club.

A full schedule of church and school activities kept the adults involved as well. In addition to the weekly meetings, each denomination held all-city mission fests, Reformation Day assemblies, Bible conferences, youth rallies, and Sunday School conventions. Even summer vacations were planned. CRC folk went to the Cedar Lake (IN) Bible Conference and campground for an exclusive retreat, whereas RCA folk preferred Billy Sunday's nondenominational Winona Lake (IN) Bible Conference and campground, which espoused typical American revivalist themes and music. The only CRC-RCA cooperation was in men's softball and (later) basketball, in the Holland Home that mainly housed widows, in regional choral societies, and occasionally in politics.

For entertainment RCA youth might patronize movie houses and dance halls with their public school friends. But CRC youth were taught to be "in the world but not of it." They were admonished to keep away from "worldly amusements," and when interviewed by the elders upon professing their faith, they were routinely asked about such activities. Adult men in both communions were likewise warned not to affiliate with masonic lodges on pain of being excluded from church membership.

Many devout CRC folk succumbed to American fundamentalism in their music, however, largely because of the reach of the only Christian radio station in the city, the voice of the Moody Bible Institute, which went on the air in 1926. Pious

Reformed homes had their radios tuned to WMBI from morning to night. "Aunt Theresa" Worman's KYB (Know Your Bible) Club program enthralled the children with her Bible stories, and the young people loved the contemporary Christian music of Homer Rodeheaver, Virginia Asher, and George Beverly Shea.[38] Children at the Timothy Christian school did not learn Dutch psalms in their daily singing exercises; they much preferred Gospel songs.

So distinct was the CRC-RCA cultural gulf that CRC parents considered their children's infrequent marriages to RCA families as "mixed" or interfaith marriages. If pressed, however, parents considered such unions preferable to mating with non-Dutch Protestants, with nonbelievers, or worst of all, with Catholics. While attending Chicago Christian High School, Peter De Vries in his autobiography tells of seriously dating an Italian girl, but he finally broke the relationship. Why? "Religious reasons," he says. "Our faith doesn't allow us to intermarry."[39] De Vries was correct.

Even in death the Dutch remained separate. Mt. Auburn, Forest Home, Mt. Greenwood, and other cemeteries set aside exclusive "Holland sections," sometimes replete with windmills, and they donated plots within these sections to the various church deaconates for indigent Dutch. In death, as in life, it was important to be near one's own. The Reformed folk preferred funeral directors who belonged to their own denomination. This is understandable because funeral services took place in church, and morticians and pastors worked closely to coordinate the services. The nonchurched used funeral chapels for their services, joined by members of their Dutch social clubs.[40] Increasingly, so do the churched, as funeral services less often bring the congregation together for worship in the sanctuary.

Politically, the Dutch Reformed were passive Republican voters who supported the party ticket and seldom ran for office themselves. The few candidates for public office, who were always RCA members, could not count on the support of their fellow ethnics, especially CRC members, unless they ran as party-backed Republicans. The editors of *Onze Toekomst* tried repeatedly to generate bloc voting for "our" Holland candidates, but they found a spirit of cooperation "non-existent among our people." Reformed and Christian Reformed would not cross religious fault lines to vote for fellow Dutch candidates.[41]

Political action groups faced the same problems. RCA leaders in 1910 founded the Christian Anti-Saloon League, which in 1911 evolved into the Dutch-American Civic League of Chicago, to promote other Progressive causes. In 1920 Reverend Broekstra and other RCA leaders formed the Christian Political Society, which essentially was a Dutch Republican Party organ. Nonchurched Hollanders on the left had in 1912 organized the Dutch Socialist Propaganda Club, and Dr. W. De Boer ran for Seventeenth Ward alderman on the Socialist ticket in 1910.[42] In the desperate 1930s RCA professionals formed the United Dutch-American Voters' League to back the Democratic mayoral reformer Anton J. Cermak.[43]

In the face of these clearly assimilated Hollanders, CRC folk sat on their hands. They were not enticed even when the Christian Political Society reached out by endorsing the controversial issue of government funds for Christian schools. Nor would they subscribe in 1928 to the ambitious Calvinistic newspaper, the *American*

Daily Standard, launched by the CRC minister J. Clover Monsma of Englewood. The daily paper was deliberately modeled after Abraham Kuyper's *De Standaard*, but it lasted only three months.[44] The CRC neo-Calvinists tried again in 1951, by creating the Christian Citizens Committee, spearheaded by Ralph Dekker of Englewood and thirty other South Siders, to promote Christian political theory and practice. After a decade of faithful effort, the Committee died a quiet death.[45] Dutch idealism had no realistic chance in Chicago's rough-and-tumble politics, and the isolation-minded Calvinists were unwilling to taint themselves.

Since many Hollanders were blue-collar workers, the one issue they could not avoid was the growing power of unions in the 1940s and 1950s. But they dealt with unions in the same way as politics, passively. They joined only when pressured to do so, but would not participate. One had to eat, they rationalized. But it was no easy decision. The CRC had long condemned "worldly" labor unions for their "socialistic," ungodly principles and violent tactics. Yet many Reformed teamsters, garbage men, and building tradesmen succumbed to threats and acts of violence and joined the Teamsters union and the AFL-CIO. The capitulation, however, could cost them a seat on the church consistory bench.[46] The solution was to found locals of the Grand Rapids–based Christian Labor Association, as did Calumet area CRC building tradesmen and grocery clerks (Locals 12 and 32, respectively). But the CLA never gained more than lukewarm support from Chicago's Dutch Reformed tradesmen, and the teamsters gave it no thought at all, because the brass-knuckled Teamsters union would tolerate no rival.[47]

Thus, despite being invisible among the city's nationality groups, Chicago Groningers, especially those affiliated with the Christian Reformed denomination, continue to maintain an ethnocultural identity seventy-five years after immigration ceased in the 1920s.[48] The West Siders, in contrast to those in Roseland and South Holland, lacked the critical mass to "Dutchify" the institutions and culture of the community. The alternatives were separation or assimilation. Christian Reformed folk chose separation and held the forces of assimilation at bay because of their schools, although the ethnic glue has loosened since the 1950s. Reformed Church members chose quasi-separation, an ethnic church but an American school. Their outward looking, revivalist emphasis put them on the fast track to Americanization and they were largely assimilated by the third and fourth generations.[49]

Urban Dutch of Cleveland

In Cleveland, as in Chicago, the churches gave form and substance to community life. They served as the cultural and religious centers of each Dutch enclave, and their presence had much to do with the rate of settlement and pace of assimilation. Dutch Calvinists there fulfilled the maxim that they "stick together not primarily on the basis of ethnicity or nationalism but on the basis of their religion."[50] Dutch Catholics and Calvinists lived in the same neighborhood in Cleveland but had no social contact, despite speaking the same language and sharing the same nationality. Their lives reflected the cultural localism of the Old Country, in which the area north of the Rhine River was heavily Reformed after the War with Spain in the sixteenth and seventeenth centuries, and the Flemish southern provinces remained Roman Catholic after holding off the Protestant upsurge.

For the first thirty years of the Dutch presence in Cleveland, from 1835 to 1865, more Catholics than Protestants came because German Catholic parishes welcomed them from the outset, but there was no Dutch Reformed church until 1864. At first, the few Reformed pioneers had to worship in the Evangelical German Reformed Church.[51] Even after 1864 the Calvinists did not find Cleveland a magnet, believing it lacked the critical population mass needed to support a full panoply of parochial schools and ethnic societies. Transiency in Cleveland remained high. In the censuses from 1850 through 1880, only 37 percent of Dutch residents stayed in the city from one census to the next.[52] Reformed immigrants preferred the solid rural colonies farther west. As a result, Cleveland attracted relatively few Dutch, despite its strong industrial base and advantageous location as a lake port. By 1880 the city counted only 2,500 first- and second-generation Hollanders. The population rose very slowly thereafter, reaching 2,900 in 1930 (Table 8.3). Adding those with multiple Dutch ancestry, the total number today in the greater Cleveland area is about 25,000.[53]

The first Dutch immigrants in Cleveland were several Catholic families from the Gelderse Achterhoek (literally, "back corner") near the German border, who in 1835 settled on the southeast side near the city limits south of Woodland Avenue.[54] Most prominent was the family of Hermanus Bernardus Wamelink, a textile dyer in the village of Aalten who helped organize St. Mary's Church "on the Flats" in 1838.[55] Wamelink offered financial assistance to his friend Johannes Gerhardus Jansen, a ropemaker from the nearby village of Groenlo, who emigrated with his wife and four children. The Wamelink Piano Store on Superior Avenue, founded by son John and brother-in-law Frances A. Nolze, made this a well-known name in the city. Cleveland's dominant westside Dutch Catholic community began in 1849

TABLE 8.3 Dutch in Cleveland (Cuyahoga County), 1850–1930

	FOREIGN-BORN		NATIVE-BORN		
YEAR	NUMBER	%	NUMBER	%	TOTAL
1850	162	76	52	24	214
1860	372	62	227	38	599
1870	559	50	560	50	1,119
1880	811	42	1,152	58	1,963
1900	804	33	1,631	67	2,435
1910	1,076	45	1,340	55	2,416
1920	1,055	38	1,723	63	2,778
1930	933	32	1,948	68	2,881

SOURCE: Robert P. Swierenga, comp., "Dutch in Cleveland, 1850–80," derived from Federal Manuscript Population Censuses, 1850–80; Bureau of the Census, *Census of the United States*, 1900 Vol. I, *Population* (Washington, 1901), 797; 1910 Vol. I, *Population* (Washington, 1913), 854, 942; 1920 Vol. I *Population* (Washington, 1922), 927, 935; 1930 Vol. III, Part I *Population* (Washington, 1932), 502, 506.

with the arrival of a group of thirty-seven friends and relatives from Winterswijk, also in the Achterhoek, led by the blacksmith John (Gerrit Jan) Te(n) Pas.[56]

The first wave of Reformed immigrants arrived in the decade 1847–57 to form the nucleus of a permanent community on the east side. They brought with them a deep pietism and religious orthodoxy that was typical in their native province of Zeeland.[57] In 1870 and 1871 an even larger group came to the west side from the Gelderse Achterhoek. Alarmed by Dutch mobilization in the face of the Franco-Prussian War (1870–71), they sought to avoid the draft and a possible conflict in their region. By 1870 about one half of the Dutch in Cleveland traced their roots to the Achterhoek and one third to Zeeland. In general, Reformed from Zeeland lived on the east side, whereas both Reformed and Catholics from Gelderland inhabited the west side. The linkage between these regions of the Netherlands and the neighborhoods in Cleveland illustrates the general pattern of chain migration and cultural transplanting that characterized much of the European transatlantic movement.

Initially the Dutch clustered in three neighborhoods each on the east and west sides (Figure 8.3). The east side locales were: at East 35th and Cedar Avenue around the First (Holland) Reformed Church and the East Side Christian (True Holland) Reformed Church; along Lexington and Wade Park avenues around East 55th Street; and to the south on Woodland Avenue along East 75th Street in an area dubbed "Dutch Alley" by local residents.[58] Cleveland's east side was more industrialized and its upwardly mobile families moved more quickly to newer subdivisions. Thus, the east side never developed the stable, ethnic neighborhoods that characterized the west side for generations.

The three west side neighborhoods were: near the City Infirmary between West 14th (Jennings) and West 25th (Pearl); farther south along the hillside of Holmden Avenue that was popularly known as "Dutch Hill"; and an area farther west nicknamed "Wooden Shoe Alley," along Lorain Avenue from West 54th (Courtland) to West 65th (Gordon) Streets. These original Dutch neighborhoods hosted the usual range of Dutch stores, shops, and businesses to serve their countrymen.[59]

"Wooden Shoe Alley," the area of greatest Dutch concentration in Cleveland from 1870 to 1940, was religiously segregated in the typical Dutch manner. The Reformed settled south of Lorain Avenue between West 58th (Waverly) and West 65th (Gordon) streets, and Catholics gathered north of Lorain Avenue between West 54th and West 57th streets, where they affiliated with the German-language St. Stephen Parish (1870) on West 54th (Courtland). Content to intermingle with the Germans, Dutch Catholics never formed an ethnic parish with a Dutch-speaking priest, as they did in Cincinnati, Chicago, Grand Rapids, and other cities.

The Reformed churches began relatively late and had a precarious existence for decades. Their working-class members, barely able to support one congregation, required four, because they were divided geographically by the Cuyahoga River, culturally by the differing provincial origins, and religiously between the more orthodox "Dutch church"—the True Holland Reformed Church (later CRC), and the more latitudinarian "American church"—the (Dutch) Reformed Church in America (RCA).

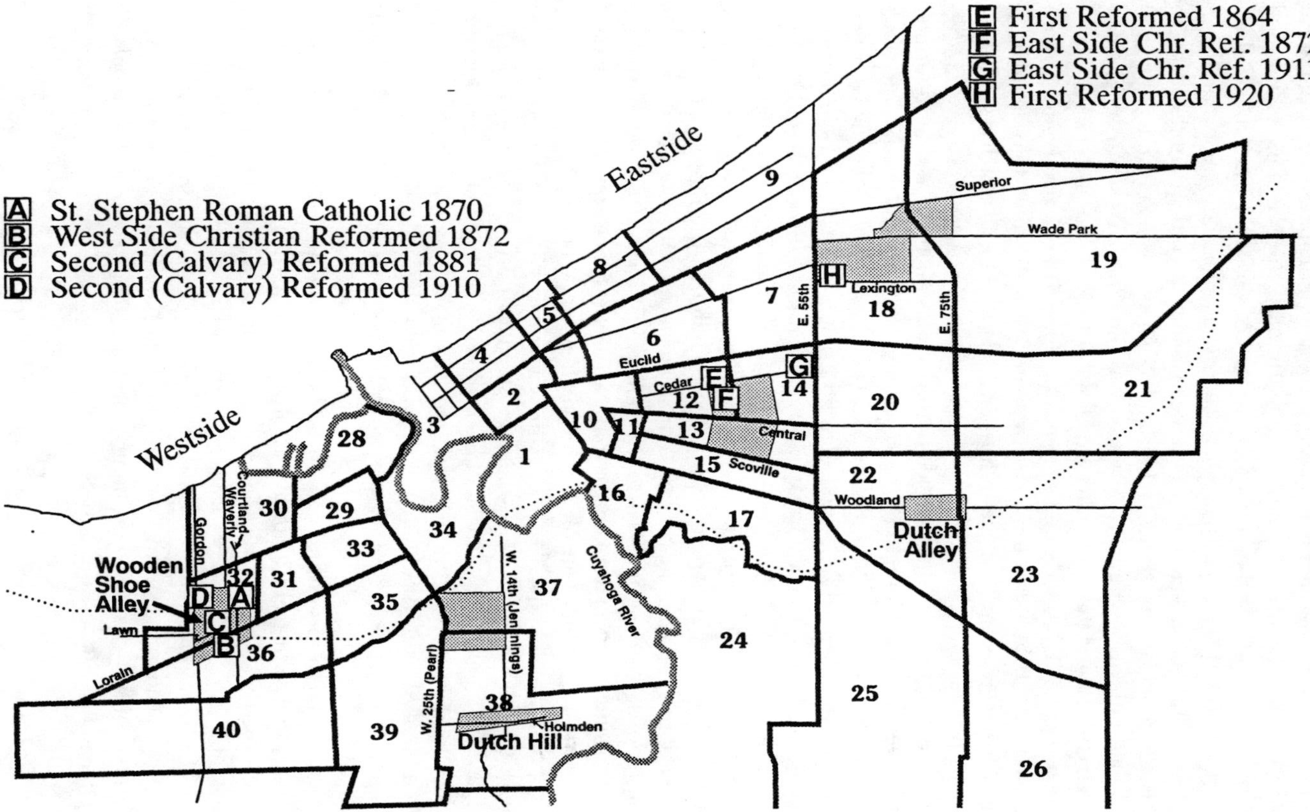

Figure 8.3 Churches and Original Areas of Dutch Settlement, Cleveland Ward Map, 1893

SOURCE: Created by Graphics Department, Kent State University.

First Dutch Reformed church was built on the east side in 1864 on Blair (East 33rd) Street near Cedar Avenue (E, Figure. 8.3). Westsiders had to go by buggy or on foot six to seven miles for worship services because the streetcars did not operate on Sunday. In 1872 some forty conservative member families seceded to form the True Holland Reformed congregation. Initially, the seceders established churches on both side of the city, on West 58th Street (B, Figure 8.3) and on Calvert (East 35th) Street (F, Figure 8.3), sharing a single pastor between them. But the conjoined congregation "experienced much discord," doubtless due to cultural clashes between west side Gelderlanders and east side Zeelanders. In 1880 they decided to form separate groups, the West Side (later West Park) Christian Reformed Church and the East Side Christian Reformed Church.[60]

Some west side Reformed families found the local True Holland church more convenient than the distant Reformed church on East 35th Street. In order to forestall further defections, in 1881 the Reformed leaders arranged worship services in a small chapel at Aspen (West 61st) Street and Lawn (later Colgate) Avenue (C, Figure 8.3). The venture flourished and led to the establishment of Second Reformed (later renamed Calvary) Church. In 1910 the congregation erected a spacious brick building on West 65th Street (D, Figure 8.3) a few blocks away from the Christian Reformed Church. Second Reformed adopted English from the outset in the Sunday school and in the afternoon worship service, but until 1918 retained Dutch in the primary morning service for the sake of the elderly and recent immigrants.[61]

The larger West Side Christian Reformed Church, located until 1950 on West 58th Street, obtained trained pastors more successfully than did East Side Christian Reformed Church, which remained for more than eleven years, until 1891, without a leader. Indeed, twice—from 1887 to 1888 and from 1895 to 1901—the two congregations again shared a pastor, but as in the 1870s the arrangement "was marked with difficulties."[62] Pastors were often reluctant to come. When the Reverend Jacob Bolt accepted the call to the West Side congregation in 1903, it was noted that he had "been asked before to visit Cleveland but steadfastly refused, having no desires to see Cleveland, much less to live and labor there."[63] Bolt's initial reluctance perhaps reflected the general attitude among Dutch Calvinists around Cleveland, who perceived themselves at risk of being swallowed up by the Yankee culture.

The process of chain migration, more than any other factor, nurtured the small Dutch settlement. Early residents appealed to relatives and friends in the Netherlands to join them, promising help in finding housing and jobs. Over the next years a "constant influx" of friends and relatives heeded the call, which reassured church leaders that "the reports concerning our city as a place to make a living, were favorable."[64]

One of the new immigrants, J. H. Brinks of Almelo, came at the invitation of his three sons who had found steady jobs and good living conditions in Cleveland. The elder Brinks, in turn, wrote to his family and friends in the homeland about his reception and first impressions of the city:

> "On the 14th of the month [September 1904] we arrived in New York. . . . And then, after twenty hours in the train, we arrived in

> Cleveland at 6:00 PM the 16th. And there were our children all around the train, and more people from Almelo. Then we went to my son Hendrick's house, and the house was full of people to welcome us. Among them the Dominie [Dutch for minister, literally lord] and the two elders.... This country is so big, that it would take 100 years to travel all over it. But it is a blessed land. A young man, and especially one with skills, can earn much here. Our son Hendrick [a bricklayer] earns 24 dollars a week, 8 hours a day. Albert a painter earns 18 dollars. Jan has been here one and a half years and has money in the bank.... Gossen is a tailor; tailors here are very busy, at home and in the shops or factories. It is not so good for a farmer here. He should go to a different place.... I think about the people of Rijssen [a village 5 miles from Almelo] that they must toil for a few cents and what little that puts on the table. Here the country is not perfect but the people eat well."[65]

The Dutch immigrants preferred to be self-employed and they generally enjoyed steady economic improvement, although like everyone else they suffered in the periodic economic downturns.[66] From the earliest years, they favored the skilled crafts, particularly in the building construction trades. In 1860 42 percent of the Dutch workforce were craftsmen (e.g., carpenters, masons, painters), 47 percent unskilled laborers and factory workers, and 11 percent shopkeepers, clerks, small-scale manufacturers, business managers, and professionals (Table 8.4).

Over the next four decades, the proportion of craftsmen held steady at about 40 percent, while white-collar workers more than doubled from 11 to 25 percent and unskilled laborers declined by nearly one fifth from 47 to 39 percent. From 1880 to 1900 the number of Dutch professionals (doctors, teachers, ministers, lawyers, etc.) tripled, increasing from 4 to 12 percent. Some immigrants had to take factory jobs, however; 10 percent worked as factory laborers and 13 percent as machinists in 1900 (Table 8.4).[67]

By 1880 the Dutch in Cleveland had coalesced into two core areas around the Reformed churches and St. Stephen Catholic parish (A, Figure 8.3). "Wooden Shoe Alley" (Wards 32 and 36) on the west side was the most populous Dutch neighborhood in the city and had the highest proportion of foreign-born. The

TABLE 8.4 Dutch Workforce in Cleveland, 1860–1900

	Occupational Status		
Year	White Collar	Skilled*	Unskilled
1860	11%	42%	47%
1880	17%	42%	41%
1900	25%	36%	39%

* Proportion of skilled in construction and building trades, 1860 40%, 1880 38%, 1900 46%.

SOURCE: Federal manuscript population census of Cleveland, 1860, 1880, 1900; De Vries, "Dutch Settlement and Assimilation," Figure 3.

Dutch on the east side, while more dispersed, were still concentrated in the three original neighborhoods: along Central (Ward 12 and 13), Lexington (Wards 18 and 19), and Woodland avenues (Wards 22 and 23).[68]

The west side neighborhood was always more cohesive and stable than the dispersed east side neighborhoods. More industrial development on the east side caused older neighborhoods to be displaced or overrun by ethnic groups that the Dutch disliked, such as blacks and Italians. The upwardly mobile Dutch fled to newer subdivisions farther east. In 1919 the East Side Christian Reformed Church followed its members to the far southeast city limits at 127th and Union. By contrast, the west side of Cleveland long remained a patchwork quilt of white ethnic neighborhoods. In 1920 Hollanders in that area still resided in a compact block of nine census tracts, each with twenty or more Netherlands-born residents, while "Dutch Alley" on the east side south of Woodland Avenue, also had twenty or more Hollanders. By 1930 the process of suburbanization had begun, but the original Dutch pockets remained.[69]

Typically, the newer residential areas on the outskirts attracted recent immigrants and younger, second-generation families. Older residents, half of whom owned their homes in 1900, remained in the original settlements anchored by the churches. Because foreign-born parents had a lifetime to accumulate wealth, they had a higher rate of home ownership than did their native-born children. Almost one half of native-born homeowners continued to live in the original wards, as did 60 percent of native-born renters. This indicates that the second- and third-generation Dutch made a continuing commitment to remain within the ethnic community rather than move to the city fringes and suburbs. In an automobile culture, geographic dispersal proved less significant than religious declension and intermarriage.[70]

The rate of Americanization among the Dutch varied according to religious affiliation. The isolationist-minded Christian Reformed churches maintained their ethnic identity for four and five generations (until the 1980s), the Reformed Church members held on into the third and fourth generations (until the 1960s), but Catholics could barely preserve their Dutch culture into the second generation (until the 1890s). Fissures in the Reformed churches began showing up during World War I. In 1914 the Second Dutch Reformed Church eliminated its overt ethnic identity by changing its name to Calvary Reformed and also gave women voting privileges at congregational meetings in an effort to attract non-Dutch members and retain its own members, who had been dropping out in droves. Membership records indicate that 38 percent of 378 communicant members who joined the church from 1890 to 1915 either let their membership lapse or transferred to non-Reformed churches.[71]

Calvary's mother church, First Dutch Reformed on the east side, was declining even more rapidly at this time. Consistory minutes for the year 1915 report that "by reason of death and moving outside its borders, the church has been losing in point of membership as also financially, our people being widely scattered and living at considerable distances from the church, its work is seriously crippled. It is to be considered that the spirit of the times is secular and that the distractions of a large city are many." Two years later the consistory again lamented the continuing loss of members because of Americanization: "Many through marriage have left to go to other Christian churches. Others, owing to the fact that the English language was introduced rather late, left because they preferred the English as used in other churches.... Moreover, Hollanders no longer settle here."[72] The church council's concern proved real when only twelve years later, in 1929, the congregation disbanded.

The Christian Reformed churches staved off ethnic diffusion for another two generations, and both the east and west side congregations survive to the present day. Between 1903 and 1917 West Side Christian Reformed Church lost only six families and fourteen adults (mainly second generation) to non-Reformed (mainly Presbyterian) churches in the Cleveland area. Most left when they moved to the western suburbs, beyond reasonable commuting distance from the mother church.[73]

Membership and baptism records of the Reformed and Christian Reformed churches provide additional evidence. In the West Side Christian Reformed Church only 2 out of 91 couples in the first thirty years (1872–1903) had non-Dutch spouses. In the World War I era, the number of mixed-ethnic marriages increased to 10 percent (9 out of 96), which was the same rate as the nearby Second Reformed church (8 out of 81) in the years 1890–1910. In both congregations the 10 percent who outmarried were second-generation members. Infant baptism records of Second Reformed Church from 1890 to 1939 also reveal an increasing rate of outmarriage among second- and third-generation immigrants after 1900. Prior to that 99 percent of the parents presenting infants for the sacrament were both Dutch, but in the next four decades (1900–39) the rate dropped to 64, 49, 29, and 32 percent, respectively.[74] The decade 1910–19 clearly marked a watershed in the process of Americanization.

Catholics lost command of their native tongue earlier, and they married non-Dutch spouses to a much greater extent than did the Reformed. The marriage records of St. Stephen Catholic Church for the years from 1870 until 1910 reveal a high and rising rate of marriages between Dutch and non-Dutch, primarily Germans. By decades, the rates of mixed nationality marriages were: 1870s, 65 percent; 1880s, 74 percent; 1890s, 89 percent; and 1900s, 96 percent.[75] After 1900 virtually all Dutch-born Catholics or their children married non-Dutch.

The difference can be attributed to the cultural, linguistic, and ethnic heterogeneity of the Roman Catholic congregations, in contrast to the homogeneous Reformed churches. There were no priests in Cleveland who could conduct religious services or instruct the youth in the Dutch tongue. However, every Reformed clergyman had that ability, and their worship services, as well as educational and social programs, were conducted in Dutch for many decades.

Beginning in 1890, one by one the Reformed congregations introduced English-language services, first in the Sunday afternoon or evening services. Then, during the World War I era, English was adopted in the primary morning service, with the second service still in Dutch. The last weekly Dutch service took place in 1936 in the West Side Christian Reformed Church, although quarterly services of Holy

Communion continued there until 1949. The progressive Second Reformed Church, which had led the way in adopting English in 1890, was also the first to discontinue Dutch services entirely in 1922. But the more conservative Christian Reformed congregations on both sides of the city clung to the mother tongue for another generation or two, even though it caused problems for its youth who spoke English in the public schools and on the streets.[76]

A Cleveland Foundation educational survey in 1915 found that among Dutch youngsters only about one third (36 percent) of elementary students and a little more than one half (56 percent) of secondary students could still read Dutch.[77] The percentages were higher, of course, among the Christian Reformed youth and lower among the Reformed children. Nevertheless, in 1903 the pastor of the West Side Christian Reformed Church found it necessary to use English in his Catechism classes, and in 1910 Sunday School teachers were recruited who knew English, although it proved difficult to staff all the classes with men fluent in the adopted tongue. The language changeover in the years 1890 to 1930 was a highly emotional and controversial issue, and fortunate was the congregation that could make the transition without schism. It pitted parents against children and the first generation against the second and third. Only the passing of the pioneers finally resolved the problem.

The substitution of English for Dutch in worship services and youth programs is a marker of acculturation, but it does not necessarily indicate assimilation. Acculturation is the ability to pass as an American in the workplace or in school. Assimilation requires the rejection of an immigrant mentality that espouses a segregated life in which all primary relationships, especially marriage, are lived within the ethnoreligious community. Many members of the Reformed Church rejected such a "fortress mentality," whereas Christian Reformed folk continued to believe in the motto "In isolation is our strength." With that in mind, the latter established day schools and a panoply of social organizations, recreational and sporting activities, and economic services within the church community.

As early as 1896 the West Side Christian Reformed Church formed a Christian School Society in an attempt to teach their children Dutch and to prevent an excessive exposure to "English-speaking sects." After several delays in 1909 they launched a summer school program of Bible instruction in the Dutch language that continued intermittently. The East Side Christian Reformed Church established the Cleveland Christian School (kindergarten through eighth grade) in 1937 at its church on Union Avenue. The West Side group followed suit in 1951 with a day school at its new facility on Triskett Road. By then the instruction was in English, but more importantly, they indoctrinated the children into the Reformed faith and ingrained in their minds the dangers of "worldliness," Catholicism, and even Yankee Protestantism. Both schools closed before their twenty-fifth birthdays.[78]

The Christian Reformed churches also issued guidelines for the workplace and social life in general. In 1879 members were warned, on pain of excommunication, not to join Masonic lodges or any oath-bound secret societies. Labor unions such as the Knights of Labor and affiliates of the American Federation of Labor came under the same injunction in 1886. Not only did unions require oaths of allegiance, according to the church, but they were given to murderous strikes, such as the Haymarket riot of 1886, and they followed humanistic, socialistic, or even worse, communistic principles. The Reformed Church lost many members to the Christian Reformed Church in the 1880s because the former took a neutral stand on secret societies and refused to discipline members who were Knights or Masons. A few Christian Reformed members who belonged to these institutions, on the other hand, transferred to the Reformed Church, spurred on in part by strong pulpit denunciations of the Knights of Labor by the Reverend Hermanus Tempel, pastor of the West Side Christian Reformed congregation (1888–93). At the time several leading members of his congregation belonged to such groups and "some took offence," an anonymous report later indicated. "Bitter feeling and partisanship sprung up. A few left the church. And in the hearts of others, tho they remained, ill feeling long lingered."[79]

Even the isolationist-minded Christian Reformed churches could not entirely ward off worldliness. From 1900 to 1910 the church council admonished its members against frequenting saloons and abusing alcohol in their homes, and of desecrating the Christian Sunday by buying milk (in an era without refrigeration), riding the streetcars, or taking joy rides in "newfangled" automobiles. One church member owned a car and periodically tempted the young people to ride with him. In 1920 the consistory warned a young man about attending "picture shows," and a number of young men confessed to a "bootlegging incident."[80] Popular culture and material prosperity had won over a number of the children and grandchildren of the pioneers.

Church leaders lamented the defection of the youth. A historical sketch, written for the commemoration of the East Side Christian Reformed Church's fiftieth anniversary in 1922, stated: "A number of baptized members from those days are still living, the greater number of which, alas, have forsaken the church that their pious parents loved so dearly and would gladly have sacrificed everything to defend. How much larger our congregation would have been if all those boys and girls, educated in the church and so much prayed for, would have continued in the fellowship of their old church home."[81] Some years earlier, a report on the congregation by one of its leaders had likewise complained that "for lack of pastoral care, many of our youth have drifted away into the world, and some in the numerous American churches in our city."[82]

By the 1950s most of the Dutch in greater Cleveland had migrated to the outskirts and suburbs, where the Reformed churches were also relocated. West Side (now West Park) Christian Reformed moved in 1950 from its original building in Wooden Shoe Alley on West 58th Street to Triskett Road at 152nd Street in West Park. Calvary Reformed chose to remain in the old neighborhood and serve the changing population, but it mothered five new suburban congregations for its scattered members: Riverside, Brooklyn, Parkview, Parma Park, and Brunswick (in order of formation). Current church directories indicate that less than 10 percent of the estimated 1,300 members of these six Reformed churches are of Dutch ancestry. Dutch Americans provided the nucleus, but the congregations grew as community churches of mixed nationalities. In comparison, two thirds of the West

Park Christian Reformed membership remains Dutch in birth or ancestry, as does that of the East Side Christian Reformed, which relocated to Warrensville Heights in 1960. Those two congregations today total about 650 members.

In the 1990s people of Dutch ancestry can be found throughout the greater metropolitan area. Calvinists remain the primary self-conscious group and still cluster within easy driving distance of their suburban churches. They, together with the small but active Netherlands American Society, a secular social club formed in 1964, preserve what little remains of Dutch group life and culture on the North Coast.

Rural Indiana Enclaves

Indiana because of its strong southern heritage and pattern of settlement from the south attracted the smallest immigrant population of any state in the Old Northwest. Only a few thousand Dutch immigrants settled in the state, mainly in the north. Calvinists farmed near Lafayette, Goshen, De Motte, Munster, and Highland, while Catholics entered the urban industrial workforce in Evansville, Fort Wayne, Indianapolis, and especially South Bend and Mishawaka. All these cities had well-established Catholic churches and schools.

An enterprising farmer from Groningen, Klaas Janszoon Beukma, was one of the first to reach Lafayette in 1835. A widower with three sons and a daughter, Beukma chose Tippecanoe County because it lay astride the Wabash Canal project, which would link Lake Erie with the Ohio and Mississippi River systems. He purchased for $995 an improved 282-acre farm covering rich river-bottom land and raised corn, oats, potatoes, and garden vegetables for the growing urban market of Lafayette.[83]

Indiana offered opportunities aplenty for the poor farm tenants and laborers of the grain region of the northern Netherlands. Beukma wrote lengthy and enthusiastic letters offering to assist friends and relatives "provided they were solid people" and not afraid to work. "Here I have found what I was looking for—bread and freedom; now I have no worry about the future of my children," Beukma wrote on 4 July 1836. Three years later he bought another farm for $500 only two miles from Lafayette and moved there, placing one of his sons on the old place.[84]

Beukma's numerous "America letters" fell on deaf ears until 1847 when the mass emigration spearheaded by the Dutch Calvinist Seceders brought six Frisian families and singles (18 persons) to the Lafayette area.[85] The newcomers, in turn, enticed others to follow. One wrote: "Because of the language barrier we would be pleased to have a Holland preacher and medical doctor here."[86] Their wish was fulfilled, but not immediately because the colony grew slowly, reaching a total of 148 Dutch born by 1850. Lafayette thus boasts the oldest Dutch Reformed settlement in Indiana.

The lack of a Reformed Church turned the more devout away from Lafayette for several decades. Finally, in 1861 the Groningers Jan Balkema and his son Edward, together with Luite Boelkens, organized Dutch-language services in

Balkema's home.[87] Three years later the Reverend John R. Schepers, also a Groninger, who had affiliated with the United Presbyterian (Scottish) Church in Michigan, agreed to organized a Dutch congregation, Second Presbyterian. The church began with twenty-two charter members, but quickly doubled and tripled in size as Schepers gathered the Hollanders in the community and the new arrivals from the Netherlands. The congregation worshiped until 1889 in a small frame structure built in 1866 on Hartford Street at Fourteenth in the northwestern section of the city. In 1896 the once enlarged building was moved one block to Fifteenth Street and Hartford and another large wing was added to accommodate the growing flock.[88]

In 1869 the congregation left the English-speaking denomination for the ethnically homogeneous True Holland (later Christian) Reformed Church. By 1880 it counted 146 "souls," and reached 530 in 1910, 600 in 1924, 700 in 1957, and 575 in 1991. The congregation nearly succumbed in the 1880s. In 1880 twelve influential farm families moved to Fowler twenty-five miles to the northwest, and more seriously, in 1888 twenty-seven families—more than one half of the congregation—seceded to join the more Americanized sister denomination, the Reformed Church in America. First Reformed Church, located on east Fifteenth Street, in turn mothered congregations in Seafield and Goodland in the 1890s, but neither survived. The Fowler CRC congregation also disbanded in 1890 because all the families moved back to Lafayette. Seven Dexter (Americanized from Dijkstra) families from Friesland were the major clan in Goodland, settling in a "chain migration" that began in 1861 and continued until 1893. They were supporters of the Goodland Reformed Church.[89]

The main growth spurts in Lafayette came in the years immediately after the First and Second World Wars. The high point was in 1920, when 1,500 persons of Dutch birth or ancestry lived in Tippecanoe County. The Christian Reformed Church then totaled 500 and the Reformed Church in America 300. These two congregations included more than half of the Hollanders in the county. Church services continued in the Dutch language but in 1913 an afternoon English service was introduced. By the 1930s the morning service was in English, and Dutch died out in the 1940s. The opening of a Christian school in 1950 helped hold the community together, as did the customary church societies for men, women, and youth.

In 1900, according to the federal manuscript census, half of the Dutch in Tippecanoe County farmed in the rural townships, primarily in Fairfield some twelve miles north, and the rest lived and worked in Lafayette. Of 265 Dutch in the city labor force in 1900, 45 percent were unskilled laborers including female domestics, 25 percent were skilled craftsmen led by carpenters, and 13 percent were semiskilled workers. No more than a dozen men can be identified as factory workers. Businessmen comprised only 12 percent, and 4 percent were professionals (clerics, teachers, a professor, etc.). All but eight men could speak English, most were naturalized citizens, and more than one third owned their own homes. The Lafayette Dutch began at the bottom rung of the socioeconomic ladder and gradually worked their way up into the middle class. Lafayette also served as an immigrant beacon that led to Dutch Reformed settlements in counties to the north—Benton and White in the 1870s, Newton in the 1880s, and Jasper in the 1890s.

While the Groningers in the Lafayette region came in hopes of economic improvement, a colony of more than fifty Frisian Mennonites, who settled in the Goshen area in 1853–54, left the Netherlands because of their religious convictions. As pacifists, they sought to escape compulsory military service and the high taxes to support the same. Two pastors of these "plain people," Ruurd J. Smit (changed to Smith) and Ruurd J. Symensma, both farmers, came with the group, which comprised more than half of the congregation in the village of Balk in Friesland.[90]

After landing in Philadelphia, they followed the trail of the German Mennonites westward to Zoar and Waynesburg, Ohio, and then on to Goshen. There with the help of German fellow believers they purchased in Jackson Township a block of 320 acres for $3,200, 50 acres of which was cleared and in crops. The property was ten miles south of Goshen, along what became known as "Holland Settlement Road" near the village of New Paris.[91] Over time the small farm colony attracted other family and friends from the Balk congregation.

Because the "Amish" Frisian colony in New Paris was too small to support a full-fledged church, it met monthly and later biweekly in private homes, and Pastor Ruurd Smith conducted worship in the Frisian language. On alternating Sundays the Frisians worshiped with the local German-speaking Mennonite congregation. Pastor Smith preached at the Frisian services for more than thirty-five years until his retirement in 1889. This brought an abrupt end to the ethnic services, and the Balkers joined with the Germans to form the Salem Mennonite Church of New Paris.[92] Thus, the Dutch Mennonites at the passing of the first generation lost their national identity and went over to the Amish. Most remained with the very conservative Old Mennonites, while a few families joined the more liberal Mennonite Brethren faction.

That some shred of ethnic identity remained with the second generation is evident from the 1878 family history of Hiram Benjamin Ferverda of North Webster, who closed with the exclamation: "We are proud of our Dutch heritage." But neither Hiram's father nor any of his siblings married Hollanders, and the descendants scattered throughout north-central Indiana where no Hollanders lived.[93] The Frisians prospered greatly as farmers and were simply absorbed into the larger Mennonite community of the region.

In the 1880s a second group of Hollanders settled in nearby Goshen. These were a dozen orthodox Calvinist families from the province of Zeeland who developed celery farms on the muck land east of town. Whether they learned of Goshen from the Frisian Mennonites is not known, but the groups considered each other to be theologically misguided and certainly kept their distance. In 1904 9 families (50 persons) formed the East Goshen Christian Reformed Church. The church grew slowly over the decades, and today it numbers about 250 persons.

Dutch Catholic immigrants preferred the cities rather than the countryside, even though most hailed from the rural Achterhoek region of Gelderland on the German border. Some began filtering into Evansville (Vandenburgh County) on the Ohio River in the late 1840s and 1850s, settling among German Catholics from Prussia, Oldenburg, and Hannover. They increased in numbers from 150 to 200 between 1860 and 1880 but then declined by 1890 to only 100. In 1930 there were 131 persons of Dutch birth or ancestry in the county. Clearly, Evansville never became a Dutch center; the immigrants there intermarried with Germans and quickly lost their identity. Following the Civil War Catholic families from the province of Overijssel came to Fort Wayne where they found factory work, while others went to Indianapolis and Terre Haute.

The major Dutch Catholic center in Indiana developed among the Flemish Belgians in Mishawaka and South Bend (St. Joseph County) in the 1880s and 1890s. The main wave arrived after 1900, especially between 1920 and 1930, when the number of Dutch Catholics almost doubled from 300 to 550. Since most worked in the Ball-Band glass jar factory, it is clear that the attraction was the booming economy and employers who favored Flemish workers.

Orthodox Dutch Calvinists built their largest settlement in the Calumet district, centered in the twin towns of Munster and Highland (Lake County). This area, like most of northwest Indiana at the time, was classified as "swampland" or "low prairie" by the federal government, and the heavy clay soil required drainage ditching systems before it could be farmed. By 1930, 1,650 persons of Dutch birth or ancestry lived in northern Lake County (Table 8.5) and today the number surpasses 5,000. The four Reformed churches in 1990 alone counted 2,500 members.[94]

The first families, led by Peter Jabaay, moved into Munster between 1854 and 1857 as a spillover from the earlier colonies of Roseland, South Holland, and Lansing, Illinois. They opened farms on a fertile lowland strip running for five miles along the north side of a ridge (now Ridge Road) stretching to the Little Calumet River. When the Cady Marsh south of the ridge was reclaimed in 1871, the Hollanders expanded there too. Drawing upon their traditional skills of draining and tiling swamp land, they built a prosperous settlement that a visitor described as a proverbial "Happy Valley."[95]

The founding families originated in the old country village of Strijen near Rotterdam in the province of Zuid-Holland. They crossed the ocean together in 1855 and headed for the cheap but fertile lands along the Calumet River. Jacob Monster (who fortunately changed his name before giving it to the village of Munster) ran a general store and post office and served on the town council, school board, and as road supervisor. With oxen and sled he also deepened the Hart Ditch cut through the sand ridge, which hastened the drainage of Cady Marsh. The next years brought more Dutch families.[96] Munster became the church village for 60 to 70 farm families along the Ridge. Hammond, the larger city to the north, was the market center, although for everyday needs the Hollanders patronized the general store of Munster and Klootwijk in the Dutch village. Surprisingly, two saloons run by Americans survived in this "puritan" village, but no orthodox Hollander would deign to cross the thresholds.

The founding of the Dutch Reformed Church in Lansing, Illinois, in 1861 enhanced the settlement in nearby Munster. However, within a decade, in 1870, the entire Munster contingent of the Lansing church (except Jacob Munster and

Table 8.5 Dutch in Indiana by County, 1850–1940

County	1850	1860	1870	1880	1890	1900	1910	1920	1930		1940
									FB	NB	
Adams				2	1	1	2	6	2	15	
Allen		4	17	145	17	33	40	49	42	171	35
Bartholomew			1	4		3	3	2		6	
Benton		2	1	39	21	9	9	13	7	24	4
Blackford				1	1					1	
Boone				1				13		9	1
Brown							1		2	5	1
Carroll			6	4	4	1	5	5	6	14	3
Cass			2	4	1	12	2	9	6	35	8
Clark		2	1	3	1			1	2	9	
Clay		1	10	5	6	5	2	3	1	10	
Clinton		2	9	3	2	2	2		2	11	5
Crawford		1	1	1		1					
Daviess	2	2		11					1	2	
Dearborn	5	17	4	20	4	1	2	2	2	10	1
Decatur	2	3	4	9	1	3	2	1		10	
Dekalb			3	1		2	3	3	2	10	
Delaware				2	2	47	35	27	22	37	19
Dubois		6	1	11	10	6	4	3	2	7	1
Elkhart		36	99	105	121	102	104	90	117	283	90
Fayette	1	2	1	1	1		6	2	1	10	3
Floyd		3		7	2	1	3	6	1	9	2
Fountain		3		1	9	43	74	58	55	127	36
Franklin	2	4	11	8		1		5	1	9	1
Fulton		4				2				4	
Gibson		1	3	5	4	2		6	3	7	2
Grant				8		6	6	10	6	15	12
Greene		1								4	
Hamilton				1		2				4	1
Hancock			2			1		1	4	10	
Harrison		1	1			1	1		1	5	
Hendricks				2	1		4	3	16	28	19
Henry				1			14			10	1
Howard				1	1	1	3	10	4	14	1
Huntington			6	2	3	5	5	4	6	17	2
Jackson	1	14	8	11	3	3	6	5		9	
Jasper				69	52	141	156	195	181	414	174
Jay			1	1			2			6	
Jefferson	1	2	1	6	3	3	5	3	1	9	2
Jennings			9	3	1	1		1		4	
Johnson	2	1	2	2	4	7	8	4	15	18	13
Knox		9	8	23	6	3	2	2	1	26	
Kosciusko			12	11	12	27	22	18	13	47	5
Lagrange		1		1	1	7	1		2	8	1
Lake		28	76	117	151	230	477	415	437	1221	344
Laporte		38	18	16	9	17	17	47	43	82	37
Lawrence							1		2	10	1
Madison			1	21		19	12	5	7	38	6
Marion	1	13	32	63	88	120	220	268	262	520	188

Table 8.5 *(Continued)*

County	1850	1860	1870	1880	1890	1900	1910	1920	1930		1940
									FB	NB	
Marshall		7	11	10	4	5	7	8	11	33	10
Martin										1	
Miami	1		2	2	3	3	3	4		9	5
Monroe				1	2	2	4	6	3	7	2
Montgomery			3	8	4	4	2		1	11	2
Morgan										5	1
Newton			5	9	66	95	94	55	39	82	44
Noble		1	3	2	1	4	6	4	5	9	8
Ohio	2					1			2		
Orange		1								1	
Owen			1	1	3			1		2	
Parke					1	1	1	1		2	
Perry	6	11	15	18	12	6	4		1	19	
Pike		1		1					1	2	1
Porter			2	5	10	25	14	7	9	33	23
Posey	5		21	15	5	4	3	1	7		
Pulaski		1	2	1				4	1	8	1
Putnam		1								4	2
Randolph			1							2	
Ripley		2	21	13	3	4	2	1		11	
Rush		1			2	4	3	4	2	12	
St. Joseph	2	8		17	17	27	112	137	234	316	190
Scott			4	1						1	
Shelby		2	7	1	2	5	1	1		4	3
Spencer				5	1	1		1			7
Starke		5		6	3	8	24	10	4	15	9
Steuben		2	5	2				1		6	
Sullivan		1		2			1	1	1		1
Switzerland							1				
Tippecanoe	27	148	248	273	369	443	437	368	25	940	228
Tipton		1		2						4	
Union			19							2	1
Vanderburgh	1	81	73	92	28	27	19	17	17	114	8
Vermillion				1			2		2	4	1
Vigo	2	24	28	67	36	53	57	51	33	139	29
Wabash						1	4	4	1	4	4
Warren		3	1	4	7	18	20	8	4	9	3
Warrick				3	1	2	1			5	4
Washington		1									
Wayne		5	4	6			1	2	4	25	4
Wells		1	3		1			1	1	5	1
White		3	22	48	31	63	40	26	14	63	13
Whitley			1	1	2	2	1		1	7	3
Totals	63	513	878	1,344	1,157	1,678	2,126	2,018	1,992	5,286	1,620

FB = Foreign Born

NB = Native Born

Source: Published federal population censuses, 1850–1940. The 1880 figures are based on an actual count of the manuscript census. The published total is 1,338.

his wife) organized their own congregation in town and seceded from the Reformed denomination by affiliating with the more isolationist-minded Christian Reformed Church (CRC). At the turn of the century, the Munster CRC grew rapidly with immigrants fresh from the Netherlands and others moving out from Chicago. It reached its apogee in 1915 with 650 members, after mothering in 1908 a daughter church in Highland ten miles east that already numbered 466 members in 1915. Dutch settlers had moved into Highland in the 1890s led by Jacob Schoon.

The Dutch Calvinists in northern Indiana generally eschewed factory work, finding the shop floor confining, hostile, and un-Christian. They bought their own farms and kept things "Dutch." At first they raised the typical American field crops of hay, corn, and wheat. In the 1870s the muck farmers along the ridge discovered their destiny, the intensive truck farming of vegetables and fruits for the south Chicago markets—cabbages, cauliflower, pickles, tomatoes, sweet corn, potatoes, melons, and after 1900 primarily onions, onion sets, and sugar beets. The Chicago food processing firm of Libby, McNeill & Libby opened a plant in Highland about 1904 to take the tomatoes, cabbages, and pickles of the Dutch and other farmers. At harvest time the plant processed sixty tons of cabbage daily into sauerkraut.[97] The kraut plant of Herman Meeter, a Highland Hollander, and Schrum's dill pickle plant also bought Dutch produce. Beets went to the Holland Sugar Beet Company and later to railroad receiving stations for processing elsewhere.

The huge Chicago market provided the Dutch truck farmers the opportunity for prosperity. First by ox cart, then by horse and wagon, and after World War I increasingly by motor truck, they brought their vegetable crops in season daily (except Sunday) to the Chicago commission houses at the South Water market and later to the Randolph Street market and the 71st Street Market in Englewood. Alternatively, they raised their crops under contract to commercial food processors, set up farm stands, or peddled their produce from house to house in the steel mill towns of Hammond, Whiting. East Chicago, and Gary.

The most typical Dutch crop in the ridge communities was onion sets. For thirty years, 1920–50, the farmers from South Holland to Highland devoted more than 3,000 acres (one third of all cropland) to onion sets, of which they gained a virtual national monopoly with over 75 percent of the market. The labor-intensive, onerous handwork seemed to suit the Dutch temperament, although only the most successful survived the Great Depression.[98]

Edna Ferber's novel *So Big* (1924) forever immortalized these Dutch truck farmers at the apogee of this business in the 1920s.[99] They were poor folk struggling to achieve financial security on the land and in their own communities. By 1900 40 percent owned their own farms, two-thirds free of mortgages. But 60 percent were yet tenant farmers trying to climb the agricultural ladder. Gradually, the penetration of Chicago industry and residential suburbs into the Calumet region brought Munster and Highland into the metropolitan orbit. In 1905 the National (later American) Brick Company opened a factory near town to exploit the "blue" clay soil. Some Hollanders worked seasonally as day laborers at the kilns that provided most of the "Chicago common" bricks for the booming metropolis. Such off-farm earnings enabled many families to survive the early "lean years."

Because of the large concentration of Hollanders, Munster and Highland boasted of Dutch social and civic organizations—a community band and chorus, a commercial club and agricultural societies, and sporting activities. But most social activities were church-centered, such as the Young Men's and Young Women's societies and their adult counterparts. Dutch Calvinists were a staid lot compared to their Dutch Catholic compatriots in Mishawaka and South Bend with their dance halls, carnivals, bicycle racing, and pigeon fanciers.

The Munster and Highland Calvinists separated themselves "from the world," i.e., the alien culture, by establishing Christian day schools to educate their youth in biblical perspectives.[100] As a supporter noted many years later, these "hardy pioneers" had "no means, no money, no experience, no background, nothing but sincere convictions that this was a way of life they wanted for their children and children's children."[101] This practice opened them to "reproach" from Americans and even from the more Americanized fellow Dutch. But as a defender stated later, "it was forced on us to a great extent by our immigrant ways, but also by the militant mind of the church." During their first decade instruction in English gradually became the norm. Until the 1930s the Dutch private schools in Lake County had larger enrollments than the tax-supported public schools, which served the non-Dutch and the Reformed Church in America families who rejected the separatist principle.[102]

World War I hastened the Americanization process and in the 1920s and 1930s the Dutch language gave way to English in the churches and on the streets. In historian Lance Trusty's apt words, "the old tongue inevitably faded away in Munster, victim of time and the times."[103]

As urban life encroached on the market gardeners of the Calumet region and land values shot upward, some Dutch moved south thirty-five miles to De Motte in Jasper County, a town on the Illinois Central Railroad line, where a Dutch farm colony was founded in the 1870s. The Otis brothers of Chicago, Charles and Lucius, foresaw the remarkable opportunities in the prairie counties of northern Indiana where absentee landlords had retarded settlement.[104] They purchased thousands of acres southwest of De Motte near Thayer and recruited dozens of Dutch immigrants as sharecroppers by furnishing milk cows and farm equipment on favorable terms. Pioneers on the Otis Estates were a dozen Groningen and Frisian families.[105]

By 1880 sixty-nine Dutch–born lived in Keener Township, Jasper County (Table 8.5). The number doubled by 1900 because in the early 1890s a second wave of Dutch arrived from Roseland, Lansing, and Highland. They were spurred by the Roseland real estate dealers and promoters, John Cornelius Ton and his brother Richard, who purchased a large parcel of recently drained swamp lands north of De Motte and advertised it heavily in Roseland and surroundings as an ideal Dutch truck gardening colony. Within a year they began "buying out the American farmers of that vicinity" in order to create a "large and enterprising" Dutch settlement. "The outlook is cheering," reported a visiting Dutch Reformed Church organizer, but several crop failures later tried the faith of the farmers and caused some to leave. Besides raising cabbages and pickles, the Dutch specialized in asparagus and later in dairying and chicken and turkey hatcheries.[106]

The founding of a Dutch Reformed church in 1893 ensured De Motte's growth by providing "solid" preaching and psalm singing. The church building site was selected two miles west of town at "Dutch Corner" to draw in the families from Roselawn and Thayer. First Reformed Church had 450 persons in 1920 and the Christian Reformed Church had 200 in 1935. It had begun in 1932 when 32 families seceded from First Reformed for the more "Dutchy" denomination. Previously, in 1920 26 families (100 persons) had withdrawn to form the English-speaking American Reformed Church, after First Reformed refused "so radical a change" as to allow English in the second service. Half of De Motte's population of 200 became members of the new church.[107]

By 1930 700 Dutch-born lived in De Motte. It experienced a second growth spurt in the 1950s when "white flight" from the Chicago neighborhoods of Englewood and Roseland brought thousands more Dutch-Americans. In 1990 De Motte's four Calvinist churches (two Reformed and two Christian Reformed) surpassed 2,750 members, making the town the second largest Dutch Protestant settlement in Indiana today.[108] De Motte, like Munster and Highland, has a Christian day school and the usual panoply of church societies, music clubs, and leisure activities. For years a community band provided music for Fourth of July picnics and ice cream socials. The town's relative geographic isolation has preserved a stronger sense of Dutchness in De Motte than in the Lake County towns.

Several hundred Dutch Protestants also settled in and around Indianapolis (Marion County) in the years after 1890. They were primarily dairy farmers from Friesland.[109] By 1911 seventeen families organized a Dutch Reformed Church to carry on the faith. Christian Park Reformed Church also serves several hundred second- and third-generation families. In 1930 Marion County counted 262 Dutch-born and 520 of Dutch ancestry out of a population of 425,000.[110]

Conclusion

The Dutch in Chicago, Cleveland, and northern Indiana had to cope with an essentially American environment. Catholics chose the rising urban centers where they worshiped in multiethnic parishes and quickly intermarried, but the Calvinists established their own churches, led by Dutch-speaking pastors who taught their flock to remain separate from the world. Religion slowed the rate of Americanization for the Calvinists, and their enclaves survive to the present day. But few traces of the Catholic Dutch can be found; they are fully assimilated.

Notes

1. In 1900 the total number of persons of Dutch birth or parentage (either father, mother, or both) and their children, excluding approximately 3,000

non-Dutch spouses or parents, was 20,100; this was 1.1 percent of Chicago's population of 1.8 million (derived from Robert P. Swierenga, compiler, "Dutch in Chicago and Cook County 1900 Federal Census" [Kent, Ohio, 1992]). In Grand Rapids in 1890, 16,000 of the 80,000 inhabitants were Dutch-born or their children (Cornelius Bratt, "Our Churches in Grand Rapids," *The Christian Intelligencer*, 9 July 1890, 11).

2. A brief history is Amry Vandenbosch, *The Dutch Communities of Chicago* (Chicago: Knickerbocker Society of Chicago, 1927). See also Jacob Van Hinte, *Netherlanders in America*, Robert P. Swierenga, ed., Adriaan de Wit, chief translator (Grand Rapids: Baker Book House, 1985), 153–156, 308–09, 346–49, 352, 792–94, 829–30; and Henry Lucas, *Netherlanders in America* (Ann Arbor: University of Michigan Press, 1955; repr. Grand Rapids: Wm. B. Eerdmans, 1989), 227–32, 325–26. Henry Stob, *Summoning Up Remembrance* (Grand Rapids: Wm. B. Eerdmans, 1995), is essential to understanding the Old West Side in the 1920s and 1930s. See also Hans Krabbendam, "The West Side Dutch in Chicago," *Origins* 9, No. 2 (1991): 4–8; William Dryfhout, "Chicago's 'Far West Siders' in the 1920s," ibid., 18–22; "Chicago" (summary of travel account of Netherlanders Van Dyke and A. Gelders), ibid., 1 No. 2 (1983): 10–15; "And Now, About Chicago" (letter of Eisse H. Woldring, 2 June 1912), ibid., 6 No. 2 (1988): 16–18.
3. Vandenbosch, *Dutch Communities of Chicago*, 2.
4. In Bratt's terms, they were "post-Enlightenment Reformed sectarians (the old Seceders)" and not "post-Enlightenment Calvinists (the neo-Calvinists)." See *Dutch Calvinism in Modern America: A History of a Conservative Subculture* (Grand Rapids: Wm. B. Eerdmans, 1984), 3–54, quotes in text and note on 31.
5. Vandenbosch, *Dutch Communities of Chicago*, 79.
6. Nearly 20 percent of the Middelstum congregation emigrated at the time De Bey left, with more than half settling in Chicago.
7. Herbert J. Brinks, "The Americanization of Bernardus De Beij (1815–1894)," *Origins* 6, No. 1 (1988): 28.
8. I am indebted to Herbert J. Brinks and Marinus Goote for providing information on the religious spirit of the Chicago CRC pastors.
9. "Dr. John Van Lonkhuyzen," obituary, *The Banner*, 8 January 1943, 38. Vander Heide likewise had an independent "philosophic" mind shaped by the writings of Kuyper ("Rev. S. S. Vander Heide," obituary, ibid., 27 September 1929, 36); Lucas, *Netherlanders in America*, 851, 920, 936, 917.
10. Bratt, *Dutch Calvinism*, 51.
11. Van Hinte, *Netherlanders in America*, 938–42.
12. Harold M. Mayer and Richard C. Wade, *Chicago: Growth of a Metropolis* (Chicago: University of Chicago Press, 1969), 63–64.
13. Lucas, *Netherlanders in America*, 232, says: "These Hollanders, few of whom were Seceders, lacked the religious faith of the people who settled in Roseland and South Holland."

14. First Reformed Church of Chicago, "A Century for Christ, 1853–1953," *100th Anniversary Booklet* (Chicago, 1953), 3, 5; *Chicago City Directory*, 1856. The congregation worshiped for a year in an empty store on Randolph and Desplaines streets and then for a year or two in the Seeley Building on Randolph and Clinton streets two blocks to the east.
15. First RCA, "Century for Christ," 305; First Christian Reformed Church of Chicago, *Seventy-Fifth Anniversary, 1867–1924* (Chicago, 1942), 11; Bernardus De Bey, letter in *Provinciale Groninger Courant*, 10 Dec. 1869.
16. A detailed account of De Bey's career is Hans Krabbendam, "Serving the Dutch Community: A Comparison of the Patterns of Americanization in the Lives of Two Immigrant Pastors" (M.A. thesis, Kent State University, 1989), 48–93. See also Brinks, "Americanization of Bernardus De Beij," 26–31.
17. Vandenbosch, *Dutch Communities in Chicago*, 17.
18. De Bey's invaluable letters about Chicago in the *Provinciale Groninger Courant* are in the Calvin College Archives. The Chicago Fire letter is published in English translation in *Origins* 1, no. 1 (1983): 10–13. An English-language typescript of all of these letters by Dirk Hoogeveen of Regina, Saskatchewan, is in the writer's possession. The quote in the text is from the issue of 8 June 1870.
19. De Bey letter in *Provinciale Groninger Courant*, 13 February 1869; *Petah-Ja*, "Church Historical Notes," October, 1975.
20. Peter Moerdyke, "Chicago Letter," *Christian Intelligencer*, 11 November 1891, 11; ibid., 3 March 1893, 10. Moerdyke predicted correctly that the language issue was the "irrepressible conflict [that] will ere long be the burning question of the majority of our Western churches" (ibid., 20 January 1892, 11).
21. Peter Moerdyke, "Chicago Letter," *Christian Intelligencer*, 25 May 1892, 11.
22. As Peter Moerdyke lamented: "The Seceders are strong and grow rapidly, and its church has fattened on defections from our church. For years it gathered in nearly all the Holland immigrants; it has profited by the presence of English in our First Church, in Sunday school and other work, from which fresh arrivals have turned away to a purely and thoroughly Dutch Church" (ibid., 11 November 1891, 11).
23. Van Hinte, *Netherlanders in America*, 382–85. Chicago had no schisms over the lodge issue as in western Michigan. As late as 1935, First RCA refused membership for lodge members to which "no true Christian could belong." See First Chicago RCA Consistory Minutes, 30 April 1935, Book 7 1935–1938, at First Reformed Church, Berwyn, IL, and on microfilm at the Joint Archives of Holland, Hope College.
24. First RCA, "Century for Christ," 5; First CRC, *Seventy-Fifth Anniversary*, 11; John Vander Velde, "Our History," Ebenezer Christian Reformed Church, *Centennial Booklet* (Berwyn, IL, 1967), 5. When First CRC moved from Ashland Avenue to Berwyn in 1945, the congregation

changed its name to Ebenezer CRC. The last regular Dutch worship service was held in 1955.

25. Stob, *Summoning Up Remembrance*, 21–25; "Recollections," *Origins* 9, no. 2 (1991): 14; 10, no. 2 (1992): 18.
26. Vander Velde, "Our History," 607; Stob, "Recollections," *Origins* 9 (1991): 15–16; Peter De Vries, *The Blood of the Lamb* (New York: Little, Brown, 1961), 23.
27. Timothy Jacobson, *Waste Management: An American Corporate Success Story* (Washington, D.C.: Gateway Business Books, 1993); Robert P. Swierenga, compiler, "Chicago Dutch Garbage Companies: A Complete Listing, 1890–1991."
28. West Side (Cicero) RCA was organized in 1911; First Cicero CRC in 1924; and Second Cicero CRC (formerly Douglas Park CRC) in 1927. In 1933 Fourth CRC relocated to the suburb of Oak Park, immediately northwest of Cicero. Additional outlying churches were established in the western suburbs of Des Plaines (1929) and Western Springs (1933).
29. The following section relies heavily on the Chicago Dutch-language weekly newspaper *Onze Toekomst*, 1897–1953; and its successors *The Illinois Observer* (monthly) 1954–1959, and *The Church Observer* (monthly) 1960–1964. Files of *Onze Toekomst* are incomplete. Prior to 1920, all issues are now lost and only selected articles and items are available in English translation in the Chicago Foreign Language Press Survey, Chicago Public Library Omnibus Project, Works Progress Administration (Chicago, 1942). This WPA translation file includes the years 1906–13 and 1919–27, and is available on microfilm. John Meyer, assisted by M. J. Pinzke, did the translation in 1937–38, when the pre-1920 issues of the weekly were yet available. All issues after 1938 are also lost. The extant files of *Onze Toekomst* and complete runs of the *Observer* are available at the Trinity Christian College Library, Palos Heights, IL, and at the Calvin College Archives.
30. *Onze Toekomst*, 9 February, 27 August 1906; 1 February 1907; 7 August 1908; 5 February, 30 April, 10, 24 September, 1909; 4 February 1910; 17 February 1911; 23 January 1920; *Illinois Observer*, 15 April 1954.
31. The complete records (25 vols.) of the Roseland Mutual Aid Society (Roselandsche Ouderlinge Hulp Vereeniging) are in the Trinity Christian College Library, Palos Heights, IL. See also Ross K. Ettema's synopsis of the records (1990).
32. *Onze Toekomst*, 29 June, 21 September 1906; 1 March 1907; 19 June, 3 July 1908; 2 February, 3 July 1909; 15 July, 23 September 1910; 14 April 1911; 7 March 1913; 20 January 1920; 23 December 1921; 27 June, 17 October 1923; 24, 28 May 1924; 4 March, 30 September 1925; 26 October 1926; 6 April, 7 December 1927; 11 March 1931.
33. Robert P. Swierenga, "Promoting Ethnic Pride: The Dutch Social Clubs of Chicago," *Origins* 14, No. 2: 30–37.

34. *Christian Intelligencer*, 3 December 1890, 11; 25 March 1891, 11; *Onze Toekomst*, many issues.
35. *Onze Toekomst*, 23 July 1909; 26 August 1910.
36. *Christian Intelligencer*, 4 November 1891; *Onze Toekomst*, 25 December 1908.
37. *Onze Toekomst*, 8 January, 10 December 1909; 9 December 1910.
38. Bernard R. De Remer, *Moody Bible Institute, A Pictorial History* (Chicago: Moody Press, 1960), 121–22.
39. De Vries, *Blood of the Lamb*, 30.
40. *Onze Toekomst*, 3 June, 29 April 1925; 30 January 1930.
41. Ibid., 7 September 1906; 26 February (quote in text), 3 July 1909; 18 March, 1 April 1910.
42. P. Court Van Woerden of First Englewood RCA headed the Anti-Saloon League, which had chapters in Englewood, Roseland, and the West Side (*Onze Toekomst*, 18, 25 March, 24 June, 23 September 1910; 27 January 1911; 28 February 1913). Reverend S. C. Nettinga of First Englewood RCA led in forming the Civic League (ibid., 28 October 1910; 20 January, 3 March 1911); Lucas, *Netherlanders*, 573–74. The Christian Political Society began with 45 charter members (ibid., 1 October 1920).
43. *Onze Toekomst*, 7 January, 1 April 1931.
44. Ibid., 1 October 1920; Van Hinte, *Netherlanders in America*, 938–42.
45. *Illinois Observer*, 15 February 1954; January, March, December 1955; November 1956; November 1958.
46. Ibid., 15 March, 15 October 1954; February 1956; November 1957; July, August 1958.
47. Ibid., February, March, June, July 1956; January, April, October 1957; September 1958.
48. In 1900 86 percent of the Dutch in Chicago were naturalized and only 6 percent could not speak English (derived from Swierenga, "Dutch in Chicago and Cook County 1900 Federal Census").
49. Church membership records, while incomplete, are instructive. First RCA between 1860 and 1900 lost 9 percent (67 of 730) of its confessing members—a third to the CRC, a third to American denominations, and a third to oblivion (erased or excommunicated). Fully one third of 200 baptized adult members were similarly erased. First CRC, by contrast, lost only 3 percent (22 of 691) of its confessing members between 1890 and 1920 and one fifth of its adult baptized members, the latter mainly by erasure. The RCA thus experienced a loss rate three times as high as the CRC, and this was in the early period before the full impact of Americanization hit after World War I. The records of First RCA are in the Joint Archives of Holland, Hope College Library, and those of First CRC are in the Calvin College Archives.
50. Lucas, *Netherlanders in America*, 473, 623–25; David De Vries, "Dutch Settlement and Assimilation in Cleveland" (seminar paper, Kent State University, 1987). The author wishes to acknowledge his indebtedness to

De Vries's research. See also Swierenga, "Dutch," in *Encyclopedia of Cleveland History*, ed. John J. Grabowsky and David Van Tassel (Bloomington: Indiana University Press, 1987).

51. Gerrit Dragt, "One Hundred Years, Christian Reformed Church, Cleveland, West Park, Ohio," in *West Park Christian Reformed Church 100th Anniversary 1872–1972, Cleveland, Ohio* (1972), 1–4.
52. De Vries, "Dutch Settlement," 11.
53. Howard Whipple Green, *Population Characteristics by Census Tracts, Cleveland, Ohio, 1930* (Cleveland: Plain Dealer Publishing Company, 1931), 28–29.
54. "Peoples of Cleveland," WPA Writers Program typescript (Cleveland, 1942), 76, Cleveland Public Library.
55. William R. Coates, *A History of Cuyahoga County and the City of Cleveland*, 3 vols. (Chicago: American Historical Society, 1924), 1:393; Samuel P. Orth, *A History of Cleveland, Ohio*, 3 vols. (Chicago and Cleveland: S. J. Clarke Publishing Co., 1910), 3: 431–32; Lewis Publishing Company, *Memorial Record of the County of Cuyahoga and City of Cleveland* (Chicago: Lewis Publishing Company, 1894), 107, 483–84, 487–88; Federal Manuscript Population Census, Cleveland, 1850.
56. *Memorial Record*, 765.
57. Lucas, *Netherlanders*, 241–42, 681; Reverend J. Kremer, "Hollanders in Cleveland and Detroit," in Henry S. Lucas, ed., *Dutch Immigrant Memoirs and Related Writings*, 2 vols. (1955; reprinted in a one-volume revised edition by Wm. B. Eerdmans, 1996), 2:574–75. Adriaan de Wit translated this document into English.
58. Cleveland *Plain Dealer* [1961?], in Cleveland Press Collection, Cleveland State University Library; "Cleveland," Church File, Calvin College Archives.
59. "Peoples of Cleveland," 76–77; Geraldine Javor, "Skillful Dutch Have Left Mark," Cleveland *Plain Dealer*, 18 January 1965, Cleveland Press Collection.
60. Dragt, "One Hundred Years"; Ella Terbeek, "Historical Sketch of Calvary Reformed Church," typescript, 10 February 1965, in author's files, courtesy of Donald L. Deunk, Cleveland; *Fiftieth Anniversary Jubilee of the Christian Reformed Churches, East Side and West Side, at Cleveland, April 9, 1922* (Cleveland, 1922), 13; "Dutch Churches Here Mark 60th Anniversaries," *Cleveland Press*, 8 April 1932, Cleveland Press Collection. The East Side Christian Reformed Church members worshiped at five locations: 33 East 35th (Calvert) Street between Cedar and Central (Garden) (F, Figure 8.3) (1872–1890); East 39th (Osborne) Street (1890–1910); East 55th and Thackery (G, Figure 8.3) (1911–1919); 12706 Union Avenue (1919–1960) in Newburgh Heights; and 23600 Emery Road in Warrensville Heights (since 1960). The West Side (later West Park) Christian Reformed Church worshiped at two locations: 2067 West 58th Street (formerly 414 Hodge, later Waverly) (B, Figure 8.3),

1872–1950, and 15135 Triskett Road. First Reformed Church was located on East 33rd (Blair) Street between Cedar and Central (Garden) (E, Figure 8.3), 1864–1910, and 5807 Lexington Avenue (H, Figure 8.3), 1910–1929, when it disbanded; Second (Calvary) Reformed members worshiped at West 61st (Aspen) and Lawn (later Colgate) Avenue (C, Figure 8.3), 1881–1910, and 1918 West 65th (D, Figure 8.3), since 1910.

61. Calvary Reformed Church, *Golden Jubilee Anniversary Celebration, Cleveland, Ohio, February 11 to 14, 1940* (Calvary Reformed Church, 1940); *Ebenezer! 1890 Feb. 1, 1900, Memorial of the Tenth Anniversary of the Second Reformed Dutch Church of Cleveland, Ohio* (Calvary Reformed Church, 1900); Michael A. Weber, "Calvary Reformed Church History," typescript, Calvary Reformed Church, Cleveland.
62. *Fiftieth Anniversary Jubilee of the Christian Reformed Churches*, 13, 22; *Seventy-Fifth Anniversary of the Christian Reformed Churches of Cleveland* (Cleveland, 1947), 11.
63. Jacob Bolt, "The Cleveland West Side Chr. Ref. Church," Part 1, *The Banner*, 15 March 1905, 390.
64. J. Goudzwaard, "Cleveland Christian Reformed Churches, I, The East Side Congregation," *The Banner*, 5 August 1909, 512; *Fiftieth Anniversary Jubilee of the Christian Reformed Churches*, 23.
65. J. H. Brinks to H. Gossen, September 1904, translated typescript, Calvin College Archives; "75 Years Marked by Two Churches," *Cleveland Press*, 10 April 1947, Cleveland Press Collection.
66. Dragt, "One Hundred Years," 2–9. In a 1965 Cleveland *Plain Dealer* interview, John Dykeman stated that "the Dutch have never gone into businesses for themselves in large numbers," preferring instead to work in large companies. This suggests a major shift took place after 1900, when the Dutch adapted to urbanization and experienced upward mobility.
67. De Vries, "Dutch Settlement and Assimilation," Figure 3 and p. 15; Federal Manuscript Population Census, Cleveland, 1900.
68. De Vries, "Dutch Settlement and Assimilation," 22–25.
69. Green, *Population Characteristics*, 28–29, 124–51, 219–30.
70. De Vries, "Dutch Settlement and Assimilation," Figure 5.6.
71. Membership records, Second Reformed Church, 1890–1915, Calvary Reformed Church, Cleveland.
72. Consistory Minutes, 1915, 1917, First Dutch Reformed Church, Calvary Reformed Church, Cleveland.
73. Membership records and council minutes, West Side Christian Reformed Church, 1872–1917, Cleveland.
74. Data compiled from Second Reformed Church marriage records, 1890–1910, and baptism records, 1890–1939, at Calvary Reformed Church, Cleveland; and marriage records, 1872–1920, West Side Christian Reformed Church, Cleveland.
75. Data compiled from St. Stephen Roman Catholic Church Marriage Records, Cleveland, vol. 1.

76. East Side Christian Reformed Church introduced an afternoon English service in 1908; West Side did so in 1912. East Side switched the English service to the primary morning worship in the late 1920s; West Side did so in 1928, but compromised by having two morning services, the first in Dutch and the second in English (*West Park Christian Reformed Church, 100th Anniversary 1872–1972*, 11–12).
77. Herbert Adolphus Miller, *The School and the Immigrant* (Cleveland: 1916; repr., New York: Arno Press, 1970), 29–30.
78. *Fiftieth Anniversary Jubilee of the Christian Reformed Churches*, 24; Dragt, "One Hundred Years," 11–12; *Cleveland Press*, 12 April, 30 May 1950; 1 August 1942, Cleveland Press Collection.
79. Bolt, "Cleveland West Side Chr. Ref. Church," Part 2, *The Banner*, 1 September 1905, 369; Dragt, "One Hundred Years," p.6.
80. Dragt, "One Hundred Years," p. 6.
81. *Fiftieth Anniversary Jubilee of the Christian Reformed Churches*, 15.
82. J. Goudzwaard, "The East Side Congregation," *The Banner*, 5 August 1909, 511.
83. Lucas, *Netherlanders in America*, 35–36.
84. Ibid., 36–37; Willem Beukma's Travel Diary, 1847–1863, translated typescript, Calvin College Archives.
85. Lucas, *Netherlanders in America*, 37–38.
86. Van Hinte, *Netherlanders in America*, 119.
87. *Lafayette Christian Reformed Church, 100 years of God's Grace, 1865–1965* (Lafayette, 1965), 9.
88. *100 Years*, 9–11; *History of Tippecanoe County and the Wabash Valley* (Dayton, 1928), 283; Richard P. DeHart, *Past and Present of Tippecanoe County, Indiana*, 2 vols. (Indianapolis, 1909) 1:260.
89. *100 Years*, 11–18; First Reformed Church *100 Years, 1888–1988* (Lafayette, 1988), 3–9; *Christian Intelligencer*, 11 June 1890, 11; 1 October 1890, 11; "The Dexter Families," clipping from an anonymous newspaper published at Boswell, Indiana.
90. Marie Yoder, "The Balk Dutch Settlement Near Goshen, Indiana, 1853–1889," *Mennonite Historical Review* 30 (January 1956): 33–34; Lucas, *Netherlanders in America*, 247–48; Van Hinte, *Netherlanders in America*, 167–73.
91. Yoder, "Balk Dutch," 36; Van Hinte, *Netherlanders in America*, 170–71; Lucas, *Netherlanders in America*, 248.
92. Yoder, "Balk Dutch," 38–42; Van Hinte, *Netherlanders in America*, 172–73.
93. Hiram and Eva Ferverda family memoirs, "Early Beginnings," 3–4, published in 1978, Calvin College Archives.
94. Superb local histories are Lance Trusty, *Town on the Ridge: A History of Munster, Indiana* (Hammond, 1982); David L. Zandstra, "The Calumet Region," *Origins*, 4 No. 1 (1986):16–21, and No. 2, (1986):48–54. See also Reformed Church in America Yearbooks, 1900, 1920, 1990; Christian Reformed Church Yearbooks 1935, 1990; Munster Christian Reformed

Church, *Diamond Jubilee Anniversary Book, 1870–1945* (Munster, 1975), 1; Munster Christian Reformed Church, *Centennial of the First Christian Reformed Church, Munster. Indiana, 1870–1970* (Munster, 1970); 1, Trinity Reformed Church, *Dedication December 1, 1957* (Munster, 1957), 1. For Highland see *Diamond Jubilee Committee, Highland Indiana Diamond Jubilee. 1910–1985* (Highland, 1985); Henry Bakker, *Highland First Christian Reformed Church, Seventy-Five Years of History, 1908–1983* (Highland, 1983). The author also benefited from David L. Zandstra's detailed information about historic Munster in a letter of 14 June 1992.

95. *Diamond Jubilee*, 1.
96. Trusty, *Town on the Ridge*, 6–8.
97. *Highland Indiana Diamond Jubilee*, 8; Bakker, *Highland*, 5–6.
98. Ibid., 51–53, provides a detailed description of onion set cultivation.
99. Zandstra, "Calumet Region," 16–20.
100. The Munster Christian School was established in 1906 and the Highland Christian School in 1909; see "A History of Highland Christian School," *Highland Christian School 75th Anniversary, 1909–1984* (Highland, 1984). Highland's charter stated that the instruction would be "according to the Calvinistic Principals [sic] of the tenets of the Christian Reformed Church, both in the Holland and American Language." See "Happy 75th Birthday Highland Christian School," Highland Historical Society *Newsletter*, 7 (Feb. 1984):4.
101. *Illinois Observer*, Apr. 1957.
102. First CRC Highland, *Fiftieth Anniversary, 1908–1958* (Highland, 1958), 9; Trusty, *Town on the Ridge*, 19–21.
103. Trusty, *Town on the Ridge*, 16–17.
104. Paul W. Gates, *Landlords and Tenants on the Prairie Frontier: Studies in American Land Policy* (Ithaca, NY, 1972), chaps. 4, 6.
105. *Centennial History of De Motte, 1876–1976* (De Motte, 1976), 13–14; *50th Anniversary of First Christian Reformed Church, De Motte, Indiana, 1932–1982* (De Motte, 1982).
106. Lucas, *Netherlanders in America*, 327–28; Van Hinte, *Netherlanders in America*, 553; *The Christian Intelligencer*, 21 Feb. 1894, 10; First Reformed Church [of De Motte], *Centennial Booklet, 1893–1993* (De Motte, 1993), 5–7.
107. *The Christian Intelligencer*, 18 Apr. 1900, 252; Minutes, Classis of Wisconsin, Reformed Church in America, 1895, and Chicago Classis (RCA) Minutes, 1919–22, 1932–33, The Joint Archives, Hope College; "De Motte Church Still Growing," *De Motte Citizen*, undated clipping (c. 1970); *The First Reformed Church, De Motte, Indiana, 1893–1953*; *Seventy-Fifth Anniversary, 1893–1968, First Reformed Church, De Motte, Indiana*; *Fiftieth Anniversary, 1920–1970, The American Reformed Church, De Motte, Indiana*; RCA Yearbooks, 1900, 1920; CRC Yearbook, 1935.

108. RCA Yearbook, 1990; CRC Yearbook, 1990.
109. Kathleen Van Nuys, "Dutch Influence Lives On," *The Indianapolis News*, 7 Oct. 1977, reprinted in Kathleen Van Nuys, *Indy International* (Indianapolis, 1978), 9–11.
110. Park Christian Reformed Church, Indianapolis, *Dedication Services, September 11–12. 1949*; Van Nuys, "Dutch Influence Lives On," 9; Federal population censuses, Marion County, 1930.

PART III

WORK AND POLITICS

CHAPTER 9

Migration and Occupational Change

THE ECONOMIC PROGRESS of European immigrants to the United States is one of the major questions in the literature.[1] Using occupation and wealth as indices of socioeconomic status, researchers have developed cross-sectional and longitudinal data sets to compare American ethnic groups spatially at one point in time or to follow wage earners over time once they were established in the United States.[2]

But few studies have explored occupational change as a result of the overseas emigration process itself. To do so requires a comparison of the "last job" in the country of origin with the "first job" in the country of destination. The social geographers and historians have demonstrated the feasibility of such international occupational mobility studies in a number of Scandinavian and German case studies.[3] But their data bases were small and usually limited to a few Old World villages that were tied through chain migrations to particular Midwestern frontier communities.

This chapter examines occupational changes among overseas emigrants for an entire nationality group, the Dutch, for the years 1840 through 1870. All officially registered emigrants throughout the Netherlands who were bound for the United States in these thirty years are included. Emigrants can thus be compared by decadal cohorts, age, rural-urban origin, social class, religion, and geographic region. In short, by studying a total immigrant population one can capture the full diversity of the group rather than be limited to subgroups that may be homogeneous.

Mobility Models

Migration scholars have hypothesized that, all things being equal, international migration is likely to result in downward occupational mobility, at least in the short run, because of language difficulties and the imperfect transferability of credentials and job skills.[4] Within a few years, as the new arrivals gain a tolerable competency in English, adapt to American job practices, and obtain needed credentials, they begin to experience upward mobility. This model posits a U-shaped pattern of immigrant occupational change, with an initial sharp decline followed by steady advance, until the newcomers reach and even surpass their original level.

The extent of occupational change in the migration process, however, is directly dependent on the labor and land market opportunities and the similarity of occupational structures in the sending and receiving countries and particularly in the local communities involved. The greater the differences, the sharper the decline. If the two countries are alike in most respects, we can hypothesize that occupational skills are readily transferred and that immigrants would suffer little status loss and might actually improve their position from the outset. Immigrants from English-speaking countries (the British Isles and Canada) have generally followed this pattern. But when the two countries differ substantially in language and culture, as is the case of emigrants from Continental countries, the initial deterioration would be more intense.

This hypothesis, which derives from modern studies of occupational status change among emigrants, must be modified to take into account the greater land and labor opportunities in the United States in the nineteenth century that stood in stark contrast to overcrowded, stagnant Europe. Until the closing of the farmers' frontier in the 1890s, European peasants and rural day laborers frequently were able to obtain their own farms because of generous American land policies. In such situations, despite wide differences between countries of origin and destination, emigrants would experience an immediate rise in status from landless laborer to farm proprietor. Indeed, in such circumstances, the U-shaped pattern might be inverted. If the first immigrants could monopolize the available land, they would experience a sharp rise in status, whereas latecomers, closed out by high land prices, would suffer an initial decline.[5]

The comparative economic opportunities and level of development in the respective sending and host communities thus affect job transferability and status changes. The Netherlands, for example, lagged behind the United States in industrial development in the mid-nineteenth century, but this affected Dutch immigrants only slightly because they did not enter the American labor market in the conventional two-stage process. Rather, the Dutch bypassed eastern seaboard factories, opting instead to go directly to the farmlands of the Midwest.[6]

Empirical Analysis

The data base is a linked nominal file of Dutch overseas emigrants in the years 1835–70 and Dutch-born households in the United States population censuses of 1850, 1860, and 1870.[7] The Dutch records are the official emigration lists compiled annually by local officials beginning in the mid-1840s under the direction of the Interior Ministry (see chapter 12 on sources). They provide a wealth of social, economic, and geographical data, including name, place of last residence, age, religion, occupation, social class, and destination. When the premigration biographical data are combined with the postmigration information in the United States population census manuscripts, the resulting profile of individual immigrant families is rich indeed.

Approximately 15,000 Dutch families and single adults emigrated to the United States in the thirty years of this study. By searching the manuscript population censuses of all counties and cities with at least 50 Dutch-born persons, I was able to trace about 4,000 households (almost one third). The linkage procedure is explained in Chapter 12.

The biases in the linked file are not fully known. As in other studies, however, the most likely missed links involved isolated immigrant families or single adults living outside of known Dutch communities, especially those who settled in the large cities where the census marshals were extremely careless in spelling names. If names are incorrect, linkage is problematic. Single persons were also more difficult to link than families, because of the lack of comparable data for other family members. The "lost" immigrants ranged in numbers from 14 percent in 1850 to 38 percent in 1870. Many were single young men. Others were fringe types—unchurched, adventurous, malcontents, and members of racial and religious groups with an international institutional character, specifically Roman Catholics and Jews. Thus, the linked file is biased toward Protestants and especially those who emigrated in family or community groups and followed common migration streams to rural colonies or urban Dutch neighborhoods.

Comparing Last and First Occupations

The linked file of Netherlands emigration records and U.S. census lists permits tracing the occupational progress of the immigrants at three stages in the period 1841–70: within ten years after the transatlantic move; between ten and twenty years; and from twenty to thirty years after the removal. The data analyzed here are for male household heads and single adults active in the labor force. Female heads, mainly widows, numbered only 1 percent of the linked file and were omitted from the analysis.

The primary records include specific occupations, but for purposes of comparison these were classified into an a priori seven-category, vertical ranking based on occupational prestige. The categories, ranked from higher to lower, are high white collar (professional, owner, manager, gentleman), low white collar (clerk, merchant, shopkeeper, peddler), farmer (or farm operator), skilled and semiskilled laborer, unskilled nonfarm laborer, farm laborer, and jobless.[8]

The findings show a marked degree of occupational change and rising occupational status among the Dutch immigrants.[9] In the first emigrant cohort (1841–50) portrayed in Table 9.1, 52 percent of 700 household heads and single adults changed from one major occupational group to another between their last position in the Netherlands and their "first" occupation reported in the 1850 census. Of these, 32 percent climbed and 20 percent skidded to a lower rank. The most notable change was the shift into the farmer class: one half of the 31 farm laborers became farmers, as also did one third of the 181 skilled craftsmen and 40 percent of the 183 unskilled nonfarm laborers. The lure of the land is indeed striking. The number of farmers among the emigrants nearly doubled (from 195 to 347, including 22 jobless emigrants who became farmers). On the other hand, one fifth of

Table 9.1 Occupational Mobility from Last to First Job, 1850: Immigrant Male Household Heads and Single Adults, 1841–50

	Level of "First" Job													
Level of "Last" Job	High White Collar	Low White Collar	Farmer	Skilled	Unskilled	Farm Laborer	Jobless	N	Percent Unchanged	Percent Climbing	Percent Skidding	Total Person/Ranks Climbing	Total Person/Ranks Skidding	Total Person/Ranks Gain
High White Collar	7	2	6	1	2	0	0	18	39	—	61	—	25	–25
Low White Collar	3	4	28	5	15	0	0	55	7	5	87	3	83	–80
Farmer	0	3	149	6	36	0	1	195	76	2	25	3	82	–79
Skilled	2	3	61	76	39	0	0	181	42	36	22	73	39	34
Unskilled	1	0	66	18	97	0	1	183	53	46	1	154	2	152
Farm Laborer	0	0	15	1	15	0	0	31	0	100	0	62	—	62
Jobless	2	1	22	2	10	0	0	37	0	100	—	131	—	131
Totals	15	13	347	109	214	0	2	700	48%	32%	20%	426	231	195

N.A. 135 C = .58 tau – b = 25 gamma = .34

Source: R. P. Swierenga, Netherlands Emigration and U.S. Census Linked Data File.

the immigrant farmers and skilled craftsmen fell to the rank of unskilled day laborers by 1850. The low white-collar group suffered the largest loss in status, with 48 out of 55 moving down. However, 28 of these 48 became farmers who doubtless considered this change a positive one.[10]

The 1851–60 emigrant cohort (N=1,195) had a more sanguine outcome than the 1841–50 group (Table 9.2). Again 52 percent changed occupations, but 38 percent climbed in job status, compared to 32 percent in the first cohort. The chief gainers were unskilled day laborers, farm workers, and the jobless, who moved up to the farmer class. None of the 95 farm laborers or unemployed in the Netherlands remained in that status after emigrating. Everyone moved up, with a third or more becoming farmers or farm operators, a fifth joining the skilled workers or low white-collar groups. The relatively small number of white-collar emigrants again suffered extreme losses, with 93 percent of the high white-collar group and 84 percent of the low white-collar group skidding. A fifth of the farmers and skilled workers also skidded.

The 1861–70 cohort (N=1,447) had somewhat fewer occupation changes and fewer immigrants climbed, but the difference was only 4–5 points (Table 9.3). The pattern of change was virtually identical to that of the earlier cohorts. Those in the three lowest ranks climbed, and those in the top three ranks skidded, with the number of farmers growing by a third. Again, all 99 farm laborers escaped that lowly status; nearly half became farmers or skilled craftsmen.

When occupational changes of immigrants living in the United States 0–9 years are compared with those in the United States 10–19 years and 20–29 years (i.e., the 1840–50 cohort in 1860 and in 1870, and 1851–60 cohort in 1870), the results show a marked improvement in occupational status (Table 9.4). The percentage of immigrants climbing the status ladder increased from a third to a half, and those skidding decreased by nearly one half to 10–12 percent. The ratio of "person-ranks" climbing to those skidding rose from 1.8:1 to 4.4:1 to 6.5:1 for the 1841–60 emigrant cohort in 1850, 1860, and 1870, respectively, and from 2.7:1 to 6.3:1 for the 1851–60 emigrant cohort in 1860 and 1870, respectively. Thus, within ten years after emigration, half the Dutch in the United States had improved their occupational status compared to their premigration status, and a third remained in the same rank as before emigrating.

Farmers always had the highest degree of occupational stability. The various cohorts ranged between 64 and 87 percent persistency. The first emigrant cohort had 76 percent persisting in farming in 1850, 78 percent in 1860, and 87 percent in 1870 (Table 9.5). The second cohort of 1851–60 had 77 percent persisting among farmer emigrants in 1860 and 80 percent in 1870. The latest cohort, 1861–70, had the lowest rate of farmer persistence at 64 percent.

The other blue-collar emigrants also consistently climbed the agricultural ladder to farm operator, especially those in the first two cohorts, who emigrated before 1860 at a time when farmland remained available in or near the Dutch colonies. Among farmer laborers in the 1841–50 emigrant cohort, 90 percent had become farm operators by 1860. And 71 percent of the 1851–60 cohort also became farmers by 1870. The unskilled laborers and jobless emigrants had similar successes.

TABLE 9.2 Occupational Mobility from Last to First Job, 1860: Immigrant Male Household Heads and Single Adults, 1851–60

	Level of "First Job"													
Level of "Last" Job	High White Collar	Low White Collar	Farmer	Skilled	Unskilled	Farm Laborer	Jobless	N	Percent Unchanged	Percent Climbing	Percent Skidding	Total Person/Ranks Climbing	Total Person/Ranks Skidding	Total Person/Ranks Gain
High White Collar	1	1	3	4	4	0	1	14	7	—	93	—	41	–41
Low White Collar	5	4	18	12	19	0	0	51	7	9	84	5	99	–94
Farmer	1	3	191	6	48	0	0	249	77	1	22	5	102	–97
Skilled	2	11	82	144	50	0	1	290	50	33	18	110	52	58
Unskilled	1	7	180	73	228	0	0	489	47	53	0	458	0	458
Farm Laborer	0	2	24	15	27	0	0	68	0	100	0	137	0	137
Jobless	1	4	11	4	7	0	0	27	0	100	—	96	—	96
Totals	11	32	509	258	383	0	2	1,195	48%	38%	14%	811	294	517

N.A. = 36 C = .52 tau – b = .19 gamma = .26

SOURCE: R. P. Swierenga, Netherlands Emigration and U.S. Census Linked Data File.

Table 9.3 Occupational Mobility from Last to First Job, 1870: Immigrant Male Household Heads and Single Adults, 1861–70

	Level of "First Job"													
Level of "Last" job	High White Collar	Low White Collar	Farmer	Skilled	Unskilled	Farm Laborer	Jobless	N	Percent Unchanged	Percent Climbing	Percent Skidding	Total Person/Ranks Climbing	Total Person/Ranks Skidding	Total Person/Ranks Gain
High White Collar	7	0	3	5	2	0	0	17	41	—	59	—	29	–29
Low White Collar	4	6	12	9	23	0	1	55	11	7	82	4	104	–100
Farmer	1	1	175	16	78	0	1	272	64	1	35	3	176	–173
Skilled	1	5	56	136	60	2	2	262	52	24	24	69	70	–1
Unskilled	2	12	161	128	420	3	2	728	58	42	1	494	7	487
Farm Laborer	0	1	22	22	54	0	0	99	0	100	0	168	0	168
Jobless	0	3	2	6	2	0	1	14	7	93	—	45	—	45
Totals	15	28	431	322	639	5	7	1,447	52%	33%	15%	783	386	397

N.A. = 26 C = .58 tau – b = .23 gamma = .33

Source: R. P. Swierenga, Netherlands Emigration and U.S. Census Linked Data File.

TABLE 9.4 Summary Occupational Mobility Data, Last to First Job: Immigrant Male Household Heads and Single Adults, 1841–70

	1850	1860	1870
Emigrant Cohort 1841–50			
Percentage Unchanged	48	38	35
Percentage Climbing	32	49	55
Percentage Skidding	20	12	10
Ratio Climbing: Skidding (person/ranks)	1.8:1	4.4:1	6.5:1
Number	700	643	551
Statistics			
Pearson's C	.58	.51	.46
Kendall's tau-b	.25	.17	.10
Gamma	.34	.26	.16
Emigrant Cohort 1851–60			
Percentage Unchanged		48	39
Percentage Climbing		38	51
Percentage Skidding		14	10
Ratio Climbing: Skidding (person/ranks)		2.7:1	6.3:1
Number		1,195	1,032
Statistics			
Pearson's C		.52	.48
Kendall's tau-b		.19	.14
Gamma		.26	.21
Emigrant Cohort 1861–70			
Percentage Unchanged			52
Percentage Climbing			33
Percentage Skidding			15
Ratio Climbing: Skidding (person/ranks)			2.0:1
Number			1,447
Statistics			
Pearson's C			.58
Kendall's tau-b			.29
Gamma			.33

SOURCE: R. P. Swierenga, Netherlands Emigration and U.S. Census Linked Data File.

Within ten years 60 percent of the unskilled workers in the 1841–50 cohort had become farm operators and within twenty years 76 percent had gained this coveted status. Even a third to a half of the skilled craftsmen became farm operators within twenty years.

Conversely, as Table 9.5 also shows, the white-collar workers benefited far less from migration to the United States. Over two thirds of both the high and low

TABLE 9.5 Occupational Mobility, Premigration Job to U.S. Farm Operator: Immigrant Male Household Heads and Single Adults, 1841–70 (in percent)

	U.S. FARMERS AND FARM OPERATORS		
PREMIGRATION OCCUPATIONS	1850	1860	1870
Emigrant Cohort 1841–50			
High white collar	23	33	31
Low white collar	51	44	56
Farmer	76	78	87
Skilled	34	51	54
Unskilled	56	60	76
Farm Laborer	48	90	87
Jobless	59	72	78
Emigrant Cohort 1851–60			
High white collar		21	36
Low white collar		31	40
Farmer		77	80
Skilled		28	35
Unskilled		37	54
Farm laborer		35	71
Jobless		41	44
Emigrant Cohort 1861–70			
High white collar			18
Low white collar			22
Farmer			64
Skilled			21
Unskilled			22
Farm laborer			22
Jobless			14

SOURCE: R. P. Swierenga, Netherlands Immigration and U.S. Census Linked Data File.

white-collar workers skidded. Many, however, became farm operators, probably by choice, as is clear from the fact that 51 percent of the low white-collar workers entered farming from the 1841–50 cohort and 40 percent of the 1851–60 cohort were farming within ten to twenty years.

Old Country social background characteristics may also have influenced occupational mobility (Table 9.6). The factors of religion, agriculture and culture region, social class, and age were analyzed in terms of occupational ranking changes. Religion proved to be irrelevant. Dutch Reformed and Roman Catholic emigrants had identical rates of job changes and also identical proportions climbing and skidding within the first ten years. Concerning the regional and class variables, the groups that had the most to gain from the decision to emigrate had a higher proportion rising in job status and a lower rate of status loss. Immigrants from the hard-pressed, commercial farming regions (clay soils) did 5–6 points better than

TABLE 9.6 Summary Occupational Mobility Data, Last to First Job: Immigrant Male Household Heads and Single Adults, 1841–70 (0 to 9 years since emigration)

	Ratio				
Socioeconomic Variables	Percent Unchanged	Percent Climbing	Percent Skidding	Climb: Skid*	Number
Religion					
Protestant	49	35	16	2.2:1	2,967
Catholic	49	35	16	2.4:1	360
Agricultural Regions					
Commercial Farming	49	38	13	2.8:1	1,934
Mixed Farming	49	32	19	1.9:1	1,122
Dairying	48	27	25	1.1:1	273
Cultural Regions					
Urban	43	31	26	1.1:1	319
Rural	50	35	15	1.4:1	3,022
Social Class					
Well-to-do	60	22	19	1.3:1	631
Middling	44	41	14	3.0:1	2,547
Needy	41	51	8	5.8:1	1,020

* The ratio is based on the total "person ranks" climbing and skidding. The number of persons climbing or skidding one rank is multiplied by 1, the number moving two ranks is multiplied by 2, etc., up to 7 ranks.
SOURCE: R. P. Swierenga, Netherlands Emigration and U.S. Census Linked Data File.

those from the more stable, mixed farming (sandy soils) regions and 11–12 points better than those from the prosperous dairy regions. Half as many emigrants from commercial crop regions skidded as did those from dairy areas (25 percent compared to 13 percent). Similarly, urban emigrants fared much worse than did rural folk; 26 percent skidded compared with 15 percent of the rural emigrants. Among social classes, the well-to-do likewise had the highest rate of status loss and the needy the highest rate of status gain. Fifty-one percent of all emigrants classed as needy, that is, on the public dole, gained one or more occupational status ranks within ten years after arriving in America.

Within each of the emigrant cohorts, age also strongly affected occupational change in the migration process. The youngest emigrants consistently fared better than the middle aged, and the middle aged did better than the older ones (Table 9.7). Of those under thirty years of age at the time of emigrating, 40 percent of the 1841–50 cohort experienced status improvement compared to only 23 percent of those over forty years of age. In the 1851–60 cohort, 52 percent of those under thirty were upwardly mobile, in contrast to only 29 percent of the over-forty age group. Similarly, in the 1861–70 emigrant group, the figures were 45 percent and 26 percent, respectively. The percentage of emigrants losing status likewise varied by age at emigration, with about 10 percent of those under thirty years and 17

TABLE 9.7 Summary Occupational Mobility Data, Last to First Job, by Age Cohort: Immigrant Male Household Heads and Single Adults, 1841–70

	1850 COHORTS			1860 COHORTS			1870 COHORTS		
	–30	31–40	41+	–30	31–40	41+	–30	31–40	41+
1841–1850 Cohort									
Percent unchanged	41	47	51	32	38	46	26	36	46
Percent climbing	40	37	23	63	49	35	65	54	39
Percent skidding	19	16	25	6	13	19	9	10	14
1851–1860 Cohort									
Percent unchanged				38	52	53	32	41	47
Percent climbing				52	33	29	64	49	36
Percent skidding				10	15	17	4	10	17
1861–1870 Cohort									
Percent unchanged							43	54	57
Percent climbing							45	29	26
Percent skidding							12	16	17

SOURCE: Robert P. Swierenga, Netherlands Emigration and U.S. Census Linked File.

percent of those over forty years slipping in occupational ranking. The thirty-one to forty-year-old emigrants had occupation shifts more similar to those over forty than to those under thirty years of age. Among all emigrant cohorts, the under-thirty age group improved in occupational ranking more than the over-forty group by a range of 17 to 28 points—a spread of 42 to 45 percent in favor of the young. The younger emigrants also skidded by 6 to 13 points (32 to 76 percentage points) less than the over-forty age group.

The age differential was even more pronounced among emigrants in the United States more than ten years. The longer the period after emigrating, the better the younger emigrants fared in their occupational status. By 1860, 63 percent of the 1841–51 emigrant cohort under thirty years of age had risen in job status; only 6 percent had skidded. Among the 1851–60 emigrants, 64 percent had improved by 1870, and only 4 percent had declined. The comparable mobility figures for emigrants over forty years old are 35 percent climbing and 19 percent skidding for the 1841–50 cohort by 1860, and 36 percent climbing and 17 percent skidding among the 1851–60 emigrants by the year 1870. Emigration was clearly a young man's game, judging from these statistics.

From this evidence, it is no surprise that the young, rural, lower-class, day laborers emigrated eagerly and in larger numbers than did the wealthy urban, middle-aged, and elderly. Nonetheless, the salient fact is that all social and economic subgroups benefited from emigration. Consistently, the proportion enjoying a rise in occupational status was twice as great as those suffering a decline. And always, about half—mostly farmers—held their ground and did not change from one occupational group or rank to another.

Destination and Job Change

The place of settlement doubtless influenced occupational mobility as much as timing and behavioral characteristics. Labor and land opportunities differed in each settlement community. However, since more than three fourths of the mid-nineteenth century Dutch immigrants settled in frontier communities with similar structural characteristics, the major distinctions can be found between urban and rural settlements.

Three different midwestern Dutch communities have been studied, namely Holland and Grand Rapids, Michigan, and Pella, Iowa.[11] Grand Rapids was a major light industrial and commercial center; Holland was a small commercial and service village integrally related to surrounding Dutch farms; and Pella was a rural farm settlement with a central village. In Holland "at least half and more commonly 60 percent or more experienced occupational movement," according to Kirk; in Grand Rapids, the rate of change ranged between 50 and 57 percent in the three census years 1850–70.[12] In the farming community of Pella, however, less than 40 percent changed occupations.[13] Doyle attributed the higher job retention rate in Pella to Dutch conservatism and the more open circumstances of settling in a new farm settlement. As a closed community with limited opportunities for land ownership after the first settlers had monopolized the available land, however, Pella may have had a lower rate of job change precisely because it offered fewer opportunities than the more diverse western Michigan economy.

Most of the upwardly mobile Dutch immigrants in Holland, Michigan, were blue-collar workers in the Old Country who became farm owners in America. The percentage of blue collar emigrants before 1850 who achieved this cherished goal of farm ownership increased from 3 percent in the 1850 census to 27, 44, and 47 percent, respectively, in 1860, 1870, and 1880 (Table 9.8). The rates for the 1850s cohort were 10, 27, and 28 percent, respectively, in 1860, 1870, and 1880. The 1860s cohort fared better, with 20 and 38 percent achieving farm ownership by 1870 and 1880, respectively. Obviously, the major avenue for upward mobility among Dutch immigrants in the Holland colony was from blue-collar jobs to farm ownership. Most of the upwardly mobile were under thirty years of age.

Grand Rapids, a predominantly native-American community, also attracted Dutch immigrants from manual and skilled occupational backgrounds, but more than half of these took up jobs at similar or lower status levels (Table 9.9). By 1860, after a decade of adjusting to American life, one third of the Dutch immigrants in Grand Rapids had advanced to higher status jobs. The vast majority (70 percent) had been unskilled laborers in the Old Country. Unlike the Holland colony, therefore, where numerous blue-collar workers became farm owners, their counterparts in Grand Rapids remained blue-collar workers after migrating overseas. Holland was a Dutch settlement carved out of virgin forests. Grand Rapids was a thriving city of native Americans, surrounded by developed farms. The Grand Rapids Dutch, therefore, lacked the opportunity to obtain cheap farms in the early years. But long-run prospects in the growing industrial city of Grand Rapids were superior to those of Holland. After two to three decades, Dutch rates of upward

TABLE 9.8 Summary Occupational Mobility Data of Dutch Immigrants, Holland, Michigan, 1850–80 (in percent)

	1850	1860	1870	1880
Pre-1850 Immigrants:				
Mobile	60	68	65	70
Upwardly mobile	2	7	9	11
Downwardly mobile	26	10	4	0
Urban to rural	3	9	51	55
Urban laborer to farmer	3	27	44	47
Rural to urban	3	3	2	4
Sample	90	73	57	47
1850–59 Immigrants				
Mobile		55	36	64
Upwardly mobile		0	4	36
Downwardly mobile		10	0	0
Urban to rural		45	32	29
Urban laborer to farmer		10	27	29
Rural to urban		0	0	0
Sample		20	22	14
1860–69 Immigrants				
Mobile			57	54
Upwardly mobile			10	4
Downwardly mobile			7	8
Urban to rural			23	38
Urban laborer to farmer			20	38
Rural to urban			17	4
Sample			30	26

SOURCE: Gordon W. Kirk, Jr., *The Promise of American Life: Social Mobility in a Nineteenth Century Immigrant Community, Holland, Michigan, 1847–1894* (Philadelphia: American Philosophical Society, 1978), Table 27, 90.

mobility increased in Grand Rapids more than in Holland. The large city offered more opportunity for occupational advancement than the rural village on the shores of Lake Michigan.

In the isolated frontier community of Pella, Iowa, changes in occupational status were less frequent than in either Michigan settlement. The clerical leader of the colony of 1,000 souls had deliberately selected the region because cheap land was available for the many farmers in his group. The high proportion of adult males who took up occupations similar in status to their Old Country positions reflects the fact that many Pella colonists were Dutch farmers who intended to farm in America, hopefully on a larger scale, by taking advantage of cheap prairie land prices. More than one third of the Pella settlers were Old Country farmers who continued their professions in Pella. Only one tenth of the Pella farm operators had been blue-collar workers before emigrating (Table 9.10). In the Holland colony, this proportion was several times higher.

TABLE 9.9 Transoceanic Dutch Occupational Mobility: Netherlands and Kent County (Grand Rapids), Michigan, 1850–70 (in percent)

	1850 CENSUS	1860 CENSUS	1870 CENSUS
Upwardly mobile	17.4	32.7	22.9
Downwardly mobile	34.8	24.3	26.5
Same status	47.8	43.0	50.6
Sample number	23	107	354

SOURCE: David Gordon Vanderstel, "The Dutch of Grand Rapids, Michigan: A Study of Social Mobility in a Midwestern Urban Community, 1850–1870" (M.A. thesis, Kent State University, 1978), Tables 5.16, 5.17, and 5.18, pp. 126, 127, 129.

TABLE 9.10 Transoceanic Dutch Occupational Mobility, Entry Occupation Only, Netherlands and Lake Prairie Township (Pella, Iowa), 1850–95

	IMMIGRANT COHORTS			
	1847–50 (%)	1851–60 (%)	1861–70 (%)	1871–95 (%)
Upwardly mobile*	9 (7)	20 (10)	27 (27)	14 (7)
Downwardly mobile	14	18	13	14
Same status	77	63	60	71
Sample N	43	51	15	14

* Figures in parentheses represent the proportion of immigrants who moved from a blue-collar position in the Netherlands to being farm operators in the Pella community.
SOURCE: Compiled from research data of Richard J. Doyle, "The Socio-Economic Mobility of the Dutch Immigrants to Pella, Iowa, 1847–1925," Ph.D. Diss., Kent State University, 1982.

These three local studies suggest several conclusions. First, the economic composition of the intended destination attracted particular types of emigrants. Farmers sought opportunities for land ownership on a larger scale than the small family plots in the Netherlands. Some blue-collar workers sought land, too, but closer to villages and cities where they could combine farming with other jobs. Other unskilled workers chose to settle in larger cities where industrial jobs were available. More important, the effect of immigration on occupational status was largely determined by the economic nature of the receiving community. Growing industrial towns attracted blue-collar workers, and farm settlements drew farmers and farm laborers. In the first decades of settlement the rural migrants enjoyed greater stability and had a minimal loss of status. But within a generation the Dutch in the expanding cities surpassed their kin in the rural colonies. By 1880 Grand Rapids offered more opportunity for advancement than Holland, and Holland held out more promise than Pella. Land was expensive and in short supply by 1880 in the Dutch colonies, and the only remedy was to found daughter colonies.

Conclusion

The research findings reported here do not support the U-shaped model of short-run, downward mobility among non-English-speaking emigrants, followed by a steady advance until they reach and surpass their original level. Even though the U.S. economy was more diverse and advanced than the Dutch economy, and hence the hypothesized status decline should be all the greater, nevertheless, 80–90 percent of the Dutch immigrants either remained in the same occupational category or improved their status. Of the first emigrant cohort of 1841–50, the proportion of those climbing in rank, in relation to those skidding in status, increased from 3:2 in 1850 to 4:1 in 1860 to 5:1 in 1870. The initial status decline on the part of 20 percent of the emigrants was greater by 10 points than was the case twenty years later, but there was no overall decline.

Neither does the inverse U-shaped pattern fit the Dutch experience, at least within the first thirty years after emigration. Each passing decade saw a growing proportion within each cohort rising in occupational status. Within ten years, one third climbed; within twenty years, one half had improved themselves; and within thirty years, more than half did so. The trend line is steadily upward, without a decline. This was the fabled "turnabout!" (*kentering*) or "about face" in their status that immigrants touted in their letters to the homeland.[14]

In individual communities, such as Pella, Iowa, where farmland had become scarce and expensive within twenty years, the inverse U-shaped pattern occurred, but so long as cheap land remained available elsewhere, new Dutch colonies were founded for latecomers and the children of the first arrivals. For most of the Dutch immigrants at midcentury, the American dream of success became a reality.

Notes

1. Joseph P. Ferrie, "'We are Yankees Now': The Economic Mobility of Two Thousand Antebellum Immigrants to the United States," *Journal of Economic History* 53 (1993): 388–91; Ferrie, "The Entry into the U.S. Labor Market of Antebellum European Immigrants, 1840–60," unpublished paper, 1993; Brinley Thomas, *Migration and Economic Growth: A Study of Great Britain and the Atlantic Economy*, 2d ed. (Cambridge: Cambridge University Press, 1973); Gordon W. Kirk, Jr. and Carolyn Tyirin Kirk, "The Immigrant, Economic Opportunity and Type of Settlement in Nineteenth Century America," *Journal of Economic History* 38 (1978): 226–34; John C. Hudson, "Migration to an American Frontier," *Annals, Association of American Geographers* 66 (1976): 242–65.
2. Stephen Thernstrom, *The Other Bostonians: Poverty and Progress in the American Metropolis, 1880–1970* (Cambridge, MA: Harvard University

Press, 1973), 220–61; Theodore Hershberg, *Philadelphia: Work, Space, Family, and Group Experience in the 19th Century* (New York: Oxford University Press, 1981), 461–91.

3. Robert Ostergren, *A Community Transplanted: The Transatlantic Experience of a Swedish Immigrant Settlement in the Upper Middle West* (Madison, WI: University of Wisconsin Press, 1988); Jon Gjerde, "The Effect of Community on Migration: Three Minnesota Townships, 1885–1905," *Journal of Historical Geography* 5 (1979): 403–22; Walter D. Kamphoefner, *The Westfalians: From Germany to Missouri* (Princeton, NJ: Princeton University Press, 1987); Kathleen Neils Conzen, *Immigrant Milwaukee: 1836–1860: Accommodation and Community in a Frontier City* (Cambridge, MA: Harvard University Press, 1976); Hudson, "Migration to an American Frontier;" Theodore Hershberg, et al., "Occupation and Ethnicity in Five Nineteenth-Century Cities: A Collaborative Inquiry," *Historical Methods Newsletter* 7 (1973): 174–216.
4. Barry R. Chiswick, "A Longitudinal Analysis of the Occupational Mobility of Immigrants," 20–26, in *Industrial Relations, Research Association Series, Proceedings of the Thirtieth Annual Meeting, December 28–30, 1977* (New York City, 1977).
5. Richard L. Doyle, *The Socio-Economic Mobility of the Dutch Immigrants to Pella, Iowa, 1847–1925* (Ph.D. diss., Kent State University, 1982).
6. Robert P. Swierenga, "Exodus Netherlands, Promised Land America: Dutch Immigration and Settlement in the United States," 127–47, in J. W. Schulte Nordholt and Robert P. Swierenga, eds., *A Bilateral Bicentennial: A History of Dutch-American Relations, 1792–1992*, (New York: Octagon Books, 1982).
7. Robert P. Swierenga, *Dutch Emigrants to the United States, South Africa, South America, and Southeast Asia, 1835–1880: An Alphabetical Listing by Household Heads and Independent Persons* (Wilmington, DE: Scholarly Resources, 1983); Swierenga, *Dutch Households in U.S. Population Censuses: 1850, 1860, 1870: An Alphabetical Listing by Family Heads*, 3 vols. (Wilmington, DE: Scholarly Resources, 1987).
8. On the problematics of occupational classification to measure social mobility, see Theodore Hershberg and Robert Dockhorn, "Occupational Classification," *Historical Methods Newsletter* 9 (1976): 59–98; Michael B. Katz, "Occupational Classification in History," *Journal of Interdisciplinary History* 3 (1972): 63–88; and Donald J. Treiman, "A Standard Occupational Prestige Scale for Use with Historical Data," *Journal of Interdisciplinary History* 7 (1976): 283–304. The social-occupational class categories follow Lynn Hollen Lees, "Patterns of Lower-Class Life and Irish Slum Communities in Nineteenth-Century London," in Stephen Thernstrom and Richard Sennett, eds., *Nineteenth-Century Cities: Essays in the New Urban History* (New Haven: Yale University Press, 1969), 359–85. Semiskilled workers were combined with skilled workers because they comprise only 8 percent of the skilled/semiskilled category

and mainly include apprentices in the skilled trades, plus a few shovel workers.

9. As a check against the possibility that some immigrants in the first year or two after arrival may have reported to census marshals their Old Country occupation, while actually holding a different occupation at the time of the census, I compared job changes among immigrants who had been in the United States two years or less, two through five years, and six through nine years. The results show such a similar pattern of stability and change across the various occupational levels for the three immigrant cohorts, that the possibility of widespread misreporting of occupations is unlikely. The percentage of immigrants whose occupational levels remained unchanged declined by only 7 points (52 to 45 percent) between immigrants of two years and those of six through nine years. The percentage climbing in prestige level rose from 28 to 41 percent, and the proportion declining dropped from 19 to 14 percent. The trends in both directions are to be expected, given the longer period of time in which to become established in the new environment.
10. Doyle, "Dutch Immigrants to Pella," 188.
11. Gordon W. Kirk, Jr., *The Promise of American Life: Social Mobility in a Nineteenth-Century Immigrant Community, Holland, Michigan, 1847–1894* (Philadelphia: American Philosophical Society, 1978); David Gordon Vanderstel, "The Dutch of Grand Rapids, Michigan: A Study of Social Mobility in a Midwestern Urban Community," (M.A. thesis, Kent State University, 1978); Doyle, "Dutch Immigrants to Pella."
12. Kirk, *Promise of American Life*, 89–90; Vanderstel, "Dutch of Grand Rapids," 126–29.
13. Doyle, "Dutch Immigrants to Pella," 185–88.
14. Jacob Van Hinte, *Netherlanders in America: A Study of Emigration and Settlement in the Nineteenth and Twentieth Centuries in the United States*, Robert P. Swierenga, ed., Adriaan de Wit, chief trans. (Grand Rapids: Baker Book House, 1985), 175.

CHAPTER 10

Pella Dutch Voting in the First Lincoln Election

SCHOLARS, PARTICULARLY THOSE interested in the impact of ethnic groups on key national elections, have long been intrigued by Abraham Lincoln's victory in 1860. Ever since Professor William E. Dodd's classic article, it has been axiomatic in the works of historians that the foreign born of the Old Northwest, voting in solid blocs according to the dictates of their leaders, cast the decisive ballots. Lincoln could not have won the presidency, Dodd suggested, "but for the loyal support of the Germans and other foreign citizens led by Carl Schurz, Gustav Koerner, and the editors of the *Staatszeitung* of Chicago."[1]

A decade later, taking his cue from Dodd, Donnal V. Smith scrutinized the immigrant vote in 1860 and confidently declared that "without the vote of the foreign born, Lincoln could not have carried the Northwest, and without the Northwest ... he would have been defeated." Smith's statistics also confirmed the premise that the social solidarity characteristic of ethnic groups invariably translated itself into political solidarity, and that because of the language barrier the immigrants needed leaders to formulate the political issues for them. "The leaders who were so trusted," Smith maintained, "were in a splendid position to control the political strength of the foreign born." And in the election of 1860, he continued, even to the "casual observer," the ethnic leaders in the Middle West were solidly Republican.[2] Therefore, except for isolated, insignificant minorities, the foreign born of the Old Northwest voted Republican.

Most midwestern ethnic leaders, it is true, were predominately in the Republican camp in 1860. Foreign-language newspapers generally carried the Lincoln-Hamlin banner on their mastheads and prominent immigrants campaigned actively for Old Abe and played key roles at the Chicago convention.[3] It is also widely conceded that the antislavery movement, the free homestead idea, and the Pacific railroad issue were key factors attracting ethnic leaders to the Republicans.[4]

The really crucial question, however, concerns not the foreign-born leaders but the masses that they supposedly represented. Did the naturalized immigrants vote as their spokesmen desired? Except for Dr. Joseph Schafer's deathbed protest in 1941 that the Wisconsin Germans did not fit the pattern,[5] the Dodd-Smith thesis has stood unchallenged.[6] But a recent analysis of the 1860 election statistics for Iowa suggests that the foreign born, and particularly the Germans, may not have supported Lincoln as strongly as historians have long assumed to be the case.[7]

A possibly critical factor thus far ignored in studies of the ethnic impact on the first Lincoln election is the time gap between the date of immigrant settlement and the year 1860. That ethnic leaders initially influenced the ballots of their countrymen is highly probable. Yet it seems reasonable to assume that a leader's power would steadily wane as the rank-and-file newcomers attained a measure of economic security and cultural acclimatization. If true, the student of ethnic voting must be careful when relying on what spokesmen said as an indication of how the foreign born voted, particularly if ten or fifteen years had elapsed since the transatlantic migration. The collective experience of the Netherlanders who migrated to central Iowa in the mid-nineteenth century, in illustrating this danger, is a case study of the complex influences actually molding immigrant political patterns in the years immediately preceding the Civil War.

In 1847 the Hollanders—some 800 strong—established their colony, with the new town of Pella at its center, in Lake Prairie Township, Marion County, Iowa. To ensure complete control of the area, the colony's leaders had earlier bought up the claims and improvements of almost all pioneer squatters in the township. Along with the purchase of vacant government land the Netherlanders were thus able to engross some 18,000 choice acres between the Des Moines and Skunk rivers. Through the antebellum years the settlement grew rapidly under a continuing Dutch immigration, augmented by a growing minority of native Americans. In the decade of the fifties potential voters in the township increased by 340 European-born and 152 native-born men. With a maximum voting majority of 85 percent in 1850 and 72 percent in 1860, therefore, the Dutch clearly dominated local parties.[8]

The Reverend Mr. Henry Peter Scholte (pronounced *Skol'-tuh*), founder of the Pella colony, was one of the ethnic leaders cited by Donnal Smith as typical of those who led the foreign born into Lincoln's camp.[9] The basis of Scholte's political influence, dating from the Old Country, was his position as president of the "Netherlandish Association for Emigration to the United States," formed at Utrecht in 1846 and consisting mainly of members of his religious congregation. Having seceded from the state-supported Dutch Reformed Church because of its alleged lack of spirituality, Scholte and his flock suffered a mild persecution from government officials. This, coupled with economic distress, prompted the Dutch minister to lead his followers to America.

Until his death in 1868, the "Dominie," as his followers affectionately addressed him, played an important part in the intellectual, economic, and political life of Pella, Marion County, and the state of Iowa. His versatility was truly remarkable. He served as minister, editor of the English-language Pella *Gazette*, lawyer, real estate developer, justice of the peace, school inspector, and mayor *ex officio*. Scholte was also an energetic capitalist. Besides owning almost one third of the land in and around the town of Pella, he had substantial investments in local industry. He owned a brick kiln, steam flour mill, and limestone quarry, founded the Pella National Bank, and was a benefactor and trustee of the local college.

Although he failed in his bid for nomination as state senator in 1852, he served as delegate-at-large and vice president of the 1860 Republican national convention at Chicago. In 1864 President Lincoln appointed him United States minister to Austria, although the Senate refused to confirm the nomination because he was not a native-born American.[10]

The early political views of the Pella leader were decidedly Whig. Idolizing Henry Clay while still in the Netherlands, Scholte espoused the Whig cause upon his arrival in Iowa. Like Clay, he possessed a typical Whig attitude toward slavery and the important economic questions of the day. While no admirer of the Peculiar Institution, he condemned abolitionism more than slavery since it embodied the greater threat to the survival of the Union.[11] The American economy, he divined from his study of recent history, "always flourished" under Whig administrations and slumped during Democratic misrule. Moreover, the Whigs were "more respectable and more intellectual," while the Democrats were "poorer and slower-witted citizens." The only explanation for the Democrats' ascendancy in Iowa since the state's birth in 1846, he convinced himself, was the constant influx of "poor folks from other states and from abroad. . . . All the poverty-stricken Irish and Germans that arrive are immediately incorporated by the Democrats who inform them that the Whigs are the wealthy aristocrats and blood-suckers of the common man."[12]

Political observers assumed that the Pella Dutch would follow the usual pattern and line up with the other immigrants behind the Democratic standard.[13] But they failed to contend with the Dutch leader and his Whig sympathies. The presidential election of 1852, the first in which the newcomers were eligible to vote,[14] clearly demonstrated the Dominie's power over his immigrant band. Contrary to all expectations, over 80 per cent of the new voters cast Whig ballots (Table 10.1).[15] The thumping Whig majority can largely be explained in terms of Scholte's influence. The language barrier isolated the Hollanders from their neighbors and rendered unintelligible the newspaper editorials of the day. Therefore, they were completely dependent on the few bilingual leaders like Scholte.[16]

Dutch ethnic antagonism toward native Americans in the immediate locale apparently aided Scholte's effort to indoctrinate his followers with Whig dogmas. Such cultural conflict was by no means unique to Marion County. New York State, originally settled by the Dutch, had long witnessed bitter antagonism between "Yankees" and "Yorkers," as Professors Dixon Ryan Fox and Lee Benson have shown. Fox traced nineteenth-century Yankee–Dutch antagonisms back to the seventeenth century and Benson demonstrated that in the Jacksonian period the Dutch "ranged themselves politically against the Yankees and Negroes—and voted accordingly."[17] The Pella settlers soon fell into this pattern. A bitter county seat contest, for example, evoked native American–Dutch ill will.[18] Even such seemingly minor concerns as different conceptions of proper farming techniques and animal husbandry, and proper dress and domestic habits of women, proved irritating.[19]

Between the national elections of 1852 and 1856 the political patterns in the state, as well as in Lake Prairie Township, changed radically. In the so-called revolution of 1854 the Iowa Whigs finally overturned the Democratic ascendancy in the

TABLE 10.1 Election Statistics, Lake Prairie Township, Iowa, 1851–60

	WHIG/REPUBLICAN		DEMOCRATIC		KNOW-NOTHING	
ELECTIONS	NUMBER	%	NUMBER	%	NUMBER	%
1851 State	9	18.0	41	82.0		
1852 National	89	60.1	59	39.9		
1854 State	52	34.9	97	65.1		
	(For)		(Against)			
1855 Prohibition	31	11.1	250	88.9		
1856 State	98	24.7	299	75.3		
1856 National	136	27.7	345	70.3	10	2.0
1857 County (spring)	55	20.4	214	79.6		
1857 County (fall)	58	17.1	282	82.9		
1857 State	56	16.3	287	83.7		
1858 County	102*	27.8	265	72.2		
1859 State	146	28.6	364	71.4		
1860 National	199	33.9	388	66.1		

* Includes 66 (18 percent) Independent votes.
SOURCE: Marion County newspapers and published county histories.

state. Among the Dutch, however, the trend was in the opposite direction, as Scholte and more than 80 percent of the Lake Prairie voters now switched to the Democratic party.[20]

Why did most of the Iowa Hollanders defect to the Democrats? Scholte's newspaper editorials perhaps provide the answer. The final plank in the 1854 platform of the Iowa Whigs pledged the party to enact a state liquor prohibition law. Scholte and his people bitterly opposed prohibition, which they viewed as an unwarranted intrusion into their traditional way of life.[21] Comparable to the liquor issue in generating anger and anxiety was the nativist movement then gaining ground in the United States—a crusade against Roman Catholicism in particular but all recent immigrants in general. By 1856 almost one in every ten voters in Marion County supported ex-President Millard Fillmore, candidate of the American (or "Know-Nothing") party, which had pledged itself to limit the political rights of naturalized citizens.[22] The Iowa Democrats, on the other hand, promised in their platform to resist "every attempt to abridge the privilege of becoming citizens," a plank that obviously appealed to the Dutch.[23]

Following their 1854 election victory, the new Whig majority in the Iowa legislature immediately pushed through a proposed constitutional amendment "for the suppression of intemperance" and in early 1855 submitted it to the electorate for approval.[24] The Dominie campaigned heatedly against the measure. From February through April 1855, every issue of the Pella *Gazette* devoted itself almost exclusively to this subject. On February 15, editor Scholte printed the bill in its entirety and promised to "dissect the corpse" in subsequent editorials. He emphasized that "no man in the State of Iowa" was more strongly opposed to intemperance and the "debasing practice of drunkenness" than he. The "Whig law," however, was "an abomination" which would "subvert ... the principles of common justice.... We [must not] try to effect by law," he reasoned, "what can only be effected by the Gospel."[25]

A counterattack by the prohibition forces was immediate. Levi Leland, popular agent of the Iowa Temperance Society, lectured in Pella on two successive evenings. Besides issuing other inflammatory statements, he charged Scholte with advocating "intemperance and drunkenness" and remarked that judging from the faces he had seen about town the Dutch used too much alcohol.[26] Native Americans throughout central Iowa joined the anti-liquor clamor, specifically attacking Scholte.[27] The Dutch leader, possibly anticipating real trouble, advised his "Christian soldiers" to "Put your trust in God and keep your powder dry."[28]

On March 10, a group of native Americans at Pella, led by Francis A. Barker, warden of the state penitentiary, met and drew up resolutions charging Scholte with "retarding the progress of the temperance cause." Unless the Dutchman capitulated on the issue, they threatened to urge readers to cancel their subscriptions to the *Gazette*. Scholte disdainfully replied that to him "Pecuniary profit is a secondary thing."[29]

Politicians from Knoxville, the local county seat, staged the next rally in Pella. William M. Stone, a future Republican governor of Iowa, was the main speaker. He not only charged the Dominie with injuring the anti-liquor movement, but he ridiculed "Father Scholte's" foreign birth and asserted that the Dutch leader was scheming to open a "saloon or doggery" in Pella for the sale of imported liquors. Stone's attack on Scholte was the beginning of a bitter personal vendetta. The feud took the form of a newspaper war, since Stone edited and published the Knoxville *Journal*. More important, Stone's blatant prejudice against foreign-born citizens demonstrated to the Dutch in a most personal way that the emerging Republican party was no place for them, thoroughly permeated as it was with nativism.

The next issue of the *Gazette* contained a four-column letter charging that Scholte merely wanted a law that was harsh on the drinker but lenient on the seller—the former being mostly native Americans and the latter German and Dutch. In reply Scholte labeled this charge "Know-Nothingism" and declared that "It would perhaps be difficult to find ten beer shops kept by Dutchmen; they are commonly Germans. In the cause of temperance," he continued, "it is perfectly wrong to set the Hollanders or Dutchmen on the side of favoring drunken[n]ess, it is just the contrary." He ended by demanding that native Americans never lay upon the Netherlanders "what they will never bear."[30]

Scholte's bitterness was now open. He considered all antagonists to be Know-Nothing types and grew overly sensitive to references to his European birth. In one sarcastic editorial he wrote:

> Some men have sneeringly alluded to the foreign birthplace of one of the editors of our Paper. Men tainted with, or immersed in Know-Nothingism have in their native presumption supposed that they had only to open their native babbling instrument, and bellow out their native wind-pipe, and the foreign-born citizen would tremble upon his

> feet, his hearer would shudder for fear of the native ignoramuses.... They are mistaken.[31]

Election day proved Scholte a correct judge of the local temper. Lake Prairie Township rejected the prohibition law by an overwhelming 89 percent, although statewide the voters approved the law by a small majority. Nearby Knoxville Township, consisting mainly of native Americans, also rejected prohibition, but by only 51.5 to 48.5 percent. Significantly, on the liquor issue as on the county seat question, Pella and Knoxville were sharply divided.

An important county election that occurred shortly afterward further increased the Democratic sympathies of the Dutch and prompted Scholte openly to endorse a Democratic slate. The contest pitted the Democratic machine which controlled the courthouse at Knoxville against a slate of ex-Whigs who styled themselves "Independents" but who were in fact incipient Republicans.

A secret midnight political caucus of the Independents at Pella on a July evening in 1855 became a crucial event. Several Dutch Democrats learned of the meeting and immediately declared it to be a Know-Nothing conclave. They strengthened their charge by swearing an affidavit before a Pella justice of the peace. "In our Government," Scholte observed,

> it is unfair, unmanly, and unchristian to so work in the dark, and to shun open contest with political opponents.... Is it a wonder that the people begin to have strange thoughts about men, who ... resort to such secret policy? No! It is no wonder, true and genuine Democrats must detest such an organization.

The Dutch leader demanded that the Independent candidates pledge under oath that the charge of the affidavit was not true. The aspirants promptly refused, claiming Scholte was merely

> the tool of certain party managers, who exult in their power of wielding at their pleasure the votes of our Holland fellow-citizens.... We most emphatically deny the right of any man, or set of men in the town of Pella or elsewhere to establish a censorship over the minds of our people.

At the same time, the men denied that they were members of the Know-Nothing Party. In reply Scholte argued that the candidates, if innocent, should have taken the oath because "the voters have a right to know.... To ask citizens of foreign birth to vote for men who are bound to exclude such citizens from office is more than an insult, it is to ask them to commit political suicide."[32]

The Dominie's editorial remarks soon bore fruit. The Dutch remained convinced that the Pella "midnight meeting" provided a clear indication of the linkage of Know-Nothingism and Republicanism. Anyone who claimed otherwise, said Scholte, committed an "open, bare-faced falsehood." From now on, he concluded, the Pella Dutch had a clear-cut choice between the nativist and Democratic parties and the decision would "not be difficult" to make.[33] On election day the colonists flocked to the polls and delivered a heavy majority against the Republican ticket.[34]

Following the two emotion-charged elections of 1855, the Dutch and their leader clearly and consistently espoused the Democratic cause. In the local election of April 1856, the Democrats carried the county by two hundred votes, the largest majority ever. A few days before the election a Knoxville citizen had predicted that Pella did not have enough wooden shoes to gain the victory. Afterward Scholte reported prophetically: "The men with wooden shoes . . . kicked the Know-Nothing Republicans badly now, and they will do it [again] next August."[35]

As the citizens prepared for the important state election of 4 August 1856, just three months prior to the presidential contest, Scholte worked hard to gain another Democratic victory. He delivered a series of lectures in Pella in the final week of the campaign in both the English and Dutch languages. So forceful were these speeches that an anonymous nativist charged him with driving the citizens of Lake Prairie to the polls "like cattle to the slaughter."[36] Despite the complaint, the great bulk of the Dutch inhabitants applauded Scholte's zeal. On election day, Lake Prairie went Democratic by 75.3 percent, enough to put the entire county in the Democratic column.

To swell this majority for the Democratic presidential nominee, Scholte inserted three political columns in the weekly *Gazette* in the Dutch language for the duration of the national campaign. Since Republican politicians considered victory in Lake Prairie a prerequisite for gaining Marion County, they countered by importing their most prestigious personality, Governor James W. Grimes. The governor's rhetoric proved of little help. After the Pella rally Scholte observed that Grimes had gained very few converts and that "the demonstration was a total failure." This prediction proved correct. In one of the largest turnouts in the decade Lake Prairie gave Democrat James Buchanan 70.3 percent of their ballots. Republican John C. Frémont attracted 27.7 percent and Millard Fillmore of the nativist American party 2 percent. The increased total vote reflected Scholte's heated editorials in the Dutch language, and his efforts to have all eligible aliens naturalized so as to cast ballots. In response to his urging some fifty Hollanders had appeared at the August session of the district court.[37]

Politically, the years 1857–58 saw little change in Lake Prairie. Citizens balloted five times, with the Democrats consistently garnering 70 to 80 percent of the vote. These impressive majorities placed Marion County well within the Democratic fold, whereas neighboring counties returned strong Republican votes in all these elections.[38] Scholte, however, was beginning to have second thoughts about the Democracy. He blamed President Buchanan for the sectional violence in Kansas and expressed dissatisfaction with the increasingly proslavery complexion of the party.[39]

Disillusionment with the Buchanan administration in no way aided local Republicans, however, for in the spring of 1858 the Republican-controlled legislature proposed an election law that discriminated against naturalized citizens whose ballots were challenged at the polls.[40] Scholte declared the bill an "outrageous affront" which clearly illuminated the nativist bias of the new party. "We did not dream," he wrote,

> that the stupidity and recklessness of our Iowa Nativists would go so far.... Native puppyism was never better illustrated.... It is a narrow mind indeed that cannot devise a law to preserve the purity of elections without exposing naturalized citizens to repeated insults. The proposed outrage will sink deep into the minds of Hollanders, and they will take care to resent it.... The Hollanders were nursed and cradled under the enjoyment of Republican liberties for centuries and ... will not, without a remonstrance submit to the ignominy of begging for a vote ... at the pleasure of any Know-Nothing demagogue that may choose to challenge them!... But we know also that the day of reckoning is coming.... Whenever there is an opportunity ... the despised wooden shoe nation will be at hand to kick would-be despots and exclusivists into the abyss of political oblivion.[41]

The statistics of the 1858 election, in which Lake Prairie voters gave almost three fourths of their ballots to the Democrats, prove that Scholte's desire to "kick would-be Republican despots" was shared by most Pella Dutchmen. This was the fourth straight year that the community returned solid Democratic majorities, but their convictions would soon be put to a severe test.

In 1859 the overconfident Democratic party of Marion County was rocked by two jarring blows that all observers predicted would change the political complexion of the county. In April a longtime Democrat, Sebra U. Hammond, editor of the *Democratic Standard* of Knoxville, bolted his party with an editorial blast in which he labeled the local Democratic leadership a "selfish and unprincipled clique."[42] The second jolt came with the defection of the man who was believed to control the crucial Dutch votes of Lake Prairie Township—Henry Scholte. The Dominie had planned his move carefully to obtain maximum newspaper coverage and squeeze out the last ounce of propaganda value. On June 18, the county Democratic convention named the Pella leader as one of its thirteen delegates to the state convention at Des Moines on June 23.[43] To the astonishment of all, however, on June 22 Scholte appeared at the Republican convention (also meeting in the capital city) at the head of the Marion County delegation. Eager to publicize this coup, the state's Republicans honored Scholte with the convention vice presidency.

Almost every prominent newspaper in Iowa commented on this "Incident at the Convention." The Republican press reported that Scholte had fallen in with a number of Republican delegates on the steamer en route for Des Moines. These partisans supposedly had convinced him of the error of his way. On the morning of the convention, the story went, the Marion County Republicans elected him as a delegate since he had "privately declared himself a Republican, and wanted to have done with modern Democracy forever."[44] The Democratic journals lamely asserted that Scholte had "wandered into the Republican Convention by mistake."[45] Scholte himself ambiguously explained that "the foolish and unreasonable action of the Democrats of nominating me as a delegate to their State Convention, against my will and without my knowledge, has accelerated my decision to take an active part in the Republican Convention, where I did belong in reality."[46]

That the Dominie belonged in the Republican fold is obvious from his editorials. Whig even before coming to America, he had adhered to that dying party until convinced that abolitionists and Know-Nothings had captured it. Thereafter, along with many former Whigs, he supported the Buchanan administration "for the purpose of saving the Union."[47] But the President's support of the fraudulent proslavery Kansas constitution and the eruption of violence in the Sunflower State disillusioned him. Scholte, in short, had joined the Democrats only as a last resort and soon grew disenchanted.

The most important question is not why Scholte changed his party allegiance, however, but whether the Pella Dutch would follow his lead. Opinions of contemporaries varied widely, depending on political viewpoint. Typical of Republican editors was a flat statement that "the accession of Mr. Scholte and those he represents will give us Marion County, with a gain of two Representatives and one Senator."[48] The Knoxville *Journal* editor assured his readers that Scholte's defection was "likely to work a complete revolution in the political character of Marion County. The feeling and conviction that led Scholte to abandon the black democracy, has also induced most of his countrymen to take the same step."[49] Democratic newspapers, on the other hand, predicted that "Mr. Scholte will take with him into the Republican party exactly four men, himself one of the number. And a number of Hollanders, whose dislike to Scholte has placed them with the Republicans, will now come over to the Democracy."[50] The Oskaloosa editor labeled Scholte "another Benedict Arnold," whose "unprincipled course" would result in a larger majority for the Democracy of Lake Prairie "than they ever yet had."[51] A Netherlander from Muscatine, professing some acquaintance with the Pella colony, also judged that Dutchmen "possess a mind of their own," and could not be "turned by the voice of a traitor.... Hollanders are not such a set of fools as to change their political principles at the bidding of a man in whom they have no confidence."[52]

Republican politicians, particularly ex-Governor Grimes and the gubernatorial nominee, Samuel J. Kirkwood, were unwilling to accept this verdict. On July 29 Grimes encouraged Kirkwood to discount rumors that the Republicans were losing strength in Iowa, as just the reverse was true. "I just saw an intelligent man from Marion County," Grimes wrote. "He says the Hollanders are nearly all going with Scholte and that we shall carry the county by as large a maj[ority] as the democrats have usually done it, viz. 200."[53]

Because of the wide publicity given to Scholte's defection, winning the Dutch vote became a matter of prestige for both parties. A Knoxville editor spoke for many when he noted the election was "one of unusual importance because all eyes are turned on Marion."[54] Maintaining the support of the Hollanders was a must for the

Democrats. Should the Dutch defect, other Iowa immigrant groups, particularly the Germans, might be influenced to follow suit.

The politicians worked diligently as the gubernatorial election of 1859 approached. Scholte sponsored several Republican caucuses in Lake Prairie, thereby affecting the first permanent Republican organization in the township.[55] As in previous contests, the key issues seemed to be ones affecting the Dutch as an ethnic group. Instead of squatter sovereignty, free land, and a transcontinental railroad, local attention centered on the nativist Massachusetts naturalization law and the protection of naturalized Americans abroad.[56] The Massachusetts Act, an expression of eastern Republicanism which other states were being urged to emulate, banned foreign-born citizens from the polls of that state for a minimum of two years after gaining citizenship. Iowa Democrats, citing this issue, argued that for the Dutch to vote Republican was tantamount to "putting the rope around their own necks."[57] Republicans, however, countered by stressing the refusal of Buchanan's Secretary of State, Lewis Cass, to protect naturalized citizens from induction into foreign military service while temporarily visiting their old homelands.[58]

The balloting took place on 10 October 1859. Despite Scholte's strongest urgings, Lake Prairie citizens again cast Democratic votes in undiminished numbers. Over 71 percent of the total went to the Democrats whereas in 1856, with Scholte campaigning ardently for the Democracy, the party had captured but 70.3 percent. The turnout in both contests varied little—491 in 1856 to 510 in 1859. Instead of wholesale desertions to the Republicans, therefore, the Democrats actually showed a slight net gain. The Knoxville *Standard* editor was obviously correct when he concluded that "H. P. Scholte does not control the Hollanders."[59]

Scholte's loss of power highlights a significant fact—that the initial power of the ethnic leader to control the ballots of the immigrant could be short-lived. It is difficult, however, to pinpoint when the Dominie's political influence began to decline. A few disgruntled colonists had criticized him and dissensions already had erupted within his church in the early years, and by 1855 a group of "young Turks" had pushed through the municipal incorporation of Pella and taken office against Scholte's wishes.[60] Undoubtedly he had made enemies. Yet this probably had little impact on the outcome of the 1859 election. The voting pattern had been set, and, regardless of attitudes toward Scholte, the people continued to think in terms of prohibition and nativism, as the Dominie subsequently complained.[61] No doubt the bitterness of these issues, both associated with Republicanism, still smarted within the rank and file. The sophisticated Scholte, his political contacts transcending the local scene, apparently proved to his own satisfaction that the Republican Party had purged itself of nativism and that prohibition had become a relatively minor issue. But the mind of the average Dutchman, still largely isolated by the language barrier, could not easily be changed. "I don't bother much about politics," remarked a Dutch carpenter. "I put a Democratic ticket in the box and leave the rest to God."[62]

Seemingly not discouraged, Scholte labored for the Republicans throughout 1860. Returning full of enthusiasm from the national convention in Chicago, he penned splendid tributes to Lincoln and castigated Democratic leaders.[63] He also publicized the Republican platform planks on the supposedly key issues—no extension of slavery into free territory, a homestead bill, and a transcontinental railroad.[64] The homestead principle, in particular, should have appealed to the Dutch of Marion County. By 1860 most of the vacant land within seventy miles of Pella had been taken up and the community considered itself overcrowded.[65] Colonists were discussing the feasibility of a mass migration to northwest Iowa where government land was still available. The idea of free—or at least cheap—land should have been decisive. Yet the Hollanders rejected both the Republican platform and the party's rough-hewn candidates.[66] In November 1860, Lake Prairie Township awarded Lincoln only 33.9 percent of its ballots.[67]

Scholtes postelection editorials gave no indication that the Pella colony had repudiated his political leadership; other politicians and editors continued to treat him as an important ethnic leader. Only the township statistics now contradict the assumption by historians that the Dominie continued to deliver the Dutch vote.[68] Scholars might well be cautious of other immigrant spokesmen who professed political leadership of their people.

But there is a larger lesson to be learned from the case of the Pella Dutch. In recent years some students of the ethnocultural approach to voting—in stressing nativism and prohibition as hidden issues—have implied that immigrants "rationally" defended their Old Country ways of life at the ballot box. The case of the Pella colony, however, suggests that after the first few years sheer political inertia governed—as Scholte himself discovered. Influenced by personal attacks on himself and his followers (attacks that he translated to the rank and file), the Dominie created such a staunch tradition of Democratic voting that he was unable to alter it. Hence, while Scholte in 1860 fulminated against Democrats as slavemongers, opponents of the Pacific railroad and homestead bills, and destroyers of the Constitution, the Dutch citizens blithely ignored him and the national issues he propounded and voted against nativism and prohibition—the issues of 1854–56.

One suspects that if Scholte had initially championed slavery abolition and had refrained from emphasizing the Know-Nothing and anti-liquor movements, he might have created a Whig-Republican tradition. Indeed, in failing to gravitate to Lincoln's support in 1860, the Pella Hollanders apparently ran counter to what occurred in Dutch settlements in Michigan, Illinois, and Wisconsin.[69] Lake Prairie Township, in fact, has been in the Democratic column in every national election since 1860 except for the Eisenhower and Kennedy contests.[70] For those who would understand this longtime rejection of the party of Lincoln, the peculiar historical circumstances within which the tradition began provide the decisive insight.

Notes

1. William E. Dodd, "The Fight for the Northwest, 1860," *American Historical Review* 16 (1910): 786. The idea was quickly accepted. See, for example, Arthur C. Cole, *The Era of the Civil War* (Springfield, 1919), 341–42.

2. Donnal V. Smith, "The Influence of the Foreign-Born of the Northwest in the Election of 1860," *Mississippi Valley Historical Review* 19 (1932): 204, 193, 202. See also F. I. Herriott, "Iowa and the First Nomination of Lincoln," *Annals of Iowa*, 3rd Ser., 8 (1907): 196.
3. Besides Schurz of Wisconsin and Koerner of Illinois, prominent foreign-born campaigners included Frederick Hassaurek of Ohio, Theodore Hielscher of Indiana, and Henry P. Scholte and Nicholas Rusch of Iowa. See M. Halstead, *Caucuses of 1860: A History of the National Political Conventions* (Columbus, OH, 1860), 123, 127; Reinhard H. Luthin, *The First Lincoln Campaign* (Cambridge, MA, 1944), 185–87; Charles W. Emery, "The Iowa Germans in the Election of 1860," *Annals of Iowa*, 3rd. Ser., 22 (1940): 421–33.
4. Luthin, *First Lincoln Campaign*, 187; Paul W. Gates, *Fifty Million Acres: Conflicts Over Kansas Land Policy, 1854–1890* (Ithaca, NY, 1954), 104–05.
5. "Who Elected Lincoln?" *American Historical Review* 47 (1941): 51–63. Schafer's revisionist view was quickly rebutted in a brief nonstatistical article: Jay Monaghan, "Did Abraham Lincoln Receive the Illinois German Vote?" *Journal of the State Historical Society of Illinois* 35 (1942): 133–39. Support of Schafer's viewpoint came from Hildegard B. Johnson, "The Election of 1860 and the Germans in Minnesota," *Minnesota History* 28 (1947): 20–36, but this article has been virtually ignored.
6. For textbook examples see Carl N. Degler, *Out of Our Past: The Forces that Shaped Modern America* (New York, 1959), 287; Ray Allen Billington, *Westward Expansion: A History of the American Frontier*, 2d ed. (New York, 1960), 611.
7. George H. Daniels, "Immigrant Vote in the 1860 Election: The Case of Iowa," *Mid-America* 44 (1962): 146–62.
8. Voting population figures were compiled from the 1860 manuscript federal census on microfilm at the State Historical Society of Iowa, Iowa City. Lake Prairie was the only township in Iowa in this period (1850–60) in which the Dutch held a clear majority over native American voters.
9. Smith, "Influence of the Foreign-Born," 193, 196.
10. Biographical data in Scholte Collection, Central College Archives, Pella, Iowa. The only full-length biography, by Lubbertus Oostendorp, *H. P. Scholte: Leader of the Secession of 1834 and Founder of Pella* (Franeker, Netherlands, 1964), is mainly concerned with Scholte's theological ideas and his religious career. But see also Jacob Van der Zee, *The Hollanders of Iowa* (Iowa City, 1912); Henry S. Lucas, *The Netherlanders in America: Dutch Immigration to the United States and Canada, 1789–1950* (Ann Arbor: University of Michigan Press, 1955; repr. Grand Rapids: Wm. B. Eerdmans, 1989); Lenora Scholte, "A Stranger in a Strange Land: Romance in Pella History," *Iowa Journal of History and Politics* 37 (1939): 115–203.
11. Unpublished autobiographical sketch, Scholte Collection. The best expression of Scholte's views on slavery is in his pamphlet, *American Slavery in Reference to the Present Agitation of the United States* (Pella, 1856),

5. George M. Stephenson, *A History of American Immigration, 1820–1924* (Boston, 1926), errs in maintaining that Scholte affiliated with the Democrats "shortly after his arrival in this country" (130).

12. A. E. Dudok Bousquet to John Bousquet, 1 Jan. 1851, in "Letters of Abraham Everardus Dudok Bousquet to His brother, John, 1849–1853," trans. Elizabeth Kempkes, Scholte Collection. For a similar expression of sentiment see Kommer Van Stigt, *Geschiedenis van Pella, Iowa, en Omgeving*, 2 vols. (Pella, 1897), 2:81.

13. "Marion County will shortly become an important part of the Democracy of the State, for, besides being thoroughly democratic ever since her organization, she is about to receive an acquisition of a thousand Hollanders," Davenport *Gazette*, 17 Oct. 1847.

14. Iowa law prescribed a five-year naturalization period, except with respect to voting in township elections. Iowa *Revised Code*, 1851, 562–63.

15. In the August 1851 election, when only native American settlers in Lake Prairie Township participated, the Democrats captured forty-one out of fifty ballots (or 82 percent), demonstrating a solid Democratic predilection for this group. In the presidential contest of 1852, with ninety-eight additional votes cast, the Democrats gained eighteen and the Whigs eighty. There is no evidence that the native Americans switched parties; and since the Dutch monopolized the land of the township (refusing as a matter of policy to sell to incoming Americans), it is safe to assume that almost all the new voters of 1852 were Hollanders.

16. Historians of the Pella colony were later unable to comprehend the magnitude of Scholte's early power. Failing to consult the township vote, they assumed that the native Americans led their Dutch neighbors into the Democratic fold immediately upon their arrival. See Van Stigt, *Geschiedenis van Pella*, 2:81–2; Cyrenus Cole, "Pella—A Bit of Holland in America," *Annals of Iowa*, 3rd Ser., 3 (1898), 257–58; Van Der Zee, *Hollanders of Iowa*, 231; Lucas, *Netherlanders in America*, 542.

17. Dixon Ryan Fox, *Yankees and Yorkers* (New York, 1940), passim; Lee Benson, *The Concept of Jacksonian Democracy: New York as a Test Case* (Princeton, 1961), 301.

18. A. E. Dudok Bousquet to John Bousquet, 14 July 1852, "Letters," Scholte Collection.

19. One Dutchman reported to friends in the Netherlands that American farmers had no regard for their animals and that their women "are terribly lazy." Moreover, he said, American consumption of whiskey was "scandalous." Quoted in Sjoerd Aukes Sipma, *Belangrijke Berigten uit Pella* (Dockum, Netherlands, 1849), 14–15. This document is translated and published with an introduction in Robert P. Swierenga, ed., "A Dutch Immigrant's View of Frontier Iowa," *Annals of Iowa*, 3rd. Ser., 38 (Fall 1965): 81–118, quotes on 96–97.

20. There were 343 more votes cast in 1856 than in 1852. Of this increase, 283 (or 83.6 percent) were new Democratic votes and 57 (16.4 percent) were new Republican votes.

21. Scholte, in one of his early promotional broadsides, asserted that Pella needed a brewery. He added, however, that "I would not encourage a distillery, since I think that an increase in strong drink would be bad for the Colony." *Tweede Stem Uit Pella* (Bosch, Netherlands, 1848), 32. This document is translated and published with an introduction in Robert P. Swierenga, "A Place of Refuge," *Annals of Iowa*, 3rd Ser., 39 (Summer 1968): 321–57, quote on 354.
22. Fillmore collected 225 out of 2,616 votes cast, or 8.8 percent. *Census of Iowa*, 1869, 261.
23. Herbert S. Fairall, ed., *The Iowa City Republican Manual of Iowa Politics* (Iowa City, 1881), 36.
24. Dan E. Clark, "History of Liquor Legislation in Iowa, 1846–1861," *Iowa Journal of History and Politics* 6 (1908): 55–87.
25. Pella *Gazette*, 1 Mar. 1855. The only extant file of this newspaper is in the Scholte Collection.
26. Ibid., 8 Mar. 1855.
27. The Eddyville *Free Press*, 8 Mar. 1855, published a bitter three-column editorial, and a Knoxville resident, Charles Burnham, sent Scholte a lengthy letter-to-the-editor which leveled a variety of charges. See Pella *Gazette*, 8 Mar. 1855. Native Americans, of course, harbored similar opinions of their Dutch neighbors. Recalled one pioneer Marion County resident: "The writer will never forget the Hollanders coming into Pella—strange people, at least strange at that time, in their appearance, their strange ways, their forms of dress and language." Pella *Chronicle*, 18 July 1912.
28. Pella *Gazette*, 8 Mar. 1855.
29. Ibid., 29 Mar. 1855.
30. Ibid., 17 May 1855. The letter was written by S. N. Lindley of Monroe, Jasper County.
31. Ibid., 29 Mar. 1855.
32. Ibid., 2 Aug. 1855.
33. Ibid., 29 Nov. 1855.
34. Ibid., 9 Aug. 1855.
35. Ibid., 17 Apr. 1858.
36. Ibid., 21 Aug. 1858.
37. Ibid., 21 Aug., 4 Sept. 1858.
38. Knoxville *Journal*, 27 Oct. 1857; 2 Feb. 1858.
39. Pella *Gazette*, 3, 24 Dec. 1857; 7, 14 Jan., 11 Feb., 11 Mar. 1858.
40. Naturalized citizens would have to swear under oath they were indeed naturalized, then prove it by presenting their papers, and then swear to the veracity of the papers. Iowa *House Journal* 7th General Assembly (1858), 233.
41. Pella *Gazette*, 18 Feb. 1858.
42. Knoxville *Democratic Standard*, 5, 14 Apr. 1859.
43. Ibid., 14 Apr. 1859; Pella *Gazette*, 22 July 1859.
44. Muscatine *Weekly Journal*, 1 July 1859; Des Moines *Iowa Citizen*, 29

June, 13 July 1859; Keokuk *Des Moines Valley Whig*, 4 July 1859; Dubuque *Daily Times*, 30 June 1859.

45. Dubuque *Express and Herald*, cited in Burlington *Hawk-Eye*, 30 July 1859.
46. Pella *Gazette*, 22 July 1859.
47. Scholte, *American Slavery*, 78.
48. Burlington *Hawk-Eye*, 28 June 1859. See also Iowa City *Republican*, 6 July 1859.
49. Cited in Des Moines *Citizen*, 6 July 1859.
50. Des Moines *State Journal*, reprinted in Davenport *Daily Iowa State Democrat*, 3 July 1859.
51. Oskaloosa *Times*, 28 July 1859.
52. Davenport *Democrat*, 6 July 1859.
53. "Correspondence of James W. Grimes," *Annals of Iowa*, 3rd Ser., 22 (1941): 556.
54. Knoxville *Standard*, 12 Aug. 1859.
55. Pella *Gazette*, 17 Aug., 14 Sept., 5 Oct. 1859.
56. Ibid., 14, 21, 28 Sept. 1859.
57. Ibid. 17 Aug., 14 Sept., 5 Oct. 1859; Knoxville *Standard*, 14 June 1859.
58. Pella *Gazette*, 22 July 1859; Oskaloosa *Times*, 28 July, 4 Aug. 1859.
59. Knoxville *Standard*, 22 Oct. 1859. Scholars, entirely ignoring the township vote, have assumed that Scholte's defection had a tremendous influence on his countrymen. See Stephenson, *History of American Immigration*, 130; Frank I. Herriott, "Republican Presidential Preliminaries in Iowa, 1859–1860," *Annals of Iowa*, 3rd Ser., 9 (1910): 253.
60. Sipma, *Belangrijke Berigten*, 27–30; Pella *Gazette*, 9, 16 Aug. 1855; Oostendorp, *H. P. Scholte*, 168–73; "The Garden Square Controversy, April 1855," Scholte Collection.
61. "The Democratic leaders," wrote Scholte, "are continually trying to influence foreign-born citizens . . . [to think] that the Republican party is under the control of the party generally known as the Know-Nothing or Native Americans." This was "slander," he concluded. Pella *Gazette*, 25 Jan. 1860.
62. Quoted in John Scholte Nollen, *Grinnell College* (Iowa City, 1953), 249.
63. The Pella *Gazette* succumbed to financial difficulties in February 1860, and thereafter Scholte published his views in the Burlington *Hawk-Eye* and the Sheboygan (WI) *Nieuwsbode*, a Dutch-language paper read by many Pella Hollanders.
64. Burlington *Hawk-Eye*, 3 Nov. 1860.
65. Lucas, *Netherlanders in America*, 333.
66. There is other evidence in addition to this negative Dutch vote that Buchanan land policy and the homestead issue may have been overemphasized by historians such as Paul W. Gates ("The Homestead Law in Iowa," *Agricultural History* 38 [1964]: 73). Many northwest Iowa newspapers welcomed Buchanan's land sales of 1858–60 and ignored his homestead bill vetoes, while Stephen A. Douglas ran far ahead of his ticket in the same area.

67. Although this was a net Republican gain of 5.3 percent over the gubernatorial contest of 1859, the Republican increase was likely due to the influx of native Americans attracted to Pella by Central Iowa University, which opened its doors in 1857. A comparison of the 1850 and 1860 population censuses in Lake Prairie Township shows that nearly two thirds of the non-Dutch newcomers of the fifties were from the New England, Middle Atlantic, and Upper Ohio Valley states. Daniels, "Immigrant Vote," table II, demonstrates that most migrants to Iowa from these areas voted Republican in 1860.
68. See Stephenson, *History of American Immigration*, 131, Van Stigt, *Geschiedenis van Pella*, 3:44; Van Der Zee, *Hollanders of Iowa*, 229, 408n. Lucas alone concluded the reverse. "In Pella," he wrote, "the majority still stubbornly adhered to the Democratic position and were suspicious of the abolitionist elements in the new party" (*Netherlanders in America*, 562). The "official abstract" of the Marion County vote was printed in the Knoxville *Republican*, 20 Nov. 1860. The only issue of the newspaper for that year known to be extant, it now reposes in the State Historical Society of Iowa.
69. Lucas, *Netherlanders in America*, 529ff; Daniels, "Immigrant Vote," Table II and Appendix A, lists the Iowa Dutch as strong Lincoln supporters. This conclusion resulted from an examination of the Hollanders of Black Oak Township, Mahaska County. Although the largest ethnic group in that township, these Dutch were outnumbered by native American voters by a more than two-to-one margin. It is likely, therefore, that the native Americans, rather than the Dutch, accounted for the heavy Republican vote there. The Black Oak Netherlanders represented a contiguous segment of the Pella colony.
70. In gubernatorial races the township has voted Democratic in every election except in 1930. The Pella city wards, separated from the rural precinct since the turn of the century, remained consistently Democratic until 1928. Since then a two-party trend has emerged. All votes are in the yearly editions of the *Iowa Official Register*.

PART IV

STATISTICS AND SOURCES

CHAPTER 11

Dutch International Migration Statistics 1820–80

INTERNATIONAL MIGRATION STATISTICS in the mid-nineteenth century are notoriously meager and haphazard.[1] Brinley Thomas, the acknowledged authority on transatlantic migration, has remarked that "the era of free international migration was nearly over before the countries concerned began to give serious attention to their statistical records ... It was not until migration itself became the object of national planning that this branch of statistics was developed for its own sake."[2] The nations of the Atlantic community developed the modern system of recording migration statistics in the decade after the Napoleonic wars, under the impact of the massive peasant migration to America. England in 1815 and the United States in 1820 first established comprehensive procedures to document the transatlantic population flow.[3]

Despite its administrative policy goals, the immigration figures compiled by United States authorities in the nineteenth century are as problematic as those of Western European governments.[4] American officials did not employ a uniform reporting year and the statistical unit varied, according to the definition of an immigrant.[5] In the early years from 1820 to 1855, customs collectors were also notoriously careless in compiling accurate reports, and officials in the State Department, where the reports were to be forwarded, did not systematically review and scrutinize them.[6] Moreover, an undetermined number of immigrants disembarked at Canadian ports and entered the United States at interior border points where officials were not obliged to take special notice.[7]

The extent of the shortfall in U.S. immigration statistics is indicated by the fact that major port cities such as New York made their own yearly tally of immigrant arrivals in the mid-nineteenth century and these figures often exceeded federal totals for all East Coast ports.[8] Foreign government statistics of United States–bound emigrants in some instances also exceeded the federal totals for some nationality groups. This gross method of comparison of emigrants and immigrants assumes that both governments were reporting on the same individual, which is an unproven assumption at best.

For the statistics that were reported officially, scholars customarily rely on the work of Imre Ferenczi, which was compiled under the auspices of the International Labor Office in the early 1920s and published in 1929 by the National Bureau of Economic Research under the editorship of Walter Willcox. The Ferenczi-Willcox volume brings together between two covers all official data series on post-1820 international migration then available in published form or supplied by governments at the behest of the I.L.O. Textbook writers routinely have relied upon this "bible of the trade," which contains quinquennial totals of alien arrivals and immigrants to the United States from 1820 to 1924, broken down by nationality.[9]

Migration specialists know the many deficiencies and gaps in these official statistics.[10] Instructive in this regard is the series of diagrams in Willcox that compare migration from six European countries to the United States by juxtaposing official statistics of sending countries and U.S. data. The diagrams show that prior to 1900 each of these countries, except England, reported far fewer emigrants than the number of arrivals of the same nationality counted by U.S. port officials. These crude aggregate comparisons, coupled with conceptual biases, have been the basis for the conventional wisdom that migration statistics of receiving countries (notably the U.S.) are more reliable than those of sending countries.[11] Host countries such as the United States, it was assumed, took a greater interest in the arrival of immigrant peasants and laborers than the home governments did regarding their departure.

J. D. Gould recently challenged the a priori character of these conclusions and their implicit "U.S.A.-centric bias." He suggested that sending country data may often be superior in both principle and practice.[12] For example, where the emigration was passport-based, as in the Scandinavian countries, the statistics of sending countries might be more reliable. Whether one measures the population flow from one end of the migration stream or the other, however, the aggregate serial data remain unreliable.

Willcox's technique of comparing aggregate statistical series of sending and host governments may suggest which set of figures is more reliable in a given instance. It may even reveal gaps and deficiencies in the published data. But source biases will not yield so readily to superficial comparisons. The ideal method of source criticism is to compare linked, nominal files of immigrants in sending and receiving nations.[13] If each America-bound migrant reported by the home government and each immigrant arrival reported by the U.S. authorities could be traced in the nominal record files of the other nation, it would be possible to determine with a high degree of accuracy the biases and omissions in the official migration statistics of the two nations. Given the magnitude of European overseas migration in the nineteenth century, such record linkage could best be accomplished for small migrant populations who originated in Old World countries or regions where adequate emigration records were compiled and preserved. The Low Countries, Scandinavian nations, and Germany are likely examples. The results of this methodology may not be generalized to apply to all nationality groups, but it would suggest possible structural deficiencies in the published statistics.

This chapter provides a critical analysis of international migration statistics in the nineteenth century based on the method of nominal record linkage of multinational sources. The population considered is all Netherlands emigrants to the United States in the period 1835–80. Hence, this is the first attempt to measure the "true" rate for an entire immigrant population. The two nominal sources utilized are the official Dutch municipal emigration lists, "*Staat der landverhuizers naar Noord-Amerika of andere overzeesche gewesten*" (List of emigrants to North America and other overseas places), and, second, the U.S. ship passenger manifests that ship captains provided to the customs collectors of all major East Coast ports (see Chapter 12).

The Dutch *Landverhuizers* records are 95 percent complete for the period of the study, and include 21,500 families and single adults (55,700 persons) bound for the United States. The ship manifests, which are the basis for the published U.S. statistics of all foreign immigration, provide proof of arrival on American shores of the Dutch emigrants. All Dutch nationals in the passenger manifests have been identified by a careful search of the extant records, and the biographical data on each have been abstracted. This file includes 23,000 Dutch families and single adults (54,500 persons). It is assumed that most arriving Dutch were permanent immigrants. Only 10 percent were first- or second-class passengers, and a mere 450 (.08 percent) were merchants, visitors, and diplomats.

The findings are reported in three steps. First, I compared the official published statistics of the two governments with the tabulations of unpublished individual-level data. Second, the two files were linked name by name to produce four subfiles or "classes:" (1) emigrant families and individuals bound for North America who are listed in the Netherlands emigration records but not in the U.S. ship manifests; (2) those listed in the U.S. ship manifests but not in the Dutch records; (3) those who are truly linked in both records, and (4) those not recorded in either list.[14] Third, the linked and nonlinked records in each file are compared to each other to determine if there are structural differences over time between the recorded and unrecorded (or "unofficial") Dutch emigration.

Official Dutch Migration Statistics

Table 11.1 provides annual statistics on Dutch immigration to the United States in the years 1820–80, drawn from official published and unpublished sources. Column A is the official tally of overseas Dutch emigrants compiled by the Netherlands Ministry of Home Affairs and published annually in the Amsterdam *Nederlandsche Staats-Courant*. Prior to 1876, this series does not designate overseas continental destinations. Thus, the extent of Dutch emigration to North America cannot be determined from the published series. Column B is derived from the unpublished *Landverhuizers* manuscripts that *gemeente* (municipal) officials in 1847 compiled retrospectively to 1831 and which became mandatory in 1848 under a Royal Decree (see Chapter 12). These manuscripts designate the country or specific destination point of each emigrating household or single adult.

TABLE 11.1 Annual Netherlands and U.S. Statistics of Dutch Overseas Immigration, 1820–80

	NETHERLANDS RECORDS				U.S. IMMIGRATION RECORDS					
	ALL		NA DEST		ALL ARRIVALS			BONAFIDE IMMIGRANTS		
	A	B	C	D	E	F	G	H	I	J
YEAR	N	N	N	%	N	N	N	N	N	N
1820					49	75	68			68
1821					56	33	27			27
1822					51	25	11			11
1823					19	46	34			34
1824					40	27	25			25
1825					37	22	18			18
1826					176	23	16			16
1827					245	37	30			30
1828					263	132	124			124
1829					169	45	34			34
1820–29					1,105	465	387			387
1830					22	115	112			112
1831	1				175	41	40			40
1832	1				205	275	272			272
1833	0				39	141	130			138
1834	0				87	33	30			30
1835	6	6	6	100.0	124	48	46			49
1836	13	13	9	69.3	301	102	86			90
1837	1	1	1	100.0	312	123	115			110
1838	0	0	0	—	27	59	47			45
1839	9	13	13	100.0	85	74	63			72
1830–39	31	33	29	87.9	1,377	1,011	941			958
1840	2	2	2	100.0	57	112	110			107
1841	0	5	5	100.0	214	105	103			103
1842	24	23	23	100.0	330	121	117			127
1843	67	73	72	98.6	330	250	246			296
1844	171	176	176	100.0	184	245	242			321
1845	680	485	445	91.8	791	441	437			858
1846	1,755	1,072	1,059	98.9	979	1,855	1,853			2,824
1847	5,322	3,401	3,319	97.6	2,631	5,111	5,106		3,611	8,052
1848	2,160	2,168	1,997	92.1	918	2,435	2,432		1,560	2,932
1849	2,078	2,080	1,855	89.2	1,190	2,242	2,231		2,447	2,918
1840–49	12,259	9,518	8,953	94.1	7,624	12,917	12,877		7,618	18,538
1850	774	775	680	87.7	684	953	946		1,174	1,204
1851	1,196	1,215	1,113	91.6	352	1,129	1,127		1,798	1,669
1852	1,184	1,176	1,112	94.6	1,719	1,528	1,525		1,223	1,887
1853	1,646	1,631	1,565	95.1	600	1,604	1,601		1,085	2,587
1854	3,611	3,629	3,365	92.7	1,534	2,600	2,599		1,466	4,810
1855	2,077	2,065	1,827	88.5	2,588	2,379	2,340		822	2,849
1856	1,924	1,929	1,778	92.2	1,395	2,080	2,079		1,666	2,899
1857	1,663	1,654	1,475	89.2	1,775	2,097	2,059		1,734	2,665

(Continued)

TABLE 11.1 *(Continued)*

	NETHERLANDS RECORDS				U.S. IMMIGRATION RECORDS					
	ALL		NA DEST		ALL ARRIVALS			BONAFIDE IMMIGRANTS		
	A	B	C	D	E	F	G	H	I	J
YEAR	N	N	N	%	N	N	N	N	N	N
1858	1,177	1,184	406	34.3	185	376	374		348	585
1859	490	493	193	39.2	290	315	314		261	413
1850–59	15,742	15,751	13,514	85.8	11,122	15,061	14,964		11,577	21,568
1860	860	858	341	39.7	351	443	440	440		646
1861	757	761	287	37.7	283	272	265	331		389
1862	825	832	549	66.0	432	281	274	456		648
1863	1,054	1,049	833	79.4	416	638	634	407		1,117
1864	740	737	603	81.8	708	516	509	615		902
1865	1,681	1,682	1,464	87.0	779	491	485	729	99	1,596
1866	3,295	3,221	3,006	93.3	1,716	1,645	1,638	1,506	65	3,512
1867	4,187	4,139	3,967	95.8	2,223	2,050	2,040	2,156	453	4,751
1868	2,972	3,003	2,883	96.0	345	1,173	1,165	1,265	269	3,400
1869	3,412	3,480	3,330	95.7	1,134	1,067	1,065	1,247	413	3,868
1860–69	19,783	19,762	17,263	87.3	8,387	8,576	8,515	9,152	1,299	20,829
1870	1,644	1,896	1,795	94.7	1,066	681	674		113	2,198
1871	2,036	1,921	1,828	95.2	993	962	956		326	2,451
1872	3,486	3,548	3,412	96.2	1,909	1,952	1,938		27	4,311
1873	3,867	3,865	3,793	98.1	3,811	4,146	4,125		63	5,529
1874	1,042	1,089	991	91.0	2,444	1,357	1,352		0	1,621
1875	585	682	537	78.7	1,237	936	917		0	1,100
1876	106	356	222	62.4	855	748	736		0	741
1877	200	245	180	73.5	591	501	497		0	538
1878	385	234	223	95.3	608	634	623		0	824
1879	899	761	738	97.0	753	1,174	1,161		0	1,549
1880	3,041	2,510	2,425	96.6	3,340	3,467	3,444		0	4,654
1870–80	17,291	17,107	15,944	93.2	17,607	16,558	16,423		529	25,516
1820–80	65,106	62,171	55,703	89.6	47,222	54,588	54,107		1,828	87,796
1835–80	65,104	62,171	55,703	89.6	45,589	53,518	53,136		1,828	86,817

NOTES: Column A: Official statistics of Dutch overseas emigration published annually in the *Nederlandsche Staats-Courant*, 1847-80.

Column B: Swierenga file based on unpublished Landverhuizers manuscripts.

Column C: North American emigrants in unpublished Landverhuizers manuscripts.

Column D: Percent of North American emigrants among all Dutch overseas emigrants (Column C as a percentage of Column B).

Column E: Number of Netherlanders admitted yearly to the United States, 1820-80, based on fiscal year ending June 30. Figures for 1820-67 represent alien passengers arrived; those for 1868-80 are immigrant aliens arrived. Lucas, *Netherlanders in America*, Appendix, Table I.

Column F: Dutch nationals listed in U.S. ship passenger lists, 1820-80, for all East Coast ports.

Column G: Bonafide Dutch immigrants listed in U.S. ship passenger lists, 1820-80 (see end note 20).

Column H: Dutch emigrant arrivals at the port of New York, 1847-69 (Kapp, *Immigration and the Commissioners of Emigration of the State of New York*).

Column I: Quebec City ship passenger lists, 1865-80, Microfilm Reel Nos. C-4520-C-4530, Public Archives of Canada, Ottawa.

Column J: Swierenga's estimate of "true" Dutch immigration to North America.

Comparing columns A and B, it is readily observed that the Netherlands lists are generally complete. They total only 5 percent fewer persons in the forty-five year period than the published figures. The two periods of incomplete manuscripts are in the years prior to compulsory reporting (1835–47) and after 1876 when the Central Bureau for Statistics (CBS) became the official reporting agency. CBS unfortunately discarded the municipal emigration lists after completing its annual compilations and publishing the results in official documents such as the *Staats-Courant*.

In the early period the names of some 2,780 emigrants (23 percent) are unavailable, and in the latter years 1876–80, 775 emigrants (19 percent) are unknown. (After 1880, the manuscript sources are less than 50 percent complete; hence, 1880 is the terminal date of this study). What is not apparent in either the official published or manuscript records, of course, is the extent of unreported or "clandestine" migration. Dutch scholars have long debated the magnitude of such migration and estimates range from 20 to 100 percent.[15] Only record linkage with U.S. files can answer this knotty problem.

Column C includes only North America–bound emigrants and provides the first published figures on this highly significant movement. Column D gives the annual percentages of Column C (North American emigrants) in relation to Column B (all overseas emigrants). The overall proportion of Dutch overseas emigrants who opted to settle in the United States was 89.6 percent.[16] In the mid-1840s and early 1850s, and again in the post–Civil War decade, the "America-centeredness" ranged as high as 98.9 percent. Only in two brief periods, 1858–64 and 1875–77, when emigration was at a low ebb due to adverse political and economic conditions in the United States, was the Dutch immigrant stream diverted to South America, Southeast Asia, and South Africa.

United States immigration data reported by the State Department and after 1867 by the Treasury Department are contained in column E. The year is the fiscal year ending June 30. Figures for 1820–67, inclusive, represent alien Dutch passengers arrived; those for 1868–80 include immigrant aliens arrived. Presumably, only a very few arrivals were rejected by U.S. immigration authorities. Despite the inclusion until 1867 of nonimmigrants, such as consular officials and businessmen, the U.S. figures seriously underreport Dutch immigration. Column E totals 8,500 fewer persons than Column C, based on the Dutch municipal records of emigrants destined for North America.

This difference cannot be explained by Dutch immigration to Canada, which before 1900 is conceded to have been very small—under 500, or by booking passage to Quebec or Halifax and crossing into the United States at inland ports such as Oswego, Niagara, or Detroit.[17] The Quebec ship passenger lists in the Public Records Office in Ottawa include only 1,828 Dutch nationals in the years 1865–80 (Table 11.1, Column I), which is less than 6 percent of those bound for North America during that period (Table 11.1, Column C).[18] Unfortunately, the total number of Dutch transits through Canada cannot be determined because Canadian ship manifests are incomplete before 1865. But the minimal levels of Dutch arrivals in the 1865–80 period, when Liverpool-Quebec passage was on the rise, suggests that

Canadian ports were not primary staging areas for Dutch immigrants to the United States. There was no appreciable difference between Quebec and New York fares, and transport inland was more difficult and costly than from New York. Also, inferior ships generally plied the Quebec route, which meant more sickness and accidents en route.[19]

The U.S. figures on Dutch immigration in columns F and G of Table 11.1, which were compiled by the author from the actual U.S. ship passenger manifests, conform closely in gross totals to the Dutch figures. Column F includes all Dutch aliens arriving at East Coast ports; Column G includes only immigrant aliens.[20] These figures, which are derived from disaggregate manuscript sources, total 7,000 more persons than the official U.S. published statistics in Column E. Moreover, an unknown number of passenger manifests are now lost or misplaced.

The "True" Dutch Immigration Flow

The comparison of gross migration totals reported by national governments cannot yield accurate statistics of American immigration. The federal customs records of individual immigrants must ultimately be collated with foreign emigration records to ascertain the actual migration flow. Nominal linkage of old handwritten records has proved to be extremely difficult, but several researchers have successfully linked large files of social data electronically, such as census manuscripts and city directories.[21] But none has connected large files of immigrant records on both sides of the Atlantic in which language differences cause spelling variations in names, and social customs differ, such as in reporting maiden names of widows in one country and married names in another. On the other hand, immigrant records permit "same year" linkage, which appreciably minimizes missed links.[22]

International record linkage has been accomplished for all Dutch immigrants to the United States in the period 1835–80 by collating the Dutch *Landverhuizers* and U.S. ship lists (see Chapter 12). The results are fruitful and provide a firm basis for correcting the official statistics of the two nations. The class 1 group—those reported in Dutch records but not U.S. records—totals 34,460 (Table 11.2). This figure must then be adjusted upward by 1,240 to account for the prorated share (35 percent) of the 3,550 persons in the missing Dutch records in the years 1835–47 and 1877–80 that would not likely have been linked to the ship lists. The class 1 total must also be adjusted downward by an estimated 30 percent (10,700): 10 percent for ship lists no longer extant and 20 percent for illegible ship manifests and errors in names and nationality designations in the manifests. Taking account of the upward and downward adjustments, the total for class 1 immigrants is 25,000.

Class 2—those immigrants listed in U.S. records but not Dutch records—totals 31,700. This figure must be adjusted downward to account for 450 alien arrivals who were not bona fide immigrants and a 20 percent error margin (6,250) due to illegible records and clerical errors. The adjusted total for class 2 is 25,000. Class 3—the truly linked pairs—totals 22,700 but this must be adjusted upward by 2,300, which is the estimated portion (65 percent) of the 3,550 missing Dutch records in

TABLE 11.2 Computation of Adjusted Dutch Immigration, 1835–80

CLASSES	UNADJUSTED TOTAL	UPWARD ADJUSTMENTS	DOWNWARD ADJUSTMENTS	ADJUSTED TOTAL
1	34,460	1,240	3,500	25,000
2	31,700	—	450 + 5,250	25,000
3	22,700	2,300	—	25,000
Lower bound estimate (class 1 + class 2 + class 3)				75,000
4 "Phantom fourth cell"				25,000
Upper bound estimate (all four classes)				100,000

SOURCE: Study data.

the years 1835–47 and 1877–80 that could have been linked if the records were extant. The adjusted total for class 3 is thus 25,000. The sum of the three adjusted totals, or cells, is 75,000.

Immigrants in the "phantom fourth cell" were, by definition, invisible to officials of both governments. But probability theory says that if the chance of omission from one list is independent from the chance of omission from the other list, then the total omission from both lists is the product of the probabilities of omission from each of the lists. The chance of persons registered in the *Landverhuizers* lists being omitted from the U.S. passenger lists is 0.499 [class (1) / class (1) + (3)], and the chance of persons recorded in the passenger lists being omitted from the Dutch lists is 0.501 [class (2) / class (2) + (3)]. The cross product of 0.499 and 0.501 is .025, which indicates that 25 percent of the migrants were not recorded by either government system.[23] Thus, the fourth cell of 25,000 must be added to the three-cell sum of 75,000, giving a total emigration of 100,000 in the period 1835 to 1880 (Table 11.2).

The lower bound total of 75,000 is 16,400 (28 percent) more than the official Netherlands government figure of 58,600 North America–bound emigrants (see Table 11.1, Column A: 65,104 minus 6,471 emigrants not bound for North America). After deducting the 1,828 Canadian arrivals, who would not be included in the U.S. port reports, the revised total is 23,700 (46 percent) more than the unofficial U.S. ship list totals (Table 11.1, Column G, 1835–80 total); it is 29,400 (65 percent) more than the official published U.S. statistics of Dutch immigration (Table 11.1, Column E, 1835–80 total).[24]

The upper bound estimate of 100,000 means Dutch officials undercounted by 41,400 (70 percent) and U.S. officials missed 54,400 (119 percent). These findings bring into question the old adage, noted above, that migration statistics of receiving countries are more reliable than those of sending countries. This certainly is not true of Dutch immigrants in the nineteenth century.

Is it possible that one quarter of the emigrants are missing in the Dutch and U.S. records? The assumption of independence between the two registration systems suggests that this was the case. After all, as Gemery and Schofield note, the two sets of records "were compiled by different authorities in different jurisdictions, and for different purposes."[25] While Dutch draft evaders, for example, might leave their villages clandestinely, ship captains put themselves under oath to account to customs officials for every person in steerage they delivered to U.S. ports.

But the computation of the fourth cell rests on soft assumptions in calculating the other three cells. At present, it is unknown how many passenger manifests (cell 1) were lost before the National Archives catalogued and microfilmed them in the 1930s. Whether I identified all of the potential matches (cell 3) is also problematic, since my linkage rate was only 36 percent. Hence, the lower bound figure of 75,000 may be closer to the mark than the upper bound figure of 100,000.

Interestingly, two Dutch scholars have estimated immigration to the United States through 1880 on the basis of aggregate U.S. census figures of Dutch born, adjusted for Netherlands death rates and remigration, but not for census undercounting. Stokvis set the number at 94,552, but the U.S. mortality rate was higher than the Netherlands rate because the immigrants suffered deaths at sea and succumbed to poverty and disease in city slums and hardships on the frontier.[26] Pella's 900 colonists had a loss rate of one in six; Holland had to establish an orphanage.[27] Oomens, a statistician at the Central Bureau of Statistics in The Hague, estimated Dutch emigration to the United States 1820–80 at 80,800 (see Table 11.3). He also used published U.S. census figures and calculated death rates according to Netherlands national mortality tables, but he used the actual age structure of the immigrants.[28]

Whether one accepts the lower or upper estimate, the magnitude of the unregistered Dutch migration over such an extended time period is startling and indicates that clandestine departures from the Netherlands were commonplace. American customs procedures (or perhaps reporting procedures) were also woefully inadequate. How one of every two Dutch arrivals were omitted in the official U.S. immigration statistics is a mystery that demands further study. Should such underreporting apply to other immigrant groups, the figures on total immigration in the nineteenth century would require drastic revision.[29]

When the "true" rate of Dutch immigration is compared year by year with official figures, it is apparent that the extent of underreporting varied widely over time (Table 11.4). The ratio of the true flow (Table 11.1, Column J) to the official

TABLE 11.3 Estimates of Dutch Immigration to the United States, by Decade, 1835–80

	Swierenga (1995)		Swierenga (1981)	Gemery (1989)	Stokvis (1985)	Oomens (1988)
Decade	Lower	Upper				
1835–49	16,849	19,846	18,904	27,000	13,060	18,500
1850–59	18,711	24,620	21,568	31,000	24,459	20,100
1860–69	17,444	26,152	20,829	30,000	29,272	19,400
1870–80	22,155	29,659	25,516	37,000	27,761	22,800
1835–80	75,159	100,278	86,817	125,000	94,552	80,800

SOURCES: Swierenga, "Dutch International Migration Statistics," Table 1, Col. J; Gemery and Schofield, "Mystery of the Fourth Cell," 1594–95; Stokvis, "Dutch International Migration," Table 2.7; Oomens, *Emigratie*, Table 9.

TABLE 11.4 Annual "True" Dutch Immigration to the U.S. as a Ratio of the Landverhuizers and Passenger List Totals, 1835–80

YEAR	"TRUE"RATE: LANDVERHUIZERS	"TRUE" RATE: U.S. SHIP LISTS	YEAR	"TRUE"RATE: LANDVERHUIZERS	"TRUE" RATE: U.S. SHIP LISTS
1835	817	107	1850–59	160	144
1836	1,000	105	1860	189	147
1837	1,100	96	1861	136	147
1838	—	96	1862	118	236
1839	554	114	1863	134	176
1840	5,350	97	1864	150	177
1841	2,060	100	1865	109	329°
1842	552	109	1866	117	214°
1843	411	120	1867	120	233°
1844	182	133	1868	118	292°
1845	193	196	1869	116	363°
1846	267	152	1860–69	171	245°
1847	243	158	1870	122	320°
1848	147	121	1871	133	256°
1849	157	131	1872	126	222°
1840–49	207	151	1873	146	134
1850	177	127	1874	164	120
1851	150	148	1875	205	120
1852	170	124	1876	334	101
1853	166	162	1877	299	108
1854	143	185	1878	370	132
1855	156	122	1879	210	133
1856	163	139	1880	192	135
1857	181	129	1870–80	160	155°
1858	144	156			
1859	214	132	1835–80	156	163°

° Including Quebec arrivals, the ratios are 1865, 273; 1866, 206; 1867, 191; 1868, 237; 1869, 262; 1860–69, 212; 1870, 278; 1871, 191; 1872, 219; 1873, 133; 1870–80, 150; 1835–80, 158.

SOURCE: Table 11.1, Columns C, G, and J.

Netherlands lists of U.S.-bound emigrants (Table 11.1, Column C) indicates that the most severe gaps occurred in the period immediately before the national reporting system was implemented in 1848, and again in the late 1870s when the system degenerated. The ship list data are most inadequate in the eight years from 1865 to 1872, when the actual flow, even taking into account Quebec arrivals, was two to three times higher than can be documented from extant passenger manifests. Apparently, a larger number of manifests have been lost or destroyed for these years.

Biases in International Migration Statistics

The fact that nearly twice as many Netherlanders migrated to the United States in the years from 1835 to 1880 than is indicated in official published U.S. statistics (or

Table 11.5 Comparison of Social Characteristics, Linked and Nonlinked Ship Passenger Lists, 1835–80

Social Characteristics	Nonlinked	Linked	Pearson's C
Single	40.6%	12.5%	.29*
Male	61.2	54.7	.06
Below mean age (24 Yrs.)	51.9	58.6	.07
White collar	11.8	3.6	.17
Farmer/farm laborer	39.0	54.3	.17
Dutch embarking port	96.4	98.4	.06
New York disembarking port	87.0	93.2	.10
Cabin accommodations	12.1	7.3	.08

* Statistically significant at .01 level
Source: U.S. ship lists study data.

one third more, if Dutch statistics are used) raises the question of bias in immigration statistics in general. If precise information on the "missing" migrants were known, would the picture of transatlantic migration, based on currently available records, be significantly changed? The answer is "probably yes," especially for northern European emigration, which is usually viewed as a family migration, in contrast to the more individual migration of southern Europeans.

Cross tabulations of the social variables in the linked and nonlinked ship passenger lists indicate that the nonlinked records (i.e., class 2 above) included nearly four times more single individuals. In the nonlinked file 40 percent were single, compared to only 12 percent in the linked file (class 1). It is moot whether this deficiency is the result of contemporary administrative problems or modern-day linkage problems. Probably both factors are contributory. The nonlinked file also included slightly more males (by 7 percentage points), more white-collar occupations (by 8 points), and more passengers traveling in cabin accommodations (by 5 points), but none of these differences is statistically significant (Table 11.5). Analysis of the numerous singles who escaped the attention of Dutch municipal officials, or who could not be linked, shows that 80 percent were males and 75 percent were in the 16–36 age group. White-collar workers and professionals comprised 17 percent of the group, compared to 13 percent of all nonlinked adult immigrants. Thirty percent worked in agriculture, 47 percent in blue-collar jobs, and only 5 percent gave no occupation or were unemployed. The unregistered singles thus were composed primarily of young working-class males who may have migrated clandestinely to avoid compulsory military service and secondarily of professional people who traveled to the United States for business or pleasure and were not bona fide immigrants.

Apart from the large number of singles, the linked and nonlinked passenger records do not differ significantly in any other variables: sex, age of adults, occupation, port of embarkation and arrival, and passage accommodations. The yearly proportion of linked to nonlinked records also remained stable, except in the 1870s when the number of clandestine emigrants increased markedly. The proportions for the three major emigration periods are: 1849–57, 77 percent; 1858–68, 76 percent; and 1869–80, 64 percent.

TABLE 11.6 Comparison of Social Characteristics, Linked and Nonlinked Dutch Landverhuizers, 1835–80

SOCIAL CHARACTERISTICS	NONLINKED	LINKED	PEARSON'S C
Single	52.9%	36.1	.16
Females	15.0	9.3	.08
Below mean age (35 Yrs.)	58.5	53.5	.05
White collar	9.6	6.3	.05
Farmer/farm laborer	22.2	23.0	.05
Protestant	76.9	84.8	.09
"Well-to-do"	14.1	9.7	.07
Assessed for taxes	21.8	30.6	.09

SOURCE: Dutch Landverhuizers lists study data.

One possible explanation for the higher incidence of unregistered emigrants in the 1870s is that the nature of Dutch emigration changed from the largely family hegira of the pre–Civil War era to a more individualistic migration. This created problems for the efficient Dutch system of recording and reporting emigrants. Families could seldom depart for North America without the fact eventually coming to the attention of local officials, but singles could easily leave virtually unnoticed. The net of a voluntary registration system thus caught the families, but only mandatory passport regulations could snare the singles. A secondary explanation is that internal urban migration began on a large scale in the 1870s. Local officials may have confused the two types of movers and reported as urban migrants people who had actually removed overseas.

For students of American immigration the major question is the reliability and completeness of the passenger manifests rather than the inadequacies of European registration systems. Those 6,600 America-bound households (32,100 persons) in the Dutch municipal records (class 1 above) who cannot be located in the extant ship lists are the persons of concern. Were they significantly different in ecological characteristics from the linked emigrants? The answer appears to be negative, although there were several noticeable differences. Fifteen percent of the nonlinked household heads or single adults were females, in contrast to only 9.3 percent among linked households (Table 11.6). The percentage of nonlinked household heads and singles below the median age of 35 years was 58.5 compared to 53.5 for the linked. Religiously, nonlinked households were 76.9 percent Protestant, compared to 84.8 percent for the linked. None of these differences is statistically significant. In social class and occupation there was virtually no distinction. Thus, the comparative analysis shows that although the official statistics underreport Dutch emigration by at least one half, nevertheless, the surviving serial records provide relatively unbiased sources for the structural analysis of transatlantic migration. The notable exception is the omission of three out of four single immigrants.

Given these findings for Dutch immigration statistics, the inference is strong that official statistics underreport the migration flow of other European peoples in the mid-nineteenth century. The smaller and less distinctive the nationality group, the greater is the likelihood of such oversight. Belgians, Swiss, Danes, and Scots, in addition to the Dutch, were all likely candidates for official oversight and misrepresentation. It is also the case that the more dense and urbanized the population of the emigrant communities, the more likely that underreporting occurred. Only by ferreting out individual-level records and linking European and American sources can the actual extent of clandestine migration and official error be determined.

Conclusion

Although all European governments instituted a registration system for overseas emigrants, their official records in the nineteenth century underreport the full extent of such emigration because governments were unable, or made no attempt, to secure their borders against their own citizens. The task of immigration scholars, therefore, is to identify the clandestine or unrecorded emigrants and to measure the bias in official figures as a result of the omissions.

Dutch government records of annual emigration to the United States in the years from 1820 to 1880 are more accurate than the series of the U.S. Departments of State and Treasury. But neither governments' official figures are reliable. U.S.-published statistics of Dutch immigration underreport the actual number by 90 percent and official Dutch records fall short by 48 percent. Moreover, these deficiencies are not readily apparent in available sources. Dutch-published statistics before 1876 do not specify the number of North America–bound emigrants. Even a comparison with U.S. figures of the unpublished Dutch record series is misleading, because the Dutch and U.S. unadjusted totals in the period 1820-80 differ by only 4 percent and the annual figures roughly correspond. Hence, the technique of nominal record linkage is the sole means of accurately determining the actual migration rate.

This methodology is widely applicable for immigration to the United States after 1820 (and to Canada after 1865) from any European nation for which individual-level nominal records exist on external population movements. Such countries include Belgium, the Scandinavian nations, Germany, France, Switzerland, and Italy. Immigration from England, Scotland, Ireland, and Wales unfortunately cannot be measured in this way because no nominal emigration records exist. Even if such material were available, record linkage with U.S. passenger manifests would be unreliable, because it is estimated that upward of one half of all immigrants from the British Isles came to the United States through Canada in the period before 1865.[30]

If we must acknowledge that European immigration to the United States before 1880 was substantially greater than the official figures have led us to believe, what are some possible implications for scholars? The first issue is whether certain immigrant populations were more "at risk" of underreporting; i.e., omissions were randomly distributed. It would now appear that the more urban and densely populated the sending community, the less familial the out-migrant population, and the fewer the police restrictions on foreign emigration; hence, the greater the risk of being "invisible" to government officials. Second, immigrant scholars who make use of serial records for social or economic research must be alert to the possible bias caused by the underreporting or clandestine movement of single immigrants. This is a social structure problem that surpasses the issue of the relative size of the various immigrant groups. Until more statistical studies are completed of nominally linked and unlinked record files, one can take refuge in the results presented here: apart from the singles, social structural biases are minimal in the available disaggregate nominal records, such as the passenger manifests. Students of international migration have yet to exploit fully the massive, individual-level record files of external migrants that are available in European and North American archives.

Notes

James W. Savery of the Kent State University Computer Services department provided extensive computer programming assistance, and Ira A. Glazier, Yda Schreuder, and Pieter R. D. Stokvis read the chapter and offered expert advice.

1. Henry A. Gemery, "Disarray in the Historical Record: Estimates of Immigration to the United States, 1700–1860," *Proceedings of the American Philosophical Society* 133 (June 1989): 123–27; Farley Grubb, "The Reliability of U.S. Immigration Statistics: The Case of Philadelphia, 1815–1830," *International Journal of Maritime History* 2 (June 1990): 29–54.
2. Brinley Thomas, *Migration and Economic Growth*, 2d ed. (Cambridge: Cambridge University Press, 1973), 35.
3. W. F. Willcox, ed., and I. Ferenczi, comp., *International Migrations, Volume 1, Statistics* (New York: National Bureau of Economic Research, 1929), 81; Edward P. Hutchinson, "Notes on Immigration Statistics of the United States," *Journal of the American Statistical Association* 53 (Dec. 1958): 970–71.
4. Hutchinson, "Notes on Immigration Statistics," 968–96.
5. W. F. Willcox, ed. *International Migrations, Volume 2, Interpretations* (New York: National Bureau of Economic Statistics, 1931), 645–57.
6. Hutchinson, "Notes on Immigration Statistics," 977–81, gives the following reasons for underreporting of immigrant arrivals in the years before 1876: (1) careless collection of ship manifests by port officials; (2) failure of customs collectors to forward Passenger Abstracts quarterly to the Department of State; (3) failure of State Department clerks to include all Passenger Abstracts in their annual published statistical reports; (4) ship arrivals during early days of sailing vessels and shallower drafts at lesser coastal towns without customs houses; (5) smuggling or surreptitious entry of aliens to avoid ports such as New York, Philadelphia, Baltimore, and New Orleans, where the states levied a head tax on immigrants or required ship owners to post bond to indemnify local authorities in the event that immigrants became public charges (the Supreme Court struck down this law as

unconstitutional in 1876); (6) immigrant aliens traveling in cabin class were not consistently counted as immigrants; and (7) arrival via Canadian ports. Only the latter reason had a demonstrable impact on the statistics.

7. Ibid., 980–81, 985–89.
8. Between 1847 and 1869, for example, New York City officials reported the arrival of 28,347 Dutch nationals; federal authorities in the same years reported 24,248 (or 4,000 fewer) Dutch nationals arrived at New York, Baltimore, Philadelphia, New Orleans, Boston, and other lesser ports. For the annual statistics and sources, see Freidrich Kapp, *Immigration and the Commissioners of Emigration of the State of New York* [1880] (reprint, New York: Arno Press, 1969), Table 1.
9. J. D. Gould, "European Inter-Continental Emigration 1815–1914: Patterns and Causes," *Journal of European Economic History* 8 (1979): 596 (quote), 598; Willcox, *International Migrations, Volume 1*, 230–33.
10. Gould, "European Inter-Continental Emigration," 597–98.
11. Willcox, *International Migrations, Volume 1*, 194, 79, 82; Gould, "European Inter-Continental Emigration," 602.
12. Gould, "European Inter-Continental Emigration," 602–04.
13. The Swedish scholar I. Erickson measured underreporting of emigrants from two southern Swedish parishes in 1874, but concluded that a multiyear time frame is necessary and all ship passenger lists must be included ("Passenger Lists and the Annual Parish Reports on Emigrants as Sources for the Study of Emigration from Sweden," in Sune Åkerman, ed. *Nordic Emigration Research Conference in Uppsala, September 1969* [Uppsala: Soderstrom & Finn, 1970], 3–4).
14. Henry A. Gemery and Roger Schofield pointed out the problem of the "fourth cell," i.e., those immigrants not recorded in either listing, in "The Mystery of the Fourth Cell: Linked Multi-National Files as a Measure of Under-Reporting in International Studies," *International Migration Review* 21 (Winter 1988): 123–27.
15. Robert P. Swierenga and Harry S. Stout, "Socio-Economic Patterns of Migration from the Netherlands in the Nineteenth Century," in Paul Uselding, ed., *Research in Economic History*, vol. 1 (Greenwich, Conn.: JAI Press, 1976), 10, 30.
16. This figure is lower by approximately 2 percent due to occasional misreporting by Dutch municipal officials of missionaries, soldiers, and government bureaucrats bound for Dutch overseas colonies in Indonesia, Surinam, or elsewhere, as overseas emigrants rather than colonials. In the 1850s Dutch government statisticians complained of these erroneous classifications of overseas emigrants by local officials. See *Staatkundig en Staathuishoudkundig Jaarboekje over 1854*, 272; ibid., 1856, 212; ibid., 1857, 203; ibid., 1862, 7. In the period 1835–80, 400 overseas colonials, or 1.9 percent of all emigrants, were misclassified in the official reports as emigrants. Most colonials were from the Catholic or urban provinces of Limburg, Noord-Brabant, Noord-Holland, and Utrecht.

17. Henry S. Lucas, *Netherlanders in America: Dutch Immigration to the United States and Canada, 1789–1950* (Ann Arbor: University of Michigan Press, 1955; reprint, Grand Rapids: Wm. B. Eerdmans, 1989), 459–60; Herman Ganzevoort, *A Bittersweet Land: The Dutch Experience in Canada, 1890–1980* (Toronto: McClelland and Stewart, 1988), 2; Willcox, *International Migrations, Volume 2*, 652.
18. That some Dutch emigrants to the United States entered through Canada is attested also by the Noord-Holland Landverhuizers list of 1856 which reports that 18 families (48 persons) from Amsterdam departed for the Dutch settlement of Holland, Michigan, "via Quebec." There are no official statistics prior to 1900 of arrivals of Dutch nationals at the Canadian ports of Quebec and Montreal. Immigrant arrivals at Canadian ports who were destined for the United States are not distinguished from those intending to settle in Canada. Willcox (*International Migrations, Volume* 2, 357, 363) estimated that in the years 1866–91 one half to three quarters of all ship passengers passed directly into the United States, but this is certainly an underestimate according to Ganzevoort, who found Canadian censuses reliable before 1900 (*Bittersweet Land*, 2). In order to generate the first hard data on Dutch nationals arriving in Canada in the nineteenth century, I searched for Dutch nationals in the Public Archives of Canada files of the Quebec ship passenger lists for the Montreal Ocean Steam-Ship Company, which are generally complete from 1865. The Dutch nationals were found in the column labeled "Aliens" or "Foreigners," and were identified initially by surnames and then confirmed by linking the individuals with the Dutch Landverhuizers records.
19. This information was provided by a letter dated 12 March 1979 from the British scholar Robin Bastin, a noted authority on Atlantic passenger traffic. The Noord-Holland Landverhuizers list of 1856 also describes the major travel route to North America in these words: "With the Hull steamboat from Amsterdam or Rotterdam to Hull, with the railroad to Liverpool, and by great ocean steamer to New York."
20. Nonimmigrant aliens are identified in these ways: (1) the country in which they intend to become inhabitants is other than the United States; (2) the country of last residence is other than the Netherlands, Germany, or England; (3) their occupation is that of consular official, traveler, tourist, etc.
21. Theodore Hershberg, A. Burstein, and R. Dockhorn, "Record Linkage," *Historical Methods Newsletter* 9 (May/June 1976): 137–63; Myron P. Gutmann, "The Future of Record Linkage in History," *Journal of Family History* 2 (Summer 1977): 151–58.
22. Because the migration journey sometimes occurred during the New Year period, linkage searches must be made within at least a two-year time bracket.
23. The estimates given here are less than the 124,900 total that Gemery and Schofield reported in "Mystery of the Fourth Cell," 1595, which was

calculated from my original three-cell sum of 86,900 (Swierenga, "Dutch International Migration Statistics, 1820–1880: An Analysis of Linked Multinational Nominal Files," *International Migration Review* 15 [Fall 1981]: 461, Table 4). I have since adjusted cell 1 downward by 30 percent (instead of 15 percent) and cell 2 downward by 20 percent (instead of 5 percent), in order to account for a greater number of illegible names and missing passenger manifests than I initially estimated.

24. The totals in Table 11.1, Column G, which are based on the ship manifests, exclude the 507 persons who died en route, but include infants born on the voyage. Whether the official published U.S. statistics of immigration also reflect births and deaths during the voyage is problematic (Hutchinson, "Notes on Immigration Statistics," 970–71); it is assumed in Table 11.1, Column E, that actual arrivals are included, that is, deaths are not reported but newborn infants are added.
25. Gemery and Schofield, "Mystery of the Fourth Cell," 1595.
26. Pieter R. D. Stokvis, "Dutch International Migration 1850–1910," in Robert P. Swierenga, ed. *The Dutch in America: Immigration, Settlement, and Cultural Change* (New Brunswick, NJ: Rutgers University Press, 1985), Table 2.7.
27. Lucas, *Netherlanders in America*, 103; J. Stellingwerff, *Amsterdamse emigranten. onbekende brieven uit de prairie van Iowa, 1846–1873* (Amsterdam: Buijten & Schipperheijn, 1975), 80.
28. C. A. Oomens, *Emigratie in de negentiende eeuw* (The Hague: Central Bureau for Statistics, 1989), 8–9, Table 9, 46.
29. In his study of Philadelphia passenger lists, 1815–30, Grubb found that the federal records undercounted arriving passengers at Philadelphia by 50 percent. He concluded: "If the local customs records for the other ports were incomplete by the same magnitude as those for Philadelphia, then a purely speculative estimate of total U.S. passengers arriving between 1820 and 1831 would be 216,042 higher than reported by Federal statistics, or a 122.5% increase," "Reliability of U.S. Immigration Statistics," 41.
30. Hutchinson, "Notes on Immigration Statistics," 975.

CHAPTER 12

Sources and Methods

THREE CATEGORIES OF records are vital to an understanding of the structure and process of international migration in the nineteenth century. One must know the Old Country context of the immigrants, the details of their transoceanic crossing, and the settlement in the New Country. The data sources that best provide such information for Dutch immigrants are the official Netherlands emigration lists (*Landverhuizerslijsten*), the United States and Canadian customs ship passenger lists, and the federal manuscript population censuses. The linkage of these sources for each emigrant household or single individual provides pertinent information on all phases of the life cycle before, during, and after migration. This procedure is not without problems, given deficiencies in the records themselves and in the linkage procedure. Nevertheless, these sources provide a rich font of information about the anonymous common folk who comprised the vast majority of Dutch immigrants.

Netherlands Emigration Records

The European governments first began recording biographical information on emigrants in the 1830s and 1840s when the migration of peoples to the New World began in earnest. Their concern was to monitor the population outflow in order to assess the possible harmful consequences on the home society, and, if necessary, to enact restrictive legislation. For many decades the bureaucracies were inefficient and their statistics meager and haphazard. As Brinley Thomas noted: "The era of free international migration was nearly over before the countries concerned began to give serious attention to their statistical records.... It was not until migration itself became the object of national planning that this branch of statistics was developed for its own sake." Philip Taylor observed correctly that the closer "we approach districts and individuals, the nearer our study will be to the truth."[1]

Fortunately, the Netherlands records are available at the individual level. Beginning in 1848, municipal officials were required to register all overseas emigrants, although some compiled lists retroactively to 1831. By order of the Minister for Home Affairs of 21 December 1847, the municipal governments were required each year to send to the provincial governors for forwarding to the ministry in The Hague a "List of Emigrants to North America and Other Overseas Places" (*Staat der landverhuizers naar Noord-Amerika of andere overzeesche gewesten*).[2] If there were no emigrants the previous year, officials also had to report that fact, which they faithfully did, although some persons were missed because of the complexities of the system.[3]

The original *landverhuizers* lists for the period 1848–77 are preserved in the National Archives (Algemeen Rijksarchief) in The Hague, and microfilm copies are available at the Calvin College Archives. After 1877 the Central Bureau for Statistics (CBS) systematically destroyed the lists after compiling and publishing summary statistics in *Bijdragen tot de Algemeen Statistiek van Nederland* (Compilation of the General Statistics of the Netherlands). Some lists after 1877 have been found in provincial and municipal archives, while others have been reconstituted from population registers and census records.[4] Altogether, the extant emigration records for the years 1831–80 include 21,810 families and single persons, for a total of 62,000 persons.[5]

The emigration lists (see facsimile in Figure 12.1) contain much vital information, including for each household head or single adult the name, age, occupation, religious denomination, socioeconomic standing, municipal tax assessment class, family size and status, presumed or stated reason for emigrating, and (if known) intended destination.

A "remarks" column occasionally contains further details about the financial resources or social reputation and character of the departing person. Officials here noted family relationships (sister of so-and-so, servant of so-and-so, "widower, no children," "a bachelor," etc.), whether an emigrant carried a large sum of money ("took 7000 fl. with him"), had an ill-fated voyage ("dead at sea"), or was a remigrant ("went to N. America in 1856, returned in 1857, somewhat discouraged").

Most interesting are the many snide comments by Dutch officials concerning the character, behavior, or reputation of emigrants. In Utrecht Province, municipal officials were especially scurrilous. Concerning one man, with a wife and eight children, who was a Seceder from the state church, the official noted: "Enabled to leave thru donations. Was a dangerous man." Of another Seceder, he wrote: "A follower of H. P. Scholte [a Seceder cleric]. Otherwise well-behaved." Others, it was noted, "left many debts," "had debts due to irregular interest in work," "sometimes led a questionable life," or "was married but moved away without family." The official noted that one emigrant who had left a wife and four children, had "promised three times already to send money for their passage. Has not done it." A few emigrants received encomiums: "a well-behaved person," "left no unpaid debts. Had good reputation," or "had reputation for sound judgment." Thus did local functionaries have the last word in the official emigration records on those who chose to depart the fatherland.

The emigration records are deficient in several respects for both historical and generic reasons. First, the Dutch government myopically required local officials to

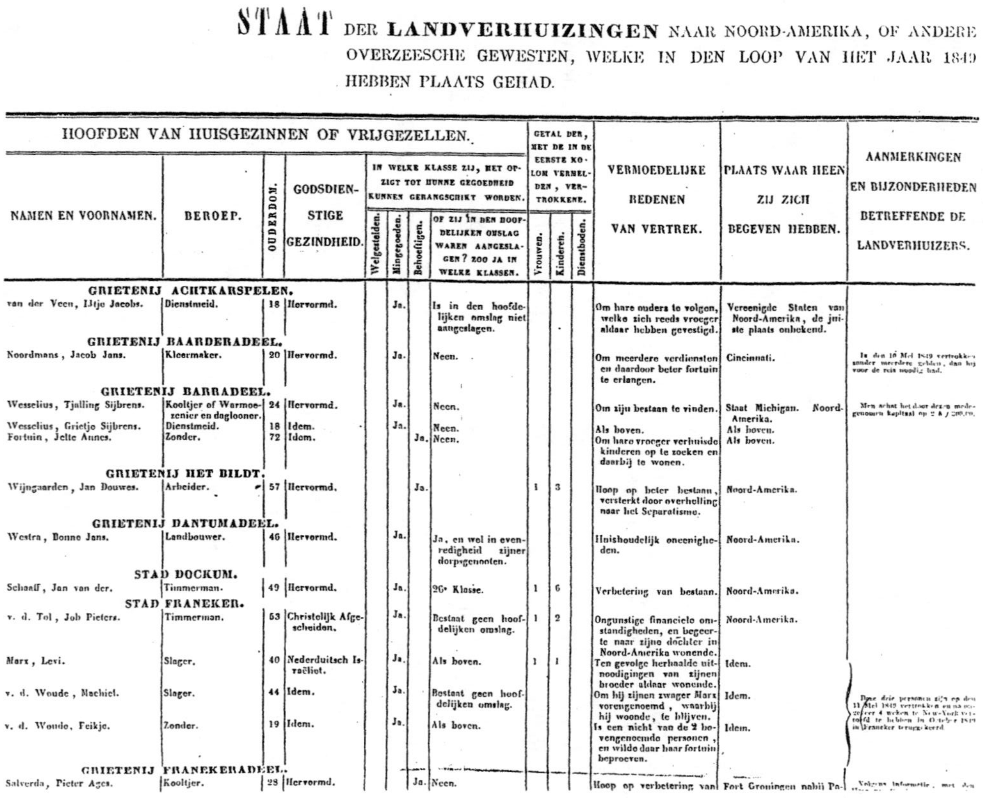

STAAT DER **LANDVERHUIZINGEN** NAAR NOORD-AMERIKA, OF ANDERE OVERZEESCHE GEWESTEN, WELKE IN DEN LOOP VAN HET JAAR 1849 HEBBEN PLAATS GEHAD.

HOOFDEN VAN HUISGEZINNEN OF VRIJGEZELLEN.								GETAL DER, MET DE IN DE EERSTE KOLOM VERMELDEN, VERTROKKENE.			VERMOEDELIJKE REDENEN VAN VERTREK.	PLAATS WAAR HEEN ZIJ ZICH BEGEVEN HEBBEN.	AANMERKINGEN EN BIJZONDERHEDEN BETREFFENDE DE LANDVERHUIZERS.
NAMEN EN VOORNAMEN.	BEROEP.	OUDERDOM.	GODSDIENSTIGE GEZINDHEID.	IN WELKE KLASSE ZIJ, HET OPZIGT TOT HUNNE GEGOEDHEID KUNNEN GERANGSCHIKT WORDEN. Welgestelden.	Mingegoeden.	Behoeftigen.	OF ZIJ IN DEN HOOFDELIJKEN OMSLAG WAREN AANGESLAGEN? ZOO JA IN WELKE KLASSEN.	Vrouwen.	Kinderen.	Dienstboden.			
GRIETENIJ ACHTKARSPELEN.													
van der Veen, IJtje Jacobs.	Dienstmeid.	18	Hervormd.		Ja.		Is in den hoofdelijken omslag niet aangeslagen.				Om hare ouders te volgen, welke zich reeds vroeger aldaar hebben gevestigd.	Vereenigde Staten van Noord-Amerika, de juiste plaats onbekend.	
GRIETENIJ BAARDERADEEL.													
Noordmans, Jacob Jans.	Kleermaker.	20	Hervormd.		Ja.		Neen.				Om meerdere verdiensten en daardoor beter fortuin te erlangen.	Cincinnati.	In den 16 Mei 1849 vertrokken zonder meerdere gelden, dan hij voor de reis noodig had.
GRIETENIJ BARRADEEL.													
Wesselius, Tjalling Sijbrens.	Kooltjer of Warmoezenier en daglooner.	24	Hervormd.		Ja.		Neen.				Om zijn bestaan te vinden.	Staat Michigan. Noord-Amerika.	Men schat het door dezen medegenomen kapitaal op [illegible]
Wesselius, Grietje Sijbrens.	Dienstmeid.	18	Idem.		Ja.		Neen.				Als boven.	Als boven.	
Fortuin, Jelte Annes.	Zonder.	72	Idem.			Ja.	Neen.				Om hare vroeger verhuisde kinderen op te zoeken en daarbij te wonen.	Als boven.	
GRIETENIJ HET BILDT.													
Wijngaarden, Jan Douwes.	Arbeider.	57	Hervormd.			Ja.		1	3		Hoop op beter bestaan, versterkt door overhelling naar het Separatisme.	Noord-Amerika.	
GRIETENIJ DANTUMADEEL.													
Westra, Bonne Jans.	Landbouwer.	46	Hervormd.		Ja.		Ja, en wel in evenredigheid zijner dorpsgenooten.				Huishoudelijk oneenigheden.	Noord-Amerika.	
STAD DOCKUM.													
Schaaff, Jan van der.	Timmerman.	49	Hervormd.		Ja.		26ᵉ Klasse.	1	6		Verbetering van bestaan.	Noord-Amerika.	
STAD FRANEKER.													
v. d. Tol, Job Pieters.	Timmerman.	53	Christelijk Afgescheiden.		Ja.		Bestaat geen hoofdelijken omslag.	1	2		Ongunstige financiele omstandigheden, en begeerte naar zijne dochter in Noord-Amerika wonende.	Noord-Amerika.	
Marx, Levi.	Slager.	40	Nederduitsch Israëliet.		Ja.		Als boven.	1	1		Ten gevolge herhaalde uitnoodigingen van zijnen broeder aldaar wonende.	Idem.	Deze drie personen zijn op den 11 Mei 1849 vertrokken en na ongeveer 4 weken te New-York vertoefd te hebben in October 1849 in Franeker teruggekeerd.
v. d. Woude, Machiel.	Slager.	44	Idem.		Ja.		Bestaat geen hoofdelijken omslag.				Om bij zijnen zwager Marx vorengenoemd, waarbij hij woonde, te blijven.	Idem.	
v. d. Woude, Feikje.	Zonder.	19	Idem.		Ja.		Als boven.				Is een nicht van de 2 bovengenoemde personen, en wilde daar haar fortuin beproeven.	Idem.	
GRIETENIJ FRANEKERADEEL.													
Salverda, Pieter Ages.	Kooltjer.	28	Hervormd.			Ja.	Neen.				Hoop op verbetering van	Fort Groningen nabij Pa-	Volgens informatie, met den

Figure 12.1 Annual Emigration List, Province of Friesland, 1849

SOURCE: Friesland *Verslagen*, 1849.

record only the names of heads of households when entire families emigrated. Moreover, only initials of given names were sometimes inscribed. In order to determine family structure and demographic details, modern scholars must link the emigration records with other local record sources. This becomes problematic in the numerous cases of common patronymics, such as Vanden Burg and De Jong, when one person cannot be positively distinguished from another of the same name and perhaps initials.

More importantly, the emigration lists are incomplete. Lists are lost or destroyed containing the names of 3,555 persons, or 5.7 percent of the registered emigrants through 1880. About three quarters of the missing lists are for the earlier years 1831–48 before the systematic registration system was created, and one quarter are for the years 1877–80, after the government changed the system.[6] The quality of the surviving 95 percent of the records also varies over time and from place to place. Irresponsible local officials in a few instances failed to submit reports to the provincial governors, as the law of 1847 required. Others included persons who were clearly not emigrants, in the technical sense of the word, such as missionaries, soldiers, and government bureaucrats bound for the Dutch overseas colonies in Indonesia, Surinam, or elsewhere. In the years 1835–80, 400 persons (2 percent of all emigrants) were so misreported; they mainly hailed from the Catholic and urban provinces.

Although the 1847 law required reports only on *overseas* emigrants, i.e., other continents, some officials included persons who departed for other European countries, including England, which was, after all, across the North Sea. By the same token, many Dutch nationals went to England and after some months and even years emigrated to the United States. Invariably, these persons are omitted from the official Netherlands emigration records. As is explained in Chapter 11, more bona fide emigrants were omitted due to oversight or error than were improperly included in the *landverhuizers* lists.

A much greater problem with the emigration lists is the failure of many families or individuals emigrating overseas to notify municipal officials, as they were legally required to do. In comparing the names of persons on the Netherlands emigration lists with Dutch nationals recorded in the United States and Canadian customs passenger lists of all east coast ports, including Halifax, it has been found that as many as 44,000 more Dutch immigrants landed in North America between 1835 and 1880 than the 56,000 persons that Netherlands officials had recorded as emigrating to North America (see Chapter 11).

Of the unreported or "clandestine" emigrants, 60 percent departed in family units and 40 percent as singles. Conversely, among the registered emigrants, families comprised 80 percent and singles only 20 percent. Thus, single persons, especially young males, had the greatest propensity to emigrate "illegally."[7] Some were doubtless businessmen and professional persons who traveled to the States on business or for pleasure and then decided to remain. A larger group were young men who left to avoid onerous and compulsory military service. For example, in the province of Zuid-Holland, from 1851 through 1877, 815 young men failed to appear for military induction after being selected in the annual lottery (Table 12.1).

TABLE 12.1 National Militia Reports, Zuid-Holland, 1851–77

YEAR	TOTAL INDUCTED	TOTAL NONREPORTING	IN AMERICA		DESERTED MARINE		UNKNOWN	
1851	135	33	2		—		6	
1852	230	24	3		—		3	
1853	178	44	3		4		5	
1854	723	60	18		3		3	
1855	285	58	10		7		7	
1856	347	56	6		10		10	
1857	121	52	4		6		14	
1858	84	60	18		7		11	
1859		48	17		2		5	
1860	na	57	23		1		8	
1861*								
1862	na	64	na		na		na	
1863	na	76	na		na		na	
1864*								
1865	298	38	9		—		6	
1866	760	42	11		—		3	
1867	313	34	13		—		5	
1868	283	25	3		2		2	
1869	265	25	9		—		2	
1870	160	22	8		—		1	
1871	263	22	4		2		5	
1872	374	19	8		—		2	
1873	354	21	7		1		1	
1874	45	18	4		—		4	
1875	97	20	3		—		4	
1876	36	18	5		—		1	
1877	23	19	7		—		2	
TOTALS	5,421	815	195	24%	43	5%	111	14%

* No report

SOURCE: Compiled from Zuid-Holland Provincial *Verslagen* (Annual Provincial Reports), 1852–78.

The stated reason for 195 (24 percent) was: "naar Amerika vertrokken" (departed to America). Another 43 men (5 percent) were seamen who had either deserted or were left behind in America. Yet another 111 (14 percent) simply were reported as "missing," and one can assume that many of them had also gone to America. Thus, nearly one half (43 percent) of the men who refused to serve had become overseas emigrants. All these "draft dodgers," however, comprised only 6 percent of the total annual group of inductees; 94 percent dutifully reported for service.

Most of the unregistered emigrants, however, simply slipped through the cracks in a cumbersome administrative system. Local government clerks inscribed the annual emigration lists from information contained in the population registers (*Bevolkingsregisters*) of each municipality. These registers were established by Royal decree of 14 November 1849, on the basis of the 1849 population census

(*Volkstelling*), although in many towns officials began the system five or more years earlier based on previous censuses. The population registers included pertinent vital information of interest to the state and public on all family members by household (name, sex, relation to head of family, date of birth, birthplace, status, religious affiliation, and occupation, plus the crucial geographical facts of last place of residence and date of in-migration, and the date and destination of those departing. The population registers thus form a continuous record in the municipality, identical to the Belgian system and similar to the Scandinavian parish books.[8] The population registers locate the emigrants in their precise neighborhoods within the municipalities. This information is useful for determining local factors in the decision to emigrate.

The Dutch government in 1861 (*Staatsblad* no. 94) sought to tighten the system by instituting local registers of in- and out- migration (*Registers van Vestiging en Vertrek*).[9] When persons moved from one place to another, they had to obtain a "migration certificate" from local authorities to present to officials at the new residence. The certificate included the full name of the family head or single individual, the number in the household by sex, and the intended place of settlement. A duplicate of the certificate provided the source of information for the registers of out- and in-migration. Only law-abiding persons and men who had fulfilled their military obligations could obtain these certificates, which made it all the more likely that draft evaders and petty criminals would emigrate overseas without registering.

The registers of in- and out-migration prepared from these certificates, if diligently copied into the population registers, provided a reliable source for local officials to consult, when in early January they compiled the lists of all the previous year's overseas emigrants for forwarding to the provincial and national governments. If inhabitants departed without giving notice and local officials later learned of the fact, they were to strike the names off the population register and include them in the register of out-migration. The officials were also to include such names in the next annual migration report.

Despite these intricate procedures, then, some emigrants were overlooked by record keepers because the system had a major flaw; it was entirely voluntary. No exit visas or passports were required to buy overseas tickets until the twentieth century, and no police checkpoints were in place at the nation's borders and seaports. Thus, citizens could depart overseas without emigration certificates. The completeness of the migration reports, therefore, was inversely related to the size and type of municipality. In small towns and rural communities, with their intricate communication networks, few inhabitants could migrate overseas without the fact sooner or later becoming public knowledge. However, in the large cities where social relations were more impersonal, individuals and even families might leave the country without the fact ever coming to the attention of city officials. This fact may account, in part, for the much lower emigration statistics from cities than from rural areas, although social structural factors, as we will note later, suggest an overwhelmingly rural exodus. In addition, those who emigrated in stages—from rural homes to larger cities and then abroad—may especially have been overlooked, if the move to the city was intended to be temporary. Single young men were more likely than any other group to emigrate in this way.

Moreover, local officials lacked the financial incentive to maintain the register of outmigration as carefully as they did the register of in-migration. Since they were obligated by law to collect taxes and dispense welfare and poor relief, they would understandably have a greater need to maintain careful records of local residents than of departed citizens. By the same token, since Dutch poor laws required that a welfare applicant not born in a community must present a migration certificate to prove legal residency, the registers of in-migration would be more complete. Conversely, draft evaders and criminals would likely move without migration certificates, because these were issued only to men who had fulfilled their military obligation and had not broken the law.[10]

In sum, the constraints of the registration system and the accidents of history have conspired to weaken a most valuable source of information for migration research. Yet, as we will describe below, the Netherlands emigrant records are more complete and trustworthy than the U.S. customs passenger lists or any other source. The emigrant lists are the only records that report last place of residence in the Netherlands and thus they are indispensable for linking place of origin with place of settlement in the United States.

U.S. Ship Customs Passenger Lists

The ship passenger manifests of vessels arriving at East Coast and Gulf ports (Baltimore, Boston, New Orleans, New York, and Philadelphia) form the basis for the official U.S. immigration statistics beginning in 1820.[11] They also supply additional valuable information on those who immigrated to the United States. These manifests had their origin in an act of Congress of 2 March 1819, *Regulating Passenger-ships and vessels*,[12] which reflected the humanitarian desire to improve shipboard conditions in the great wave of emigration following the close of the Napoleonic wars. This act was an unexpected boon to students of immigration, because it provided for the first time a regular supply of statistics on the subject. The fourth section of the law specified that beginning on 1 January 1820 ship captains upon arrival from any foreign port must deliver to the Collector of Customs a sworn manifest containing the names of all passengers who had embarked at a foreign port.

The passenger manifests consisted of printed forms that were revised periodically to meet changes in the laws (Figure 12.2). At the head of the register are data on the ship itself: name of the vessel, its place of registry, tonnage burthen and captain's name, and the port of arrival. The port of embarkation is listed on the outside of the manifest. The columns, from left to right, contain the name of each arriving passenger, age, sex, occupation, "the country to which they belong" and the country in which they intend to settle, and "remarks relative to any that may have died or otherwise left the vessel during the voyage." In 1855, Congress augmented the 1819 act to require the captain to designate on the manifest "the part of the vessel occupied by each during the voyage."[13] This latter data may be considered as a

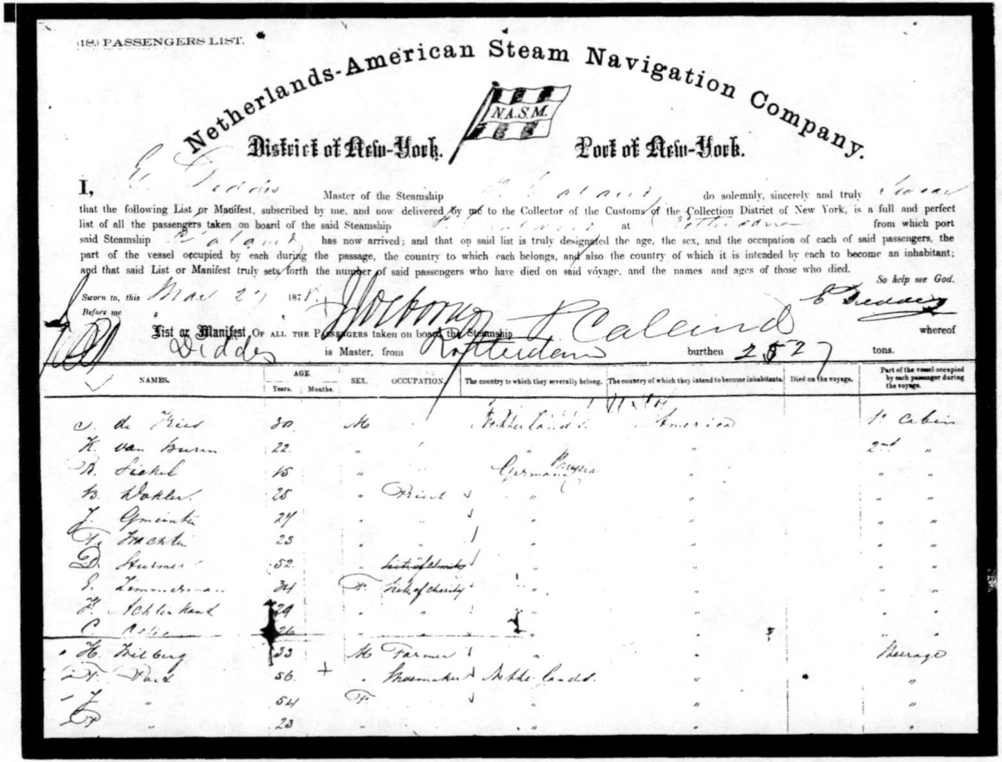

(18) PASSENGERS LIST.

Netherlands-American Steam Navigation Company.

N.A.S.M.

District of New-York. Port of New-York.

I, Master of the Steamship do solemnly, sincerely and truly that the following List or Manifest, subscribed by me, and now delivered by me to the Collector of the Customs of the Collection District of New York, is a full and perfect list of all the passengers taken on board of the said Steamship at from which port said Steamship has now arrived; and that on said list is truly designated the age, the sex, and the occupation of each of said passengers, the part of the vessel occupied by each during the passage, the country to which each belongs, and also the country of which it is intended by each to become an inhabitant; and that said List or Manifest truly sets forth the number of said passengers who have died on said voyage, and the names and ages of those who died.

So help me God.

Sworn to, this 187

Before me

List or Manifest of all the Passengers taken on board the Steamship Calend whereof is Master, from Rotterdam burthen 2527 tons.

NAMES.	AGE Years.	AGE Months.	SEX.	OCCUPATION.	The country to which they severally belong.	The country of which they intend to become inhabitants.	Died on the voyage.	Part of the vessel occupied by each passenger during the voyage.

Figure 12.2 U.S. Ship Passenger Manifest, *Jan van Brakel*, at New York, 3 February 1853

SOURCE: U.S. ship passenger lists, New York 1853, National Archives.

general proxy for the socioeconomic status of the immigrant. By law, port officials processed these manifests and submitted copies and quarterly abstracts to the Secretary of State (after 1874 the Secretary of the Treasury), who in turn made annual reports to Congress.

The ship passenger lists are a vital link in immigration research for many reasons. They contain information about the "clandestine" emigrants who failed to register before leaving Europe. They provide proof of the arrival of specific individuals in an American port and weed out immigrants who indicated they intended to settle here but went elsewhere. Most important for social and demographic historians, they contain data on *all* family members, women and children included, and not simply on heads of families or independent persons. Moreover, from the ship manifests it can be determined whether migrants traveled together, either in church, family, or neighborhood groups. The individual impact of the uprooting would, of course, be substantially affected by the degree of group cohesiveness maintained in the decision to leave, in the transatlantic passage, and in the process of resettlement in America.

The U.S. customs passenger lists, as do the Netherlands emigration records, also have limitations and deficiencies. They report the "**country** of last residence" and not (except very rarely) the province and municipality. Thus, unless the names are linked to the Netherlands emigration records, it is impossible to determine the local origin and background of particular immigrant families and individuals. Similarly, the lists indicate the country of destination but not the specific city or village. Only the U.S. census records confirm the specific place of settlement.

Despite the historical significance of the customs passenger lists, very little is known concerning the method by which they were prepared. The law itself is entirely silent on the administrative procedures; hence, an ad hoc system developed. All manifests were handwritten on printed forms, but in the early years some lists were crudely filled out on hand-ruled paper. The printed forms varied widely in format among the various ports of embarkation and shipping companies, and, more important, they differed greatly in completeness and reliability. Ships embarking at Dutch and German ports—Rotterdam, Amsterdam, Hamburg, and Bremen—presented the most detailed and accurate manifests; those from English, Scottish, and Scandinavian ports—Liverpool, London, Glasgow, and Stockholm—exhibited less concern for clarity; and those from Belgian and French ports—Antwerp and Le Havre—were most deficient. The penmanship was poor in these lists, names were spelled phonetically with only the initials of given names, and occupations were often not designated.

Customarily, all manifests were prepared before a ship left port in Europe. This is evident from names blotted or lined out, with the notation in the remarks column "decided not to embark" or "died en route." Hence, persons who died on the crossing are known, but not those few who may have died before booking passage. Since different manifests from the same port display the same handwriting during a period of time, one can conclude that professional clerks prepared the lists before departures. The Dutch and German clerks again deserve pride of place for their calligraphy and accuracy. Nils Olsson, who examined some 33,000 New York ship lists for the period 1820–50, said of the German and Dutch vessels: "The unusual calligraphy, the flawless spelling of the names and the exactness with which each person's birthplace was recorded—all point to the work of professional clerks."[14] Such clerks were doubtless active at Liverpool, Dublin, and other major ports as well.

On poorer quality manifests, the likelihood is far greater that captains, ship agents, or literate passengers filled out the required form while at sea. Or perhaps harried customs agents or their clerks had to prepare the manifest at dockside from a crudely written list furnished by an uneducated captain or even by semiliterate passengers themselves.[15] The process of immigration overwhelmed customs agents. A Dutch migrant, who entered in 1881 at Castle Garden, reported that the commotion was indescribable: "We had arrived in the period with about 6,000 emigrants, so that the officials hardly knew what to do first."[16] Officials were simply spread too thin. Fortunately for this study, the clerks were more conscientious at the primary ports of Dutch embarkation in the Netherlands and Germany.

There is some evidence of deliberate fraud in recording of misinformation, but most errors are likely honest ones.[17] For example, the nationality of German immigrants was occasionally denoted by the common American misnomer "Dutch" or "Dutchmen." Flemish-speaking Belgians arriving on Dutch ships were sometimes accounted as Dutch. Swiss and Swedish immigrants were also confused, as were Swedes with Norwegians and Scots with Englishmen.[18] Confusion also stemmed from the fact that many European emigrants transshipped via Liverpool. On these interrupted voyages, the English captains or American clerks frequently had difficulty with family names and nationalities of the Continentals, and errors resulted.

Administrative procedures of the federal government created problems as well. Little care was taken over the years to preserve the passenger lists and perhaps 10 percent or more were lost or damaged by careless officials.[19] Clerks subsequently recopied them from the quarterly compilations forwarded to the Secretary of State, but with many errors. On the redrawn manifests, marked "Copy," names are usually illegible and data on sex, nationality, and occupation were often disregarded or carelessly noted by indiscriminate ditto marks down the page. Since these are the only surviving manifests for many ships, they must be used with extreme caution.[20]

Additionally, prior to 1867, U.S. immigration regulations did not require that shipping companies distinguish immigrant aliens from alien tourists, consular officials, and businessmen. But fewer than 450 nonimmigrant Dutch aliens arrived in the United States between 1820 and 1861, so this is a relatively minor distortion.

Considering the inadequate staffing at customs houses, especially when immigration reached floodtide proportions in the years 1846–56, 1865–73, and 1881–87, one is struck by the general accuracy of the ship lists, especially for vessels from Dutch and German ports. For all their flaws and omissions, they provide scholars with indispensable information about immigrants at the moment of the transplanting. When linked with official European records such as the Dutch emigration lists, the combined data provide an unparalleled wealth of specific biographical information on hundreds of thousands of immigrants.

United States Manuscript Censuses

The third record series in the triad of sources linking the Old World to the New in the study of Dutch immigration is the U.S. decennial population censuses, which reveal the settling-in process of the first generations. The census questionnaire, compiled by a house-to-house canvass of the entire American population, documents the place of settlement of the new arrivals and details their socioeconomic status at ten-year intervals. Since few emigrants knew (or reported) their exact destination before they left the fatherland, the census records alone document the final destinations.[21]

The census questionnaires differ slightly in 1850, 1860, and 1870, but basically they report for each resident the full name, age, sex, birthplace (or nationality if foreign born), occupation of male adults at least 14 years of age (in 1870 occupations of females are also provided), value of real estate and (in 1860 and 1870) personal property, school attendance, illiteracy, citizenship (1870 only), whether married in the census year, and severe physical and mental disabilities (Figure 12.3). The designated country of birth is the key datum for identifying Dutch immigrants, for whom the census marshal usually recorded "Holland" or Netherlands, or occasionally "Dutch," Rotterdam, Amsterdam, or the name of some other large city or province.

Nominal Record Linkage

As do most large-scale statistical studies, the two steps involved data *preparation*—abstracting, coding, checking, and modifying files—and data *manipulation* or "number crunching" to generate the desired factual information. The Netherlands emigration records (1835–80) include 21,810 families and single adults; the U.S. ship manifests (1820–80) contain 56,000 Dutch nationals whose names were culled from 250,000 individual manifests; and the censuses of 1850, 1860, and 1870 include 67,000 Dutch-born individuals and their children (of which approximately 40 percent are "repeaters," that is, their names appear in more than one census).

The method of creating the data files involved a three-step process. First, the three primary nominal sources—the Dutch emigration records (file 1), ship manifest (file 2), and census lists (file 3)—were converted into electronic format. The data files were then checked by human eyes and validated with specially written computer programs to eliminate as many transcription and data-keying errors as possible. Second, the ship manifests and census records, which contained multiple records per family, were converted into single-record files to make them compatible with the Netherlands emigration records, which are single-record units per family. Third, these newly generated "family" files of the ship manifests (file 4) and censuses (file 5) were alphabetically sorted and linked, in turn, with the Netherlands emigration list (file 1), which was also ordered alphabetically, and then all three files were linked together. This produced a combined emigration–ship manifest series (file 6), a combined emigration–census series (file 7), and a combined

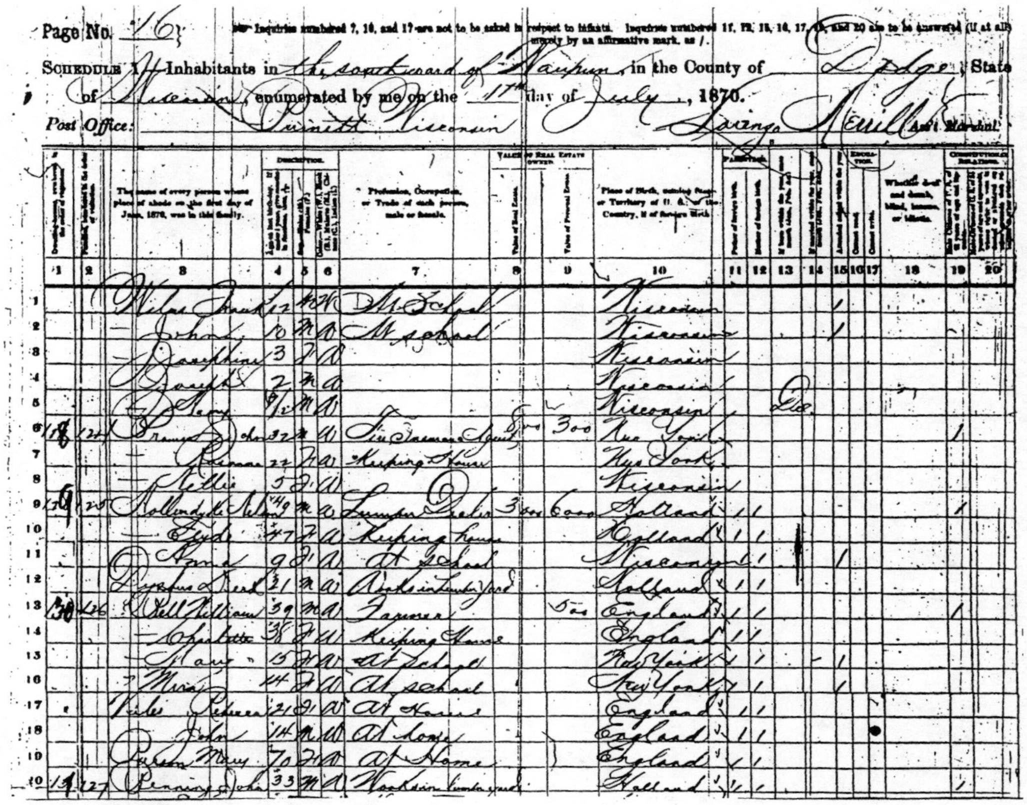
Page No. 16
Inquiries numbered 7, 16, and 17 are not to be asked in respect to infants. Inquiries numbered 11, 12, 15, 16, 17, 18, and 20 are to be answered (if at all) merely by an affirmative mark, as /.
SCHEDULE 1.—Inhabitants in the south ward of Waupun, in the County of Dodge, State of Wisconsin, enumerated by me on the 17th day of July, 1870.
Post Office: Waupun, Wisconsin
Ass't Marshal.

Figure 12.3 U.S. Manuscript Population Census Schedule, Dodge County, Wisconsin, 1870

SOURCE: National Archives.

emigration–ship manifest–census series (file 8). These eight files contain a vast amount of personal information that was summarized, cross-tabulated, and broken down for detailed analysis.

The linchpin of the study is the international record-linkage of Netherlands and America immigrant files in the period of 1835–80. The linkage was accomplished by hand, according to established rules, after arranging the files in alphabetical order and modifying first and last names according to a set of rules specifically developed for Dutch names.[22] The success of record linkage is enhanced by the large number of identification points, and the two series share nine categories of information: surname, first name or initial, sex, age, occupation, year of migration, nationality, and size and type of municipality of last residence.

The major linkage problems occurred because of spelling variations of the Dutch names in the various record series, although gaps in the records (noted earlier) also created missed links. The spelling of the names in the Netherlands emigration list, of course, is presumed to be accurate and to provide the linkage base. Dutch clerks in the local courthouses compiled the lists from *written* records (the population registers), and provincial clerks recopied them only once into provincial lists for forwarding to the royal government in The Hague. Very few copying errors swept in, and the lists are neat and readable.

Unfortunately, the same cannot be said for many ship manifests and U.S. census schedules which were based on *oral reports* taken by non-Dutch clerks. The rule is that records prepared by same nationality clerks and census takers are far more accurate than those prepared by non-natives. Manifests of ships sailing from Rotterdam and Amsterdam, which were prepared by Dutch clerks, were highly reliable and accurate in reporting on the Dutch passengers. But nearly half of the Dutch traveled on non-Dutch ships in which spelling of names was often inaccurate. Similarly, in the case of major Dutch colonies, where the immigrant leaders and teachers themselves served as census marshals, such as Henry Peter Scholte, the founder of the Pella (Iowa) colony, and Henry Hospers, the founder of the Orange City (Iowa) colony, the census schedules are legible and the names are spelled correctly. German census takers also accurately recorded Dutch names.

Since Liverpool was the major rival to Rotterdam as a Dutch port of embarking, the shipping clerks were English and most U.S. census enumerators were native American. Given the language barrier between these English speakers and Dutch immigrants, who at best had a rudimentary command of English, it is understandable that spelling of names was a problem. Spelled phonetically, Dutch names often bore little resemblance to the genuine article, and only a stroke of genius could unscramble the twisted result. The problem was always the worst in the large cities such as Chicago, New York, St. Louis, Cincinnati, Cleveland, Rochester, and the like. Single individuals were also less often identified than families, especially in the heterogeneous urban places.

Because all three record series are in handwritten form, transcription errors arose because letters of the alphabet that *look* alike were easily confused. Although ship captains and census enumerators had to testify in writing and under oath that their listings were accurate and complete, many listings were in fact very carelessly drawn by individuals who had little tolerance of thick-tongued or illiterate foreigners. Hence, the linkage procedure had to be designed to minimize both aural and visual types of errors. This was done by allowing for the transliteration of consonants that sound or look alike.

A problem related to phonetic spelling was the Americanization of Dutch names, either inadvertently by American officials, which was usually the case, or deliberately by the immigrants themselves, which was seldom the case. Jansen might be changed to Johnson, Smit to Smith, Visser to Fisher, Kuiper to Cooper, Groeneweg to Greenway, Groenhout to Greenwood, etc. If the new name was a phonetic equivalent, such as Smit to Smith, it was likely an inadvertent alteration, but when Dutch names are translated, such as Kuiper to Cooper, the change was likely deliberate on the part of the immigrant.

Common patronymics also caused missed linkages. In the Netherlands emigration records for the period 1835–80, there are 138 families or single adults with variants of the surname De Jong, 135 with Jansen, 131 with Vanden Burg, 117 with Smit, 99 with Bos, 77 with Visser, and 64 with (De)Boer. Many of these men have the same Christian name or initials. For example, there are 34 entries under J., Jan, or Johannes De Jong(e). In such case, a definite linkage could be established, if at all, only by comparing the year of migration, marital status, number of children, occupation, and place of last residence.

The fact that the emigration lists provide household data, and the ship lists contain individual data also creates linkage problems. Fortunately, shipping clerks usually listed families together in the manifests, with the family head first, then the wife, and the children in order from oldest to youngest. When clerks failed to be consistent, the household was recorded in this way. Even this adjustment, however, failed to solve the problem of split-family migrations. Since the emigration lists were compiled at the end of each calendar year, and the ship manifests were continuous, if husbands emigrated first and the wife and children followed later in the year, the family would be listed as one migrating unit in the Dutch records but two units in the ship lists.

Other minor linkage problems stemmed from differing social customs. Dutch officials recorded maiden names of widows and married women not accompanied by their husbands, whereas shipping clerks used married names. Usually such women could be identified and linked based on first names, children's surnames, or other clues. Similarly, Dutch officials considered as the head of the emigrating household a father or mother accompanied by married children and grandchildren or by unmarried adult children. Shipping clerks recorded the eldest son as the household head, if he was the primary breadwinner. In such cases, the household ordering in the ship manifest was rearranged to conform to the Dutch practice. Finally, in the few cases of Dutch immigrants who returned to their homeland for visits and were therefore included more than once in the ship manifests, only the first entry was considered.

The methodology of Dutch-American record linkage provides a firm basis for studying all phases of emigrant family behavior—premigration, migration, and postmigration. But one must always take into account the bias in the linked files that favor rural over urban localities, homogeneous Dutch colonies over heterogeneous settlements, and families over singles.

Notes

1. Brinley Thomas, *Migration and Economic Growth: A Study of Great Britain and the Atlantic Economy*, 2d ed. (Cambridge, MA: Cambridge University Press, 1954), 35; Philip Taylor, *The Distant Magnet: European Emigration to the U.S.A.* (New York and London: Harper, 1971), 27.
2. Clerks in the provincial governors' offices actually recopied the individual municipal lists onto a master list for the entire province, which they forwarded to the ministry in The Hague.
3. Yda Schreuder, *Dutch Catholic Immigrant Settlement in Wisconsin, 1850–1905* (New York and London: Garland, 1989), 167–74, analyzed the municipal emigrant reports of Uden, province of Noord-Brabant, and found total compliance.
4. The provinces with emigrant lists after 1877 are Groningen to 1901 (except the years 1878 and 1889), Overijssel to 1918, Utrecht to 1905, Zeeland to 1901, and Zuid-Holland to 1899. Annemieke Galema of the history department, University of Groningen, reconstituted from the *Bevolkingsregisters* of all the northern *grietenij* of Friesland the emigrant lists for the years 1880–1914. Additional emigration lists are available in municipal archives, especially for the years before 1848. For specifics, see Robert P. Swierenga, "Archival Materials and Manuscripts in the Netherlands on Immigration to the United States," in *Guide to the Study of United States History Outside the U.S., 1945–1980*, Lewis Hanke, ed., 6 vols. (Washington: American Historical Association, and Amherst: University of Massachusetts, 1985), 3: 198–200.
5. *Dutch Emigrants to the United States, South Africa, South America, and Southeast Asia, 1835–1880: An Alphabetical Listing by Household Heads and Independent Persons* (Wilmington, DE: Scholarly Resources, 1983). The late William K. Reinsma and Elly Kramer Hulst, then on the Calvin College Archives staff, assisted in translating and coding these records.
6. Specifically, 2,780 names of household heads and singles are omitted in the period 1831–47 and 775 in the years 1877–80.
7. In the municipality of St. Kruis, Zeeland, in the period 1847–1924, there were 379 emigrants recorded in the *Bevolkingsregisters*, and 320 in the *Landverhuizerslijsten*, but lists were missing for several years during which 27 persons emigrated. Thus, if complete, the total of the latter source is 347, or 32 (9.2 percent) short. A comparison of occupations in the two sources shows that most unregistered persons were male and female servants and farmers' sons. See Georges A. C. van Vooren, "De emigratie naar Noord-Amerika vanuit Sint Kruis-bij-Ardenburg, 1847–1924," *De eik. Drie maandelijks gewestelijk tijdschrift voor familiegeschiedenis* 4 (1979): 160–210, esp. 162, 166. In the municipality of Wisch, province of Gelderland, from 1840 to 1850, only 41 of 49 emigrant

households (82 percent) were recorded in the *Landverhuizerslijsten* compared to the *Bevolkingsregisters*.

8. Myron P. Gutmann and Etienne van de Walle, "New Sources for Social and Demographic History: The Belgian Population Registers," *Social Science History* 2 (Winter 1978): 121–43; Harald Runblom and Hans Norman, ed., *From Sweden to America: A History of the Migration* (Minneapolis: University of Minnesota Press, 1976).
9. Schreuder, *Dutch Catholic Immigrant Settlement*, 168–9.
10. Ibid., 169.
11. The customs passenger lists, 1820–97, and card indexes prepared in 1935–37 by Works Progress Administration workers were originally in the National Archives, Records of the Bureau of Customs, Record Group 36. This entire record group was moved in the late 1970s to the American Immigration Archives of Temple University, located at the Balch Institute for Ethnic Studies, Philadelphia. Alien passenger lists for the years 1897–1942 are in the Records of the Immigration and Naturalization Service, Record Group 85. The lists in Record Groups 36 and 85 are available on microfilm from the National Archives. For each Atlantic and Gulf Coast port, the lists are arranged chronologically by date of the ship's arrival and thereunder by the name of the ship. The following customs passenger lists were utilized in this study: Baltimore, Series M-255, 1820–80; Boston, Series M-277, 1820–80; New Orleans, Series M-259, 1820–80; New York, Series M-237, 1820–80; Philadelphia, Series M-425, 1820–80; Atlantic, Gulf, and Great Lakes Ports, Series M-575, 1820–73.
12. Copies of the 1819 act and all subsequent acts pertaining to immigrant passengers are conveniently published in William J. Bromwell, *History of Immigration to the United States* ... ([New York]; repr., New York: Arno Press, 1969), 206–25. The 1818 law is on 208–09. The 1819 law and subsequent amendments remained in force until 1897, when the Immigration and Naturalization Service of the Justice Department was given jurisdiction over all passenger entries into the United States.
13. Bromwell, *History of Immigration*, 221. The entire act is on 216–33.
14. Nils William Olsson, *Swedish Passenger Arrivals in New York, 1820–1850* (Chicago: Swedish Pioneer Historical Society, 1967), xiii.
15. For example, in a sworn statement of Captain Timothy B. Perry affixed to the manifest of the ship *Vermont* from Dublin, which arrived at New York on 14 January 1851, the captain declared: "I also swear that the List of passengers presented at the Custom House on Entry, *was made out in Dublin*" (italics mine). See "Passenger Lists of Vessels Arriving in New York, 1820–97," Microfilm Series M-237, Reel 95, Manifest 47.
16. C. de Smit, *To America? Sketches from the Portfolio on the Trip to and Through the New World*, 2d ed. (Winterswijk: Bulens, 1881), 16.
17. Friedrich Kapp, one of the prominent New York Commissioners of Emigration in the period 1867–70 and a student of the city's immigration history, explained that bondsmen encouraged intentional inaccuracies on the

ship lists regarding names, ages, and nationalities of passengers, with the objective of transferring legal responsibility from the carriers and their bondsmen for those immigrants who might subsequently become public charges. Kapp cites the example of one bonded passenger over 50 years of age who applied at the mayor's office for poor relief, and it was discovered that his age had been "set down in the passenger list at twenty years." Kapp, *Immigration and Commissioners of Emigration*, 56, 49. The practice of deliberate errors, if it existed to any extent, was limited to the early years of the 1840s. In 1847 the New York Commissioners of Emigration were given overall supervision of the bureaucracy; by 1855 all immigrants were processed through the Castle Garden facility, and the brokerage business was abolished. The story is described in ibid., chaps. 4–6.

18. William S. Petersen, *Planned Migration: The Social Determinants of the Dutch-Canadian Movement* (Berkeley: University of California Press, 1955), 45–46, discusses these and other difficulties with the U.S. statistics. The nationality of German immigrants was occasionally denoted by the common American misnomer "Dutch" or "Dutchmen," and, conversely, Hollanders were designated as German. Such confusion was most likely for Hollanders who sailed from Belgian and French ports or who transshipped via Liverpool. Belgian, English, and French civil functionaries frequently had difficulty with the Germanic tongue and language. The 47 percent of the Dutch who arrived in non-Dutch ships in the years 1820–1880 also had a higher incidence of misspelled names. Nationality errors are frustrating, especially when the names are clearly not Netherlanders, but for the sake of consistency, all such entries were abstracted and included in the study. An example is the ship *Northumberland* from London, 29 January 1855, where, under the heading "Germans," 15 individuals are listed as of "Dutch" nationality (Series M-237, Reel 150, Manifest 59); Olsson, *Swedish Passenger Arrivals*, xii.

19. Until the registry of passenger ship arrivals is collated with the extant copies of passenger manifests in the various public and private archives, we can only estimate the extent to which the ravages of time have taken their toll on the manifests. The 10 percent figure is a rough estimate of two categories: passenger manifests destroyed or lost, and passenger manifests that may yet be in existence in the National Immigration Archives at the Balch Institute at Temple University, the National Archives, or elsewhere, but were not microfilmed by the National Archives and incorporated into the Passenger Lists microfilm series on which this study is based.

20. Some 2–3 percent of the manifests in the microfilm series are stamped with the words "Copy/Filmed because of poor condition of the original" or "original missing." These manifests were prepared by the Collector of Customs from the quarterly reports of original manifests, which under the Act of 1819 were forwarded to the U.S. Secretary of State for statistical compilation and reporting. On the manifests marked "Copy," names are usually illegible and data on sex, nationality, and occupation were often

disregarded or carelessly noted by indiscriminate ditto marks down the page. For example, an entire page containing names of persons of different nationalities is designated at the top as "Germany," or the occupation column is listed simply as "mechanics and farmers."

21. 6,752 of 16,433 (41 percent) heads of families and independent persons who registered to emigrate to the United States, 1845–77, designated a specific state or city. Many of the 2,558 family heads or individuals who specified "New York," however, probably intended only to pass through the port en route to the Midwest. Others who designated a western terminus may have stayed in East Coast cities because they lacked sufficient funds or energy to move inland.
22. The rules, adopted from Hershberg (1976): 141–43, are explained in detail in Appendix I in Swierenga, "Dutch International Migration Statistics 1820–1880: An Analysis of Linked Multinational Nominal Files," *International Migration Review* 15 (Fall 1980): 468–70.

BIBLIOGRAPHIC ESSAY

Dutch overseas emigration to North America had three phases: the seventeenth-century *commercial* colonization of New Netherlands by the Dutch East India Company, the *free* emigration of the nineteenth and early twentieth centuries, and the *planned* or government-promoted emigration following World War II. Of the three eras, the post-1945 era is least studied; the early colonization of New Netherlands is much better described; and the New Migration (1820–1920) is thoroughly documented. The latter period is the primary focus of this essay.

Primary Works —Archival Holdings

Dutch archives contain important materials, although the major collections of primary documents on Dutch overseas migration are in the United States. The National Archives (Algemeen Rijksarchief) in The Hague has the official lists of overseas migrants for the period 1847–77, and a complete copy is in the Calvin College Archives. The Koninklijk Bibliotheek in The Hague is moderately strong in serials, pamphlets, and early books. The Nederlands Historical and Economic Archives in The Hague houses the records of Dutch emigration societies in the twentieth century, and the Ministry of Social Affairs Library in The Hague contains the best collection of post-1945 materials.

An annotated bibliography of the holdings of the National Archives and the Central Bureau for Genealogy (Centraal Bureau voor Genealogie) is Liesbeth Beelen-Driehuizen and Jan H. Kompagnie, eds., *Landverhuizers: Aanwijzingen voor het doen van onderzoek naar Nederlandse emigranten (2e kwart 19e eeuw—1940)* (The Hague, 1996). For the post-1945 emigration see Maarten van Harten, "List of Archives Specifically Concerning Dutch Emigration to U.S. Since 1945" (typescript, The Hague, March 1983). Much of the post-1945 material is confidential for thirty years and can be consulted only by permission of the keeper of the records.

A complete listing of Netherlands archival holdings, now somewhat dated, is Herbert J. Brinks, "Sources for the Study of Migration in the Archives of the Netherlands," in Francis X. Blouin Jr. and Robert M. Warner, eds. *Sources for the Study of Migration and Ethnicity: A Guide to Manuscripts in Finland, Ireland, Poland, The Netherlands, and the State of Michigan*, ch. 4, 255–85 (Ann Arbor: Bentley Historical Library, 1979). A companion piece is Robert P. Swierenga, "Archival Materials and Manuscripts in the Netherlands on Immigration to the

United States," in *Guide to the Study of United States History Outside the U.S., 1945–1980*, 6 vols. (Washington: American Historical Association, and Amherst: University of Massachusetts, 1985) 3:195–215. For names and addresses of all Netherlands archives, consult the latest edition of the Central Bureau for Genealogy, "Lijst van Nederlands archieven, genealogische vereningen enz."

The most complete materials of the New Netherlands immigration are at the New York Public Library and the New York Historical Society Library at Albany. The major collections for the New Migration are the Heritage Hall Collection at the Calvin College Library, which houses voluminous materials relating to Dutch immigration in general and the Christian Reformed Church in particular; The Joint Archives of Holland, Hope College Library, Holland, Michigan, which is the depository for most documents relating to this original Dutch-American colony; and the extensive Scholte Collection, which is in the Central College Library, Pella, Iowa. Smaller regional archives are at the Trinity Christian College Library, Palos Heights, Illinois (for the Chicago area), and at the Northwestern College Library, Orange City, Iowa (for the upper Midwest). Herrick Public Library in Holland, Michigan, and the Michigan Room of the Grand Rapids Public Library specialize in Dutch genealogy and local records. There is no central repository of Dutch Catholic materials, but St. Norbert College in De Pere, Wisconsin, is strong for the Norbertine Order of Noord-Brabant.

Essential sources for the free migration, such as the Netherlands population registers, land records, and tax lists, remain scattered in more than a thousand municipal courthouses. The Mormons fortunately microfilmed most of these records, but Dutch officials and archivists usually failed to retain a copy of the films and place them in a central repository. They are available at Salt Lake City or can be borrowed through Mormon Stake libraries around the United States.

America Letters and Pamphlets

The best collection of "America Letters," numbering over 5,000 missives accumulated between 1976 and 1990, is the Dutch American Letter Collection at Calvin College. Archivist Herbert J. Brinks published a representative sampling of several hundred items in English translation in *Dutch American Voices: Letters from the United States, 1850–1930* (Ithaca, N.Y.: Cornell University Press, 1995). This work augments the same author's *Schrijf spoedig terug: Brieven van immigrants in Amerika, 1847–1920* (The Hague, 1978), and the English translation, *Write Back Soon: Letters from Immigrants in America, 1847–1920* (Grand Rapids: CRC Publications, 1986), which includes forty letters.

Since 1970 the Calvin College Archives also produces a booklet series, Heritage Hall Publications, that has made available in English translation historic documents: Albertus C. Van Raalte's *Stemmen uit Noord-Amerika* (1847) in 1992; the immigrant guide of R. T. Kuiper, *A Voice from America About America* (1881; reprint, Grand Rapids: Wm. B. Eerdmans, 1970); Van Raalte's sermon notes in Gordon J. Spykman, *Pioneer Preacher, Albertus Christiaan Van Raalte* (Grand

Rapids: Wm. B. Eerdmans, 1976); and Leonard Sweetman, ed. *From Heart to Heart: Letters from the Rev. Albertus Christiaan Van Raalte to His Wife, Christina Johanna Van Raalte-De Moen, 1836–1847* (Grand Rapids: Heritage Hall Publications, 1997).

Annemieke Galema extensively quotes from Frisian letters in *Frisians to America: 1880–1914: With the Baggage of the Fatherland* (Groningen: REGIO-Projekt Uitgevers, and Detroit: Wayne State University Press, 1996). A remarkably complete and lengthy family correspondence of another Frisian emigrant is published in Brian W. Beltman, *Frisian Farmer in the Missouri Valley: The Life and Letters of Ulbe Eringa, 1866–1950* (Urbana: University of Illinois Press, 1996). A specialized letter series is Jan Stellingwerff, *Amsterdamse emigranten. Onbekende brieven uit de prairie van Iowa* (Amsterdam, 1975), which contains eighty-eight of the most important letters from the Höveker-Wormser Archive at the Library of the Free University of Amsterdam, relating to the founding of the Pella, Iowa, colony. Recent Dutch-Canadian immigrant letters are provided in Gordon Oosterman, Adrian Guldemond, et al., *To Find a Better Life: Aspects of Dutch Immigration to Canada and the United Status 1920–1970* (Grand Rapids: CRC Publications, 1975).

Henry S. Lucas's priceless two-volume collection, *Dutch Immigrant Memoirs and Related Works* (Assen: Van Gorcum, 1955; reprint, Wm. B. Eerdmans, 1997), is an indispensable source for memoirs and pioneer accounts of the first generation before 1890. Other reports, available singly, include H. P. Scholte, *Eene stem uit Pella* (Amsterdam, 1848) in Jacob Van der Zee, ed. and trans., "The Coming of the Hollanders to Iowa," *Iowa Journal of History and Politics* 9 (1911): 527–74; H. P. Scholte, *Tweede stem uit Pella* (s' Hertogenbosch, 1848) in Robert P. Swierenga, ed., and Albert and Henry Raap, trans., "A Place of Refuge," *Annals of Iowa*, 3rd Ser., 39 (1968): 321–57; Sjoerd Aukes Sipma, *Belangrijke berigten uit Pella* (1849) in Robert P. Swierenga, ed., and R. John Vander Borgh, trans., "A Dutch Immigrant's View of Frontier Iowa," ibid. 38 (1965): 81–118; and W. A. E. Sloet tot Oldhuis's 1866 analysis of emigration factors in Robert P. Swierenga, ed., and Dick Hoogeveen, trans., "The Causes of Dutch Emigration to America: An 1866 Account," *Michigana* (1979). This last item is a perceptive analysis by the foremost Netherlands rural economist. Dozens of other important pamphlets and memoirs by pioneer immigrants are available in English translation in typescript at the Calvin College and Hope College Archives.

Two published sets of letters concerning early Roman Catholic emigration and settlement in Wisconsin are Mathias van den Elsen, "Letters of Arnold Verstegen," *Annals of St. Joseph* 55 (1943) and 56 (1944); and Henry S. Lucas, "De reize naar Noord-Amerika van Theodorus J. van den Broek, O.P.," *Nederlandsch Archief voor Kerkgeschiedenis* 41 (1955).

There is no central repository in the Netherlands for the many small collections of unpublished immigrant letters, and they remain largely in private hands. One noteworthy collection of approximately five hundred letters from eighteen U.S. states and Canadian provinces is housed in the Friesland Provincial Library in Leeuwarden. The letters, which originally appeared in the newspapers *Advertentieblad*,

1876–1901, and *Nieuwsblad van Friesland*, 1901–35, discuss economic and social conditions among immigrants and include a running dialogue concerning the pros and cons of migration. The *Provinciale Groninger Courant*, 1850–1900, in the National Archives center in Groningen also printed immigrant letters and occasional larger reports from the United States All provincial newspapers doubtless contain similar items, none of which are indexed by subject.

Protestant Records and Voluntary Organizations

Because 80 percent of the Dutch immigrants in the nineteenth century were Protestants, members of the Hervormde Kerk or its splinter groups, the Christelijk Afgescheidenen and later Christelijk Gereformeerden, church archives contain useful material, especially in Seceder communities where pastors and entire congregations emigrated en masse in the mid-nineteenth century. The Gereformeerde Kerken collection in the municipal archive in Zwolle (Overijssel Province), a center of Seceder emigration, contains fifteen feet of records. The municipal archive in Middelburg houses a small manuscript collection of Seceder church records from Zeeland that include six folders of letters from and about emigration to North America and official minutes and reports of church gatherings that discussed the option of emigration. The municipal archive at Kampen contains the Gereformeerde Kerk Seminary collection of twenty feet; the seminary had strong connections with the Dutch Reformed churches in America, and its founders became leaders in the emigration movement.

Similarly, two collections in the municipal archive of Rotterdam include correspondence between Dutch and American church leaders: the massive Gereformeerde Kerken collection, 1836–1970, and the Helenius de Cock Papers (four feet), 1850–1900. The church archives of the Hervormde Kerk include four feet of official minutes of church meetings and reports from colonial Dutch Reformed churches in New Amsterdam (New York) and surrounding villages addressed to the supervisory Classis [ruling ecclesiastical body of the Hervormde Kerk] of Amsterdam in the years 1620–1800. This archive also possesses records of the post–World War II Hervormde Emigratie Commissie, 1940–66. An undated finding list indicates the following material: departure lists; personal files and church reports on emigrants; spiritual care on ships and in the United States; contracts with institutions such as Church-World Service, Reformed Church in America, Board of North American Missions; correspondence to and about immigrants, e.g., about the church situation in California and Michigan; correspondence about clergymen, e.g., of Western Theological Seminary in Holland, Michigan.

Finally, the archives of several nonecclesiastical organizations hold records on emigration. The archives of the Nederlands Vrouwen Comitie, housed in the National Archives in The Hague, contain one collection of "Information materials about emigrating women (1954–1963)." The archives of immigrant aid societies—secular, Protestant, and Catholic—may include relevant material but there are no finding aids. The archives of the Algemene Centrale Emigratie, Christelijke Emigratie Centrale, and Katholieke Emigratie Centrale Stichting are located together. The Gereformeerde Emigratie Stichting is in Hardenberg and the Catholic Documentation Center is located at the University of Nijmegen. All of these emigration agencies are showing an increasing interest in the subsequent history of the immigrants they had served.

Catholic Records

Catholic emigration has attracted less attention than the Calvinist uprooting; there is no central archive or definitive account of Catholic emigration. Scholars of Catholic emigration to North America have relied primarily on official government records in public archives and church records. Henry van Stekelenburg surveyed diocesan archives in the Netherlands, as well as in the United States, and found much material on missionary activity in North America. The Diocesan Archives at 's Hertogenbosch has a file of some fifty-nine letters from American prelates and Dutch seminarists and priests addressed to Jacques Cuyten, president of the Groot-Seminarie in the years 1852–1877. Forty-two priests and theological students went as missionaries to the United States from this diocese, according to L. H. C. Schuttes, *Geschiedenis van het Bisdom 's Hertogenbosch* (1872), Part 2, 291–301. In the Generàlate in Amersfoort are letters pertaining to an attempt after 1910 to establish a second mission in the United States; and in the Milwaukee, Wisconsin, Archdiocesan Archives located in the St. Francis Seminary Library are letters from Father Henricus van den Wymelenberg to the bishop of Milwaukee (see J. Scheerder, *Henricus van den Wymelenberg: een religieus emancipator in Oost Brabant, 1800–1881* [Tilburg, 1976].

In the Norbertine Abbey of Berne, Noord-Brabant, are 346 letters to the mother house sent by abbots of the Norbertine Abbey in De Pere, Wisconsin, between 1893 and 1947, which contain illuminating reports. The library of the abbey of St. Norbert, De Pere, Wisconsin, has copies of these letters, which Walter Lagerwey translated and edited as *Letters Written in Good Faith: The Early Years of the Dutch Norbertines in Wisconsin [1893–1902]* (Green Bay: Alt Publishing Company, 1996). The Jesuit archives at Nijmegen contain letters and notes of the scholar F. van Hoeck, who in 1949 published an article in *Het Missiewerk* on "Nederlandse Jezuieten in de Verenigde Staten." The official magazine of the Capuchins order, *Uni Trinoque*, in 's Hertogenbosch, published a series of reports about the United States by Father Rildebrand, "De drang naar Amerika in de gewezen Hollandsch-Belgische Province, 1857–1871," 5 (1936–39): 107–16, 127–32, 142–44.

Widely scattered references are in yearbooks: *Jaarboek van Katholiek Nederland* (previously *Pius-Almanek*, 1874–1953), and *Handboekje voor de zaken der Roomsch Katholieke Eeredienst*, 1847–85); in periodicals: *De Godsdienstvriend* (1818–69), *Katholijke Nederlandsche Stemmen* (1835–56), *De Katholiek* (1842–1924), *Katholieke Illustratie* (1867–1940); and in national newspapers: *De Tijd* (1845–), *De Maasbode* (1868–), *Het Centrum* (1884–), and *De Volkskrant* (1923–).

Secondary Works —New Netherlands Immigration

For the history of New Netherlands colonization and the Dutch presence in the Hudson Valley area, the best one-volume treatment is Alice P. Kenney, *Stubborn for Liberty: The Dutch in New York* (Syracuse: Syracuse University Press, 1975). An outstanding narrative and analytic account is Oliver A. Rink, *Holland on the Hudson: An Economic and Social History of Dutch New York* (Ithaca and London: Cornell University Press, 1986). John P. Luidens, "The Americanization of the Dutch Reformed Church" (Ph.D. diss., University of Oklahoma, 1969), offers a lucid sociological analysis of the Dutch religious adaptation (or lack of it) to the American environment. In a similar vein, George L. Smith related the increasing secularism in the Dutch Reformed Church to the dictates of commercial enterprise, in *Religion and Trade in New Netherlands: Dutch Origins and American Development* (Ithaca, N.Y.: Cornell University Press, 1973). James Tanis, *Dutch Calvinistic Pietism in the Middle Colonies: A Study of the Life and Theology of Theodorus Jacobus Frelinghuysen* (The Hague, 1967), offers a first-rate treatment of religious developments in the Raritan Valley.

New Migration —General Histories

The earliest scholarly study was published in the United States by Dingman Versteeg, *De Pelgrim Vaders van het Westen* (Grand Rapids, 1886). Versteeg was a second-generation immigrant whose laudatory account of the midwestern Dutch colonies centered on the leading clerics. Among Netherlands historians the seminal work, which supplanted Versteeg, is Jacob van Hinte, *Nederlanders in Amerika. Een studie over landverhuizers en volkplanters in de 19e en 20ste Eeuw in de Verenigde Staten van Amerika*, 2 vols. (Groningen, 1928), a comprehensive (1,100 pages) social history written at the end of the great century of migration. Van Hinte wrote from the Dutch point of view and analyzed the causes of migration, the process of transplanting, and the early growth of the American settlements. He emphasized the religious factors and strongly lamented the extent of Americanization that he found in the settlements during his brief field research in the mid-1920s. Especially valuable is Van Hinte's extensive use of early serials and pamphlets not readily available in North America. Van Hinte's extensive personal library was sold at public auction shortly after his death, but his books and pamphlets on immigration were donated to the Royal Library where they have been integrated into the general holdings. An English-language translation of this significant work is *Netherlanders in America: A Study of Emigration and Settlement in the Nineteenth and Twentieth Centuries in the United States of America*, Robert P. Swierenga, ed., Adriaan de Wit, chief trans. (Grand Rapids: Baker Book House, 1985).

Van Hinte's 1928 tome remained the standard history for decades. The only other Netherlandic scholar to write on Dutch overseas emigration is J. A. Hartman, whose *Geschiedenis van de Nederlandse emigratie tot de Tweede Wereldoorlog* (The Hague, 1959), offered a worldwide scope. In the United States, Bertus Harry Wabeke, *Dutch Emigration to North America, 1624–1860: A Short History* (New York: Netherlands Information Agency, 1946), provided a brief survey that is useful for its extensive summary of newspaper accounts of the nineteenth-century migration.

In 1955 Henry Lucas published a detailed social history of the New Migration, *Netherlanders in America: Dutch Immigration to the United States and Canada,* 1789–1950 (Ann Arbor: University of Michigan Press, 1955; repr. Wm. B. Eerdmans, 1989), which complements Van Hinte. Lucas, whose grandfather was among the pioneer settlers of Holland, Michigan, wrote from an American perspective, in contrast to Van Hinte. Lucas also made extensive use of American sources on the historical development of Dutch communities, and, unlike Van Hinte, he viewed assimilation approvingly.

An interpretative social and religious survey that covers the entire sweep from the founding of New Netherlands to the postwar era is Gerald F. De Jong, *The Dutch in America, 1609–1974* (Boston: Twayne, 1975). The "bare facts" and some pertinent documents are provided in Pamela and Jacobus W. Smit, *The Dutch in America: A Chronology and Fact Book* (Dobbs Ferry, NY: Oceana Publications, 1972). Arnold Mulder's *Americans from Holland* (Philadelphia and New York: Lippincott, 1947) is a readable filiopietistic account that stresses immigrant idiosyncrasies and contributions.

New Migration —Specialized Histories

In the 1970s a new generation of Netherlands historians took an interest in the New Migration. J. W. Schulte Nordholt, then professor of North American history at Leiden University, initiated the development, but faculties and younger scholars in other universities soon followed Leiden's lead. The first result was the Ph.D. dissertation of Schulte Nordholt's student, Pieter R. D. Stokvis, *De Nederlandse trek naar Amerika, 1846–1847* (Leiden, 1977), which is an analytic study of the origins and social structural patterns of the first wave of the New Migration. Stokvis summarized some major conclusions in "The Dutch America Trek, 1846–1847: A Reinterpretation," *Immigration History Newsletter* 8 (November 1976), 3–5.

The Achterhoek of Gelderland, the "cockpit of Dutch emigration," is explored in four books: G. H. Ligterink, *De landverhuizers. Emigratie naar Noord-Amerika uit het Gelders- Westfaalse grensgebied tussen de jaren 1830–1850* (Zutphen, 1981); Verena de Bont, "Ik druk voor het laatst uw hand in het oude vaderland, Emigratie uit de Gelderse Achterhoek naar Noord-Amerika in de periode 1848–1877" (Ph.D. diss., Tilburg University, 1983); Liesbeth Hoogkamp, "Wisch-Scenario 1830–1850: Verslag van een onderzoek naar sociaal-economische omstandigheden, de Afscheiding en de landverhuizing in de gemeente Wisch tussen 1830 en 1850" (Ph.D.

diss., University of Utrecht, 1982); and a more genealogical work by Willem Wilterdink, *Winterswijkse pioniers in Amerika* (Winterswijk, 1990).

An innovative study of the years 1900–20 is Jeannie M. E. Worms, "Landverhuizing van uit Nederland naar de Verenigde Staten in het begin van de twentigste eeuw" (Ph.D. diss., Catholic University, Nijmegen, 1984). The most ambitious of the regional works is Annemieke Galema's linkage of population registers and U.S. census manuscripts, along with immigrant letters, in "With the Baggage of the Fatherland: Frisians to America 1880–1914" (Ph.D. diss., Leiden University, 1996). A sparkling illustrated history of the immigrant traffic is Cees Zevenbergen, *Toen zij uit Rotterdam vertrokken. Emigratie via Rotterdam door de eeuwen heen* (Zwolle, 1990). The immigrant press received attention from J. Breur in "De Sheboygan Nieuwsbode: Het eerste Nederlandstalige nieuwsblad in de Verenigde Staten, 1849–1861" (Ph.D. diss., Catholic University Nijmegen, 1991).

Research into Catholic emigration is gaining momentum. Yda Schreuder explored the migration from the northeastern region of Noord-Brabant to Little Chute, Wisconsin, in a sociographical study, *Dutch Catholic Immigrant Settlement in Wisconsin, 1850–1905* (New York: Garland Publishing, 1989). The definitive work, which emphasizes the role of missionary priests, is Henry A. V. M. van Stekelenburg's trilogy: *Landverhuizing als regionale verschijnsel van Noord-Brabant naar Noord-Amerika, 1820–1880* (Tilburg: Stichting Zuidelijk Historisch Contact, 1991); *"Hier is alles vooruitgang": Landverhuizing van Noord-Brabant naar Noord-Amerika, 1880–1940* (Tilburg: Stichting Zuidelijk Historisch Contact, 1996); and a third volume in progress to cover the recent period. Frans H. Doppen looks specifically at the role of "Theodoor J. van den Broek, Missionary and Emigration Leader: The History of the Dutch Catholic Settlement at Little Chute, Wisconsin," *The Catholic Historian* 3 (Fall/Winter 1983): 202–25.

A detailed analysis of Limburg emigration lists is Anje F. M. Koeweiden-Wijdeven, *Vergeten emigranten. Landverhuizing van noord- en midden-Limburg naar Noord-Amerika in de jaren 1847–1877* (Venlo, 1982); summarized in "Vergeten Emigranten," *Spiegel Historiael* 19 (March 1984): 120–24. This supplants H. C. W. Roeman, "Vertrek uit de province Limburg naar overzeesche gewesten in de jaren 1851–1877," *Tijdschrift voor economische geografie* (1946); and G. C. P. Linssen, "Limburgers naar Noord-Amerika," *Economische-en Sociaal-Historisch Jaarboek* (1972).

In Zeeland the provincial branch of the Netherlands Genealogical Society established an Emigration Workgroup that has published research on emigration to the United States, titled *In den vreemde* (1990–96), edited by J. H. van der Boom and his wife M. E. van der Boom-Haren. Various issues of this journal list all Zeeland emigrants by municipality from 1880 to 1899, and also those from Utrecht (1880–1905). See also S. Oudes, *Index op de namen van emigranten in de Zeeuwse "Staten van Landverhuizers," 1839–1900* (Middelburg: Rijksarchief, 1995). For a complete listing of West Zeeuws-Vlaanderen emigrants, see A. Vergouwe, *Emigranten naar Amerika uit West Zeeuws-Vlaanderen 1840–1970* (1993). This Workgroup is the most ambitious local research organ in The Netherlands promoting immigration studies.

Netherlands Academic Research Centers

Two Dutch centers promoting U.S. immigration research at the professional level are the American Studies program at the University of Amsterdam, headed by Rob Kroes, and the Roosevelt Study Center in Middelburg, headed by Kees van Minnen. The Roosevelt Center has organized several international conferences devoted to the subject, and Kroes published the papers in his book series, *European Contributions to American Studies*. See *The Dutch in North-America: Their Immigration and Cultural Continuity*, 20 (1991), co-edited by Rob Kroes and Henk-Otto Neuschäfer; Rob Kroes, ed., *American Immigration: Its Variety and Lasting Imprint* 1 (1979); *A Bilateral Bicentennial: A History of Dutch-American Relations* 5 (1982), co-edited by J. W. Schulte Nordholt and Robert P. Swierenga; and *Connecting Cultures: The Netherlands in Five Centuries of Transatlantic Exchange*, 31 (1994), co-edited by Rosemarijn Hoefte and Johanna C. Kardux.

Bibliographies, Encyclopedia Essays, and Conference Papers

In the recent flurry of interest in The Netherlands, the migrants and their progeny have described their pilgrimage and preserved their heritage, especially since the "Roots" phenomenon of the 1960s. For the entire literature, one should consult the exhaustive, annotated bibliographic and reference guide by Linda Pegman Doezema, *Dutch Americans: A Guide to Information Sources*, volume 3 in the Ethnic Studies Information Guide Series (New York, 1979). Now twenty years old, this reference work needs to be updated. Concise encyclopedic overviews are Robert P. Swierenga, "The Dutch," in *Harvard Encyclopedia of American Ethnic Groups*, ed. Stephen Thernstrom, 284–95 (Cambridge, MA: Harvard University Press, 1980); and Herbert J. Brinks, "The Dutch," in *Encyclopedia of American Social History*, 3 vols., eds., Mary K. Cayton, Elliott J. Gorn, and Peter W. Williams (New York: Scribner, 1993), 2:711–18.

International conferences in Toronto (1980) and Philadelphia (1982) hastened the maturation of the field. Both resulted in collected works: *Dutch Immigration to North America*, eds., Herman Ganzevoort and Mark Boekelman (Toronto: Multicultural History Society of Ontario, 1983), and *The Dutch in America: Immigration, Settlement, and Cultural Change*, ed. Robert P. Swierenga (New Brunswick, NJ: Rutgers University Press, 1985). A recent conference in religious history to mark the sesquicentennial of the New Migration resulted in the book, *Sharing the Reformed Tradition: The Dutch-North American Exchange, 1846–1996*, VU Studies in Protestant History (Amsterdam: VU University Press, 1996), eds. George Harinck and Hans Krabbendam.

Biographies

There is a dearth of biographies. For clerics, Albert Hyma, *Albertus C. Van Raalte and His Dutch Settlements in the United States* (Grand Rapids: Wm. B. Eerdmans,

1947), first utilized the long-closed Van Raalte collection. A popular work that places the Holland colony in the broader story of the nation is Jeanne M. Jacobson, Elton J. Bruins, and Larry J. Wagenaar, *Albertus C. Van Raalte: Dutch Leader and American Patriot* (Holland, Hope College, 1997). Lubbertus Oostendorp, *H. P. Scholte: Leader of the Secession of 1834 and Founder of Pella* (Franeker, 1964) is especially strong on Scholte's life in the Netherlands but the Pella years are sketchy. Jelle Ypma wrote the story of his ancestor, *Ds. Marten Annes Ypma, 1810–1863. Van Minnertsga (Friesland) naar Vriesland (Michigan)* (Leeuwarden, 1986).

Biographies of businessmen and politicians are also scarce. C. Warren Vander Hill, *Gerrit J. Diekema* (Grand Rapids: Wm. B. Eerdmans, 1970), traced the political career of the United States senator and minister to the Netherlands who was born of Dutch immigrant parents in Holland, Michigan. Hank (Hendrik G.) Meijer recounted the successful business career in retailing of his father in *Thrifty Years: The Life of Hendrik Meijer* (Grand Rapids: Wm. B. Eerdmans, 1984). Hans Krabbendam wrote the definitive biography of one of the most successful and prominent magazine publishers, *The Model Man: A Life of Edward W. Bok, 1863–1930* (Ph.D. diss., Leiden University, 1995). The first publication of Robert Schoone-Jongen's ongoing study of the life of the greatest Dutch frontier land promoter is "Cheap Land and Community: Theodore F. Koch, Dutch Colonizer," *Minnesota History* 53 (Summer 1993): 214–24. Elton J. Bruins, *Isaac Cappon: "Holland Foremost Citizen"* (Holland, 1987) writes of the colony's leading industrialist. Pieter R. D. Stokvis tells of "An Enterprising Bird of Passage: The Autobiography of American Hotels Founder C. A. A. Steinigeweg," in *The Dutch in America: Their Immigration and Cultural Continuity*, ed. Rob Kroes, 48–54 (*European Contributions to American Studies*, 20 [1991]).

Literary Sources

Given the salience of the religious aspects of the migration, this literature is abundant. James D. Bratt, *Dutch Calvinism in Modern America: A History of a Conservative Subculture* (Grand Rapids: Wm. B. Eerdmans, 1984) is a brilliant religious-intellectual history of the orthodox Calvinists in the twentieth century and of the impact of Americanization on religious life. This complements denominational histories by John Kromminga, *The Christian Reformed Church: A Study in Orthodoxy* (Grand Rapids: Baker Book House, 1949); Henry Zwaanstra, *Reformed Thought and Experience in the New World: A Study of the Christian Reformed Church and Its American Environment, 1890–1918* (Kampen, 1973); James C. Schaap, *Our Family Album: The Unfinished Story of the Christian Reformed Church* (Grand Rapids: CRC Publications, 1998); and Gerald F. De Jong, *The Dutch Reformed Church in the American Colonies* (Grand Rapids: Wm. B. Eerdmans, 1978). Turning points in the midwestern Dutch Reformed congregations are detailed in Robert P. Swierenga and Elton J. Bruins, *Family Quarrels in the Dutch Reformed Churches in the Nineteenth Century* (Grand Rapids: Wm. B. Eerdmans, 1999). See also Hans Krabbendam's "Serving the Dutch Community: A Comparison of the Patterns of Americanization in the Lives of Two Immigrant

Pastors" [Bernardus de Beij and R. T. Kuiper] (M.A. thesis, Kent State University, 1989). Marian M. Schoolland's *De Kolonie: The Church That God Transplanted* (Grand Rapids, CRC Publications, 1973) is a superb historical novel of the founding of the Christian Reformed Church. There is no general history of Dutch Catholic congregations and the only account of Dutch Jewish synagogues is Robert P. Swierenga, *The Forerunners: Dutch Jewry in the North American Diaspora* (Detroit: Wayne State University Press, 1994).

The fullest survey of immigrant literature, verse, and poetry is Walter Lagerwey, *Neen Nederland, 'k vergeet u niet: Een beeld van het immigrantenleven in Amerika tussen 1846 en 1945 in verhalen, schetsen en gedichten* (Baarn, 1982). The best historical novels by a Netherlands writer of the founding of the Holland and Pella colonies are those of Pieter Johannes Risseeuw, *Landverhuizers: (Part I) vrijheid en brood—(Part II) De huilende wildernis* (Baarn, 1946); and *Ik worstel en ontkom* (Baarn, 1959). American novelists of the Dutch genre are Ronald Jager, *Eighty Acres: Elegy for a Family Farm* [Missaukie County, MI] (Boston: Beacon Press, 1990); and James C. Schaap, *Sign of a Promise and Other Stories* (Sioux Center, IA: Dordt College Press, 1979). Peter De Vries, *Blood of the Lamb* (Boston: Little, Brown, 1961) is an irreverent autobiographical novel of the Chicago west side Dutch community. Life in the same community is described in a more serious vein by De Vries's classmate Henry Stob, *Summoning Up Remembrance* (Grand Rapids: Wm. B. Eerdmans, 1995).

Regional Works

Useful regional histories include the pioneer works of Jacob Van der Zee, *The Hollanders of Iowa* (Iowa City: Iowa State Historical Society, 1912); Kommer Van Stigt, *Geschiedenis van Pella, Iowa en omgeving* (Pella, 1897), typescript in English translation by Elizabeth Kempkes, Central College Archives; G. A. Stout, ed., *Souvenir History of Pella, Iowa* (Pella: Booster Press, 1922); and Charles L. Dyke, *The Story of Sioux County [Iowa]* (Orange City, 1942). This latter account of the major Dutch settlement in the upper Midwest is supplanted by G. Nelson Nieuwenhuis, *Siouxland: A History of Sioux County, Iowa* (Orange City: Sioux County Historical Society, 1983). More recent local histories are Henry Van der Pol, *On the Reservation Border: Hollanders in Douglas and Charles Mix Counties [South Dakota]* (Stickney, S.D., 1969), a volume of personal reminiscences augmented by historical sources; J. P. Dahm and D. J. Van Kooten, *Peoria, Iowa: A Story of Two Cultures, 1853–1993* (Peoria, IA, 1993); and Adrian Van Koevering's popular account of the founding of Zeeland, Michigan, in *The Story of a Mass Movement of Nineteenth Century Pilgrims* (Zeeland, MI, 1960).

Chicago-area works are Amry Vandenbosch, *The Dutch Communities of Chicago* (Chicago: Knickerbocker Society of Chicago, 1927); Richard A. Cook, *A History of South Holland, Illinois* (South Holland, 1966); Marie K. Rowlands, *Down the Indian Trail in 1849: The Story of Roseland* (Chicago, 1949), reissued by Ross K. Ettema, ed. (Chicago: Trinity Christian College, 1987); and John H. Yzenbaard

"Dutch Settlement of Great Lakes Cities in the Mid-Nineteenth Century," *Inland Seas* (1971).

Provocative ethnographic studies are Rob Kroes, *The Persistence of Ethnicity: Dutch Calvinist Pioneers in Amsterdam, Montana* (Urbana and Chicago: University of Illinois Press, 1992); and Lawrence J. Taylor, *Dutchmen on the Bay: The Ethnohistory of a Contractual Community* (Philadelphia: University of Pennsylvania Press, 1983). Hendrik J. Prakke, *Drenthe in Michigan* (Assen, 1948, and in English with the same title, Grand Rapids: Wm. B. Eerdmans, 1983), is a brief but cogent case study of a rural Calvinist emigrant colony of the 1840s in western Michigan. An older, still useful sociological study is Henry Ryskamp, "The Dutch of Western Michigan" (Ph.D. diss., University of Michigan, 1930).

Political life of the Dutch in America has been largely ignored, except for brief studies of the activities of Van Raalte and Scholte: Larry J. Wagenaar, "The Early Political History of Holland, Michigan, 1847–1868" (M.A. thesis, Kent State University, 1992); and Robert P. Swierenga, "The Ethnic Voter and the First Lincoln Election" (1965), reprinted as Chapter 10 in this volume.

Linguistic Studies

Linguistic studies of the degradation of spoken Dutch in North America are few, but two excellent books that lead the way are Jo Daan, *"Ik was te bissie": Nederlanders en hun taal in de Verenigde Staten* (Zutphen, 1987); and Philip E. Webber, *Pella Dutch: The Portrait of a Language and Its Use in One of Iowa's Ethnic Communities* (Ames: Iowa State University Press, 1988). Jaap van Maarle of the P.J. Meertens Institute, Amsterdam, is at work on a large-scale study of Dutch language declension in America, including "Yankee Dutch."

Quantitative Studies

Quantitative studies of Dutch immigration in the tradition of the "new social history," which contain much new statistical data derived from official nominal records, are Robert P. Swierenga and Harry S. Stout, "Dutch Immigration in the Nineteenth Century, 1820–1877: A Quantitative Overview,"*Indiana Social Studies Quarterly* (1975), and the same authors' "Socio-Economic Patterns of Migration from the Netherlands in the Nineteenth Century," in *Research in Economic History: An Annual Compilation of Research*, vol. 1, 1976, ed. Paul Uselding. Two occupational mobility studies of Dutch immigrants, which compare pre- and post-migrant occupations, are Gordon W. Kirk, Jr., *The Promise of American Life: Social Mobility in a Nineteenth Century Immigrant Community, Holland, Michigan, 1847–1894* (Philadelphia: American Philosophical Society, 1978); and David G. Vanderstel, "The Dutch of Grand Rapids, Michigan, 1848–1900: Immigrant Neighborhood and Community in a Nineteenth Century City" (Ph.D. diss., Kent State University, 1983). An ambitious multigenerational study is Richard Doyle,

"The Socio-Economic Mobility of the Dutch Immigrants to Pella, Iowa, 1847–1925" (Ph.D. diss., Kent State University, 1982). Irene W. D. Hecht, "Kinship and Migration: The Making of an Oregon Isolate Community," *Journal of Interdisciplinary History* (1977), has masterfully reconstructed the demographic and family links of a Dutch Catholic emigrant community that originated in Noord-Brabant, first settled in Wisconsin, and then removed to Oregon.

Immigrant Women

Suzanne M. Sinke is largely responsible for building an interest in the story of immigrant women, first in "Dutch Immigrant Women in the Late Nineteenth Century: A Comparative Analysis" (M.A. thesis, Kent State University, 1983), and then more definitively in "Home Is Where You Build It: Dutch Immigrant Women in the United States, 1880–1920" (Ph.D. diss., University of Minnesota, 1994). Two brief overviews of Sinke's graduate research are "Home Is Where You Build It: Dutch Immigrant Women and Social Reproduction," in *The Dutch in North America* (1991); and "Through Women's Eyes: Dutch Protestant Immigrant Women in the United States," in *Connecting Cultures: The Netherlands in Five Centuries of Transatlantic Exchange* (1994). Annemieke Galema has written on Frisian immigrant women and joined Sinke in publishing "Paradijs der Vrouwen? Overseas migratie naar de verenigde Staten van Friese vrouwen rond de eeuwisseling" in *Vrouwen in de vreemde: Lotgevallen van emigrantes en immigrantes* (Zutphen, 1993).

Post–World War II Research

Dutch social scientists in the 1950s mounted a coordinated effort to understand the planned emigration following World War II. They were policy-oriented sociologists and demographers who used the postwar mass exodus as a unique laboratory for testing international migration theories. The social scientists in 1954 joined with government emigration authorities to conduct a series of sophisticated survey studies of the postwar emigration. B. W. Haveman, the Government Commissioner for Emigration (1950–63), headed the committee of scholars, consisting of University of Amsterdam psychologist H. C. J. Duijker, University of Utrecht sociologist S. J. Groenman, University of Wageningen sociologist E. W. Hofstee, secretary Gunther Beijer of the Research Group for European Migration Problems (REMP), and Director B. P. Hofstede of the Government Emigration Research Bureau.

With the financial support of both the Netherlands government and the Intergovernmental Committee for European Migration (ICEM) in Geneva, the Dutch research team of Beijer, Hofstede, Hofstee, and two junior scholars, N. H. Frijda and R. Wentholt, made a detailed inquiry into the behavioral characteristics of the postwar emigrants, their motives and expectations, and how they compared with nonemigrants. Frijda and Wentholt even followed emigrants to their overseas homes. The data base consisted of survey questionnaires and interviews with thousands of departing migrants.

The research results were first published in The Hague in separate monographs under the rubric *Studies over de Nederlands emigratie*: B. P. Hofstede, *De Gaande Man* (1958); N. H. Frijda, *Emigranten—niet-emigranten* (1960); N. H. Frijda, *Emigranten overzee* (1962); and R. Wentholt, *Kenmerken van de Nederlandse emigrant* (1961). Gunther Beijer edited an abridged English-language version of these works, *Characteristics of overseas emigrants* (The Hague, 1961), which conveniently summarized the findings and conclusions. After the postwar emigration dramatically declined in the early sixties, Hofstede offered an analysis of this unexpected turn of events in *Thwarted Exodus: Post-war overseas migration from the Netherlands* (The Hague, 1964). E. W. Hofstee presented his interpretation of the significance of the postwar migration in "Emigration Countries: Netherlands" in *Economics of International Migration*, ed. Brinley Thomas (London, 1958), and in *Some Remarks on Selective Migration* (The Hague, 1952).

Several Netherlands scholars who were not members of the emigration research team also contributed to the discussion. The best overview is William S. Petersen, *Some Factors Influencing Postwar Emigrants from the Netherlands* (The Hague, 1952). J. E. Ellemers, the noted emigration theorist, published two articles in the periodical *Sociologische Gids*: "Naar een theorie van emigratieverschijnselen" (1957), and "Recente Nederlandse literatuur over emigratie" (1962). Ellemers summarized both essays (in English) in "The Determinants of Emigration: An Analyses of Dutch Studies on Migration," *Sociologia Neerlandica* (1963/1964). J. D. Wildeboer analyzed Frisian emigration where the postwar outflow was the heaviest, in *Friesland verliet zijn kinderen* (Assen, 1954), and W. Steigenga analyzed the relationship between demographic pressures and economic growth in *Industrialization—Emigration: The Consequences of the Demographic Development in the Netherlands* (The Hague, 1955). The Katholieke Centrale Emigratie Stichting also sponsored a sociological study of the Catholic post-1945 emigration, *Sociografische aspecten van de emigratie* (The Hague, 1954), by G. H. L. Zeegers, A. Oldendorff, and W. J. J. Kusters.

Dutch-Canadian Immigration

The only general study of Dutch-Canadian migration is Herman Ganzevoort's *Bittersweet Land: The Dutch Experience in Canada, 1890–1980* (Toronto: McClelland and Stewart, 1988), which is solidly researched and documented. This should be supplemented with K. Ishwaran's *Family, Kinship, and Community: A Study of Dutch Canadians* (Toronto: University of Toronto Press, 1977), which is a sociological analysis of Holland Marsh, an isolated, rural settlement near Toronto. A similar study of the entire postwar emigration is William S. Petersen, *Planned Migration: The Social Determinants of the Dutch-Canadian Movement* (Berkeley: University of California Press, 1955).

Conclusion

Until Dutch scholars take a greater interest in the history of the nineteenth century, Dutch-American scholars will continue to lead in emigration research, including the collection of immigrant letters, emigration lists, and church membership lists. The Americans will also continue to open the frontiers in migration research. The ethnic revival of the sixties is as strong among Dutch-Americans as any hyphenated groups. The first Dutch-American Historical Workshop, held at Calvin College in 1977, attracted more than eighty scholars from the United States, Canada, and the Netherlands, and resulted in a decision to form the Association for the Advancement of Dutch-American Studies (AADAS) to promote the study of Dutch immigration and life in America. AADAS holds biannual conferences, as do its counterparts, the American Association for Netherlandic Studies (AANS) and the Canadian Association for the Advancement of Netherlandic Studies (CAANS). Publications of AADAS conference papers include: *The Dutch in America* (Hope College, 1984); *Proceedings* (Northwestern College, 1985); *The Dutch in America, Perspective 1987* (Trinity Christian College, 1987); *The Dutch and Their Faith: Immigrant Religious Experience in the 19th and 20th Centuries* (Hope College, 1991); *The Dutch and Their Neighbors in Transition: The Formation, Growth, and Dissolution of Ethnic Centers in Grand Rapids, Chicago, and Other Places* (Calvin College, 1993); *A Century of Midwestern Dutch-American Manners and Mores—and More* (Northwestern College, 1995); and *The Sesquicentennial of Dutch Immigration: 150 Years of Ethnic Heritage* (Hope College, 1997). Most significantly, in 1983 the Calvin College Archives launched the semi-annual Dutch-American history journal, *Origins*, under the editorship of Herbert J. Brinks, which provides a forum for new research.

The future for Dutch migration research appears promising both in the Old and New Country. As Dutch scholars increasingly join with their American cousins and apply their considerable expertise to the questions of overseas emigration, the history of the movement will be as thoroughly understood as that of the Scandinavian emigration.

INDEX

It Started with Pizza

Variables, Expressions, and Equations

Dawn McMillan

Publishing Credits

Editor
Sara Johnson

Editorial Director
Dona Herweck Rice

Editor-in-Chief
Sharon Coan, M.S.Ed.

Creative Director
Lee Aucoin

Publisher
Rachelle Cracchiolo, M.S.Ed.

Image Credits

The authors and publisher would like to gratefully credit or acknowledge the following for permission to reproduce copyright material: cover Pearson Education/Lindsay Edwards; p.1 Pearson Education/Lindsay Edwards; p.3 Pearson Education/Lindsay Edwards; p.4 Alamy; p.5 Pearson Education/Lindsay Edwards: p.6 Pearson Education/Lindsay Edwards; p.7 Big Stock Photo; p.8 Big Stock Photo; p.9 Dreamstime; p.11 Corbis; p.12 Shutterstock; p.13 (top) Big Stock Photo; p.13 (bottom) Rob Cruse; p.14 (top left) Shutterstock; p.14 (top middle) 123 Royalty-Free; p. 14 (top right) Pearson Education/Alice McBroom; 14 (bottom left) iStock Photo; p.14 (bottom middle) Shutterstock; p.14 (bottom right) iStock Photo; p.16 Shutterstock; p.17 Photos.com; p.18 123 Royalty-Free; p.19 Shutterstock; pp.20-21 Photolibrary.com/Detlev Van Ravenswaay; 22 (left) Photolibrary.com/Gerard Fritz; p.22 (right) Big Stock Photo; p.23 (both) Big Stock Photo; p.24 NASA; p.26 (all) Big Stock Photo; p.27 iStock; p.29 Shutterstock

Teacher Created Materials
5301 Oceanus Drive
Huntington Beach, CA 92649-1030
http://www.tcmpub.com

ISBN 978-0-7439-0911-2

Reprinted 2012

Table of Contents

Math in Food

On my birthday, I invited two of my friends to a pizza restaurant for dinner. Of course, we ordered pizza. We all love pizza! We sat with Mom and Dad, and my older brother. The waiter brought two pizzas to the table.

"Two pizzas!" joked Dad. "One for Mom and me to eat, and one for the rest of you!"

"That is unfair!" I exclaimed. "That means that you and Mom will have 2 slices each, which is half of the pizza. We will only have 1 slice each. That is only one quarter of the pizza!"

"Never mind!" said Mom. "We can order another pizza. The four of you can share 2 pizzas."

Before we knew it, the waiter had delivered another pizza for us kids to share.

"So," said my older brother, who thinks he is really good at math, "if we all eat a quarter from both of the pizzas, what fraction of a whole pizza will each of us eat?"

Our pizzas

LET'S EXPLORE MATH

Variables (VAIR-ee-uh-buhls) are letters or symbols that can be used to **represent** numbers. Often, the letter *x* is used to represent a number. An **equation** is a mathematical sentence that shows 2 equal numbers or quantities. It is written with an equal sign.

Look at the pictures above. They show the pizzas that were eaten at the birthday dinner. Each pizza had 4 slices. The equation $\frac{1}{4} + \frac{1}{4} = x$ can be used to find what fraction of the pizza each kid ate.

a. What does *x* represent?

b. What does *x* equal?

I looked at my two friends. “Easy!” I said. “We each eat a quarter from one pizza, then a quarter from the other. That makes two quarters, which makes half a pizza. We will each be eating the same fraction of pizza as Mom and Dad! We could write an equation to show the equivalent fractions: $\frac{2}{4} = \frac{1}{2}$.”

2/4 = 1/2
We each ate 2 quarters of pizza.
Mom and Dad each ate half a pizza.

Later that night, back at home, I grabbed an apple for a snack. I cut the apple into slices. Quickly, my older brother ate 3 of the slices. There were 5 slices left for me. I used math to figure out how many slices I started with.

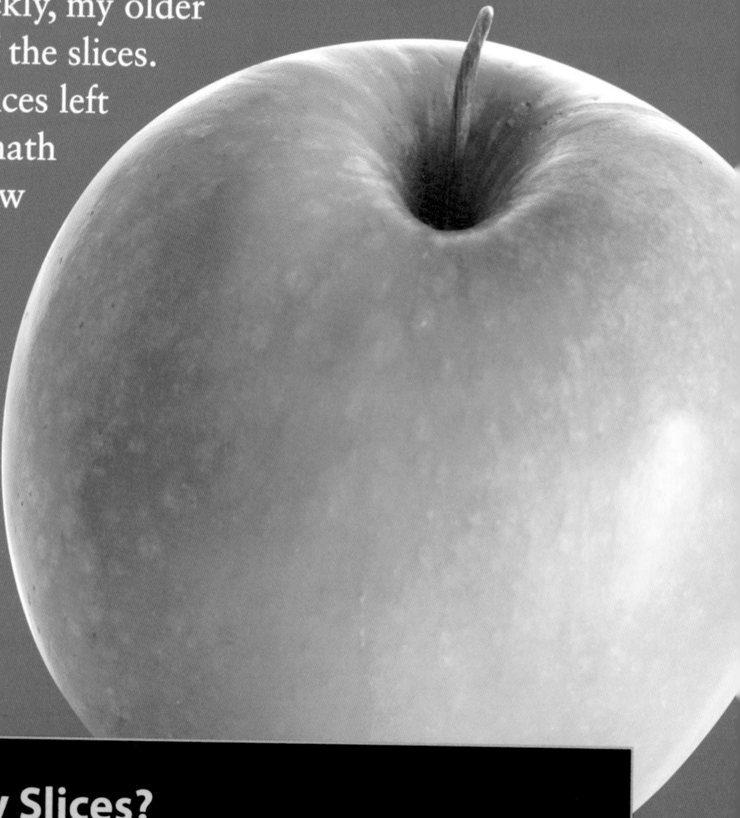

How Many Slices?

I can use the equation $x - 3 = 5$ to figure out how many slices I started with.
x represents the number of slices I started with.
3 represents the number of slices my brother ate.
5 represents the number of slices I had left.

I can add to solve for x.
$x - 3 = 5$
$5 + 3 = x$
$5 + 3 = 8$
That means I started with 8 slices.

Math Is Everywhere

My brother and I talked more about math later that night. We realized that we could use math to figure out how many hours we sleep each school night. Our bedtime is 8:00 P.M. and we wake up at 7:00 A.M. in order to get ready for school.

How Many Hours?

We go to bed at 8:00 P.M. and we wake up at 7:00 A.M. We can count up from 8:00 to figure out how many hours of sleep we get each night. We can also draw a clock and use it to solve the problem.

11 hours

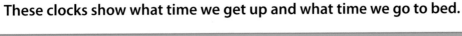

These clocks show what time we get up and what time we go to bed.

7:00 A.M. **8:00 P.M.**

As my head hit the pillow, I was still thinking about math. I thought about the **environment** and the world around me. I thought about all the things that people do. And I began to understand that math is everywhere.

I decided that tomorrow I would do a test to see how many places I could find math throughout the day.

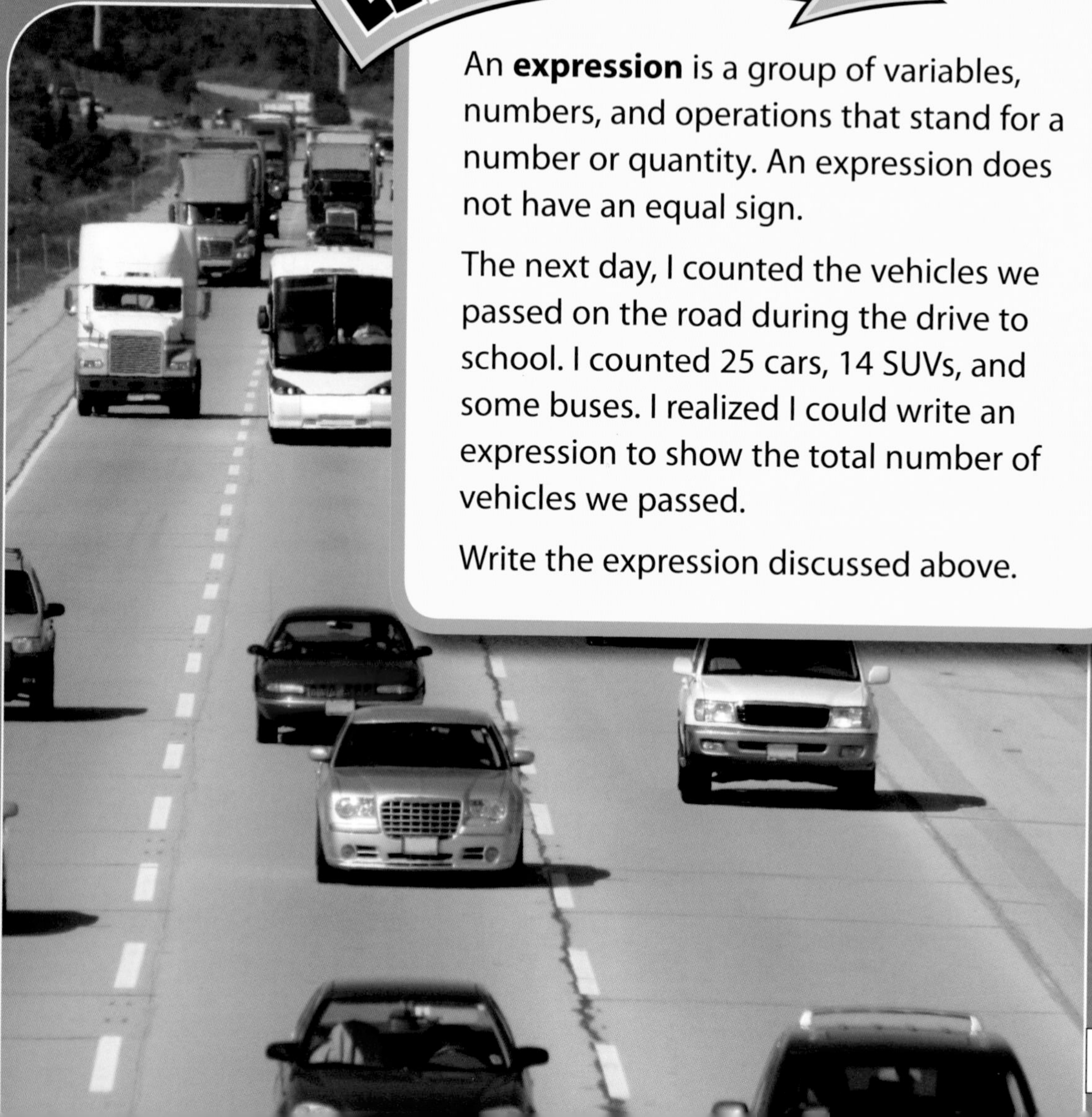

LET'S EXPLORE MATH

An **expression** is a group of variables, numbers, and operations that stand for a number or quantity. An expression does not have an equal sign.

The next day, I counted the vehicles we passed on the road during the drive to school. I counted 25 cars, 14 SUVs, and some buses. I realized I could write an expression to show the total number of vehicles we passed.

Write the expression discussed above.

Math at Home

In the Bedroom

After school, I looked around my bedroom for different examples of math. Each thing in my room takes up a different amount of space.

So I used grid paper and made a simple floor plan of my room. I sketched how much space my bed takes up. I also have a desk, a bookcase, a dresser, a night stand, and a rug. My brother helped me work out how much space each piece of furniture takes up.

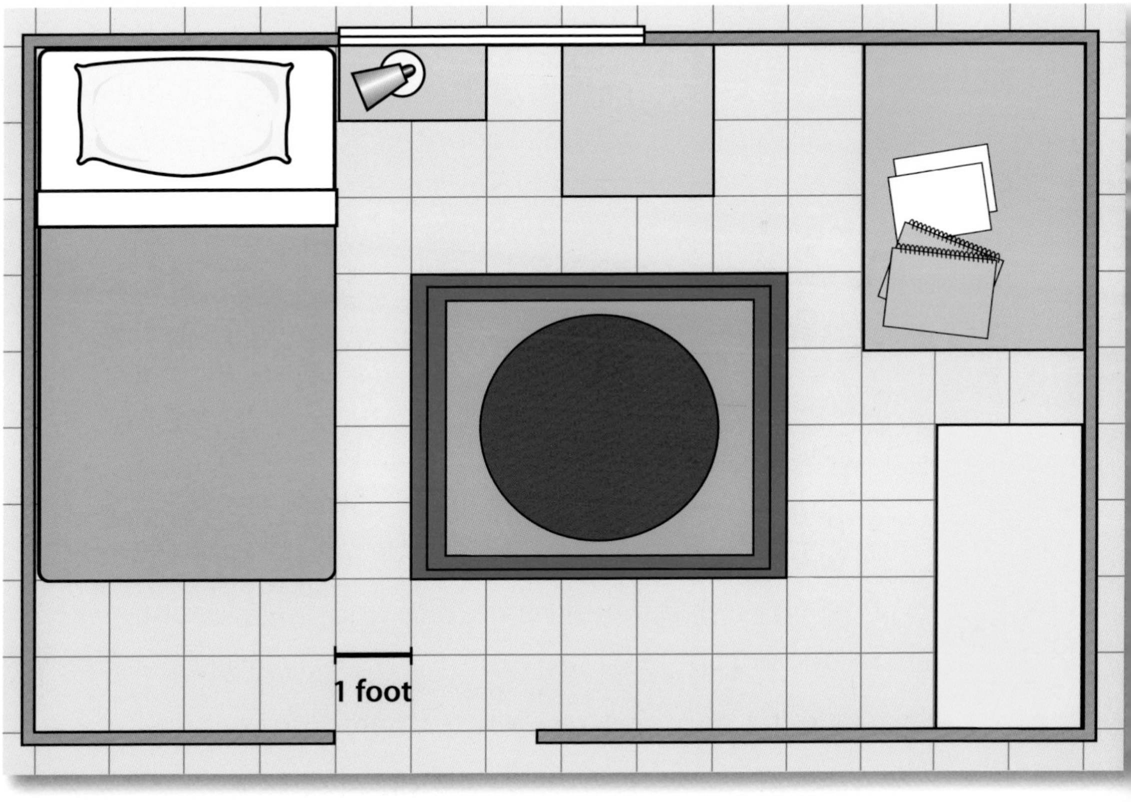

I realized that math could be shown in my floor plan. I could calculate the perimeters and areas of all of the objects in my room. I could also use the **dimensions** to rearrange my room and design a new floor plan.

LET'S EXPLORE MATH

The total area of the bedroom is 126 square feet. The bedroom furniture takes up 74 square feet. Let *x* represent the amount of unused space in the bedroom.

a. What equation could be used to find the amount of unused space in the room?

b. Solve the equation you wrote in problem **a**.

c. What would you do with the unused space?

In the Kitchen

Then I went into the kitchen to help make dinner. The kitchen is another great room for finding math. **Recipes** show measurements of ingredients. And recipe sizes can be increased or decreased using multiplication and division.

Mom's Pizza Dough
Makes 1 pizza crust

Ingredients

2 cups plain flour
$\frac{3}{4}$ cup warm water
1 teaspoon super fine sugar
$\frac{1}{2}$ teaspoon salt
2 tablespoons olive oil
8 grams of dry yeast

There are many kitchen tools that are used to measure ingredients. Measuring spoons are different sizes: $^1/_8$ teaspoon, $^1/_2$ teaspoon, and $^1/_4$ teaspoon. They are all fractions of 1 teaspoon. Measuring cups are marked with fractional measurements: $^1/_2$ cup, $^1/_3$ cup, and $^1/_4$ cup. They are all fractions of 1 cup.

measuring spoons

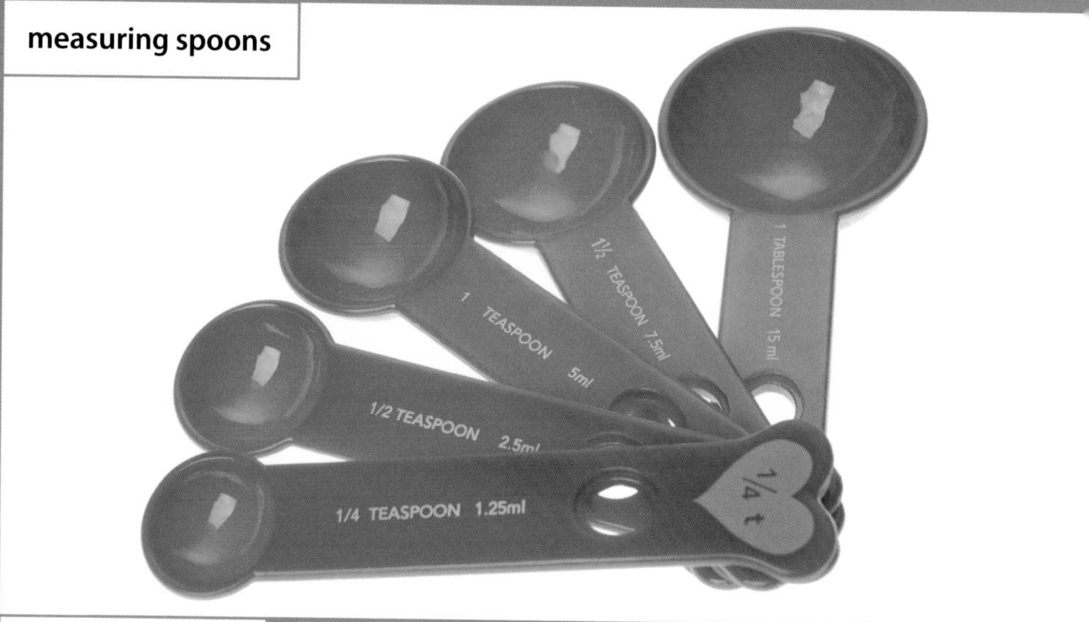

measuring cups

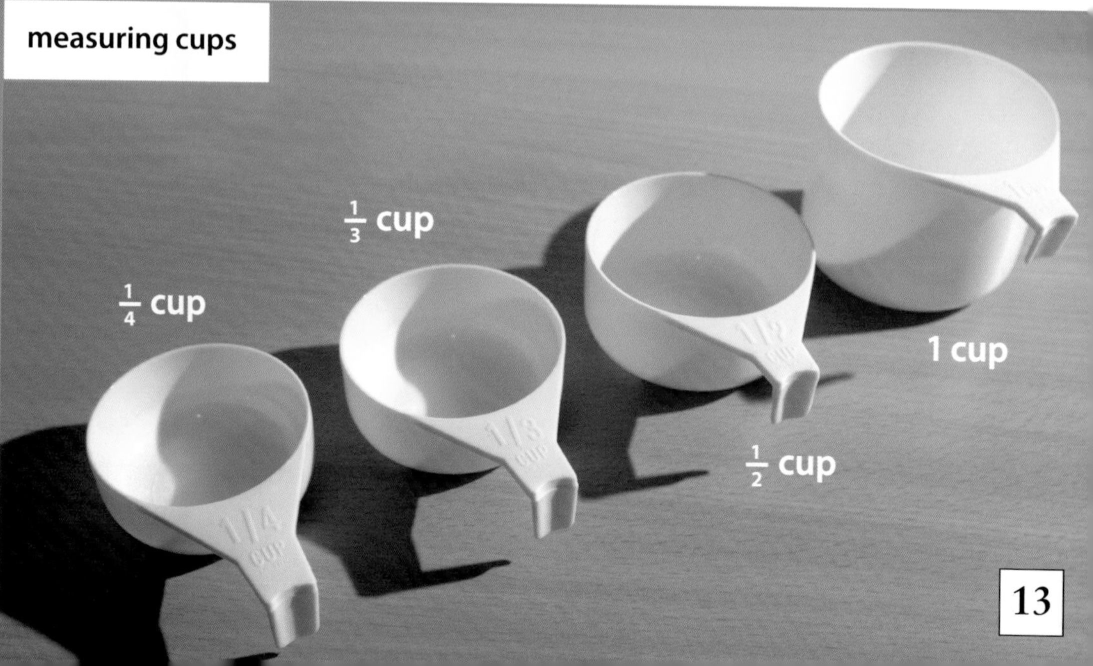

Mom and I decide to make pizza for dinner. We follow her recipe, but we have to double it to make 2 pizzas. To do this, we multiply each **quantity** in the recipe by 2.

It was easy to double the quantities of the flour, sugar, olive oil, and dry yeast. The fractions made it harder to double the amount of water and salt. Mom suggested using repeated addition instead.

Double Quantities

Water

$\frac{3}{4} + \frac{3}{4} = \frac{6}{4} = 1\frac{1}{2}$ cups warm wate

Salt

$\frac{1}{2} + \frac{1}{2} = \frac{2}{2} = 1$ teaspoon salt

Mathematical Names

As Mom and I were cooking, I realized that we can talk about numbers in different ways. I looked at our kitchen scale. Two cups of flour weighs about 8 ounces. If 8 ounces equals $^1/_2$ pound, then 8 ounces is also 50% of a pound. And 50% can also be written as a decimal number, 0.5.

The quantity remains the same. It does not matter if you use the decimal, percentage, or fractional name.

LET'S EXPLORE MATH

When we doubled the pizza-dough recipe, we calculated that we needed 16 grams of dry yeast. Dry yeast comes in packets that hold 2 grams each. We can use the variable *p* to represent the number of packets we need to use.

a. Which equation below could be used to find the number of packets needed for the recipe?

1. $2 + p = 16$ **2.** $2p = 16$ **3.** $2 \div p = 16$

b. Use the equation you chose to figure out how many packets of yeast are needed for the recipe.

Math and the Human Body

Dad came into the kitchen. "I will show you something else to do with math," he said. "Come with me!"

He led me to a full-length mirror. Then he stood in front of it. "A great example of **proportions** stares out at us from the mirror!" he said.

I looked at Dad's **reflection**. His head takes up about $1/8$ of his body. So, the human body stands about 8 heads high. That means a body is about as tall as 8 heads of that body, stacked on top of each other.

In other words, the ratio of the head to the whole body is 1 to 8; the head is $1/8$ of the height of the whole body.

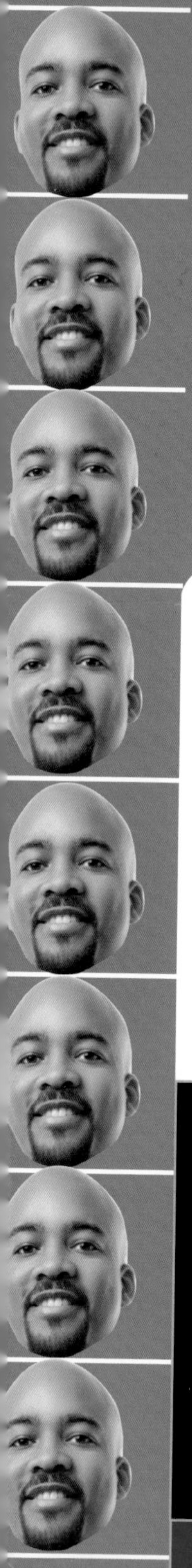

Then Dad stepped away from the mirror. "Now it is your turn," he told me. "Look closely at your face. "

I looked at my reflection. I noticed that my face was **symmetrical**.

Next, I found a magazine. I looked at some faces and saw how they were symmetrical, too.

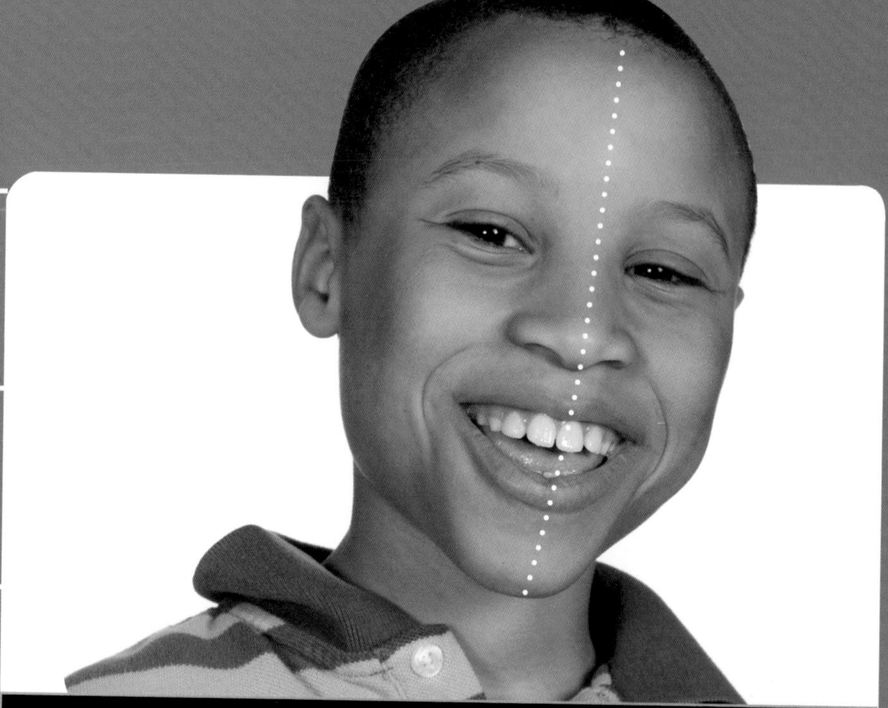

More Faces

There were 4 faces in the magazine that were not symmetrical. Those people had freckles. I wrote an expression to show the total number of faces I found in the magazine: 4 + 18.

What does the number 18 represent?

18 represents the number of people with symmetrical faces.

After dinner, I went outside to play with my neighborhood friends. I noticed my friend's younger sister, Nita, had some adult teeth growing in. She told me that she has 7 adult teeth. Altogether, she has 20 teeth. I can use the variable *t* to figure out how many baby teeth she has left.

How Many Teeth?

$7 + t = 20$

$20 - 7 = t$

$20 - 7 = 13$

Nita has 13 baby teeth left!

LET'S EXPLORE MATH

While playing, a group of my neighborhood friends are discussing how tall they are. Luis is 55 inches tall, Madeleine is 56 inches tall, and Jamie does not know her height.

a. Write an expression to show the combined height of all three friends.

The total combined height for all 3 friends is 162 inches:
$55 + 56 + x = 162$

b. What is Jamie's height?

c. Who is the tallest?

Math in Space

When I came in from playing, Mom came into my room to see what I was doing.

"What about math in space?" asked Mom. "Think about the size of the planets in our **solar system**. Maybe we could make a proportional model of some of the planets."

The planets that make up our solar system

Mom told me that **astronomers** collect proportional data about the solar system. Our solar system is huge in size and distance. There are 8 planets and a sun in our solar system. Some of the planets are smaller than Earth. Some are much larger.

LET'S EXPLORE MATH

There are 8 planets in our solar system. Mercury, Venus, Earth, and Mars are called *inner planets*. The rest of the planets are called *outer planets*.

a. Write an equation to show the number of outer planets.

b. How many outer planets are in our solar system?

Dad suggested that we **research** the size of the planets and the sun on the Internet. It was amazing. I had not realized just how large the solar system is, or how big some of the planets are. The sun is a star. It is even bigger than all the planets in our solar system combined!

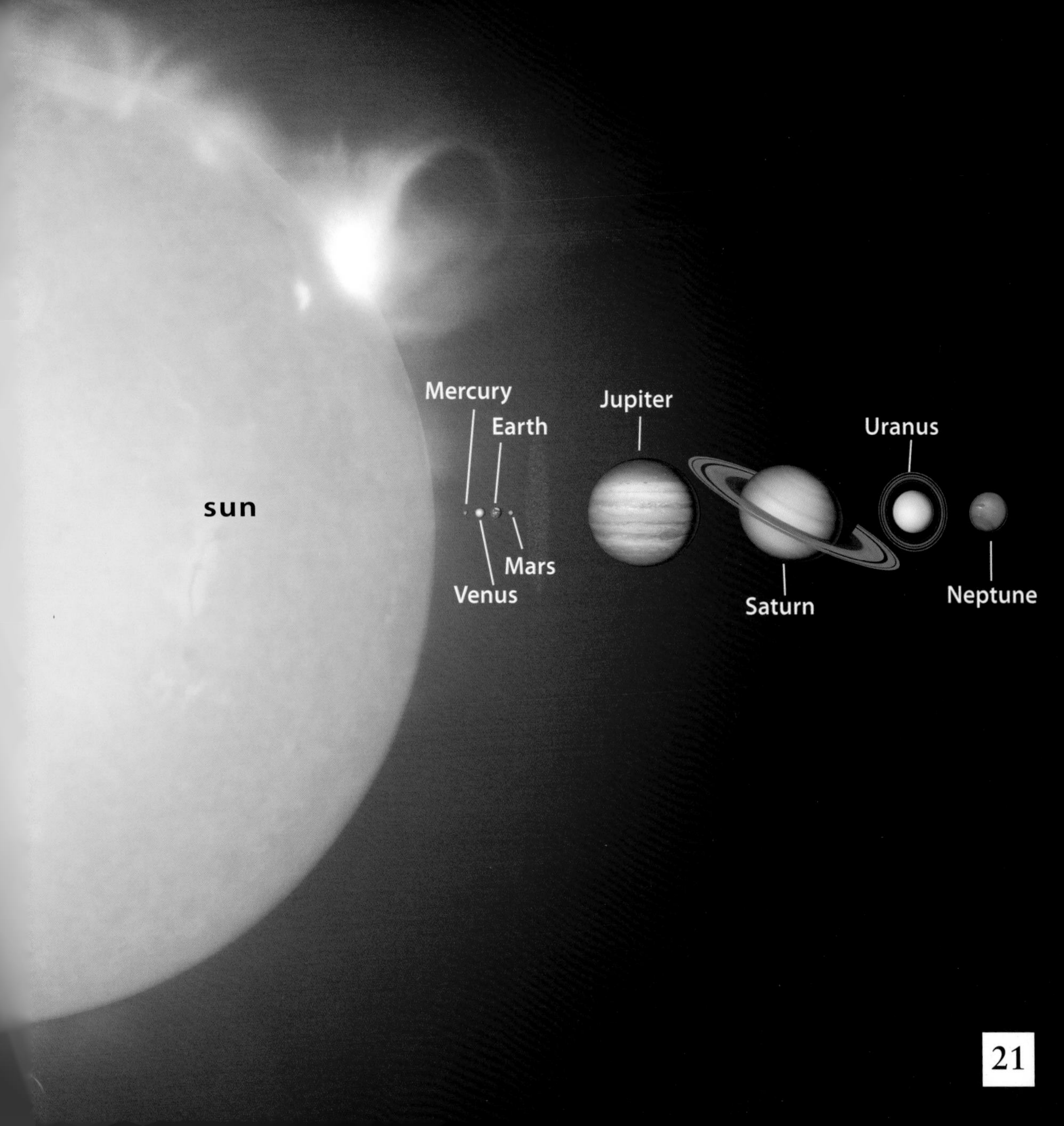

The more I thought about the solar system, the harder it was to **visualize** the size of the planets in it. So Mom helped me some more.

First, we found out the actual **diameter** of the sun and the planets. Mom got me to write them down. Then, Mom helped me change the diameter of the planets from kilometers into millimeters! Then Mom reduced that number by 100 million. So, our scale is 1 millimeter = 1,000 kilometers.

It was a lot of hard work. Mom used her calculator to help her. But it was worth it. Mom and I found a great way to make a proportional model of the planets and the sun using food.

The proportional model helped me see just how big the sun is compared to Earth. It was amazing!

Star/Planet	Actual Diameter (km)	Reduced Diameter (mm)	Food Items (in approximate proportional size)
sun (a star)	1,391,980	1,392	giant pumpkin
Mercury	4,900	4.9	coffee bean
Venus	12,100	12.1	large blueberry
Earth	12,700	12.7	cherry
Mars	6,700	6.7	pea
Jupiter	142,000	142	large grapefruit or cantaloupe
Saturn	120,000	120	very large orange
Uranus	51,800	51.8	kiwi
Neptune	49,500	49.5	apricot or nectarine

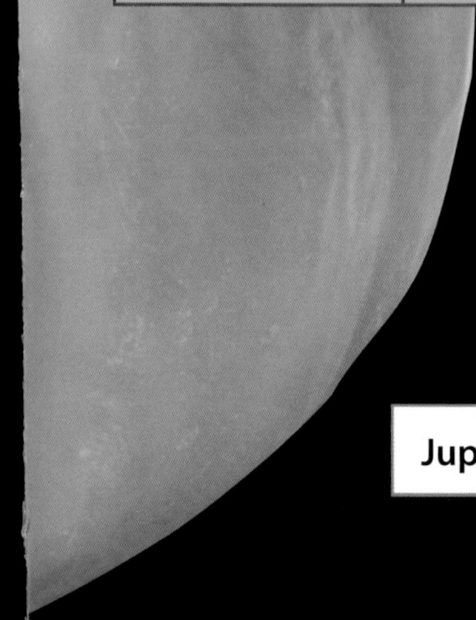

Jupiter = large grapefruit

Earth = cherry

"Now imagine trying to work out proportional distances for our solar system," said Mom.

That made me stop and think some more. During my Internet research on planet sizes, I had found the distance of each planet from the sun. I had read on the Internet that Earth is over 92 million miles (over 148 million km) from the sun. And Jupiter is around 484 million miles (779 million km) from the sun.

Jupiter is a giant planet made of gas.

LET'S EXPLORE MATH

Only 6 of the 8 planets in our solar system have moons. Saturn has 60 moons. Jupiter has 3 more moons than Saturn. Write an equation to show how many moons Jupiter has.

The table below shows the distance of each planet from the sun. The distances in our solar system are really incredible!

Planet Distances from the Sun

Planet	Distance	
	Miles	Kilometers
Inner Planets		
Mercury	35,983,093	57,909,175
Venus	67,237,912	108,208,930
Earth	92,955,819	149,597,890
Mars	141,633,262	227,936,640
Outer Planets		
Jupiter	483,682,805	778,412,020
Saturn	886,526,063	1,426,725,400
Uranus	1,783,939,419	2,870,972,200
Neptune	2,795,084,767	4,498,252,899

That's Far!

I can use variables and expressions to show planets' distances from the sun. Mars is about 4 times farther away from the sun than Mercury. The variable *m* can represent the distance Mercury is from the sun. So, the expression 4*m* can represent the distance Mars is from the sun.

Let's say my house was Earth, or the cherry. Then the sun, or giant pumpkin, would need to be about a city block away. And Jupiter, or the large grapefruit, would have to be about five blocks away from the pumpkin.

A proportional model of the distances in the solar system would not fit in my house!

Math Gives Meaning

My brain was buzzing. In just one day, I learned so much about math in the world around me. I love thinking about math. It makes my world so much more interesting. It's amazing to think that I learned so much, and it all started from eating pizza!

Problem-Solving Activity

Space Discovery

Astronomers have just discovered a new solar system in a distant galaxy. It has six planets orbiting around a sun. Some of the planets are about the size of Earth. Others are much larger. And this new solar system has a combined total of 30 moons!

The table below is missing some of the current information astronomers have learned about this new solar system.

Planets in New Solar System

Name of Planet	Approximate Diameter (miles)	Number of Moons
Zenner	z	1
Xenox	3,000	x
Axiom	a	2
Centaur	75,000	c
Yukka	36,000	17

Solve It!

For each question below, write mathematical equations using variables to help you figure out the answers.

a. Xenox has 15 fewer moons than Yukka. How many moons does Xenox have?

b. Centaur has 6 more moons than Axiom. How many moons does Centaur have?

Centaur's diameter is 68,500 miles bigger than Zenner's diameter. Axiom's diameter and Xenox's diameter total 4,000 miles.

c. What are the diameters of planets Zenner and Axiom?

Use the steps below to help you solve the problems above.

Step 1: Use the information in the table to write question **a.** as a mathematical equation. Then solve your equation.

Step 2: Use the information in the table to write question **b.** as a mathematical equation. Then solve your equation.

Step 3: Use the information in the table and above question **c.** to write mathematical equations. Then solve your equations.

Glossary

astronomers—people who study objects and matter outside the Earth's atmosphere

diameter—a line joining 2 points of a circle and passing through its center

dimensions—the measurements of shapes; 2-D objects have width and length

environment—the place in which people and other animals live, and the circumstances under which they live

equation—a mathematical sentence that shows 2 equal numbers or quantities; written with an equal sign

expression—a group of symbols or numbers standing for a number or quantity; a mathematical phrase without an equal sign

proportions—a statement that ratios are equal; $\frac{4}{8} = \frac{1}{2}$

quantity—the amount or number of something

recipes—instructions for cooking food

reflection—a mirror image of something

represent—stand in place of; to stand for

research—to study and investigate something

solar system—the part in space that is made up of all the planets that orbit the sun, including moons, comets, asteroids, and meteoroids

symmetrical—having balance in size, shape, and position on opposite sides of a dividing line

variables—symbols or letters representing unknown values

visualize—to see or form a picture of something in your mind

Index

Answer Key

Let's Explore Math

Page 5:

a. *x* represents the fraction of a pizza each child ate

b. *x* equals $\frac{2}{4}$ or $\frac{1}{2}$ of a pizza

Page 9:

$25 + 14 + x$

Page 11:

a. $126 - 74 = x$

b. 52 square feet (ft.^{2})

c. Answers will vary.

Page 15:

a. **2.** $2p = 16$

b. 8 packets

Page 18:

a. $55 + 56 + x$

b. Jamie's height is 51 inches.

c. Madeleine is the tallest.

Page 20:

a. $4 + x = 8$

b. 4 planets

Page 24:

$60 + 3 = x$

Problem-Solving Activity

a. $17 - 15 = x$

$17 - 15 = 2$ moons

Xenox has 2 moons.

b. $2 + 6 = c$

$2 + 6 = 8$ moons

Centaur has 8 moons.

c. $75{,}000 - 68{,}500 = z$

$75{,}000 - 68{,}500 = 6{,}500$ miles in diameter

Zenner has a diameter of 6,500 miles.

$3{,}000 + a = 4{,}000$

$4{,}000 - 3{,}000 = a$

$4{,}000 - 3{,}000 = 1{,}000$ miles in diameter

Axiom has a diameter of 1,000 miles.